ST. CHARLES COUNTY COMMUNITY COLLEGE
3 9835 0002
P9-CBP-714

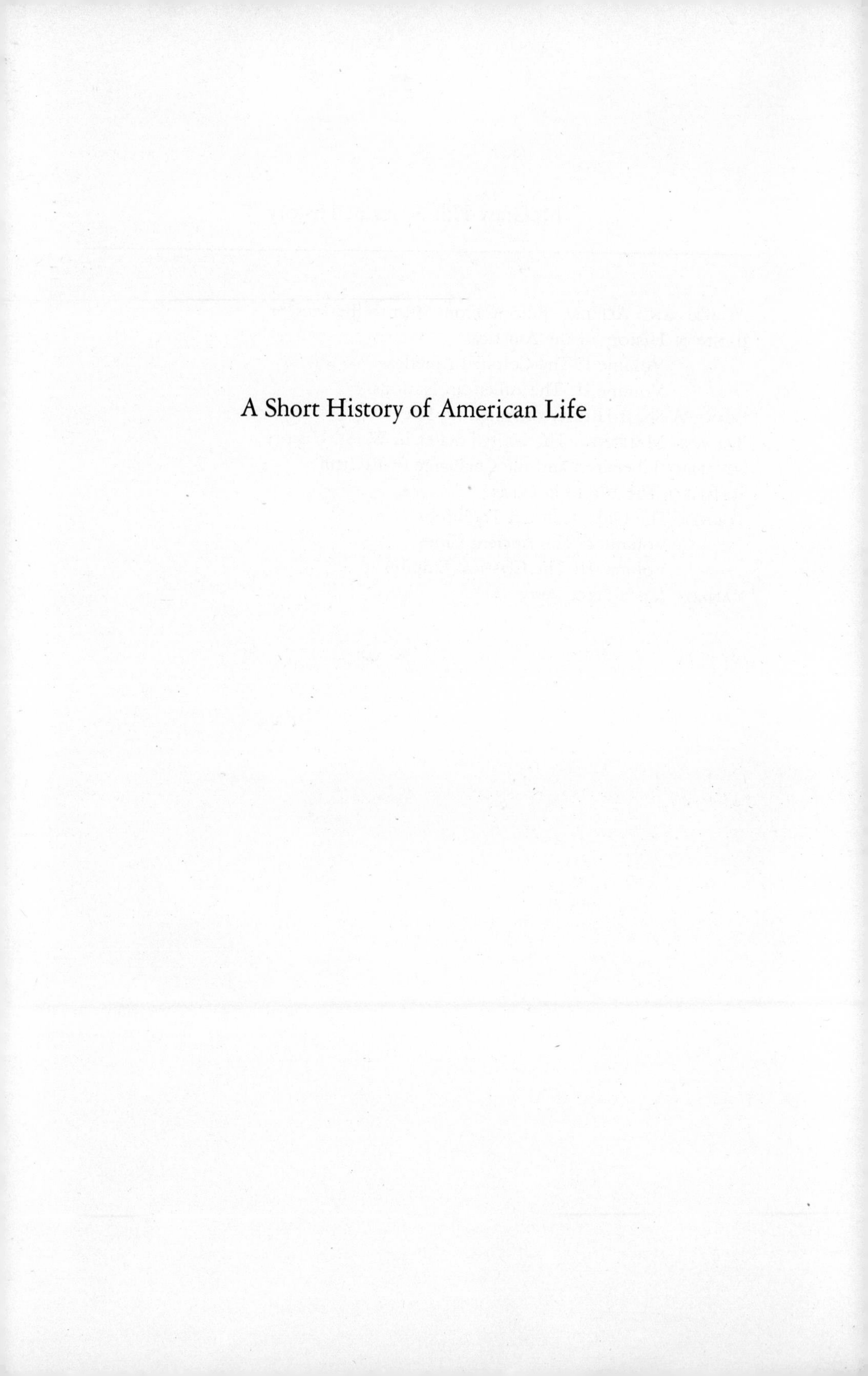

A Short History of American Life

McGraw-Hill Series in History

ALBJERG AND ALBJERG · Europe From 1914 to the Present
BANNON · History of the Americas
 Volume I: The Colonial Americas
 Volume II: The American Nations
BLAKE · A Short History of American Life
RAE AND MAHONEY · The United States in World History
SCHAPIRO · Liberalism and the Challenge of Fascism
SCHAPIRO · The World in Crisis
TURNER · The Great Cultural Traditions
 Volume I: The Ancient Cities
 Volume II: The Classical Empires
YANAGA · Japan Since Perry

91-1524

A SHORT HISTORY OF AMERICAN LIFE

Nelson Manfred Blake

Maxwell School of Citizenship and Public Affairs, Syracuse University

SCCCC - LIBRARY
4601 Mid Rivers Mall Drive
St. Peters, MO 63376
WITHDRAWN

E169.1
.B6
1972

ST. CHARLES COUNTY
COMMUNITY COLLEGE LIBRARY

FIRST EDITION

New York Toronto London

McGRAW-HILL BOOK COMPANY, INC.

1952

12.50

A SHORT HISTORY OF AMERICAN LIFE

Copyright, 1952, by the McGraw-Hill Book Company, Inc. Printed in the United States of America. All rights reserved. This book, or parts thereof, may not be reproduced in any form without permission of the publishers.

Library of Congress Catalog Card Number: 51-12587

To my mother

GERTRUDE NELSON BLAKE

Preface

Within the following pages the reader will find only the most rudimentary facts of political history. He will find no record of battles and military campaigns, diplomatic negotiations and treaties, election campaigns and legislative debates. Instead, this book has much to say of immigrants making their way to new homes, of farmers, artisans, and merchants adapting their methods to changing conditions, of preachers and priests laboring for the Lord in strange vineyards, of teachers and professors struggling to transmit the cultural heritage, of authors and artists seeking forms of expression. The general theme is the transplanting of European institutions to American soil and the modification of the Old World heritage in its new environment to produce that pattern of life which we call American civilization.

As the title of this book suggests, an attempt has been made to achieve within the bounds of a single volume a synthesis of American economic, social, and cultural history somewhat similar to that developed in the thirteen-volume *History of American Life,* edited by Arthur M. Schlesinger and Dixon Ryan Fox—a work of cooperative scholarship for which I have great respect. I wish to make it clear, however, that the following pages are by no means intended as a condensation of that series. Both in organization and in content this is an entirely independent study and one for which the editors and authors of the longer work have no responsibility.

Through the kindness of museums and private owners I have been able to use reproductions of American paintings for many of my illustrations. These have been selected not as great works of art–only a few would so qualify–but because they have helped me to visualize significant aspects of American life more clearly than could any written description. I hope that they may perform the same service for others.

Many friends and colleagues have helped and encouraged me in writing these pages. I shall not attempt to name them all, but I should like to make a particularly grateful acknowledgment to Dr. Edwin H. Cady and Dr. Oscar T. Barck, Jr., who read most of my manuscript and made many excellent suggestions. Without the devoted help of my wife, Elizabeth May Blake, in typing the manuscript, proofreading, and indexing, the book could not have been completed. Full responsibility for all errors must, however, rest with me.

NELSON MANFRED BLAKE

SYRACUSE, N. Y.
January, 1952

Contents

III. TRIUMPH OF THE BUSINESSMAN, 1861–1914

IV. THE LATEST AGE, SINCE 1914

List of Illustrations

I. Colonial Foundations, 1607-1776

Chapter 1. Early Americans

The Americans have become a distinct people. Some of them are white, some black, some red, some yellow. Their names may be as simple as Smith or as complex as Eisenhower. They may adhere to any one or none of over two hundred different religious denominations. But despite all this diversity they have many things in common. They speak the American language—to be distinguished from English by its extravagant vocabulary and its racy idiom. They believe in democracy—although they find it hard to define. They have faith in George Washington and in the Constitution. They admire good sportsmanship and are angered by foul play. They aspire to material security and applaud penicillin and plastics. They take pride in their growth to world power and are confident of their destiny. In a world where many men have lost hope, Americans maintain their basic optimism.

Americans are for the most part transplanted Europeans. Their culture is a strange amalgam of elements drawn from a score of different countries, modified by prolonged contact with a new environment. The process started over three hundred years ago. Since accurate records are lacking, it is impossible to say how many immigrants disembarked on the shores of the future United States between 1607 and 1776. They probably totaled less than one million. Compared with the one and one-third million immigrants who entered the country in a single later year like 1907, the number of colonial arrivals seems small. But in the seventeenth and eighteenth centuries men and women married young and had large families. Such are the miracles of geometric progression that an extraordinarily large proportion of the present American population—perhaps as much as one-half—is descended from this colonial stock. More important still, the span of 169 years between 1607 and 1776 accounts for almost half the years of American social development. Not until 1945 did the number of years of independence equal those spent under colonial tutelage. By 1776 not only political habits but economic patterns and social institutions of enduring influence had been established. Subsequent immigration poured human cement into a form already half erected.

The Coming of the English

It may be said, as a rough generalization, that immigration to the future United States was largely English during the seventeenth century and largely non-English during the eighteenth. Over the whole colonial period the English were probably fewer than the non-English, but once again the importance of priority is great. Coming first and raising large families despite a frightful mortality, the English element secured a dominant influence for their language and culture.

What were the reasons for this momentous seventeenth-century English migration? The force Americans like to dwell upon, the impulse for freedom, was undeniably at work. The seventeenth century was a period of political and religious ferment. On the British throne from 1603 to 1688 sat four Stuart kings, each in his way attempting to continue the strong monarchial authority so successfully exercised by the Tudors during the previous century. Opposing the absolutist policies of the Crown and drawing its strength from country gentlemen and city merchants was a faction which hoped to subordinate the King to Parliament. Particularly heated was the controversy over religion. James I and Charles I took their stand on the Elizabethan settlement. They supported the Church of England and enforced—intermittently—the laws which required religious conformity. By this policy they opposed the wishes of the Catholics, who wanted to reestablish the tie with Rome, of the Separatists, who wanted each Christian congregation to enjoy independence, and of the much more numerous and influential Puritans, who believed in an established church but wanted radical changes in church government and practice.

The influence of this situation upon the settlement of America was great. The *Mayflower* brought to a wild and dangerous country sturdy characters like William Brewster and William Bradford, who left England because they insisted on worshiping God in their bare and solemn meetinghouses instead of attending the services of the Church of England. Less radical were the Puritan leaders who settled at Boston, men like John Winthrop and the Reverend John Cotton. While they lived in England, they had both accepted and administered the sacraments of the national church—but with misgivings, since they criticized its episcopal government, its ritualistic worship, and its failure to repudiate completely the Arminian doctrine of free will in favor of the stern Calvinistic creed of predestination. Despairing of success in their campaign to capture and to purify the Church of England and disappointed also by Parliament's failure to subordinate the King to its control, they had adopted the alternative of building a Puritan Commonwealth in the New World. It is significant that the years 1629–1640, when Charles I ruled without Parliament and supported Archbishop Laud in rigorous enforcement of the religious code, are those of the first large-scale migration to America, a movement of some 20,000 Englishmen to the New England colonies—Plymouth, Massachusetts Bay, Connecticut, New Haven, and Rhode Island.

Puritan migration largely ceased from 1641 to 1660. Once again the politico-religious situation offers an explanation. These were the years of the English Civil War and the rule of Oliver Cromwell. The Puritan Commonwealth was for the time being established at home, and the impulse to emigrate was lacking. It was the turn of royalists and Anglicans to suffer persecution, and some of these found refuge in Virginia and Maryland. When the political wheel took another full turn with the restoration of Charles II in 1660, the colonies once again became a place of asylum for Puritans. The cycle was at length broken by the Glorious Revolution of 1688–1689, which finally established the supremacy of Parliament over the Crown and brought about increasing religious toleration both in law and in practice.

Meanwhile, however, religious motives had played an important role in the settlement of Catholics in Maryland and of Quakers in New Jersey and Pennsylvania. The first Lord Baltimore sought a feudal province in the New World, in part, because his conversion to Roman Catholicism had barred the way to a career of power and influence in England; and he found some of his colonists for Maryland among Catholics dissatisfied with the disabilities and penalties which they suffered in the mother country. Similar motives were at work when the Quaker William Penn promoted the colonization of Pennsylvania.

But from the beginning colonists seeking religious and political change were outnumbered by those drawn to America by other motives. Thirteen years before the settlement of Plymouth unrebellious Anglicans had provided the human material for the settlement of Virginia, and in Maryland and Pennsylvania the coreligionists of the proprietors were from the beginning outnumbered by other elements. Even on the *Mayflower* non-Separatist strangers outnumbered dissenting saints almost two to one, and in New England as a whole only a minority of the immigrants were Puritans in a strict sense. For the rank and file of the newcomers, wherever they settled, the ambition to secure a better livelihood outweighed every other motive. And so it was to be throughout the history of American immigration.

Capital for the early colonization of America was supplied in large part by wealthy merchants and nobles who hoped to derive a profit from trade. The last half of the sixteenth century had witnessed an expansion of English commerce into many new areas, and the participating merchants learned the great advantages of pooling their funds and spreading the risks through the organization of joint-stock companies like the Muscovy and East India Companies. These precedents were followed closely in the organization of the London and Plymouth Companies, and many of the same investors were involved. The new corporations, chartered by James I in 1606, had as their purpose the establishment of trading colonies in America, where sturdy employees would cut down trees for ship timber, extract ship stores like pitch, tar, and turpentine, produce potash—badly needed for English woolen manufacture—smelt iron and copper, grow silk, make wine, catch fish, and perhaps discover gold. Little importance was placed at first on sending farmers to the New World and none at all on wasting valuable ship space on women and children. Preference was given instead to English artisans and miners and to Dutch, Polish, and Italian craftsmen who would teach their skills to the English. The sounder business heads among the stockholders must have realized the speculative character of their investment, but they were induced to take the risk because of the national interests believed to be involved. The planting of colonies, it was hoped, would weaken the imperial monopoly of Spain and Portugal, invigorate the English merchant marine, and lessen British dependence on foreign sources of supply.

The struggling Jamestown colony, planted in 1607 by the London, or Virginia, Company, proved a grievous disappointment. A few samples of pitch and tar, a shipload of iron ore, a few bars of pig iron, and no glass at all constituted the miserable production record of the Virginia industries during these early years. Better days came after 1610. The planting of corn was encouraged, settlers received land grants for their own use, and—at long last—maidens were sent over for the restless colonists to marry. With the introduction of tobacco, moreover, a crop was discovered which promised to bring a living return to the inhabitants and an opportunity for the English investors to recoup their losses. The former made out better than the latter, however, since friction between rival factions within the Company led to annulment of the charter in 1624. The investors are estimated to have lost about £200,000.

Virginia was not the only colony to be financed in its infancy by English investors. A group of London merchants had the dubious business judgment to advance the funds necessary to enable the Pilgrim Fathers to settle in the New World. The arrangement whereby the colonists were to trade, to work, and to fish for the benefit of a joint account to be divided with these financial backers was so unsatisfactory to both parties that the London group agreed within a few years to write off their £7,000 investment in return for £1,800—to be paid on the instalment plan. Other projects for making money out of trade or by exploiting the labor of colonists sent to America had even less success. The Plymouth Company, founded at the same time as the London Company, completely failed. Its successor, the Council for New England, made land grants to the Plymouth Pilgrims and to the Massachusetts Bay Company under circumstances such that its stockholders could have derived no benefit, and its own halfhearted attempts to found settlements were of little consequence. Longest lived and most vigorous of all the joint-stock enterprises was the Massachusetts Bay Company. But in this case the plans of the original incorporators were diverted to other than commercial ends when the corporation was transferred to America in 1630.

Economic motivation in another form can be traced in the ambition of English aristocrats to found great estates in America. In the case of the first and second Lords Baltimore, this impulse took priority over the wish to provide a refuge for fellow Catholics. The original plan was frankly feudal. Land was to provide the basis for wealth and power. The Calverts would derive a princely revenue from their own tenants, and they would make generous grants to other English gentlemen, who, after financing the transportation of peasants, might expect to enjoy a good income from their rent payments. Similar ambitions had previously been entertained by a number of favored individuals who received large estates from the Virginia Company, and the same thinking was evident later in the calculations of the proprietors of the Carolinas, the Jerseys, and Pennsylvania. But plans for establishing baronial estates in America usually led to disappointment. Thousands of Englishmen were willing to try their fortunes in the New World, but few were willing to pass the rest of their days as humble tenants in a new country where land was abundant and cheap.

The economics of early American immigration were revealed by trial and error. Experience soon proved both the unprofitableness of transporting artisans to work for the profit of absentee stockholders and the difficulty of recruiting a stable tenantry for the maintenance of a landlord class. But all the early entrepreneurs discovered that they possessed one golden resource—land. The Virginia Company began assigning niggardly individual holdings of 3 acres in 1613–1614; it gradually liberalized its policy until in 1618 it devised the famous headright system whereby it promised each immigrant who paid his own fare across the Atlantic 50 acres for himself and 50 acres additional for his wife, each child, and each servant he brought with him. So successful was the plan that it was continued by the Crown after the government of Virginia was taken away from the Company in 1624. The second Lord Baltimore profited by this example, and the headright system was followed in Maryland from the beginning. By making individual land grants of 100 acres for each adult member of the settler's household subject only to the payment of a small annual fee, or quitrent, the Calverts discovered that they could attract settlers to their colony and also assure for themselves a respectable source of revenue. Later in the century the proprietors of the Carolinas had recourse to the headright system, although with less success. By shrewd promotion William Penn sold his land instead of giving it away. His revenues were thus derived from both sales and quitrents, but his price was low—about 1*s*. an acre or 100 acres for £5.

New England's experience was not dissimilar. Corporate land ownership proved unsatisfactory in Plymouth and private ownership became the rule after 1627. At Massachusetts Bay individual grants were made from the beginning. Each shareholder in the Company received 200 acres; the colonists who had put no capital into the corporation but who paid for the transportation of their own households received allotments which were smaller but attractive enough to encourage settlement. The exact amount depended upon the decision of the proprietors to whom townships were granted by the colonial assembly.

The settlement of all the English colonies depended to a large extent on recruitment from Englishmen of middling means, those not prosperous enough to be content in the mother country but with sufficient resources to pay for the transportation of their households and to set up as independent farmers in their new homes. Sixteenth-century England had an unusually large number of such discontented members of the lower middle class. The age was one of transition between medieval self-sufficient economy and the modern age of business. Large areas in the nation had been diverted from tillage to wool production. Land for cultivation was scarce and expensive, and tenure was still encumbered by annoying feudal survivals. Increasingly heavy taxes for the support of the poor burdened these farmers at a time when the cost of living was soaring. Gold and silver were pouring into the European economy from the Spanish Empire, and prices were rising rapidly. All groups whose income declined, remained stationary, or rose only moderately felt the pinch. The King, the nobility, and the gentry were hard hit along with the yeomen, tenants, laborers, and artisans. The same economic forces which were spelling hardship to fixed-income groups were of course enriching the merchants. But the expansion of English trade ran an irregular course. Wars on the continent closed important markets to English goods while bad crops simultaneously drove up the price of food. The years 1620–1635 witnessed a serious economic depression in the mother country and had not a little to do with the great migration to America. Economic and politico-religious motives became hopelessly intermixed. John Winthrop's embarrassed finances of 1629 undoubtedly confirmed him in his determination to transfer to Massachusetts, and similar difficulties were influential in the calculations of hundreds of other Puritans, both of the gentry and the lower middle class. Englishmen seeking better economic opportunity oftentimes preferred the West Indies to continental America. Indeed, in 1640 the population of Barbados exceeded that of any of the other colonies. Many of those who had gone to the West Indies, however, later regretted their choice, and in the later seventeenth century there was a steady influx from the overpopulated sugar colonies into the mainland settlements, especially into the Carolinas.

But if there were substantial groups of Englishmen who found it possible to escape from their discouraging status by paying their passage to America, there were many times that number whose economic plight was so desperate that the cost of transportation constituted an obstacle they could never hope to overcome from their own resources. This desperately impoverished class included the real victims of the commercial revolution. The enclosure movement had deprived thousands of small holders of their precarious stake in the soil. Nor was their labor required on the great new sheep ranches in any sufficient quantity to absorb their numbers. The army of the rural unemployed grew alarmingly, and with the interruption of the cloth trade thousands of artisans were also reduced to poverty. Increasing pauperism, vagabondage, and crime led to a widespread conviction that England was overpopulated.

What was needed was some system of assisted emigration, whereby Englishmen too poor to pay their own passage could get to America at someone else's expense. The desperate need for labor in the New World soon provided a mechanism. Individuals willing to enter upon a labor contract, or indenture, binding them to work for a stipulated term of years readily found masters willing to pay their fare across the Atlantic. The Virginia Company itself undertook to transport such servants under its charter of 1609. A servant over ten years of age who went to Virginia and served for seven years was entitled not only to his transportation and maintenance but to 100 acres of land. A further step was taken in 1617. By the policy of "particular plantations" the Virginia Company offered large tracts of land, or "hundreds," to organized groups of Englishmen who agreed to settle servants in the tracts at their own expense. Fifty such patents, each providing for the transportation of from one hundred to four hundred men, were issued during the next four years. The servants under this scheme served from three to eight years and eventually received 25 acres of land. But with the initiation of the headright system, previously described, a simpler and more effective method of facilitating immigration was provided. For each servant that the planter imported, he received 50 acres of land. Indentured servants thus recruited proved the main reliance of Virginia agriculture throughout most of the seventeenth century. The linking of headright with the importation of servile labor was later extended to Maryland and to the Carolinas.

The headright system eventually led to many abuses. The planter who obtained an indentured servant was usually more interested in getting labor than in receiving a land grant—particularly during the latter part of the seventeenth century when the land available for such grants was likely to be many miles away on the frontier. The headright certificates were accordingly signed over to speculators or to ship captains who trafficked in servants. They held the lands off the market or offered them for sale at high prices. This aroused such vast discontent on the part of actual settlers that both Virginia and Maryland eventually abandoned headright and substituted a land policy based on cash sale. But this did not interrupt the importation of laborers. Ship captains were the entrepreneurs in the trade; they secured shiploads of prospective servants, brought them to the New World, and auctioned them off to the planters. The workers thus secured were called "redemptioners."

The redemptioner system was as characteristic of the middle colonies as of the South. Sea captains engaged in this lucrative trade soon found that the poor of other nations might be recruited for sale even more readily than the English. In New England the situation was somewhat different since the elders opposed the large-scale entry of laborers of indiscriminate antecedents. But this did not mean that there were no indentured servants in the area. On the contrary, even the humble *Mayflower* saints brought a number of such persons with them, and elsewhere in New England a very substantial proportion of the immigrants came over at the expense of masters for whom they had to work for a term of years.

Not all of the indentured servants came of their own volition. Many were transported upon orders from the legal authorities. The apprenticeship of orphaned children was a standard practice in England, and numerous parishes disposed of their child wards by sending them to the colonies. Adult paupers were often similarly dealt with, and thousands of convicts were transported to the colonies as a punishment. The majority of these were not hardened criminals but unfortunates who had resorted to petty theft because of their desperate poverty. Since the criminal code of the mother country was of barbaric harshness, the sentence of transportation to the colonies often represented the impulse of a humane judge to save some wretch from the hangman. Many of the transported prisoners of the seventeenth century, moreover, were merely political offenders—Irishmen or Scotchmen who had fought against Cromwell, or Cromwellian soldiers after the Restoration. Both political prisoners and petty criminals provided a good proportion of salvageable human material for the building of a new nation. Decidedly less welcome were the murderers and other really vicious characters whom the English authorities insisted on dumping in the colonies, particularly in Maryland and Virginia. Frequent colonial protests were raised against this practice, but it was never completely abandoned throughout the colonial period. The most unfortunate immigrants were the victims of kidnaping. So lively was the demand for identured servants that a diabolical business developed of spiriting away simple victims for sale as servants in the New World. The children of the poor provided the easiest prey and as many as 10,000 are estimated to have thus been kidnaped in a single year during the reign of Charles II.

But servants who were sent to America against their will were far outnumbered by servants who came voluntarily. The bargain was not an unattractive one by seventeenth-century standards. As demand for labor increased, terms of indenture became more lenient. Whereas in the early days periods of service as long as from seven to ten years were common, after 1650 the usual term was about four years. When the servant's period of indenture had been completed, he was a free man with many opportunities. His master granted him "freedom dues," clothing, tools, and a store of food. He might become a hired farm hand, and wages, if not high by our standards, were decidedly so as compared with those prevailing at the time in England. He might become an artisan in one of the colonial towns. Very frequently he became an independent farmer, since freedom dues in Pennsylvania and the southern colonies usually included 50 acres of land granted either by the master or by the colony. Even where this practice did not prevail, land, particularly on the frontier, was not difficult to acquire.

By 1715 the first great migration of Englishmen to America was over. Political and religious issues were not very bitterly contested in the eighteenth century, and expanding industry absorbed the bulk of those who lost their stake in the soil through the continuing process of agricultural change. Reflecting the new situation, government policy now discouraged rather than facilitated emigration from the mother country. Throughout the balance of the colonial period the movement of Englishmen to new homes in America was largely confined to mercantile agents, parsons, doctors, and lawyers seeking new fields for their professional talents, and to the younger sons of the rural gentry hopeful of founding new family estates. Highly desirable though most of these eighteenth-century English immigrants were, they came as individuals and were far outnumbered by the newly arrived from other countries.

The Importation of Slaves

Next to the English the largest group added to the American population during the colonial period were African Negroes. The first 20 to come were brought by a Dutch sea captain who sold his human cargo to Virginia planters in 1619. Little is known of these humble newcomers; they may have served a term of years and earned their freedom like white indentured servants of the day, since not all Negroes imported into the colonies during the seventeenth century were treated as slaves. A small class of free Negroes appeared early in the century and continued to grow slowly throughout the colonial period. But a much different destiny awaited the vast majority of black immigrants. They and many generations of their descendants were fated to pass their entire lives in slavery.

Between 1619 and 1680 Negroes were imported into all the English colonies, but even in the South they were few in number. The slowness with which the institution of slavery took root reflected the influence of economic factors rather than moral scruples. During these years the slave trade was largely monopolized by the Dutch, who concentrated their activities in the Spanish colonies. The number of Negroes offered for sale in the English North American ports was small. So long as these circumstances prevailed, the English colonists continued to depend on white indentured servants. Even in Virginia this class was three times as numerous as Negro slaves in 1671.

After 1680 the situation was greatly altered. Wars with the English and the French had weakened the power of the Dutch, and the slave trade now became a field for large-scale exploitation by the Royal African Company, an English joint-stock enterprise. This company attempted to enforce a monopoly, but the traffic attracted many interlopers. The results were disastrous to the stockholders but highly welcome to American planters who wanted an abundant supply of labor. The unsavory business was given further stimulus when in 1713 the Treaty of Utrecht gave the asiento, or slave-trading monopoly with the Spanish Empire, to the British. Enterprising New Englanders, moreover, took an active part in the eighteenth-century trade.

Demand kept pace with increased supply. Sugar production in the British West Indies was already dependent upon the exploitation of slave labor on large plantations; the South Carolina rice growers utilized similar methods from the beginning. In Virginia and Maryland the transition from white servitude to Negro slavery was more gradual. Yet from the economic point of view the inducement to make the change was overwhelming. Indentured servants were relatively expensive. They were scarcely acclimated to the American climate and broken in to their duties when their terms of service were at an end. The planters then had to provide freedom dues for their old laborers and to undertake the expense and inconvenience of replacing them with new and inexperienced hands. In buying slaves, the planters made a somewhat larger initial investment; but with reasonable luck they were assured of many years of dependable labor, and all children born of the female slaves became the owner's property. For twenty years after 1680 the importation of slaves into the tobacco colonies showed a significant increase, and after 1700 the annual influx was huge except during periods when economic life was disrupted by war. Out of a total Virginia population of 114,000 in 1730, 30,000, or 26 per cent, were Negroes. Sixty years before, the blacks had composed but 5 per cent of the population.

This immigration trend was confined to the South. Slavery continued to be legal in the northern and middle colonies, but for the type of agriculture practiced in these areas free labor was a much better investment. Negroes were bought and sold to serve as coachmen and household servants, but the number so employed was never great. Only in the large-scale cultivation of tobacco, rice, and indigo did the slave system become thoroughly established during the colonial period.

New Population by Conquest

English imperial statesmen appraising their American empire in the mid-seventeenth century were not happy to see New England and the southern colonies separated by a belt of strategic territory ruled by their rivals, the Dutch. They were envious of New Netherland's flourishing fur trade and distressed to have Dutch ships plying out of New Amsterdam and enriching themselves on the trade of the English colonies. An opportunity to liquidate this nuisance was soon at hand. When in 1664—for the second time in the century—war broke out between England and Holland, a British fleet entered the port of New Amsterdam and compelled the surrender of the entire area. In 1673 during the third Anglo-Dutch war the Dutch reoccupied their former colony briefly but soon lost it again—this time forever.

The population which thus fell under British rule was not large, probably no more than eight thousand. Many of these, moreover, were of English or of some other non-Dutch stock. Yet, small though it was, the Dutch element was destined to have important influence on American life. Families bearing Dutch names were to have unusual prominence in the political and social life of the most populous city and state in the United States. Dutch words became a part of the American language, and Dutch styles an important influence in American domestic architecture. Secondary migration, moreover, carried the Dutch into New England, New Jersey, Pennsylvania, Maryland, Virginia, and the Carolinas.

The Dutch had begun to colonize New Netherland forty years before the English conquest. The first settlers came over in 1624 as the servants of the Dutch West India Company, a joint-stock enterprise resembling the great English companies of the day. The plan to establish forts and trading posts in the Hudson River area was subsidiary to other projects contemplated by the Company—namely, to dominate the African slave trade, to found colonies in South America, and to raid the trade of the Spanish and the Portuguese with whom the Dutch were at war. This dispersion of interests was a serious handicap to the New Netherland colony. The first 30 families sent over were divided into several settlements, of which Fort Amsterdam on Manhattan Island, Fort Orange at the present site of Albany, and Fort Nassau on the Delaware River were the most

FIG. 1. *De Peyster Boy with Deer.* Artist unknown. A charming representation of Dutch colonial aristocracy. (*Courtesy of the New York Historical Society.*)

important. These garrisons were reinforced with more personnel over the next few years, but despite the inducement of individual land grants the soldiers and Company servants usually returned to Europe after their term of service was over. In 1629 the patroon system was inaugurated. Wealthy individuals who would commit themselves to transporting 50 adult immigrants within four years were granted large estates wherein they might exact rents, exploit monopolies, and dispense justice to their tenants. But only a few patroonships were actually attempted, and all but one of them—that of Kiliaen Van Rensselaer in what is today Albany County—eventually failed. Feudal tenantry was no more attractive to Dutch farmers than to English.

The population grew very slowly. In addition to a conservative land system, the arbitrary government exercised by the Dutch West India Company and its resident governors created great resentment. The folly of one of the governors, moreover, involved the colony in a desperate struggle with the Indians. With these conditions prevailing in America and with the political, religious, and economic situation in the homeland relatively good, the wonder is that New Netherland gained any population at all. That it did so is attributable, in part, to its fertile soil. Many Dutch farms, or *bouweries*, were established on Manhattan Island, Long Island, Staten Island, and along the lower Hudson. Many New Englanders, moreover, migrated into Dutch territory and took up land on Long Island or in the short river valleys east of the Hudson, often without legal warrant. Even more important were the opportunities for trade available at New Amsterdam. Its magnificent harbor with a great river leading into the heart of the fur country was an advantage which could only be partially canceled out by the shortsighted policies of the Dutch West India Company. Small though the Manhattan settlement was when Peter Stuyvesant became governor in 1646, its fascinating cosmopolitan destiny was already foreshadowed. Eighteen languages were spoken, and the population included Dutch, Flemings, Walloons, French, Danes, Norwegians, Swedes, English, Irish, Germans, Poles, Bohemians, Portuguese, and Italians. There was a small but prosperous group of Spanish and Portuguese Jews and there were numerous Negroes, both free and slave.

Meanwhile Sweden, then one of the great powers of Europe, had also experimented in colonization. The South Company, chartered in 1637, received a land grant on the shores of Delaware Bay and founded Fort Christina in 1638 on the present site of Wilmington. From this beginning New Sweden expanded to include several settlements in areas which are now within the states of Delaware, Pennsylvania, Maryland, and New Jersey. Settlers were hard to secure and were recruited in large part from army deserters, debtors, and unfortunates caught poaching or stealing wood in the royal forests. A substantial portion were Finns. The Dutch West India Company looked upon the Swedes as interlopers but refrained from the use of force while Holland and Sweden were allies in the Thirty Years War. But in 1655 a Dutch expedition of seven vessels appeared off Fort Christina and the Swedes, recognizing the inevitable, surrendered without bloodshed. The Swedes and Finns who thus passed under the rule of the Dutch numbered perhaps no more than five hundred, but they were a sturdy stock and left an indelible influence on the area where they had settled. Moreover, enterprising individuals of Swedish ancestry moved from the Delaware to other regions in such numbers that by 1790 Swedish surnames were to be found scattered throughout the colonies from New England to the Carolinas.

Less than a decade after the conquest of New Sweden, the whole region between the Hudson River and Delaware Bay fell under the rule of the British. Enterprising Englishmen secured great land grants, and thousands of settlers moved into the region both from the mother country and from the other colonies. But the non-English elements had had two generations to establish themselves and they could never be completely submerged by the newcomers. For over a century northern New Jersey and southeastern New York were dotted by communities where Dutch was still the only language in common use and where Dutch folk-ways persisted with little change. The other non-English groups were smaller and less tenacious, but their identity was by no means lost. From the beginning, therefore, the middle colonies were to be distinguished from the rest of British North America by the rich diversity of national origins from which their population and culture derived. And nascent American civilization was destined to be fed from many other non-English sources through the immigration trends of the next century.

Exiles from France

The totalitarian impulse which impelled Louis XIV to persecute the Protestant minority among his subjects benefited France's neighbors. Louis's policy, reaching its climax in the revocation of the Edict of Nantes in 1685, resulted in an exodus of thousands of Huguenots. Countries enlightened enough to offer refuge to these exiles were invariably rewarded by the stimulus given to trade and industry, since the newcomers included some of the thriftiest merchants and best skilled artisans of Europe. The British North American colonies received an important share of these talented migrants. Several thousand of them, sailing either from France or from some other European country where they had lived for a while, made their way to America.

In 1686 a group of Huguenots undertook the hazards of frontier life on a grant of land in what is today Oxford, Massachusetts, near Worcester. The project failed because of the hostility of the Indians, and some of the settlers removed to Boston, where a few Huguenots were already living. Others went to Rhode Island, where they hoped to develop vineyards, but here too they suffered hardship and disappointment because of the jealousy of their neighbors. The Huguenots who sought refuge in New England soon dispersed and were speedily Anglicized. Such important eighteenth-century Massachusetts figures as Paul Revere, Peter Faneuil, and James Bowdoin were descendants of this French stock.

Even before the revocation of the Edict of Nantes Huguenots had begun to come to the middle colonies in significant numbers. There were French among the earliest settlers of New Amsterdam, where a French church was established in 1659 and proclamations were frequently issued in French as well as in Dutch. In 1689 New Rochelle was founded as a Huguenot colony in Westchester County and remained a center of French culture for many generations. Even more persistent was the French influence at New Paltz in Ulster County, where a number of exiles founded an important Huguenot settlement. Secondary migration carried the French from New York into New Jersey and Pennsylvania. The latter colony, moreover, received many such exiles direct from Europe.

In the South the Huguenots settled at numerous points, but it was in South Carolina that they attained greatest wealth and influence. Charles II and the titled proprietors of the colony encouraged settlement by French Protestants with the expectation that they would use their technical knowledge to develop the production of silk, wine, and olive oil. In this the proprietors were disappointed, for the Huguenots, with characteristic acumen and energy, turned instead to commerce and to the growing of rice and indigo. Indeed, several of the key improvements in the growth of the great South Carolina staples were developed by the French colonists. Huguenots were prominent from the beginning in the society of Charleston, and their plantations were so numerous along the Santee River that the region became known as French Santee. During the eighteenth century between one-tenth and one-fifth of the white population of the colony was of French origin. Along with other South Carolinians, moreover, the Huguenot element participated in the settlement of Georgia, North Carolina, and Tennessee.

The Huguenot influx was of short duration. In 1689 France and England became involved in hostilities that continued with only a brief interruption until 1713. Anti-French feeling was rampant in the colonies, and the fact that the Huguenots were religious and political exiles from their mother country did not exempt them from the suspicion of their neighbors. They became the victims of petty persecution, and this fact, together with the circumstance that those most eager to come had already done so, reduced Huguenot migration to America to negligible proportions after 1700. But enough French had entered the colonies to provide a sprinkling of French family names in every area from Maine to Georgia. The Huguenots did not constitute a distinct group in the population anywhere for very long. They tended to adopt English as their language, to Anglicize their names, to intermarry with their English neighbors, and generally to accommodate themselves to their new environment. In New England they became Congregationalist, in the South they turned Anglican, and in the middle colonies they gravitated to whatever creed was locally dominant. Few immigrant groups have been assimilated so quickly or so completely.

Not all French newcomers to British North America were Protestants. During the eighteenth century the coastal towns offered opportunities which attracted a considerable number of French doctors, professors, dancing masters, wigmakers, and the like. The English colonies also secured occasional immigrants from France's imperial possessions in Canada and the West Indies. More important was the influx of Acadians, which resulted from Britain's drastic wartime measure of 1755 deporting thousands of Catholic residents of Nova Scotia. Some of these survived the hardships of their removal to become permanent residents of the English colonies along the Atlantic seaboard, although more went to Louisiana, to France, or, eventually, back to Nova Scotia. The contest for empire had meanwhile resulted in scattered French settlements in areas ultimately to be included within the boundaries of the United States. Such was the case at New Orleans, along the lower Mississippi, and also in French frontier outposts in the future states of Michigan, Illinois, Wisconsin, Indiana, and Missouri.

The Irish and the Scotch

Far outnumbering the French were immigrants from Ireland. Life in their mother land was rendered difficult by many circumstances. Centuries of conflict between English kings and Celtic chieftains had finally subjected the country to alien rule, and wholesale confiscation of the land had made most of the Irish the impoverished tenants of English landlords. This Anglo-Irish aristocracy were further alienated from the Celtic-Irish peasantry by the fact that the former were mostly Anglican while the latter persisted in devotion to the Roman Catholic Church despite the legal disabilities thereby incurred. During the seventeenth century the situation was further complicated when large numbers of Scotch Presbyterians were encouraged to settle in Ulster. The new element suffered many bitter experiences. Their Protestantism did not save them from legislation excluding all but Anglicans from civil and military office. Like the Celtic-Irish, the Scotch-Irish soon learned to hate the political and religious system of their adopted home. But it was the country's strait-jacketed economic life that finally impelled thousands to leave. When Ireland developed a flourishing livestock industry, jealous English and Scotch landlords exerted sufficient pressure to have Irish cattle, sheep, meat, and dairy products excluded from England and Scotland. When the Irish turned to textile manufacture, the English Parliament prohibited the export of their woolens to any other country. Even in the cultivation of the soil the Scotch-Irish, like the Celtic-Irish, were exploited. In 1717 and in other years when thousands of long-term leases came due, tenants were confronted with demands from absentee landlords for double or treble their former rent. Those who refused to pay were evicted.

Celtic-Irish immigration to America began so unobtrusively that it is difficult to trace. Maryland colonial records show a number of Murphys, Kellys, and other persons with Celtic names living in that region before 1680, and a similar study reveals that by 1700 the Irish were already present in Massachusetts and other colonies. Even though small, this Celtic immigration of the seventeenth century was important. Since the colonial birth rate was so high that the population is calculated to have doubled every twenty-five years, 1,000 immigrants of a particular stock in 1700 would contribute as large a number of descendants to the future American population as 4,000 in 1750. During the eighteenth century, moreover, the rate of Celtic immigration increased sharply as the traffic in indentured servants became more highly organized and as energetic sea captains found it increasingly easy to round up their human cargoes in ports accessible to the impoverished Irish. Almost all the Celtic immigrants came in this humble capacity.

There were no group migrations to plant new Tipperarys in the wilderness, where Gaelic would be spoken and the Catholic Church would be the center of village life. The colonial Irish came as individuals, were widely dispersed, and accepted the customs and for the most part even the religion of the dominant English groups.

The case of the Scotch-Irish was different. They began to come to America in large numbers during the second decade of the seventeenth century. From 1714 to 1720, 54 ships arrived in New England from Ireland, and an even greater number landed in Delaware River ports, in eastern Maryland, and in South Carolina. Scotch-Irish immigration continued to be large throughout the balance of the colonial period, increasing and diminishing in volume in response to economic conditions in Ulster—especially in response to the falling in of leases and fluctuations in the linen industry. Although the Scotch-Irish like the Celtic-Irish usually entered America as indentured servants, their movements are much easier to trace. There was considerable group migration under ministers who made advance arrangements for their congregations to serve out their indentures in particular American localities.

The Ulster Presbyterians were for a time under the illusion that they would find their readiest welcome in Calvinist New England. But they encountered much intolerance and prejudice. Cotton Mather preached against the "formidable attempts of Satan and his Sons to Unsettle us," and the attempt of the newcomers to build a church at Worcester was frustrated by a mob which burned it down under cover of night. The Scotch-Irish found better opportunities along the New England frontier, where they established such settlements as Colerain and Pelham, Massachusetts, Londonderry, New Hampshire, and Wiscasset, Maine.

The greatest influx of Scotch-Irish was into Pennsylvania. Not only was the tradition of this colony more tolerant of strangers, but its climate and soil promised a better livelihood. Both their independent spirit and their poverty impelled the Scotch-Irish to quit as soon as possible the settled eastern counties where land was expensive. They moved on to the frontier, often squatting illegally on unoccupied land belonging to the Penn family or to eastern speculators. These proclivities, together with their aptitude for stirring up trouble with the Indians, brought upon their heads the denunciations of conservative colonists of older stock. But undeterred, the frontiersmen continued to build their cabins, to clear the land, and to found new villages. They moved along the Susquehanna River to its junction with the Cumberland Valley. The push of settlement was then southwestward across the southern boundary of Pennsylvania, through the back counties of Maryland, and down into the fertile Shenandoah Valley in western Virginia. Eventually the movement carried into the Carolinas, Tennessee, and Kentucky.

Wherever they went, the Scotch-Irish carried with them a distinctive way of life. Presbyterian churches dotted the frontier from Maine to Georgia, and the newcomers were strict in their observance of the Sabbath, but dourness did not constrain their social intercourse. No less than the Celtic-Irish did they love weddings, wakes, fairs, and whisky.

The eighteenth century witnessed also a sizable immigration from Scotland. The Act of Union of 1708, terminating the nation's nominal independence, was a boon to Scotch merchants and professional men, who now shared in all the opportunities offered by the British Empire. The Scotch commercial agent, customs official, clergyman, and schoolmaster became a familiar figure in the American colonies. Such Scotchmen were usually Lowlanders and somewhat Anglicized. The Highlanders continued to live in their ancestral clans until the coercive measures which the English took following the rebellions of 1715 and 1745 drove a considerable number into exile. Most of these colonized in the mountainous districts of North and South Carolina. About four hundred Highlanders were settled by Sir William Johnson on his great estate in the Mohawk River region of New York.

The Colonial Germans

The seventeenth and eighteenth centuries brought troubles of many kinds to Germany. From 1618 to 1648 the country was convulsed by the Thirty Years War, a religious struggle which broadened into a great international conflict. This war, even more than most, brought desolation in its train. The population was decimated, the countryside laid waste, and trade paralyzed. Recovery was difficult and so painfully slow as to require generations. Nor was this the end, for more than once the ambition of Louis XIV again turned western Germany into a battlefield.

The political and religious situations were equally bad. Hundreds of petty nobles exercised complete sovereignty, exacting heavy tolls and taxes and persecuting subjects who refused to accept whatever religion had been established. The religious persecution bore with particular gravity upon the Protestants of the Palatinate, which was now under Catholic rule, and upon the numerous radical Protestants whose nonconformity subjected them to penalties even in Lutheran and Calvinist states. Germany had had an unusual number of minor sects ever since the Reformation, and during the chaotic seventeenth century such groups won many new converts.

Thousands of Germans were impelled to emigrate from their homeland. Religious and political motives played an important part, but once again the primary impetus seems to have been economic. Feudal land tenure still prevailed and the peasantry was heavily burdened. Crop failures and local famines were frequent. To farmers thus harassed, the fertile and cheap land of America had an overpowering attraction. The enterprising William Penn was aware of this. As early as 1681 an intriguing prospectus entitled *Some Account of the Province of Pennsylvania in America* was translated into German and widely circulated.

In 1683 this advertising had its first result when a small group of Mennonites from the Rhineland led by Francis Daniel Pastorius settled at Germantown near Philadelphia—a center to which Germans soon began to come in increasing numbers.

German immigration became large-scale a generation later. After a succession of hard winters, conditions in the Palatinate became so desperate that a great exodus resulted in 1709. Over thirteen thousand impoverished Germans made their way down the Rhine to Rotterdam and thence to England. The British government headed by the tender-hearted Queen Anne gave temporary assistance. The newcomers were sheltered in barns, warehouses, and tents and were kept from starvation by private charity and public doles. But to find permanent homes for these displaced persons was a problem to strain the imagination of the statesmen. Over two thousand Catholics were sent back to Germany. Of the Protestants who remained, several thousand were permanently settled in England, about four thousand more were colonized in Ireland, and about six hundred were assisted in emigrating to North Carolina, where they founded New Bern.

A novel project resulted in the transportation of some three thousand Palatines to the colony of New York—the largest single movement of immigrants during the colonial period. Mercantilist statesmanship had formulated a plan whereby these Germans were to work off their indebtedness to the British government by manufacturing tar and naval stores and thus free Britain from dependence on the Baltic countries. The Germans involved in this transaction had a most unhappy experience. Their passage to America was unusually painful even for those days. Overcrowding, poor food, and insufficient water bred ship fever so that almost eight hundred died on the ocean or soon after arrival. The experiment in gathering naval stores proved a costly failure because of the bad administration of Governor Robert Hunter and the avarice of Robert Livingston, who sold the government 6,000 acres of indifferent land from his manor on the east bank of the Hudson and then secured a profitable contract to feed the workers. After two years the project was abandoned, and the Palatines were left to shift for themselves. Most of them settled down to successful farming along the Hudson. But the more adventurous pushed out to the frontier, where they founded a number of villages on land purchased from the Indians in the fertile Schoharie Valley. Here they prospered until they were once again victimized through the unholy alliance existing between the colonial government and the land speculators. Despite the indignant protests of the German frontiersmen the Schoharie region was granted to a syndicate of Albany proprietors. Some of the Palatines resigned themselves to the indignity of paying rent for land which they believed they owned themselves; others sought out a new frontier along the Mohawk Valley, where they became successful farmers.

But a small company of the Schoharie Palatines under the leadership of two remarkable men, Johann Conrad Weiser and his son, Conrad Weiser, left the New York colony in disgust and made their way south by the Susquehanna River into Pennsylvania. This group eventually found new homes in Berks County, thus terminating the migration which had begun in the Rhineland almost twenty years before. The tribulations of the Palatines were well known through letters and reports sent back to Germany. So striking was the contrast between the fair treatment which they experienced in Pennsylvania and their heartless exploitation in New York that most subsequent German immigration directed itself toward the former colony and avoided the latter. Unenlightened government and greedy land speculation so retarded the growth of the New York colony that at the end of the colonial period it ranked only seventh in population—behind Virginia, Pennsylvania, Massachusetts, North Carolina, Maryland, and Connecticut.

Quite independently of the Palatines the tempo of German immigration into Pennsylvania was much accelerated after 1710. German-speaking Mennonites from Switzerland settled in Lancaster County and were followed by Dunkards, Schwenkfeldians, and Moravians. But group immigration—although interesting and important in transferring distinctive sects to America and forming nuclei around which enclaves of German-derived culture have persisted to the present—had less significance numerically than the individual and family-type immigration that resulted from the great eighteenth-century traffic in indentured servants. Land speculators and shipowners prepared pamphlets in German portraying the advantages of life in America in terms so extravagant and seductive as to indicate that their authors would have nothing to learn from the writers of twentieth-century advertising copy. Agents, called "newlanders," traveled through German and Swiss villages, displaying their fancy clothes and gold watch chains as visual evidence of the wealth to be easily acquired in the New World. They received a commission for each immigrant whom they recruited and, in addition, made a good thing out of escorting immigrant companies down the Rhine to Rotterdam. Indeed, the unfortunate travelers were exploited on every stage of their journey. Many had saved their money in hopes of paying their own ship passage and buying land in America. But after the exactions of the newlanders, of the petty sovereigns who charged them tolls, and of the sharpers who sold them food and shelter, few had money left to pay their fare across the Atlantic. This suited the interests of shipowners, since there was much more profit in selling redemptioners than in merely collecting passage money. Indeed, the sea captains themselves were experts in cheating the immigrants out of the last of their savings to insure that they would arrive in America penniless. This cruel exploitation coupled with the overcrowding and disease which prevailed aboard the ships made the eighteenth-century traffic in servants scarcely more humane than the slave trade.

Nevertheless, the flow of immigration from Germany continued. Many of the newcomers had been warned of the hazards of the passage by letters from America and by counterpropaganda against emigration put out by the German princes. Yet the burdens of life at home were so heavy, the attraction of cheap, fertile land so compelling, that thousands took the great gamble. Pennsylvania was the destination of the great majority. In 1766 Benjamin Franklin estimated that German emigrants constituted one-third the population of the colony, and statistics from the latter part of the century tend to confirm this. Like the Scotch-Irish, the Germans found their land of promise near the frontier where land was cheap. They settled particularly in such south-central counties as Lancaster, Berks, and Montgomery. Since their further movement westward was barred by the Appalachian mountain ranges, they turned south and found new homes in western Maryland, in the Shenandoah Valley of Virginia, and in western North Carolina. Somewhat less adventurous and restless than the Scotch-Irish, they usually moved into areas which had already been opened up. They purchased the partially cleared land of the first pioneers and settled down to farming, while bolder frontiersmen, frequently Scotch-Irish, pushed on into the wilderness. Although the colony of Pennsylvania was the funnel through which most of this migration flowed, smaller numbers of Germans went directly to northern New Jersey, to eastern Virginia, to North Carolina, and to the southern frontier in South Carolina and Georgia.

Americans in 1790

Soon after the inauguration of George Washington, data were compiled for the first census of the United States. By present standards the work was incomplete and inadequate, but it provides, nevertheless, an important source for studying the infant nation's heritage from its colonial past. Prudently refraining from any attempt to list the Indians, the enumerators counted white and black Americans to a total of 3,929,214. Of these we may estimate that about 50 per cent were of English stock; 19.3 per cent were Negroes; 7.9 per cent were of Irish origin (about three-fifths Celtic, the rest Scotch-Irish and Anglo-Irish); 6.7 per cent were Scotch; 7 per cent German; 2.8 per cent Dutch; 1.4 per cent French; 0.6 per cent Swedish.[1] The data upon which this estimate is based are not very satisfactory, and some of the details may be incorrect. For example, the relative size of the Scotch-Irish and Celtic-Irish groups has been a matter of

[1] Conclusion based on American Council of Learned Societies, "Report of the Committee on Linguistic and National Stocks in the Population of the United States," *Annual Report of the American Historical Association for the Year 1931* (Washington, 1932), I, 124–125. The analysis there given is based exclusively on the white population, which is estimated to have consisted in 1790 of the following national stocks: English 60.9 per cent, Scotch 8.3, Ulster Irish 6, Free State Irish 3.7, German 8.7, Dutch 3.4, French 1.7, Swedish 0.7, unassigned 6.6. Note that the authors of this study do not consider the whole Ulster stock to have been Scotch-Irish; on the contrary, they assume that more than one-third of it was Celtic in origin (*ibid.*, 264–267). They estimate that 6.3 per cent of the white population of 1790 was of Celtic origin—a conclusion at wide variance with that of most students of colonial America who have assumed Celtic immigration to have been much smaller than Scotch-Irish.

most heated controversy. But at least two comments may be safely made. The English element was sufficiently more numerous than any other to ensure the general predominance of the English language and English institutions. Nevertheless, the fact that about one-half the population was non-English gave assurance that the new nation would modify its English heritage in thousands of interesting ways.

Chapter 2. Conquering the Soil

Colonial America was a land of villages and farms. Philadelphia, the largest city, had only 30,000 inhabitants in 1775 and only three other towns had populations of over 10,000. Probably 90 per cent of the population derived its principal livelihood from the soil. But this fact by no means reduced American life to a single pattern. Soil and climate conditions dictated striking differences in the agricultural evolution of New England, the middle colonies, and the South.

Learning from the Indians

The first English settlers brought over with them agricultural traditions that were often wasteful and irrational. Even in England urban markets for farm products were still limited and the incentive to get the utmost in production was lacking. Of agricultural science there was practically none, and farmers, large and small, cultivated the soil in accordance with the rules laid down by immemorial custom and superstition. In the typical agricultural village of the Old World the farmer's cottages were clustered together near the church, the mill, and the manor house, and the principal crops were grown in great open fields some distance away. The land of the individual farmer was held not in a single consolidated farm but in several separate strips interspersed with the strips of his neighbors. The system left little opportunity for experimentation, since each man had almost of necessity to grow the same crops in the same way as his fellows. The great wooden plows were cumbersome and inefficient, and sowing broadcast was wasteful of seed and permitted no cultivation to remove the weeds from the growing crops. Harvesting and threshing methods were equally conservative, having progressed little beyond the laborious use of the sickle and the flail depicted upon the walls of ancient Egyptian tombs. The principal crops were wheat and rye for bread, barley for beer, and oats for the animals. Peas and a few other vegetables were grown, although their important nutritional function was scarcely appreciated.

English villagers took miserable care of their livestock. The common pasture in which the cattle of the whole community grazed was a bad institution from almost every point of view. Breeding was entirely haphazard, and no individual's stock could be better than the mongrel type of the village. Even in summertime the animals found little to eat and were deplorably thin. Since nothing was available for winter feeding save the inadequate hay crop from the village meadow, many of the animals had to be slaughtered each fall. Scant shelter from the winter storms was provided for those that were kept. Under such conditions the cows produced milk that was small in amount and poor in quality and beef that was tough and unpalatable. They even failed to yield enough manure to maintain the fertility of the arable lands, nor was the little that they did provide utilized as it should have been. Instead, the great fields had to be restored through a rude rotation system that required one-third of the land to lie fallow each year. Sheep, swine, and horses were nondescript in breed and poorly tended.

Inefficient though they were, these English agricultural methods permitted the villagers to live without fear of starvation, except in a few bad crop years, and even to grow enough surplus to feed London and other English towns. But the transference of these traditions to the New World involved serious difficulties. The importance of the matter was scarcely appreciated by the planners of the Virginia colony. They sent over colonists who were either gentlemen, unused to manual effort of any kind, or laborers unacquainted with farming. Moreover, the site of the Jamestown settlement was poorly chosen for agriculture. The earliest attempt to grow wheat failed, and the colony would not have survived its first winter except for purchases of corn from the Indians. As it was, more than half the original settlers succumbed to malnutrition and disease. Even this grim experience, however, did not adequately underline the urgency of postponing every other activity until the colonists were successful in growing their own food. Instead, the energies of the settlers during the next year were still diverted to gathering pitch and iron ore and to exploring. A planting of wheat and peas was made, but the results were disappointing. American conditions were different from English, and the colonists sowed their seed at the wrong time and in the wrong kind of soil. Once again the winter brought hunger and misery, only partly alleviated by purchases of corn from the natives.

In the spring of 1609 the colonists finally condescended to take lessons in growing maize, or Indian corn, from two savage captives. The agricultural heritage from Europe had proved inadequate to keep the English pioneers alive; with immense profit for the future they now borrowed extensively from the agricultural tradition of native America.

Indian agriculture, like European, was based on custom and tradition rather than on science; hence it was sometimes irrational and wasteful. But it had the important advantage of long adaptation to the American environment. Squaws cleared the land by girdling the trees and allowing them to die. Breaking up the earth with crooked sticks or primitive hoes, they formed hills about three or four feet apart. In each hill they planted from four to six kernels of corn and oftentimes two or three beans as well. The growing plants were carefully cultivated; the hills were kept free of weeds, and the soil was piled up around the tender stalks. A single field was used for as many years as good crops could be grown, and when the soil showed evidences of exhaustion, the site was abandoned and a new field was cleared. Continued over many generations, this process had resulted in the clearing of much of the land on which the English eventually settled—fortunately for them.

Corn grown in the Indian manner was destined to save the Virginia colony. But salvation was not assured until after the settlement had gone through its most terrible experience. The crops grown in 1609, even in combination with the stores brought in from England, were insufficient to carry the settlers through the next winter, and this time the hostility of the Indians prevented the usual purchases. Wholesale starvation resulted, and in the spring of 1610 the discouraged colonists were in the process of abandoning the colony when Lord Delaware, their new governor, arrived with supplies and new immigrants. Under Delaware and under Sir Thomas Dale, who arrived in 1611, the cultivation of corn was undertaken in grim earnest. Impatient with the difficulty of clearing their own lands, the English seized the fields of the Indians near the mouth of the James and founded the new settlement of Henrico.

The livestock situation also required drastic steps. Horses, pigs, and chickens had been brought over in the first crossing, but practically all of them had been killed and eaten by the colonists during the starving time. Delaware and Dale met this problem by importing wild hogs from the Bermudas and cattle, horses, and poultry from England. The new stock multiplied—thanks to a favorable environment and to harsh laws forbidding, under penalty of death, any slaughtering without the governor's consent. The enlarged herds, the hundreds of acres now devoted to the growing of corn, the beginnings of individual land holding, and the gradual abandonment of the Company's industrial projects all contributed to the attainment of self-sufficiency. By 1616 the situation had so far altered that the colonists were not only feeding themselves but selling surplus corn to the Indians.

The Plymouth settlers learned the same lesson as the Virginians, although with less delay. Since the New Englanders arrived far too late in the fall of 1620 to do any planting, hunger and disease halved their numbers during the first terrible winter. But in 1621 they successfully laid the foundations for their agriculture. Having chosen their site more wisely than did the Jamestown colonists, they had the cleared and abandoned fields of the Indians available for their first planting. Although unacquainted with scientific method, the Pilgrim Fathers unwittingly conducted a most interesting controlled experiment. In 5 acres of their land they sowed English wheat and peas, and in 20 additional acres they planted Indian corn under the supervision of the friendly native Squanto, a "spetiall instrument sent of God for their good beyond their expectation." The English crop failed miserably, but the Indian one flourished. Henceforth throughout the colonial period corn was destined to be the mainstay of New England agriculture.

The difficulties in raising small grain were of a local and temporary character. Within a few years wheat and other English crops were successfully grown. But these by no means displaced maize. Throughout all subsequent American history more corn has been produced each year than any other single crop. Corn's assets were legion. With no other tool than a hoe, it could be grown on land that was only partially cleared. The yield per acre was greater than that for most of its rivals, and it was easier to harvest and to prepare for use. It could be roasted and eaten on the cob; it could be cut from the cob and boiled with meat and other vegetables in various types of stew; dried and pounded in a mortar, it provided corn meal from which bread could be baked. The American language began its differentiation from English with the addition of words descriptive of dishes prepared from corn—words like johnnycake, pone, hominy, mush, hasty pudding, hulled corn, and succotash. Some of the words, and most of the recipes, were borrowed directly from the Indians. All told, the knowledge of corn, of how to grow it and how to use it, was the most impressive contribution of aboriginal American culture to our own civilization.

The Tobacco Boom

American agriculture borrowed many other plants from the Indians. A partial list would include potatoes, both sweet and white, peanuts, pumpkins, squashes, tomatoes, watermelons, and some varieties of cotton and of beans. Many of these, originally grown in Central and South America and the West Indies, were introduced into Europe in the sixteenth century, and by this circuitous route came to North America many generations later.

Tobacco was just such a case. Although the Spaniards became acquainted with it as early as the first voyage of Columbus, Europeans did not begin to use it to any great extent until half a century later. But eventually the habit spread throughout the Continent—to the gratification of Spanish merchants. By 1585 smoking had attained substantial popularity in England. The demand was met to some extent by tobacco grown by English farmers, but the major portion had to be imported from the Spanish Empire at great expense.

Well acquainted with tobacco before they left the mother country, the Virginia colonists began to experiment with this crop as soon as their immediate food problem had been met. They could not, however, borrow as directly from the natives as they had in the case of corn. The Virginia Indians grew tobacco, but of a type much inferior to the West Indies varieties with which the English were familiar. The colonists were not successful in producing a commodity which would sell in the mother country until they imported seed from Trinidad and improvised methods of their own for properly curing the leaves. John Rolfe, who began to experiment with the crop in 1612, was the great pioneer in establishing tobacco production on a profitable basis. By 1616 the essential knowledge had been gained, and so great was the eagerness of the Virginians to gamble everything on the new crop that the hardheaded Governor Dale had to promulgate an order requiring each landholder to devote 2 of his 3 acres to the growing of corn. But after the departure of this strong disciplinarian the expansion of tobacco acreage was rapid. In 1617 tobacco was to be seen growing in the market place, the streets, and all the other spare ground of Jamestown. Under the stimulus of high prices 20,000 pounds were sent to England in 1618, and the exports climbed annually until in 1629, 500,000 pounds crossed the Atlantic.

Since this development involved a wide departure from the plans upon which the colony had been organized, there were at first some misgivings on the part of the Virginia Company and the English government. But the corporation's need to recoup its losses and the Crown's eagerness for import duties speedily overrode all scruples. The colonists were given every encouragement to devote their energies to the new staple, and official policy was shaped to derive the greatest possible revenue. The American colonists were given a monopoly of the English market, foreign importations and home production alike being prohibited.

From this time on, tobacco dominated the life of colonial Virginia. Tobacco served as money: the cost of manufactured goods imported from English merchants was calculated in tobacco; taxes were levied in tobacco; debts and other mortgages were recorded in terms of tobacco; the colony's first 90 bridgegrooms paid 120 pounds of tobacco each for their wives. So vital to the well-being of all was the maintenance of a profitable price for the great staple that drastic steps were taken on occasions when overproduction swamped the market. Attempts were made to fix arbitrary prices by law, to enforce individual production or marketing quotas, to destroy the surplus, and to encourage diversion to other crops. Despite these measures low prices in the English market resulted in frequent depressions in the tobacco colonies. During the French and Indian War and thereafter to the outbreak of the Revolution, tobacco prices fluctuated violently, and the wholesale discontent characterizing these bad years had not a little to do with the rise of anti-British feeling. The Virginia planters, who were much in debt to English merchants, tended to blame unsatisfactory prices on the mercantilist legislation of the mother country which deprived them of the opportunity to sell directly to customers on the European continent. Their grievance was a legitimate one, although a more fundamental cause of their troubles was excessive specialization. The constant tendency was for American tobacco production to expand more rapidly than its market, especially after farmers in Maryland and North Carolina came into competition with the Virginians.

The impulse to grow more and more tobacco encouraged extensive importation of indentured servants. The headright system, moreover, provided a mechanism whereby the ambitious planter could expand his landholdings in direct proportion to his purchase of laborers. But this does not mean that seventeenth-century Virginia was at once transformed into a land of huge estates. Indentured labor was not really cheap. In addition to the costs of transportation and maintenance, the employer suffered heavy losses through the frequent illness and death of unseasoned immigrants. Moreover, after some five years he was obliged to grant the individual laborer his freedom and to undergo the expense of replacing him. The number of Virginians who expanded their activities into large-scale plantation agriculture under these conditions was small. Much more rapid was the growth of the yeoman class of small farmers tilling their own soil. As late as 1680 about 65 per cent of the landholders of Virginia and Maryland belonged to this category. Deriving both from freedmen who had completed their indentures and from free immigrants of small means, the yeomanry for several generations found a comfortable living in the growing of tobacco.

All this changed rapidly near the end of the seventeenth century. Declining prices began the ruin of the yeomanry, and the wholesale importation of Negro slaves completed it. Unable to compete successfully with slave-produced tobacco, many of the small farmers of Virginia migrated either to the frontier or to other colonies—to North Carolina, Maryland, Delaware, or Pennsylvania. Of those who remained, some secured employment on the large plantations as overseers or slave drivers, and others drew a precarious subsistence from their own poor farms. A substantial number scraped together funds enough to become slave owners on a small scale themselves. A census of 1782 revealed that in one important section of Virginia about one-quarter of the citizens owned ten or more slaves, one-half held from one to nine, and the remaining quarter had none.

Although there were still many more small planters than large, the latter now dominated politics and society. Holding estates of thousands of acres with a hundred or more slaves, the Virginia aristocrats of the eighteenth century lived in a fashion far different from the pioneers who had first turned to tobacco as an answer to their economic problems.

The Expansion of Plantation Agriculture

Tobacco was not suitable for all sections of the South. Its cultivation spread from the Virginia tidewater into the Piedmont, but it could not be grown in the Blue Ridge Mountains or in the great Shenandoah Valley which lay beyond. Eastern Maryland was good tobacco country, but not western, and to the south of Virginia only the Albemarle Sound country of North Carolina competed in the production of the great staple. Elsewhere the colonists had to seek their fortunes in other crops.

The eight courtiers to whom Charles II granted the Carolinas in 1663 had ambitious plans. They hoped to enrich themselves and to strengthen the realm by encouraging the production of exotic products like cotton, sugar, rice, indigo, silk, hemp, flax, wine, and oil. The fact that England was importing most of these from foreign countries was, according to mercantilist theory, a grievous weakness. But despite extensive experimentation none of these staples was at first successful. Indian trade, forest industries, and small-scale farming permitted the colony to survive but not to thrive. The turning point came in 1696 when a superior kind of rice from Madagascar was introduced. The difficult problems of cultivation were solved, and by the turn of the century rice production was a flourishing activity.

Rice was grown in the swamps which abounded near the rivers and streams of the coastal plain. Dikes were built so that these areas could be drained or flooded at will. The work of tending the fields was arduous and unpleasant. Laborers had to wade through the pestilent mud under a broiling sun to plant the seeds, to pull out the weeds, and to harvest the crop. Threshing and separating the grain from the chaff were likewise slow and difficult hand processes. To enlist white labor for these tasks was impossible, the more so since malaria-bearing mosquitoes made it almost suicidal for whites to remain in the rice country at certain seasons of the year. Even for Negroes who were used to somewhat similar conditions in their native Africa or on the plantations of the West Indies, the mortality rate was shockingly high. So great, nevertheless, were the profits to be made from rice production that thousands of planters risked their capital in the purchase of land and slaves. By 1708 the demand for the latter had becomes so extensive that blacks were as numerous as whites in South Carolina—there being about four thousand of each in the colony—and by 1765 blacks outnumbered whites two to one.

Indigo was another crop included in the early calculations of the proprietors which was not successfully produced until much later. The pioneer in this case was a remarkable woman, Eliza Lucas, who later became Mrs. Charles Pinckney. Left in charge of Wappoo, a plantation near Charleston, while her father served as governor of Antigua in the West Indies, Eliza experimented with cotton, ginger, alfalfa, and indigo. In 1742 she successfully brought some indigo plants to maturity. Knowledge of the difficult process by which the dyestuff was extracted from the leaves was provided by a West Indian whom the senior Lucas sent back to help his daughter. The experiments at Wappoo were sufficiently successful to encourage imitation, and in 1748 the British Parliament accelerated the spread of indigo culture by voting a bounty of 6*d*. a pound on all indigo produced within the Empire. By 1770 exports of indigo from the American colonies had risen to about £131,000 as compared with tobacco exports of £900,000 and rice exports of £340,000.

The conditions under which indigo was produced were as unpleasant as those associated with rice growing. Although the indigo plants were grown on sandy soil back from the rivers and swamps, the fields had to be carefully tended and the harvesting meticulously performed to prevent the bluish tinge from being rubbed off the plants. The leaves were placed in large vats to ferment, and then the dyestuff was drawn off with the water. This solution was allowed to stand in other vats while the indigo settled to the bottom. After this the water was drawn off, and the dye was collected, pressed, dried, and prepared for shipment. The fermentation process gave off a most offensive odor, and the piles of refuse near the vats attracted innumerable flies. This industry was another depending completely on the exploitation of Negro slaves.

Like tobacco culture rice and indigo expanded beyond the limits of a single colony. Southeastern North Carolina took up the new staples relatively early. In Georgia, founded in 1732, the trustees opposed rice and indigo and sought to develop a very different type of economy through prohibiting the slave trade, insisting upon small holdings, and encouraging the production of silk and wine. But these plans failed, and, when the colony came under the direct rule of the Crown in 1752, it speedily adapted its agriculture to one closely resembling that of its prosperous neighbor.

In all the southern colonies great staples were produced for the foreign market. In all of them there was a pronounced trend toward the growth of large plantations and the employment of Negro slaves. Yet the results of evolutionary process were not everywhere the same. In Maryland, for example, white labor was not displaced by black to the same extent as in the colonies further south, and indentured servants continued to play an important role throughout the eighteenth century. Virginia plantations tended to be larger in area than plantations elsewhere, but their size was deceptive. Tobacco culture quickly exhausted the soil, and the great planters always had much more land in abandoned fields and in uncleared tracts than they did under cultivation. By contrast, the rice and indigo plantations of South Carolina were smaller but were more intensively cultivated and required a larger number of slaves. Another important difference was that between the Virginia gentleman who usually resided on his own estate some miles from his nearest neighbor and the South Carolina gentleman who—leaving his pestilent rice fields or his stinking indigo vats largely in the care of overseers—lived a pleasant life in Charleston and enjoyed the society of his peers. Contributing to a similar result was the fact that tidewater Virginia was magnificently served by navigable streams, making it possible for the planter to utilize his own wharf in exporting his tobacco and importing his purchases from England. Very little of the trade was concentrated in ports, and town life was almost nonexistent. But farther south these conditions did not prevail. Few of the streams would admit ocean vessels, and ports like Charleston and Savannah became important.

The wealthy planter who exported tobacco, rice, or indigo was a good customer for English manufactured goods. He prided himself on his imported furniture, table service, wallpaper, fine clothes, and books. But it would be very wrong to think of him as producing only a single commodity and purchasing all his other needs. On the contrary, a well-managed plantation attained a high degree of self-sufficiency. Besides his staples for export the planter grew an abundance of corn and often wheat as well. He had vegetable gardens, fruit orchards, blacksmith and carpenter shops, gristmills, and sawmills. The slaves were kept busy during the winter, cutting timber, tanning leather, and weaving cloth.

The livestock industry expanded prodigiously. With little need of shelter or care in the southern colonies, cattle and hogs wandered widely and multiplied rapidly. The maintenance of fences to keep out these beasts was the responsibility of the cultivator, and all unfenced land served as commons for grazing stock. The great plantation owners sometimes had herds of several hundred cattle feeding off the pastures and wastelands of their own and the neighbors' properties. The animals multiplied so rapidly that open seasons were occasionally proclaimed during which they could be hunted like deer. From the large surplus of plantation cattle, animals were driven west to graze on the unoccupied lands of the frontier. Salted beef and pork from the southern colonies found a profitable market in the British West Indies.

The New England Village

New England rural life was cast in a distinctive mold from the beginning. Only rarely did the Massachusetts Bay Company sell or give its land directly to individuals. Instead the General Court granted entire townships—of varying sizes but averaging about 6 miles square—to groups of proprietors. Often these grantees composed the whole or a part of some church congregation in one of the older settlements.

Although eventually all the land of the new townships was divided into individual holdings, the process took many generations. Throughout the seventeenth and well into the eighteenth century the villages contained three different categories of land—land allotted to individuals, land set aside for the common use of some or all of the inhabitants, and land still unassigned for any specific purpose. Since defense against the Indians and the proper worship of God dictated that the settlers should live close together, the first grants were home lots near the village green. In some towns these home lots might be as small as ½ acre; in others they might be as large as 30 acres; but 3 to 5 acres was the average—enough for a house, sheds, vegetable garden, and a cowyard. After this, arable land in the outlying fields was assigned. Since divisions were made at many different times and since there was some attempt to apportion different kinds of soil with rude equity, a farmer in seventeenth-century New England usually owned tracts of assorted shapes and sizes scattered over the whole area of the township. Rarely did the proprietors assign the same amount of land to each settler. Instead the allotment was large or small according to the rank of the recipient in society, his investment in the enterprise, the size of his family, and his reputation for sobriety and industry.

Commons rights were of great importance. The cattle of the village grazed together in the town pasture, each man's animals being identified by a brand or earmark recorded in the town records. Oftentimes the community employed a cowherd, who began his duties a half hour after sunrise by blowing a horn through the village streets and receiving the cows from each household at the home-lot gate. The herdsman then drove his charges out to the pasture, guarded them throughout the day, and drove them back each evening to be milked by their owners and cared for during the night. An important local institution was the town bull, concerning whose purchase and care the village fathers gravely legislated. Sheep and goats sometimes grazed in the same pasture with the cattle and sometimes in separate pastures of their own. Hogs received little care except when they were sometimes penned and fed corn prior to slaughtering. Most of the time they ranged through the woods untended, often breaking through fences and destroying crops. The townspeople also enjoyed the valuable right of taking timber and stone from the undivided common lands. Even the arable fields were sometimes administered in common, but this usually involved only the maintenance of a common fence and the practice of turning the livestock into the fields after the harvest was gathered. Within such common fields each farmer had his individual holding upon which he did the work and owned the crop.

During the eighteenth century the New England towns were greatly altered. Growing population and successive divisions gradually extinguished the commons. The process was attended by no little social friction and controversy. At first newcomers to the towns had been readily admitted so long as their character and antecedents met the approval of the original settlers. They had been allowed to participate in the land divisions and to enjoy commons privileges. But as time went on there was a tendency for the heirs of the original proprietors to construe their rights more strictly—to distinguish sharply between commoners and non-commoners and to exclude the latter from both pasturage rights and land divisions. This precipitated sharp debates and frequent litigation, in which the proprietors usually triumphed over those who challenged their privileges. These contests were particularly sharp in the frontier towns when they brought into conflict the interests of actual settlers and proprietors of a new type who often continued to live in the older towns while maintaining absentee property rights in the new.

Through another important evolution the system wherein each individual's land lay in scattered tracts gave way to one in which each usually owned a single consolidated farm. This New England enclosure movement proceeded slowly and undramatically. Marriage, inheritance, exchange, and sale were the usual agencies of consolidation. As in most great social transformations, the passing of the old-type village represented both a gain and a loss. The abandonment of the common pasture made better breeding possible; the consolidation of the individual holdings prevented the waste of time involved in going to and from the village homes to the outlying tracts; it ended controversy and litigation over the use of innumerable winding paths and rights of way. But as the farmers lived more and more on isolated farms, oftentimes several miles distant from the town church and school or even from their nearest neighbors, much of the older community spirit was sacrificed.

Yankee Farming

Rural life in New England was hard. Even after the trees had been disposed of, it was difficult to clear the land of rocks and boulders. So large were many of these that the farmer had to leave them in the fields and plow around them. Except in the Connecticut Valley and a few other favored regions, the soil was thin and of low fertility. To complete the farmer's roster of troubles, there were the unkind seasons of these northern latitudes, where winters were long and cold, springs late, and summers short. Plantation agriculture was unthinkable. Negro slaves were of no value and indentured servants or hired laborers of very little; only the owner and his family had the incentive to coax a living from this uncooperative soil.

Corn continued to be the Yankee's best friend. Still planted in hills and fertilized with fish after the Indian fashion, it gave a generous yield and served an astonishing variety of purposes. Ground into meal and baked into bread, or "johnnycake," as the Yankees called it, the white and yellow ears provided the staff of life for New England tables. In one incarnation corn became hasty pudding, in another, Indian pudding, in a third, samp. The great crop also provided feed for the livestock and a staple which the Indians would accept in exchange for their beaver skins. Like tobacco in Virginia its value was so universally recognized in the community that it was often used for money.

It was not, however, entirely by choice that New Englanders ate johnnycake instead of white bread. Soon after the first Massachusetts colonies were founded, the settlers began to grow wheat, and for a generation the European crop was reasonably successful. But soil exhaustion and poor tillage methods soon reduced the yield, and after 1660 the farmers had to deal with a new and more discouraging problem. Their wheat would appear to prosper during the early season, but it would bear no grain. The cause was a mysterious disease, known as the "blast" to the colonists, but now identified as the black stem rust. First in eastern Massachusetts and then in Rhode Island and eastern Connecticut, wheat growing had to be abandoned. By the end of the colonial period the only areas of New England where wheat was still successfully grown were the western counties of Connecticut and of Massachusetts and northern Vermont.

With other grain crops like rye, oats, and barley the Yankees had better fortune. Rye flour mixed with corn meal provided the material for "rye and Injun" bread, a great New England favorite. Oats were raised primarily to feed the horses, since the idea that oatmeal was fit for human consumption was long regarded as simply an aberration of the Scotch. Barley was grown in sufficient quantity to supply the New England brewers and also to help meet the demand in the middle colonies, where the thirst for beer was not easily quenched.

For himself the New Englander usually preferred cider. He made it in prodigious quantities from the apples of his own orchard and stored it away by the barrelful in his cellar. This was the use to which the major portion of the apple crop was put, although the fruit was also used in its natural state and was sliced and dried for winter sauces and pies. The farmer might also have a few pear and cherry trees, but the New England climate did not favor peaches. Although the orchard was an important part of the typical New England farm, scientific care of the fruit trees was unknown. Once planted, the trees were left to themselves and were easy victims for pests and disease. The Yankee also varied his diet with peas, beans, squash, pumpkins, and other vegetables from his home-lot garden. But the nutritive importance of these was not understood, and the farmer gave little care to their cultivation.

Vital to the farm family was its livestock. Oxen were the most useful beasts of burden, and most farms had at least two of these great, patient beasts to drag the plows and wagons. Horses were reserved for riding and lighter tasks. Cattle were esteemed both for their milk and their meat, although herds were small, most farms having less than ten cows. By present-day standards these were invariably wretched creatures; in life they gave little milk, and in death they provided only tough and stringy beef. Although most farm women made their own butter and cheese, there was usually little to be said for their handiwork. Fastidious town dwellers preferred to import dairy products from England and Ireland. Since salt pork was ideally suited to provide the family with meat throughout the winter, each farmer had four or five hogs which he either fed on kitchen and dairy wastes or turned loose in the woods to live on nuts and roots. An occasional surplus of salt pork had a ready sale for provisions on the fishing boats or for export to the West Indies.

Sheep growing increased in importance throughout the colonial period, and in the eighteenth century most New England farms had flocks of thirty or forty. Only in a few areas like Martha's Vineyard, Nantucket, and the Narragansett country, where the ocean provided a great natural fence were the flocks large enough for woolgrowing to be conducted on a commercial basis. Elsewhere the sheep provided only enough wool for the farmer's own spinning wheel and loom.

One of the limiting factors in raising cattle and sheep during the seventeenth century had been the shortage of natural grass. Neither the salt marshes nor the fresh-water meadows which lay along the streams in the lowlands provided enough hay to keep any large number of animals through the winter. During the eighteenth century an answer was found in the development of "artificial meadows." Upland fields were sown with grass seed, which at first had to be imported from England but later was carried from one part of America to another. The most popular of the new hay crops was herd's grass, or timothy—supposedly named for one Timothy Hansen who carried it to New York from New Hampshire where its merits had first been recognized. The evolution of the artificial meadow made it possible to work thousands of upland farms which had hitherto been worthless because of the lack of natural meadow.

Most of what the New England farm family produced, it consumed. If the farm was in the vicinity of one of the towns, the owner might sell a little surplus of corn or milk or meat in the town market, but these opportunities were limited. Nor was the sale of surplus foodstuffs to the West Indies or to the other colonies large enough to be significant. On the contrary, New England imported more food than she exported.

Absolute self-sufficiency was then as now almost impossible to achieve. The Yankee farmer needed iron, salt, sugar, and other things that he could not produce.

But since he seldom grew a surplus and lacked the incentive of good markets, he found it difficult to secure the necessary cash. It was this imperative need for money that drove the Yankee into becoming a Jack-of-all-trades. He tapped his trees and made maple sugar; he cut timber in his own wood lot and in those of his neighbors; he worked the wood into barrel heads and staves which found a market in the West Indies and in southwestern Europe; he burned trees and sold the potash; he set his traps in the nearby forests and sold the valuable beaver skins; he found part-time employment in shipbuilding or in manning the fishing fleets.

Although this type of small-scale farming prevailed in New England, there were a few larger estates farmed by laborers or tenants. The most important exception to the general pattern was in southern Rhode Island, the so-called "Narragansett country." Here the climate was much milder, and the many lagoons and streams provided natural stockades ideal for raising livestock. Here developed estates of a thousand acres or more on which vast numbers of sheep, cattle, and horses were raised for export to other colonies. The proprietors became wealthy planters living a gentlemanly life similar to that of the plantation owners of the South. They even found it profitable to hold large numbers of Negro slaves.

The Colonial Breadbasket

Between New England and the southern colonies lay the so-called "middle colonies"—New York, New Jersey, Pennsylvania, and Delaware. Generally speaking, these enjoyed a better climate and a more fertile soil than New England, and their farmers made a better living. The misfortunes which destroyed Yankee wheat fields were not unknown in the areas to the south, but they were not serious during the colonial period. The middle colonies grew enough wheat not only to provide for their own needs but also to help feed New England, South Carolina, and the West Indies. The livestock industry also flourished. Philadelphia became the focal center of the colonial meat trade. From its busy port beef and pork products were exported in large volume, particularly to the West Indies. The large estate—so frequent in the South, so exceptional in New England—was fairly common in the intermediate territory. The Penn family, which exercised proprietary rights in Pennsylvania and Delaware throughout the colonial period, reserved extensive lands for itself and made many large grants to other individuals. In New Jersey also there were numerous large estates, but the most lavish land grants were those made by the royal government of New York. In 1685 the English confirmed the manorial rights of the Van Rensselaer family over Rensselaerwyck, an area 24 miles square with Albany at its center, thus perpetuating a feudal domain which had originated as a Dutch patroonship in 1629. Further south along the Hudson and in the vicinity of New York were similar great properties—Livingston Manor, Beekman Manor, Cortlandt Manor, Pelham Manor, and others. The power to govern and to dispense justice implicit in the word "manor" did not long survive, but the right of the great landowners to demand rent from all who settled on their property was successfully maintained throughout the colonial period despite occasional challenges. Moreover, royal governors, often corrupt, allowed most of the available land west and north of the Hudson to pass in vast tracts into the hands of speculators. So difficult was it for new settlers to acquire land on reasonable terms that the growth of the New York colony was seriously retarded.

The wealthy proprietors of the middle colonies used Negro slaves both for household duties and for field labor, but their employment in cultivation was on the whole unsuccessful. Agriculture north of Maryland could rarely be reduced to the simple routine that made slave labor satisfactory. Crops were diversified and each day's work brought its particular problems. Much more useful were white indentured servants. These laborers were free after a short term of years, however, and the supply never kept up with the demand. The owners of the great estates also resorted to hired hands, but there were equal difficulties in this solution. The supply of free labor was small, and wages, by contemporary English standards, were high. For the most part, the owners of the great estates found the most satisfactory use of their property in leasing it to tenants and thus building up a good income in rents. Tenantry was common along the Hudson and to a lesser extent in New Jersey and Pennsylvania. It also had a rapid expansion during the eighteenth century into the western counties of Maryland.

But the great estates were far exceeded in number and importance by family-sized farms averaging in the middle colonies between 100 and 200 acres—slightly larger than those of New England. There were hundreds of such farms on Long Island and in Westchester County, New York, and in northern New Jersey—many of them owned by New Englanders who had come seeking better land. Farther to the south the Penn family saw the wisdom of encouraging immigration by selling land in modest-sized tracts on reasonable terms. Before 1713 a settler could obtain 100 acres for £5 with 1*s*. annual quitrent thereafter. The price was raised in 1713 and 1732, but even at its highest, land could be purchased for £15 per 100 acres with a quitrent of a halfpenny per acre. The harassed land agents, however, could never enforce their employer's rights to the full. Thousands of squatters settled on the frontier, worrying little about their lack of legal title, and even in the East the avoidance of quitrents was common.

Despite the presence of middle-sized farms, the Pennsylvania countryside presented a different appearance from that of New England. Villages were less compact; farms were more widely scattered and, on the whole, more prosperous. More land had been cleared and livestock was fatter. Many fields of corn were to be seen, but these were chiefly valued as providing food for the livestock. Wheat bread, rather than corn, provided the basic food for most of the inhabitants. Thousands of acres were sown to this favorite crop, and mills to grind the grain into flour were numerous.

Methods of cultivation were still crude. Oxen were usually needed to drag the heavy wooden plows, and even then the surface of the soil was barely scratched. Plowing was followed by harrowing and rolling—once again with cumbersome wooden implements. Wheat was sown broadcast, usually in the fall, since winter wheat was less vulnerable to disease than spring wheat. The ripe grain was cut with a sickle until late in the colonial period when the cradle was introduced; it was threshed with a wooden flail until this method was supplanted by that of using horses or oxen to trample out the grain. Little attention was paid to maintaining the fertility of the soil. It was usually worked year after year until the decreasing yield gave eloquent testimony of its loss of vitality, and then it was simply allowed to lie fallow for several years until its fertility was partially restored.

But it was only when judged by the better standards of eighteenth-century England that Pennsylvania methods seemed backward. Compared with the farmers of the other colonies, the Pennsylvanians shone. Many of them had learned to esteem manure—to collect it carefully and to spread it over the fields. Some had begun to use lime, which was first made from oyster shells and later ground from stone. They knew also the fertilizing properties of wood ashes. A way of irrigating upland meadows had been developed by guiding the water from springs down the hillsides through a system of ditches. Particularly good agriculturists were the Pennsylvania Germans. Bringing with them from Europe a knowledge of intensive methods and a tradition of hard work, they took full advantage of the superior opportunities of their new environment. They were, to be sure, superstitious. They placed great importance on such dubious practices as the backing of newly purchased pigs into their sties or the planting and slaughtering according to the shape of the moon or the signs of the zodiac. But in more important matters the Germans surpassed all other groups. They were excellent judges of soil and usually established themselves in the most fertile limestone areas. They constructed their barns with loving care on an ingenious two-story plan. Building against a hillside so that they could drive their animals onto either floor, they provided clean and comfortable quarters for their cattle and horses on the first level and used the second for their threshing floor. The great barn was impressive evidence of the superior care for livestock which most distinguished the German farmer from his fellow colonists. To the Germans also goes credit for developing the sturdy Conestoga horses, the best draft animals in America, and for building the great Conestoga wagons—the prototypes of the fabulous covered wagons of the later-day Far West. Other excellent farmers were the Dutch in New York and New Jersey and the Swedes along the Delaware.

Diverse national backgrounds together with favorable conditions of soil and climate gave agriculture in the middle colonies more variety than elsewhere. The thrifty Germans reserved most of their wheat to sell and grew rye for their own bread. Rye was also esteemed along with wheat and corn for whisky making, and barley was grown for beer. Like the Yankee the Pennsylvanian was as likely to drink his fruit as to eat it. Most of the apples were made into cider and applejack, and peaches, plums, cherries, and grapes were transformed into brandy. Orchards were more productive than in New England, and peaches grew in such abundance that they were fed to the swine. Hemp and flaxseed were produced, the latter in quantities sufficient for export. Scotch and Irish fondness for oatmeal and potatoes gave those crops more importance in the middle colonies than elsewhere. A little tobacco was grown for local use. English grasses, introduced at an early date, prospered, and the hay crop became of increasing importance.

The Colonial Frontier

But diversified crops, luxuriant orchards, well-manured fields, and grand barns were the marks of settled agriculture. None of these things were to be seen on the frontier. There crops and methods developed in England, Germany, or Holland had little relevance. Pioneer life had its own distinctive pattern—one that derived more from American experience than from European.

There was always a frontier in colonial America. Jamestown and Plymouth provided the first schools of bitter experience where Englishmen learned to live in the wilderness. For several generations the inhabitants of all the colonies chose their homes close to navigable waters. Not until after 1700 did the Virginians push into the Piedmont, and the step was taken later still in most of the other colonies. But the eighteenth century was one of rapid expansion. Many new towns were founded in the hilly country of Massachusetts and Connecticut while the frontier pushed north into Maine, New Hampshire, and Vermont. Eventually the easier mountain barriers began to be passed. Pioneers found their way into the Great Valley of the Shenandoah between the Blue Ridge Mountains and the Appalachians. In another generation they had pushed south into the back counties of the Carolinas. Many of them, although by no means all, were Scotch-Irish and Germans from the middle colonies. Soldiers who fought beyond the Alleghenies during the French and Indian War spread the news of the attractions of southwestern Pennsylvania, and frontiersmen, many of them Virginians, found their way into the new country over recently marked military roads.

The Indians sought to exterminate these intruders in the bloody conflict known as Pontiac's Conspiracy, and the British government attempted to curb frontier expansion through the proclamation of 1763. But the westward movement could scarcely be slowed up, much less halted. By 1775 when the Revolutionary War began, the Appalachian barrier was being breached to the west of Virginia and North Carolina. Pioneers had already been living five or six years along the Watauga River in what is today northeastern Tennessee, and Judge Richard Henderson had purchased 20 million acres of land from the Indians on behalf of the so-called Transylvania Company and had employed Daniel Boone to mark the Wilderness Road through Cumberland Gap and thence northwest into Kentucky. These obviously illegal transactions foretold the opening up of a vast new area of the West.

Wherever a new frontier was pushed out, the stages of settlement were roughly the same. The first white men came, not to clear the land and to settle with their families, but as solitary adventurers. Many of them were traders who secured furs from the Indians in exchange for gunpowder, rum, or trinkets. Usually they were rascals who cheated and debauched their savage customers; occasionally they were honest men serving as skillful intermediaries between the colonists and the natives. But the traders also dealt with white hunters and trappers—men who had pushed far beyond the limits of settlement to live a strange life in the wilderness, sleeping in the open, eating venison and johnnycake, and tracking game mile after mile with uncanny skill. Traders and hunters met a few other white men in the forest—soldiers in outlying military posts, Jesuits or Moravians in lonely missions.

In areas where there was natural pasturage, the next stage of frontier life was marked by the arrival of the cattlemen. Vast herds ranged both the Piedmont and the Great Valley during the eighteenth century and found good grazing amidst the grass and pea vines growing luxuriously in the extensive tracts where the Indians had burned out the forests. Here developed a routine that was destined to be carried westward across the continent. Ownership of the cattle roaming over the open range was established by distinctive brands or earmarks. Cowboys conducted an annual roundup; calves were branded and animals ready for the market were separated from the herds. The latter were driven hundreds of miles along frontier cattle trails to Philadelphia, Charleston, and other markets, where the animals were slaughtered and the salted meat shipped to the West Indies.

The traders, the hunters, and the cattlemen simply used the wilderness; it remained for other men to subdue it—to clear the land and to establish farming. This was the work of pioneer families who pushed out from the older communities to establish new homes in the forest. Oftentimes they made a journey of many miles on foot, taking with them only what they could carry on their backs—a rifle, an axe, a hoe, and a bag of seed corn. The more fortunate had a cow or two, a horse or a yoke of oxen, a wagon, and a plow. Sometimes the adventurers selected a natural clearing for their new home; but this was seldom wise, since land where trees would not grow would rarely grow good crops. Most frequently the pioneer chose his land in the midst of the virgin forest.

Every refinement of civilization was for the time being lost. Until a cabin could be built, the family found what shelter it could—perhaps in a rude hut built of boughs, perhaps in a convenient cave. For food they were dependent on fish, game, and wild fruits and berries. Unless there were neighbors to help, it was a backbreaking and tedious task to clear a site and to cut and to fit logs for a cabin. When finished, the dwelling was primitive in the extreme. Four walls of unfinished logs with the spaces between plugged with moss or straw and daubed with mud, a roof covered with split staves, a single door made of roughhewn slabs, sometimes a single window covered with greased paper—such was the

FIG. 2. *The Beginning and Completion of an American Farm.* On the left, the log cabin, rude fences, sawmill, and plow of frontier days; on the right, the large house, cleared fields, and carriage of the prosperous farmer. (*Courtesy of the New York Historical Society.*)

external appearance of the frontier cabin. Within was a single room dominated by a great stone fireplace, where all the cooking was done and from which came all the heat to warm the shivering family during the cold weather. Above the room there was often a loft reached by pegs driven into the wall. Here part of the family might sleep while others passed the night in the room below in rude bunks or on boughs spread before the fireplace.

It was not enough that the cabin should be ready by fall. It was equally important to harvest the first indispensable crop to feed the family through the winter. Even while the cabin was being built, a field was being cleared for corn. If the pioneer was a German, he might chop down the trees and pull out the roots. But most of the frontiersmen were satisfied to do things the Indian way. They killed the trees by chopping a broad girdle of bark from their trunks. This allowed the sunlight to penetrate through the leafless boughs and bring to maturity the corn planted and cultivated in hills. In a year or two the winds would bring down the dead trees which could be chopped up and burned; sometimes the process could be hastened by building fires around the roots. At last the field would be completely cleared, but there was always a second or third to be labored over.

At first, frontier families struggled for a bare subsistence. Often they failed. Flood, drought, or the ravages of animals destroyed their crops. They died of sickness brought on by malnutrition, they were killed by the Indians, or they gave up and went back to civilization. The fittest—or the luckiest—survived and achieved a reasonably secure subsistence. A few did better. They somehow found a surplus for sale—a little corn or some deerskins or beaver furs. One year they bought a few cows; another a horse; another a plow; another the seed to plant wheat, rye, barley, or oats.

But to accumulate agricultural capital in this way was a painfully slow process. It was the exceptional frontiersman who started with only his axe and hoe and bag of corn and ended up a prosperous farmer producing staples for sale in distant markets. It was much more usual for the poor man who had cleared the farm to sell it to a newcomer, a man who had already owned and sold a farm further east and was now ready to move west with his wagonload of household goods, his livestock, and some cash to invest in tools and seed. This was the final stage of settlement. Cabins gave way to more pretentious houses, stables and barns were erected, and life began to center in villages and towns with stores, churches, and schools. But when this happened, the area was no longer frontier. To the west, traders and hunters were marking out their trails in the wilderness; cattlemen were looking for good grazing grounds; pioneers were again building their cabins and clearing their fields.

Agriculture was preeminently the colonial way of life. But agriculture included everything from the frontier corn patch to the great Virginia tobacco plantation.

Chapter 3. Artisans and Merchants

Although most of the colonial population derived a living directly from the soil, the importance of the minority who did not was very great. Artisans, country merchants, and professional men played a vital role in community life. At places favorably located for ocean trade, villages grew into towns and towns into cities. Industry and commerce advanced colonial America toward economic and intellectual self-reliance—and thus toward eventual nationhood.

The Artisans

Where necessary, the rural family could supply most of its own needs. The men of the household could build a cabin and furnish it with benches, stools, and tables. With axe and knife they could fashion almost any implement. They made plows, flails, ox yokes, brooms, and dishes from wood. They made leather from deer and cattleskins and shaped it into shoes, breeches, and jackets. To assure food for the long winters, they salted, smoked, or dried meat and fish, and they made and stored away barrels of tangy cider. Sugar they provided by tapping maple trees and making syrup, or by collecting honey. The women were equally versatile. They could grind corn in a mortar and bake it into bread. They could make butter and cheese as well as soap and candles. They could perform all the laborious processes necessary to transform flax into linen or fleece into woolen cloth and then use the fabric to make clothing for the entire family. A traveler, visiting such a household on a winter evening, might find the grandmother busy carding wool, the mother spinning rolls of yarn, the father weaving at the loom, some of the children mixing dye in the indigo tub, and others whittling useful articles out of wood.

But the self-sufficiency of rural life was never complete. Even the most independent pioneer needed a gun and an axe, and his wife needed iron cooking utensils. When such things as these were lost or broken or when other similar articles were needed, the settler often made long, difficult trips to some trading post where he exchanged corn or pelts for the things that he wanted. The frontiersman could never entirely break his contact with the trader and the artisan. The country store, the blacksmith shop, the gristmill, and the sawmill were busy places wherever village life developed.

Artisans were prominent among the immigrants who landed at Jamestown in 1607 and those who came thereafter. The famous John Alden of Plymouth was not a Separatist seeking to worship unmolested but a husky young cooper who contracted to come to America to make barrels—essential for storing the saints' water and beer. Massachusetts towns often provided generous inducements to attract artisans. In 1658 Haverhill offered John Johnson a house and land if he would ply the trade of village blacksmith for seven years, and Enfield made a similar bargain with one Andrew Miller.

Artisans were welcome not only because they performed tasks for which the ordinary colonists lacked the requisite skill but because they did work which, without proper equipment, was excessively laborious. It was foolish to grind grain with primitive home implements as soon as a mill had been built where the miller would prepare corn meal and flour for a reasonable toll—often one-fourteenth of the product. To make boards with handsaws was unprofitable when a sawmill was nearby. The more prosperous colonists employed professional carpenters and masons to build their houses and skilled joiners to make their furniture. Even much humbler families were glad to have expert assistance in the finishing of their home-woven cloth. In 1643, 20 families of Yorkshire clothmakers migrated to Rowley, Massachusetts, where they established a fulling mill in which greasy matter was removed from new woolens and the cloth was soaked to shrink and to thicken it. Fulling mills were later established in many other villages. Sometimes gristmill, sawmill, and fulling mill were all to be found in the same building. Other important village industries were the tanneries and breweries.

Where the population was too sparse to support shops, itinerant artisans often appeared. An annual event, eagerly awaited, was the visit of the shoemaker, who would spend several days living in the household while he made shoes for the entire family out of its own leather. Or the visitor might be a traveling weaver, who would set up his loom and weave into cloth all the woolen yarn or linen thread which the women had spun since his last visit. These itinerants were often jovial fellows, entertaining the adults with tidbits of news and gossip and the children with songs and stories.

But where town life was well established, work was more likely to come to the artisan than the artisan to go to the work. The craftsman opened a shop, usually in his home, and worked on order for the townspeople. Oftentimes he had one or two of his own sons helping him, since there was a tendency for trades to run in families. However, the boy in the shop was as likely to be the son of some other artisan or farmer. Families were large, and it was not possible for all boys to follow their fathers' calling. A prudent parent might apprentice one son to a carpenter, a second to a blacksmith, and a third to a tailor. In cases where parents were dead or too indolent to make proper provision for their children, the public authorities often did so. Apprentices worked for their masters a stipulated term, frequently seven years, during which they received food and lodging and were taught the mysteries of the craft. Following their apprenticeship, they became journeymen, entitled to receive wages for their labor from any master who might employ them. Colonial manufacturing, therefore, was typically represented by the small shop, where a master, assisted by one or two apprentices or journeymen, produced goods on order for his neighbors. Such a master was both manufacturer and merchant, both worker and employer.

Although the artisan in colonial America enjoyed higher wages and better social status than the artisan in England or Europe, he often abandoned his

FIG. 3. *Paul Revere.* Portrait by J. S. Copley. The famous patriot-silversmith is shown with his tools and an example of his work. (*Courtesy of the Museum of Fine Arts, Boston.*)

craft to become a farmer. Ownership of land brought its own prestige, and where land was cheap, the temptation to purchase it was strong. Consequently, despite the institution of apprenticeship and the immigration of many artisans from the Old World, the number of skilled workmen in America was usually insufficient. Particularly was this true in the southern colonies, where blacksmiths and weavers felt the same compulsion as their neighbors to grow tobacco and rice.

At first the scarcity of artisans was less felt than it might have been on account of the close trade relations of the South with the mother country. The same English ships that carried the tobacco out of the colonies brought manufactured goods in. But as time went on, planters discovered that there were many disadvantages to exchanging agricultural goods for finished products. The price of the staples tended to go down while that of the manufactured articles remained high. As it became more and more difficult to pay for imports, planters sought to supply as many needs as possible from their own estates. Some shrewd plantation managers learned this lesson early. Before 1650 Captain Samuel Matthews of Virginia was growing his own hemp and flax and having it spun and woven into cloth by his servants. He had his own tannery and cobbler's shop and 40 Negro slaves trained for special trades. But this was less characteristic of the seventeenth century than of the eighteenth, when tobacco prices were so depressed that only prudent management could keep a planter out of debt. Efforts to secure white artisans were not very satisfactory, and planters resorted increasingly to the practice of training their slaves to the necessary crafts. Negroes became carpenters, blacksmiths, tanners, shoemakers, and weavers. At least 28 different trades were practiced by the slaves of South Carolina during the eighteenth century. Shrewd management sometimes permitted the planter to manufacture a surplus for sale. Exports to the West Indies of slave-produced lumber, barrel staves, and leather made the southern colonies somewhat less dependent on the older staples.

Lumbering and Shipbuilding

Since wood was the material from which almost everything from spindles to houses was made, many settlers were employed in lumbering operations. At first the logs were cut into boards in pits, where two-man teams laboriously operated great handsaws, but very soon rude sawmills employing water power were erected. American shingles, clapboards, and timber had an eager market both in the mother country and in the West Indies.

Barrels were the universal containers for shipping bulky products, whether they were New England fish, Pennsylvania flour, Virginia tobacco, or South Carolina rice. Colonial coopers and farmers working in their spare time not only supplied this large local demand but produced a surplus for export. Both from New England and the southern colonies barrel staves, hoops, and heads were shipped to the sugar planters of the West Indies and to the wine makers of southwestern Europe.

Each year vessels bore away to England valuable cargoes of ship timber—masts, bowsprits, yards, spars, and oars. Especially esteemed were the great white pines of New England, which made the world's best masts. Surveyors traveled through the public forests, marking with a broad arrow the straightest and tallest trees. These were reserved for the Royal Navy, and heavy penalties were prescribed against any person who should divert them to other uses. But trees so prized by the British government brought rich rewards from private builders, and the King's mark was often ignored.

During the early years both the Jamestown and the Plymouth settlers tried their hand at shipbuilding, but the industry had its greatest development in Massachusetts. There *The Blessing of the Bay,* built at John Winthrop's order, was launched in 1631, while other craft soon followed. By 1650 Edward Johnson could write: "Many a fair ship had her framing and finishing here besides lesser vessels, barques, and ketches; many a Master, beside common Seamen, had their first learning in this Colony." [1] The shipbuilding industry profited particularly by the Navigation Acts of 1651 and 1660, which reserved trade with the British colonies to ships built within the Empire. The colonial builders supplied not only the merchants and the fishermen of America, but many of those in England as well. Ships could be built in the colonies much cheaper than in the mother country, and by the end of the colonial period one-third of the British merchant marine had been built in America.

Many subsidiary industries were similarly encouraged. Rope yards, sail lofts, and foundries for making ships' hardware appeared. From the pines of New England and the Carolinas pitch, tar, rosin, and turpentine were made with the encouragement of bounties from the British government. Particularly in South Carolina the production of these naval supplies became an important industry.

Despite the value of the forests the colonists showed no interest in their conservation. They resented and disobeyed the laws which reserved trees for the Royal Navy. They logged the coastal belt so recklessly that residents of the port towns began to complain of a scarcity of fuel. To the frontier farmer the trees were simply an encumbrance to be girdled, allowed to die, and then burned. The wood ashes thus produced had a ready market as potash, but the pioneer—either through ignorance or because of difficulties of transportation—usually allowed them to go to waste.

Colonial Iron Industry

Although the Virginia Company succeeded in producing a small quantity of iron during the early years of the Jamestown colony, the enterprise encountered many difficulties. More permanent were the steps taken in Massachusetts, where bog ore was discovered in ponds and swamps along the Saugus River. Samples were taken to England in 1642 and John Winthrop, Jr., was active in enlisting the support of a small group of English investors. The resulting Company of Undertakers for the Iron Works received land grants and a monopoly of iron production from the Massachusetts General Court in 1644. A furnace was built

[1] Edward Johnson, *Wonder-working Providence,* ed. by J. F. Jameson (Scribner, New York, 1910), 247.

at Lynn and operated by skilled workmen imported from England. A pig iron of low quality, but satisfactory for pots and kettles, was produced. Similar iron-works were eventually established in all the colonies.

The center of the industry was at first eastern New England, but in the eighteenth century depletion both of the bog ore and the supply of wood for charcoal permitted other sections to take the lead. In the rocky hills of western Connecticut rich ore deposits were discovered, and at the end of the colonial period the best iron in the colonies, suitable for tools and guns, was produced at Salisbury, Connecticut. Another important center was the Sterling Works near West Point, New York. In Maryland large-scale operations were conducted by the Principio Company, which exported pig iron to England. In Virginia the industry was encouraged by the energetic royal governor, Alexander Spottswood, who employed the labor of German Palatines in works which he built in the Rappahannock region. In Pennsylvania rich ore deposits and expert German craftsmanship combined to develop the most flourishing ironworks in all the colonies.

By 1750 the industry was of sufficient significance to become a matter for Parliamentary consideration. The Iron Act of that year prohibited colonists from making steel or engaging in other advanced stages of manufacture but encouraged the production of pig and bar iron by providing that these might enter the mother country free of duty after 1757. Obviously, English ironmakers hoped to conserve the fast-disappearing English forests by importing unfinished iron from the colonies while reserving for themselves the manufacture of finished products. But since the law did not interfere with the making of nails and farm implements in forges and was not strictly enforced in any case, the colonists were only slightly handicapped. By 1775, indeed, more pig and bar iron was being produced in the American colonies than in England and Wales combined.

More than other colonial industries, the production of iron required capital. Usually the money was raised by companies which pooled the resources of a number of partners. These capitalists were often English, but the amount of colonial investment in such enterprises increased rapidly. In eighteenth-century Pennsylvania prosperous ironmasters like Thomas Potts, Thomas Rutter, Anthony Morris, and George McCall were representative of a new type of wealth derived from industry.

Other important colonial activities were the distilling of rum, centered in Boston, Newport, and Philadelphia, paper manufacture, particularly active in the vicinity of Philadelphia, and sugar refining in Boston, New York, and Philadelphia.

Fishing and Trading

"Let not the meannesse of the word fish distaste you," wrote Captain John Smith in 1624, "for it will afford as good gold as the mines of Guiana and

Potassie with less hazard and charge, and more certainty and facility." [1] Nor was Smith alone in perceiving the profits to be made by catching fish off the North Atlantic Coast and selling them in Europe. Long before there were any settlements in New England, Portuguese, French, and English fishing vessels were visiting its waters. Interest in the fisheries played its part both in the settlement of Plymouth and the less successful venture at Cape Ann.

It remained for the Massachusetts Bay colonists to achieve real success. "The first to set upon the trade of fishing in the bay" were the settlers at Dorchester, many of whom had come from English fishing towns in Dorset and Devon. Other villages, Scituate, Gloucester, Salem, Marblehead, and Boston itself, were not far behind. When one of the ministers attempted to tell his congregation that the worship of God had been the main end of their coming to America, he was interrupted by a realist who called out: "Sir, you are mistaken . . . our main end was to catch fish." [2] Of some coastal towns this was certainly true. Marblehead, for example, not only maintained a sturdy independence, sometimes defying both the laws of England and those of the Massachusetts General Court, but even retained a characteristic local dialect brought by early settlers from Cornwall and the Channel Islands. At first the Massachusetts fishermen confined their activities to the waters between Cape Cod and the Maine coast, but eventually they began to make profitable visits as far as the Grand Banks of Newfoundland.

The colonists early learned the profits to be made from selling the bones and oil of whales. At first they did no more than the Indians had done before them, killing right whales who ventured too far into shallow waters in search of herring. Lookouts on the beaches spied out the great creatures, which were then pursued by daring crews in rowboats. Into the whale's side would be thrust a harpoon with line and drags attached. After the wounded creature had plunged and struggled until he was exhausted, he would be killed by the whalers and towed ashore, where the carcass would be cut up and the oil and bones extracted. Some time after 1700 deep-water whaling developed. Sailing vessels searched for sperm whales which were especially prized because of the superior grade of oil to be obtained. When these speedy and dangerous beasts were sighted, skilled crews put out in small boats from the main vessels, harpooned them, and allowed themselves to be dragged on "Nantucket sleigh rides" by their injured captives. Crews frequently lost their lives when the whales sounded and dragged them under or smashed the boats with their lashing tails. But if all went well, the struggle was soon over and the carcasses were towed back to the main vessels, where the blubber was tried out in brick tryworks. Before the end of the colonial period Nantucket whalers were venturing into the Arctic Ocean to the north

[1] "The Present State of New-Plimoth," *Travels and Works of Captain John Smith,* ed. by Edward Arber (Edinburgh, 1910), II, 784.

[2] Cotton Mather, *Magnalia Christi Americana; or The Ecclesiastical History of New-England* (Hartford, 1855), I, 66.

and Brazilian waters to the south. One result of the rise of whaling was the establishment of spermaceti candlemaking as an important colonial industry. In 1760 there were 17 candle factories in Newport alone.

Although shipbuilding and fishing were established industries during the first decade of Massachusetts history, the sea first assumed prime importance in 1641. When the Puritan quarrel with Charles I resulted in civil war, immigration to New England largely ceased. The result was a serious depression, since those already established in the colony could no longer make a good living through selling cattle and provisions to the new arrivals. As John Winthrop recorded the crisis: "All foreign commodities grew scarce and our own of no price. Corn would buy nothing; a cow which cost last year £20 might now be bought for £4 or £5. . . . These straits set our people on work to provide fish, clapboards, plank, etc., . . . and to look out to the West Indies for a trade for cotton." [1]

In the sugar colonies the New England sea captains found eager purchasers. Fish, particularly the cheaper grades, had a ready sale as food for the slaves. So also did dried beef, pork, wheat, and peas. Lumber of all descriptions—barrel stock, clapboards, planks, even "houses ready framed"—always had a market, as did horses for the sugar mills. In exchange for these products the Yankees received molasses, sugar, tobacco, cotton, indigo, and Negro slaves. Many of these commodities were sold in New England; others were reexported to other markets.

The shrewd New England Protestants reserved their best fish for sale to Catholics in France, Spain, Portugal, and Italy. Colonial vessels maintained a prosperous trade with the ports of southern Europe, exchanging codfish and barrel staves for Cadiz salt, Madeira and Canary wine, Malaga grapes, Valencia oranges, and Spanish gold. Many of these products were brought directly to New England, particularly the salt which was vital to the home fisheries. But many Yankee vessels called at England to exchange wine and fruit for English manufactured goods. This helped to solve a New England problem, which was becoming increasingly serious—how to pay for imports from the mother country.

Except for furs and ship timber there was little market for New England goods in England. To pay for imports Yankee merchants had to secure either gold or goods that would have an English market. They reexported to the mother country much of the surplus sugar accumulated through their trade with the West Indies; they developed also the "sugar triangle," whereby after taking their timber and produce to the Caribbean, they carried sugar and molasses directly to England to be exchanged for manufactured goods. Much-needed specie was gained through trade with the French and Spanish West Indies—no less eager than the English islands to secure provisions and usually paying better prices. Since Negro slaves were in constant demand in all the islands, another trade soon developed. This was the "slave triangle," wherein Boston or Newport ships carried New England

[1] *Winthrop's Journal "History of New England" 1630–1649,* ed. by J. K. Hosmer (Scribner, New York, 1908), II, 31.

rum to Africa and there exchanged their fiery cargo for captive Negroes, who were carried to the West Indies to be sold for sugar, molasses, or specie, which was then brought back to New England.

The Yankee merchants were familiar figures in other colonies. They traded with the Dutch along the Hudson River; they visited Virginia where they exchanged West Indian sugar and molasses for tobacco, corn, beans, and meat—and sometimes surreptitiously bought stolen goods from the slaves. To carry American tobacco directly to Europe was strictly against the British laws of trade, but the profit was great, and many Boston, Newport, and Salem ships supposedly carrying fish to Europe actually had their holds bulging with Virginia and Maryland tobacco. It was notorious that the New Englanders obeyed the Navigation Laws only when it was profitable to do so.

The Rise of Towns

Other colonists than the New Englanders realized the profits to be secured through trade. The natural advantages of New York Harbor had been obvious since the days of Dutch settlement, and those of Philadelphia and Charleston were well recognized by the end of the seventeenth century. These places soon developed into thriving ports, where merchants gained wealth through trading in the colonial staples.

For more than a century Boston kept ahead of all rival ports. In 1730 it had a population of about 13,000 as against Philadelphia's 11,500, and New York's 8,500.[1] The continued primacy of the Massachusetts city was due both to its enterprising spirit and to its flourishing shipbuilding industry. Many of the goods which entered and left the other harbors did so in Yankee vessels. Boston was the great "mart town." The major portion of European goods went first to the Massachusetts port, whence they were carried to the other colonies. And despite growing activity in Philadelphia and New York, much of the produce of the middle colonies and the Carolinas was carried to the West Indies and to Europe in Boston ships. In its relations with the smaller New England towns Boston enjoyed similar advantages. Its merchants grew rich through exchanging imported European goods for the lumber and surplus produce of the surrounding area.

Despite its great carrying trade, however, Boston suffered certain handicaps that became more apparent as the eighteenth century progressed. As compared with the hinterlands of Philadelphia and New York, that of Boston was restricted in size and lacked great staples for foreign trade. Shipbuilding in the middle colonies was soon greatly expanded so that Philadelphia and New York merchants were able to carry produce to the West Indies and to Europe in their own vessels. Nor were they so dependent on Boston for imported goods as in the past. While Boston's population through the middle decades of the century

[1] Newport and Charleston each had a population of about 4,500.

remained nearly stationary, that of its two rivals increased steadily. At the end of the colonial period Philadelphia had a population of about 30,000, New York 22,000, and Boston 17,000.

Philadelphia's remarkable rise had begun with the settlement of the area in 1683. Well situated to serve the needs of colonists in Delaware, Maryland, and western New Jersey as well as those in Pennsylvania, the city grew with its section. When the Germans and the Scotch-Irish opened up rich agricultural regions to the west, the market city prospered all the more. Out of the port went flour, meat, and livestock. The abundance of cattle, moreover, encouraged development of the leather industry, which became a Philadelphia specialty. Shrewd Quaker merchants found legitimate profits in commerce with the West Indies, England, and southern Europe and illegal ones, still greater, in trading with pirates or with the enemy during the intercolonial wars.

New York's advance was less dramatic. Factors discussed in earlier chapters retarded the growth of the colony. But if the hinterland was less prosperous than that of Philadelphia, it nevertheless produced a good volume of flour and meat for export. From 1680 to 1694 the Bolting Act gave the city a monopoly of the bolting and packing of flour in the colony. Although the law was eventually repealed at the insistence of the country people, the flour-packing industry continued to be an important activity. New York's central location made it the headquarters of the British army during the wars with the French and brought gratifying opportunities to the colonial merchants.

By later standards colonial cities were not large, but they were big enough to raise problems unknown to villages. Fire was a constant menace. In 1711 when Mary Mors of Boston got drunk and set Captain Ephraim Savage's privy on fire, the result was a terrible disaster. Numerous lives were lost and over a hundred families were left homeless. This experience added urgency to efforts, already begun, to provide Boston with a public fire department. By 1720 the city had six hand engines, which were operated by a company of 20 men under the direction of 10 leading citizens known as "firewards." Meanwhile, the need for better trained firefighters had led to the organization of a private company, the Boston Fire Society, in 1717. Nineteen years later Benjamin Franklin organized the famous Union Fire Company in Philadelphia.

A minimum of police protection was another necessity of town life. In the daytime, enforcement of the laws was entrusted to constables. Their authority was symbolized by long black staffs, but it was by no means sufficient to insure that their orders would be respected. Defiance and resistance were so frequent as to make the constable's position an unpopular one, which was forced on artisans over their protests. At night additional protection was necessary, and citizens were compelled to take their turns at watch duty. Men drafted for this service were so prone to shirk their responsibilities to smoke or to nap that in some towns a paid watch was substituted. But these steps were quite inadequate to deal with the growing problem of crime. Although homicides were fortunately rare, thefts and assaults were common occurrences. Riots and mob violence also became increasingly serious.

Domestic Trade and Travel

In the colonial ports enterprising merchants engaged in both wholesale and retail trade. They owned or took shares in ships and built their own wharves and warehouses. They sold their imported goods in part to consumers who visited the shops which they frequently kept in their own homes. Some of these sales were for money; more were for the produce of the region—meat, grain, leather, and the like—for which the merchants had a market. But they engaged in wholesale trade as well. Country storekeepers and traders would appear at the great warehouses to exchange country goods for the sugar, molasses, and manufactured products of the importers.

During the eighteenth century there was more and more differentiation between wholesaling and retailing. The great merchant dealt in larger quantities, and more of the sales to the general public were by small shopkeepers "who bought to sell again." In towns like Boston there were stores specializing in groceries, dry goods, tobacco, or millinery, although most merchants engaged in a more general trade. Much of the retailing continued to be done in the homes of the artisans, where the goods were produced.

Trade in the towns was carefully regulated by the public authorities, acting in the spirit of medieval tradition. The price of bread and other necessities was fixed by law, and the privilege of trading was usually reserved for inhabitants of the town. Other transplanted Old World institutions were the weekly market day, when country people sold or bartered their produce with the townspeople in the public market place, and the annual fairs, particularly important for the exchange of livestock.

In the villages the country storekeeper accepted the surplus corn or meat of the farmers in exchange for sugar, buckles, gloves, and other goods with which he had stocked his shelves. Some of these he might purchase on visits to the larger towns; others he bought from inland traders who served as middlemen. In many villages the local merchant was the tavern keeper, who kept store in one of the rooms of his establishment. In the South where there were few villages, both stores and taverns were infrequent, and the planters themselves often engaged in trade, bartering English manufactured goods carried directly to their private wharves for the tobacco, grain, or furs brought in by their less prosperous neighbors. Peddlers were active in all sections despite frequent attempts to limit their activities by law.

During the seventeenth century, settlement clung to the seaboard and the navigable streams. Men and goods moved, whenever possible, by boat. For land travel the colonists were dependent at first on the narrow and deeply worn Indian trails, suitable only for horsemen and pack animals. In time these were widened to accommodate wagons and carts, but the primitive roads were almost everywhere bad—muddy in the spring, dusty in the summer, and extremely rough in all seasons. They were perhaps at their best when they were covered with the winter snow and could be traversed with sledges. Since there were few bridges, the larger streams could be crossed only where there were fords or ferries.

Although colonial roads never became good by later American standards, many were sufficiently improved by 1700 to stand comparison with the roads of the mother country. Country people still saw only wagons and horsemen passing along the highways, but coaches were beginning to appear in the towns, replacing the sedan chairs in which the wealthy had hitherto been carried. By 1732 overland travel had sufficiently increased to warrant the publication of a guidebook entitled *The Vade-Mecum for America: Or a Companion for Traders and Travellers.* It described roads stretching down the coast from Boston through Providence, New London, New York, and Philadelphia to Jamestown, Virginia—a distance of 711 miles.

Stagecoach lines between the colonial towns were beginning to operate. One of the earliest was that between Boston and Newport, Rhode Island. A fortnightly service began in 1716 and a weekly one in 1721. Another stage line ran across New Jersey from Amboy to Burlington. Since water transport was good between New York and Amboy and between Philadelphia and Burlington, the coaches served well the needs of travelers between the two principal ports of the middle colonies. The trip was not for the feeble, since the great coach lumbered over the rough roads for as much as eighteen hours before it stopped at some village tavern about ten o'clock at night. The travelers were awakened at about three the next morning and were soon on the road again.

Particularly important were the roads to the West. Boston and Hadley on the Connecticut River were connected by 1674, and carts from Chester County were able to drive into Philadelphia by 1710. In 1733 work began on a road to connect Philadelphia with the Susquehanna River, and during the French and Indian War (1754–1763) two military roads were built across the mountains to the headwaters of the Ohio—the site of the future city of Pittsburgh.

The gradual improvement of roads was of great importance in encouraging intercolonial contacts and paving the way for eventual union. Similarly important was the colonial post office, established in 1691. Since service was slow and rates were high, the institution did not at first prosper. But when Benjamin Franklin was appointed postmaster general in 1753, he applied himself with characteristic energy to improving the service. During the next twenty years the postal carriers conveyed more and more material—business letters from merchants of different cities, communications between leading politicians, scientific reports from gentlemanly amateurs, and newspapers bringing intelligence of the happenings in one colony to readers in another.

The Colonial Social Structure

The colonial upper class derived only in minute part from the English aristocracy. The peerage of the mother country was scarcely represented at all—the Fairfaxes of Virginia being unique in their right to the hereditary title of baron. A few Virginia families like the Wyatts, the Throckmortons, and the Peytons were descended from younger sons of the nobility, and a few others were more remotely connected. Much more numerous were colonial families which came from the stock of English country gentlemen, untitled but prominent in the rural affairs of the old country as squires and justices of the peace. From such ancestry descended the Randolphs and Washingtons of Virginia, the Carrolls of Maryland, and the Winthrops, Saltonstalls, and Dudleys of Massachusetts.

But the English aristocracy had always been open to new blood, and the American was still more receptive. Examples of middle-class or lower class immigrants who achieved wealth and social recognition were commonplace. William Byrd was the son of a London goldsmith, who inherited some Virginia land from an uncle and removed to America in 1671. Here he built up a great estate on his profits from trading in tobacco, fur, rum, and indentured servants. His son William Byrd II increased the family holdings from 23,231 acres to 179,440 and built the lordly mansion Westover. Even more obscure were the origins of John Carter, who arrived in Virginia in 1649 to found one of the most notable of colonial families. During the eighteenth century Robert Carter of Nomini Hall was known as "King" Carter because of his possession of 300,000 acres of land, 1,000 slaves, ironworks, a flour mill, and a magnificent private library of 1,500 volumes.

Similar great landholding families became established in the middle colonies. One aristocratic line derived from Kiliaen Van Rensselaer, an Amsterdam jewel merchant who bought a patroonship in New Netherland. Another was established by Robert Livingston, the son of a poor Scotch parson, who rose from Albany bookkeeper to great landlord by "never disbursing six pence but with the expectation of twelve pence." A third great family was established by Richard Morris, a Welsh soldier under Cromwell, who became first a merchant in Barbados and then a landed proprietor in New York.

Since wealth usually brought social recognition, the great merchants of New England, the middle colonies, and the Carolinas soon took their place in the American aristocracy. Although the first Boston gentlemen had belonged to the English gentry, successful traders soon shared prestige with the older leaders. One of the earliest of the new type was John Hull, who made a fortune in commerce and moneylending and set up the mint in which pine-tree shillings were made for the colony. During the eighteenth century Peter Faneuil, who devoted part of a fortune derived from trade in rum and slaves to the building of a public market, and Andrew Belcher, who graduated from tavern keeping to profitable, if not always legal, foreign commerce, were leading figures. Notably successful also were Thomas Hancock, uncle of the famous John, and Thomas Hutchinson, royal governor and historian. Among the rich merchants of other sections were John Watts and John Cruger of New York, Israel Pemberton and Thomas Wharton of Philadelphia, and Henry Laurens and Gabriel Manigault of Charleston.

The social structure was also influenced by the rise of professional men. From the earliest days clergymen had been treated with deference in all the colonies and held in particular esteem in New England. But lawyers and physicians had at first little place in American life. In early lawsuits both the advocates who argued the cases and the judges who heard them were unhampered by professional studies. The practice of medicine was equally the province of amateurs. In the South the planters felt no hesitation in prescribing for their retainers, and in New England pills and purges were often administered by the ministers and deacons. But in the eighteenth century things became decidedly different. First in Maryland and later in the other colonies, the pleading of cases fell more and more into the hands of men who had received legal training. Some of these like John and Edward Rutledge and Thomas and Charles Cotesworth Pinckney of South Carolina, John Dickinson of Pennsylvania, and Daniel Dulany of Maryland, studied in England at the famous London Inns of Court. But more commonly colonial lawyers learned their craft from older members of the bar. Through such apprenticeship, James Otis and John Adams of Massachusetts, William Livingston of New York, and Thomas Jefferson of Virginia became lawyers. Despite the increased emphasis on legal training standards were lax, and the famous Patrick Henry was admitted to the Virginia bar after only a few weeks of study. As these names suggest, successful lawyers achieved such prestige that they became principal spokesmen for the colonists in the controversies with the mother country. But their close association with merchants and moneylenders did not assure the lawyers' popularity with the lower classes. A contemporary verse complained:

> Annoint the lawyer, grease him in the Fist,
> And he will plead for thee, even what thou list.[1]

Somewhat similar was the evolution of a professional class of physicians. Among the immigrants of the eighteenth century were English, Scotch, and French doctors. A few colonials went to Edinburgh or London to study medicine, but many more gained what training they could as apprentices. Although doctors usually occupied a somewhat lower social status than clergymen and lawyers, a few, like Dr. Joseph Warren of Boston, Dr. Cadwallader Colden of New York, and Dr. Benjamin Rush of Philadelphia, became persons of great influence.

The class of gentlemen included a variety of individuals: royal officials, great landowners, merchants, and professional men. It was partly composed of the wellborn and partly of the conspicuously successful. Whatever its origins, it en-

[1] Quoted in Evarts Boutell Greene, *The Revolutionary Generation, 1763–1790* (Macmillan, New York, 1943), 86.

joyed important prerogatives. The most respected colonials, magistrates and members of the council, were addressed with the title "Esquire" after their names. Only slightly less deferential was the title "Mister," not then bestowed on every adult male but reserved for those who were unquestionably gentlemen. Gentlemen largely monopolized the political life of the colonies, occupied the best seats in church and other public assemblies, and wore clothes whose rich material and fashionable cut clearly distinguished their wearers from other elements in the population.

Next in the social hierarchy were the yeoman farmers and the artisans. Although deferential to the class above them, they had their own pride of station. They called each other "Goodman" and "Goodwife" and considered themselves better than journeymen and unskilled laborers, who owned no real estate and were addressed by their Christian names. Free laborers, in turn, looked down on the indentured servants, and the latter took satisfaction in the reflection that, since their status was temporary, they were at least superior to the slaves.

Colonial society was obviously undemocratic in its frank recognition of classes. These social distinctions were part of an Old World heritage that only a few Americans were ready to challenge. But New World influences were, nevertheless, corrosive of aristocratic privilege. The man of talent was again and again able to rise well above the station to which he was born. It was symbolic of the influences at work that John Adams, whose yeoman background entitled him to rank only fourteenth in his Harvard class of 25 and Benjamin Franklin, who started life as a printer's apprentice, should become the colleagues of the patrician George Washington in the struggle for independence.

Chapter 4. Worshiping God

Nothing is more characteristic of America than the extraordinary diversity of its religious life. Almost every sect of European Christianity and Judaism has had its American counterpart, and many new cults have sprung out of the fertile native soil. The process of division and subdivision began with the first generation of colonists and has never stopped.

The Religious Inheritance

Just a century before the Pilgrim Fathers landed at Plymouth, the unity of Western Christendom had been shattered by Martin Luther's assault upon the Roman Catholic Church. The Church had often been challenged before. Kings and emperors had quarreled with the popes over specific issues, and a few bold souls like John Huss and John Wycliffe had denied the papal supremacy and criticized the sacramental system. But not until Luther's day were conditions ripe for a revolt which would win the support of people from all classes. Thousands of sincerely religious individuals were shocked by clerical abuses, and others were ready to attack the old order for other reasons—to expand their own power or to enrich themselves by confiscating ecclesiastical property.

From criticism of the methods by which the Church was attempting to raise money, Luther was led to challenge Catholic doctrine as well as Catholic practice. He denied the authority of the pope, repudiated the idea that men could attain heaven through good works, and asserted that salvation was dependent on faith alone. He called upon the German nobles to extend their authority over the churches within their respective realms and to reform them in accordance with his teachings. Most of northern Germany, the Scandinavian states, and the Baltic states went over to Lutheranism.

In denying the unique authority of the Roman Church and setting forth doctrines based upon his own interpretation of the Bible, Luther had taken a step that other men could take as well. Radical Protestants disliked the retention of bishops and the close union of church and state that characterized Lutheranism. Luther's theology was too conservative for them, retaining as it did many teachings of the old church which Luther regarded as not contrary to Scripture. From the beginning of the Protestant Reformation there existed a radical wing represented by numerous minor sects. Impatient with both traditionalism and rationalism, these radicals placed primary importance on individual religious experience. Many, known as Anabaptists, condemned the baptism of infants and taught that the rite should be administered only to adults after their conversion. Drawing their strength principally from peasants and artisans, the Anabaptists suffered persecution from both Catholic and Lutheran princes. They were condemned, not only for their extreme religious views, but for the radical political and social ideas which many of them professed.

Intermediate between the conservatism of the Lutherans and the radicalism of the Anabaptists was the great Calvinist movement. Living most of his life as an exile in Switzerland, John Calvin exercised enormous power in the political and religious life of Geneva. Through his writings and personal contacts with Protestant leaders from many countries, Calvin exerted international influence. The Huguenots of France, the Presbyterians of Scotland, and the Reformed Churches of Holland and Germany were all strongly Calvinist in creed and government.

Calvin's basic doctrine was the absolute sovereignty of God. The first man, Adam, was made in the likeness of God, but from this state of purity he fell through disobedience and sin. Adam's fall involved the whole human race. Even newborn infants were sinners in the eyes of God; they had not yet brought forth the fruits of their iniquity, but the seed was shut up in them. Since human nature was utterly depraved, men were entirely without ability to do good and to win their own salvation. In his mercy, however, God had willed that some should be saved. To atone for their sins, Christ had suffered death upon the cross. Through faith in God men availed themselves of Christ's sacrifice and obtained salvation. But only a few ever attained this redeeming faith. Proceeding logically from Calvin's conception of the complete sovereignty of God was his doctrine of predestination. The few, the elect, were predestined by God for eternal life; they heeded Christ's call and knew that they were saved; they gave evidence of their redemption in their good and holy conduct. The many were predestined for eternal damnation, and usually gave evidence of their fatal destiny by their wicked behavior.

Although Calvin repudiated the rule of bishops, he believed strongly in religious discipline. Only duly ordained ministers might preach and administer the sacraments—baptism and the Lord's Supper. In supervising the morals of the congregation and in censuring evildoers, the ministers had the assistance of venerable and respected laymen, the elders. Congregations had the right to elect their preachers and elders, but preachers must be ordained and inducted in their offices by other preachers. This duty and many other functions of church government were performed by presbyteries and synods composed of the clergy and representative elders.

Calvinism appealed particularly to the rising middle classes. Businessmen had been irked by Catholic economic doctrines which deprecated avarice, condemned the taking of interest, and advocated the fixing of fair prices. Such clerical moralizing had been resented both because it seemed insensitive to the needs of nascent capitalism and because it seemed essentially hypocritical in view of the acquisitive activities of many ecclesiastics. Merchants and investors were therefore gratified by Calvin's emphasis on the virtues of industry and thrift. Although salvation was not to be won by good works, the regenerate man would demonstrate his fortunate state by sober habits and uncommon application to his calling. The Christian weaver would weave more and better cloth than his sinful competitor; the Christian merchant would sell more goods. The prosperity achieved by the Christian businessman was evidence of God's approval. Poverty was to be attributed to the idleness and wicked habits of the poor—unhappy reminders that they were not among those chosen by God for salvation. More important than specific Calvinist approval of the taking of moderate interest and other capitalist practices was the general stamp of respectability given to the newer forms of economic activity. "What reason is there," wrote Calvin, "why the income from business should not be larger than that from land owning? Whence do the merchant's profits come, except from his own diligence and industry?"

The Reformation in England was powerfully influenced by developments on the Continent. There was the same discontent with conditions in the Roman Catholic Church, and many English clergymen were eager to emulate Luther and Calvin. Indeed, there is evidence that the ferment introduced by John Wycliffe two centuries before still bubbled strongly beneath the surface of English religious life.

But the actual form of the English break from Rome was largely determined by the Tudor monarchs. Henry VIII had no sympathy with Protestant doctrine and vigorously condemned Luther's rebellion. When the Pope refused to annul his marriage with Catherine of Aragon, however, Henry demanded and received from Parliament drastic legislation renouncing the authority of the papacy and recognizing the King's supremacy over the English Church. This action was followed by confiscations of ecclesiastical lands and the introduction of English into the church services. But the doctrine of the Church of England remained fundamentally Catholic, and Henry persecuted Protestant and Catholic critics of his religious policy with fine impartiality. After Henry's death the trend of events was strongly Protestant under his sickly son Edward VI and strongly Catholic under his daughter Mary.

After Mary's death Elizabeth, Henry's Protestant daughter, undertook to settle the religious controversy on a basis broad enough to reconcile all factions. All ties with the papacy were severed, and the Anglican creed was stated in mildly Calvinist terms. But the Church was still organized along hierarchical lines with archbishops and bishops retaining their traditional powers, and the service was ritualistic, perpetuating the dignity and beauty of Catholic worship. Severe penalties were stipulated for persons who failed to attend the services of the national church or attempted to worship in unauthorized assemblies.

There were many opponents of the Elizabethan settlement. At one extreme were the Catholics, who could not accept the repudiation of papal authority; at the other were Protestants, unhappy because the national church had not departed far enough from Catholicism. These Protestant critics, or Puritans, were deeply influenced by Calvinism. Except for a small minority they had no wish to separate from the national church—a course of action which they opposed as contrary to the principle of religious uniformity in which they believed no less than their rivals. They hoped to win control of the Church and to purify it in accordance with their own ideas. They wished to substitute presbyterian or congregational government for that by bishops, to restate the creed in more explicitly Calvinist terms, and to eliminate such Catholic vestiges as the altar, clerical vestments, the liturgy of the prayer book, and the sign of the cross in the baptism service.

Few in numbers and drawing their strength largely from the lower classes were the Separatists. They too were Calvinists—Calvinists who carried the implications of the doctrine of predestination further than Calvin himself had. Since only the elect were godly, they believed that only the elect should be admitted to church membership. According to this reasoning the Church of England, all-inclusive in its membership, was no true church, and the elect had no alternative but to separate from it and form their own independent churches. Rejecting Presbyterianism as well as Anglicanism, the Separatists taught that church government should be congregational, that is, based upon the voluntary association of a group of Christians and independent of any external authority other than God's will as revealed in the Bible.

All these European varieties of Christianity were transplanted to American soil during the first century of colonization.

Colonial Anglicanism

On June 21, 1607, Chaplain Robert Hunt first administered the sacrament of communion to his Jamestown parish in the shade of an old sail hung between the trees of the Virginia forest. Later a rude church was built, to which the colonists were summoned twice daily and four times on Sunday. Commercial in purpose though it was, the Virginia Company recognized an obligation to provide for the proper worship of God. Indeed, the planting of the Church of England in heathen parts was emphasized as one of the Company's great objectives, entitling it to the support of the Crown and the nation.

The colonists were instructed as to their religious obligations in terms which they could not fail to understand. Under the code of laws proclaimed by Governor Dale in 1611, persons who failed to attend daily prayers were to be deprived of their rations for a first offense, whipped for a second, and sent to the galleys for a third. Those who indulged in gaming on the Sabbath or failed to attend Sunday worship were to be even more severely dealt with—the penalty for a third offense being death. Those who were disrespectful to the clergy were to be flogged; those who blasphemed against God were to be executed.

When the colonists gained a voice in government through the House of Burgesses, they dealt with religious affairs somewhat less drastically, but they still gave the Church strong support. Absence from worship or disparagement of the minister were punishable by heavy fines in tobacco. The clergymen were given the use of sizable estates called "glebes," and each male inhabitant was required to pay a special tax for the pastor's salary. When three Congregational missionaries from Massachusetts appeared on the scene in 1642, the crisis was met by a new law forbidding any minister to enter the colony unless he could satisfy the governor of his orthodoxy. The Puritans made some headway during the Cromwellian period, but with the Restoration the Anglican Church was once more firmly established.

However strong legally, the Anglican position was in practice somewhat weak. Institutions well adapted to the care of souls in the compact villages of England were ill suited to the scattered plantations of Virginia. Law or no law, many families lived too far from church to attend regularly, and even the most diligent pastor found it difficult to minister to the needs of a parish that might extend for 25 miles or more of river front. Sometimes marriages and funerals had to be conducted without a clergyman. Many of the Virginia dead were laid away in family cemeteries rather than in the consecrated ground of the churchyard.

Since there were no bishops in America, Anglican clergymen could be ordained only in England. Relatively few colonials overcame this obstacle, and those of the English clergy who came over were frequently second-rate men. Governor Berkeley acidly remarked that "of all commodities, so of this, the worst are sent to us." Doubtless these words did an injustice to many good men who labored faithfully in the colonial vineyard. But the Church was nevertheless handicapped by a few dissolute pastors and a larger number of careless and indolent ones. Even of second-rate men there was a scarcity. The Virginia clergy were so poorly paid that there were never enough properly ordained men in the colony to minister to all the parishes. With salaries fixed in terms of tobacco, the parsons suffered severely from the downward trend of tobacco prices. The better parishes voted extra compensation to provide the clergymen with a decent living, but many parishes were unable or unwilling to do this.

The isolation of Virginia churches resulted in divergences from strict Anglican principles. Through control of the purse, laymen gained extensive power. The vestries claimed the right to choose their own ministers and to treat them as salaried employees. The scarcity of properly ordained clergymen and the poverty of the parishes led to the widespread use of lay readers. Both parsons and lay readers often departed from the strict liturgy of the prayer book to shorten and simplify the service.

It was not until after the Restoration that responsibility for the American parishes was clearly vested in the Bishop of London. Henry Compton, who became Bishop of London in 1675, took his duties seriously and attempted a program of reform. In 1689 he began to appoint commissaries to act as his delegates in visiting colonial parishes and admonishing the clergy. The first such official was James Blair, who served in Virginia from 1689 to his death in 1743. Blair began his mission in a crusading spirit. He lectured the governors on their duties and brought about the removal of those who would not support him; he pleaded for more money for the Church; he obtained the establishment of William and Mary College. But his task was difficult. Colonial officials were often indifferent to his pleas; parishes continued to be large and vestries independent; clergymen were so scarce that discipline was avoided except in the most notorious cases.

In neighboring Maryland Anglicanism made no progress until the end of the century. The first proprietors were Roman Catholics and of course welcomed Catholic colonists. From the first, however, they also encouraged the settlement of Protestants. This was doubly expedient since it insured against the hostility which an exclusively Catholic colony might have invited and since it promoted settlement to the economic advantage of the proprietors. To meet the crisis resulting from the Puritan revolution in England, Maryland's religious policy was clarified by the Act of Toleration of 1649, which declared that no person professing to believe in Jesus Christ was to be molested in the free exercise of his religion. The same law, however, made blasphemy or denial of the Trinity punishable by death. Forty years after the founding of the colony Maryland's 2,000 Catholics and three or four priests were greatly outnumbered by Puritans, Quakers, and other Protestants. In 1692 the Baltimores lost control of the colony, and by 1715, when the proprietorship was restored, the Baltimores had become Protestants. These political events were accompanied by religious changes of far-reaching character. In 1692 the Maryland assembly made the Church of England the established religion of the colony, even though there were only three or four Anglican clergymen in Maryland at the time. Protestant dissenters were permitted to worship unmolested, but Catholics were not protected. Forbidden by law to hold political office, to vote, or to conduct religious services except in private homes, the Maryland Catholics suffered intermittent persecution for three generations. Meanwhile the Church of England received strong support from some of the Maryland governors and from Commissary Thomas Bray but failed to flourish.

The Church of England was also established by law in North and South Carolina, Georgia, and in four counties of New York. But by burdening the Church with a complacent clergy and an indifferent laity, state sponsorship appeared to handicap Anglicanism more than it helped.

The Church of England had more real vitality in the colonies where it did not depend on government support. During the eighteenth century Anglicanism made significant gains in the northern and middle colonies. As life became more settled in the colonial towns, the orderly beauty of Church of England worship began to appeal to many people, particularly to the official classes and the well to do. Two of the most famous Anglican churches were King's Chapel in Puritan Boston and Christ's Church in Quaker Philadelphia. In 1722 the Congregationalist world was shocked when Timothy Cutler, the president of Yale, and Daniel Brown and Samuel Johnson, his assistants, resigned their posts and sailed to

England to obtain ordination as priests of the Church of England. Anglicanism won another notable convert in George Keith, who had quarreled with his fellow Quakers.

Through the initiative of Commissary Thomas Bray the Society for the Propagation of the Gospel in Foreign Parts was founded in 1701. Devoted to general missionary aims, it found the first great field for its activities in America. The S.P.G., or Venerable Society, sent over three hundred missionaries to the colonies between 1701 and 1775. Missions and schools were maintained for the benefit of pauper whites, Negroes, and Indians. Anglican chapels were built in many areas where there was no Anglican establishment.

Despite its eighteenth-century gains the Church of England never overcame the handicap of being episcopal in organization but without an American bishop. Since colonials who desired ordination had to undergo the expense and hardship of a 3,000-mile ocean voyage, the Church continued to depend largely on an English-born and English-educated clergy. Failure to provide colonial bishops was at first a result of British negligence. Later the Church of England was anxious to remedy the situation, but all proposals for the establishment of bishoprics in the New World were vigorously opposed by colonial dissenters and by many colonial Anglicans as well. John Adams said:

> The objection was not only to the office of a bishop though that was dreaded, but to the authority of Parliament on which it must be founded. The reasoning was this: There is no power less than Parliament which can create bishops in America. But if Parliament can erect dioceses and appoint bishops, they may introduce the whole hierarchy, establish tithes, establish religion, forbid dissenters, make schism heresy, impose penalties extending to life and limb as well as to liberty and property.

Congregationalism in New England

The story of how a small group of English Separatists migrated first to the Netherlands and then to America is a familiar one. Settling finally at Plymouth, the Pilgrim Fathers worshiped as Congregationalists just as they had in England and Holland. But if Congregationalism in America had been dependent on Separatist migration alone, it could never have become a large movement.

Congregationalism's great expansion was assured only when it began to recruit from the Puritan faction in the Church of England. Although most of the English Puritans inclined toward Presbyterianism, the leaders who came to Massachusetts Bay belonged to a faction which had become attached to Congregational principles. Like the Separatists they had come to the conclusion that church membership should be restricted to the elect and that each congregation should be self-governing. But, paradoxically, they still condemned separation from the Church of England as a sin. These nonseparating Congregationalists continued to consider themselves members of the national church, which they regarded as a true church but one with unfortunate corruptions. In America they organized their churches on a congregational basis. They accepted advice from Plymouth on matters of detail; but they continued to draw a sharp line between the Plymouth church, which had separated from the Church of England, and their own group, which had never formally done so—although they governed themselves and worshiped in a manner far different from Anglican practice.

The leaders of the great Puritan migration were men of substance and good education. They sought not merely to worship in their own way but to demonstrate that theirs was the only way. New England was to be a Puritan model state for the instruction of all true Christians. In the Bible God Himself had fixed the laws which must control all religious and political activities, and the New Englanders believed that they were merely carrying out these clear ordinances.

According to Congregational theory a church came into existence when a group of the elect organized a voluntary association. After expressing its intention in a church covenant, the group proceeded to elect ministers and elders. The vote of the church members was necessary to admit new communicants and to excommunicate those who proved unworthy or heretical. But seventeenth-century Congregationalism was not so democratic as might first appear. Once called to a church, the minister was not regarded as the servant of the congregation. His office was not of human origin but had been ordained by Christ Himself. The minister had a clearly defined area of authority which must not be invaded by laymen. Although the individual church member might read the Bible for himself, the minister's interpretation was usually regarded as authoritative. In admitting new members or in disciplining heretics, the ordinary church members were accustomed to ratify the action which the ministers and elders indicated as the proper one in the circumstances. Following the teachings of Calvin, the Congregationalists claimed to have established a mixed form of church government. It was monarchic since Christ was its all-sovereign King; it was aristocratic since the ministers were given a predominating influence; it was democratic since it was based on voluntary association of godly men.

Congregationalism, no less than Anglicanism in Virginia, was a state religion. The ministers were supported by allotments of land and taxes levied on the entire population. As an established church, however, the Congregational Church was in a peculiar position. Although it required church attendance of all, it did not admit all to membership and participation in the sacraments. In this inner circle only those were accepted who could convince the minister and congregation that they were "saints" selected by God for salvation. Only a minority of the population appear to have passed this rigid scrutiny.

The New England Puritans derived their doctrines only in part from the great John Calvin. More immediately influential were the writings of William Ames and other English "federal" theologians who had developed the theory of the "covenant of grace." According to this, God had covenanted with mankind that whoever should have faith in Him and follow in His way would be saved. Predestination still determined which souls would benefit by this act of grace, but covenant theology modified strict Calvinism to place greater emphasis on God's justice and to stress the obligation of the elect to obey God's law. The elect did not earn their salvation by good works, but they fulfilled their part of the covenant by faith and by sincere effort, however faltering, to follow the path of righteousness. At its best, covenant theology quieted men's anxieties and stirred them to Christian action; at its worst, it encouraged complacency: the ability to live an upright life was likely to be equated with election by God.

FIG. 4. Old Brick Meetinghouse, Boston. Erected in 1713, this square meetinghouse reflects Puritanism's determination to have nothing to do with architectural conventions derived from Catholicism. (*Courtesy of the Massachusetts Historical Society.*)

Church and state were closely related. Aspiring to create an ideal state no less than an ideal church, the Massachusetts Puritans carried the same principles into effect in both spheres. The church covenant had its counterpart in the compact whereby the colonists, in the words of John Winthrop, "implicitly at least, bind themselves to support each other, and all of them that society, whether civil or sacred, whereof they are members." The voters sent their representatives to a General Court to make laws and elected magistrates to administer them. But no more than the ministers were the magistrates regarded as mere servants of the people. They too occupied an office which had divine sanction. They must be unquestioningly obeyed lest the government be brought from "a mixt Aristocratie to a meere Democratie." Only church members were permitted to vote.

The clergy and the magistracy worked in efficient partnership. In cases of heresy the church government excommunicated and the civil government imposed punishments of flogging, mutilation, or banishment. Although much of the population might be doomed to future damnation, they had no license to enjoy their sins unmolested in this life. On the contrary, the godly who dominated the government felt a special duty to repress conduct that might be displeasing to God. Traveling or playing games on the Sabbath, inattention or levity during divine worship, and the utterance of blasphemous and profane language were punishable by the stocks or the whipping post, and such major sins as adultery might bring the death penalty or the humiliating scarlet letter. The support given by the magistrates to the church was fully reciprocated. Obedience to the civil authorities was inculcated as a religious duty. Since the Bible was the fundamental constitution of the state as well as of the church, the ministers were often asked to give their opinion on important political issues.

The Rise of Dissent

Congregationalism did not long retain its New England monopoly. In 1635 Roger Williams was charged by the Massachusetts General Court with "divers dangerous opinions." Williams, an ardent Separatist, criticized the Bay churches for continuing to regard the Church of England with all her corruptions as their mother. He believed that they were wrong in summoning the unregenerate to worship along with the elect in their meetinghouses. He condemned the magistrates for their interference in the affairs of the Salem church of which he was minister. He asserted that the Massachusetts Bay charter was invalid, since America belonged to the Indians and not to the King of England. Refusing to yield to the counterarguments of the orthodox clergy, Williams was brought to trial before the magistrates and condemned to banishment. After living for a time with his Indian friends, he and a few followers began a new settlement at Providence in 1636.

The issues which divided Williams from the Massachusetts Puritans were clearly defined in an important pamphlet war during the next decade. In *The Bloudy Tenent of Persecution, for Cause of Conscience, Discussed* (1644), Williams argued that church and state should occupy separate spheres and that civil governments should not intervene in matters of conscience—to establish churches, to punish heretics, or to impose civil penalties or disabilities for any religious reason. John Cotton, the ablest spokesman for Massachusetts orthodoxy, replied in *The Bloudy Tenent, Washed, and Made White in the Bloud of the Lambe* (1647), stanchly upholding the traditional duty of the magistrates to maintain purity of religion and to punish purveyors of erroneous doctrine.

More dangerous theologically was the dissent of Anne Hutchinson. A woman of strong religious convictions and fluent speech, Mrs. Hutchinson gathered an influential following. At the height of her power Governor Harry Vane and John

Cotton showed sympathy with her position. But the Hutchinson faction was soon overthrown. The freemen returned the conservative John Winthrop to the governorship, and a synod of the Congregational clergy condemned the doctrines of Antinomianism which they attributed to the voluble Anne. This was their response to her criticism of them for preaching "a covenant of works" rather than "a covenant of grace," that is, of emphasizing the observance of external rules and commandments rather than direct communion with God. The church-state alliance worked smoothly in the crisis. Excommunicated and banished from the jurisdiction of the colony, Mrs. Hutchinson and her followers took refuge in the Narragansett Bay country, where they founded settlements at Portsmouth and Newport.

Rhode Island thus became a haven for the otherwise-minded. Some of the Rhode Islanders became Baptists, adopting the tenets of a faction of English Separatists who, like the German Anabaptists, condemned the baptism of infants. In 1639 Roger Williams and several followers were rebaptized and organized a Baptist church at Providence. Williams's tendency toward contrariety was so ingrained, however, that he did not remain long in any religious camp. His final position was that of a Seeker. Convinced that all Christendom had become so corrupt that no one was qualified to administer the sacraments, he resigned himself to waiting for the moment when Christ should send forth "new apostles to plant churches anew." Williams's misgivings did not prevent the expansion of the Baptist movement. The most vigorous Baptist church of the period was that built up at Newport under the ministry of John Clarke.

Alarmed by these events, the Massachusetts General Court in 1644 prescribed banishment for any person who should openly oppose the baptizing of infants. In 1651 John Clarke and two other Rhode Island Baptists defied the authorities by preaching at Lynn. Clarke and one of his companions were fined; the third member of the party, Obadiah Holmes, refused to pay and was severely whipped. Soon after this, orthodoxy was challenged at its very citadel when President Henry Dunster of Harvard College publicly opposed infant baptism. In 1654 Dunster was compelled to resign. Over the next generation a struggle continued between Baptists, who insisted on holding meetings, and the Massachusetts authorities, who attempted to repress the movement with fines and imprisonments.

The Quakers presented a still more troublesome problem. This movement had begun in England in 1647, when George Fox, an itinerant shoemaker, had undergone the mystical religious experience known as "the Illumination." Rejecting the doctrine of predestination, Fox became convinced that all Christians who truly loved God would be saved. Since all men and women were children of God and of equal value in His sight, Fox opposed rank and title, refused to remove his hat before the magistrates, and addressed all persons with the familiar "thou" and "thee." He believed that God revealed himself not alone through the Scriptures, but through direct communication with the individual—the "Inner Light." Hence his rejection of formal worship, his practice of interrupting the services of other sects, and his reliance upon a lay ministry. He advocated refusal to take oaths, to bear arms, and to pay taxes for the support of established churches. Fox's doctrines were as unacceptable to the Puritans as to the Anglicans. He was imprisoned eight times and his followers suffered many persecutions. But the Friends of Truth, as they liked to be called, grew rapidly in numbers. Zealous missionaries carried their message to the continent of Europe, to Palestine, and even to the Sultan of Turkey.

In 1656 the Quakers made their first attempt to bring the Inner Light to Massachusetts. But Mary Fisher and Anne Austin met a most unceremonious reception upon their arrival in Boston. Their books were publicly burned and they themselves were stripped and searched for telltale marks that might reveal that they were witches. After imprisonment for several weeks they were deported to Barbados. The authorities now hurried a drastic anti-Quaker code through the General Court. When whippings and mutilations did not halt subsequent Quaker demonstrations, the magistrates condemned three enthusiasts to death in 1659. Mary Dyer, one of those sentenced, was reprieved on the gallows, but, determined on martyrdom, she returned to Boston the following spring and was executed. A fourth Quaker was hanged in 1661. Charles II intervened to halt further killings, but Quakers were still subject to whipping and banishment. In Connecticut the new sect received similar treatment.

The Friends encountered less hostility in Plymouth Colony and Rhode Island. Although the veteran Roger Williams strenuously combated the newcomers in public disputations, no attempt was made to suppress them. By 1700 the Quakers were the most numerous denomination in the colony and were dominant in the colonial government.

During the Commonwealth period the idea of religious toleration gained ground in England, and the severity of the Massachusetts system was criticized by many English Puritans. Restored to the throne in 1660, Charles II made evident his displeasure with both the religious and political practices of the Boston oligarchy. Under these pressures the theocracy gradually weakened. The Baptists and Quakers gained a limited toleration during the 1670's. After the annulment of the old Massachusetts Bay charter in 1684 more drastic changes soon followed. Church of England services began in 1686, and the following year the Puritans were subjected to the chagrin of having one of their own meetinghouses used for Anglican worship on order of Sir Edmund Andros, the royal governor. After the Glorious Revolution in England the old regime tried to reestablish itself but gained only a limited victory. In 1691 Massachusetts received a new charter, but the old theocratic system was not permitted. Religious toleration for all Protestants was enjoined, and the franchise was based upon a property qualification rather than upon church membership.

Internally as well as externally, the old Puritan establishment was weakening. The strict limitation of church membership led to increasing criticism. In 1657 a synod of the clergy approved the so-called Half-way Covenant, whereby persons who had been baptized in infancy and had led exemplary lives might be regarded as church members and be allowed to present their children for baptism even though they had not had a distinct religious "experience." This led to the growth of a class of "Half-way" church members, who enjoyed most of the privileges of membership, including the franchise, but were not permitted to participate in the Lord's Supper. Even in admitting individuals to this last citadel, the elders became more lenient with the passing of the years.

The last great expression of Puritanism in its older, more fanatical form was the witchcraft hysteria of the late seventeenth century. Like most Europeans of the day the New Englanders took for granted the ancient belief that the devil might take residence in human bodies and compel his unhappy hosts to perform all sorts of supernatural evil. The first New England witch was hanged in Connecticut in 1647, and there were occasional subsequent executions in both Connecticut and Massachusetts. In 1692 all Salem was convulsed by hysteria. Deluded or mischievous children screamed and rolled on the ground, accusing one neighbor after another of tormenting them. The accused often confessed—either to escape torture or because they fell under the same delusion as their accusers. After 19 alleged witches had been put to death and the number of suspects began to mount into the hundreds, New England suddenly came to its senses. Trials and executions were halted and the prisoners released. Five years later Judge Samuel Sewall displayed the more admirable side of Puritanism when he stood before the congregation of the Old South Church in Boston and acknowledged repentance and shame for his part in the shedding of innocent blood. The excesses of the witch trials seriously discredited the old religious order.

Liberal seams were clearly visible in the Puritan granite during the early eighteenth century. In 1699 a group of wealthy and influential Bostonians organized the Brattle Street Church with more lenient standards of membership than the older churches. Supported by the royal governor, this latitudinarian faction soon gained control of Harvard College to the dismay of Increase and Cotton Mather and other conservatives.

The Mathers suffered a further defeat when they attempted to fortify orthodoxy through the establishment of regional associations of ministers.[1] Opposing this program as tending toward Presbyterianism, John Wise of Ipswich defended the traditional Congregational polity in two able works, *The Churches Quarrel Espoused* (1710) and *A Vindication of the Government of New England Churches* (1717). Wise's argument, largely derived from the German philosopher Samuel Pufendorf, emphasized the idea that government originates in the consent of the governed. Since principles of popular sovereignty were as applicable to political affairs as to religious, Wise's books were reprinted later in the century to justify colonial resistance to Parliamentary taxation. Meanwhile,

[1] An earlier and more drastic step had been taken in Connecticut, where the Saybrook Platform of 1705 gave legal status to regional consociations of ministers and elders—thereby transforming Connecticut Congregationalism into a "semi-Presbyterianism."

on the immediate issue the Mather proposal failed, and Congregational churches retained complete autonomy. Congregational ministers could stray far from conventional orthodoxy so long as they retained the support of their own parishioners. This was evident in the strongly rationalist tendencies of the preaching of Jonathan Mayhew and Charles Chauncy.

Religion in the Middle Colonies

The system of uniformity which Virginia and Massachusetts struggled to enforce never secured a foothold in the middle colonies. The complex factors that led to that region's settlement resulted in great religious diversity from the beginning.

To be sure, the Dutch Reformed Church enjoyed the privileges of an established church in New Netherland. Pastors were sent out by the Dutch West India Company, and the settlers were obliged to pay taxes for their support. But toward other denominations the government, despite occasional lapses, followed a policy of toleration. After the British conquest the Dutch Church continued in a strong position. Its privileges had in general terms been guaranteed by the instrument of surrender, and for a time this was interpreted to mean that the Dutch clergy were still entitled to support from public taxation.

Late in the seventeenth century some of the English governors attempted to establish the Church of England. In 1693 the colonial assembly ordered that in each community of New York, Westchester, Queens, and Richmond counties, wardens and vestries should be elected and provision made for the support of the clergy through taxation. But since neither the Book of Common Prayer nor the Church of England was specifically mentioned, Dutch congregations continued to elect Dutch Reformed clergymen. In the end the Church of England secured a precarious establishment in communities where the local sentiment supported it; elsewhere, the town church was usually Dutch Reformed. The Dutch clergy, however, found it impossible to collect the old church dues, and a system of support through subscriptions and voluntary contributions had to be substituted.

For many years the Dutch Reformed Church suffered from handicaps similar to those of the Church of England. Since ministers had to be ordained by the Classis of Amsterdam, the rise of a native clergy was inhibited and many parishes found it difficult to obtain pastors. After a long controversy between conservatives and liberals an American governing body with power to license ministers was finally established. Although conservatives insisted that the service should be exclusively in Dutch, a younger generation criticized this practice. By the time of the Revolution many of the sermons were being preached in English.

The Dutch Reformed and the Anglican communions were not permitted to monopolize the field. New England Congregationalists had begun to settle in New York and New Jersey during the Dutch period, and they came in increasing numbers after the conquest. Many settled on Long Island and in Westchester County; others founded villages in northeastern New Jersey. When the Connecticut charter of 1662 merged New Haven with the slightly more liberal colony of Connecticut, many old-line Puritans removed to New Jersey to keep their institutions undefiled. Their most ambitious settlement was at Newark (New Ark). They attempted to transplant the New England system in all its characteristic features—the compact village with its land allotments in the outlying fields, government by Congregational church members, the exclusion of other religious groups, legislation in accord with harsh Old Testament principles. But as settlers with different backgrounds and beliefs flooded into the area, the narrow exclusiveness of the New Englanders was soon broken down.

New Jersey had a great attraction for groups eager to practice their faith in the favoring environment of a new country. Baptists, persecuted in Massachusetts and New Hampshire, founded settlements at Middletown and Piscataway, while the Quakers erected their first New Jersey meetinghouse at Shrewsbury. The way was cleared for more extensive Quaker settlement when wealthy Friends purchased proprietary rights in both West Jersey and East Jersey.

The Quakers, however, found their best opportunity in Pennsylvania. On the banks of the Delaware William Penn made his "holy experiment"—the creation of a model state dedicated to the ideals of religious toleration, political liberalism, and the renunciation of war. In accordance with Penn's wishes the early settlers passed laws guaranteeing freedom of worship to all law-abiding persons who "acknowledged an Almighty and Eternal God to be the Creator, Upholder, and Ruler of the world." Quaker tolerance did not extend to sinners, however, and strict laws were passed against the theater, gambling, drunkenness, and profanity.

In 1700 it seemed possible that the Friends might become the leading American denomination. Their influence was great in Rhode Island and New Jersey, and in Pennsylvania they had erected a commonwealth wholly dedicated to their principles. Better understood by a new generation, they no longer suffered persecution. They were admired for the earnestness of their religious life and their generosity toward good causes.

During the eighteenth century, however, the Quakers made little progress. Individual Friends like John Woolman and Anthony Benezet gained respect for their piety and noble humanitarianism, but the sect itself grew only slowly. Quaker pacificism was dangerously unpopular during the period of the French and Indian War. Quaker tenacity in Pennsylvania politics antagonized other groups which were underrepresented in the assembly. Quaker wealth and material success damped the zeal that had characterized the movement during its heroic age. Repugnance to compulsion resulted in loose organizational ties that put the Friends at a disadvantage in the competition for souls, and emphasis on the Inner Light obstructed the growth of a professional clergy. Unlike the Calvinists and the Anglicans, the Quakers felt no need to establish colleges to train leaders.

Meanwhile Quaker tolerance made Pennsylvania the ideal refuge for persecuted religionists of many faiths. Especially did Penn's policy attract the minor sects of Germany, which were harassed by Catholic, Lutheran, and Calvinist princes alike. Many of these groups were derived from the Anabaptists of Reformation days. Like the English Baptists they usually opposed infant baptism and practiced some form of immersion. In mystic piety and opposition to war they resembled the Quakers.

Among the earliest of these sects to arrive were the Mennonites—so named because they followed the teachings of Menno Simons, originally a Dutch Catholic priest. The first Mennonites to come to America settled at Germantown near Philadelphia in 1683. Later groups went further west, especially to the country near Lancaster. The Mennonites differed in the rigidity of their practices. Some of the earliest became easy converts to the Quakers. But the stricter Mennonites stuck stubbornly to their own faith. They paid taxes and obeyed the laws, but would not hold public office, take oaths, nor bear arms. The most conservative of all were the Amish. Two hundred years after their arrival in America the Amish still wore their characteristic loose-fitting garments fastened with hooks and eyes and abstained from the use of any of Satan's later-day snares like electric lights, radios, and automobiles.

The German Baptist Brethren or Dunkers settled in the same general areas as the Mennonites but maintained their separate identity with such practices as immersing their converts face forward, washing each other's feet, and anointing themselves with oil. The most influential Dunker was Christopher Sauer, who set up a printing press in Germantown, where he published a newspaper and many books in the German language. In 1728 a group of dissident Dunkers, led by Conrad Beissel, established a unique community at Ephrata in Lancaster County. Most of Beissel's followers renounced marriage and consecrated themselves to celibate life in separate dormitories for men and women. The Brothers and Sisters dressed in monastic robes, slept on hard beds in narrow cells, and ate their simple meals in silence off wooden tables with wooden utensils. They gathered several times each day for services in which they sang hymns of weird beauty composed by themselves. Well-tilled fields, fine handicraft, and numerous mills brought prosperity to the community for several generations.

The Moravian Brethren, who appeared in Pennsylvania in 1740, were sent over by Count Zinzendorf of Saxony. This remarkable nobleman had thrown open his great estates to several of the persecuted sects. Among those to whom he had offered shelter were the survivors of a group which had maintained its identity since the days of John Huss. Under the protection of Zinzendorf the Moravian Brethren were reorganized and won many converts. They made their first effort to establish an American mission in Georgia in 1735, but the exposed position of this frontier colony in the war between England and Spain resulted in their removal in 1740 to Pennsylvania, where settlements were soon made at Bethlehem and Nazareth. Imbued with zeal during a memorable visit of Count Zinzendorf, the Moravians undertook an ambitious program of missionary work among the Indians—an activity which they pursued with greater success than any other American denomination.

Even less than the Quakers, however, were the minor German sects destined to become popular American faiths. The great majority of the eighteenth-century German immigrants came for economic rather than religious reasons. In the old country they had been Lutheran, Reformed, or Catholic. In America they often

FIG. 5. Chapel in the sisters' house, Ephrata Cloisters. Suggests the austere piety of this Pennsylvania German sect. (*Courtesy of Library of Congress.*)

went to no church at all, since the pace of settlement was more rapid than the extension of organized religion. But the clerical authorities in Europe at length recognized the need for sending out ministers. Especially notable were the efforts of Henry Melchior Mühlenberg, a young Lutheran minister who arrived in 1742 and began the work of organizing the widely dispersed Lutherans into parishes. By 1776 Mühlenberg was supervising some seventy Lutheran congregations in Pennsylvania and the adjacent colonies. A comparable work for the German Reformed Church was done by Michael Schlatter, sent over by the Classis of Amsterdam in 1746. German Jesuits organized Catholic parishes.

While German immigration to America resulted in the growth of many separate denominations, the great eighteenth-century influx of Scotch and Scotch-Irish benefited chiefly one, the Presbyterian. In 1700 there were only a few scattered Presbyterian churches in the colonies; by 1776 the Presbyterians outnumbered all other religious groups but one, the Congregationalists. The history of the church in America really begins with the activities of Francis Makemie, a Scotch-Irish missionary, who began to work among the unorganized Presbyterian immigrants of Maryland in 1683. Makemie traveled widely, getting as far south as South Carolina and as far north as New York, where he suffered arrest and imprisonment by the Anglican governor for preaching without a license. In 1706 a small group of ministers from Maryland, Delaware, and Pennsylvania organized the Presbytery of Philadelphia with Makemie as moderator. In 1716 this body was reorganized as the Synod of Philadelphia with four subordinate presbyteries. The Synod grew in prestige and influence. Into its orbit were eventually drawn most of the Congregational churches of New Jersey and New York. Many of the former New Englanders hesitated to accept Presbyterianism but overcame their scruples in view of the need for closer church organization under the conditions prevailing in the middle colonies. But the Scotch-Irish and the New England-derived Presbyterians found it difficult to remain in harmony. Differences over the degree to which the local churches and ministers should be under the authority of the synods became so bitter at times as to result in schism.

Meanwhile, the great Scotch-Irish immigration had set in. Presbyterianism was carried into the frontier counties of Pennsylvania, down the Great Valley of Virginia, and into the Carolinas along with the various denominations of the other great migrating group, the Germans.

The Great Awakening

In all the colonies there was an extraordinary outbreak of religious enthusiasm during the 1730's and 1740's. A new generation of ministers, shocked at the lethargy of the churches, stirred their congregations with descriptions of the future punishment in store for the damned; religious excitement was aroused in one community after another; and thousands announced their conversion under highly emotional circumstances.

Several streams converged to form this mighty torrent of revivalism. One may be traced to the preaching of Dominie Theodorus J. Frelinghuysen, who about 1720 began a highly successful revival in the Dutch Reformed churches of New Jersey. Frelinghuysen's work provided inspiration for a similar ministry by William Tennent and his four sons among the Presbyterians of New Jersey and eastern Pennsylvania. William Tennent, a graduate of the University of Edinburgh, was even more influential as a teacher than as a preacher. First training his own sons for the ministry, he later expanded his activities to educate other young men. In 1735 he erected at Neshaminy, Pennsylvania, a rude school building, derisively named Log College by Tennent's critics. Although this small academy was maintained for less than ten years, it provided the Presbyterians with twenty or more young preachers with an extraordinary passion for saving souls. Gilbert Tennent, William's oldest son, began a revival at New Brunswick, New Jersey, in 1729. The fame of his preaching spread widely. In 1741 he spoke to great crowds in Boston and New Haven. In 1743 he became minister of a new Presbyterian church in Philadelphia.

The Great Awakening was powerfully influenced by a parallel movement in England. In 1738 John Wesley, an earnest young Anglican clergyman, felt his

FIG. 6. *Jonathan Edwards,* about 1750. Portrait by Joseph Badger. (*Courtesy of Yale University Art Gallery.*)

heart "strangely warmed." Developing a zeal for evangelism so intense that he was no longer content to minister to the comfortable congregations of the regular churches, Wesley began to preach an emotional gospel to English miners and workers in private houses, foundries, and open fields. Thus began the great Methodist movement. Although organized Methodist activity in America did not begin until the 1760's, one of Wesley's friends, George Whitefield, played a dramatic part in the earlier Awakening.

In a generation of great preachers Whitefield was in many ways the most extraordinary of all. An extreme individualist, he did not remain long within the Anglican fold where he began his ministry or with the Methodist group with which he was for a time associated. He preached from the pulpit of any church that would open its doors to him and was particularly successful in great outdoor meetings. In 1738 he visited the recently founded colony of Georgia and made plans for the establishment of an orphan's home, a philanthropy in which he maintained a lifelong interest. In 1739 he visited Philadelphia and began an evangelistic tour that took him to New York, Maryland, Virginia, the Carolinas, and back to Georgia. In 1740 he preached in Boston and other New England towns. Everywhere Whitefield went, his fame preceded him. Great crowds listened to him in an atmosphere electric with religious excitement.

In New England the Great Awakening centered around the person of Jonathan Edwards. When Edwards became minister of the Congregational church at Northampton, Massachusetts, in 1727, he was distressed at the condition of his parish. Religious observance was perfunctory, the younger generation were addicted to "mirth and jollity," and parental discipline was lax. As in other New England towns, growing interest in the pleasures and profits of this world had diluted the old Puritan preoccupation with the world to come. Not of a temperament to acquiesce in this state of affairs, Edwards in the spring of 1735 preached so powerful a series of sermons on man's utter dependence on God for salvation that religion became for some months the town's principal topic of conversation. Over three hundred professed conversions took place, and news of the Northampton revival spread widely, partly by word of mouth and partly through Edwards's own description in his *Faithful Narrative of the Surprising Work of God* (1736).

The excitement of Edwards's first revival soon subsided, but a much greater explosion was touched off by Whitefield's visit to New England in 1740. For two years highly emotional scenes were enacted in one town after another. At Northampton and other Connecticut Valley towns Edwards delivered highly effective sermons. His best remembered effort, "Sinners in the Hands of an Angry God," was preached to a weeping and groaning congregation at Enfield, Connecticut, in 1741.

In greater or less degree the Great Awakening affected every colony. Besides the famous preachers of the day scores of itinerants took to the road, often holding services in defiance of the regular ministers. Log College-trained evangelists invaded Anglican Virginia and enjoyed a great success in the Piedmont and the Great Valley. Even more effective were the Baptist and Methodist itinerants who came in later decades.

To the influence of the Great Awakening could be attributed many good things. Schools and colleges were established; Indian missions and charitable institutions like Whitefield's orphanage were founded; moral standards were elevated. Many of the lower classes heard for the first time preaching that stirred them deeply. The more evangelical denominations had a phenomenal growth.

This was particularly true of the Baptists, who won thousands of new members in New England and the middle colonies but had their greatest success in the South.

Revivalism had its less admirable aspects. In many communities religious emotionalism rose to such a pitch that its manifestations bordered on the psychopathic. Susceptible individuals shrieked, groaned, shook, and fainted. A few committed suicide. Many clergymen were disturbed by these exhibitions. They doubted whether such excitement served any sound spiritual purpose, and they called attention to the frequency with which the weeping convert reverted to his sins once the revival was over. Charles Chauncy of Boston condemned these excesses with vigor in his book, *Seasonable Thoughts on the State of Religion* (1743). Both the Presbyterians and the Congregationalists were seriously divided between the New Lights who favored the revivals and the Old Lights who opposed them. Jonathan Edwards himself was a victim of the reaction against the Great Awakening. Dismissed from his Northampton pastorate in 1750, he served for eight years as a missionary among the Indians at Stockbridge, Massachusetts. In 1758 he was called to the presidency of Princeton but died of smallpox soon after taking up his new duties.

Religion in 1775

At the close of the colonial period America was already a land of many faiths. According to one reckoning there were 3,105 local churches. Of this total the Congregationalists had 658, mostly in New England, the Presbyterians 543, the Baptists 498, the Anglicans 480, the Quakers 295, the German and Dutch Reformed 251, the Lutherans 151, and the Catholics 50. In such cosmopolitan communities as Charleston, New York, and Newport there were Jewish congregations. The principle of religious toleration for Protestants received willing assent in the middle colonies and in Rhode Island and grudging acquiescence elsewhere. Most of the colonies still forbade public worship by Catholics. Although Anglicans in the South and Congregationalists in the North no longer maintained a religious monopoly, they enjoyed many legal privileges. In Virginia dissenters were taxed along with conformers for the benefit of the Anglican clergy, and for marriages and burial in the churchyard the services of an Anglican clergyman were required. In all New England colonies except Rhode Island the Congregational clergy were still paid out of public funds. In Massachusetts and Connecticut members of Baptist and Quaker churches were now exempted from the church taxes, and those paid by Anglicans went to their own ministers. But with these exceptions all persons were still required to pay the old taxes.

Of growing importance among the highly educated was the movement known as Deism. The Deists had been deeply impressed by the evidence of natural law implicit in the findings of Newton and other seventeenth-century scientists. They believed in a Divine Being who created the universe and set it in motion but who did not interfere with the cosmic machine thereafter. They discarded all religious teachings that seemed to be inconsistent with the reign of universal law. This meant not only a rejection of belief in special interventions by God in contemporary affairs but skepticism regarding the miracles recorded in the Bible. Deism had been strong in England during the first half of the eighteenth century; it was at its height in the American colonies during the generation of the Revolutionary War. Thomas Jefferson and Benjamin Franklin adhered to this school of thought, and John Adams, although less advanced in his views, deviated from Calvinist orthodoxy. But Deism was by no means universal among the colonial leaders. Such radicals in politics as Patrick Henry and Samuel Adams were conservatives in religion, and the great majority of the colonial population was untouched by the rationalism of the intellectuals.

Chapter 5. The World of the Scholar

For many generations America was colonial in culture as well as in politics. Ships from the mother country brought not only manufactured goods but newspapers, books, and tutors. Colonial boys attended English grammar schools and universities. But at the same time the colonists were laying the foundations for a vigorous intellectual life of their own. Culturally, as well as politically, long strides toward nationhood had been taken before the climactic year of 1776.

Educational Traditions

The early settlers brought with them ideas about education derived from the English mother country. There a national system of schools supported by public taxation lay two centuries in the future. Education was primarily the responsibility of parents. Those who could afford it provided schooling for their children. For the poor the government, the Church of England, and private philanthropists all manifested some concern, but not enough to prevent widespread illiteracy.

The fortunate child destined to receive a thorough education began his training by learning to read either at home or in a so-called "dame school." He was then ready for a Latin grammar school where he spent seven or eight years preparing for the university. Facility in reading and writing Latin was still the most cherished possession of the scholar, and most of the time of the grammar schools was devoted to drill in the ancient tongue. When the youth had learned enough Latin for advanced study and had made a beginning in Greek—usually at about the age of fifteen—he was admitted to one of the Oxford or Cambridge colleges.

For bright boys unable to pay the regular fees of the grammar schools and the universities, certain opportunities were provided. Through the generosity of English kings and other wealthy patrons these institutions had acquired endowments which enabled them to offer free tuition and board to a limited number of poor scholars. Others might earn their way by serving the more privileged students and the masters. But this door to learning was not wide enough to accommodate any large number of lower class youth. Moreover, the type of education provided, although well adapted to serve the needs of those who intended to enter the Church or the learned professions or those who could live the lives of country gentlemen, was of little use to boys who would have to earn their living in trade or industry. In the towns private masters set up schools where children might learn to write, to do arithmetic, and to keep accounts. Such schools served the needs of middle-class families who could afford to pay the fees. Free education of this character was also provided in a few charity schools maintained by the Church or by private endowment.

But the needs of the poor were more generally met by the apprenticeship system, whereby children were bound out to masters for a term of years while they learned a trade. It was, indeed, in the matter of apprenticeship that the English government made its most significant intervention in the field of education. In the case of orphans or of children whose parents were too ignorant or too indolent to arrange their apprenticeship, responsibility was placed upon the county authorities. The overseeers of the poor were required to bind these children out to masters, and in cases where hemp, flax, or other materials were necessary for the work, these might be purchased out of funds raised through taxation. Apprenticeship often involved more than training in the craft of the master. Conscientious masters felt a responsibility to teach their charges to read and write. Indeed, this obligation was sometimes made explicit in the terms of the indenture.

Education in Virginia and the South

During the first decade of Virginia history there was no educational problem. The colony was primarily an adult male community struggling desperately to survive. But when the planters began to marry and raise children, the need for schools was soon recognized. One hopeful early plan called for the building of a college in the Virginia forest to teach the classical curriculum to both whites and Indians. Funds were accumulated, a one-man faculty imported, and buildings erected at Henrico on the James River. All was well in progress when the whole enterprise was liquidated by a terrible Indian massacre in 1622. Later attempts to found a college were even less successful. Not until 1693 were effective steps finally taken.

Less ambitious projects were brought to earlier fruition. During the 1640's the Symes Free School began to function in Elizabeth City County. This derived its support in part from the bequest of Benjamin Symes, who had endowed it with 200 acres of land and the milk and increase of 8 cows. Even more generous was Dr. Thomas Eaton of the same county, who left 500 acres of land stocked with 2 Negroes, 12 cows, 2 bulls, and 20 hogs for the establishment of a free school. Similar institutions were to be found elsewhere.

More common were the "old field schools." Several families on neighboring properties would cooperate in erecting a rude building, often in an abandoned tobacco field. Here a master hired by the parents would teach reading, writing, and arithmetic during the months from April to September. The government exercised no control over these schools except that it required that the teacher have a license—usually a perfunctory act on the part of the governor once the stipulated fee in tobacco had been paid. Most frequently the teacher was the Anglican clergyman or lay reader of the parish attempting to augment his meager salary with tuition fees. But the Virginia plantation system, which so handicapped the colony's religious life, laid even greater obstacles in the way of education. In many areas distances between neighbors were so great that any type of community school was impossible.

Wealthy parents employed tutors for their children. During the seventeenth century these were usually young Oxford and Cambridge graduates; during the eighteenth century they were more likely to be products of the Scotch universities or of northern colonial colleges like Harvard, Yale, and Princeton. The tutors were provided with comfortable quarters, ate at the table with the family, and

FIG. 7. Christopher Wren building, William and Mary College, Williamsburg, Virginia. (*Courtesy of Library of Congress.*)

accompanied them to church and social gatherings. Sometimes they held classes for their young charges in the family mansion; sometimes they were provided with a small separate building. They might have in charge not only children of their employer but children from neighboring estates as well. Girls as well as boys received instruction, although it was not usually considered desirable to burden their fragile minds with the same weight of classical training. They were more likely to study English literature, elocution, music, and embroidery. These special needs led eventually to the increasing employment of female tutors or governesses.

Young Virginians were sometimes sent to England to attend the historic grammar schools and the universities. Many parents believed that only thus could their sons be transformed into finished gentlemen. But other parents refused to send their boys on a hazardous ocean trip, to be separated from them so long and to run the risk of acquiring more bad habits than sound learning from an education abroad. Although the establishment of William and Mary eventually provided not only a college but a good grammar school, not all Virginians were satisfied. To some the new institution seemed too provincial, and they continued to send their sons abroad to gain fastidious tastes and fine manners. Others accused the William and Mary professors of skepticism and indolence and refused to entrust their boys to them, depending instead on tutors or on private grammar schools conducted by Anglican clergymen.

For the poor, opportunities were very limited. There were a few endowed free schools and a few charity schools maintained by the Church. But the most important institution for providing elementary education was apprenticeship. Laws similar to those of England required the apprenticing of orphans and children whose parents were unable to provide properly for them.

Elsewhere in the southern colonies the situation was much the same. No real system of schools developed. The children of the wealthy were educated by tutors and in private schools, many boys receiving a part of their education abroad. The children of the poor sometimes gained the rudiments of education through charity schools or apprenticeship. A majority probably received no formal learning at all. In a few places like Charleston, where town life was well developed, the situation was somewhat better. Although there were no public schools, there were numerous private schools for those who could pay the fees, and the needs of the poor were partially met by the Society for the Propagation of the Gospel and by other Anglican agencies.

Schools in New England

Although the man of the twentieth century may find little else to attract him in the harsh political and religious system of early New England, he can hardly fail to admire the zeal of the Puritans in the field of education. The motivation for their efforts was partly stated in *New England First Fruits,* published in 1643:

> After God had carried us safe to *New England,* and wee had builded our houses, provided necessaries for our liveli-hood, rear'd convenient places for Gods worship, and setled the Civill Government: One of the next things we longed for, and looked after was to advance *Learning* and perpetuate it to Posterity; dreading to leave an illiterate Ministry to the Churches, when our present Ministers shall lie in the Dust.

But the religious motivation was not the only one. An early law of New Haven provided for "the better trayning up of youth of this towne, that through God's Blessinge, they may be fitted for publique service hereafter, either in church or commonweale."

In 1636 the Massachusetts General Court appropriated £400 "towards a schoale or colledge." Two years later Professor Nathaniel Eaton began to instruct the first classes of the new institution humbly housed in Cow Yard Row, Newtown. That same year the Reverend John Harvard died at Charlestown leaving his library and half of the rest of his estate—about £800—to the college. In gratitude the General Court ordered that the institution should be called Harvard College. Symbolic of their aspirations for the infant seat of learning was the decision to change the name of Newtown to Cambridge in honor of the great English university which had been the alma mater of many of the colony's ministers and leaders.

Even older than Harvard College was the Boston Latin School, which dates from 1635 when a town schoolmaster was appointed. His salary was at first paid through voluntary contributions of some of the wealthier inhabitants, but by 1643 the town itself had assumed responsibility for the support of the school. Similar provision for public schools was made in neighboring towns.

Attendance at these schools was by no means compulsory, but parents were required to make some provision for the instruction of their children. In 1642 the Massachusetts General Court took note of "the great neglect of many parents & masters in training up their children in learning & labor, & other implyments which may be proffitable to the common wealth." The selectmen in each town were charged with the responsibility of investigating the situation, especially the children's "ability to read & understand the principles of religion and the capitall laws of this country." The selectmen were empowered to apprentice the children of such parents or masters as shall "not be able & fitt to employ and bring them up." This law was obviously modeled on English apprenticeship laws, but it introduced a new principle in insisting that all children should be taught to read. A law of 1648 explicitly required instruction in reading and religion in all indentures of apprenticeship.

Whether these minimum essentials of education should be imparted in the school, the shop, or the home was left to the decision of the individual parent or master. But the General Court attempted to assure that schools would be available to those who wanted them through the famous law of 1647. It "being one chief project of ye ould deluder, Satan, to keep men from the knowledge of ye Scriptures," towns having 50 householders or more were to appoint one within their town "to teach all such children as shall resort to him to write or reade"; towns having 100 householders or more were to maintain schools where boys could be prepared for college.

These laws set an ideal that was but imperfectly realized. Some New England parents neglected to provide their children with even the rudiments of knowledge; some villages were too poor to fulfill the letter of the school laws. The schoolmasters were shamefully underpaid and sometimes had to supplement their incomes by serving as cowherds or doing odd jobs. Despite shortcomings and evasions, however, enough money was scraped together in most communities to keep the schools alive. The seventeenth-century pattern of settlement with the homes of the settlers built near the village green gave vitality to the school as well as to the church. The town school became a distinctive institution in both Massachusetts and Connecticut.

Usually the public schools did not accept children who had not learned the alphabet and the first rudiments of reading. This primary training was provided either in the home or in a dame school, where some woman of the neighborhood, in return for a small fee from the parents of each child, would initiate seven or eight youngsters into the fraternity of letters. The child learned his first lessons from a hornbook—a single page of printed matter mounted on a wooden frame and covered with transparent horn to protect the paper from dirty fingers. In this way he studied the A B C's and the Lord's Prayer. Sometimes this was all; sometimes the dame schools taught a little writing, counting, simple reading, and the catechism.

Boys preparing for college went directly from the dame school to a Latin grammar school. But others went to town schools offering a less ambitious curriculum—either to the common schools of the smaller communities or to the schools for writing and ciphering established in Boston during the 1680's. Here the child studied reading, writing, spelling, a little arithmetic, and a great deal of religion. His first exercises were usually in a primer, a collection of simple verses and stories. At first these primers and all other textbooks were imported from England, but by the end of the seventeenth century American printers were entering this profitable field. Published originally in 1690, the *New England Primer* went through many editions and was the leading book in its field for a century and a quarter. The hornbooks were no longer needed after their contents were included in the primer's illustrated alphabet. Each letter had its appropriate verse. That for *A*—"In Adam's Fall we sinned all"—provided the proper beginning for good Calvinist instruction, although that for *F*—"The idle Fool is whipt at School"—was more immediately useful. Page by page religious indoctrination kept pace with secular instruction. When the town minister visited the school, as he did regularly, a favorite subject for oral examination was the sermon of the preceding Sabbath.

The pride of Boston was the Latin School. Here boys were admitted at seven or eight and drilled until they were ready to enter Harvard at fourteen or fifteen. The curriculum is sufficiently suggested by the Harvard entrance requirements: "When any Schollar is able to understand *Tully,* or such like classicall Latine Author *extempore,* and make and speake true Latine in Verse and Prose. . . . And decline perfectly the Paradigm's of *Nounes* and *Verbes* in the *Greek* tongue: Let him then and not before be capable of admission into the College." From 1670 to 1708 Ezekiel Cheever, who had previously taught in New Haven and elsewhere in New England, was master of the Boston school. His reputation for thoroughness was such that Cotton Mather wrote:

> Do but name Cheever, and the Echo straight
> Upon that Name, Good Latin, will repeat.

Cheever's *Accidence,* published in 1709, was the most popular Latin textbook of the eighteenth century. Scarcely less renowned than the Boston Latin School were the grammar schools at Cambridge, Dorchester, and Roxbury in Massachusetts and at Hartford and New Haven in Connecticut.

But elsewhere the Latin grammar schools languished. Their curriculum was too narrowly classical to be useful to boys who could not expect to go to college. The demand for instruction in the practical arts was so great that many private schoolmasters began to teach in Boston and the larger towns. Advanced arithmetic, navigation, bookkeeping, modern languages, and even shorthand were available to those who could pay the fees of the private schools. More ambitious in program were the academies which began to function after the middle of the eighteenth century. The earliest such private secondary schools in Massachusetts were Dummer Academy in South Byfield, founded in 1761, and Phillips Academy at Andover, founded in 1778. Such institutions prepared students for college, but their curriculum was much broader than that of the old Latin grammar schools.

Meanwhile, the public-school system tended to deteriorate. To the extent that the Congregationalists lost their monopoly in the religious field, they lost also their zeal for the maintenance of the town school as an agency for religious indoctrination. Moreover, when the old-type village with its compact system of settlement gave way to the later type of dispersed settlement, the town school and the town church both suffered. The town school sometimes became a moving school, meeting a term first in one part of the town and then in another. The final result was to decentralize the public-education system. Separate public schools began to develop in the various sections. Thus began the evolution of the district school—the small country school serving the needs of a particular neighborhood rather than the whole town. The system was picturesque and democratic, but, educationally, the results were often pathetic. Attendance was irregular and standards were lax.

The public-school system was as characteristic of Puritan Connecticut and New Hampshire as of Massachusetts. In general Rhode Island made less adequate provision for education than its neighbors, but this judgment should not be extended to its larger towns. Newport had an excellent system of public schools rivaling those of Boston.

Education in the Middle Colonies

In New Netherland somewhat similar provisions to those of New England were at first made for education. The Dutch West India Company sent out teachers along with its other servants. The first public school in New Amsterdam was established in 1638 and continued to be the official school throughout the period of Dutch rule. In ten or eleven other villages schoolmasters were also employed. They were supported by small salaries paid by the community and by tuition fees of beaver or bearskins paid by the parents of all except the charity pupils. The school was usually kept in the master's own home—a house that had sometimes been provided by the village. Like the village minister the teacher had to be licensed by the Classis of Amsterdam. In addition to his duties in the schoolroom, he served as the reader, the chorister, and the sexton of the church. A Latin grammar school was established at New Amsterdam in 1659.

The conquest of New Netherland by the English disturbed the evolution of the school system. The Dutch elementary schools survived—but not as public institutions. They became parochial schools, managed and supported by the Dutch Reformed Church and providing instruction only in the Dutch language. The English and other non-Dutch groups had to secure education for their children through private schools maintained by itinerant schoolmasters or through other agencies. A limited number of poor children attended the charity schools maintained by Trinity Church and the Venerable Society, and others learned to read during their apprenticeships.

Even among the more fortunate classes education received little emphasis. In the bustling town of New York most parents were satisfied if their boys were taught enough writing and arithmetic to transact business. The Latin grammar school of Dutch days expired during the early period of English rule; subsequent attempts to maintain grammar schools were short-lived. Classical training could be secured only from private masters or in the schools of the other colonies. In other New York communities conditions were even worse.

In Pennsylvania a different system had been originally projected. At the initiative of William Penn the assembly in 1683 laid upon the council the duty of fostering education and ordered that "all persons in the Province . . . having children . . . shall cause such to be instructed in reading and writing, so that they may be able to read the Scriptures and to write by the time they attain to twelve years of age." Enoch Flower was employed as teacher in Philadelphia that same year. But in 1689 the public school was discontinued, and education was left to the initiative of private groups, especially the churches.

Although indifferent at first to college education, the Quakers maintained some of the best elementary and secondary schools in America. Their meetinghouses served as schools as well as churches. Teachers were carefully selected and well paid, at least by contemporary standards. The support of such schools by subscription and endowment was a favorite Quaker philanthropy. A large majority of the pupils paid tuition, but the poor, both Quaker and non-Quaker, were allowed to attend without paying fees. Particularly notable was the William Penn Charter School, founded in 1689. There taught such able men as George Keith, Francis Daniel Pastorius, Thomas Makin, and Anthony Benezet. Two separate courses of study were offered: the Latin School gave the traditional classical curriculum of the Old World grammar schools, and the English, or Mathematical, School taught the practical studies particularly esteemed by Quaker merchant families. The Charter School drew pupils from as far away as Barbados.

The Germans clung to their own parochial schools. Sending their children to classes in the church or in the separate schoolhouse nearby, they believed that knowledge of German and indoctrination with the particular tenets of their sect would both be assured. In the poorer parishes the minister himself served as schoolmaster; in the more prosperous he had an assistant to teach the children and to help in the church services on Sunday. Such was the general system under which all the German denominations operated. Some, like the Moravians, were much interested in education; others, particularly the Amish, were negligent.

Since many Germans who entered the colony as redemptioners and took up land along the frontier were out of contact with organized religion, they were beyond the limits of the parochial schools as well. Both Mühlenberg and Schlatter were shocked by the situation and gave their attention to the establishment of schools no less than churches. Schlatter was particularly active in this field, and his reports of the widespread illiteracy of the Germans aroused English philanthropists to organize in 1754 the Society for Propagating Christian Knowledge among the Germans in America. Benjamin Franklin, Conrad Weiser, and other prominent Pennsylvanians were appointed trustees, and Schlatter was engaged to act as supervisor. The plan was to found community schools to be managed by local trustees chosen from the Lutheran and Reformed denominations as well as from any English denominations prominent in the town. Children of all Protestant churches might attend these schools, but their primary object was to instruct the Germans in the use of the English language. On this rock the project eventually foundered. Although at one time 750 pupils were receiving instruction through the society's efforts, the opportunity to have their children taught English did not appeal to most German parents. In 1763 the movement was abandoned.

The Scotch-Irish were in general more interested in education than the Germans. In Ulster the town school was an accepted institution, and the Presbyterians were energetic in establishing parochial schools in America. Particularly notable was the support given to secondary education. William Tennent's Log College taught not only evangelical piety but also the traditional subjects of the classical curriculum. During the 1750's such important Presbyterian academies as Pequea and Blair were established.

Although the denominational schools were the most characteristic feature of the Pennsylvania situation, there were various departures from this pattern. In the interior counties where the establishment of church schools was often delayed, neighborhood schools were sometimes organized. These resembled the old-field schools of Virginia. The families of an isolated community would form a voluntary association and raise funds or contribute labor for the building of a rude log schoolhouse. Entirely controlled by the whims of their rustic patrons, such schools were not likely to attract competent teachers nor to maintain adequate standards. But the alternative was no education at all, and the neighborhood schools with all their shortcomings were considerably better than that. There were even a few towns in the Wyoming Valley near present-day Wilkes-Barre where the settlers, Congregationalists from Connecticut, taxed themselves for the support of education after the New England fashion. In Philadelphia numerous private masters took pupils for fees and taught any course of studies for which there was a demand.

The Colonial Colleges

For some sixty years after its founding in 1636, Harvard College was the only degree-granting institution in British America. The institution had its vicissitudes. Its first professor, Nathaniel Eaton, was dismissed in disgrace when it developed that his fondness for flogging extended not only to his scholars but to his assistant as well, making him "fitter to have been . . . master of a house of correction than an instructor of Christian youth." Contributing to the scandal was the revelation that Mistress Eaton had been skimping on the students' bread, beef, and beer. For almost a year after this false start Harvard had neither faculty nor students. But in 1640 Henry Dunster, a Cambridge graduate recently arrived in Massachusetts, was appointed president, and the college really began to function. For fourteen years Dunster toiled devotedly—much of the time teaching all the courses offered in the curriculum—but in 1654 he was compelled to resign because of his public espousal of Baptist principles. He was succeeded by the learned and pious Charles Chauncy, who served until his death in 1672. There followed another period of difficulties. The zeal for religion and learning which so characterized the first generation of Massachusetts Puritans was less evident in the second. Materialism and indifference in the seaboard towns and poverty and ignorance on the frontier threatened the existence of the college. In 1672 it granted no degrees, in 1673 only four, in 1674 only two. King Philip's War (1675–1676) added still more to its difficulties. During the last two decades of the century student enrollment was better, but the college became the center of controversy between Massachusetts conservatives and liberals. The conservative faction was led by Increase Mather, president of the college; the liberals by tutors John Leverett and Thomas Brattle. The latter eventually won out; Increase Mather resigned the presidency and John Leverett succeeded him.

Meanwhile several hundred young New Englanders had received a Harvard education—a course of studies closely patterned on that of the great English universities. It included Greek and Hebrew grammar, rhetoric, logic, divinity, and a smattering of arithmetic, geometry, and Aristotelian physics. Latin was absent from the list only because its use was taken for granted. Both the students' textbooks and the professors' lectures were in Latin. Student disputations in Latin were a weekly fixture for the course in logic, and declamations in Latin gave an opportunity to practice the principles of rhetoric derived from textbooks and the classics. Although the desire to train ministers had been the most important motive for founding the college, Harvard was never merely a theological seminary. Only about half its graduates entered the ministry, and they received their special training in graduate work. The undergraduate course was intended to provide the intellectual equipment needed by every Christian gentleman, whether he entered the ministry or followed some secular calling.

In addition to carrying the bulk of the teaching burden, the early Harvard presidents had to struggle with college finances. During the 1650's students were charged £2 for tuition and about £10 annually for board. The total cost of four years in college, £50 to £75, seems low indeed by present-day standards, but it represented great sacrifice to seventeenth-century parents. Collecting these sums in cash was so nearly impossible that the college had to accept wheat, malt, meat, firewood, lumber, tallow, turnips, live goats—even boots and shoes. Much of this the college steward put to direct use for the sustenance of faculty and students; the rest he had to sell. But the college could never have survived on the payments made by the students and their parents. In a variety of ways additional support was found. The colonial government granted land, made occasional cash contributions, and eventually assigned the tolls of the Boston-Charlestown ferry to the struggling institution. Soon after the New England Confederation was formed in 1643, it requested every family under its jurisdiction to give annually ¼ bushel of wheat, 1*s.* in money, or the equivalent in wampum "for the mayntenance of poore Schollers at the Colledg at Cambridg." For a number of years these annual contributions of "college corn" from New England farmers were the main reliance of the Harvard faculty.

Although the idea of a college in Virginia had often been discussed, the project was long delayed. Finally in 1693 Commissary James Blair secured a charter for an institution to be named William and Mary after the reigning monarchs. He brought back to Virginia an order for £2,000 and plans drawn by the great Christopher Wren for a beautiful building in the Renaissance style. Both the British and the Virginia governments assigned certain revenues for the college, and an additional endowment was secured through private subscription.

The college still had a period of struggle ahead. Blair found it difficult to collect the funds that had been promised, and the first building was destroyed by fire soon after its completion. For two decades William and Mary resembled an academy more than a college. But by 1729 there were six professors, and the institution was equipped to give a variety of courses.

William and Mary reached a high point of influence during the generation preceding the American Revolution. Pleasantly located at Williamsburg, the colonial capital, the college was the focal point of a highly cultured community. Many of its graduates went to England for ordination and came back to infuse badly needed American blood into the Anglican Church. Other graduates entered the professions or lived the lives of plantation aristocrats. At William and Mary such great Virginians as Thomas Jefferson, James Monroe, and John Marshall received their education.

Yale College was founded soon after William and Mary. In 1701, 10 Congregational clergymen, all Harvard graduates, received from the colonial government of Connecticut a charter for "a collegiate school"—so designated to avoid dangerous questions as to the legality of the legislature's action. The project had the strong support of Increase and Cotton Mather and Judge Samuel Sewall of Boston after the failure of the conservatives to retain control of Harvard. For several years the new institution was without a fixed abode. Its students boarded and studied with a rector and tutors in several different towns. But in 1718 the collegiate school acquired both a name and a building in New Haven through the

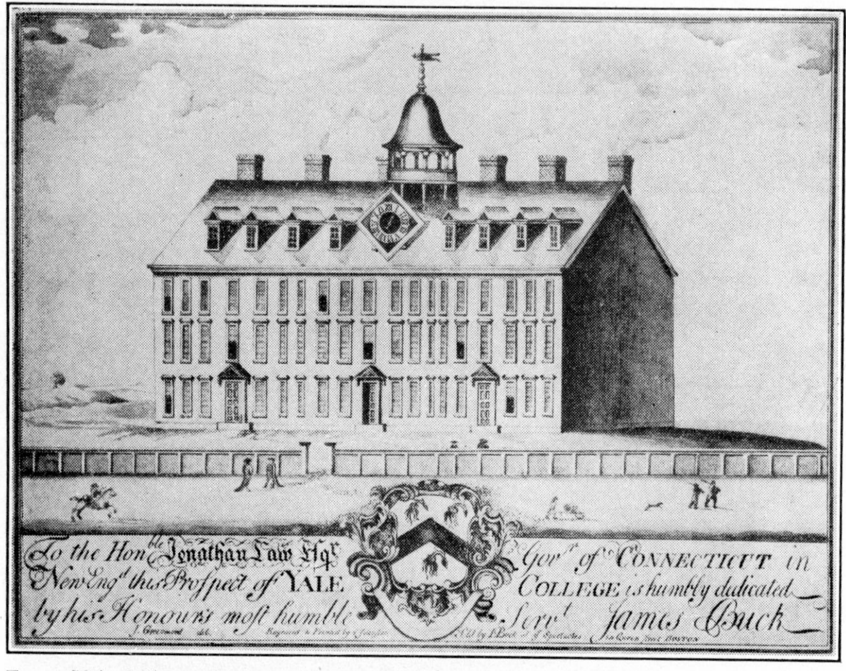

FIG. 8. Yale College, New Haven, Connecticut, about 1749. Engraved by Thomas Johnston after John Greenwood. (*Courtesy of Yale University Library.*)

generosity of Elihu Yale, a New Englander who had gained wealth in the British East India Company. For many decades Yale enjoyed the reputation of being a citadel of Calvinist orthodoxy.

The College of New Jersey was founded by the Presbyterians in 1746. The new institution was housed in the home of its first president, Jonathan Dickinson, in Elizabethtown, New Jersey. After Dickinson's death the college moved to Newark, where its second president, Aaron Burr, was minister. In 1755 it became permanently established at Princeton and eventually became known by that name. More evangelical than either Harvard or Yale, Princeton drew students from New England, the middle colonies, and the South. Its influence was thus less localized than the other colonial colleges. Only about half of its graduates were to be found in the middle colonies; the other half went to New England or to the South—usually as Presbyterian ministers or schoolteachers.

The College of Philadelphia, the future University of Pennsylvania, resulted from a characteristic project of Benjamin Franklin. As early as 1743 Franklin had proposed the establishment of an academy, but the times had been unpropitious. Six years later he renewed the project in one of the most effective of his pamphlets, *Proposals Relating to the Education of Youth in Pennsylvania.* Not only did he state the need for an academy, but he outlined his very original ideas on the general subject of education. The useful subjects which all students should study were writing, drawing, mathematics, English, history, and science. These subjects would arouse the curiosity and lead naturally to the study of such related subjects as geography, morality, oratory, politics, law, logic, agriculture, and mechanics. Though all should not be compelled to learn Latin, Greek, and the modern foreign languages, none that had an ardent desire to learn them should be refused—"their English, Arithmetick, and other Studies absolutely necessary, being at the same Time not neglected."

Franklin's proposal brought a good response. Funds were raised, trustees appointed, and the great hall originally built for George Whitefield's revival meetings was purchased to house the new institution. In 1751 instruction in the Philadelphia Academy and Charitable School began. A college where the A.B. degree might be earned was added to the institution in 1755. Although the final program of study was less novel than Franklin's *Proposals*, the College of Philadelphia was in many ways more liberal than the other colonial colleges. The trustees and faculty were drawn from different religious groups; English and natural science received more attention than elsewhere; and in 1765 the institution pioneered by setting up a medical department.

The nondenominational character of the College of Philadelphia was exceptional. The needs of particular religious groups continued to give higher education its principal impetus. Anglicans founded King's College, later Columbia, at New York in 1754, Baptists took the lead in the establishment of Brown at Providence in 1764, and the Dutch Reformed started Queen's College (Rutgers) in New Jersey in 1766. The ninth and last of the colonial colleges was Dartmouth, chartered in 1769—a Congregational venture originally intended as an Indian school but soon diverted to the education of the white youth of New Hampshire.

Clerical Literature

The most energetic American scholars of the seventeenth century were to be found among the New England clergy. The first group of these had been trained in the best educational institutions of old England; later generations were subjected to the rigid intellectual discipline of Harvard. Their education completed, the Congregational clergy employed their rhetoric in frequent and lengthy sermons to their congregations. Pulpit oratory seems to have been genuinely enjoyed by New England laymen. So popular were the midweek sermons, or lectures, that many families attended not only those of their own town but those of neighboring towns as well. When the magistrates, disturbed by the absenteeism from work that this entailed, tried to discourage the practice, the sermon-hungry New Englanders protested effectively against this interference with their pleasure. Most of these sermons have survived only in the manuscripts of the ministers or in the notebooks of conscientious listeners. But a certain number—especially those delivered to select groups like the assembled magistrates or the Ancient and Honorable Artillery Company—found their way into print.

In addition to sermons the New England clergymen wrote many able books and pamphlets in defense or explanation of their church organization and doctrine. The Puritan revolution in England provided the occasion for much of this activity, since the American Congregationalists were eager to have their system adopted in the mother country. Outstanding examples were Richard Mather's *Platform of Church Discipline,* Thomas Hooker's *Survey of the Summe of Church Discipline*, and John Cotton's *Way of the Congregational Churches Cleared.* New England dissent was vigorously championed in the works of Roger Williams.

The royal family of seventeenth-century American intellectual life was that descended from John Cotton and Richard Mather. Cotton began his career in Boston, England, and brought it to a fruitful climax in Boston, Massachusetts, where he was the most respected minister from 1633 to 1652. Not least in influence among his many published works was his catechism entitled *Milk for Babes, Drawn out of the Breasts of Both Testaments, Chiefly for the Spiritual Nourishment of Boston Babes in either England, but may be of like Use for any Children* (1646). Richard Mather too was a well-known preacher in England before he came to America in 1635. He became minister of the Dorchester church and played a leading part in Congregational affairs until his death in 1669. Increase Mather, Richard's youngest son, had an excellent education at Harvard and at Trinity College, Dublin. He married John Cotton's daughter Maria, and as preacher at the North Church in Boston, he soon gained a reputation equal to that of either his father or his father-in-law. A conservative in religion, politics, and education, Mather did effective writing in defense of his principles. Cotton Mather, Increase's eldest son and the grandson of John Cotton and Richard Mather, took his intellectual heritage most seriously. He graduated from Harvard at the age of fifteen and became assistant to his father in Boston at eighteen. Like his forebears he exerted great influence both as preacher and as counselor on public affairs. Busy though he was with these matters, he found time to produce 450 published works. Most of these with their heavy style, their painful puns, their ostentatious use of Latin, Greek, and Hebrew quotations, and their lapses into bad poetry repel the modern reader. This is true of Cotton Mather's most ambitious work, *Magnalia Christi Americana: or the Ecclesiastical History of New England* (1702). Most of it is prolix and conceited, but certain parts like the biographical sketches of John Eliot and William Phips reveal that Mather was capable of writing direct and vigorous prose.

New England clerical scholarship reached its culmination in Jonathan Edwards. As a preacher the Northampton minister was only one of a great generation, but as a writer and theologian he was uniquely gifted. He possessed an extraordinary mind, capable of posing fundamental questions and attacking them with brilliant logic. But he was no ice-cold intellectual. He had a poet's sensitivity to beauty and a mystic's love of God. Although he published much throughout his career, his greatest writings were produced during the last eight years of his life, while he was ministering to the Indians at Stockbridge. Here he wrote such works as *Original Sin, The Nature of True Virtue,* and *The Ends for Which God Created the World.* Most influential of all was *On the Freedom of the Will,* published in 1754. This was a powerful defense of Calvinism against the attacks of the Arminians. Liberty Edwards defined as freedom from constraint, "the power . . . that any one has to do as he pleases." This liberty man had, but his choice of action was inevitably determined by his motives or inclinations, which were predestined by God. Edwards's mind was too original to be content with a mere restatement of Calvinism. His approach and emphasis were new. He clothed the old creed in a rationality and beauty that made it more acceptable to a more sensitive and humane generation.

Such was Edwards's prestige that he restored vigor to New England intellectual activity. The so-called New Divinity had as its later disciples such Congregational clergymen as Joseph Bellamy, Samuel Hopkins, and Jonathan Edwards the younger. Although claiming the great theologian as their master, they advanced to new positions—some of which he might not have approved.

Colonial Science

While the New England divines were struggling with problems of theology, the main stream of intellectual life in Europe was breaking its way into a new channel. The discoveries of Copernicus, Galileo, Harvey, Newton, and Locke were changing men's conception of the universe in a way that was to put the old orthodoxies to severe strain.

The clerical scholars of colonial America were much more receptive to the new knowledge than might have been expected. In 1683 Increase Mather organized the Philosophic Society, a club of Boston intellectuals who met in the pastor's study to discuss a broad range of topics. The club did not long survive, but the interest of Increase and Cotton Mather in astronomy and other sciences continued throughout their lives. The glories of the universe revealed through the microscope impressed Cotton greatly. Man's wonder and love of God should increase, he believed, with knowledge of nature. Unfortunately, the Mathers' enthusiasm for science took as one of its forms an ambition to investigate the phenomena of witchcraft. Increase Mather's *An Essay for the Recording of Illustrious Provi-*

dences (1684) and Cotton Mather's *Memorable Providences* (1689) stimulated New England's curiosity about witches and helped to bring on the Salem hysteria. But the Mathers were no more superstitious than other educated men of their day, and in the end, although they did not renounce their belief in the reality of witches, they helped to convince the authorities of the need for greater caution in handling witchcraft cases. The Mathers appear in a much better light a few years later when we discover them resolutely defending smallpox inoculation against the opposition of some leading Boston physicians. Jonathan Edwards was also greatly influenced by the new psychology of John Locke.

The clergy were not alone in developing a lively interest in science. John Winthrop, Jr., who was for many years governor of Connecticut, experimented extensively in chemistry, prospected for minerals, assayed ores, and built the first New England ironworks at Lynn, Massachusetts. He was an early and active member of the Royal Society of London. No narrow specialist, he dabbled in alchemy, optics, and astronomy. He procured for Harvard College its first telescope. The new instrument was put to good use, and Thomas Brattle's observations of the comet of 1680 were considered worthy of commendation in Isaac Newton's *Principia*.

The leading New England scientist of the eighteenth century was another John Winthrop who taught natural philosophy at Harvard from 1738 to 1779. An expert in mathematics, physics, geology, and astronomy, he experimented with electricity, advanced a theory to explain earthquakes, and led a scientific expedition to Novia Scotia in 1761 to observe the transit of Venus across the sun.

But colonial America's most original scientific mind was that of a young man who had forsaken his native Boston to seek his fortune in Philadelphia. Once Benjamin Franklin had become securely established as a printer and publisher, he began to divert more and more of his energies to the acquisition of knowledge. He read much, but developed his intellectual powers even more by discussion and correspondence with kindred spirits first in his own city, then in other colonies, and finally in London and in Paris. Thus in 1727 he organized the Junto, a club of 12 Philadelphians who met weekly to eat, to drink, and to discuss questions of politics, business, practical philanthropy—and occasionally of science. In 1744 Franklin organized the American Philosophical Society as a sort of intercolonial Junto. Men interested in the advancement of knowledge in the various colonies were invited to become members and to send communications to the society's headquarters at Philadelphia. Not many of the members had Franklin's drive, and the society languished until its reorganization twenty-five years later. But even in its early years it had sufficient vitality to provide fruitful contacts between Franklin and men with similar interests. Especially did the Philadelphian enjoy his correspondence with Cadwallader Colden of New York, a conservative in politics but a bold and original scholar. Colden's *History of the Five Indian Nations* (1727) was a pioneer work in American anthropology, and his numerous published and unpublished investigations in the fields of plant science, physics, and medicine gave additional evidence of his brilliant talents.

Franklin himself was beginning to advance scientific knowledge in extremely practical ways. His invention of the Franklin stove in 1740 began a revolution in domestic heating. During a visit to Boston in 1746 he witnessed some crude experiments in electricity. He was intrigued by this curious phenomenon, and upon his return to Philadelphia he and his friends conducted extensive experiments of their own. Franklin soon began to make valuable contributions to the understanding of the mysterious force. His "single-fluid" theory was a more useful hypothesis than any which had preceded it, and his designation of "positive" and "negative" electricity was a help to clear thinking. Indeed, Franklin contributed in extraordinary degree to what was particularly needed at this point in the history of science—an adequate vocabulary in which to discuss electrical phenomena. He appears to have been the first to use—at least in print in English—such terms as armature, battery, brush, condense, charge, discharge, Leyden bottle, conductor, nonconductor, and several others still in common usage.

Franklin's experiments became known to the European scientific world through his letters to Peter Collinson, a London friend. In 1751 Collinson had these published under the title *Experiments and Observations on Electricity, Made at Philadelphia in America.* This account aroused much interest both in London and in Paris. At the latter capital the savants were particularly intrigued with Franklin's conjecture that lightning was electricity. The idea had occurred to earlier thinkers, but Franklin suggested how it might be proved experimentally. Acting upon the suggestion, D'Alibard successfully drew lightning from the clouds in May, 1752, thus proving Franklin's theory. The next month, apparently before he heard the news from Paris, the Philadelphian conducted his own famous experiment—that of the electrical kite. This work with lightning was sufficiently dramatic to capture the imagination of the reading public everywhere, and within very few months Franklin became the most famous man in the colonies. Practical as ever, Franklin had suggested the use of lightning rods as a protective device even before his theory of the nature of lightning had been proved.

The intellectual atmosphere of Philadelphia proved stimulating to other minds as well. David Rittenhouse, a clockmaker without formal education, became a learned mathematician and astronomer. Putting his mechanical skill to good use, he made important improvements in astronomical instruments, and in 1767 constructed an orrery—a machine which simulated the motions of the planets and their satellites. Dr. Benjamin Rush joined the faculty of the College of Philadelphia as America's first professor of chemistry. He did much to improve the training of physicians and was a pioneer student of diseases of the mind. In 1718 the first botanical garden in the colonies was begun near Philadelphia by John Bartram, a Quaker farmer who traveled widely in search of specimens.

The southern colonies also witnessed a rising interest in science. Dr. John

Mitchell, a Virginia physician, contributed to a better knowledge of yellow fever, to the improvement of agriculture, and to the classification of American plant life. In 1746 he made one of the most important maps of British North America. The wealthy planter, William Byrd II, pursued science as one of his many avocations. Two Charleston physicians, Dr. Alexander Garden and Dr. John Lining, gained recognition as students of natural science and climatology.

Newspapers and Books

The first printing press in the English colonies was established at Cambridge in 1639. Its most ambitious product was John Eliot's Indian translation of the Bible, but it also printed a steady stream of sermons, catechisms, primers, psalm books, law books, and almanacs as well as pioneer New England efforts in history, biography, and poetry. A second New England press was established at Boston in 1675. Philadelphia gained its first printing establishment in 1685, New York in 1693, and New London in 1709. Freedom of the press was not yet an American principle, and printers often ran into trouble with the authorities. The first attempt at a Boston newspaper, *Public Occurrences both Foreign and Domestik,* was killed by the magistrates after the publication of only one issue in 1690, and two years later the Philadelphia printer, William Bradford, was imprisoned by Quaker officials for publishing matter displeasing to the ruling order.

Despite these difficulties the printers gained steadily in influence, particularly through their newspapers. The *Boston News-Letter,* established in 1704, managed to survive by avoiding controversial topics and confining itself to news from Europe, customhouse clearings, and other colorless material. In 1719 the *Boston Gazette* and the *American Weekly Mercury* of Philadelphia began publication. Benjamin Franklin's brother James started the *New England Courant* in 1719, and William Bradford, who had moved his printing press to New York after his trouble with the Philadelphia authorities, founded the fifth colonial newspaper, the *New York Gazette,* in 1725. By 1765, 43 newspapers, 3 of them German, had been established. Some were short-lived, but others attained vigor and helped to break down the provincialism of the individual colonies.

Freedom of the press was given substantial impetus in 1733 by the acquittal of John Peter Zenger, a New York printer who had been brought to trial on a charge of criminal libel for having attacked Governor Cosby in the columns of the *New York Weekly Journal.* Zenger's able lawyer, Andrew Hamilton of Philadelphia, convinced the jury that, despite English precedents to the contrary, a printer ought not to be punished for making damaging statements about a public official provided the truth of the statements could be established.

Although colonial readers purchased many books and pamphlets printed in America, they continued to rely mainly on publications imported from England. In all the larger towns there were thriving bookshops, and many colonists had extensive private libraries. Particularly was this true of the Virginia planters.

At Westover, William Byrd II built up a collection of almost four thousand volumes, Robert Carter had over fifteen hundred, and George Washington over nine hundred. The New England preachers were likewise great book purchasers, and the library of Cotton Mather contained some three thousand volumes. But books were expensive and the usual collections were much smaller.

Here and there attempts were made to provide access to books for those who could not afford to purchase them. A small collection was bequeathed to the town of Boston in 1656 for the establishment of a public library, and this was maintained in the Town House until the building was destroyed by fire in 1747. In several other colonial towns, small public libraries were established. Thomas Bray, the Anglican commissary of Maryland, regarded the difficulty of securing books as one of the principal handicaps of the poorer clergy. He sought to provide a library for each parish. Intended at first only for the parsons, the project was later broadened to include circulating libraries for laymen as well. So long as Bray lived, the movement had great vitality, and parish libraries became common both in the North and in the South. Unfortunately the collections were usually scattered and lost with the passing of the years.

Much more successful were the eighteenth-century subscription libraries. Here the organizing zeal of Benjamin Franklin found another characteristic outlet. Members of the Junto and other interested individuals organized the Library Company of Philadelphia in 1731. Each member paid in 40*s*. and promised to contribute 10*s*. annually thereafter. Although the company's books might be read in the library quarters by any "civil gentleman," only subscribers were allowed to draw them out. Similar libraries were organized in several other towns. One of the most successful was the Library Society of Charleston, South Carolina, founded in 1748, which built up a collection of six or seven thousand volumes before the Revolutionary War.

Like private collectors the libraries bought mostly books of English or European authorship. But a few colonial authors gained recognition. The first American best seller was *The Day of Doom* by Michael Wigglesworth. This was a terrifying picture of the Last Judgment, written by a Congregational minister of Malden, Massachusetts. First published in 1662, the poem had an extraordinary immediate sale and retained its popularity for generations. Although the bliss of heaven was depicted as well as the tortures of hell, it was the latter which gave the ballad its macabre fascination. Of the many verses descriptive of the plight of the damned, these may be taken as characteristic:

> As chaff that's dry, as dust doth fly
> before the Northern wind,
> Right so are they chaséd away
> and can no refuge find.
> They hasten to the Pit of Woe,
> guarded by Angels stout,
> Who to fulfil Christ's holy Will,
> attend this wicked Rout;

With Iron bands they bind their hands,
 and cursed feet together,
And cast them all, both great and small,
 into that Lake forever,
Where day and night, without respite,
 they wail, and cry and howl
For tort'ring pain which they sustain
 in Body and in Soul.

Less popular than Wigglesworth's vivid doggerel but more enduring was the poetry of another New Englander, Anne Bradstreet. Her early work was published in London in 1650 under the pretentious title *The Tenth Muse Lately Sprung Up in America, By a Gentlewoman in Those Parts.* But her best and most original poems were written later and published after her death. Much of her work had a religious theme, but its tone was distinctly different from *The Day of Doom.* In lovely verse like the following, she marveled at God's handiwork in Nature:

I wist not what to wish, yet sure thought I,
If so much excellence abid below;
How excellent is he that dwells on high?
Whose power and beauty by his works we know.
Sure he is goodness, wisdome, glory, light,
That hath this under world so richly dight:
More Heaven then Earth was here no winter and no night.

Even more effective were the simple poems in which she spoke of her devotion to her home and family.

Edward Taylor, minister at Westfield, Massachusetts, during the latter part of the seventeenth century, wrote poems of remarkable vigor in manuscripts which were discovered and published two centuries later. God's mighty power was depicted in verses like the following:

Upon what Base was fixt the Lath, wherein
He turn'd this Globe, and rigalld it so trim?
Who blew the Bellows of his Furnace Vast?
Or held the Mould wherein the world was Cast?
Who laid its Corner Stone? Or whose Command?
Where stand the Pillars upon which it stands?
Who Lac'de and Filleted the earth so fine
With Rivers like green Ribbons Smaragdine?
Who made the Sea's its Selvedge, and its locks
Like a Quilt Ball within a Silver Box?
Who Spread its Canopy? Or Curtains Spun?
Who in this Bowling Alley bowld the Sun? [1]

Other colonials tried their hand at poetry, but their work is largely forgotten —mercifully so in most cases. Some of the early prose has survived better. The struggles of the colonists were recorded in local histories that occasionally rose to real excellence as in the case of William Prince's *Chronological History of New*

[1] *The Poetical Works of Edward Taylor,* ed. by T. H. Johnson (Princeton University Press, Princeton, N. J., 1943), 31.

England (1736), William Stith's *History of the First Discovery and Settlement of Virginia* (1747), and Thomas Hutchinson's *History of the Colony of Massachusetts Bay* (1764). The finest of all colonial histories, William Bradford's *History of Plymouth Plantation*, existed only in manuscript throughout the colonial period. During the Revolutionary War it disappeared and was not finally found and published until late in the nineteenth century.

The earliest best seller in American prose was the *Narrative of the Captivity and Restauration of Mrs. Mary Rowlandson* (1682). Mrs. Rowlandson, the wife of the minister at Lancaster, Massachusetts, had seen the Indians attack that frontier town, burning the houses and killing the villagers. She herself had been taken captive and enslaved, but after many adventures had secured her freedom again. Her unadorned but vivid description of these episodes was reprinted many times and became exceedingly popular both in America and in the mother country. The success of Mrs. Rowlandson's book encouraged the publication of many similar narratives. The most notable of these were Jonathan Dickinson's *God's Protecting Providence* (1699), recounting the experiences of a Quaker merchant's family following a shipwreck off the Florida coast, and the Reverend John Williams's *The Redeemed Captive* (1707), another sensational account by a New Englander who had been captured by the Indians.

Wherever we probe eighteenth-century American intellectual life, we discover the influence of the genial and versatile Benjamin Franklin. And so it is with colonial literature. Franklin made no pretense of being a literary man, yet his shrewd wisdom embodied in the proverbs of *Poor Richard's Almanack* has outlived hundreds of ponderous volumes, and the *Autobiography* is one of the few colonial writings that is still widely read.

Thus were laid the simple foundations of American intellectual life. Nine struggling colleges; a rudimentary public school system in one part of the country and various private and parochial schools in the rest; numerous clergymen continuing to drop their buckets down a theological well that was patently running dry; a few amateur scientists, petty newspapers, and modest libraries; a handful of poets and prose writers, few of whom had real talent—it was not an impressive record for a nascent nation. But the American colonials were learning many lessons in the school of experience. On the frontier they learned hardihood and self-reliance; in the towns they learned the practical lessons of business; in town meetings and legislatures they learned more of political science than any professor of the day could have taught them. Moreover, the Americans lived on no Robinson Crusoe island. They read all the most influential English writers of the day and many of the French. The proof of their intellectual maturity was their response to the challenge of the quarrel with the mother country and the launching of a new government. Those tremendous events brought forth a political literature of which any country would be proud. The finest tribute that can be paid to colonial culture is merely to point out that George Washington, Thomas Jefferson, Alexander Hamilton, James Madison, John Marshall, and John Adams were its products.

Chapter 6. Arts and Amusements in Colonial America

The first settlers ordered their lives by the stern rule of necessity. Requiring immediate shelter, they built hastily with little thought for either permanence or beauty. Similar preoccupation with essentials governed their making of furniture and household utensils. But after the first battle for survival was won, other impulses had their opportunity. Men proud of their position in the community demanded larger houses built to last and to please the eye. In these more pretentious homes they placed fine furniture, silver table service, delicate china, and beautiful glassware. In the more sophisticated society of eighteenth-century America portrait painters, musicians, and actors found employment.

Seventeenth-century Homes

The first houses built at Jamestown and Plymouth survive neither in remains nor in drawings, but their crudeness is eloquently suggested in the early chronicles. References to the "wigwams" of the early settlers suggest that they frequently built conical huts of branches and turf. Others found shelter in rude lean-tos built against hillsides or in shanties made of branches, turf, and earth. More ambitious pioneers constructed palisaded houses, the walls of which were fashioned from vertically placed logs or roughhewn planks. The space between the timbers was filled with mud and twigs, and the roof was covered with thatch.

The log cabin—so hallowed in later tradition—was unknown to the early English settlers. Such houses, ingeniously constructed of horizontally placed logs, they had never seen in England, nor did their Indian neighbors build them. The first Americans to erect this type of shelter were probably the Swedes and Finns who were accustomed to such log cabins in Europe and carried their knowledge to the Delaware Bay region. Thence the log cabin spread to other groups until it eventually became the standard architecture of the frontier.

Both in Virginia and in Massachusetts the colonists soon sought better shelter. In 1654 Edward Johnson wrote: "The Lord hath been pleased to turn all the wigwams, huts, and hovels the English dwelt in at their first coming, into orderly, fair, and well built houses." [1] These new dwellings were modeled upon the frame houses of English yeomen of the day. At their simplest they had a

[1] Edward Johnson, *Wonder-working Providence, 1628–1651,* ed. by J. Franklin Jameson (Scribner, New York, 1910), 211.

single room, with a great chimney and fireplace at one end, and above—under the steep, sloping roof—a loft or garret. As more space was needed, the colonists often built onto this original structure. Another room was added beyond the chimney, which was thus enclosed. Still more space was gained by the addition of a lean-to—an appurtenance which was found so useful that it became almost universal. Houses also became higher; 2½ stories was the prevailing fashion during the later seventeenth century.

Features characteristic of the New England home were the great central chimney into which all the fireplaces of the house opened, the narrow staircase rising

FIG. 9. Parson Capen House, Topsfield, Massachusetts. Note the high gables, central chimney, casement windows, overhanging upper stories, and pendants of this typical seventeenth-century house, built in 1683. (*Courtesy of Library of Congress.*)

sharply out of the small entrance hall, and the steep roof sweeping down to within a few feet of the ground over the lean-to at the rear. In order to conserve heat, ceilings were low and windows were few and small. The poorer houses used simple wooden shutters; the better had casements with small panes of leaded glass. The second floor often projected over the first. This overhang, like the high gables, was evidence of the medieval origins of seventeenth-century architecture.

But New World conditions brought about important modifications. Outer walls finished in the usual English way, that is, with exposed half timbers filled with clay and straw, were not suited to the severe American climate. Very early,

American builders learned the necessity of enclosing the frame with clapboards. Somewhat more slowly they discovered the disadvantages of English-style thatched roofs, so vulnerable to both weather and fire. Shingles, which were too expensive for the poor in England, eventually won general acceptance in America.

The interiors were simple. Exposed beams and great fireplaces were the first features that caught the eye. In some of the earliest houses the interior walls were merely daubed with clay—with a finishing coat of lime added in districts where this was available. Soon it became customary to follow English practice by sheathing the interior walls with wide boards, grooved together and often molded at the joints. This wainscoting was done with increasing care, and at the end of the seventeenth century carpenters began to fasten wooden strips over the sheathing to form a simple paneling.

Although extensively used in the mother country, brick-and-stone construction was avoided at first in the colonies. Even the early chimneys were built of wood with a lining of clay to make them fireproof. But within a few years brickyards became common, and the use of masonry for chimneys, fireplaces, and foundations became general. Brick houses were built as early as 1638 in Virginia and somewhat later in Massachusetts. By the end of the century there were many such homes in the South and a few in New England. In the middle colonies brick and stone found their widest use. Philadelphia was a town of brick houses from its earliest days, and in New York the use of masonry was also widespread. In appearance these seventeenth-century brick houses had much in common with the wooden ones. They too displayed such medieval features as steep gables and small casement windows. But there were interesting differences. The great central chimney of the wooden houses was abandoned in favor of chimneys at either end—an obvious economy since the masonry work of the chimneys could serve for part of the outer walls as well. Toward the end of the century the medieval roofs and gables began to give way to new styles—gambrel roofs, hip roofs, and pediment gables. Notable also were the greater size and pretentiousness of the houses. Particularly in the South the colonial mansion was beginning to appear.

Seventeenth-century public buildings displayed similar features. Anglican churches in the South resembled the small parish churches of England with their pointed arches, buttressed walls, and square entrance towers. But New England Puritans renounced the architecture of Anglicanism along with its ritual. Even the name "church" they avoided, preferring to call their places of worship "meetinghouses." The meetinghouse was square, or nearly so, and was topped by a four-sided roof with a belfry over the center of the edifice.[1] The interior was severely plain, with great exposed beams as its most striking feature. At first, churches provided the only halls large enough for town meetings and legislative sessions. When the earliest town halls and statehouses were built, they were unpretentious structures similar in appearance to the meetinghouses.

[1] See Fig. 4, p. 65.

Although English models provided the most important influence on colonial architecture, refreshing local variations derived from other immigrant groups. Towns like New York and Albany retained their Dutch appearance long after the English conquest. Gables, often stepped or otherwise ornamented, were prominent, since the houses were built with their ends toward the street. Dutch farmhouses were characterized by their long, low lines and by their great sloping roofs whose eaves projected well beyond the walls. This feature, probably more Flemish than Dutch, had been necessary to protect the clay walls of European cottages from the weather. In America, where more durable materials were available, the overhanging roof served no comparably important function; but it did provide a pleasant shelter for the long benches placed against the front of the house, where the genial householders sat by the hour and exchanged greetings with passers-by. Both the Dutch and the Germans built fine barns which contrasted sharply with the casually constructed outbuildings of the English. German religious groups often built churches and schoolhouses in quaintly different Old World styles.

Eighteenth-century Architecture

A line of influence destined to transform colonial architecture can be traced back to Renaissance Italy. Among the enthusiastic students of the classical tradition was Andrea Palladio (1518–1580), who made important measurements and drawings of many Roman buildings which had survived to his day and himself designed a number of churches and palaces in the classical style. A richly illustrated manual, prepared by the Italian architect and translated into many foreign languages, influenced the evolution of building design throughout western Europe. An English edition of Palladio's work was prepared by Inigo Jones (1573–1651), an English architect who had studied in Italy and returned to England to become famous in his own right as a designer of palaces and country houses. The new style, based upon a repudiation of the Gothic, gained further prestige through Sir Christopher Wren (1632–1723), the greatest of English architects. Given a unique opportunity during the rebuilding of London after the great fire of 1666, Wren performed so magnificent a job in the designing of St. Paul's Cathedral and other churches that a new standard of architectural taste was set. During the eighteenth century, churches, public buildings, and country houses throughout England were built in a generally consistent style which became known as Georgian after the monarchs who occupied the English throne.

Georgian architecture crossed the Atlantic at an opportune moment, for there were then throughout the colonies families with sufficient money and pride to build stately homes. Mansions in the Georgian style were soon to be found in every section. Almost all were built without the help of professional architects. Colonial masons and carpenters were given their general directions by the wealthy patrons who employed them; they derived their ideas of ornamental detail from numerous books on practical architecture which were published in England early in the century and had a ready sale in the colonies.

Approached from the outside, the Georgian mansion was first to be identified by its balance and symmetry. Whereas the seventeenth-century home in its arrangement of doors, windows, and wings frequently reflected the peculiar needs or whims of its owner, the eighteenth-century house paid almost religious deference to form. The long side of the house usually faced the street and the prin-

FIG. 10. Westover, Charles City County, Virginia. Famous mansion in the Georgian style, built by William Byrd II about 1730. (*Courtesy of Library of Congress.*)

cipal doorway was placed in its exact center. If there was a wing at one end of the house, it was balanced by a similar structure at the other end. Instead of the small casements of the seventeenth century there were now large sash windows placed with careful symmetry. The sharp-pitched roof and the high gables of the older houses were out of fashion. With flatter slopes the eighteenth-century roof was much less conspicuous. Instead of terminating in a ridge, it was frequently topped by a flat deck enclosed by a balustrade. Often the balustrade was built at the level of the eaves, thus concealing the roof almost completely. Great attention was given to ornamental detail. A cornice was an almost universal feature, and the front of the house was frequently broken by pilasters or engaged columns in one of the classical orders. The corners of the house were often given emphasis by the use of quoins.

The doorways became increasingly elegant as the century proceeded. The doors themselves were attractively paneled, and the need for light in the halls led to the use of transoms, first rectangular and later fan-shaped. The classical influence was reflected in the use of columns at either side of the door and in an arch or pediment above it. A pleasing divergence from slavish adherence to the classical tradition came in the use of broken and scroll pediments—baroque liberties for which the great Wren himself had provided precedents. Although one-story porticoes were common, very few which rose to the full height of the building were erected during the colonial period.

Coming into increasing use about the middle of the eighteenth century was the so-called "Palladian window"—a large window with a central arch rising above the rectangular windows which flanked it on either side. This attractive arrangement was often placed above the front doorway.

The interiors of eighteenth-century mansions adhered with equal exactness to the canons of formal beauty. Rooms were arranged according to carefully symmetrical floor plans. In this they differed strikingly from the casually arranged interiors of seventeenth-century homes. The new houses had more rooms and higher ceilings. The central chimney was abandoned in favor of two or more chimneys concealed in the ends of the house or in the partitions. This arrangement opened up the center of the building for the great entrance hall which became characteristic of the Georgian mansion. No longer did the stairs serve a merely utilitarian function; on the contrary, colonial carpenters took particular pride in building fine stairways with elaborately turned balusters and newel posts. Cornices, pilasters, and doorways topped by arches or pediments carried out the classical tradition. Paneling, which gave rooms a rich but somewhat heavy appearance, began to pass out of fashion about the middle of the eighteenth century. Occasionally, as at Jefferson's Monticello, rooms now achieved classical simplicity with austere plastered walls; more often they were brightened by fine imported wallpapers. Eighteenth-century householders were as dependent on fireplaces for heat as had been their ancestors, but the fireplaces in the new homes were smaller in proportion to the rooms and were framed in beautifully carved chimney pieces.

Though derived from the same English models and books, colonial architecture developed interesting regional variations. On southern plantations in districts where inns and taverns were infrequent, traveling gentlemen felt no embarrassment in accepting the hospitality of distant relatives or even that of chance acquaintances. The presence of guests in the house was the usual rather than the exceptional thing. Provision had also to be made for the family tutor and any cousins or neighbors who might be staying in the household. Obviously the planter needed to build his house along generous lines with as many rooms as possible. Plantation life, moreover, made the great house the center of a community. Separate quarters had to be built for the slaves, and numerous barns, stables, and shops were needed for the plantation industries. Even the cooking for the planter's household was usually done in a separate building. The location of the outbuildings with relation to each other and to the mansion itself carried out the eighteenth-century love for symmetry. Also carefully arranged were the flower and vegetable gardens, the lawns, the hedges, and the shade trees. Although the finer houses were now almost universally built of brick, wood continued to be used for many of the less pretentious homes. In Charleston, South Carolina, the main floor was built high above the ground because of the damp-

FIG. 11. Hancock Mansion, Boston. An example of northern Georgian architecture, built in 1737. (*Courtesy of Massachusetts Historical Society.*)

ness, and porches to provide relief from the heat came into use much earlier here than elsewhere. Williamsburg and Annapolis were other towns notable for their fine mansions and public buildings.

Although brick was also employed for many New England houses in towns like Boston, Salem, Portsmouth, and Newport, its use was nowhere nearly as common as in the South and in the middle colonies. Wood remained the favorite northern building material, and its extensive use continued to give architecture in this section a character all its own. Apparently ashamed of their material at first, New England carpenters sought to imitate the English stone forms in wood, sometimes going so far as to groove the clapboards to simulate masonry. But better taste soon prevailed. Wood was used without concealment, and the Georgian features were modified to exploit the full possibilities of this material. Eighteenth-century New England houses became notable for their dignity and simplicity, for their solid, substantial construction, and for the delicacy and appropriateness of their ornamentation.

New England churches were now strikingly different from the spare meeting-houses of the early days. These changes reflected the softening of the Puritan creed together with a growing sophistication in the towns. Significantly, the first Boston church to be built in the new style—the style of Sir Christopher Wren's London churches—was Christ (Old North) Church, dedicated to Anglican worship in 1723. Six years later a Congregational body ventured to accept the new style, and the Old South Church was built. Destined to influence ecclesiastical architecture throughout the section, these Boston churches differed from the old in their oblong shape, in their cornices, arched windows, and pedimented doors, and—most strikingly—in their great square entrance towers topped with graceful belfries and lofty spires.

In the middle colonies brick and stone construction prevailed. The local practice of alternating light and dark bricks and the use of white shutters gave Philadelphia homes a unique charm. Mansions here were usually larger and heavier in detail than in New England. As befitted the largest of colonial towns, Philadelphia had particularly outstanding churches and public buildings. Masterpieces of Georgian architecture were Christ Church, an Anglican church begun in 1727 and completed in 1754, and the Pennsylvania State House (Independence Hall), constructed during the same period.

Arts and Crafts

Having gained some shelter from the rain and the cold in their simple houses, the early colonists were not fastidious about their household furnishings. They sat without complaint on rude stools and benches. They ate their meals thankfully from a few cherished dishes brought with them from the mother country or from new ones hastily fashioned out of wood. But a desire for finer things was not long in asserting itself. The more prosperous imported much from England—furniture, chair cushions, window curtains, pewter or silver plate. Such imported luxuries were beyond the reach of the humbler classes, but they too soon felt the impulse to fill their houses with articles pleasing to the eye as well as useful. Many farmers became excellent furniture makers, and their wives became skilled with loom and needle.

Good though amateur craftsmen became, they yielded more and more to professionals. From the beginnings of settlement cabinetmakers, silversmiths, and blacksmiths found profitable employment. These busy artisans were not only manufacturers; they were often true artists exhibiting imagination and intelligence in filling their orders. Since furniture was too bulky for large-scale importation, American cabinetmaking developed with great vigor. The prevalent styles of the mother country determined the basic trends in the colonies, but, as in architecture, distinctively American refinements often developed. The "joiners," as the seventeenth-century furniture makers were called, at first did their work in the heavy Gothic style that had persisted in Tudor England. Oak was a favorite material, and from this sturdy wood were fashioned great wainscot chairs with solid and elaborately carved backs. Although these ornate pieces might well serve family pride, they did little for comfort. For common use simpler types with spindle or slat backs were developed. To be seen also in every colonial home were great chests serving a variety of uses. The front and sides of these offered an extraordinary opportunity for the woodcarver's art. At first English decorative designs were carefully reproduced, but soon there was evidence of refreshing originality. Particularly beautiful were the chests made in Hartford, Connecticut, and in Hadley, Massachusetts.

The late seventeenth and eighteenth centuries were a golden age for English cabinetmaking. Furniture styles changed with the monarchs. Jacobean gave way to William and Mary, which was followed in turn by Queen Anne and early Georgian. During the middle of the century the dominant influence was that of the great Thomas Chippendale. Almost every development in the mother country had its impact on the colonies, but with fascinating variations. Although the highboy, a tall chest of drawers mounted on legs, passed out of fashion in England before 1725, it achieved a durable popularity in America. Similarly, the Windsor chair, introduced from England about 1736, remained a favorite American style for a hundred years and was modified and refined by American furniture makers in many ways.

Chippendale's book, *The Gentleman and Cabinet Maker's Director* (1754), had a great influence in the colonies. The decorative effects of the English master —his use of curved lines instead of straight and his elaborate carving—were imitated by American cabinetmakers, but by no means slavishly. The chairs and lowboys of William Savery of Philadelphia and the desks of John Goddard of Newport gave evidence that American craftsmen were capable of placing the stamp of their individual genius on work done within the general Chippendale style.

Even more esteemed than fine furniture as visible evidence of worldly success was beautiful silverware. Plantation aristocrats usually imported their plate from England, but in the North the demand was largely met by resident craftsmen, many of them immigrants from Holland or France. Particularly fine work was done in New York and Boston. More than other artisans, silversmiths were likely to rise to wealth and social distinction. One of the first New England silversmiths was John Hull, who became a rich Boston merchant and a man of great influence in the government. More famous still was Paul Revere, who had long been respected by his fellow Bostonians as an expert craftsman in silver—practicing an art which he had learned from his Huguenot father, Apollos De Revoire—before he gained immortality through a midnight ride and a poem.

The tables of the wealthy were also graced by beautifully decorated porcelain and delicate glassware. Almost all of this was imported. The finest porcelain came from China, but the great vogue for such ware during the eighteenth century led to the building of English potteries capable of making a very fine product as well as many cheaper grades. In the colonies numerous local potteries were established to supply earthenware at a price which the poorer classes could afford. Although intended to be useful rather than beautiful, the product of the colonial potters often pleased the eye with its brilliant color and fine glaze. There were many attempts to establish colonial glassworks, but most of the establishments failed after a few years and, in any case, confined themselves to making window glass and dark bottle glass instead of fine tableware. Not so, however, with the fabulous "Baron" Henry William Stiegel, an ingenious German who came to America in 1750 at the age of twenty-one and became a wealthy ironmaster in Lancaster County, Pennsylvania. Aspiring to repeat his success in another field, Stiegel not only sank all his own resources but borrowed heavily to build a great glassworks at Mannheim, Pennsylvania. In 1773 when Stiegel's speculative venture reached its greatest expansion, it employed about 130 men—many of them highly skilled craftsmen who had been induced to come to America from England and continental Europe. Stiegel's product was extensively advertised and distributed through agents in Philadelphia, New York, Boston, and Baltimore. The Baron—whose title had its warrant only in the awe which his sumptuous mode of living inspired in his simple Pennsylvania-German neighbors—failed so completely in 1774 that he landed in debtor's prison; but during the eleven years in which he was in the glass business, he manufactured thousands of tumblers, wineglasses, decanters, and cruets, which fairly met the claim of his advertisements—"to be equal to most imported from England."

Even the village blacksmith took pride in fashioning his useful products in shapes that caught the eye. The iron weathervanes, which topped houses and barns throughout the country, showed ingenious collaboration between the houseowner who ordered them and the smiths who fashioned them. Sometimes the vane was fashioned as an arrow or an Indian or a soldier; at other times the owner's initials were worked into the pattern. Andirons, hinges, door handles, and knockers were likewise fashioned in graceful and often highly original shapes. The introduction of stoves in the eighteenth century provided another opportunity for craft art. The cast-iron stove plates were ornamented with floral and geometrical designs, with mottoes, and with the names of the builders.

The aesthetic impulse that led male workers to give their products a simple and honest beauty was reflected equally in the handiwork of the women. Little girls learned their letters by embroidering samplers and carried the ability to do fine needlework through life. Many lovely things came from the household looms. Particularly attractive were the hand-woven bedspreads, which displayed a great variety of designs and color combinations.

Colonial folk art was enriched by German immigration. The Pennsylvania Germans brought to America not only knowledge of all the traditional crafts but also a love for color and pattern much more highly developed than that of the English. Their affection for red was almost an obsession, and they spread red paint over everything that would take it—barns, houses, furniture, and even stoves. For variety they sometimes used other colors like orange and blue, provided always that the substitutes were sufficiently bright. Even a red barn required additional decoration in the form of geometrical designs, ingeniously drawn with compass and straightedge and made vivid with white, red, yellow, green, and blue paint. German potters showed great ingenuity in fashioning not only pots and dishes but candlesticks, lampstands, inkwells, and mantel ornaments, often elaborately decorated with birds, flowers, or geometrical designs. Even the German clergymen and schoolmasters practiced a decorative art. The tradition of the illuminated manuscript was brought over from the Old World, and a cherished possession in almost every home was a birth or baptismal certificate beautifully written and ornamented with drawings of birds, flowers, and heraldic designs. Such manuscripts were known as Frakturs.

Painting

Although few early Americans loved color as passionately as did the Pennsylvania Germans, taste everywhere was less austere than we are likely to imagine from our preconceptions of the colonial scene. Even in Puritan New England color was cherished. Chair cushions, table covers, and wall hangings broke the monotony of New England interiors, and furniture was often painted in ornamental designs. Shops and inns were universally identified by gaily painted signs. Since this demand for color increased with the growth of a wealthier and more sophisticated society, artisans who could paint were much in demand. The craft was by no means specialized: furniture painting, house painting, sign painting, and coach painting were often practiced by the same individuals. The cleverest of these added limning, or portraiture, to their accomplishments, since the desire to have their likenesses preserved was a vanity which not even the Puritans denied themselves. Some of the limners were third-rate English artists who either visited America to practice their craft for a few years or transferred permanently to the New World. Others were men born in the colonies who saw an opportunity to make a living and picked up the requisite skill as best they could.

The native painters worked under great handicaps. Largely self-trained, they had little opportunity to see good art. They were of humble origin, quite unable to afford a trip to study abroad. The great art treasures of Europe they knew through black-and-white engravings, if at all. Nor could they learn much from the English artists who visited America, since these were almost invariably men who had been unsuccessful at home. Most colonial portraits were crude things, lifeless and reflecting a pathetic attempt to imitate the conventions of contemporary European art. The men who painted them are for the most part unknown.

The anonymous work of the early colonial limners is not, however, without interest. Again and again these pioneer American painters achieved results that have striking appeal because of their very ingenuousness. This is true, for example, of the portrait which some unknown Boston artist painted of Ann Pollard in 1721. Successfully depicted are the shrewdness and roguishness found only in lively old women who are proud of having lived over a century. It is true as well of the work of the so-called Patroon School—limners painting members of the old Dutch families of New York colony in the early eighteenth century.[1]

Much more is known of later artists. John Smibert, who arrived in America in 1729, was a better trained painter than the colonies had seen before. He had achieved a modest success in London and gained the friendship of Dean Berkeley, the great Anglican philosopher, who brought him to Newport, Rhode Island, en route to Bermuda. There Berkeley aspired to found a college with the artist as a member of his faculty, but expected funds failed to materialize and the party never reached its destination. Berkeley returned to England after spending three years in America—time by no means wasted since the good man wrote one of his finest books here—but Smibert remained in America. Taking up his residence in Boston, he achieved a success much greater than he had known in his native country. He painted portraits of the leading citizens and married into a wealthy provincial family.

Some of the finest colonial portraits were painted by Robert Feke between 1741 and 1750. Biographical details are very uncertain. According to some students Feke was the son of a Long Island Baptist minister and followed the sea during his youth. At all events, during the period of his success as a painter he lived at Newport and visited both Boston and Philadelphia. His work achieved a highly individual character. Beautifully gowned ladies and proudly attired gentlemen with idealized features and graceful poses dominated Feke's canvases. Such people and such portraits suited well an age of Georgian houses and Chippendale furniture.

During the last half of the eighteenth century two American-born painters displayed sufficient talent to win a high place in the world of international art. The first of these was Benjamin West, who was born in 1738 to a rural Pennsylvania innkeeper and one-time tinsmith. As a child West's talent for drawing was so pronounced that he excited the interest not only of the neighboring villagers but also of traveling strangers who gave him oil paints and engravings to copy. From William Williams, a competent English artist then residing in the colonies, young West learned some of the tricks of the trade, but for the most part he was self-taught. At the age of eighteen he was well established as a portrait painter in Philadelphia. Three years later he left the colonies to study in Italy. His expenses were paid by a group of wealthy Pennsylvania merchants, who believed, as one of them wrote, that it was "a pity such a genius should be cramped for the want of a little cash." West's good fortune continued. Settling in London after his Continental studies, the American achieved a brilliant success. He enjoyed the

[1] See Fig. 1.

special favor of George III and received generous patronage for the grandiose type of historical painting in which he now specialized. In 1792 he was elected to the presidency of the Royal Academy. Later generations have thought less highly of West's work than did his contemporaries, but his influence on American art was great. Many earnest young colonials were inspired to emulate him. They crossed the Atlantic to study with the famous master, and West's London studio became the seminary for the next generation of American artists.

Born in the same year as West was John Singleton Copley. His father disappeared about the time of his birth, and he was brought up by his Irish mother, who kept a tobacco store on the Boston water front. When he was ten, the mother married Peter Pelham, an engraver and occasional painter. The latter died three years later but not before he had instructed Copley in the rudiments of his craft. Thereafter, the youth apparently taught himself, studying eagerly the work of Smibert and other local artists. At sixteen Copley was painting portraits that showed great promise. Ten years later he was not only the busiest artist in America but incomparably the best. Unversed in many of the conventional techniques that eased the work of European artists, Copley solved problems in his own painstaking way, working many hours to secure results which satisfied him. His portraits were impressively honest, showing his sitters without flattery exactly as Copley saw them. Nor was their realism superficial. The New England genius studied his subjects so intensively that he seemed able to transmit their very characters to canvas.[1]

In 1774 Copley left Massachusetts never to return. He had long felt the need to travel abroad to study the Old World masters, but his final decision was hastened by political factors. The artist was in the middle of the struggle between the Boston radicals and the Tories. His father-in-law was a wealthy Tory merchant; many of his friends and clients were Whigs. Distressed by the apparently inevitable conflict, Copley settled permanently in England. Here he changed his manner of painting to the heroic mode which West had made popular. Although this new work was greatly admired, Copley's reputation still has its surest foundations in the painstaking portraits of his early career in America.

Today we must study colonial painting almost entirely in portraits which have been preserved through family pride even when their artistic merit was small. No such instinct has preserved other types of painting; but despite this neglect a few examples have survived, and many more are mentioned in contemporary letters and diaries. Colonial artists experimented with almost every type of subject and in all the different mediums. They painted landscapes and seascapes, classical and religious scenes, pictures of public buildings and of the water fronts of colonial ports. They depicted gentlemen riding to the hounds and mariners carousing in taverns. They painted in oils, water colors, and pastels and on canvas, paper, silk, and glass. There was a lively market for all kinds of pictures and a numerous company of eager, if inexpert, artists.

[1] See Fig. 3.

Music

In the southern colonies love of music seems to have been widespread. The common people handed down from one generation to another hundreds of folk songs, partly Old World in origin and partly American. Villagers who could play the fiddle or some more archaic instrument were popular at rural dances and on other festive occasions.

On the great plantations music had its place in both the slave huts and the mansion. Music for dancing in the great house was often provided by talented slaves. But gentlemen and ladies were by no means dependent upon the skill of their retainers. On the contrary, ability to play a musical instrument was a genteel accomplishment highly esteemed among both sexes. Music was "the darling amusement" of Colonel Robert Carter of Nomini Hall in Westmoreland County, Virginia. The Colonel owned a harpsichord, a pianoforte, a German flute, and a guitar. George Washington played the flute, and Thomas Jefferson was an accomplished violinist who regarded music as "the favorite passion" of his soul. Charleston was a musical center, where public concerts are known to have been given as early as 1733 and where the St. Cecilia Society was organized in 1737.

In the middle colonies the musical tradition was also strong. The Quakers disapproved, but in this as in other things they were soon a minority in their own colony. The Pennsylvania Germans preserved the rich heritage that they had brought from the Old World. Perhaps the best music to be heard in colonial America was in the Moravian town of Bethlehem, Pennsylvania, where Washington, Franklin, and other distinguished visitors were thrilled by masterpieces of German choral and instrumental music beautifully performed. Unorthodox but possessing a haunting fascination was the music composed and sung by the Brothers and Sisters at the Ephrata Cloisters.

In eighteenth-century New York and Philadelphia there were frequent public concerts as well as much private enjoyment of music. Benjamin Franklin learned to play the harp, the guitar, the violin, and the so-called "harmonica." This harmonica was not the mouth organ as we know it today, but an invention of Franklin himself. With characteristic ingenuity he arranged 37 glass hemispheres, specially blown for the purpose, on an iron spindle set in a wooden frame. To play the instrument he revolved the spindle with a treadle and touched the edge of the moving glass with his fingers. Between 1760 and 1800 the harmonica gained great popularity, particularly in Germany and in Austria. Among the composers who wrote music for the new instrument were Mozart and Beethoven. Although the tone produced by Franklin's invention was pleasing to the listener, its vibrant quality was so harrowing to the performer that the instrument was at length abandoned.

In New England, music encountered serious obstacles. The Puritans had no objection to secular music, and the wills and inventories of many settlers, even those of divines, mention viols and other instruments. Samuel Sewall wrote: "I am a lover of music to a fault." But the New Englanders cherished a strange prejudice against instrumental music in their churches. This was one of the popish elements to which they had objected in the Church of England. The singing of psalms had abundant Scriptural warrant and was an important part of Puritan worship. Indeed the *Bay Psalm Book* (1640) was one of the pioneer colonial attempts both at poetry and printing. But no music appeared in the book. The psalms were sung to a few tunes remembered from the English homeland. One of the deacons would sing the first line, and the congregation would carry on from there. In the early days, when memory of the old melodies was strong, this procedure worked tolerably well, but each generation's singing became worse. The congregations soon found it difficult to identify the tune which the precentor was trying to establish and harder still to keep it. The following eloquent opinion has been found scribbled on one of the old pews:

> Could poor David but for once
> To Salem Church repair,
> And hear his Psalms thus warbled out,
> Good Lord, how he would swear.

As a cautious step of reform the Reverend John Tufts of Newbury suggested that the psalm books should indicate the tunes. Since the New England presses possessed no musical type, Tufts devised a scheme for indicating the melody with letters and punctuation marks. About 1712 he published a work entitled *An Introduction to the Singing of Psalm Tunes in a Plain and Easy Method with a Collection of Tunes*. By this time, however, the disharmonies of the traditional singing had become so dear to many conservatives that they pronounced Tufts's suggestion dangerously popish. But, on this issue, Cotton Mather sided with the liberals, and a gratifying improvement in New England singing was eventually to be noted.

The introduction of musical instruments was still stoutly resisted. In 1713 the Brattle Street Congregational Church rejected the bequest of Thomas Brattle who had left it an organ, "which he dedicated and devoted to the praise and glory of God." Boston Anglicans had no such scruples, and the Brattle organ was eventually installed in King's Chapel. The controversy over the use of instrumental music in the churches continued throughout most of the eighteenth century, but the conservatives were gradually forced to give ground. From the gallery of New England churches there was now occasionally heard a medley of stringed and wind instruments, which were accepted as the equivalent of the sacred trumpets and shawms mentioned by King David. Even the unscriptural organ at length won a place. When a committee consulted Charles Chauncy of First Church, Boston, just after the venerable pastor had delivered his farewell sermon in 1785, he replied sadly that they might do as they pleased, that he would soon be in his grave, and that before his head was cold, they would have an organ anyway. Thus did the old order give way to the new.

Not until nearly the end of the colonial period did Americans attempt to compose music. Francis Hopkinson, lawyer, judge, and later signer of the Declaration of Independence, was an accomplished amateur musician of Philadelphia, who is known to have been writing sentimental songs as early as 1759. James Lyon, Presbyterian pastor and graduate of Princeton, published *Urania,*

FIG. 12. New England choral singing. An engraving by Paul Revere to illustrate William Billings' *New England Psalm Singer* (1770). (*Courtesy of Boston Public Library.*)

or A Choice Collection of Psalm-tunes, Anthems and Hymns in 1761. William Billings, one-eyed, misshapen Boston tanner, wrote words and music for numerous "fuguing pieces," which he published in the *New England Psalm Singer* (1770), *Billings' Best* (1778), and four other collections. Enthusiastic about his own work, Billings declared that his fuguing pieces were "more than twenty times as powerful as the old slow tunes."

Colonial Amusements

In 1611 when Sir Thomas Dale arrived at Jamestown and found the settlers merrily engaged in bowling, he rebuked them sternly and ordered them to stick to their work. His action was natural, since the idleness of the colonists was threatening the Virginia Company with bankruptcy and the pioneers themselves with starvation. But another motive was probably at work. During the seventeenth century there were many persons who regarded all play—except possibly that of infants—as sinful. This point of view was of course particularly strong among the Puritans and reflected their middle-class origins. Generally sober and hard-working themselves, they disapproved strongly of the worldly wickedness of the English upper classes. Beginning with a condemnation of the excesses of the pleasure-loving aristocrats, they soon extended their censure to idleness and gaiety under any conditions. Particularly sinful were sports or recreations that desecrated the Sabbath.

Many of the early Virginia clergymen and leaders were strongly influenced by Puritanism. Dale and his successors set severe penalties for idleness and non-attendance at church. In 1618 Governor Argall banned Sabbath-day dancing, fiddling, card playing, hunting, and fishing. Nor were the colonial representatives less severe when they began to make their own laws in the House of Burgesses. Among their first enactments were measures penalizing idleness, drunkenness, gambling, "excesse in apparell," and Sabbath breaking.

The New Englanders repressed unseemly hilarity with a strong hand. Governor Bradford rebuked sternly a group whom he found "pitching ye barr" and playing "at stoole-ball" in the streets of Plymouth on Christmas Day, 1621. Any observance of Christmas was regarded as dangerously popish, but it was particularly disturbing to Bradford's conscience that some should play while others worked. In 1628 the godly were upset by reports that the New England Falstaff, Sir Thomas Morton, had set up a Maypole at his settlement at Merry Mount around which he and his fellow rogues sported for many days, "inviting the Indean women for their consorts, dancing and frisking togither, (like so many fairies, or furies rather,) and worse practises." [1] Governor Endecott of the newly founded Salem colony rode over to investigate, had the offending "idoll Maypole" cut down, and threatened to make the "merry mount but a woful mount" if there were any more such revels.

New England lawmakers worked industriously at the task of specifying each of Satan's numerous wiles and providing an appropriate penalty. Cards and dice were forbidden together with bowling and shuffleboard. Drinking was legal, but the drinking of toasts was not, and drunkenness was punishable by fines or public whippings. The tithingman was the scourge both of boys found swimming when they should be working and of men found smoking under the same circumstances. Increasingly severe laws protected the sanctity of the Sabbath. All youths and maids over fourteen and all elder persons who profaned the holy day by "playing, uncivil walking, drinking, traveling from town to town" were to be

[1] William Bradford, *History of Plymouth Plantation,* ed. by William T. Davis (Scribner, New York, 1910), 238.

admonished or fined. If unable to pay the fine, they were to be whipped by the constable. Parents were liable to similar penalties for Sabbath breaking by children over the age of seven—"not that we approve younger children in evil," the magistrates carefully pointed out. Sabbath legislation was by no means peculiar to New England, but this section enforced its laws more rigorously than any other.

The instinct to play was, however, too strong to be long suppressed. In Virginia the crust of Puritanism was thin and soon broken. The dispersion of the population weakened all attempts to regulate by law the personal life of the settlers, and the Virginia clergy had neither the opportunity nor the inclination to censure their parishioners for trivial offenses. In the end, the growth of plantations produced a leisure class which enjoyed life without apology and with few inhibitions.

Colonial America was a hunter's paradise. For the adventurous there was really dangerous prey—wolves, bears, and panthers. For the more discreet there was such smaller game as deer, foxes, rabbits, squirrels, raccoons, opossums, partridges, turkeys, geese, and ducks. The Virginia gentlemen were expert horsemen and often trained their mounts to stand motionless while unsuspecting deer moved within gunshot. The pursuit of wild horses over the rough countryside was one of the most exciting sports of the late seventeenth century.

During the eighteenth century southern gentlemen devoted still more of their time and energy to outdoor sport. George Washington was an enthusiastic hunter, importing from England fine guns and elegant riding costumes and filling his stables with excellent horses and his kennels with clever hounds. His diary reveals that he hunted fifteen times during January and February, 1769, and that he engaged in this favorite sport six days in one week.

Pride in horseflesh led also to a great vogue for racing. There were five courses in Henrico County, Virginia, and many others elsewhere. Sizable stakes were offered to the winners, and the spectators backed their favorites with generous bets. When famous horses like Young Fire and Smoker raced, the rivalry was sometimes so heated that charges of foul play were carried into the law courts. Horse racing was at first considered to be one of the prerogatives of the aristocrats. In 1674 a tailor was fined in York County, Virginia, for "having made a race for his mare to run with a horse belonging to Mr. Matthew Slader for two thousand pounds of tobacco and cask, it being contrary to Law for a Labourer to make a race, being a sport for Gentlemen." [1] But racing was so popular that all attempts to restrict it to the upper class failed.

Virginia gentlemen played cards and danced with the same enthusiasm that they hunted and raced. Playing for stakes was at first prohibited by colonial law, but soon this restriction was so far relaxed that players sometimes resorted to

[1] Philip A. Bruce, *Economic History of Virginia in the Seventeenth Century* (New York, 1895), II, 473.

court action to collect their gambling debts. In southern towns like Charleston, Williamsburg, and Annapolis gay and brilliant balls were frequent, and on the plantations there were many less pretentious affairs. Guests were invited from neighboring plantations and often remained for several days, feasting, drinking, playing cards, and dancing. The clergyman of the parish was not infrequently a member of the party. Far from holding aloof from the balls and dances of his section, George Washington appears to have attended as many as possible and to have thoroughly enjoyed himself.

The lower classes of the South loved a good time as keenly as the rich. Cock-fights, boxing matches, and turkey shoots entertained the men, and gay country dances attracted merrymakers of both sexes.

The flesh and the devil were combated much more resolutely in New England. But even here the attempt to confine all the energy of the community to work and religious exercises was never entirely successful and became less so with each generation. From the beginning Puritan practice was less exacting than Puritan theory and Puritan legislation would suggest. Stories of the first Thanksgiving at Plymouth and of other feasts remind us that the early New Englanders permitted themselves to eat for pleasure as well as for sustenance. Since it was drunkenness rather than drinking which was a sin, the Puritans imbibed moderate quantities of cider, beer, and rum without fear of reproach. When the occasion was one obviously in the service of God, as at the ordination of a minister or the raising of the walls of a church, the pious might visit the punch bowl more times than usual without being accused of overindulgence.

The New Englanders often compensated themselves for their renunciation of other amusements by getting pleasure out of occasions intended to be serious. The celebration of Christmas and saints' days was prohibited, but the colonists made the most of civic holidays like Election Day and Training Day. On the latter occasion, when all the able-bodied men of the town gathered on the green to drill for the militia, the atmosphere was like that of a country fair. There was eager competition in shooting at a realistically stuffed dummy with prizes offered for the best marksmanship. After the exercises the amateur soldiers were served a bountiful dinner, and many of them spent the balance of the day resting from their exertions at the town tavern. Funerals were community events during which the villagers crowded the streets to watch the procession to the graveyard ride past in macabre pageantry. But the excitement of an ordinary funeral could not compare with that aroused by a public execution. Fascinated spectators crowded around the gallows to listen to the powerful sermon which was a regular feature of such an event. For once, however, the minister had to yield the center of the stage to another. The condemned man usually performed his part magnificently—even to the delivery of an edifying speech pointing out the obvious morals to be drawn from his melancholy fate.

Some of the amusements which seventeenth-century New England had condemned eighteenth-century New England learned to tolerate. The first generation of colonists had weighed seriously the problem of dancing. Such careful students of the Old Testament as the Puritans were well aware that King David and other Israelities had danced before the Lord. The Reverend John Cotton concluded that not all dancing was wrong, only "lascivious dancing to wanton ditties, and in amorous gestures and wanton dalliances." But since most of those who wanted to dance wanted to do so with members of the opposite sex, all dancing soon fell under condemnation. Shocked to discover that many of the townspeople were indulging in this forbidden pastime, Increase Mather issued a pamphlet entitled *An Arrow against Profane and Promiscuous Dancing, drawn out of the Quiver of the Scriptures* (1684). The Boston ministers appealed to the magistrates to take action against one Francis Stepney, who opened a dancing school, and the offending professor was compelled to stop his instruction. But Boston society was changing rapidly. After the loss of the old charter in 1684, the royal governors became the centers of a more sophisticated social life than New England had hitherto seen. Rich Boston merchants now entertained their guests with music and dancing despite clerical disapproval. Advertisements reveal that dancing masters were teaching their art unmolested as early as 1717, and after 1725 public balls were tolerated.

And so it was with other diversions. Although taverns had been licensed in New England since the earliest days, there were at first strict regulations against the traditional tavern sports. But strict supervision was gradually relaxed, and the eighteenth-century taverns were not only the scenes of much heavy drinking, but of the singing of ballads, the playing of innumerable games, frequent contests where customers could shoot at turkeys or bears, and occasional cockfights.

In the middle colonies town life was particularly gay. The Dutch introduced sports like skating and bowling, which continued to be popular in the section after it passed under English rule. New York was a lively town, where the well to do dressed ostentatiously and went on gay coaching parties in the summertime or sleighing in the winter. They would drive out to the Bowery or Harlem, spend the day at some tavern drinking, dancing, and playing cards, and return in the evening. Or they would ferry across the East River to watch and to place bets on the horse racing at Hempstead. The first New York coffeehouse was opened shortly before 1700 and became a popular place to meet friends, to enjoy good talk, and to hear the latest news.[1]

The serious-mindedness of the Quakers inhibited the social life of Philadelphia very little. The Pennsylvania capital became noted for its brilliant dancing assemblies, its elaborate banquets, and its pleasant fishing parties on the Schuylkill. The residents had a particular liking for clubs and societies. Franklin's Junto was as much recreational as educational, and similar clubs were numerous. The first Masonic body in America was St. John's Lodge, organized at Philadelphia in 1730.

[1] The first coffeehouse in the colonies was that opened in Boston in 1676.

The Theater

Despite the fact that the settlement of America began during the golden age of the English theater, the early colonists regarded actors and stage productions with extreme suspicion. In 1619 the Virginia legislature banned the entry of actors into the colony "because we resolve to suffer no Idle persons in Virginia." The Connecticut legislators provided that 15 stripes upon the bare back should be the punishment for anyone who should attempt to "set up and practice common plays, interludes, or other crafty science." Congregationalists, Quakers, Lutherans, and other sects agreed at least in this—that the stage was of the devil and to be vigorously combated.

Although the ruling order was strong enough to keep the theater out of New England throughout the colonial period, elsewhere the opposition soon lessened. In 1665 when three actors—probably amateurs—presented a play called *Ye Bare and Ye Cubb,* they were haled before a Virginia court and required to submit the text of their drama. But the authorities decided that the play was innocent, and the complainant was required to pay the costs of the case. As early as 1703 one Tony Aston, an itinerant English actor, landed at Charleston, South Carolina, according to his own description, "full of Shame, Poverty, Nakedness, and Hunger." Aston apparently performed in several other colonial towns, and his example was followed by other adventurous English actors during the early eighteenth century. In the absence of theaters these itinerants performed in taverns, coffeehouses, courtrooms, council chambers, and barns. In 1716 a building was erected at Williamsburg, Virginia, which was used both as a theater and as a dancing academy. The Quakers for a time prevented the presentation of plays within the city of Philadelphia, but in 1723 and 1724 rude theaters were erected on the outskirts. By 1732 there was a theater in New York and by 1735 one in Charleston.

The colonial theater for many years operated on a feast-or-famine regime. A company of English actors would spend several months touring such towns as Charleston, Williamsburg, New York, and Philadelphia. Then it would move on, and, except for an occasional amateur effort, there would be no plays for several years. But this situation was greatly improved after 1750. The colonial towns were now large enough to attract more competent English actors and longer tours. The new day may be dated from September 15, 1752, when a London company, headed by Lewis Hallam, presented *The Merchant of Venice* at Williamsburg. Members of the Hallam family were to be familiar figures on the American stage for the next fifty years.

The first of the Hallam tours lasted for two years, after which the company moved on to the apparently greener pastures of Jamaica. But in 1758 most of the group returned to the mainland colonies, where under the name of the American Company they remained for many years. The elder Hallam was now dead, and the company was under the direction of David Douglass, who had married Hallam's widow. The leading man was the youthful Lewis Hallam, Jr.

Not content with touring the colonies from Albany to Charleston, Douglass attempted to invade New England, where in 1762 he gave performances in Newport and Providence. But even in Newport, the least Puritan of New England towns, this was dangerous business. Douglass ingeniously advertised *Othello* as a "Moral Dialogue, in Five Parts, Depicting the Evil Effects of Jealousy and other Bad Passions. . . . Proving that Happiness can only Spring from the Pursuit of Virtue." The characters were delicately described as "a noble and magnanimous Moor," "a young and thoughtless officer," and "a young and virtuous wife, who, being wrongfully suspected, gets smothered (in an adjoining room) by her husband." The dialogue was to conclude by ten-thirty so that "every spectator may go home at a sober hour, and reflect upon what he has seen, before he retires to rest." But the Rhode Island assembly was unimpressed; they countered the American Company's invasion by a new law prohibiting theatrical performances and setting a penalty of £100 fine for each actor. In this action Rhode Island was belatedly locking a door that had been slammed shut long before elsewhere in New England.

The hazards of the acting profession were by no means confined to New England. In New York and Philadelphia actors were still regarded with suspicion and from time to time encountered difficulties with the authorities. In 1766 a New York mob, angry with all things British because of the quarrel over taxation, demolished the theater which Douglass had built on Chapel Street. Conditions became so impossible after the outbreak of the Revolutionary War that the veteran actor-manager retired to Jamaica where he died.

Despite these vicissitudes the theater became more and more an established American institution. On a visit to Charleston in 1773 the New Englander Josiah Quincy was surprised to learn that even the most respectable ladies attended the theater, and the playhouses at Williamsburg and Annapolis were honored by frequent visits by George Washington. The ramshackle buildings of earlier days now gave way to more pretentious structures like the Southwark Theater in Philadelphia, opened in 1766, and the John Street Theater in New York, opened in 1767. There were even a few attempts at writing drama, such as Thomas Godfrey, Jr.'s *The Prince of Parthia,* which was published in 1765 and given a public presentation in 1767.

The rise of the theater during the eighteenth century was another evidence that colonial life had escaped from the rather narrow pattern which earlier conditions, frontier poverty and provincial prejudice, had forced upon it. By 1775 American life displayed fascinating variations. Some of these arose from immigration, which had woven across the prosaic English web bright-colored threads representing the influence of the Dutch, the Swedes, the French, the Irish, the Scotch, the Germans, and the Negroes. Others reflected wide differences in soil and climate, evident in the contrasts of the rocky farms of New England, the fertile fields of Pennsylvania, and the great plantations of the South. Still others were the result of industry and trade, which added to American society the stimulating influence of artisans and merchants. The variety of colonial life was shown in its religions: God was honored with the cold and carefully calculated respect of the Deists, with the ritualistic worship of the Catholics and the Anglicans, with the sober meditation of the Quakers, and with the lengthy preaching of the Calvinists. Colonial architecture ranged all the way from the rude cabins of the frontier to the Georgian mansions of the seaboard; colonial music, from the simple folk songs of isolated villagers to the stately minuets of the ballrooms.

The more life in the American colonies is examined, the more obviously does it fail to conform to any single pattern. But at least it may be said that it *was* colonial and it *was* American, that is, it was a transplanted culture, whose origins might in almost every phase be traced to the Old World. The prestige of Europe remained great. Colonists traveled and studied abroad; whether on architecture or agriculture they accepted the authority of European manuals. But in crossing the Atlantic all Old World institutions suffered a sea change. The isolation of many colonial communities, the circumstances of their settlement, the influence of soil and climate modified the European heritage in hundreds of ways. A new, an *American*, way of life was in the process of evolution.

II. The New Nation, 1776-1861

Chapter 7. Independence and Nationhood

The American Revolution was decisive both for American political development and for its social evolution. In response to the challenge of the quarrel with Great Britain and the need for framing new constitutions, Americans thought more seriously about fundamental problems of government than ever before or since. The times called both for theorizing and for putting theories to the test of action. From what source should governments derive their powers? How much—or how little—government was required? How should individual liberty be protected against the arbitrary action of the state? How should power be distributed between central and local authorities?

Socially, the Revolution weakened the old aristocracy and laid the basis for a readjustment of classes. Thousands of the gentry fled the country; those who remained shared prestige with new men thrust up in the social upheaval. Landholding was disrupted by confiscations and new laws of inheritance. Large estates by no means disappeared, but the number of family-sized farms multiplied. New opportunities opened for merchants and speculators. Artisans and journeymen became discontented with their traditional status. Old institutions and modes of thought were widely challenged.

Revolutionary Thought

The mercantilist theory of empire required that colonies be a source of strength to the mother country. The British Parliament regulated the trade and shipping of the colonists, taxed their imports, and limited their manufactures. Some of these laws appeared to benefit the colonies as much as the mother country; others did not. The Navigation Acts greatly stimulated colonial shipbuilding and the carrying trade. On the other hand, the requirement that various enumerated products like tobacco must be exported only to England was not so clearly beneficial. Although the colonials enjoyed a monopoly of the English market, they were dependent on English prices and barred from foreign markets that might be more profitable. The requirement that most European products destined for the colonies first be carried to England worked to the profit of English merchants at the expense of the colonists. The limitations on colonial manufacturing were irritating in principle although scarcely felt in practice.

The Americans had long been accustomed to extensive powers of self-government. Either by charter or by royal permission each colony had its own assembly. In British theory these bodies were narrowly limited in power. Their enactments required the consent of the councils, conservative bodies of wealthy colonials; they were subject to the absolute veto of the governors; and they might be disallowed by the Privy Council in England. Despite these limitations, however, the colonial assemblies steadily gained in prestige. Most colonial governors deferred more to the local bodies that voted their salaries than to the distant authority that had appointed them.

Long experience trained colonial leaders in all the arts of practical politics. American political maturity was matched by the economic and cultural progress which has been described in earlier chapters. A bustling society of planters and farmers, merchants and artisans, lawyers and ministers grew yearly in wealth and assurance.

British imperial control provoked no dangerous protests so long as it was lightly felt. The colonists acknowledged the right of Parliament to regulate their trade and to impose tariff duties, but they tacitly reserved a right to disobey laws which seemed to run counter to their own interests. Smuggling, carrying enumerated articles to forbidden ports, and trading with the enemy during wartime laid the basis for many colonial fortunes.

When the British government sought to tighten the administration of its laws during and after the French and Indian War, a warning growl of discontent arose from the colonial merchants. When this step was followed by an attempt to tax the colonists, the Americans protested with unexpected violence. Resolutions, memorials, boycotts, riots, and hangings-in-effigy threw the colonies into turmoil. Repeal of the Stamp Act resolved the first crisis, but subsequent Parliamentary legislation revived the controversy. Colonial resistance led to British coercion; British coercion led to war.

In denying Parliament's power to tax the colonies, the American spokesmen talked much of their rights as Englishmen under the British Constitution. They professed sincere loyalty to King and Parliament but asserted that they could be taxed only by their own assemblies. The Resolutions of the Stamp Act Congress of 1765 thus expressed their position:

> That it is inseparably essential to the freedom of a people, and the undoubted right of Englishmen, that no taxes be imposed on them but with their own consent, given personally or by their representatives.
>
> That the people of these colonies are not, and from their local circumstances cannot be, represented in the House of Commons in Great Britain.
>
> That the only representatives of the people of these colonies are persons chosen therein by themselves, and that no taxes ever have been, or can be constitutionally imposed on them, but by their respective legislatures.
>
> That all supplies to the Crown being free gifts of the people, it is unreasonable and inconsistent with the principles and spirit of the British Constitution, for the people of Great Britain to grant to His Majesty the property of the colonists.

This early statement of the colonial position, probably drafted by the moderate Philadelphia lawyer, John Dickinson, stressed two points that were long to dominate American political thought. The state should not exercise arbitrary power but should rule within a framework of fundamental law known as the Constitution. No principle should be so jealously upheld as that which provided that the people should not be deprived of their property without their own consent. Since a tax was a grant of property, consent to its imposition could only be given by a body in which the property holders were represented. This tenderness for the rights of property was deeply rooted in English history and had its classic rationalization in the writings of the great Whig philosopher, John Locke. Summarized by Samuel Adams in the Massachusetts Circular Letter of 1768, the constitutional argument ran thus:

> That in all free States the Constitution is fixed; & as the supreme Legislative derives its Power & Authority from the Constitution, it cannot overleap the Bounds of it, without destroying its own foundation; That the constitution ascertains & limits both Sovereignty and allegiance, and therefore, his Majesty's American Subjects, who acknowledge themselves bound by the Ties of Allegiance, have an equitable Claim to the full enjoyment of the fundamental rules of the British Constitution: That it is an essential, unalterable Right, in nature, ingrafted into the British Constitution, as a fundamental Law, & ever held sacred & irrevocable by the Subjects within the Realm, that what a man has honestly acquired is absolutely his own, which he may freely give, but cannot be taken from him without his consent. . . .

These early American arguments were essentially conservative. Although denying the constitutionality of the Parliamentary taxes, James Otis of Massachusetts wrote in 1764: "Let the parliament lay what burdens they please on us . . . it is our duty to submit and patiently bear them, till they will be pleased to relieve us." In his famous *Letters from a Farmer in Pennsylvania* (1767–1768) John Dickinson counseled: "Let us behave like dutiful children, who have received unmerited blows from a beloved parent. Let us complain to our parent; but let our complaints speak at the same time the language of affliction and veneration."

But the constitutional argument encountered serious difficulties. Since the British Constitution had its only existence in tradition and precedent, men might differ widely on its contents. As interpreted by the British Parliament in the Declaratory Act of 1766, the Constitution provided that

> . . . the King's majesty, by and with the advice and consent of the lords spiritual and temporal, and commons of Great Britain, in parliament assembled, had, hath, and of right ought to have, full power and authority to make laws and statutes of sufficient force and validity to bind the colonies and people of America . . . in all cases whatsoever.

Even more disruptive to the constitutional argument was the fact that precedents were against the colonial claims. Parliamentary supremacy had been assumed in a long line of laws regulating the economic affairs of the colonies and imposing tariff duties upon them.

At length convinced of the futility of arguments that conceded the power of Parliament to legislate for the colonies in some matters but not in others, the Americans shifted their emphasis from appeals to the British Constitution to an assertion of their rights under the "laws of nature." In 1774 James Wilson, a Philadelphia lawyer, wrote:

> All men are by nature equal and free: no one has a right to any authority over another without his consent: all lawful government is founded on the consent of those who are subject to it: such consent was given with a view to ensure and to increase the happiness of the governed, above what they could enjoy in an independent and unconnected state of nature. The consequence is, that the happiness of the society is the first law of every government.[1]

Such arguments were not entirely new. They were clearly foreshadowed in earlier writings of James Otis, Samuel Adams, and John Adams. But Wilson, an incisive Scot, first forced the natural law argument to its logical conclusion—a denial of the legislative authority of the British Parliament over the colonies in every instance.

The developing American philosophy cannot be adequately understood without some reference to John Locke, from whom Wilson and other colonial spokesmen borrowed copiously. Locke's *Two Treatises of Government* (1690) had been a defense of the Glorious Revolution of 1688. For this purpose reliance on the British Constitution was hardly adequate. It might have been unconstitutional for James II to suspend the laws, but was it not even more unconstitutional for the Parliamentary leaders to invite a foreign invasion of England, to depose the King, and to grant the crown to someone else? Could it be that the British Constitution itself was but an imperfect reflection of some higher law—a law that might sometimes justify revolution? Sir Isaac Newton had profoundly impressed the intellectual world of Locke's day by demonstrating the existence of a universal law of gravitation. Were there not, asked Locke, comparable laws of nature upon which all government was based?

In order to find out what these laws were, Locke speculated upon what the relations of men would be in a state of nature where there was no organized government. In such a society all would be perfectly free and equal, but all would be bound by the "law of nature." Locke went on to explain: "The state of nature has a law to govern it, which obliges every one: and *reason, which is that law,* teaches all mankind, who will but consult it, that being all equal and independent, no one ought to harm another in his life, health, liberty, or possessions. . . ."

Since these natural rights were insecure, individuals agreed to the establishment of governments. In the words of Locke:

> Men being . . . by nature all free, equal, and independent, no one can be put out of this estate, and subjected to the political power of another, without his own consent. The only way whereby any one divests himself of his natural liberty and puts on the bonds of civil society, is by agreeing with other men to join and unite into a community, for their comfortable, safe and peaceable living one amongst another, in a secure enjoyment of their properties and a greater security against any that are not of it. . . . When any number

[1] Benjamin F. Wright, Jr., *A Source Book of American Political Theory* (Macmillan, New York, 1929), 69.

of men have so consented to make one community or government, they are thereby presently incorporated, and make one body politic, wherein the majority have a right to act and conclude the rest.[1]

If these were the premises on which government was based, the conclusions which should follow were obvious. Laws should be made only with the consent of the majority expressed through representative institutions. The minority was under obligation to obey the laws enacted by the majority, but even so the laws must not defeat the ends for which government was instituted—the protection of the individual's natural right to life, liberty, and property. When a government became destructive of those ends, it was the right of the people to alter or to abolish it. Locke was cautious in asserting this right of revolution, insisting that it was only to be taken as a last resort when efforts to secure the people's liberties through the ordinary channels of government had failed.

The growing prominence of the natural-rights argument and the denial of Parliamentary supremacy greatly disturbed colonial Tories. In pamphlets and sermons the Whig position was vigorously denounced. In a series of letters to the *Massachusetts Gazette* Daniel Leonard, a wealthy Boston lawyer, condemned the seditious activities of the radicals and asserted: "Two supreme or independent authorities cannot exist in the same state. It would be what is called imperium in imperio, the height of political absurdity. . . . If then we are a part of the British empire, we must be subject to the supreme power of the state, which is invested in the estates of parliament. . . ." Jonathan Boucher, an Anglican parson in Virginia and Maryland, ridiculed the idea that the whole human race was born equal and that government had its basis in the consent of the governed. "Any attempt . . . to introduce this fantastic system into practice would reduce the whole business of social life to the wearisome, confused, and useless talk of mankind's first expressing, and then withdrawing, their consent to an endless succession of schemes of government." Kings, according to this stubborn and courageous Tory, received their authority not from the consent of men but from God, the source and origin of all power.

The upholders of the old system could not stay the rush of events. The American destiny was in the hands of men who denied Parliamentary supremacy. Most of them, however, professed loyalty to the King and denied that their object was independence. Replying to Daniel Leonard's charges, John Adams wrote:

That there are any who pant after "independence," (meaning by this word a new plan of government over all America, unconnected with the crown of England, or meaning by it an exemption from the power of parliament to regulate trade,) is as great a slander upon the province as ever was committed to writing. The patriots of this province desire nothing new; they wish only to keep their old privileges.

[1] John Locke, *Two Treatises of Government,* ed. by T. I. Cook (Hafner Publishing Co., New York, 1947), 168–169.

Even after the battles of Lexington and Concord, the Second Continental Congress declared:

> Lest this declaration should disquiet the minds of our friends and fellow-subjects in any part of the empire, we assure them that we mean not to dissolve that union which has so long and so happily subsisted between us, and which we sincerely wish to see restored. . . . We have not raised armies with ambitious designs of separating from Great Britain, and establishing independent states.

With such conservatism, Thomas Paine, an English radical who had come to the colonies in 1774, had no patience. In *Common Sense* (1776) he argued that the logic of events demanded American independence: "All plans, proposals, &c. prior to the nineteenth of April, *i.e.* to the commencement of hostilities, are like the almanacks of last year; which, though proper then, are superseded and useless now." Appealing to self-interest, he contended that independence would encourage American trade and free the New World from involvement in the endless wars of the Old. He belittled the British Constitution, so blindly venerated by colonial lawyers. The Constitution, in Paine's analysis, was an incongruous composite of two ancient tyrannies, represented by the King and the House of Lords, with some new republican materials, represented by the House of Commons. For the monarchy, an institution still commanding the nostalgic respect of most Americans, Paine had only contempt. English kings traced descent to William of Normandy, but who was he? "A French bastard, landing with an armed Banditti, and establishing himself king of England against the consent of the natives, is, in plain terms, a very paltry, rascally original. It certainly hath no divinity in it."

In an argument destined to echo in America for many generations, Paine declared that the least government was best:

> Society in every state is a blessing, but Government even in its best state is but a necessary evil; in its worst state an intolerable one; for when we suffer, or are exposed to the same miseries *by a Government,* which we might expect in a country *without Government,* our calamity is heightened by reflecting that we furnish the means by which we suffer. Government, like dress, is the badge of lost innocence; the palaces of kings are built upon the ruins of the bowers of paradise. For were the impulses of conscience clear, uniform and irresistibly obeyed, man would need no other lawgiver; but that not being the case, he finds it necessary to surrender up a part of his property to furnish means for the protection of the rest; and this he is induced to do by the same prudence which in every other case advises him out of two evils to choose the least. Wherefore, security being the true design and end of government, it unanswerably follows, that whatever *form* thereof appears most likely to insure it to us, with the least expence and greatest benefit, is preferable to all others.[1]

Most extraordinary was Paine's feeling of the cosmic importance of the American struggle. "'Tis not the concern of a day, a year, or an age; posterity are virtually involved in the contest, and will be more or less affected, even to

[1] *The Writings of Thomas Paine,* ed. by M. D. Conway (New York, 1894–1896), I, 69.

the end of time, by the proceedings now." The freedom of the whole world seemed to hang in the balance:

> O! ye that love mankind! Ye that dare oppose, not only the tyranny, but the tyrant, stand forth! Every spot of the old world is overrun with oppression. Freedom hath been hunted round the globe. Asia, and Africa, have long expelled her—Europe regards her like a stranger, and England hath given her warning to depart. O! receive the fugitive, and prepare in time an asylum for mankind.[1]

Paine's words fell on fertile soil. Months of war with their inevitable stories of American heroism and British cruelty stimulated American patriotism and chilled affection for the old connection. To the impact of changing loyalties were added many factors of practical politics. A declaration of independence would resolve many internal problems, clear the way for the creation of new agencies of government, and fulfill a necessary prerequisite for the negotiation of foreign alliances. On July 2, 1776, the Continental Congress committed itself to the principle of independence by accepting a resolution introduced by Richard Henry Lee of Virginia. On July 4 a formal Declaration of Independence was agreed to and signed by John Hancock, president of the Congress. The Declaration was magnificently adapted for its principal purposes: to resolve the doubts of still hesitant Americans and to appeal to liberal sentiment abroad. Setting forth the causes that had impelled "the United States of America" to assume "the separate and equal station to which the Laws of Nature and of Nature's God entitle them," the Declaration epitomized the Revolutionary philosophy in these familiar words:

> We hold these truths to be self-evident, that all men are created equal, that they are endowed by their Creator with certain unalienable Rights, that among these are Life, Liberty and the pursuit of Happiness. That to secure these rights, Governments are instituted among Men, deriving their just powers from the consent of the governed. That whenever any Form of Government becomes destructive of these ends, it is the Right of the People, to alter or to abolish it, and to institute new Government, laying its foundation on such principles and organizing its powers in such form, as to them shall seem most likely to effect their safety and Happiness. . . .

Thomas Jefferson, the principal author of this famous document, never claimed for it any originality of thought. The ideas, so felicitously expressed, were those of John Locke and other seventeenth-century English philosophers. They echoed familiarly in American ears because of the increasing frequency with which James Wilson, John Adams, Alexander Hamilton, and other colonial pamphleteers had resorted to the natural-rights argument. Jefferson's emphasis on the pursuit of happiness as a primary right to be secured by government had been foreshadowed by James Wilson and Tom Paine. The great strength of the Declaration was that it said so well what this generation of Americans had come to believe. This philosophy became a part of living tradi-

[1] *Ibid.*, 100–101.

tion. Observing differences in human intelligence and talents, men might smile at the naïveté of a statement that all men are created equal, but Americans tried through their institutions to promote equality before the law and equality of opportunity. Governments based on force rather than consent, governments that were destructive of life and liberty were destined to enjoy scant respect in American opinion.

Social Consequences of the Revolution

The Revolution was not a simple war for independence in which all Americans made common cause against the mother country. It was a civil conflict, dividing colonies, communities, and even families.

Throughout the years of controversy which preceded hostilities, the colonists divided into Whig and Tory factions. Party loyalties did not become finally fixed until well after the war began. Many of the merchants who had been most opposed to the Stamp and Townshend Acts became frightened by the radicalism of the lower classes and turned Tory. On the other hand, conservatives like John Dickinson, John Jay, and Robert Morris opposed the assertion of independence but acquiesced in the decision and supported the American cause. In the end perhaps one-third of the population were Whigs, one-third were Loyalists, and one-third were not actively committed to either side. That the Whig minority was able to dominate the situation and to commit the colonies to the establishment of a new nation is impressive testimony to its determination and zeal.

The Tories included many of the wealthiest and most influential colonists. Royal governors and councilors almost always remained loyal to the Crown. Of the Anglican clergy practically all those of the North and many in the South were Tory. Many of the leading lawyers and physicians of the northern towns took the King's side, as did also a number of the wealthy merchants of every colony. Some of the largest landholders of the northern and middle colonies were also Tory. Yet it would be a mistake to think that the Loyalists were all gentlemen and the Patriots all yeomen and artisans. Some of the King's stanchest supporters were to be found among the common people: the Worcester blacksmiths, the New York house carpenters, the Baltimore printers, the frontier farmers of North and South Carolina were Tory in sympathy.

The Whigs were also drawn from every class. Strongly committed to independence were the greater part of the artisans and small farmers. The western counties of most colonies except the Carolinas were defiantly Whig. Yet the Revolutionary leaders were almost all men of education and culture. John Adams, John Dickinson, James Wilson, Patrick Henry, Edward Rutledge, Thomas Pinckney, and C. C. Pinckney were lawyers; Joseph Warren and Benjamin Rush were physicians; John Hancock, Thomas Mifflin, Robert Morris, and Henry Laurens were wealthy merchants. Most impressive of all was the Revolutionary prominence of southern planters like George Washington,

Thomas Jefferson, Richard Henry Lee, and Charles Carroll. Congregational and Presbyterian clergymen were almost always strong supporters of the American cause, as were also the preachers of most of the minor sects.

The Revolution was obviously not a rising of the lower classes against the upper. Yet its result was to weaken the position of the aristocracy. How many Loyalists left the country is unknown: 35,000 are believed to have gone into exile from New York alone; for the whole country the number may have reached 100,000. Some came back after the war, but more did not. American Loyalists settled in large numbers in Upper Canada and the Maritime Provinces; smaller numbers took up their residence in England or elsewhere in the British Empire. The removal of so many prominent merchants, landowners, and professional people reduced the ranks of the gentry. The immediate result was to create opportunities for the upper middle class, who gained wealth through speculation in trade and land and wielded decisive political power over the next generation. But the long-range result was more drastic. Small farmers and artisans felt the yeasty spirit of the times. Acquiescence in government by the rich and wellborn lessened. The mounting wave of Jeffersonian democracy was clearly visible during the Revolution; the Jacksonian swell was still far out at sea, but its coming could be predicted by the more discerning.

The weakening of the aristocracy was intensified by Revolutionary land policy. Tory estates of tremendous size were confiscated. The Penn family was deprived of holdings valued at almost 1 million pounds; the Philipse family of New York lost about 300 square miles; the famous Wentworth estate in New Hampshire, the Pepperell estate in Maine, the Fairfax estate in Virginia, and the Johnson estate in New York all passed into the hands of the Revolutionary governments. Scores of smaller properties were similarly confiscated. The older aristocracy suffered a paralyzing blow, and the American yeomanry was strengthened by the addition of hundreds who purchased family-sized farms when the great properties were broken up.

The revolution in land tenure took other forms as well. Royal restrictions on western settlement were swept away; crown lands fell under the administration of the states; the reservation of white pine trees for the Royal Navy was ended. Quitrents were abolished with promptness and enthusiasm. Particularly important was the Revolutionary attack upon entail and primogeniture, two of the main supports of the prewar aristocracy.[1] Although several of the colonies had legislated against these institutions earlier, entail and primogeniture flourished in New York, New Jersey, Virginia, North Carolina, and Georgia until outlawed by legislation during or soon after the Revolution.

The trend toward more democratic land tenure was irresistible. To be sure, plantation agriculture continued in the South; and in the North a new group of

[1] Entail was a legal device for maintaining the integrity of an estate: entailed property could be neither sold nor given away but must pass intact to the heir. Primogeniture provided that in the absence of a will the eldest son was sole heir.

large landholders arose through the activities of speculators like Robert and Gouverneur Morris, General Henry Knox, and John Cleves Symmes, who profited by the postwar situation to buy up land scrip from the veterans or large tracts from the governments of the day. But the speculators bought the land to sell again, and the ultimate result was to multiply the number of family-sized farms. Even if the franchise had continued to be reserved to real-estate owners, the basis would have been laid for a broad expansion of the governing class.

The Revolution brought irregular conditions which impoverished some merchants and enriched others. For the cautious businessman the deluge of paper currency, naval seizures, British occupation of American ports, and the loss of British Empire markets brought intolerable hardships. For the daring, however, there were opportunities for sudden riches in privateering, provisioning the army, and trading in France, Holland, and other new markets. Elias Derby of Salem, William Duer of New York, and Robert Morris of Philadelphia were among those who acquired fortunes during the war.

American manufacturing, already stimulated by prewar boycotts against British imports, expanded greatly during the period of the Revolution. The need for weapons resulted in the establishment of an armory at Springfield, Massachusetts, and new business for the ironmakers of Pennsylvania, New Jersey, and Maryland. Even more than the demands of Revolutionary finance the wartime avidity for news, reflected in the establishment of many new journals, led to the expansion of the paper industry. Salt making, glassmaking, and leathermaking likewise prospered under wartime conditions.

The intellectual results of the Revolution were far-reaching. Besides the stimulus to political thought the great war quickened the spirit of nationalism. Soon forgotten were the less heroic aspects of the war: the wrangling of the Continental Congress, the wholesale desertions from the army, the weather-vane politics of those who changed their allegiance with the shifting fortunes of war, the bad administration which left Washington's army shivering and hungry in a rich agricultural country, and the repudiation of the colonial currency. The war that passed into American memory was an epic of exalted patriotism—wherein Patrick Henry cried, "Give me Liberty, or give me death!" Ethan Allen demanded the surrender of the redcoats "in the name of the great Jehovah and the Continental Congress," and Nathan Hale regretted that he had "but one life to lose for his country." Myth or fact, such episodes were destined to implant love of country in the hearts of millions of American schoolboys. For half a century or more the cult of nationalism had visible heroes in Revolutionary veterans, who with pardonable exaggeration related their memories of the famous contest. Nascent nationalism found expression in patriotic poems and sermons, state histories, and biographies of the Revolutionary leaders.

Although the war years were difficult ones for schools and colleges, the end of hostilities found widespread interest in education. Eight colleges were established during the 1780's, and Jefferson and other statesmen formulated plans for ambitious public-school systems. The development of education will be discussed in a later chapter as will such other results of the Revolution as its impact on religion, on the treatment of criminals, and on the institution of slavery.

The State Builders

Revolutionary political thought, as we have seen, was not strikingly original. The American publicists borrowed freely, not only from John Locke, but from a score of other sources—English authorities like John Milton, James Harrington, and Sir William Blackstone, Germans like Samuel Pufendorf, and Frenchmen like the Baron de Montesquieu and Jean Jacques Rousseau. The novelty of American political thought was the extent to which it served as the basis for immediate political action. The Declaration of Independence linked familiar abstractions with practical conclusions of unique importance.

The Americans demonstrated not once but again and again how men might literally carry out Locke's prescription for putting on the bonds of civil society by agreeing with other men to join and unite into a community. The year 1776 was one of earnest constitution writing, with eight of the states adopting frameworks of government. Two more states took action in 1777 and one in 1780.

The first state constitutions reveal the political ideas upon which the Revolutionary leaders were building a new nation. Recent unhappy experience led them to place more stress on what governments might not do than on what they might. Significantly, the Virginia patriots adopted a Declaration of Rights before they drafted an instrument of government. In 16 clauses this famous document, largely the work of George Mason, spelled out the inherent rights of men entering upon a state of society: magistrates should be the trustees and servants of the people; office holding should not be hereditary; there should be rotation in office and frequent elections; persons accused of crime should receive speedy and impartial trial by jury; all men should enjoy freedom of the press and the free exercise of religion.

The unanimity with which the states founded their governments upon written constitutions was further proof of the American belief that the powers of the state should be carefully limited and defined. "To the end it may be a government of laws, and not of men," the Massachusetts constitution of 1780, like that of other states, provided for a strict separation of powers among the legislative, executive, and judicial departments. Reflecting Revolutionary experience, the first constitutions carefully hedged the governor's power but were more liberal with that of the legislature. The force of tradition was to be seen in the almost universal adherence to bicameral legislatures and property qualifications for voting and office holding. The radical Pennsylvania constitution of 1776 was unique in providing for a unicameral legislature, a plural executive, and a broad franchise.

Political thinkers, both in America and Europe, studied these pioneer constitutions with keen interest. In his *Notes on the State of Virginia* (1782) Thomas

Jefferson criticized the Virginia constitution on a number of scores: the franchise was too restricted in that it excluded half the taxpapers and militiamen; the western counties were underrepresented; the senate too homogeneous with the house of delegates. But his most serious misgivings were aroused by the excessive power entrusted to the legislature:

> All the powers of government, legislative, executive, and judiciary, result to the legislative body. . . . An *elective despotism* was not the government we fought for, but one which should not only be founded on free principles, but in which the powers of government should be so divided and balanced among several bodies of magistracy, as that no one could transcend their legal limits, without being effectually checked and restrained by the others.[1]

Even more zealously committed to a belief in checks and balances was John Adams. Stung by the words of the French savant Turgot, who had criticized the American constitutions for slavishly imitating English institutions, Adams wrote his ambitious treatise entitled *A Defense of the Constitutions of Government of the United States of America* (1787–1788). The significance of the American achievement was thus stated by the Massachusetts statesman:

> Thirteen governments thus founded on the natural authority of the people alone, without a pretence of miracle or mystery, and which are destined to spread over the northern part of that whole quarter of the globe, are a great point gained in favor of the rights of mankind. The experiment is made, and has completely succeeded; it can no longer be called in question, whether authority in magistrates and obedience of citizens can be grounded on reason, morality, and the Christian religion, without the monkery of priests or the knavery of politicians.[2]

Adams, a student of the English philosopher Harrington, believed that the basis of political power was economic. The peculiar virtue of the American constitutions was their careful balancing of the interests of the propertied and propertyless classes. It must be remembered, argued this hardheaded conservative, that

> . . . the rich are *people* as well as the poor; that they have rights as well as others; that they have as clear and as sacred a right to their large property as others have to theirs which is smaller; that oppression to them is as possible and as wicked as to others; that stealing, robbing, cheating, are the same crimes and sins, whether committed against them or others. The rich, therefore, ought to have an effectual barrier in the constitution against being robbed, plundered, and murdered, as well as the poor; and this can never be without an independent senate. The poor should have a bulwark against the same dangers and oppressions; and this can never be without a house of representatives of the people. But neither the rich nor the poor can be defended by their respective guardians in the constitution, without an executive power, vested with a negative, equal to either, to hold the balance between them, and decide when they cannot agree.[3]

From the beginning the Revolutionary leaders had recognized that their edifice of state governments must be capped by some kind of government for the United

[1] Thomas Jefferson, *Notes on the State of Virginia* (Boston, 1829), 123–124.

[2] *The Works of John Adams,* ed. by C. F. Adams (Boston, 1850–1856), IV, 293.

[3] *Ibid.,* VI, 65.

States as a whole. But the drafting of a constitution for the central authority proved exceedingly difficult. The Articles of Confederation, although agreed to by Congress in 1777, did not receive the consent of all the states until 1781. In many details this document was a progressive one, representing lessons in co-operation learned during the conflict with England. To Congress were entrusted exclusive control over foreign affairs, Indian relations, the establishment of post offices, and the fixing of standards for weights and measures and for the value of coins. Other provisions, however, reflected an excessive fear of central authority, bred by the long controversy with the mother country. The Articles specifically reserved the sovereignty of the states, granted equal representation to large and small states, required the consent of nine states to all important measures and unanimous agreement for amendments to the Articles themselves. Congress was given no power to tax, to regulate foreign and interstate commerce, or to enforce its decisions on recalcitrant states or individuals.

The seriousness of these deficiencies in the powers of the central government were soon demonstrated. The states, struggling with their own financial problems, paid only a small portion of the requisitions fixed by Congress. Without an adequate revenue the central government could neither pay the interest charges on the Revolutionary debt nor provide adequately for defense. An object of contempt in foreign eyes, Congress could not secure the free use of the Mississippi from Spain, the evacuation of the Northwest post from England, or satisfactory commercial treaties. The weakness of the central government was a matter of despair for the holders of the defaulted government securities, for speculators in western lands, and for merchants unable to trade profitably in the disordered postwar markets.

Equally a cause of concern to the business community was the radicalism of many of the state governments. Not only did they burden interstate commerce with exasperating duties and regulations, but they enacted inflationary issues of paper money, "stay laws" interfering with the foreclosure of mortgages, and other measures favoring debtors over creditors. In Massachusetts where conservative control of the state government made such measures impossible, radical mobs under Daniel Shays intimidated the courts and threatened to capture the Springfield armory before being overawed by the militia.

Conservative alarm at this state of affairs resulted in the Philadelphia Convention of 1787. Convinced that tinkering with the Articles of Confederation could provide no adequate remedy, the delegates boldly decided to write an entirely new document—one that would give the central government adequate power and provide a check on the action of the states. The resulting Constitution recognized property interests by prohibiting the states from emitting bills of credit, making anything but gold and silver coin legal tender, or passing any laws impairing the obligation of contract. Since the evils of the day were attributed to an excess of democracy, careful safeguards were erected against too much popular power. Only the House of Representatives was to be elected directly by the people. The

Senate was to be elected by the state legislatures; the President was to be chosen through an electoral college; the judges were all to be appointed. As a further safeguard against gusts of popular passion, the Representatives were to serve two years, the Senators six, the President four, and the judges during good behavior.

The Constitution obviously represented a return to conservative principles and a reaction from the radical implications of the Declaration of Independence. But the Philadelphia framers were intelligent and patriotic men, not disposed to push their counterrevolution too far. Even Hamilton, who would have preferred a president for life with an absolute veto, a powerful senate composed of distinguished persons serving during good behavior, and state governors appointed by the general government, recognized that such authoritarian institutions would never be accepted by the voters. The conservatism of the Convention was more accurately reflected in the opinions of James Madison, its most influential member. In a pamphlet published just before the opening of the Philadelphia meeting, Madison said:

> The great desideratum in Government is such a modification of the sovereignty as will render it sufficiently neutral between the different interests and factions, to controul one part of the society from invading the rights of another, and at the same time sufficiently controuled itself, from setting up an interest adverse to that of the whole Society.

Although diplomatic duties in England prevented John Adams from attending the Convention, he was delighted with its results. In the Constitution he later discovered no less than eight of the balances which he so much admired: (1) states against the central government, (2) House of Representatives against Senate, (3) President against Congress, (4) judiciary against Congress, (5) Senate against President in appointments and treaties, (6) the people against their Representatives, (7) the state legislatures against the Senate, and (8) the Electoral College against the people.

The true greatness of the Constitution did not lie in its checks and balances—rather too ingeniously contrived, it sometimes later appeared, for the efficient operation of government. The Philadelphia framers did their best work in creating a workable basis for federalism by reconciling the demands of vigorous central authority with the ideal of local self-government. The national government was endowed with ample means and power not only to deal with foreign nations but to enforce its laws upon individuals. But although the Constitution, the laws made in pursuance thereof, and all treaties made under the authority of the United States became the supreme law of the land, the sphere of operations of the central government was carefully defined, and the states were left with power over all other subjects.

The Great Debate

The ratification of the Constitution by nine states, the necessary condition for its going into effect, was not accomplished without a sharp struggle. Although the creditor and mercantile classes enthusiastically supported the proposal, the debtor and small farmer groups were hostile. Leadership in the antifederalist cause was forthcoming from many veterans of the Revolutionary agitation who regarded the Constitution as a revival of the threat of centralized despotism which they had renounced in 1776.

Richard Henry Lee, in *Letters from the Federal Farmer to the Republicans* (1787), rebuked the advocates of the new Constitution for their attempts to rush the project through:

> It is natural for men, who wish to hasten the adoption of a measure, to tell us, now is the crisis—now is the critical moment which must be seized or all will be lost; and to shut the door against free enquiry, whenever conscious the thing presented has defects in it, which time and investigation will probably discover. . . . The fickle and ardent, in any community are the proper tools for establishing despotic government. But it is deliberate and thinking men, who must establish and secure governments on free principles. . . .[1]

Lee conceded grave weaknesses in the Articles of Confederation and many excellent features in the proposed Constitution, but he argued that the new plan should not be accepted until the powers of the central government were circumscribed more narrowly and the liberties of the people protected by a Bill of Rights. He warned that

> . . . when power is once transferred from the many to the few, all changes become extremely difficult; the government, in this case, being beneficial to the few, they will be exceedingly artful and adroit in preventing any measures which may lead to change; and nothing will produce it, but great exertions and severe struggles on the part of the common people.[2]

The struggle over ratification in Virginia was notable for the quality of leadership in both parties. The new document was powerfully supported by George Washington, James Madison, and the youthful John Marshall. It was opposed not only by Richard Henry Lee but by George Mason and Patrick Henry. Mason had been a delegate to the Philadelphia Convention but refused to sign the Constitution. In a pamphlet in which he set forth his objections, he criticized the proposal for its inadequate protection of the rights of the people. "This government," he predicted, "will commence in a moderate aristocracy; it is at present impossible to foresee whether it will, in its operation, produce a monarchy, or a corrupt oppressive aristocracy; it will most probably vibrate some years between the two and then terminate in one or the other." [3] The veteran radical, Patrick Henry, who had declined to serve as a delegate to the Convention because he "smelt a rat," found his suspicions confirmed by the document now proposed. In the Virginia ratifying convention, he declared:

[1] Alpheus T. Mason, ed., *Free Government in the Making: Readings in American Political Thought* (Oxford, New York, 1949), 259.

[2] *Ibid.,* 262–263.

[3] *Ibid.,* 255.

> That this *is* a consolidated government is demonstrably clear; and the danger of such a government is, to my mind, very striking. I have the highest veneration for those gentlemen; but, sir, give me leave to demand, What right had they to say, *we, the people*? My political curiosity, exclusive of my anxious solicitude for the public welfare, leads me to ask, who authorized them to speak the language of, *we, the people,* instead of *we, the states? States* are the characteristics and the soul of *a confederation.* If the *states* be not the agents of this compact, it must be one *great, consolidated, national government of the people of all the states.*[1]

Although the antifederalist leadership elsewhere—embodied in such men as the captious Elbridge Gerry of Massachusetts and the calculating Governor George Clinton of New York—was less admirable than that of Virginia, the debates of the ratifying conventions reveal honest misgivings on the part of many obscure country delegates. One in Massachusetts shrewdly observed: "We contended with Great Britain, some said for a threepenny duty on tea; but it was not that; it was because they claimed a right to tax us and bind us in all cases whatever. And does not this Constitution do the same?" Another opposed the Constitution because, "as it now stands, Congress will be vested with more extensive powers than ever Great Britain exercised over us; too great, in my opinion, to intrust with any class of men, let their talents or virtues be ever so conspicuous, even though composed of such exalted, amiable characters as the great Washington. . . ."[2]

Among the publications issued to gain support for the Constitution, the most important was the series of public letters known as *The Federalist.* The work was originally planned by Alexander Hamilton as a means of influencing opinion in New York, a key state in the ratification struggle. Enlisting the cooperation of James Madison and John Jay, Hamilton secured publication for the first number, written by himself, in the *Independent Journal* for October 27, 1787. Subsequent articles appeared over the course of the next six months in other New York newspapers. Despite their local purpose the *Federalist* papers soon commanded the respect of readers in other states. They were reprinted in various newspapers, and in 1788 the first edition in book form appeared.

As political propaganda *The Federalist* was extremely skillful. The tone was one of calm persuasion. Without resort to invective the objections of the antifederalists were one after another patiently reviewed in the light of history and right reason. The Constitution, it was conceded, probably fell short of absolute perfection, but it was the best that could be achieved under existing circumstances. Sensible procedure was to adopt the new instrument and then amend it rather than to prolong the precarious state of national affairs "in the chimerical pursuit of a perfect plan."

The Federalist, however, was more than propaganda for an immediate purpose. Its enduring importance was recognized from the first. In a letter to Madison, Jefferson praised the work as "the best commentary on the principles of govern-

[1] William Wirt, *The Life of Patrick Henry* (New York, 1835), 284.

[2] Wright, *op. cit.,* 253–254.

ment ever written." Extravagant though this seems, the American historian, Henry Steele Commager, writing 160 years later, goes almost as far:

> The substance has significance far beyond the immediate use to which the papers were directed, beyond even American history. For here is the first distinctly modern treatise on government—a treatise which turns from abstractions and theories to realities and practicalities. Here is the first close, hard analysis of the nature of political power, of the executive, the legislative, the judiciary. Here is the first realistic consideration of the economic background of politics. Here is the first thorough consideration of the character of federalism—a question of deep concern to the modern world.[1]

Hamilton with sharp intelligence and lucid language cut through the verbiage of the contemporary debate to fundamental issues. "The great and radical vice in the construction of the existing Confederation," he asserted in his No. 15, "is in the principle of LEGISLATION for STATES or GOVERNMENTS, in their CORPORATE or COLLECTIVE CAPACITIES, and as contradistinguished from the INDIVIDUALS of which they consist." From this consideration he drew the obvious conclusion that "we must extend the authority of the Union to the persons of the citizens—the only proper objects of government." In No. 70 Hamilton argued that "energy in the Executive is a leading character in the definition of good government." The ingredients which constitute energy in the Executive are "first, unity; secondly, duration; thirdly, an adequate provision for its support; fourthly, competent powers." With characteristic boldness he asserted the power of the courts to declare acts of Congress unconstitutional—an issue on which the Constitution had been significantly silent:

> The complete independence of the courts of justice is peculiarly essential in a limited Constitution. By a limited Constitution, I understand one which contains certain specified exceptions to the legislative authority, such for instance, as that it shall pass no bills at attainder, nor *ex-post-facto-laws,* and the like. Limitations of this kind can be preserved in practice no other way than through the medium of courts of justice, whose duty it must be to declare all acts contrary to the manifest tenor of the Constitution void. . . .[2]

Madison's contribution to *The Federalist,* although less in quantity than Hamilton's, was equally remarkable in quality. No. 10, written by the great Virginian, is indeed the most famous essay in the entire series. In this Madison argued that one of the chief merits of the Constitution was the promise that it offered of breaking and controlling the violence of faction. A faction he defined as "a number of citizens, whether amounting to a majority or minority of the whole, who are united and actuated by some common impulse of passion, or of interest, adverse to the rights of other citizens, or to the permanent and aggregate interests of the community." The causes of faction are sown in the nature of man.

[1] Introduction in H. S. Commager, ed., *Selections from The Federalist: A Commentary on the Constitution of the United States* (Appleton-Century-Crofts, New York, 1949), x-xi.

[2] No. 78. H. C. Lodge, ed., *The Federalist: A Commentary on the Constitution of the United States* (New York, 1895), 484–485.

They may be brought forth by differences over religion, forms of government, or personal loyalties.

But the most common and durable source of factions has been the various and unequal distribution of property. Those who hold and those who are without property have ever formed distinct interests in society. Those who are creditors, and those who are debtors, fall under a like discrimination. A landed interest, a manufacturing interest, a mercantile interest, a moneyed interest, with many lesser interests, grow up of necessity in civilized nations, and divide them into different classes, actuated by different sentiments and views. The regulation of these various and interfering interests forms the principal task of modern legislation, and involves the spirit of party and faction in the necessary and ordinary operations of the government.[1]

Factions were inevitable, but their effects could be to a large extent neutralized by increasing the size of the republic, thus balancing one interest against another.

The influence of factious leaders may kindle a flame within their particular States, but will be unable to spread a general conflagration through the other States. A religious sect may degenerate into a political faction in a part of the Confederacy; but the variety of sects dispersed over the entire face of it must secure the national councils against any danger from that source. A rage for paper money, for an abolition of debts, for an equal division of property, or for any other improper or wicked project, will be less apt to pervade the whole body of the Union than a particular member of it; in the same proportion as such a malady is more likely to taint a particular county or district, than an entire State.

In the extent and proper structure of the Union, therefore, we behold a republican remedy for the disease most incident to republican government.[2]

In the end, the ratification of the Constitution was attributable more to the adroit political generaliship of the Federalists than to the persuasiveness of their arguments. Perhaps the decisive factor was their promise to add a Bill of Rights to the Constitution as soon as the new government should go into operation. The pledge was kept, and in 1791, 10 amendments, guaranteeing the liberties of the citizens and the states against invasion by the Federal government, went into effect. By this happy compromise the new nation secured a double birthright. From the conservatives of the day it received adequate provision for strong and effective government; at the insistence of the radicals it received a cherished charter of liberties.

[1] *Ibid.,* 54.
[2] *Ibid.,* 59–60.

Chapter 8. Agriculture and the Frontier

When Great Britain acknowledged the independence of the United States in 1783, the new nation received generous boundaries. Although few Americans yet lived beyond the Appalachian mountain chain, the United States became sovereign over a vast area extending from the Atlantic Ocean to the Mississippi River and from the thirty-first parallel on the south to the Great Lakes. Even this did not long satisfy the American yearning for territory. By diplomatic skill and luck, by bluster and war, by the insistent pressure of frontier migration, the boundaries of the United States were pushed west during the next three generations until they reached the Pacific Ocean.

Annexations of territory provided new frontiers to be settled after each of the old had been passed. Fertile land, abundant and cheap, assured the continuance of farming as the leading economic activity of the nation and preserved the village as the characteristic American community. But the agriculture of 1860 was not the agriculture of colonial days. Illinois wheat and Mississippi cotton made their way to distant markets over highways, railroads, rivers, canals, and oceans. Regional specialization, new methods of transportation, and complex commercial organization reflected the growth of cities and the development of capitalism. Better breeds of livestock, better methods of cultivating the soil, and the introduction of agricultural machinery gave evidence of the application of reason to activities long chained to tyrannical custom.

The Trans-Appalachian Frontier

In the decade before the Revolutionary War hunters began to push their way across the mountains of western Virginia and North Carolina into the future states of Kentucky and Tennessee. Here they found mile upon mile of forest and heavy brush in which buffalo, bears, deer, and wild turkeys abounded. Particularly sought after were the deer, whose skins were worth about a dollar apiece. The pelts were half dressed by the hunters, placed on poles to protect them from ravaging animals, and finally baled into packs weighing about 50 pounds each. When enough were accumulated, they were carried back to the settlements. The "long hunters," as these far-ranging adventurers were called, usually organized in bands of from ten to forty men for protection against the Indians and for convenience of transportation. But the boldest went out in smaller groups or singly. The famous Daniel Boone traveled alone through the wilderness for months, delighting in stratagems to outwit the savages and the wild animals. Not avoiding the Indians but seeking them out were the traders, who exchanged rum and other merchandise for valuable furs.

After the hunter and the trader came the squatter, who brought wife and children, built a rude cabin, and cleared a corn patch in the forest. After the French and Indian War frontiersmen moved into western Pennsylvania and Virginia. Farther south a small settlement was made on the Watauga River in what is today eastern Tennessee. This soon attracted disgruntled North Carolina frontiersmen, defeated in their attempt to obtain a redress of grievances from corrupt eastern officials in the battle of Alamance in 1771. In 1775 Daniel Boone, as the agent of the North Carolina land speculator Judge Richard Henderson, blazed a trail through Cumberland Gap into Tennessee and thence north into central Kentucky. This famous Wilderness Road provided the route by which thousands of pioneers made their way to new homes. Not sufficiently improved to permit wagon traffic until about 1800, the trail was usually traveled by companies organized for protection. First came livestock driven by the older boys, then pack horses laden with all the worldly goods of the migrating families. Some of the women walked; some rode with their babies in their arms. The older children trudged along on foot; the younger were tied to the horses and sometimes cooped in baskets made of hickory withes. The able-bodied men, carrying loaded guns, spread out on the front, flanks, and rear of the caravan to serve as scouts and guards. At night the company formed a camp, built fires around its circumference, and posted sentinels to watch while the rest slept.

A somewhat easier route ran overland across western Pennsylvania to the headwaters of the Ohio River at Pittsburgh. Here the migrating family either purchased or built a flatboat. About 15 feet wide and 50 long, the boat had a rectangular deck enclosed by a plank bulwark, pierced with loopholes, for protection against the Indians. Part or all of the boat might be covered by a roof. Often called "arks," these clumsy craft, crowded with two or three families and all their horses, cattle, hogs, and chickens, had more than a little resemblance to Noah's famous vessel. Until 1788 West Virginia or Kentucky was the destination of this stream of migration. After that time a growing number settled in Ohio—particularly after the Federal government had subdued the Indians and provided for the organization of the territory.

In Tennessee and Kentucky the savages were a grave menace throughout the period of the Revolutionary War and only slightly less so until their power was finally broken in the 1790's. The wiser pioneers therefore settled in or near well-protected "stations" like Watauga, Nashboro, Boonesborough, and Harrodsburg. Land near the fort was divided among the settlers, who took turns working in the fields and standing guard. At night the company would return to the stockade and the great gates would be closed. But this regimented existence irked the land-hungry frontiersmen. More and more of them staked out claims at some distance from the station, built cabins upon them, and moved their families.

Many were scalped for their rashness; others owed their lives to hairbreadth escapes to the stockade during Indian attacks.

A pioneer farm was easily acquired, though not so easily retained. In Kentucky and Tennessee—under the government of Virginia and North Carolina respectively until they achieved statehood in 1792 and 1796—land policy was generous but chaotic. There was no regular survey prior to settlement, and pioneers could claim tracts by raising a crop of corn or by cutting their initials on trees. These claims gave valid title upon payment of a small registry fee to the proper authorities. But boundaries were vague, and conflicting and overlapping claims led to frequent lawsuits. The squatter often lost the land he had improved to some claimant who had fulfilled the legal requirements earlier or more carefully than he.

In the Northwest Territory and in Alabama and Mississippi the Federal government controlled land policy. Here, except in certain large tracts sold to land companies or reserved by eastern states, orderly procedures were laid down. Survey was to precede settlement; minimum prices and areas were fixed; land was sold at auction to the highest bidder and the unsold portions conveyed by later sales at the minimum price. But squatters held the law in light regard. They built their cabins and cleared their fields despite the danger that they might lose the land when it was surveyed and put up for sale. Speculators frequenting the auctions often bid the price of the improved tracts so high that their occupants could not afford to purchase them. Sometimes the squatters prevented this by organizing "claim clubs" to prevent any rival bidding at the auctions, thus enabling each member to buy his land at the minimum price. So strongly were squatter rights asserted that Federal law had eventually to be amended, first by partial preemption acts and finally by the general preemption act of 1841. Even the minimum price was too much for many squatters to pay, and these drifted west ahead of the official surveyors. Poverty, restlessness, and will-o'-the-wisp rumors of better land created perennial squatters, staying only a few years in each location.

The squatter lived as his colonial prototype had lived. Often his family dwelt in a cave or rude lean-to while he and his neighbors built a log cabin. This was still a rough one-room dwelling, dominated by a huge fireplace, sometimes wide enough to take 12-foot logs. In the South the windows and doors were sometimes unprotected openings through the walls; in colder climates heavy greased paper or deerskins scraped thin covered the windows. If the pioneer prospered sufficiently, he might build a second cabin and connect the two by a covered passage called the "dog trot." Log architecture permitted many other refinements. Additional rooms and a second story might be added, a long veranda might be built across the front, or the logs might be hewn or enclosed with weatherboards.

Fields were still cleared by cutting down and burning the smaller trees and by girdling the larger ones. Great bonfires were a feature of the process—by no means a dead loss since potash and pearl ash had a ready sale if they could be moved to market. Corn continued to be the great frontier crop, since it was easily grown in the partially cleared fields and provided food for both human beings and livestock. Many of the squatters were indifferent farmers, spending as little effort as possible in clearing the land and growing food. They liked better to hunt and to trap or to collect beeswax or ginseng—an aromatic root readily accepted in trade by frontier merchants, who sold it to easterners for export to China, where it was highly esteemed for its supposed medicinal value.

Pioneer agriculture aimed first at self-sufficiency. Corn and, later, rye and wheat provided breadstuff, and cattle, hogs, and chickens assured meat, milk, butter, and eggs. Although sheep were hard to protect under frontier conditions, a small flock was usually kept to provide wool for the family clothing. Almost every frontier farm had also its field of flax, since linen and the linen-woolen mixture known as "linsey-woolsey" were favorite materials. When the farmer became permanently located, he started an orchard. The peregrinations of John Chapman or "Johnny Appleseed," who planted apple trees throughout frontier Ohio, have become a part of American folklore.

But growing crops for home use would not raise the cash necessary to meet instalment payments on the land or to buy salt, iron, gunpowder, lead, and other necessities that the farm could not produce. If he was to succeed, the pioneer had to produce a surplus and to get it to market. This was the reason that emigrants on the Wilderness Trail met occasional caravans moving in the opposite direction. Ten or twelve plodding pack horses, tied one to another and each carrying about 200 pounds of produce, would be driven over the mountains by two or three men, entrusted with marketing the goods of several frontier families. In the earliest days the packs usually contained hides, pelts, beeswax, bear oil, and ginseng. Later, the animals might be carrying tobacco, flour, or whisky. These products were too bulky to transport with much profit on pack animals, but when the trails were widened into roads, they were moved slowly to eastern markets in great covered wagons.

Livestock multiplied rapidly, and the surplus had a ready sale in the East. Cattle, hogs, and horses from Kentucky were driven hundreds of miles to markets as far north as Baltimore and as far south as Charleston. Similar drives from Ohio brought livestock to Philadelphia, Baltimore, and New York.

Overland routes to market were difficult, and the trans-Appalachian districts responded eagerly to the diplomatic victories which opened the great Middle Western waterways to American trade. During the early nineteenth century the Ohio, the Cumberland, and the Tennessee were crowded with flatboats, floating down to the broad Mississippi and thence to the thriving port of New Orleans. Through the new artery of commerce flour moved both to eastern cities and to Europe, where the Napoleonic wars had created a lively demand. Down the rivers also came corn, livestock, salt pork, apples, potatoes, tobacco, whisky, hemp, and cotton.

The growing volume of staples moving out of the West was eloquent testimony that in many districts the day of the squatter had passed. The more industrious pioneers had paid for their land, conquered their initial handicaps, and cleared enough fields to become established farmers. The unsuccessful but still hopeful had moved on to new frontiers. The least ambitious had resigned themselves to a precarious livelihood on hilly, infertile holdings. Meanwhile, there was emerging an enterprising agricultural class with farms of 200 or 300 acres, producing staple crops for distant markets. This class was derived in part from successful pioneers but more characteristically from eastern farmers who moved west after the forest had been conquered and purchased the best land. The most remarkable representatives of this class were the cotton planters of the Deep South.

Westward to the Pacific

The westward movement of the population persisted generation after generation, carrying the area of settlement ever farther from the Atlantic seaboard. Periodically the stream of emigration would swell to unusual dimensions. One such wave at the end of the eighteenth century populated the western counties of Pennsylvania, New York, and Georgia and brought the new states of Kentucky (1792), Tennessee (1796), and Ohio (1803) into the Union. A greater wave followed the War of 1812—a conflict that gave many eastern soldiers an opportunity to see the West for themselves. The roads of New York and Pennsylvania were crowded with migrating families and their wagons and livestock responding to the "Ohio fever"—a fever that not only doubled the population of Ohio between 1810 and 1820 but also created the states of Indiana (1816) and Illinois (1818). The southern frontier with the cotton boom now in full force was no less active and brought into the Union, Louisiana (1812), Mississippi (1817), Alabama (1819), and Missouri (1820). A third great wave of migration rose during the thirties. It was a period of buoyant optimism, speculation, and inflation, which culminated in the ruin of thousands in the depression of 1837. But it left its permanent achievement in the new states of Arkansas (1836), Michigan (1837), Iowa (1846), and Wisconsin (1848).

Whence came the thousands to populate these new communities? Some of the settlers before 1840 and many more afterwards were immigrants from Europe. But the majority were natives of the older states moving west in search of better opportunities. The decennial census reports told the story. Although the birth rate was so high that none of the older states declined in absolute population, the growth of many of them became slow, and they lost in relative importance. Virginia, still first in population as late as 1810, fell to fifth place by 1860. Connecticut, eighth among the states in 1790, was twenty-fourth in 1860, and South Carolina fell from seventh to eighteenth during the same period. Meanwhile, the new districts grew with astounding rapidity. Ohio was third among all the states in 1860, Illinois was fourth, and Indiana sixth.

New England contributed heavily to each wave of the frontier movement. By 1860 families of Yankee origin abounded in western New York and northern Pennsylvania and in all the states of the Old Northwest. The result was to spread across this whole area a culture belt where New England patterns of speech, habits of thought, and distinctive institutions prevailed. But Virginia and the older southern states were equally prodigal in dispersing their people and their culture. Not only did they populate the Old Southwest, but a large element crossed the Ohio River from Kentucky to settle in the southern counties of Ohio, Indiana, and Illinois. There they clung to their distinctive idiom and customs. In politics they were aggressively proslavery. Sometimes indeed they were actual slaveholders despite the laws prohibiting the institution in the Northwest.

After 1840 the frontier movement took its most extraordinary form when long caravans of emigrants began to move across the continent from Missouri to Oregon 2,000 miles away. To most Americans the vast area of plains and mountains across which the covered wagons were now passing was the "Great American desert"—a place of mystery and terror. But it was familiar terrain to fur traders and trappers, who had been living in this country for many years.

The trans-Mississippi fur trade had begun under French and Spanish direction before the American purchase of the Louisiana Territory. Americans became deeply involved in the trade immediately after the annexation. When Lewis and Clark made their way down the Missouri in 1806 on their return from the Pacific Coast, they met a number of small parties already venturing far up the river in search of furs. In 1809 the Missouri Fur Company was organized at St. Louis to exploit the trade of the upper valley.

Shortly after this the Napoleonic figure of John Jacob Astor began to operate in the western fur trade. From 1811 to 1813 he made an abortive attempt to maintain an American fur post at Astoria in the Oregon country at the mouth of the Columbia River. The project failed—in part because of the War of 1812, but more because British fur-trading interests were already firmly entrenched in this area. While the venture lasted, however, it spurred American exploration of the West. Astorian overland expeditions crossed the Continental Divide at South Pass and marked out other stretches of what was eventually to become the famous Oregon Trail. Farther east, Astor had abundant success. His American Fur Company profitably exploited the trade of the Great Lakes area and then pushed its domination further west. During the twenties it gained control of the Missouri River trade, establishing its posts as far north as Fort Union at the mouth of the Yellowstone in present-day Montana. The trade was greatly facilitated when the American Fur Company steamboat *Yellowstone* began its annual voyages up the river in 1831.

Between the British-dominated posts of Oregon and the region controlled by Astor lay the magnificent fur country of the Rocky Mountains. The trade of this area was first exploited by General William Ashley and his employees—intrepid figures like Jedediah Smith, William and Milton Sublette, and Jim Bridger. After Ashley retired, his men continued the trade and eventually organized the Rocky Mountain Fur Company in 1830. Although some of their furs were purchased from the Indians, most of them were taken by white trappers, who lived in the wilderness a thousand miles from civilization. These "mountain

FIG. 13. *Fur Traders Descending the Missouri.* Painting by G. C. Bingham. (*Courtesy of the Metropolitan Museum of Art, New York.*)

men" were so devoid of formal schooling that few of them could write their own names, but they knew every landmark of the mountains and the plains. They ranged over areas of hundreds of miles, seeking virgin districts in which to set their traps. During the winters they slept in lodges made of skins; in the summers they lay on buffalo robes under the stars. Some Indian tribes were their enemies, against whom ceaseless vigilance must be maintained; others were their friends, whose villages they visited and whose women they often married.

Once a year the mountain men made their way to a prearranged rendezvous at some prominent landmark like the Green River in present-day Wyoming. Here they met caravans of traders, who had brought out from St. Louis pack animals laden with whisky, gunpowder, lead, knives, bells, beads, and other goods to be exchanged for the year's accumulation of furs. The rendezvous was a wilderness fair attracting trappers, traders, and Indians from vast distances. It was a time of vigorous trading and even more vigorous drinking, gambling, and carousing.

In the thirties the American Fur Company moved into the Rocky Mountain country and took over the bulk of the trade, but the best days of the business were already past. Too many trappers were now in the field, and prices were falling ruinously because of the whim of fashion which was throwing the beaver hat out of style and bringing in the silk topper to replace it. But the mountain men had done their work. They had learned the best crossings of mountains and rivers and had established the routes across which the emigrants of the forties would pass both to Oregon and to California.

Despite the joint occupancy agreement between the United States and Great Britain, Oregon had fallen during these years more and more under British control. The "King of Oregon" was the patriarchal Dr. John McLoughlin, the chief factor of the Hudson's Bay Company. But in the thirties American interest in the Pacific Northwest suddenly mounted. In 1831 a delegation of Flathead Indians visited St. Louis seeking knowledge of the white man's religion. News of this event was given prominent place in the religious press and brought a speedy response. In 1834 Methodist missionaries under Jason Lee crossed the Oregon Trail with a fur-trading caravan, and a year later the Presbyterians sent out Samuel Parker and Dr. Marcus Whitman. Catholic missionaries arrived in Oregon in 1838 and 1840.

The pious men who went out to the Northwest garnered no large crop of Indian souls, but they discovered a goodly country. The farms and cattle ranches established at the Willamette Valley missions prospered, and the missionaries became energetic promoters of emigration. They wrote letters to the religious press and returned to the East to lecture and to write books. Oregon became a fever, as Kentucky and Ohio had been fevers in earlier generations. The religious spur to emigration soon became subordinate to political and economic motives. Settlers were needed to make Oregon an indisputably American territory. A new start in a new country appealed powerfully to many Mississippi Valley farmers discouraged by the hard times that followed the panic of 1837. In 1841 a company of nearly seventy emigrants passed over the Oregon Trail; in 1842 a hundred made the journey. In 1843 occurred the "great migration" of 260 men, 130 women, and 610 children—a total of 1,000 persons. Thereafter a thousand or more crossed the trail each year.

Emigrants making their way across the continent put to use knowledge accumulated in a century and more of frontier experience. Their wagons were of a type first developed in pioneer Pennsylvania; their organization in companies was similar to that of earlier frontiersmen in Kentucky. But the Oregon Trail posed new problems and required new answers. It was formidably long—some 2,000 miles—and required six months for passage with slow-moving wagons and cattle. In the spring, when the migration began, swollen streams and floods were a serious menace. In the summer, when the caravans moved across the Great Plains and the deserts beyond, the problem changed to that of too little water and water so full of alkali that it could not be drunk. Whitened bones lay along the trail, the remains of livestock that had died of thirst, and an occasional shallow grave gave testimony that human beings might also succumb. In the hot, dry atmosphere axles shrank, and wagon wheels came off or fell apart. In the mountains the trail was so narrow and precipitous that many wagons were wrecked. Household goods often had to be abandoned, and the emigrants sometimes arrived in the promised land with no possessions except those they could carry on their backs. If too many delays were encountered, the pioneers might be caught in the mountains by the snows of early winter and be doomed to perish or to suffer incredible hardships before spring brought relief. To the hazards of nature were added those provided by the Indians. Thefts by the savages were more common than attacks, but the latter were an ever-present danger in hostile territory.

Yet hard though the migration was, thousands made it safely and even looked back upon it as a happy adventure. The emigrant companies often achieved admirable organization. Emigrants would meet for the first time on the prairies of western Missouri, where they assembled in the early spring to wait for the floods to recede sufficiently to make it safe to start the trip. Practicing frontier democracy, they would elect a captain and other officers. In motion the company formed a long line that might stretch along the trail for 2 or 3 miles. First came the pilot and his guards, and then the great covered wagons pulled by plodding oxen and guided by teamsters who either rode on the wagons or walked beside them. The women and children usually rode but often chose to walk a part of the day for exercise. There was rivalry for positions in the line, because the clouds of dust thrown up by the moving column made the rear positions very unpleasant. Behind the wagons came horses, driven by a few men and boys, and at the rear moved hundreds of cattle, often refractory and controlled with difficulty by the men assigned this unwelcome task.

At night the wagons were arranged in a great circle and tightly fastened to each other to form an effective fortification. The animals were allowed to graze outside the circle while the emigrants slept either in the wagons or in tents pitched within the corral. Sentinel duty was carefully organized. All men able to bear arms were divided into three companies, each of which was responsible for guarding the camp every third night. The company in turn was divided into four groups to watch in two-hour shifts.

At four o'clock in the morning the sentinels discharged their rifles, stirring the company into instant activity. To round up a thousand or more livestock, some of which might have wandered 2 miles from the corral, was a long task. Young and old were busy, preparing and eating breakfast, striking the tents, reloading the wagons, and yoking the oxen so that all would be in readiness when the seven o'clock bugle signaled the beginning of the day's march.

On the trail life went on with all its vicissitudes. Deaths were a frequent occurrence, but so were births. By evening campfires tall tales were exchanged, songs sung, and fiddles played. Young couples danced and fell in love. Men and women had frequent opportunities to display courage and fortitude and equal opportunities to cheat, to steal, and to quarrel. Strife was common, and rebel groups frequently left the main company and went their separate ways.

At Fort Hall in present-day Idaho the California Trail branched off from the Oregon Trail, crossed the present state of Nevada and the lofty Sierra Mountains, and eventually reached the Sacramento Valley of California. More and more emigrants, fascinated by the reports of the trappers, left their Oregon-bound companions and sought their destiny in the area to the south. This of course brought them onto Mexican soil, but the days of Mexican rule over this area were numbered.

During the forties American expansionism developed explosive pressures. Even before the northern frontier movement had brought the Oregon question to diplomatic boil, southern settlement in Texas had caused an eruption there. Revolt against Mexico resulted in the establishment of the Republic of Texas in 1836. In 1844 James K. Polk was elected President on an expansionist platform, and events moved rapidly thereafter. In 1845 Texas was admitted to the American Union; in 1846 Great Britain recognized United States sovereignty over all of Oregon south of the forty-ninth parallel; and in 1848 the peace treaty which followed the Mexican War brought under the American flag not only California but the vast southwestern territory of New Mexico. To complete the drama of the decade, the Mormons began the settlement of Utah in 1846, and gold was discovered in California in 1848. In 1849 thousands of adventurers swarmed into the territory, and in 1850 California achieved statehood.

The Agricultural Revolution

During the eighteenth century English agriculture had been strikingly reformed. Careful drainage had expanded the acreage available for cultivation, and the fertility of the soil had been increased by the systematic application of manure and lime in various forms. Scientific rotation and the introduction of new crops like turnips and clover had served the double function of preserving the fertility of the soil and providing fodder for livestock. Seed was now carefully selected and planted in rows with drills, and the growing crops were carefully cultivated to keep them free of weeds. While yields per acre were thus being increased, English livestock was also greatly improved. Abandonment of the common pasture, scientific breeding, and better feeding meant cows that gave more milk and beef and sheep with more wool and mutton.

The striking results to be obtained by applying rational methods to agriculture made a strong impression upon American gentlemen-farmers. They compared the new English practices with those prevalent in America and realized that the latter were shockingly wasteful. As George Washington wrote to Arthur Young, one of the key figures in English agriculture: "Our lands . . . were originally very good, but use and abuse have made them quite otherwise." [1] On his own estate Washington introduced new crops, applied fertilizers of different types, and sought to improve the breed of his livestock. When Lafayette and the King of Spain sent him jackasses from Europe, the gifts were gratefully received and put to good use, bringing the great general new fame as a mule breeder. Thomas Jefferson also carried on an extensive correspondence on agricultural matters, made many experiments, and directed his mechanical skill to the problem of designing an improved plow.

A few of the gentlemen-farmers gained an extensive influence through their writings. John Beale Bordley, a Maryland lawyer who operated a 1,600-acre farm on an island in Chesapeake Bay, wrote a number of pamphlets calling for scientific crop rotation and the use of clover. John Taylor of Caroline, one of the most successful Virginia planters, published a volume of agricultural essays under the title *Arator* (1812). Taylor's gospel was based on deeper plowing, a four-field system of crop rotation, and the enrichment of the soil by a mixture of corn stalks and cow dung. Edmund Ruffin, also of Virginia, became the most energetic crusader for better agricultural methods. He investigated the properties of marl—mixed deposits of clay and lime from sea shells. These proved a sovereign remedy for many of the acid soils of the Upper South, contributing to the agricultural revival of the fifties. Ruffin wrote books and articles, edited an influential farm magazine, and helped organize agricultural societies and fairs. Other gentlemen-farmers experimented with new breeds of livestock, improved seeds, and systems of crop rotation. They recognized the dangers of erosion and devised systems of cross plowing and terracing to check it.

But the dirt farmers of the nation were at first little influenced by these innovations. They did not read the new books and would not have believed them if they had. The old practices persisted, not only because they were hallowed by custom, but because the need for change was not imperative. Many of the new methods were developed in England, where land was expensive and labor was cheap. In the United States, where conditions were the reverse with land abundant and labor scarce, these practices had much less appeal. From the American point of view it was often cheaper to cultivate a new field than to restore an old one. Moreover, subsistence agriculture was still much more prevalent than commercial. So long as the frontier farmer fed and clothed his family and had a small surplus for exchange, he was satisfied. Larger surpluses would have done him no good. Transportation facilities were inadequate, and the cities were too small to create much of a demand.

In the twenties and thirties conditions began to change. The Industrial Revolution resulted in the growth of a large urban population dependent on the rural

[1] Letter of Nov. 1, 1787, *Letters from General Washington to Arthur Young* (London, 1801), 12.

districts for food. At the same time it diminished the self-sufficiency of the farms. More and more the rural population came to depend on factory-made clothes, shoes, and tools, and, to buy these, money crops had to be grown. City and country became more dependent on each other with each new road, canal, and railroad.

Fig. 14. *Country Fair,* 1824. Painting by J. A. Woodside. (*Courtesy of Harry T. Peters, Jr.; photograph by the Metropolitan Museum of Art, New York.*)

Knowledge of the new methods was popularized by agricultural fairs and farm journals. The fairs were an outgrowth of the old colonial fairs where livestock was bought and sold. When the practice of offering prizes for the best animals developed, the commercial fair evolved into the agricultural exhibition. Fairs of the new type were held in the District of Columbia as early as 1804. But their most active promoter was Elkanah Watson. In 1807 Watson purchased some Merino sheep—an imported breed beginning to have a great vogue among the gentlemen-farmers. Since these were the first Merinos in western Massachusetts, Watson exhibited them on the Pittsfield town green. So successful was this experiment that a neighborhood cattle show and a county agricultural society soon followed. By 1810 the Berkshire Agricultural Society had developed the type of annual fair that was to be an American institution for many generations. Men competed eagerly for the prizes offered for the best livestock and produce; women, for the best handicraft. As an annual social event the fair featured community singing, dancing, and oratory. Watson, who presently moved to Albany, assisted in the establishment of some fifty other fairs, and many more were founded independently.

The fair movement languished during the thirties but revived strongly in the forties. More generous state aid was now forthcoming, and the introduction of horse racing stimulated new interest. In addition to hundreds of local and county fairs, there were great state fairs and for a time during the fifties a national fair sponsored by the United States Agricultural Society. For the majority of visitors the fairs were a place of entertainment rather than instruction, but to the more alert the exhibits were an incentive to better agricultural practice.

A quieter but more pervasive influence was agricultural journalism. Perhaps the first American periodical devoted to the needs of the farmer was the *Agricultural Museum,* which began publication in the District of Columbia in 1810. This lasted only two years, but the *American Farmer,* established in 1819 by John P. Skinner, the postmaster of Baltimore, continued publication for many years. During the next decade many other farm journals were started. Most were of local influence only, but a few like the *Cultivator,* established at Albany by Jesse Buel in 1834, attained a national circulation. These periodicals brought into thousands of farm families practical information about better agricultural methods. The circulation of such papers in 1860 was estimated to be 233,600 in the free states and 32,250 in the slave states.

The long-delayed agricultural revolution, when it came, was largely mechanical. The American farmer, often owning more land than he could cultivate with the labor of his family and one or two hired hands, was interested in new tools and machines that would make his work easier.

Eighteenth-century plows had been crude wooden affairs, so heavy that they sometimes required eight or ten oxen to drag them yet scarcely scratching the surface of the soil. More efficient iron plows had been developed in Scotland and a few of these were imported. Jefferson demonstrated mathematically the curvature that the moldboard should have for greatest efficiency, and Charles Newbold of Burlington, New Jersey, invented an all-iron plow in 1797. But except for a few individuals, farmers still clung to wooden plows, improved only to the extent of iron tips or iron plates along the sides. The popular opinion that cast-iron plows poisoned the soil was ignorant prejudice, but there was more validity in the objection that Newbold plows were cast in one piece and therefore easily broken and impossible to repair. In 1819 Jethro Wood, a New York Quaker, perfected a plow made of standard iron parts bolted together. Since this could be repaired in case of accident, it gradually came into favor. In the prairie country, however, cast-iron plows were unsuccessful. They would not cut through the heavy turf properly, nor would they keep clean of the clinging soil. To meet these new conditions John Deere developed his famous "prairie breaker" in 1837. Twenty years later over ten thousand of these polished steel plows were being produced each year at the Deere plant in Moline, Illinois.

The need for better methods was particularly acute in the harvesting of wheat. When the grain was ready, it was imperative that it be cut, bound, and gathered without delay. The amount of wheat that any farmer could afford to plant was rigidly limited by the labor which he could command during the crucial few days of the harvest. Late in the eighteenth century the sickle, which had been the tool of the reaper since the days of the Pharaohs, began to give way to the scythe and

FIG. 15. Farmer using cradle, near Reading, Pennsylvania. Long after mechanical reapers were in common use, many American farmers continued to rely on older methods. (*Courtesy of the Historical Society of Berks County, Reading.*)

the cradle. The scythe with its long blade and long handle permitted the reaper to cut the grain in a wide swath as he moved through the field. The cradle, a scythe fitted with long forklike prongs, was even more useful, since it deposited the grain in neat piles where it could be easily bound. Most of the nation's wheat in the first half of the nineteenth century was cut with cradles. Simple though the new tool was, its use permitted one man to cut $2\frac{1}{2}$ times as much grain in a day as he could reap with a sickle.

But village inventors were fascinated with the idea of a horse-drawn machine that would reap the grain as it was pulled through the fields. Agricultural societies offered prizes for the best models, and at least fifty different reapers were built between 1786 and 1831, but none of these proved to be practical in actual use. In 1833 Obed Hussey of Ohio patented a reaper that attained some popularity during the next decade. More famous was the reaper patented in 1834 by Cyrus H. McCormick of western Virginia. Both the Hussey and McCormick machines and numerous other reapers developed in the United States and Europe were at first too clumsy and inefficient to gain many customers. The invention came into extensive use only after McCormick opened his Chicago factory in 1847. By 1851 he was turning out 1,000 reapers a year; by 1856 his annual production was 4,000. By 1860 the machines were in such common use among the larger farmers of the Middle West that a diligent observer, equipped with a spyglass, counted 146 of them at work at one time in the fields of northern Illinois.

One machine's success made others necessary. The speedier reaping of the fifties called for better threshing methods. Although threshing machines had been used in Scotland during the eighteenth century, American threshers did not come into general use until after 1850. During the next decade itinerant machines went from farm to farm through the prairie country, each preparing 300 or more bushels of wheat a day. Similar innovations reduced the labor of planting wheat as better plows, harrows, and seed drills came into use.

Nor did the inventors concentrate exclusively on wheat. Corn growers had the benefit of planters, cultivators, cutters, huskers, and shellers, and farmers raising hay now used mowing machines and horse rakes. The more prosperous southern planters used seed drills, cultivators, gins, and balers; but the picking of cotton remained a slow hand process, and southern agriculture remained much less mechanized than the agriculture of the Middle West.

Although here and there attempts were made to operate agricultural machinery with steam engines, the great revolution was for the most part a substitution of horsepower for man power. Particularly in the Middle West it had the effect of greatly increasing the acreage that could be cultivated in the family-sized farm and greatly increasing agricultural production.

Regional Specialization

Newer land, larger farms, more machinery, and improved transportation gave the western farmer distinct advantages over his eastern brother. The center of wheat growing moved inexorably west. Even though Pennsylvania and New York retained their leadership through the first quarter of the nineteenth century, new districts within those states like the Genesee country of western New York supplanted the older centers. Ohio became an important rival in the thirties. In 1850 the leading wheat states were Pennsylvania first, Ohio second, and New

York third. But the most striking changes came during the next decade. In 1860 Illinois was the greatest wheat producer with Indiana second and Wisconsin third.

In a similar way the corn belt moved west. In 1840 the leading corn states were Kentucky, Tennessee, and Virginia. Twenty years later these were surpassed by Illinois, Ohio, Missouri, and Indiana. The livestock industry followed the corn belt. Drovers from the trans-Appalachian states started their cattle drives to the East in the spring and continued through the summer, halting each night in drove stands where food and shelter could be purchased. After 1825 some of the cattle were moved by canal and river; after 1850 they were mostly shipped by railroad. In 1858 over 58,000 bullocks from Illinois were marketed in New York City, smaller numbers coming from Ohio, Indiana, Kentucky, and other states. Although hogs were also driven to distant markets, sometimes in droves as large as five thousand, a large proportion were slaughtered in the Middle West and shipped to the East and South as salt pork. The center of this industry was Cincinnati—known as "Porkopolis."

As production of the great staples concentrated in the West and South, eastern farmers had to adapt themselves to the new conditions. For a generation, sheep seemed an answer to their problems. The introduction of Merinos and other improved breeds together with the establishment of American woolen mills excited the most extravagant hopes. During the thirties eastern woolgrowing enjoyed its golden age with thousands of farmers in New England and the Middle Atlantic states devoting most of their energies to it. But falling prices and the growth of the West made eastern sheep raising generally unprofitable after 1840. The industry passed to the newer territories, where cheap and extensive pasturage was available.

Eastern farmers found their most profitable specialties in perishable produce, for which proximity to the urban markets was essential. Near each of the great cities market gardening and dairying increased. New York State became a center of butter and cheese manufacture; Maine and Long Island specialized in potatoes. Since horses pulled thousands of carriages and wagons in the cities as well as in the villages, the northeastern hay crop became increasingly valuable. Even in the livestock industry easterners kept a profitable hand, since their proximity to the cities was advantageous for buying cattle from the western drovers and fattening them for slaughter. The feeding business became important in the Connecticut and Hudson valleys and in southeastern Pennsylvania.

Under the influence of regional geography and climate American agriculture had evolved patterns even more variegated than those of colonial days. A southern plantation where cotton was picked by gangs of singing slaves differed strikingly from a Middle Western farm where wheat was reaped and threshed by horse-driven machines. Unlike either were eastern dairy farms or California vineyards.

Chapter 9. The Old South

The conditions of soil and climate which had set the South apart during colonial days as a distinct region with its own type of agriculture and society operated with even greater force in the early national period. Cotton, never an important American crop until after the Revolution, became the dominant staple. Rapidly expanding demand from England, France, and the industrial North led to the extension of cotton culture into the new states of the Old Southwest. Slavery, a decadent institution during the latter part of the eighteenth century, was revitalized. Believing that its continuance was essential to their section not only economically but socially, southern spokesmen protested energetically when the institution fell under the violent condemnation of northern abolitionists. The tone of apology was soon lost, and the organization of southern society was praised as ideally adapted for the promotion of Christian charity, social justice, and republican virtue.

The Cotton Boom

By a series of English inventions during the last half of the eighteenth century, the spinning of cotton thread had been mechanized and its cost so reduced that cotton textiles came into common use. This revolution created an enormous demand for the raw material. English cotton imports, which had amounted to only 5 million pounds in 1775, rose to 56 million pounds by 1800. Before 1790 these supplies came from the Mediterranean countries, the West Indies, and Brazil. The United States had no share in the trade. Although cotton was widely grown on southern farms for use in household manufactures, the species in common cultivation with its short-staple lint clinging tenaciously to the seed could not be profitably marketed.

About 1786 planters on the Georgia coast began to experiment with seed obtained in the Bahamas. This produced "sea-island cotton"—a species with long staple and smooth seed, which could be removed by a roller "gin" (engine) developed in the West Indies. The fiber was delicate and required careful handling, but despite its high production cost sea-island cotton was a valuable product, commanding an excellent price in the English market, and its cultivation expanded rapidly between 1790 and 1801. Its profits, however, were available only to planters who enjoyed the special climatic conditions of coastal Georgia and South Carolina. On the great interior uplands sea-island cotton could not be grown.

In 1791 and 1792 southern planters, aware of the great English demand, increased their production of short-staple cotton and waited hopefully for some mechanic to devise a machine that would do for their product what the roller gin was doing for the sea-island species. The eagerly awaited inspiration finally came to a visiting Connecticut Yankee. Like many another young college graduate Eli Whitney, fresh from Yale, had traveled south in pursuit of a position as tutor. Finding the job in Savannah that he expected to get already filled, he accepted the invitation of General Nathanael Greene's widow to become a guest on her Georgia plantation. There he became acquainted with the short-staple cotton problem and began the experiments which resulted in his famous invention of 1793. Fixing wire spikes like porcupine quills into a wooden cylinder, he rotated them against the slatted sides of a box of cotton. The spikes picked up the lint and left the seeds. With the addition of a rotating brush to remove the lint from the spikes, the essential principles had been discovered. Whitney hoped to get rich by patenting his invention and ginning cotton on a toll basis, but the machines were too easily made by local mechanics for such a monopoly. By 1795 gins had been set up in various parts of the South as far west as the Mississippi, and the conflicting assertions of those who claimed to have improved upon the crude original model resulted in a legal tangle that ruined Whitney's ambitions. He had won fame without fortune.

Although there was some initial prejudice against the new "saw-ginned" cotton, this was soon overcome. By 1810 exports of the short-staple species were ten times as great as those of sea-island. The case of Wade Hampton, who in 1799 produced a cotton crop worth $90,000 on his plantation near Columbia, South Carolina, was exceptional, but fabulous profits were common until overproduction halved the price between 1800 and 1807. Embargo and war ruined the market until 1815, when the return of peace brought good prices and rapidly expanded production.

The first region to profit from the cotton boom was interior South Carolina and Georgia. Virginia and North Carolina planters attempted to raise the new staple, but early frosts proved too great a hazard. To the west, however, the new cotton kingdom had ample opportunity for expansion. Louisiana, brought under the American flag in 1803, proved good cotton territory, as did parts of Tennessee. But the great frontier area between Georgia and Louisiana offered the most exciting opportunities. In 1810 there were only 40,000 inhabitants in the whole region. By 1817 Mississippi was ready for statehood and Alabama followed closely in 1819. The two boasted a population of 200,000 in 1820 and nearly a million in 1840.

The expansion of the cotton kingdom was recorded in impressive statistics. In 1814 American production was less than 150,000 bales; by 1835 it had reached 1,000,000 bales; in 1842, 2,000,000; in 1852, 3,000,000; in 1859, 4,500,000. It was a crop grown largely for export. Despite the growth of manufacturing only one-fifth of the 1859 crop was used in the United States. More than one-half of it went to England and the rest to continental Europe. In 1860 the value of American cotton exports was $192,000,000—considerably more than one-half the value of all American exports. The great cotton kingdom centered in Mississippi, Alabama, Louisiana, and Georgia, where 68 per cent of the crop was grown. Most of the rest came from the peripheral states of Texas, Arkansas, South Carolina, and Tennessee.

Although cotton was a crop well adapted to the needs of the struggling frontiersman, who could raise a bale or two and sell it for a little welcome cash, it was even more inviting to the planter who could afford slaves. Plowing, planting, thinning, hoeing, and picking under the broiling sun were tasks which white men could do if they had to but which they gladly relinquished to Negroes. Moreover, the labor, though tedious, was fundamentally simple and might be satisfactorily performed by gangs of slaves working under the direction of a few foremen.

Thus it was that many planters from Virginia, the Carolinas, and Georgia, discouraged by soil exhaustion and unprofitable crops in the eastern districts, sold their old estates and purchased new ones in the cotton belt. Able to offer high prices, they accumulated most of the best land cleared by the pioneers along the river valleys.

Patterns of Southern Agriculture

Northern opinion tended to oversimplify its picture of the Old South. Despite its economic and political importance the great cotton plantation was not the whole thing. Except for indigo, which soon passed out of commercial production, the colonial staples continued to be grown. Although tobacco raising declined sharply in the tidewater districts of Virginia, Maryland, and North Carolina, it increased in the Piedmont counties and found a new home in Kentucky, Tennessee, and Missouri. Total tobacco production for the country, which had remained almost stationary from 1800 to 1850, suddenly doubled during the next decade—largely through the vogue of "bright yellow," a new light variety, grown on the sandy soils of southern Virginia and northern North Carolina and cured by a charcoal process. Rice growing continued in coastal Georgia and South Carolina in about the same volume as in late colonial days. Expansion was retarded by the high cost of slaves and the hazards of employing them in an unhealthful industry.

Sugar growing began near New Orleans during the 1790's while the area was still under Spanish rule. After Louisiana became part of the United States, production expanded under the stimulus of a growing domestic market and tariff protection. Although a little sugar was eventually grown in Texas, Florida, and other states of the Lower South, climatic conditions made it largely a Louisiana specialty. The extraction of sugar from the cane was a difficult process, which required much labor and machinery. Even small sugar plantations represented an average investment of some $40,000, and the largest had an average capital value of over $300,000. Sugar plantations were larger in area, had more slaves, and were more highly organized than those devoted to any other staple.

Cotton, tobacco, rice, and sugar by no means absorbed all the attention of southern farmers. Although containing less than 30 per cent of the population of the United States in 1859, the 15 southern states produced 52 per cent of the country's corn, 87 per cent of its hemp, 80 per cent of its peas and beans, and

FIG. 16. *A Southern Planter's Home in Alabama.* Suggests the frontier simplicity of many small plantations. (*Courtesy of the Boston Public Library.*)

29 per cent of its wheat. In livestock the situation was similar. About 50 per cent of the country's cattle, 60 per cent of its swine, and 45 per cent of its horses were to be found in the South. These statistics emphasize a number of facts. General farming rather than plantation agriculture prevailed over large districts, particularly in the border states. Moreover, despite their concentration on staples most planters attempted to meet some of the food needs of their slaves by growing corn and livestock on their own estates. They supplemented these supplies with purchases elsewhere in the South or with produce sent down the Mississippi from the Middle West.

The large planters were a much smaller group than commonly believed. Millionaire agriculturists like Nathaniel Heywood of Charleston with his 14 rice plantations and 2,000 slaves were few. If ownership of 50 or more slaves be taken as the mark of a large planter, fewer than 11,000 southerners—about 3/4 of 1 per cent of the total free population—fell in that category. Middle-class planters, owning 10 to 50 slaves, numbered about 100,000. The largest number of slaveowners, about 270,000, owned fewer than 10 slaves and could hardly be considered planters at all. Many were small farmers who worked in the fields beside their slaves; others were merchants and professional men who owned a few household servants. Even including these small holders, only about one-quarter of the white population belonged to slaveholding families.

The most numerous class in southern society was that of sturdy yeoman farmers, tilling their acres without the help of slaves. Another substantial group was composed of town and village artisans. Finally, there were the poor whites, whose shiftlessness sometimes reflected discouragement with the unpromising soil on which they had settled and sometimes the weakened physical constitutions associated with malaria or hookworm. A paradox of southern politics was the general acceptance of the institution of slavery by the nonslaveholding majority. Only isolated rebels like Hinton Rowan Helper in *The Impending Crisis of the South* (1857) protested against "the lords of the lash," whose wealth and prestige were enjoyed at the expense of the whites who owned no slaves. The vast majority of the underprivileged defended slavery even more aggressively than did the slave owners. Many looked forward to the day when they would be able to purchase a slave or two and enter the charmed circle. Others found in the plantation system a market for their surplus produce or an opportunity for employment as overseers or slave drivers. Even those who lacked these ambitions were fiercely proud of their superiority to the blacks and resentful of the leveling program of the abolitionists.

Revival of Slavery

At the end of the eighteenth century slavery had appeared to be a slowly dying institution. On religious and rational grounds enlightened opinion condemned it in the South as well as in the North. Many slave owners provided in their wills for the manumission of their slaves, and projects for gradual emancipation received consideration in the legislatures of Maryland, Virginia, and Kentucky. Sentiment against slavery was strengthened by the evidence that in many areas it had become unprofitable. Soil exhaustion and unsettled market conditions resulted in many Virginia and Maryland planters' shifting their production from tobacco to wheat and other crops. For this more diversified agriculture slave labor was poorly adapted. Many large proprietors found themselves in the predicament of George Washington, who had more slaves than he could profitably employ yet had scruples against selling or hiring them out except in families.

The antislavery sentiments of such leaders as Washington, Jefferson, Madison, and Mason are, to be sure, somewhat misleading. Majority opinion in the South still opposed emancipation, and the rice and indigo growers of South Carolina and Georgia were particularly outspoken on the issue. However, even though opinion was by no means ready for abolition, the trend of events prior to 1793 seemed to favor slavery's eventual end. Not only were the old staples declining in profitableness, but the ratio of blacks to whites and of planters to small farmers was being steadily reduced by the frontier movement. In South Carolina, for example, the census of 1790 revealed a white population of 140,000 and a Negro population of only 107,000 in striking contrast to the situation in 1765 when there were about 40,000 whites as compared to 90,000 blacks.

The cotton boom reversed these trends. As the new staple became the mainstay of the economy of the Lower South, plantation agriculture again offered enticing possibilities. Slave prices fluctuated with the market for cotton, but the general trend was sharply upward. Prime field hands, rarely valued at more than $500 in 1800, were bringing $1,500 or more in 1860. During the fifties the smuggling of slaves into the country became extensive, and some southerners agitated for a reopening of the foreign slave trade, prohibited since 1808.

Since there were almost four million slaves in the South in 1860, generalizations as to their condition are dangerous. Slavery on a Georgia rice plantation might be much more rigorous than on a Virginia tobacco plantation, and slavery under the personal supervision of a benevolent master was likely to be far different from slavery on property managed by a hardhanded overseer.

The slaves were divided into household servants and field hands. The former usually enjoyed excellent treatment and were proud of their positions of trust as cooks, maids, nurses, coachmen, and butlers. Treatment of the field hands varied more widely. The larger planters usually hired white overseers, who in turn employed either white or slave foremen to lead the field gangs. Sometimes the hands were kept at their tasks through fear of the lash. Sometimes they were managed through a system of inducements. On the Mississippi plantation of Thomas Smith Dabney awards, ranging from a first prize of one dollar down to numerous prizes of a few cents each, were made each week to the best workers. In this way Dabney induced many of his Negroes to pick 500 or more pounds of cotton a day, although elsewhere 300 to 400 pounds were considered a good day's work. On many other plantations labor was organized on the task system. A daily stint was set for each slave, and when that was done, his time was his own.

Normal slave conditions differed greatly from the lurid picture of northern abolitionists. Although Negroes were sometimes whipped for refusal to work or for other infractions of discipline, they were rarely seriously injured—if for no other reason than that each of them represented an investment of several hundred dollars. The same economic interest assured that the slave was provided with clothes and shelter, enough corn meal and salt pork to keep him in good health, and medical attention when he needed it. And as the slave owners never tired of pointing out, unlike the northern employer who assumed no responsibility for his employees when they were unable to work, the planter fed and cared for both the slave children and the disabled and aged. Indeed the planter sometimes asked whether he or his Negro servant was really the slave. As one of them related:

> In a year or so we, by learning to manage ourselves, could easily manage our servants—or slaves if you will have it so, but in truth we were the slaves. We had to do the nursing in time of sickness, to supply food and clothing. Upon us was all the care and anxiety. We had a hard and slavish time of it . . . and it was about all we could do to make the income meet the outgo. . . . Negro children now came piling in on us. . . .[1]

Fig. 17. *A Slave Market, Richmond, Virginia,* about 1853. Painting by Eyre Crowe, an English artist. (*Courtesy of Mr. and Mrs. Samuel J. Henry; photograph by the Corcoran Gallery of Art, Washington.*)

Yet the abolitionist's view of slavery was not entirely fallacious. When laborers were property, many abuses were possible. Negroes might be overworked and mistreated. Slave women might become the paramours of overseers or masters. When the mulatto children of such unions took their place among the slaves of a plantation, one of the ugliest facets of slavery was revealed. The slave trade was particularly nasty business. Although conscientious owners often refused to sell their slaves or sold them only in family groups, others had no such scruples. Husbands were often separated from their wives and children from their parents. Since slave marriages were not recognized by law and since many of them were casual in the extreme, these separations were frequently accepted with indiffer-

[1] Quoted in Everett Dick, *The Dixie Frontier* (Knopf, New York, 1948), 83.

ence; but other Negro families were bound by close ties of affection and displayed poignant grief when they were broken up through sale. Respectable opinion in the South regarded the professional slave trader with contempt but defended the trade itself as necessary, since there was an oversupply of slaves in Virginia and other sections of the older South and an almost insatiable demand for them in the cotton belt.

But the most damaging indictment of slavery did not rest on its occasional cruelty. Slavery was a bad institution for the slave, because it deprived him of both the opportunities and the responsibilities of freedom. It was a bad institution for the owner, because it was an incubus to progress, encouraging excessive dependence on a few staples and perpetuation of wasteful methods of cultivation. Since large investments in labor as well as land were required, plantation agriculture encouraged excessive borrowing and burdensome debts. To the vast majority of southern whites who owned no blacks, slavery was a curse, because plantation agriculture forced down the price of staples and made it more difficult for the small grower to gain a livelihood. It greatly restricted opportunities to earn wages not only in agricultural labor but in other occupations as well, since investment in land and slaves absorbed most of the available capital and inhibited the building of factories and railroads.

After 1830 the laws relating to slaves became more rigorous. Slave codes had existed since colonial days, but they were now strengthened out of fear that abolitionist agitation would incite servile insurrection. Slaves rebelling or plotting revolt were subject to the death penalty. Slaves were forbidden to leave their plantations without written passes or to assemble except in the presence of white men. Slaves might not own firearms, horses, horns, or drums. They might not purchase whisky nor administer medicine to a white person. Except in Maryland, Tennessee, and Kentucky they might not be taught to read and write. They were restricted to their quarters after curfew, and white militia companies were to patrol the countryside by night. In normal times these laws were not enforced. Slaves assembled for church services and dances, roamed the countryside, and were often taught to read and to write by their own mistresses. Patrol duty was an unpleasant task seldom strictly performed. But periodically whole districts would be thrown into panic either by news of actual revolts like those of Denmark Vesey in South Carolina in 1822 or Nat Turner in Virginia in 1831 or by the more frequent rumors of imminent revolts that never occurred. Repressive measures would be taken and vigorous patrolling would be continued until the excitement died down.

In addition to almost four million slaves in the South in 1860, there were about 260,000 free Negroes, about half of them in Virginia and Maryland. Some of these were prosperous farmers, occasionally owning slaves themselves. Others were hard-working artisans in the towns. But the majority were occasional laborers, ignorant, poor, and often involved in vice and crime. The misfortunes of this group tended to harden the slavery system, which was defended as a necessary instrument of social control whatever its economic shortcomings. Manumissions were made more difficult, and free Negroes were subjected to regulations similar to those limiting the activities of slaves. Many states forbade the entry of free Negroes, and Arkansas even went so far in 1860 as to require all free Negroes either to leave the state or to become slaves.

Slavery and Southern Thought

Slavery cast a blight on the intellectual life of the South. The planters were usually well educated and prided themselves on their cultural attainments, often asserting that they were the only true gentlemen to be found in the nation. But aristocratic society reserved its advantages for a privileged minority. The small farmers were poorly schooled at best and often completely illiterate. They were exceptionally provincial, knowing little of the world beyond their own villages. Even among the upper classes intellectual life was rooted in thin soil. Southern writers were few in comparison with those of other sections and received scant recognition. Southern literary magazines and publishing ventures struggled for existence.

To the relative sterility of southern intellectual life slavery contributed both directly and indirectly. By perpetuating rural conditions, slavery retarded the growth of cities, where libraries, lyceums, and clubs might have encouraged the exchange of information. Southern repugnance to abolitionism tended to create an intellectual blockade against all northern ideas. Southerners prided themselves on their immunity to feminism, socialism, pacifism, transcendentalism, and all the other isms of these years of intellectual ferment.

More directly, the existence of slavery stifled freedom of thought. Whereas eighteenth-century southerners had criticized slavery with vigor and impunity, nineteenth-century writers and speakers felt impelled, not merely to defend the "peculiar institution" as a necessary evil, but to praise it as a positive good. The vigor of the proslavery argument reflected both resentment against the activities of northern abolitionists and the growing financial stake in slave property, estimated to amount to some four billion dollars in 1860. For a southerner to oppose publicly this powerful interest became increasingly dangerous.

That the South did not lack for vigorous minds is evident from an examination of the extensive literature in praise of the slave system. In their industrious search for new arguments southern publicists turned to the Bible, the Constitution of the United States, the classical philosophers, the pages of history, and the records of contemporary society.

One of the earliest elaborations of the proslavery argument was contributed by Thomas Roderick Dew, professor of history, metaphysics, and political law at William and Mary. Rebuking in 1832 the efforts of western representatives in the Virginia legislature to secure gradual abolition, Dew contended that the institution of slavery was one of the principal factors in the rise of civilization.

"Slavery," he argued, "was established and sanctioned by divine authority, among even the elect of heaven, the favored children of Israel. Abraham, the founder of this interesting nation, and the chosen servant of the Lord, was the owner of *hundreds* of slaves." [1] Slavery was the chief means of mitigating the horrors of war: whenever barbarous nations had so far advanced in civilization as to understand the use which might be made of captives by converting them into slaves, there the cruelties of war were lessened. The institution also raised the status of woman.

She ceases to be a mere *"beast of burden;"* becomes the cheering and animating centre of the family circle—time is afforded for reflection and the cultivation of all those mild and fascinating virtues, which throw a charm and delight around our homes and firesides, and calm and tranquillize the harsher tempers and more restless propensities of the male. . . .[2]

To Dew the contention that slavery was inconsistent with republican institutions was absurd. Aristotle and the great men of antiquity believed slavery necessary to keep alive the spirit of freedom. Burke had observed that the people of the southern colonies were more strongly attached to freedom than those of the North, "because freedom is to them not only an enjoyment, but a kind of rank and privilege." Besides, added Dew, slavery made it possible for a perfect spirit of equality to prevail among the whites. "The menial and low offices being all performed by the blacks, there is at once taken away the greatest cause of distinction and separation of the ranks of society. . . . Color alone is here the badge of distinction, the true mark of aristocracy, and all who are white are equal in spite of the variety of occupation." [3]

The idea that southern society was ideally constituted for the promotion of republican virtue was repeated many times. William Gilmore Simms, the Charleston novelist, writing a reply to Harriet Martineau's criticisms of slavery, contrasted "the fever and phrensy" of French politics with the high tone of those of the South:

Perhaps, the very homogeneousness of a people is adverse to the most wholesome forms of liberty. . . . For that most perfect form of liberty, which prompts us to love justice for its own sake, it requires strange admixtures of differing races—the combination and comparison of the knowledge which each has separately arrived at—the long trials and conflicts which precede their coming together; and their perfect union in the end, after that subjection on the part of the inferior class, which compels them to a knowledge of what is possessed by the superior.[4]

Chancellor William Harper of South Carolina touched upon the delicate issue of the influence of slavery upon the female slaves. He acknowledged that "the morals of this class are very loose . . . and that the passions of men of the superior caste, tempt and find gratification in the easy chastity of the females."

[1] *The Pro-slavery Argument; As Maintained by the Most Distinguished Writers of the Southern States* (Charleston, 1852), 295.

[2] *Ibid.*, 339. [3] *Ibid.*, 461–462. [4] *Ibid.*, 268.

But he considered these connections less injurious than those resulting from prostitution in other societies. In the case of the Negro woman he added: "Is not the evil less in itself, and in reference to society—much less in the sight of God and man?" Want of chastity among slaves "hardly deserves a harsher term than that of weakness." One of its happy results, moreover, was to protect the virtue of white women:

Never, but in a single instance, have I heard of an imputation on the general purity of manners, among the free females of the slaveholding States. . . . And can it be doubted, that this purity is caused by and is a compensation for the evils resulting from the existence of an enslaved class of more relaxed morals? [1]

The southern spokesmen contended that the transfer of the Negroes from barbarous Africa to the Christian civilization of the South was evidence of divine providence. As President E. N. Elliott of Planters' College, Mississippi, viewed the matter:

That the negro is *now* an inferior species, or at least variety of the human race, is well established, and must, we think be admitted by all. That by himself he has never emerged from barbarism, and even when partly civilized under the control of the white man, he speedily returns to the same state, if emancipated, are now indubitable truths. Whether or not, under our system of slavery, he can ever be so elevated as to be worthy of freedom, time and the providence of God alone can determine. The most encouraging results have already been achieved by American slavery, in the elevation of the negro race in our midst; as they are now as far superior to the natives of Africa, as the whites are to them. In a religious point of view, also, there is great encouragement, as there are twice as many communicants of Christian churches among our slaves, as there are among the heathen at all the missionary stations in the world.[2]

The most effective proslavery arguments were those in which the security and good treatment of the average Negro servant were contrasted with the insecurity and hardship of the industrial worker of the North or of England. Particularly skillful was the development of this theme in William J. Grayson's long poem *The Hireling and the Slave* (1854). Grayson, a well-read public official of Charleston, depicted with grim realism the plight of the English "hireling":

Hard work and scanty wages still their lot,
In youth o'er laboured, and in age forgot,
The mocking boon of freedom they deplore,
In wants, cares, labours never known before.[3]

In contrast to this was the happy lot of the southern slave:

Far other fortune, free from care and strife,
For work, or bread, attends the Negro's life,

[1] E. N. Elliott, ed., *Cotton Is King, and Pro-slavery Arguments* (Augusta, Ga., 1860), 582.

[2] *Ibid.*, xiii.

[3] William J Grayson, *The Hireling and the Slave, Chicora, and Other Poems* (Charleston, 1856), 22.

And Christian Slaves may challenge as their own,
The Blessings claimed in fabled states alone—
The cabin home, not comfortless, though rude,
Light daily labour, and abundant food,
The sturdy health that temperate habits yield,
The cheerful song, that rings in every field,
The long, loud laugh, that freemen seldom share,
Heaven's boon to bosoms unapproached by care. . . .[1]

The contrast between the rival systems was set forth with equal vigor by George Fitzhugh, a Virginia lawyer, in books whose very titles were provocative, *Sociology for the South, or, The Failure of Free Society* (1854) and *Cannibals All! or, Slaves without Masters* (1857). Free society, Fitzhugh contended, was "a monstrous abortion" and slavery "the healthy, beautiful and natural being" which northern reformers were trying unconsciously to adopt. In so-called "free society," white workers were the slaves of the capitalists. The white slave trade, Fitzhugh charged, "is far more cruel than the Black Slave Trade, because it exacts more of its slaves, and neither protects nor governs them." When the day's labor is ended, the slave of capital is free, "but he is overburdened with the cares of family and household, which make his freedom an empty and delusive mockery." In contrast to this "the Negro slaves of the South are the happiest, and in some sense, the freest people in the world. The children and the aged and infirm work not at all, and yet have all the comforts and necessaries of life provided for them. They enjoy liberty, because they are oppressed neither by care nor labor." [2]

Fitzhugh saw proof of the failure of free society in the efforts of the workers to form labor unions and in the agitation of socialists for the establishment of utopian communities. Everywhere the need was felt for a social system that would provide full employment and security. But, said the Virginian:

Slavery alone can effect that change; and toward slavery the North and all Western Europe are unconsciously marching. The master evil they all complain of is free competition—which is another name for liberty. Let them remove that evil, and they will find themselves slaves, with all of the advantages and disadvantages of slavery. They will have attained association of labor, for slavery produces association of labor, and is one of the ends all Communists and Socialists desire. A well-conducted farm in the South is a model of associated labor that Fourier might envy.[3]

One of the tragedies of the proslavery intellectual effort was that it caused so many southerners to reject the fine heritage of Thomas Jefferson. Some weakly explained away the Declaration of Independence by asserting that it was only intended to define the rights of white men; others openly rejected its fundamental philosophy. Simms dismissed the disturbing words, "All men are created equal,"

[1] *Ibid.,* 51.

[2] Alpheus T. Mason, ed., *Free Government in the Making: Readings in American Political Thought* (Oxford, New York, 1949), 507.

[3] Benjamin F. Wright, Jr., *A Source Book of American Political Theory* (Macmillan, New York, 1929), 473–474.

as simply a fine-sounding phrase, "significant of that sentimental French philosophy, then so current." Chancellor Harper asserted: "Man is born to subjection. Not only during infancy is he dependent, and under the control of others; at all ages, it is the very bias of his nature, that the strong and the wise should control the weak and ignorant. . . . "[1] Fitzhugh ridiculed the idea that governments derived their powers from the consent of the governed. "All governments must originate in force, and be continued by force. The very term, government, implies that it is carried on against the consent of the governed."

> The ancient republics were governed by a small class of adult male citizens, who assumed and exercised the government, without the consent of the governed. The South is governed just as those ancient republics were. In the county in which we live, there are eighteen thousand souls, and only twelve hundred voters. But we twelve hundred, the governors, never asked and never intend to ask the consent of the sixteen thousand eight hundred whom we govern. Were we to do so, we should soon have an "organized anarchy."[2]

Particularly vigorous denunciation of Jeffersonian democracy came from John C. Calhoun, the great political leader of South Carolina. To believe that all people were equally entitled to liberty was, in Calhoun's words, "a great and dangerous error." Liberty was a reward to be earned, not "a boon to be bestowed on a people too ignorant, degraded and vicious to be capable either of appreciating or of enjoying it." As for the state of nature, there never was such a state and never could be. Men, instead of being born in the state of nature, were born in the social and political state; "and of course, instead of being born free and equal, are born subject, not only to parental authority, but to the laws and institutions of the country where born, and under whose protection they draw their first breath. . . ."

The proslavery advocates were the spokesmen for a doomed cause. Their dream of the South as a Greek democracy, where an elite citizenry freed from menial labor would practice civic virtue and cultivate the arts, was shattered by the hard realities of the nineteenth century. Elsewhere in America were gathering new economic and cultural forces too dynamic for an essentially anachronistic feudal society to resist.

[1] *Cotton Is King, and Pro-slavery Arguments,* 555.

[2] Mason, *op. cit.,* 510.

Chapter 10. Revolution in Industry

In 1800 most Americans were attired in homemade clothes, which were fashioned from wool grown on the family's own farm, carded and spun by the women, woven and dyed either within the household or by village artisans. For the fastidious, tailor-made clothes of fabrics imported from England were the only alternative. Other needs were similarly met. Shoes were made by the local cobbler from leather produced at the village tannery, and hardware was secured on order from the village blacksmith.

On the eve of the Civil War things were strikingly different. Men wore shirts made from cloth manufactured in the mills of Lowell, suits from woolens produced in Lawrence, and shoes fashioned in Haverhill. They told time by clocks made in Connecticut and worked their fields with plows manufactured in Illinois. The new system meant cheaper goods and a higher standard of living. It meant also the growth of cities and slums, the exploitation of women, children, and immigrants, loss of independence and status by artisans, and new conflicts between workers and employers. It meant, in short, both greater wealth and greater social problems.

Beginnings of the Factory

Like most historical events the American Industrial Revolution did not occur as suddenly as often appears in retrospect. Although the nineteenth-century transformation of manufacturing was rapid and far-reaching, many of the elements of the new system had been the result of gradual evolution.

The employment of power-driven machinery was by no means without precedent before 1800. Long before that time ingenious men had learned to build water wheels and windmills, which they used to grind grain, to saw wood, to full cloth, and to work the bellows for furnaces and forges. Improving on European models, American ingenuity had developed methods of transmitting power so that several machines could be run from the same water wheel. During the 1780's the milling of flour was so organized by Oliver Evans of Philadelphia that the grain was mechanically conveyed from one part of the mill to another while it was being cleaned, ground, cooled, bolted, and packed into barrels. Six men, mainly employed in closing the barrels, supplied all the labor necessary to grind 100,000 bushels of grain a year.

Nor were colonial industrial processes invariably free of capitalist control. Enterprises like the refining of iron or the manufacture of glass, which required too great an investment for the individual artisan, were often owned by partnerships or companies. Not infrequently the funds were supplied by English or foreign investors. The so-called "domestic" or "putting-out" system, well established in England, had its occasional American counterpart when merchants invested their capital in wool or flax which they placed in farm households to be spun into thread or woven into cloth.

There were precedents also for taking industry out of the home and into special buildings where artisans plied their crafts under supervision. As early as 1646 the colony of Virginia had built two spinning houses where groups of poor children were taught to spin. Similar establishments were maintained elsewhere. In 1769 William Mollineux opened a school in Boston where three hundred women and children were reputed to have been taught to spin in a single season. Since Mollineux also managed weaving and other operations, he had in effect established a woolen factory, although all the processes were still performed by the old methods. Further steps in the organization of the textile industry were taken by the United Company of Philadelphia, which during the Revolutionary War employed as many as five hundred persons at one time in the production of cotton cloth. Most of them worked in their own homes, but others were assembled in a central building. The United Company used horsepower for some of its processes and owned a few spinning jennies—the first of the new English inventions destined to revolutionize the industry. Jennies were also used in a cotton-textile factory opened in 1787 at Beverly, Massachusetts.

The jenny was little more than a glorified spinning wheel, but later English inventions like Arkwright's frame and Crompton's mule were heavy machines requiring water power for their operation. With their adoption the spinning of cotton yarn passed irrevocably out of the home and into the factory.

By prohibiting both the exportation of machinery and the emigration of artisans, the British government tried to secure an English monopoly in the new technology. But the secret of the water frame proved no easier to keep than the secret of the jenny. In 1789 Samuel Slater, a shrewd young English mechanic of twenty-two who had learned the textile business as an apprentice of Arkwright's partner, concealed his identity and slipped out of England. After a brief period of employment in New York, he went to Rhode Island, where he formed a partnership with William Almy and Moses Brown, merchants already engaged in manufacturing coarse cotton cloth in a factory using jennies. By a remarkable feat of memory Slater was able to reproduce the Arkwright machinery, and in 1790 or 1791 the first American spinning mill to employ water power began operations.

Located on the Blackstone River at Pawtucket, Slater's factory was at first a small affair, employing only nine persons—all children between the ages of seven and twelve—but it achieved a success that encouraged imitation. Within the next few years attempts were made to establish spinning mills in many different parts of the country. Only in New England did these at first succeed. Of eight such factories running in 1800, four were in Rhode Island, three in Connecticut, and one in Massachusetts.

The heavy mortality in the industry was the result of many factors. Since investment in the new machinery was regarded as highly speculative, most men of

FIG. 18. *Pat Lyons, Blacksmith.* Portrait by John Neagle. Expresses the sturdy independence and self-assurance of the old-time artisan. (*Courtesy of the Boston Athenaeum; photograph by the Metropolitan Museum of Art, New York.*)

means preferred to put their money into commerce or into land. Labor was likewise difficult to secure. Although English artisans continued to cross the Atlantic to seek their fortunes and American mechanics began to learn the trade, skilled operatives were for many years scarce, and the unskilled showed at first some reluctance at entering the mills. Markets for new manufactures were limited by poor transportation facilities and by the superior appeal of goods imported from England.

The country's continued dependence on imported manufactures was a cause for misgiving on the part of many citizens. Societies of mechanics and tradesmen in various cities were active in the movement to secure a national government able and willing to protect home industry. One of the early acts of Congress under the new Constitution was a patent law for the encouragement of invention (1790). In the *Report on Manufactures* (1791) Secretary of the Treasury Alexander Hamilton gave Congress an illuminating survey of the situation and argued for the support of industry through protective tariffs and bounties. These proposals had for the moment only a limited response. The tariff of 1789, which had been intended primarily as a revenue measure, remained the basis of national policy. Agriculture and commerce were still regarded as the country's principal interests, and manufacturing occupied a clearly secondary place.

Positive steps to assist manufactures were largely a matter of local effort. State legislatures gave occasional help with bounties for new machinery, tax or militia exemptions, and loans or outright grants to new factories. In several cities special societies for the encouragement of industry were organized. The most ambitious of these was the Society for Establishing Useful Manufactures, formed upon a plan drafted by Hamilton and incorporated with generous privileges by the New Jersey legislature in 1791. The company selected an excellent power site along the falls of the Passaic River and began to develop the town of Paterson. Much money was spent in blasting rocks, digging a canal, erecting buildings, and organizing a cotton-spinning mill. The Society overreached itself in these initial efforts and failed, with serious losses to all concerned. But in 1807 the project was revived, and this time Paterson's advantages were so successfully exploited that within twenty years it boasted 12 cotton mills, 3 woolen factories, 3 machine shops, and several foundries.

Government patronage had its greatest influence on the manufacture of firearms. In 1792 Congress authorized the establishment of two national armories, and a few years later it began to subsidize private contractors making muskets, pistols, and rifles for the national government. This opportunity to turn out guns for an assured market stimulated important manufacturing experiments. Although the armories and the private contractors pooled their information to such an extent that credit cannot be exclusively assigned to any individual, the famous inventor Eli Whitney did the most to secure acceptance for the new methods.

Disappointed in his hope of making a fortune through the manufacture of his cotton gins,[1] Whitney secured in 1798 a contract to make 10,000 muskets for the government. The usual method of fitting together guns out of parts specially made for each weapon was so slow and laborious that the shrewd Yankee contractor decided upon a radically different technique. He sought to make

[1] See Chap. 9.

the same parts of different muskets so nearly identical that the final completion of the guns became a simple matter of assembly. The idea was not new, since as early as 1785 Thomas Jefferson had been greatly impressed by a French experiment along the same lines. But the practical difficulties were so great that French and British manufacturers had abandoned the idea. Similar skepticism prevailed in Washington, although Whitney converted some of the doubters in a demonstration before the Secretary of War and other officials in 1800. Choosing at random from piles of identical parts, the Yankee assembled 10 perfectly fitted muskets. The principle of standard interchangeable parts provided the magic key for American mass-production methods of the future, but its application continued to present many problems. Despite Whitney's ingenuity in devising new tools and in training workmen to use new methods, the completion of his contract required eight years instead of the specified two and brought him scarcely any profit.

Meanwhile another Connecticut gunmaker, Simeon North, was advancing quietly and independently along the same lines. Born in the same year as Whitney (1765), North outlived him by twenty-five years. When he died in 1852, he had been manufacturing guns for fifty-three years. Perhaps no other individual did more than he to develop practical techniques of interchangeable manufacture.

Triumph of the Factory

American manufacturing enjoyed its first great boom during the period from 1807 to 1815, when commerce was seriously handicapped first by the experiments with embargo and nonintercourse and then by the war of 1812. Although imports from Great Britain did not entirely cease, their volume was sufficiently reduced to offer a rare opportunity for American manufacturers. Merchants, no longer able to venture their money in ships and trade, began to turn to industry. By the end of the war the investment in cotton manufactures was estimated to be 40 million dollars with 100,000 workers engaged in the industry. Woolen manufacture was also much expanded.

With the final coming of peace English manufacturers made a determined effort to recapture their American markets. They sold the surplus of goods which they had accumulated during the conflict at bargain prices. This threat to American industry aroused the concern of nationalists from every section. The first American tariff to be based frankly on the protective principle was enacted in 1816, and further protection was provided in the tariffs of 1824, 1828, and 1832. Despite these measures American manufacturers were hard hit by postwar conditions, and many failed during the crisis of 1819. During the next decade a new and sounder advance began.

Textile manufacturing was radically reorganized along lines laid down by Francis Cabot Lowell. The son of a distinguished Massachusetts jurist, Lowell became a Boston merchant after his graduation from Harvard in 1793. By taking shrewd advantage of the opportunities for trade during the European wars, he became wealthy. In 1810 after his business had been hampered by the commercial policies of Jefferson and Madison, Lowell began an important residence in England. Ostensibly abroad for his health, he seized the opportunity to learn all that he could about the British textile industry. In particular, he studied power looms, which were only then becoming sufficiently reliable to do the work of the hand-loom weavers. Returning to America, Lowell tried to

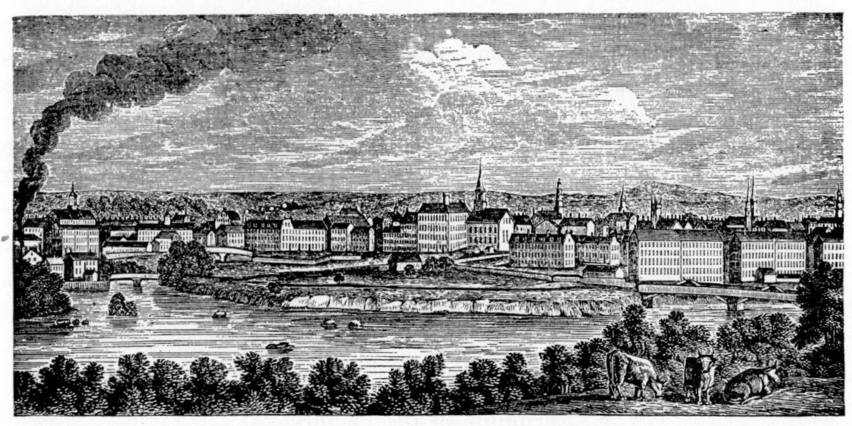

FIG. 19. East view of Lowell, Massachusetts, early center of the New England textile industry.

build a power loom from memory. His effort was none too successful until he joined forces with Paul Moody, an ingenious American mechanic. With this reinforcement Lowell not only built looms which were superior to most others, but he proceeded to apply his capital and managerial skill to an important experiment in textile manufacturing. At the Boston Manufacturing Company, opened at Waltham, Massachusetts, in 1814, all operations of clothmaking were performed by power at a central plant. When Lowell died in 1817 at the age of forty-two, he was both wealthy and famous, and factories on the Waltham model were soon attempted in many other places.

The location of the new factories was at first largely determined by their need for water power. The small rivers of southern New England were harnessed with extraordinary thoroughness. In 1840 the Blackstone River, running from Worcester, Massachusetts, to Providence, Rhode Island, was providing power for 94 cotton mills, 22 woolen mills, and 34 machine shops and ironworks. For the most part the factories were not in cities but in towns or villages. New communities often sprang up around a good power site. The success of the Boston Manufacturing Company at Waltham encouraged its proprietors to develop the power resources at the falls of the Merrimack River in northeastern Massachusetts. In 1822 the Merrimack Manufacturing Company was incorporated, and in 1826 a township, appropriately named Lowell, was organized. In 1840 the new town boasted nine large textile mills as well as numerous subsidiary industries and the largest machine shop in the United States. The same capitalists achieved similar success twenty-five years later a few miles to the south of Lowell where they built a tremendous granite dam across the Merrimack and organized the town of Lawrence, named for another great textile magnate. The factories at Lawrence, specializing in woolens, were among the largest industrial establishments of the world during the 1850's.

Since water power was subject to interruption by drought or by ice, the steam engine gradually came into use. Although primitive engines had been occasionally used to pump water out of mines even before the Revolution, their application to mill machinery did not begin until after 1800. Some engines were imported from England, others were built in American foundries like that of Oliver Evans, where a popular high-pressure type was developed. At first wood was employed as a fuel, but gradually the superior efficiency of coal was recognized. Steam engines were more common in Pennsylvania, where coal was abundant, than in New England. Nevertheless, woolen mills exclusively dependent on steam power were operating in Rhode Island and Connecticut as early as 1812. Cotton-textile factories deriving their power entirely from steam engines were in successful competition with the water-driven mills after 1830. Many factories assured themselves of continuous operation by using both water and steam power.

The Iron Age

The progress of the Industrial Revolution depended upon an enormous expansion of iron production and increased skill in metalworking. Wooden textile machinery was soon replaced by iron, wooden water wheels by iron turbines, steam engines made largely of wood by new all-iron ones. Housewives now cooked with iron utensils on iron stoves. The new trains puffed mile after mile over iron rails.

The transformation of the iron industry proceeded less rapidly in America than in England. The substitution of coal for charcoal in the smelting process seemed less important in America, where wood was plentiful, than abroad, where the forests had largely disappeared. But new English techniques in the refining process, whereby pig iron suitable only for casting was transformed into malleable bar iron ready for village blacksmiths, aroused more interest. Labor in America was scarce, and the older method of refining iron by heating it repeatedly on an open forge and pounding out the impurities under a water-driven trip hammer required many skilled workers. The new methods, introduced into western Pennsylvania in 1817, were based upon puddling and rolling. The iron was heated in reverberatory furnaces, stirred to remove impurities, and then passed through grooved rolls to produce the desired bars. Since these new furnaces kept the fuel separate from the molten metal, coal could be substituted for charcoal without injury to the product. The new rolling mills, freed from dependence on wood, brought the iron industry to the cities for the first time. Pittsburgh, already an important industrial town with glassworks, textile factories, and machine shops, was an early rolling-mill center. Even more important before the Civil War were eastern Pennsylvania cities like Philadelphia and Scranton. Fall River, Massachusetts, Troy and Albany in New York, Baltimore, Maryland, Richmond, Virginia, and Cincinnati, Ohio, also had important rolling mills.

Smelting remained a rural industry for some time longer. But as wood eventually became scarcer, the incentive to use the country's abundant coal resources increased. In eastern Pennsylvania the new type of smelting dates from 1833, when the Reverend Frederick W. Geissenhainer, a Lutheran minister, patented a process utilizing anthracite. The method's efficiency was greatly increased the following year by the introduction of the hot-blast principle which had been developed in Scotland. For the next generation the anthracite regions of eastern Pennsylvania were the center of the smelting business.

An industry based upon the use of bituminous coal grew more slowly. One reason for this was the abundance of timber beyond the Appalachians; another, more important, was that blacksmiths serving the agricultural needs of the West continued to prefer charcoal-smelted iron. But with the great expansion of the railroads the situation was radically altered. Only by using coke could iron be produced in the volume needed for the rail mills. Great plants like the Cambria Works erected in 1857 at Johnstown, Pennsylvania, now brought together coke furnaces, puddling furnaces, and rolls—all the processes necessary to transform iron ore into finished rails.

In 1860 more than half the pig iron of the country still came from the anthracite furnaces of the East, but the forces that were to move the center of the industry across the Alleghenies were already evident. In 1855 the Sault Sainte Marie Canal was opened, and the rich ore of the Lake Superior region began to move by water and by rail to the bituminous districts of western Pennsylvania and eastern Ohio.

Greatly expanded also were the plants where objects made of iron and other metals were fabricated. Steam engines were built in the local foundries of nearly all the states, but particularly in those of New York, Pennsylvania, Ohio, and Massachusetts. Three-quarters of the locomotives made in the United States in 1860 came from the shops of Philadelphia and Paterson. Stoves, which were rapidly displacing fireplaces, were manufactured in the Albany-Troy district of New York, in Pennsylvania, and in Ohio.

Ingenious automatic machinery revolutionized the manufacture of many small products. In 1860 one-third of the nation's nails came from the factories of eastern Massachusetts, and many of the rest came from northern New York and northwestern Virginia. Three-quarters of the country's brass pins came from Connecticut, particularly from the Waterbury district. Another Connecticut specialty was the clock industry. Manufacturers like Eli Terry and Seth Thomas, who had been making wooden clocks for many years, substituted brass parts about 1840. Even watches could now be made under factory conditions, as was proved at Waltham, Massachusetts, during the fifties. The invention of the sewing machine by Elias Howe in 1846 opened up another branch of precision manufacturing. By 1860 factories in New York, Bridgeport, and other places were turning out over 100,000 machines a year.

Shoes and Clothing

Although the transition to the machine was slow in many industries, new conditions of trade radically altered the status of the hand workers.

Early in the nineteenth century shoes and boots were still made in small shops by masters employing a few journeymen and apprentices. The finest work was done on order for individual customers, and a somewhat lower grade of shoes was made in advance and stocked for the retail trade. But improved methods of transportation soon opened a broader market. The shoe shops of Massachusetts towns like Lynn and Haverhill began to produce coarse shoes to be sold at wholesale to the merchants of other sections. This business became increasingly dependent on merchant-capitalists who purchased leather and had it made into shoes in various shops. Since competition was sharp, the employers sought to reduce their labor costs to a minimum. Journeymen's wages were cut. either directly or by compelling them to take their pay in store orders or bank notes of dubious value. Through division of labor the sewing and binding could be done by apprentices, half-trained workers, convicts, and women, and fully trained craftsmen were needed only to cut the leather. Manufacturing was organized around a central warehouse where the leather was cut and the finished shoes were stocked. For the intermediate processes carriers took the material out to hundreds of shops and homes, but eventually more and more of the work was performed in the warehouse. This transformation of the central establishment into a factory was accelerated during the fifties by the invention of machinery for cutting, pegging, and sewing. Not until after 1860, however, were the shoe factories harnessed to power.

A somewhat similar evolution occurred in the clothing industry. During the early nineteenth century men's suits and shirts were made either in the home or by tailors working on order. But enterprising merchants developed a market for cheap, ready-made clothing for western farmers and southern slaves. In New York and other cities they organized production on a large scale. Through abuses of the apprenticeship system children were employed for a pittance and taught only a portion of the craft. Thousands of women slaved on piecework in their homes at niggardly rates. As in the shoe industry, factories took over a large proportion of the production, particularly after the invention of the sewing machine.

Condition of the Workers

Craftsmen felt desperately insecure as one after another of the old skilled trades was either mechanized or so simplified that special competence was no longer necessary. Spinners and weavers saw their work performed by machines, largely tended by women and children. Shoemakers and tailors watched helplessly while industry was so reorganized that much of their work could be done by the unskilled. Printers felt similarly threatened when most of the newspaper and book-publishing business fell under the control of enterprising capitalists who introduced power-driven presses and other new methods. Men who had once been able to look forward to being masters in their own shops were now destined to spend their lives as wage earners and felt keenly their loss of status.

Hours were long and wages were low. The working day was from sunrise to sunset—thirteen or fourteen hours in the summer, ten or eleven during the winter. Although traditional in agriculture, these long hours were more and more resented by town and city workers who wanted a little leisure for recreation or self-improvement. Even highly skilled craftsmen in the iron trade received less than $20 a week, and most wage earners were paid far less. Carpenters were among the more fortunate; yet as late as 1851, at a time when the *New York Tribune* estimated the minimum needs of a family of five at $10.37 a week, they were receiving about $10.25 a week. Women binding shoes earned less than $2.50 for an eighty-hour week; women in the needle trades averaged less than $2.

In southern New England and in the Middle Atlantic states textile factories followed the so-called Fall River system. Entire families, men, women, and children, were employed in the mills. At first these conditions encountered little criticism. Indeed, Alexander Hamilton in his *Report on Manufactures* assumed that the employment of women and children "who would otherwise be idle" was one of the great advantages of expanded industry. In 1835 almost one-third of the factory workers of Paterson were under sixteen years of age. Child labor was particularly characteristic of Rhode Island, where in 1853 there were 1,857 children under the age of fifteen at work in the factories. Of these 680 were under twelve and 59 were under nine. A Massachusetts law of 1842 forbade the employment of children under twelve for more than ten hours a day, but neither this nor other state laws requiring children to have a certain minimum amount of schooling were well enforced. A Massachusetts worker, recalling his early years, said:

> When I began as a boy in a mill, I worked fifteen hours a day. I used to go in at a quarter past four in the morning and work till quarter to eight at night, having thirty minutes for breakfast and the same for dinner, drinking tea after ringing out at night. But I took breakfast and dinner in the mill as the time was too short to go home, so that I was sixteen hours in the mill. This I did for eleven years, 1837–48.

In northern New England the so-called Waltham, or Lowell, system prevailed. The textile mills recruited their labor force largely from unmarried girls in their late teens or early twenties. In order to quiet parents' fears that their daughters might be corrupted, the employers instituted an elaborate set of rules. Unless they lived with approved relatives, the girls were required to sleep and eat in company boardinghouses where they were under the supervision of the boardinghouse keeper. They had to be in their quarters by 10 P.M. and were subject to dismissal for unseemly conduct. This paternalistic policy was so successful in its first trial at Waltham that it was extended to Lowell and other new factory towns. English travelers like Harriet Martineau and Charles Dickens were deeply impressed. Describing Waltham in 1834, Miss Martineau wrote:

> Five hundred girls were employed at the time of my visit. The girls can earn two and sometimes three dollars a week besides their board. The little children earn one dollar a week. Most of the girls live in houses provided by the corporation. . . . When sisters come to the mill it is a common practice for them to bring their mother to keep house for them and some other companions, in a dwelling built by their own earnings. . . . I saw a whole street of houses built with the earnings of the girls; some with piazzas and green venetian blinds, and all neat and sufficiently spacious. The factory people built the church which stands conspicuous on the green in the midst of the place. . . . The corporation gave them a building for a Lyceum which they have furnished with a good library and where they have lectures every winter, the best that money can procure. The girls have, in many instances, private libraries of some value.[1]

From 1840 to 1845 a magazine was published called *The Lowell Offering,* which contained articles, stories, and poems written by the mill girls. This periodical, indirectly subsidized by the corporations, won the praise of Dickens, Whittier, and other well-known personages of the day. It did much to convince the general public that the Lowell workers were happy with their lot.

Although now and again a dissident voice was to be heard, the factory girls of the twenties and thirties did appear to enjoy their life. Brought up on the farms of nearby villages, they found the experience of living in the boardinghouses and working in the factories as exciting as going away to school. They were used to long hours and the work was not hard by farm standards. Girls who had never had much money of their own gratefully accepted their $2 or $3 weekly wage. After a year or two most of the girls left to get married. The factory represented but a brief episode in such lives.

After 1840 discontent with the system became more common. The first generation of factory owners, who, however eager for profit, were sincerely concerned for the workers' welfare, disappeared from the scene. Control of most of the great textile corporations now passed to men of tougher fiber, who administered the Lowell system less as an experiment in philanthropy than as a convenient device for ensuring the docility of their operatives. But the factory girls also belonged to a different generation, a generation less naïve and more likely to feel itself exploited. The girls complained of manipulation of the piecework rates which compelled them to work harder for their money. Girls who had tended two looms were now required to tend four, and the pace of factory life

[1] Harriet Martineau, *Society in America* (New York, 1837), II, 57–58.

became more rapid and exhausting. Long after the ten-hour day became common elsewhere, factory workers were required to work from 11½ to 13½ hours according to the season. Since they worked every day except Sunday, this meant sixty-nine to eighty-one hours of labor each week. The girls had little chance of bettering their lot by changing jobs, since the various companies followed a common policy on hours and wages. A worker discharged at one mill found it impossible to secure a job at another. Ostensibly instituted to protect the morals of the girls, the black list was a perfect weapon to exclude "agitators."

As the glamour of factory life wore thin, it became more difficult to maintain the labor force. Employers tried to reduce the turnover by refusing an honorable discharge to any girl who quit her job within a year. They sent agents into the more remote country districts of Vermont and New Hampshire, promising them a dollar a head for each girl induced to work in the factories. More was paid for girls from faraway than from nearby places because these would find it more difficult to go home. But even these "slaving" expeditions could not long supply enough workers for the expanding mills. First in southern Massachusetts and Rhode Island during the forties, then in northern Massachusetts during the fifties, the factories turned to immigrant laborers. A witness to the change reported:

> On September 24th (1861) Prince Jerome Napoleon, with his consort, the Princess Clothilde . . . visited Lowell, having doubtless been recommended to do so by his friend Michel Chevalier. More than a quarter of a century had elapsed since Chevalier's visit; the New England girls on whom he then gazed so admiringly had passed away, and their places were now filled by a motley crowd of Americans, English, Scotch, Irish, Dutch, and French Canadians, who were hardly likely to arouse that exquisite poetic sentiment which Chevalier felt for the factory girls of 1834.[1]

The Labor Movement

Under the earlier industrial system there had been little reason for wage-workers to organize against their employers. Since the market was local, the price of goods could be fixed to provide both a reasonable profit for the master and a fair wage for the journeyman. Masters and journeymen had many interests in common: they both wanted to maintain prices and to discipline masters who cut them; they wanted to protect the home market against cheaper goods that came in from outside; they wanted to maintain rigid standards of apprenticeship and to protect the good name of the craft. To achieve such ends and to provide benefits in case of illness or death, many "societies of mechanics and tradesmen" were founded late in the eighteenth century. Masters and journeymen sometimes belonged to the same organization, sometimes to separate organizations, but even in the latter cases the societies were not the equivalent of modern labor unions, since their purpose was not to maintain or raise wages.

[1] Quoted in Norman Ware, *The Industrial Worker, 1840–1860* (Houghton Mifflin, Boston, 1924), 105.

As economic changes came, however, the wageworkers began to recognize certain interests peculiar to their status. Journeymen sought from time to time to fix a wage schedule which all masters would be required to pay. In 1786 the printers of Philadelphia secured a minimum wage of $6 a week through the first well-authenticated strike of American wage earners. Similar local strikes occurred occasionally during the next generation. Some of these were orderly; others were riotous, as in New York in 1800 when a mob of striking sailors tried to board a vessel in the harbor and were three times repulsed with broken heads and bloody noses.

Although the early strikes were usually fought by temporary combinations of workers, a few attempts at permanent organization were made. In 1792 the Philadelphia shoemakers organized a society, but it failed in less than a year. A second attempt in 1794 was more successful, and the resulting union, the Federal Society of Journeymen Cordwainers, maintained its existence for over a decade. In New York the printers took the lead. The Typographical Society, founded in 1794, lasted 2½ years, and successor organizations were maintained between 1799 and 1804 and between 1809 and 1819. After 1800 printers and shoemakers organized societies not only in Philadelphia and New York, but in Pittsburgh, Boston, Albany, Washington, and New Orleans. These early unions were entirely local, although they sometimes corresponded with similar bodies in other cities. They usually combined the functions of benevolent societies paying benefits in case of the sickness or death of the workers with those of trade-unions seeking to improve wages and conditions of labor. Few of them could stand the loss of prestige caused by an unsuccessful strike or the scrambling for jobs that accompanied an economic depression. Bad times from 1815 to 1820 gave the final blow to almost all of them. Most of those which survived did so by abandoning their trade-union program and reorganizing as benevolent societies.

The return of prosperity during the 1820's led to new attempts to form unions. Hatters, tailors, carpenters, house painters, stonecutters, weavers, nailers, and cabinetmakers all tried to organize on a permanent basis. There were numerous strikes, usually for better wages but occasionally for shorter hours, as in 1825 when the Boston house carpenters tried without success to secure a ten-hour day. The ten-hour demand was taken up also in Philadelphia and in New York and was a principal factor in the formation in 1827 of the short-lived Mechanics' Union of Trade Associations in Philadelphia—the first union of all the organized workers in any city.

Wage-and-hour issues were not the only preoccupation of the workers. They wanted free public schools, the abolition of imprisonment for debt, mechanics' lien laws that would protect workers' wages when employers were insolvent, an abolition of licensed monopolies, and a revision of the militia system, which was more burdensome to the poor than to the rich.

Since the abolition of property qualifications had by now enfranchised most of the workers, they attempted political action. A Working Men's party, organized in Philadelphia in 1828, held the balance of power in the election of 1829 and contributed to the success of several candidates who had accepted its endorsement as well as that of one or another of the older parties. But this advantage was soon lost. Wily professional politicians manipulated the workers' party for their own advantage, and its influence was destroyed.

In New York City a Working Men's party was organized in 1829. In the elections of that year they secured 6,000 votes and elected two of the candidates whom they had endorsed. Despite this promising start the new party was soon beset by troubles. One schism occurred when Thomas Skidmore, an earnest advocate of the confiscation and equal distribution of property, seceded with his "Agrarian" faction. Another occurred over the plans of Frances Wright and Robert Dale Owen for "state guardianship," an educational project which would have placed all children in boarding schools to receive not only equal instruction but equal food and equal clothing. Despite these controversies workers' parties were founded in Albany, Troy, and several other upstate cities and achieved a number of local successes. In August, 1830, a workingmen's convention with delegates from 13 New York counties met in Syracuse and nominated candidates for the various state offices. But the divisions within the Working Men's party nullified its influence and the Democrats carried the election without difficulty.

Events took a similar turn elsewhere in the country. Workingmen's parties appeared in Delaware, New Jersey, and Ohio. In New England such parties campaigned in the elections of 1830 and 1831, and in the latter year a regional movement called the New England Association of Farmers, Mechanics and Other Working Men was organized. The most effective labor spokesman was Seth Luther of Providence, who delivered impassioned speeches in most of the New England cities. Luther was a bitter critic of the factories, deriding the complacent acceptance of the Waltham system. He regarded child labor as brutal and advocated manual-labor schools to improve the lot of the poor. The New England association sought to secure the ten-hour day both through memorializing the legislature for appropriate legislation and through pledging its members not to work the longer hours.

Nowhere did the workingmen's parties achieve sufficient success to become a permanent factor in politics. By the middle thirties most of them had disappeared. But their influence was by no means negligible. The aggressiveness of their demands for public schools, abolition of imprisonment for debt, mechanics' lien laws, reform of the militia system, and state regulation of banking impressed the old-line politicians, and eventually most of this program was achieved. The political agitation of the thirties was particularly important in inducing a reorientation of the Democratic party in the states of the Northeast. In 1837 the success of the so-called Equal Rights party, based upon an alliance of Locofocos, or antimonopoly Democrats, and workingmen resulted in a significant change in Tammany tactics. From then on, the New York City Democratic organization tried to base its power upon the labor vote.

The rising cost of living and the abundance of work during the economic boom of the thirties renewed the laborer's interest in unions. Shoemakers, printers, tailors, carpenters, and other craftsmen organized not only in the eastern cities, but in western centers like Louisville, Cincinnati, and St. Louis. Even women shoebinders and seamstresses formed unions with temporary success. In 1833 a General Trades' Union, which federated the various craft unions of New York City, was organized, and similar central labor organizations were formed in Baltimore, Philadelphia, and other cities.

The movement assumed a national aspect in 1834 when the central labor unions of six cities sent delegates to New York to found the National Trades' Union. The new organization agitated for the ten-hour day, universal education, sale of public land only to actual settlers, child-labor laws, and repeal of the laws under which trade-unions were being prosecuted as illegal combinations. In addition to this movement at least five crafts—the shoemakers, printers, combmakers, carpenters, and hand-loom weavers—held national conventions during 1835 and 1836.

Strikes were frequent: no less than 173 are known to have taken place between 1833 and 1837. An almost universal demand was for the ten-hour day. Most of the workers of New York City had secured this in 1829, but elsewhere the old sun-to-sun hours continued. In 1835 members of the building trades in Boston began a strike, which continued for seven months before the men finally acknowledged defeat. In the meantime, the ten-hour movement had spread to other eastern cities as far south as Baltimore. In Philadelphia public opinion, even among the professional classes, supported the demand for shorter hours, and the workers were successful. Six to six with an hour off for breakfast and an hour off for dinner became the standard working day not only in Philadelphia but in most of the other cities except Boston.

The longer day still survived in the navy yards and other government works. In 1835 the National Trades' Union memorialized Congress to introduce the ten-hour system, but neither this nor other labor petitions could overcome conservative resistance. The workers had better success when they transferred their pressure to the executive branch. In 1836 President Jackson prescribed the shorter day for the Philadelphia Navy Yard, and in 1840 Van Buren issued an Executive order providing for the ten-hour day without reduction in wages on all government works.

The rise of the unions and their successful strikes for shorter hours and higher pay alarmed employers. Associations to combat these demands were formed. Striking workers were discharged and black-listed. Frequently the employers sought to have union members prosecuted for criminal conspiracy. As early as 1806 a Philadelphia court had found a shoemakers' society guilty on this charge, and prosecutions were numerous thereafter. A few judges ruled that any combination to raise wages was illegal under the common law; more of them held that such a combination was criminal when it resorted to "coercive and arbitrary" means. Particularly vulnerable were the journeymen shoemakers who refused to work with nonunion men and demanded the discharge of workers who failed to pay union fines. A heavy blow to organized labor was the decision of Chief Justice Savage of the New York Supreme Court in the so-called "Geneva shoemakers' case" (*People v. Fisher,* 1835). Not only did the judge rule that strikes to enforce the closed shop violated a New York statute forbidding acts injurious to trade or commerce, but he expressed his strong disapproval of any combination to enhance or to reduce the price of labor.

The workers were not always defeated in their court battles. Their most striking victory occurred in 1842, when Chief Justice Shaw of the Massachusetts Supreme Judicial Court strongly asserted the general legality of labor unions and ruled that a strike to enforce the closed shop was not unlawful if it were conducted in a peaceable manner (*Commonwealth v. Hunt*).

In 1837 the bubble which had been inflated by speculation and overexpansion in every field—western land sales, railroad and canal building, banking and manufacturing—suddenly burst. The resulting depression was both severe and long. Most of labor's gains were swept away. Unemployment and wage cuts were the rule everywhere. Lost in the debacle were the National Trades' Union, the national associations of the crafts, the city central organizations, even most of the local unions. Trade-union activity remained feeble for over a decade.

During the 1840's the workers were subjected to the preaching of many middle-class reformers, each with his own panacea for the ills of the new industrialism. Albert Brisbane, Horace Greeley, and others were spreading the gospel of "association"—utopian socialism on the Fourier plan. Few mechanics and laborers were inclined to seek their salvation through founding phalanxes in the wilderness, but more modest efforts to escape the control of the capitalists had labor support. Many consumers' cooperatives were attempted as well as producers' cooperatives like those of the Lynn shoemakers, the New York seamstresses, the Cincinnati iron molders, and the Boston tailors. But bad management and bad planning brought most of these experiments to an unhappy end. The mobility of the American population made cooperation much less successful here than in England. One of the most doctrinaire of the reformers was George Henry Evans, who taught that salvation would come only through "land reform"—the allotment of the public domain in equal, free, and inalienable tracts to actual settlers.[1]

The factory workers, unorganized almost everywhere, had not benefited by the ten-hour agitation of the thirties. Men, women, and children still worked a day that varied in length with the seasons but averaged about 12¼ hours a day or 73¼ hours a week in New England and a little longer in the middle and southern states. It was even alleged that some factory managers tampered with the clocks

[1] These reform movements are treated in greater detail in Chap. 15.

in order to steal fifteen or twenty minutes more from the operatives. During the forties these abuses aroused the protest not only of the workers themselves but of many middle-class sympathizers. The demand for state laws limiting the working day became one of the crusades of the humanitarians.

In Massachusetts the reformers besieged the legislature with petitions bearing hundreds of names. In 1846 the petition from Lowell was 130 feet long and bore 4,500 signatures. In this citadel of the new industrialism agitation was aggressively pressed by the Lowell Female Reform Association, led by Sarah Bagley and supported by many of the factory girls. Similar organizations sprang up in other mill towns both among the men and the women. Active in the ten-hour movement but dispersing its energy among various other reform agitations as well was the New England Working Men's Association, which held several conventions between 1844 and 1847. Numerous labor papers were started, the most influential of these being the *Voice of Industry.* The pressure of the workers and their allies was sufficient to prompt the legislature to appoint an investigating committee in 1845, but the report dealt very gently with the corporations. Of Lowell the committee said:

> Grass plots have been laid out, trees have been planted and fine varieties of flowers in their season are cultivated within the factory grounds. In short, everything in and about the mills and boarding-houses appeared to have for its end, health and comfort. . . . Your committee returned fully satisfied that the order, decorum, and general appearance of things in and about the mills could not be improved by any suggestion of theirs or by any act of the legislature.

There were a few abuses, to be sure. But "the remedy does not lie with us. We look for it in the progressive improvement in art and science, in a higher appreciation of man's destiny, in a less love for money, and a more ardent love for social happiness and intellectual superiority." [1]

The ten-hour issue continued to be agitated in Massachusetts politics over the next decade. Many ambitious politicians pledged their support during the early fifties, but corporation influence was so adroitly brought to bear that the proposal was finally defeated. The factory employers, however, bowed slightly to public opinion. They cut the working day by about twenty minutes in 1847 and more drastically in 1853 so that it averaged about eleven hours thereafter.

In other states events took a somewhat different turn. In 1847 the New Hampshire legislature enacted a law making ten hours a legal day's work in the absence of special contract. The textile corporations promptly prepared special contracts in which their employees gave their assent to the old hours. Those who refused to sign were discharged and black-listed. The legislatures of Pennsylvania, Maine, New Jersey, Ohio, and Rhode Island followed the example of New Hampshire by passing ten-hour laws which were of little effect because of the special-contract provision. In Pittsburgh employers in the textile mills closed their gates for six weeks, throwing out of employment 2,000 operatives who had

[1] Quoted in Ware, *op. cit.,* 137–138.

insisted on working only ten hours a day as provided in the law. The factories finally reopened on the ten-hour basis, but the employees were compelled to take a 16 per cent reduction in wages.

The discovery of gold in California was the signal for another economic boom which continued throughout most of the fifties. The workers sought to take advantage of the brisk demand for their labor by again organizing and pressing for higher wages. The new unions usually restricted membership to those actually working in a particular craft. Employers and middle-class reformers were excluded. Rejecting such slogans of the forties as association, cooperation, and land reform, the trade-unions concentrated their energy in a struggle to secure more pay and better working conditions. Mechanics of Boston and other New England cities at last achieved the ten-hour day; workers elsewhere gained higher wages. In 1850 the National Typographical Union was organized, and later in the fifties other crafts like the molders, the hatters, and the machinists attempted national organization.

Like their prototypes of the thirties the unions of the fifties proved exceedingly fragile. Employers cooperated to resist the movement, and the large-scale immigration of the period strengthened their hands. But once again the fate of the unions was more influenced by the economic cycle than by anything else. Many of them were ruined by the short depression of 1854; more went under during the serious collapse of 1857. Nothing perhaps was more suggestive of the position of labor under the new industrial conditions than the rise and fall of their protective organizations under the impact of the economic cycle. Although the long-run effect of change was to raise the standard of living, the individual worker often felt himself a chip borne along by a tide whose ebb and flow he could not control.

Chapter 11. Transportation and the Rise of Cities

Shortly after George Washington had laid down the responsibilities of his Revolutionary command, he set out on horseback to visit the great country beyond the Appalachian chain. His interests there were both personal and patriotic. As one of the great speculators in western lands he hoped to see the country opened up to settlement as rapidly as possible. As a patriot he perceived sooner than most of his countrymen that the problem of transportation was fundamental to nationhood. To "open all the communication which nature has afforded between the Atlantic States and the Western territory and encourage the use of them to the utmost" was, Washington believed, the only tie by which the West would "long form a link in the chain of Federal Union."

The importance of communications increased with each decade as the relatively simple economy of Washington's day became complicated by commercialized agriculture and mechanized industry. Improved means of transportation were the necessary condition for every step of national progress. And as transporation improved and commerce grew, the inevitable result was the growth of cities.

The Old Merchant Marine

The coming of peace after the Revolutionary War brought a period of difficult adjustment for American merchants. Deprived of their wartime opportunities they could not slip back easily into the old channels of trade. By gaining independence from the British Empire, the Americans had excluded themselves from their most profitable prewar business—carrying provisions to the British West Indies to exchange for sugar and molasses. In practice the exclusion was far from complete. Yankee ships "in distress" would put into British colonial ports, where obliging officials would grant permission for them to land their cargoes "to relieve the starving population." Limited trading rights extended to the Americans in the French, Spanish, Dutch, and Danish Caribbean possessions presented opportunities to engage in illicit trade with the British islands as well.

Such loopholess, however, were not enough to restore prosperity to the merchants, who complained bitterly at the inadequate protection provided for their interests by Congress under the Articles of Confederation. Equally matters of lament were the clashing fiscal and commercial policies of the various states.

The difficulty in restoring the old lines of trade was not without its compensations, since it led Americans into ventures that they had never undertaken before. Out of New York on February 22, 1784—scarcely three months after the British evacuated the port—sailed the *Empress of China* on a voyage that carried her across the North and South Atlantic, around the Cape of Good Hope, across the Indian Ocean and the China Sea to Canton. Here she exchanged her cargo of ginseng for tea, retraced her route, and returned to New York, successfully completing a fifteen-month voyage with 25 per cent profit to her owners. The first American visit to India also occurred in 1784, when the *United States*, a Philadelphia ship, reached Madras and Pondichéry. Elias Hasket Derby of Salem, who had made a fortune in Revolutionary privateering, soon saw the possibilities of the new trade. His ship, the *Grand Turk,* returned from its first China voyage in 1787 with profits so fabulous that a score of other Salem and Boston merchants were inspired to follow Derby's example.

One of the great problems was to find cargoes that the Chinese would accept in return for their tea, silk, furniture, and chinaware. Silver coin, welcome in the Orient, was too scarce at home to be used extensively. Ginseng served well during the earliest voyages, but neither the supply nor the demand was adequate to support a large trade.

Much more dependable was the Chinese market for furs. The possibilities of this trade became manifest when a group of Boston merchants financed a voyage by the *Columbia* around Cape Horn to the Pacific Northwest. Exchanging trinkets for sea-otter furs gathered by the Indians, Captain Robert Gray obtained a cargo that had a ready sale when he crossed the Pacific to Canton. Returning around the Cape of Good Hope, the *Columbia* sailed into its home port on August 9, 1790, after a thirty-four-month voyage of almost 42,000 miles. On a second trip in 1792 Gray discovered the Columbia River and laid the basis for an American claim to the Oregon country.

Boston and Salem merchants developed different specialties in trade. Boston ships usually followed the Cape Horn route, trading not only with the Northwest Indians but with the natives of the various Pacific islands and with the Spanish-American colonists—in defiance of Spanish laws. At Canton their cargoes of otterskin, sealskin, and sandalwood logs were exchanged for teas and textiles. Salem ships continued to use the Cape of Good Hope route, trading in the ports of southern Europe, Africa, Mauritius, India, and the Dutch East Indies as well as China. Pepper from Sumatra was one of the most profitable Salem imports.

Salem was a fascinating place during her glory days. Wealthy merchant families like the Derbys and the Crowninshields lived in substantial mansions close to their warehouses and wharves. The sons of the merchants began to study navigation as soon as they had learned to read and to write and were sent to sea in their early teens as cabin boys or clerks. Their period of apprenticeship was short, and they often became captains of their own vessels before they were old enough to vote. Salem ships, necessarily small because of the shallow harbor, were built mostly by skillful local craftsmen. A woman, brought up in nearby Beverly, remembered that men talked about a voyage to Calcutta or Hong Kong as if it were not much more than going to the next village. Women of well-to-do families donned Canton shawls, Smyrna silks, and Turkish satins to attend church. All kinds of foreign coins passed into common use. Green parrots, Java sparrows, canaries, and monkeys capered about outdoors as well as in. In many households lived wanderers from distant countries—Mongolians, Africans, and waifs from the Pacific islands, who were always known by distinguished names like Hector, Scipio, Julius Caesar, or Christopher Columbus.

Meanwhile, changing conditions opened up nearer and more profitable, though less romantic, markets. Ratification of the Constitution aided the commercial revival, already well begun. By some of the first laws enacted under the prompting of Alexander Hamilton, American ships were given decisive preference over foreign vessels in American ports. In response to this stimulus shipbuilding began an extraordinary boom. Ships owned in Massachusetts tripled in tonnage between 1789 and 1792.

These ships and many launched later found golden opportunities in the war between France and England that broke out in 1793. The laws excluding American shipping from the British West Indies became a dead letter as Yankee vessels eagerly returned to the familiar ports. Particularly inviting avenues to profit were opened up when the French Republic lifted all barriers to neutral trade between French colonial ports and France. By a subterfuge which the British long permitted, American ships brought the products of the French West Indies to American ports and then carried them across the Atlantic. American merchants carried provisions and lumber to the belligerents of both sides, picked up goods in one European port and sold them in another, gained new markets in the Baltic and the Mediterranean, and often sold their ships as well as their cargoes in the inflated wartime market.

Neutral trade involved many hazards. Protests arose, first from Republican, then from Federalist quarters, as the British and the French seized American ships and cargoes. One diplomatic crisis followed another, adding to the anxieties of George Washington, John Adams, Thomas Jefferson, and James Madison during their respective terms of office.

However irritating to American opinion, foreign seizures did not greatly injure American trade. If one ship were lost, the profit on the next was all the greater. The port of New York, benefiting particularly from this extraordinary situation, grew rapidly in importance. Its registered tonnage tripled between 1792 and 1807, and its exports jumped from an annual total of $2,500,000 to $26,300,000 over the same fifteen-year period.

The first serious check to this commercial boom was Jefferson's embargo of 1807. A newspaper of Newburyport, Massachusetts, expressed the sentiments of Federalist New England thus:

> Our ships all in motion once whitened the ocean,
> They sailed and returned with a cargo;
> Now doomed to decay, they have fallen a prey
> To Jefferson—worms—and embargo.[1]

Although the embargo was repealed in 1809, the trade boom received another and longer interruption when Madison's faltering diplomacy involved the country successively in nonintercourse, embargo, and war. The return of peace in 1815 brought a surge of optimism, but some of the consequences of the difficult period between 1807 and 1815 were far-reaching. In New England, Salem and other secondary ports entered upon a period of slow decline, while Boston with its superior harbor, larger market, and more extensive financial facilities gained an increasing share of the regional shipping.

New York, the leading American port since 1797, when its imports and exports first exceeded those of Philadelphia, profited hugely by the dumping of British manufactures after the War of 1812. The bargains to be obtained in Pearl Street auction rooms attracted American storekeepers from hundreds of miles away. The habit of visiting New York to obtain the best prices on imported goods became so firmly established that it continued long after the special conditions of postwar trade were over.

Although New York enjoyed unusual geographical advantages, its greatest asset was the imaginative boldness of its merchants. A typical exploit was the establishment of ocean-packet service between New York and Liverpool by the Black Ball Line in 1818. Prior to this, ships had sailed without any attempt at regular schedule. Passengers waited impatiently while captains delayed their passage until they filled their holds or liked the smell of the weather. Businessmen never knew when their letters or goods would start the transatlantic crossing. Full or empty, fair weather or foul, the packets sailed on a fixed day each month. Once skeptics were convinced that the schedule would be kept, the new line did a flourishing business, carrying mail, news, specie, cabin passengers, and "fine freight." In 1822 the Black Ball increased its service to two ships a month, and rival lines began to compete in the transatlantic shuttle.

The volume of imports entering New York expanded so rapidly that shipowners found it difficult to obtain cargoes for the eastbound vessels. Since the South was the great producer of export commodities, New York merchants sent scores of agents—often Connecticut Yankees—to buy large quantities of these goods. Brought by coasting vessels to New York, they helped fill the holds of ships bound for England and Europe. In 1822 about 55 per cent of the exports

[1] Quoted in Samuel Eliot Morison, *The Maritime History of Massachusetts, 1783–1860* (Houghton Mifflin, Boston, 1921), 187.

from New York consisted of cotton, tobacco, naval stores, and rice from the South. Even on the large volume of cotton exported directly from such southern ports as New Orleans and Mobile, New York exacted toll. Many of the ships engaged in the direct trade were New York-owned; the cotton was often sold on commission by New York merchants; much of the marine insurance was carried by New York companies. Southerners complained that 40 cents out of every dollar paid for cotton went to the North—most of it to New York. Equally profitable was the dominant position that the Manhattan merchants secured in handling imports destined for sale in the South. A Charleston commercial convention in 1839 complained: "The South thus stands in the attitude of feeding from her own bosom a vast population of merchants, shipowners, capitalists, and others, who without the claims of her progeny, drink up the life-blood of her trade."

New York was equally vigorous in reaching out for the trade of the West. The completion of the Erie Canal in 1825 gave the port a decisive advantage over such rivals as Philadelphia, Baltimore, and Boston. The other ports hoped to divert much of this business by railroads, but New York's own rail connections with the West, completed in the fifties, assured its continued dominance.

Although river steamboats came into rapid use after 1807, sailing vessels continued to dominate ocean commerce for another generation. Despite the transatlantic crossing in 1819 of the *Savannah,* propelled partly by steam, partly by sail, steam's conquest of the seas did not really begin until April 23, 1838, when by a dramatic coincidence two British steamships, the *Sirius* and the *Great Western,* arrived in New York Harbor within a few hours of each other. In 1840 the Cunard Line, recipient of generous mail subsidies from the British government, began scheduled passages between Boston and Liverpool. In 1848 Cunard service was extended to New York.

Since American national pride—in an expansive mood following the Mexican War—could not tolerate the Cunard supremacy, Congress voted mail subsidies for several American steamship companies. The most ambitious of these was the Collins Line, which opened service between New York and Liverpool in 1850. The new American line spared no expense to build larger, faster, and more luxurious ships than its English rival. Americans cheered as Collins's *Baltic* set a transatlantic record of nine days and eighteen hours in 1851. Unfortunately, the Collins's financial record was not so impressive as its speed. The line lost money from the start, forfeited the confidence of the public by two great sea disasters, and finally received its death blow when Congress abandoned the subsidy policy in 1858.

Meanwhile, American sailing vessels were writing a final glorious chapter to their romantic history. The annexation of California and the subsequent gold rush provided the stimulus for perfecting the clipper ship. Sacrificing cargo space for speed, the clippers had sharper ends, were longer in proportion to their breadth, and carried more canvas than ordinary ships. The most famous shipbuilder of the day was Donald McKay, a Nova Scotian who had worked in the shipyards of New York and Newburyport before opening his own establishment in East Boston. On her maiden voyage in 1851 McKay's masterpiece, the *Flying Cloud,* sailed from New York around Cape Horn to San Francisco in eighty-nine days and twenty-one hours—a record that stood until 1854 when the *Flying Cloud* herself bettered it by thirteen hours. From San Francisco the clippers generally sailed west across the Pacific, proving their speed anew in voyages between the China ports and England.

However much the clipper ships contributed to American pride, they added little to American pocketbooks. The sad truth was that the age of poetry in maritime commerce was rapidly passing. Even in the California trade a lion's share of business was secured by prosaic steamship lines. They ran from New York to Colon, where passengers and freight were shuttled across the Isthmus to Panama and then carried by other steamships to San Francisco. Although shrewd businessmen like Commodore Cornelius Vanderbilt gained fortunes in the steamship business, Americans as a people made a faltering transition to the new conditions. The American merchant marine, which had almost equaled the British in tonnage in 1854, lost ground during the last years of the decade and then suffered a decisive setback during the Civil War.

Turnpikes and Bridges

The French traveler Brissot, describing a trip from Wilmington to Baltimore in 1788, wrote:

> The road in general is frightful, it is over a clay soil, full of deep ruts, always in the midst of forests; frequently obstructed by trees overset by the wind, which obliged us to seek a new passage among the woods. I cannot conceive why the stage does not often overset. Both the drivers and their horses discover great skill and dexterity, being accustomed to these roads. But why are they not repaired? [1]

A similar indictment might have been brought against most of the highways of the nation. Rocks, stumps, mud, sand, and deep holes made each passage of the roads an adventure. Only the narrowest of streams were spanned by bridges. Many others could be forded, but accidents were frequent during periods of high water. For the crossing of deeper rivers travelers were dependent upon the irregular service provided by ferries.

A better day dawned with the chartering of the Philadelphia and Lancaster Turnpike Road Company in 1792. Through sale of stock this private corporation obtained the nearly $500,000 required to build a stone-surfaced road from Philadelphia to Lancaster, 62 miles to the west. Completed in 1794, the new turnpike proved highly profitable to the stockholders. From the revenue flowing in through

[1] J. P. Brissot de Warville, *New Travels in the United States of America* (London, 1794), I, 364.

nine tollgates were paid dividends running as high as 15 per cent. Over the road passed a colorful procession of fine family carriages, bright-colored stage-coaches, and lumbering Conestoga wagons, heavily loaded with freight.

The success of the Lancaster Turnpike encouraged similar investments elsewhere. New England capitalists entered the field early: by 1814 Massachusetts had chartered about one hundred such companies, and the port of Boston had gained good road connections with an extensive hinterland. In this activity,

FIG. 20. *The Yankee Peddler.* Engraved from a painting by T. W. Wood. The Yankee peddler was a familiar figure, selling pots, pans, brooms, pails, and the like to rural customers in all parts of the country. (*Courtesy of the Boston Public Library.*)

however, the Massachusetts city was surpassed by Baltimore, whose growth had been dramatic. Only a village before the Revolutionary War, Baltimore had gained commerce at the expense of Philadelphia during the period of hostilities and then profited greatly by the postwar passage of provisions down the Susquehanna River from frontier New York and Pennsylvania. Participating vigorously in the turnpike movement, Baltimore became the center of seven trunk roads.

Turnpike construction was at a peak during the first two decades of the nineteenth century. By 1820 all major cities in the eastern and northern states were linked by reasonably good roads. Construction methods varied greatly. Many turnpikes were surfaced with crushed stone according to methods developed abroad by such road builders as the French Trésaguet and the British Telford and Macadam. Others used earth, plank, or corduroy.

The need for bridges was almost as great as that for roads. In 1785 the Boston-Charlestown ferry was replaced by a long wooden bridge supported on piles; similar bridges followed elsewhere, including one a mile in length across Lake Cayuga in central New York. But pile bridges had serious limitations, since they impeded navigation and dammed up ice floes in the spring. A type of bridge ideally suited for American conditions was the wooden truss bridge so constructed that it needed only one or two piers for support. The first important wooden truss bridge was built across the Connecticut River at Bellows Falls, Vermont, in 1792. Some particularly large ones were built soon after in the vicinity of Philadelphia. When the bridges were roofed to protect them from the weather, the familiar covered type was the result. Many were toll bridges, built and operated by private corporations.

Although the earliest turnpike and bridge corporations were given perpetual charters with little provision for public regulation, the legislatures soon learned to make their grants more carefully. Later charters protected the public by requiring reasonable tolls and by providing conditions under which the roads and bridges might be taken over by the state. After 1825 private capitalism played a role of diminishing importance. Public highways and bridges, maintained through taxation, replaced most of the turnpikes and toll bridges.

The improvement of communications between the new trans-Appalachian states and the eastern seaboard was considered important enough to justify action by the Federal government. In 1802 Congress provided that a twentieth of the proceeds of Federal land sales in Ohio should be set aside for "making public roads leading from the navigable waters emptying into the Atlantic, to the Ohio. . . ." In 1811 the first contracts were let for the construction of a National Road from Cumberland, Maryland, on the Potomac, to Wheeling, Virginia, on the Ohio. Completed in 1818, this highway became at once the most popular route to the West. Vehicles of every description were to be seen passing over it. Particularly important were the huge wagons, each pulled by six horses and carrying loads of from 2 to 5 tons. Since Cumberland was linked by an excellent turnpike with Baltimore, the latter became for the next few years the most important eastern market for the produce of the Old Northwest.

Rivers and Canals

Although good roads speeded the mails and made stagecoach travel more comfortable, freighting for long distances was intolerably expensive. To transport a ton of goods from Pittsburgh to Philadelphia cost $70; to do so from the Great Lakes to New York cost $100. For most western products such charges were prohibitive.

Wherever possible, therefore, goods were moved by water. A flourishing coasting trade carried cargoes from one seaport to another, and every river and lake that would float a boat was in use. All through the winter, produce would accumulate in the warehouses at Albany, awaiting the breaking up of ice in the Hudson for transport to New York. Every year heavily laden flatboats floated down the Ohio and the Mississippi to New Orleans. The rivermen who handled these cargoes were rough fellows, given to boasting, like the fabulous Mike Fink who could "out-run, out-hop, out-jump, throw down, drag out, and lick any man in the country."

Floating downstream was not difficult, but backbreaking labor was required to move boats by sails, oars, and poles in the other direction. Most rivermen bringing provisions to New Orleans did not attempt to return by water. Selling their boats for lumber, they traveled home over the long and dangerous Natchez Trace and other frontier trails.

It was in serving the needs of this upstream traffic that steamboats proved most useful. Behind Robert Fulton's famous voyage of 1807 lay many decades of experimentation. Eccentric genius in France and England had found outlet in planning and building steamboats throughout much of the eighteenth century. By 1800 these experiments had proved sufficiently promising to gain the financial support of wealthy British canal owners.

American mechanics took an early interest in the problem. During the 1780's James Rumsey built a steamboat that moved slowly along the Potomac, and John Fitch offered regular service between Delaware River ports in 1790. But these pioneers and others were handicapped by lack of financial support and general skepticism.

The fame that eluded other steamboat builders fell in abundant measure to Robert Fulton. A Pennsylvanian, Fulton went to England in 1786 to study painting with Benjamin West. Becoming interested in engineering, he was employed in various English canal projects and later in designing submarines and other war machines for the French and British governments. That so ambitious a mechanic should dream of building steamboats was to be expected; that he should meet a man able to give him ample backing was a stroke of good luck.

Chancellor Robert Livingston, Jefferson's minister to France, was wealthy and politically powerful. He was, moreover, enthusiastically committed to the development of steamboats. In 1798 he had induced the New York legislature to grant him the exclusive privilege of steam navigation on all waters within the state, provided that he should build a boat capable of moving at 4 miles an hour. In 1803 Livingston and Fulton built a steamboat, which they tried out on the Seine. In 1806 Fulton returned to America, determined to fulfill the conditions for the steamboat monopoly.

Profiting by the experience of his predecessors and adequately backed with funds, Fulton was in a position to transfer steamboating from the world of visionary experiment to the practical world of business. In August, 1807, his new boat, the *Clermont*—named after Livingston's estate—steamed up the Hudson from New York to Albany in thirty-two hours. Within the next few years Fulton and Livingston had a number of other steamboats in operation on eastern waterways, while competing owners attempted to challenge the monopolies granted by New York and other states. Although Livingston died in 1813 and

FIG. 21. *The Belle Creole at New Orleans,* about 1850. Artist unknown. Depicts the golden age of the river steamboats. (*Courtesy of Mrs. E. S. Chadbourne; photograph by the Corcoran Gallery of Art, Washington.*)

Fulton in 1815, their heirs and successors continued to claim exclusive rights. A tangle of litigation handicapped steamboat operation until the knot was finally cut by the famous Supreme Court decision, *Gibbons v. Ogden* (1824), which asserted the supremacy of the Federal government over navigation on the inland waterways.

The first steamboat to navigate the great trans-Appalachian river system was the *New Orleans*, built by Nicholas Roosevelt, a partner of Fulton and Livingston. Leaving Pittsburgh in September, 1811, the new ship had an adventurous passage down the Ohio and the Mississippi but finally established service between New Orleans and Natchez. A flat-bottomed type of steamboat, better adapted for western conditions, was developed by Henry M. Shreve, whose *Washington* delighted the frontier in 1817 by pushing its way up from New Orleans to Louisville—1,440 miles—in twenty-five days.

By 1830 about two hundred steamboats were operating on the western rivers.

From his own boyhood days of the 1840's Mark Twain recalled the excitement attending the daily arrival of the river boat at a small Mississippi port:

> The town drunkard stirs, the clerks wake up, a furious clatter of drays follows, every house and store pours out a human contribution, and all in a twinkling the dead town is alive and moving. Drays, carts, men, boys, all go hurrying from many quarters to a common center, the wharf. Assembled there, the people fasten their eyes upon the coming boat as upon a wonder they are seeing for the first time. And the boat *is* rather a handsome sight, too. She is long and sharp and trim and pretty; she has two tall, fancy-topped chimneys, with a gilded device of some kind swung between them; a fanciful pilot-house, all glass and "gingerbread," perched on top of the "texas" deck behind them; the paddle-boxes are gorgeous with a picture or with gilded rays above the boat's name; the boiler-deck, the the hurricane-deck, and the texas deck are fenced and ornamented with clean white railings; there is a flag gallantly flying from the jack-staff; the furnace doors are open and the fires glaring bravely; the upper decks are black with passengers; the captain stands by the big bell, calm, imposing, the envy of all; great volumes of the blackest smoke are rolling and tumbling out of the chimneys—a husbanded grandeur created with a bit of pitch-pine just before arriving at a town; the crew are grouped on the forecastle; the broad stage is run out over the port bow and an envied deck-hand stands picturesquely on the end of it with a coil of rope in his hand; the pent steam is screaming through the gauge-cocks; the captain lifts his hand, a bell rings, the wheels stop; then they turn back, churning the water to foam, and the steamer is at rest.[1]

Out of his later experiences, Mark Twain left other vivid pictures of steamboating—of the extraordinary skill of pilots who knew every detail of a capricious 1,200-mile-long river, of the passion for speed that found its outlet in exciting races between rival favorites, and of the frequent catastrophes when steamboats ran aground, burned up, or exploded.

Many eastern rivers were spoiled for navigation by falls, rapids, or shallows. Projects for improving transportation, therefore, frequently took the form of building canals around these obstacles. In 1785 the Virginia legislature chartered the Potomac Company for improving the navigation of that river as the first link in a communications system between the Atlantic Coast and the West. With George Washington as president and James Rumsey, the steamboat enthusiast, as engineer, the new company undertook to build a number of projects, including an ambitious system of locks around the Great Falls. Inexperience, inadequate funds, and frustrating delays prevented the Potomac Company from fulfilling the ambitions of its founders, but it served to inspire more successful projects elsewhere. In 1794 short canals were completed around South Hadley Falls on the Connecticut River and through the Dismal Swamp of North Carolina. More ambitious undertakings were the Santee Canal in South Carolina, completed in 1800, and the Middlesex Canal between the Merrimack River and Boston, completed in 1803. The Western Inland Lock Navigation Company, chartered by the New York legislature in 1792, sought to improve the Mohawk River route to the West.

[1] Mark Twain, *Life on the Mississippi* (Harper, New York, n.d.), 33–34.

These pioneer canals and others like them were built by private enterprise, which was organized in corporations like the contemporary turnpike and bridge companies. But the experience of most canal investors was an unhappy one, for the projects were usually more expensive than their optimistic promoters counted on. Capital began to shun canal investments in favor of turnpikes and bridges, and canal building lagged until the state governments took direct action.

The idea of building a canal from the Hudson River to Lake Erie took shape over several decades. After unsuccessful attempts to gain assistance from either the Federal government or neighboring states, New Yorkers at length became convinced that the canal would have to be built by state initiative if at all. For several years the project was vigorously debated. Skeptics, aware of the financial difficulties of earlier canals only a few miles in length, scoffed at the thought of building one 350 miles long.

Although many shortsighted residents of New York City opposed the canal project as of benefit only to the western counties, Mayor De Witt Clinton became an enthusiastic convert to the idea. After Clinton became governor in 1817, legislative authorization was obtained and the first shovelful of earth for the great ditch was lifted at Rome, New York, on July 4, 1817.

Engineering problems, more challenging than Americans had ever faced before, were intelligently and energetically handled. Impatient with slow traditional digging methods, the contractors devised means of excavating with plows and scrapers. The felling of trees and pulling of roots was expedited by ingenious machines. Faced with the problem of constructing watertight locks, the canal builders discovered stone from which an excellent cement could be made. At Rochester the canal was carried across the Genesee River on an aqueduct 750 feet long; at Lockport it was raised nearly 60 feet within 2 miles by a double system of five locks.

On October 26, 1825, news of the opening of the canal was carried from Buffalo to New York by a relay of cannons, placed from 8 to 12 miles apart across the state. This was the start of ten days of festivities, during which a procession of canal boats moved triumphantly through the new waterway. In the first, the *Seneca Chief,* rode Governor Clinton and other dignitaries, drawn by four gray horses; in another boat were a bear, two eagles, two fawns, two Indian boys and several other creatures typical of the West. Down the Hudson from Albany to New York the canal flotilla was towed by steamboat. While the populace of the city celebrated enthusiastically, Governor Clinton ended his voyage at Sandy Hook, where he solemnly poured a keg of Lake Erie water into the Atlantic.

Nor were these jubilations inappropriate. The success of the Erie Canal surpassed the fondest hopes of its promoters. Collecting tolls of over a million dollars a year, the state soon recouped its initial investment of 7 million dollars and took in enough more to maintain and to enlarge the waterway. The western part of the state enjoyed a tremendous boom. To move a ton of goods from

Buffalo to New York City had formerly cost $100 and taken three weeks; now the cost was $15 and the trip took only eight days. Rochester, a village in 1820, became a thriving city and the leading flour-milling center of the country; Syracuse, Utica, and a dozen smaller places along the canal enjoyed a growth almost as remarkable. To Ohio and the other new states bordering on Lake Erie, the canal also brought important benefits—better prices for agricultural products, cheaper manufactured goods from Europe and the East, and a stimulus to westward migration.

The success of the Erie stimulated a score of similar projects, both state and corporate. Canal building continued in New York until Lake Champlain, Lake Ontario, Lake Seneca, and most other parts of the state were connected with the main Erie Canal–Hudson River artery. Pennsylvania, jealous of its neighbor's prosperity, committed itself to an ambitious scheme of public works to link Philadelphia and Pittsburgh.

Constructed between 1827 and 1834, the Pennsylvania system was an extraordinary affair. Since the Allegheny Mountains presented an obstacle too formidable to be surmounted with locks, canal passengers and freight were transferred across a 37-mile stretch between Hollidaysburg and Johnstown by an ingenious portage railroad. Charles Dickens, fascinated like many another traveler, thus described the experience of journeying over it:

> There are ten inclined planes; five ascending and five descending; the carriages are dragged up the former, and let slowly down the latter, by means of stationary engines; the comparatively level spaces between being traversed, sometimes by horse, and sometimes by engine power, as the case demands. Occasionally the rails are laid upon the extreme verge of a giddy precipice; and looking from the carriage window, the traveler gazes sheer down, without a stone or scrap of fence between, into the mountain depth below. . . . It was very pretty travelling thus, at a rapid pace along the heights of the mountain in a keen wind, to look down into a valley full of light and softness; catching glimpses, through the tree-tops, of scattered cabins . . . and we riding onward, high above them, like a whirlwind.[1]

But the Pennsylvania system, however picturesque, never enjoyed the financial success of the Erie. Similarly doomed to disappointment were western states like Ohio, Indiana, Illinois, and Michigan that went heavily in debt in their attempts to build ambitious canal systems. Caught by the panic of 1837, the state governments had so difficult a time extricating themselves that state enterprise in such works became unpopular, but despite these mishaps several public works of great benefit to the section were constructed. The growth of Ohio was greatly stimulated by the opening of the Ohio and Erie Canal from Portsmouth to Cleveland in 1832 and of the Miami Canal between Cincinnati and Toledo in 1845, and the completion of the Illinois and Michigan Canal in 1848 contributed mightily to the growth of Chicago.

[1] Charles Dickens, *Pictures from Italy and American Notes* (2 vols. in one, New York, 1868), II, 184–185.

Railroads

Americans, already deeply indebted to Europe for principles of turnpike and canal engineering, took a keen interest in English railroad experiments during the early nineteenth century. The railroad represented the final linking of two lines of development, originally quite separate. The older evolution had been that of tramways. As early as the sixteenth century, English mineowners had begun to lay planks in the ruts worn into the roads by coal carts moving their heavy loads from pit heads to waterways. The wooden planks gradually gave way to wooden rails sheathed with iron along which carts equipped with flanged wheels were drawn. So greatly did these tramways reduce friction that a single horse could pull loads of several tons. The second line of experimentation was in steam-propelled land vehicles. The first of these, built in France and England in the late eighteenth and early nineteenth centuries, attempted to use the ordinary highways but encountered two serious obstacles: rough surfaces and sharp grades held the vehicles down to a crawl, and the terrifying noises emitted as they labored along caused indignant carriage drivers to insist that they be banned from the public highways.

The transfer of the steam vehicles to the tramways, a seemingly obvious step, was a development that investors were slow to support. Although one or two English mineowners used locomotives before 1820, the engines were not efficient enough to arouse much confidence. Even when the first railroads for the general use of the public were being planned during the 1820's, conservative opinion advocated reliance on either horsepower or stationary steam engines. Not until George Stephenson built successful locomotives for the Stockton and Darlington Railway in 1825 and for the Liverpool and Manchester in 1829, did English opinion finally recognize that a new, speedy means of transportation had been developed.

Each phase of railroad development had its American repercussions. Between 1796 and 1828 several tramways were built in various parts of the country. Although none of these attempted to use steam power, American mechanics were interested in the locomotive from an early date. Some time about 1802 Oliver Evans, pioneer in improved flour milling, built a steam-propelled amphibian, which crawled through the streets of Philadelphia and then paddled along the Schuylkill and the Delaware Rivers. But investors did not care to risk their funds in the development of such an outlandish machine, and Evans turned to other interests. Similarly, Colonel John Stevens of New Jersey, unable to secure financial backing for railroad projects that he had been agitating since 1811, had to content himself with building a miniature locomotive, which he operated on a circular track on his own property. In 1829 the Delaware and Hudson Canal Company, impressed by events in England, imported the *Stourbridge Lion* to try out on its railroad, which had been recently constructed to transport coal between Carbondale and Honesdale, Pennsylvania. The British-built locomotive performed well enough, but the directors decided that it was too heavy for regular service over the company's flimsy trestles, and stationary engines were used instead.

Meanwhile, the citizens of Baltimore, aroused by the challenge of the Erie Canal and the projected Pennsylvania canal system, had formulated a bold project for a railroad over which horses would draw passengers and freight from Baltimore to the Ohio River. Chartered in 1827, the Baltimore and Ohio Railroad began construction the next year. In 1830 it offered a regular passenger service in horse-drawn carriages along the 13 miles of track then built. Experiments, more curious than practical, were made in propelling vehicles with sails and horse-driven treadmills. Prevailing opinion was that the sharp curves of the railroad made steam locomotives impractical, but this judgment was proved erroneous. During the summer of 1830 a number of successful runs were made by the *Tom Thumb,* a tiny locomotive constructed by Peter Cooper, ingenious New York glue and iron manufacturer. Despite its makeshift character the *Tom Thumb* performed well enough so that the railroad was induced to purchase more substantial engines and to institute regular service by steam in July, 1831.

In this step, however, the Baltimore and Ohio had been anticipated by the South Carolina Railroad, which had tried out the American-built locomotive *Best Friend of Charleston* in December, 1830, and placed it in regular service in January, 1831. Pushing construction more rapidly than its northern contemporaries, this pioneer line in 1833 extended 136 miles from Charleston to Hamburg. For a brief period it could boast of being the longest railroad in the world.

Many other lines were in construction during the early thirties. The Mohawk and Hudson, spanning the 16 miles between Schenectady and Albany, began to operate in 1831, and a number of other short New York lines soon followed. Railroads were particularly adapted to the transportation needs of New England, where distances between cities were short. By 1835 Boston had rail connections with Lowell, Worcester, and Providence. Travel between New York and Philadelphia was speeded by the Camden and Amboy, built across New Jersey. Local lines were particularly active in Pennsylvania, where almost 1,000 miles of track were laid down before 1840—making Philadelphia one of the first important railroad centers. Nor was the South to be outdone in this first burst of construction: Virginia gained 363 miles of railroad during the thirties, Alabama 308, North Carolina 246, and other states smaller amounts.

The railroad fever, spreading to the Middle West together with the canal mania, resulted in many ambitious schemes. Railroads, east and west, suffered a crippling blow in the panic of 1837, but construction was again pushed forward rapidly during the late forties.

Trunk lines between the East Coast and the Middle West—long delayed by financial difficulties, engineering problems, and legislative obstructions created through the lobbying of jealous turnpike and canal interests—were finally completed during the early fifties. New York, grown complacent through the advantages gained by the Erie Canal, received a jolt when the Western Railroad of Massachusetts pushed across the Berkshires to Albany in 1841. Threatened with a serious diversion of western traffic to Boston, New York investors rallied to the support of projects that would help ensure the supremacy of their own great market. The Erie Railroad, begun in 1836, was finally completed in 1851. The formal opening of this 446-mile line from Piermont on the Hudson River to Dunkirk on Lake Erie was a national event of such importance that President Millard Fillmore and Secretary of State Daniel Webster were present for the occasion. In 1851, moreover, New York gained direct rail connections with Albany by the Hudson River Railroad. Albany was already clumsily linked with Buffalo by some ten small connecting lines, but service was immeasurably improved when these were merged in the New York Central Railroad Company in 1853.

While New York was gaining the advantage of two rail routes to the West, Philadelphia and Baltimore were rushing rival projects to completion. The Pennsylvania Railroad, chartered in 1846, completed a line from Harrisburg to Pittsburgh in 1852. Additional construction and purchase of a state-owned railroad gave the Pennsylvania a through line from Philadelphia to Pittsburgh in 1858. The Baltimore and Ohio finally fulfilled the ambitions of its promoters by reaching the Ohio River at Wheeling, Virginia, on Christmas Eve, 1852.

Stretching out to meet these iron fingers from the East were such western railroads as the Lake Shore, the Michigan Southern, the Atlantic and Western, and the Pittsburgh, Fort Wayne, and Chicago. The importance of the new transportation lines was emphasized by the doubling of the population of Illinois between 1850 and 1860. In this growth the Illinois Central Railroad, recipient of the first large Federal land grant, played a leading part through its program of land sales and colonization. Terminus of a dozen railroads, Chicago's preeminence as a railroad center was clearly established before the Civil War.

A curiosity in 1830, the railroads were a vital part of American life by 1860. Important technical improvements had added to their speed and convenience, although their provision for safety and comfort still left much to be desired. American conditions had forced American railroads into a somewhat different pattern from European. Although English locomotives had been extensively used during the early days, American types developed by such builders as Baldwin of Philadelphia and Rogers of Paterson proved better adapted to American curves and grades. The cowcatcher was a characteristically American innovation, as was the all-iron "T rail." Unlike European coaches, which provided small compartments in which passengers rode in splendid isolation from most of their fellows, the American passenger car was a miniature public hall in which several dozen travelers occupied rows of seats on either side of a long central aisle.

To a degree greater than any previous innovation the railroad gave the country a national economy. Wherever the iron roads appeared, the need for local self-sufficiency was no longer left. Household manufactures were abandoned as farmers began to grow staples for distant markets and depend on store purchases for their clothing and tools. With a national market opened for the products of the factories, simpler forms of merchandising gave way to a more complex system in which wholesalers, brokers, advertisers, and traveling salesmen played their specialized roles.

Although all but a few of the railroads were owned and managed by private corporations, their relations with government were particularly intimate. Requiring charters and franchises, the railroads were deeply involved in politics from the start. They were, moreover, the recipients of many forms of government aid. In order to encourage construction, state and local governments bonded themselves to subscribe for railroad stock, made grants of land, and gave tax exemptions. Federal land grants to railroads, following precedents established in the turnpike and canal eras, began modestly in the thirties and became substantial during the fifties.

Telegraph

As the properties of electricity became better understood during the early nineteenth century, European and American scientists experimented with various devices for sending messages by wire. Particularly important were the researches of the American scholar Joseph Henry. To make primitive telegraphs that would operate over short distances was not difficult; to develop a system that would provide instantaneous communication between one city and another was not so simple a matter.

Samuel F. B. Morse, who patented the first electric telegraph suitable for practical use, was the son of the Reverend Jedidiah Morse, famous both as a defender of Congregational orthodoxy and as the author of school geographies. Like Robert Fulton, the younger Morse studied painting with Benjamin West in London. Unlike the steamboat specialist, however, Morse practiced his art with marked success for two decades before attempting a new career in invention. Becoming interested in electricity during the 1830's, Morse constructed his first crude telegraphs in 1836 and 1837. A period of discouragement followed, as the artist-inventor applied in vain for support from the United States and foreign governments. Finally, in 1843, Congress by a close vote appropriated $30,000 to enable Morse to build an experimental line from Washington to Baltimore.

On May 24, 1844, from the chamber of the national Capitol Morse transmitted to his partner in Baltimore the famous words, "What hath God wrought"—a sentiment that did credit to the inventor's good Congregational upbringing. Although official Washington was impressed by this demonstration and even more by later messages received from Baltimore while the Democratic national convention was in session there, Morse was unsuccessful in convincing Congress that the telegraph should be developed by public rather than private enterprise. Cave Johnson, who became Postmaster General in 1845, agreed with Morse. "The use of an instrument so powerful for good or evil," he asserted, "cannot with safety to the people be left in the hands of private individuals uncontrolled by law." But the opportunity to develop the telegraph as a part of the postal system was allowed to pass, and Congress authorized the sale to private interests of the government-financed Washington-Baltimore line.

Although investors were at first wary of the new communications medium, the Magnetic Telegraph Company was organized in 1845, and numerous other corporations licensed to use the Morse patents soon afterward. By the end of 1846 Washington was linked to Philadelphia and Newark, New York to Boston and Buffalo, and Philadelphia to Harrisburg and Pittsburgh. Thereafter the electrical network was extended with remarkable speed. In 1852 there were over 23,000 miles of telegraph lines in the country. From Washington messages could be sent halfway across the continent to New Orleans, Chicago, or Dubuque, Iowa. On October 24, 1861, a telegram from the head of the Overland Telegraph Company to the President of the United States read:

> I announce to you that the telegraph to California has this day been completed. May it be a bond of perpetuity between the states of the Alantic and those of the Pacific.

Newspapers, eager for the latest reports, were excellent customers for the infant telegraph companies. The eagerness of the press to secure news of the Mexican War undoubtedly encouraged a more rapid expansion of the telegraph network than would have occurred otherwise. The New York Associated Press was organized in 1848 for cooperation in securing dispatches by telegraph, and similar organizations were soon formed in other sections.

In the days before the telegraph, railroad passengers were subjected to exasperating delays. Most of the lines were one-track affairs, and trains could pass only at stations where sidings had been provided. Often a train would sit on a siding for hours, not knowing what had delayed the train coming in the other direction or when it might be expected. In 1851 Charles Minot of the Erie Railroad, one of the ablest rail executives of the day, introduced the system of running trains by telegraphing orders to station agents, and the practice was soon adopted by other lines.

For the general business life of the country the telegraph was similarly useful. Dealers in stock or grain bought or sold on the basis of reports brought to their desks from all parts of the country. In 1855 William F. Channing, a Boston physician, aptly described the influence of the new medium of communication:

> The electric telegraph is the nervous system of this nation and of modern society by no figure of speech, by no distant analogy. Its wires spread like nerves over the surface of the land, interlinking distant parts, and making posible a perpetually higher cooperation among men, and higher social forms than have hitherto existed. By means of its life-like

functions the social body becomes a living whole, and each of its new applications marks a step in the organization of human life.[1]

At first the telegraph business was wildly competitive. Rival companies fought over the right to use certain routes and to enter important centers. Many cities were connected by two or more lines with resultant rate wars. Litigation involving rival patent and license rights gave profitable employment to the lawyers. But a tendency toward consolidation and monopoly soon became evident. The Western Union Telegraph Company, chartered in 1856, rapidly gained dominance in the West. Ten years later it absorbed the American Telegraph Company, the leading unit in the East. Capitalized at over 40 million dollars, Western Union became the largest corporation of the day.

The Cities

The passing of rural self-sufficiency and the development of industry and commerce, made possible by the revolution in transportation, had its inevitable consequence in the rapid growth of cities. In 1790 only 3 per cent of the population of the United States lived in places of 8,000 inhabitants or more; in 1860 about 16 per cent did so. The number of such urban communities had increased from 6 in 1790 to 141 in 1860.

The largest concentrations of population were at the great seaports. Between 1790 and 1810 New York's population grew from 33,000 to 96,000, enabling it to pass Philadelphia, whose population grew from 42,000 to 91,000 over the same period. Baltimore's rapid growth made it the third largest American city in 1810 with 35,000 inhabitants as compared with Boston's 33,000. Charleston gradually lost ground: fourth in rank in 1790, it fell to sixth in 1810 and twenty-sixth in 1860. The other great seaports held tenaciously to their relative positions. In 1860 New York had 813,000 inhabitants, and 279,000 more lived across the East River in neighboring Brooklyn; Philadelphia had a population of 565,000; Baltimore, 212,000; Boston, 177,000; and New Orleans, 168,000.

Next in rank among the cities was a group that profited by traffic over rivers and canals. In 1830 Cincinnati, Albany, Pittsburgh, and Louisville, with populations of between 10,000 and 25,000, were seventh, eighth, ninth, and tenth among the cities of the nation. Of these western centers only Cincinnati and Pittsburgh had the same relative importance in 1860. Cincinnati then had 161,000 inhabitants and was the sixth largest city in the country. Her leading western rival were St. Louis with 160,000 inhabitants, Chicago with 109,000, Buffalo with 81,000 and Pittsburgh with 77,000.

The newer cities exhibited many of the crudities to be expected on the frontier. The fastidious English traveler Mrs. Trollope knew not whether to be angry

[1] Quoted in Robert L. Thompson, *Wiring a Continent: The History of the Telegraph Industry in the United States, 1832–1866* (Princeton University Press, Princeton, N. J., 1947), 253.

with the herds of hogs she saw running through the the streets of Cincinnati or to be grateful to them for devouring the garbage, which would have otherwise clogged the uncleaned streets. Although the New York City fathers were also struggling with the pig problem, the general appearance of the city was improving. Mrs. Trollope could find little to criticize in 1831.

> The extreme point is fortified towards the sea by a battery; but in these piping days of peace, it is converted into a public promenade, and one more beautiful, I should suppose, no city could boast. From hence commences the splendid Broadway, as the fine avenue is called, which runs through the whole city. This noble street may vie with any I ever saw, for its length and breadth, its handsome shops, neat awnings, excellent *trottoir,* and well-dressed pedestrians. It has not the crowded glitter of Bond-street equipages, nor the gorgeous fronted palaces of Regent-street; but it is magnificent in its extent, and ornamented by several handsome buildings, some of them surrounded by grass and trees.[1]

But in New York, as in other great cities of both the Old and New Worlds with their fine avenues and public parks, the majority of the population lived in conditions of squalid poverty. In 1850 over 18,000 persons were living in damp, dark, vermin-infested cellar rooms. Others were crowded together in flimsy tenement houses thrown up by the thousand. Some of the poor had to patronize the three-class boardinghouses of the day. The first class paid $1.50 a month for board and lodging, sleeping on straw thrown loose over the floor; the second class paid 75 cents and slept on the bare floor; the third class paid 36 cents and slept on the floor on sufferance, being turned out when second-class lodgers were available. Food was obtained either from children sent out to beg or from professional beggarwomen with whom the boardinghouse keepers made contracts. The whole mass of food was thrown on a long table, and the first-class boarders were given the first picking, to be followed in turn by the second- and third-class boarders.

Such degrading poverty was not peculiar to New York. In 1847 an investigator in industrial Lowell discovered a family composed of a man, his wife, eight children, and four adult boarders sharing a one-room lodging with another family. In Boston's notorious Half-Moon Place a doctor, visiting a patient in a cellar room, found that the tide had risen so high that he had to approach the sick man's bedside by means of a plank laid across two stools while the body of a dead infant sailed about the room in its coffin.

That the cities should be periodically ravaged by terrible epidemics was inevitable. In 1793 a plague of yellow fever paralyzed Philadelphia and drove all who could to flee the city. Recalling the terrible event, a local historian wrote:

> Look, then, in which way you would through the streets, and you saw the exposed coffins on chair-wheels, either in quick motion, or you saw the wheels drawn before houses to receive their pestilential charge. Then family, friends, or mourners scarcely ever accompanied them; and no coffins were adorned to please the eye; but coarse, stained

[1] Frances Trollope, *Domestic Manners of the Americans,* ed. by Donald Smalley (Knopf, New York, 1949), 337.

wood, of hasty fabric, received them all. The graves were not dug singly, but pits, which might receive many before entire filling up, were opened. In the streets you met no cheerful, heedless faces, but pensive downcast eyes and hurried steps, hastening to the necessary calls of the sick.[1]

To the perils of yellow fever were added frequent epidemics of smallpox, typhoid fever, and other diseases. Between 1849 and 1854 plagues of cholera swept much of the country—taking as many as 2,500 lives in a single year in New York alone.

Although medical opinion was much divided on the cause of such diseases, contaminated water fell increasingly under suspicion. "There was little or no desire expressed by the citizens of Philadelphia," recorded the local annalist, "for any other than their *good* pump-water, till after the yellow fever of 1793. Then, when the mind was alive to every suggested danger of ill health, the idea of pump-water being no longer good found its increasing supporters." [2]

Benjamin Latrobe, one of the best known architects of the day, devised a scheme for forcing water from the Schuylkill River by steam engine into a central reservoir and thence distributing it throughout the city of Philadelphia. Despite much popular skepticism a company was organized to carry out Latrobe's plan. Eager to confound those who had doubted him, Latrobe opened all the hydrants of the city on the night that the project was completed and set his steam engine going. When the good burghers awoke, they found their streets flowing with water from gushing hydrants. The water works, completed in 1801, at once became an object of civic pride, to which visitors were unfailingly taken.

New York's response to the water problem was less bold. During the 1790's many families were still drinking water from their own wells, and others purchased the highly esteemed "tea water," pumped from a spring at Chatham Street and peddled from door to door in horse-drawn carts. In 1799 the Manhattan Company, organized by Aaron Burr, built a system whereby water was pumped from wells into a reservoir at Chambers Street and then widely distributed through bored wooden logs. For a generation the Manhattan Company's pumps were favorite meeting places for young lovers, but the water that they supplied became increasingly contaminated by seepage from sewers and graveyards. Not until 1835 did the city of New York abandon dependence on private enterprise and authorize the construction of an ambitious public system. From the Croton River, 40 miles to the north, water was carried to the city in a closed aqueduct. Crossing the Harlem River on the strong and beautiful High Bridge, the aqueduct delivered its contents to two large reservoirs—one on the present site of Central Park, the other where the New York Public Library now stands. From there the water was distributed through iron pipes to the rest of the city.

Elsewhere the water problem was similarly dealt with. The usual evolution was from wells and springs to privately owned systems and thence to public ones.

[1] John F. Watson, *Annals of Philadelphia and Pennsylvania* (Philadelphia, 1843), II, 390.
[2] *Ibid.,* 457.

In 1861 there were 80 private water systems and 68 public ones in the country. The maintenance of a pure and adequate supply became increasingly difficult. As the cities grew, they had an inevitable tendency either to contaminate their water resources or to make excessive demands upon them. The New York system, completed in 1842 at a cost of 12 million dollars, required radical enlargement by 1858.

The problem of water supply demanded serious attention, not only because of its relation to public health, but because of the growing fire hazard in the great cities. Visiting New York in 1828, John F. Watson commented: "The frequency of fires, and their alarms, is one evil of over large population. The cry occurred every day or night I dwelt in the city." A traveler of the forties called fires "that national disease." To combat this dangerous enemy, the cities still placed their faith in volunteer companies. The firemen brought to their task exuberant high spirits and a fierce ambition to outdo their rivals. A pamphlet of the forties well captured the spirit of the enterprise:

> Short of a battle, there is nothing more exciting than a fire; and there is this delightful consideration, that while it brings into requisition all the nerve, muscle and stalwart manhood, which are demanded in the fiercest engagement by land or sea, all these qualities are exerted, not for the destruction, but for the preservation of property and life.[1]

Unfortunately the volunteers frequently paused from their heroic labors to fortify themselves at the whisky keg, to pocket valuables salvaged from the burning building, or to fight with rival companies for possession of the hydrants.

The cities found equal difficulty in dealing with the growing problem of crime. During the 1850's a wave of robberies, assaults, and murders shocked the country. New York was alleged to be the most crime-ridden city in the world with Philadelphia, Baltimore, and Cincinnati not far behind. Gangs of "Bowery Boys," "Plug-Uglies," "Swipers," and "Dead Rabbits" roamed the streets, assaulting peaceful pedestrians, fighting with each other, and flocking to fires, where they found rich opportunities for plunder. To deal with these rowdies, the cities maintained poorly disciplined police forces. Wearing no uniforms, the officers of the law were more likely to pocket their badges and to slink away than to assert their authority in time of trouble. In 1853, against indignant protests, the New York commissioners finally compelled the policemen to don official uniforms consisting of a blue cap, a blue swallow-tailed coat with brass buttons, and gray pantaloons. A similar reform was shortly forced upon the protesting police of Philadelphia and Boston.

The city with its noise and confusion repelled many Americans. In 1828 a Philadelphian wrote:

> There is something in New York, that is a perpetual ideal London to my mind, and therefore more a gratification to visit, than to abide. The stir and bustle; the perpetual

[1] *The Young Men of Cities Urged to the Work of Mental Improvement* (New York, 1849), 4.

emulation to excel in display; . . . the various contrivances, by signs and devices, to allure and catch the eye . . . the imitations of London, and foreign cities and foreigners; rather than our own proper republican manners and principles, struck my attention everywhere. The very ambition to be the metropolitan city, like London, gave them cares which I am very willing to see remote enough from Philadelphia. . . . I am fully willing, ours shall long be "the peaceful city of Penn." Why do we want our cities, and even our country, dense with foreign population? . . . Is there no maximum point, beyond which our comforts and ease must proportionably diminish? I fear so.[1]

But such laments were futile. For better or worse, irreversible economic and social forces were at work that would eventually stamp all America with many of the characteristics already associated with New York.

[1] Watson, *op. cit.,* Appendix, 74.

Chapter 12. Coming of the Foreigners

Between 1790 and 1860 the population of the United States was multiplied by eight—rising from less than 4 million to almost 31½ million. In part, this extraordinary growth could be explained by the reduced death rate, which nineteenth-century America shared with Europe; in part, it resulted from the high American birth rate. But even with this large natural increase the nation's growth would have been much slower had it not been for large-scale immigration. About one-eighth of the population of 1860 was foreign-born.

Impact of War and Revolution

Immigration depended on many factors—expulsive causes in the Old World, attractive conditions in the New, and opportunities for obtaining passage. Between 1775 and 1815 these factors were not present to any large extent. It was a period of wars in America and Europe. When the United States was at war, few foreigners wanted to involve themselves by migration. When Europe was at war, it was difficult to leave.

Despite these adverse conditions a small flow of newcomers continued. Of the German mercenaries whom George III employed to fight against his rebellious colonists, several thousand remained in America as permanent residents. The Revolutionary War served also to interest Frenchmen in the new nation. When the Scioto Company wanted colonists for its western lands, it found at first an enthusiastic response in France. Six hundred Parisians attempted to settle at Gallipolis, Ohio, in 1791, but their unhappy encounter with fever, Indians, and frontier hardship discouraged others from following their example.

During the French Revolution there were many turns in the wheel of fortune, each resulting in the removal to America of a new group of refugees. All shades of political opinion were represented from stanch supporters of the old regime to passionate apostles of "liberty, equality, and fraternity." For one reason or another such well-known figures as Talleyrand, Chateaubriand, Volney, Jerome Bonaparte, and Joseph Bonaparte all took up brief residences in the United States. For several years it was a common thing to point out to sight-seers the lowly dwelling where some impoverished duke or marquis was making his temporary home. Louis Philippe, a future king, slept in a straw bed over a Philadelphia barroom.

Not all of the refugees were of the aristocracy. Thousands were colonial planters and merchants fleeing from a violent uprising of Negro slaves on the island of Haiti. Leaving behind all their possessions, the terrified whites made their way to such American ports as Charleston, Norfolk, Baltimore, Philadelphia, and New York. Their plight so touched American sympathy that relief funds, totaling about $250,000, were contributed from public and private sources. Included in this was a $20,000 appropriation by Congress.

Although most of the nobles returned to their homeland when political conditions became stabilized, thousands of humbler refugees became permanently established as physicians, dentists, or market gardeners. Even the French transients left their mark on the young nation. The upper circles of society learned a new esteem for fine food, witty conversation, and elegant manners. The impact of the visitors on sober Philadelphia was described by a contemporary in these words:

> Our city thronged with French people of all shades from the colonies and those from Old France, giving it the appearance of one great hotel, or place of shelter for strangers, hastily collected together from a raging tempest. The characteristic old school simplicity of the citizens, in manners, habits of dress, and modes of thinking and speaking . . . began to be broken in upon. . . . French boarding houses . . . multipled in every street. The one at the south east corner of Race and Second Streets, having some 40 windows, was filled with colonial French to the garret windows, whistling and jumping about, fiddling and singing, as fancy seemed to suggest, like so many crickets and grasshoppers. Groups of both sexes were to be seen seated on chairs, in summer weather, forming semi-circles near the doors, so displayed as sometimes to render it necessary to step into the street to get along; their tongues, shoulders and hands in perpetual motion, jabbering away, "all talkers and no hearers." . . . Instrumental music abounded in the city everywhere, by day as by night, from French gentlemen, . . . on the hautboy, violin and clarionet, exquisitely played—and seemingly intended to catch the attention of neighboring fair ones, at opposite windows.[1]

Far-reaching in its consequences, the French Revolution brought immigrants to America from other countries as well. In England, where fear of change became an obsession, any criticism of existing institutions was likely to be construed as dangerous Jacobinism. Dr. Joseph Priestley, clergyman, scientist, and political philosopher, moved to America in 1794 after his Birmingham house had been destroyed by a reactionary mob. A number of other English reformers followed him across the Atlantic. Reaction also laid its heavy hand on Wales. Methodist and Baptist preachers and newspaper editors were jailed on charges of sedition. Since times were also bad economically, many Welshmen migrated to American communities like Utica, New York, Cambria County, Pennsylvania, and Paddy's Run, Ohio. In 1798 the United Irishmen rose in a spirited but ill-fated attempt to win Irish independence. With the failure of the rebellion came another influx of refugees. Many of these were men of wealth and education who became influential persons in their new homes. They organized lodges of United Irish-

[1] John F. Watson, *Annals of Philadelphia and Pennsylvania* (Philadelphia, 1843), II, 169–170.

men in all the principal coastal cities, became leaders in the rising Jeffersonian party, and encouraged later more extensive immigration from Ireland.

The tendency of recent arrivals from Europe to throw themselves actively into American politics, usually on the side of the Jeffersonian Republicans, aroused Federalist resentment and led to the first attempt to discourage immigration by hostile legislation. Taking advantage of widespread indignation with France over the X Y Z affair, the Federalist majority in Congress enacted laws raising the residence requirement for naturalization from five to fourteen years and empowering the President to order out of the country any alien whom he judged dangerous to the peace and safety of the United States. But these laws, part of the Alien and Sedition Acts of 1798, were not long in force. When the Republicans came to power, the residence requirement for naturalization was restored to five years, and the alien law expired by limitation.

Although the American government quickly returned to a liberal immigration policy, the annual influx remained small. From 1790 to 1815 the total of new arrivals was only about 250,000.

A generation of relatively small immigration fostered an Americanization of the older stock. Although even after the Revolution Dutch had persisted as the language of everyday affairs in many sleepy villages along the Hudson and on Long Island, Dutch culture suffered a steady attrition during the next generation. First in the market place, then in church, and finally in the home, English displaced the old tongue.

The Germans, more numerous and more recently arrived, clung to their language more tenaciously. In the regions where the Germans were a minority—in New York State, in most of the South, and in the West—English won an early victory. But in Pennsylvania, Maryland, and the Great Valley of Virginia German culture had sent down deeper roots. In 1829 the author of a guide for German immigrants estimated that there were in the United States a thousand German-speaking parishes and a million Germans not yet Anglicized. In some regions—especially the so-called "Pennsylvania Dutch country"—the old ways persisted into the twentieth century.

But the proportion of the non-English-speaking elements to the whole population became constantly smaller. Any danger that the United States would be a mere patchwork of different cultures disappeared as a strong sense of American nationality began to develop.

Rising Tide

With the return of peace immigration immediately increased in volume. Between 1815 and 1819 about 100,000 foreigners arrived in American ports. At first they were easily absorbed, but those who came in 1819 had a disillusioning experience. The postwar boom collapsed suddenly, throwing thousands of laborers out of work. Unable to get jobs, immigrants who still had funds returned to Europe, and thousands of others were kept alive only through private and public charity. America's reputation as a land of limitless opportunities suffered severely.

The nation came back strongly after this economic setback. The late twenties and the thirties witnessed a buoyant optimism that found its expression in the establishment of factories, the building of canals and railroads, and extensive investment in land. A rekindled faith in the American future crossed the Atlantic and invaded hundreds of remote European villages.

The American dream was all the more enticing because of the situation abroad. A fear that Europe was becoming overpopulated obsessed this generation. Although the Old World rate of increase was far smaller than that in the New, it was large by comparison with that of preceding centuries. The total population of Europe, which increased only 30,000,000 in the seventeenth century and 60,000,000 in the eighteenth, more than doubled during the nineteenth century—rising from 187,000,000 to 400,000,000. The immediate consequence of this rise in population was to create an insatiable demand for land. The reclamation of swamps and mountain slopes and the clearing of forests, which had relieved agricultural pressure in earlier generations, offered little hope for this one. One region after another suffered a fragmentation of holdings until millions of Europeans were dependent on plots of a few acres to keep them alive. Land hunger had its inevitable consequence in high land prices and rents. The lower classes suffered also through the oversupply of agricultural workers and resultant low wages.

Adverse economic conditions were accompanied by unwelcome political and social developments. The Irish became increasingly resentful of English rule, blaming the dominant power for every misfortune. The Germans, still divided into petty states and principalities, engaged in futile attempts to achieve unity and constitutional government. Although the number of Old World liberals who emigrated to America to escape oppression was not large, it included professional people and journalists who became influential in their new homes. Religious persecution was fortunately less than in earlier centuries, but Irish-Catholic resentment at the Anglican establishment and German peasant hostility to the collection of tithes were not without influence in encouraging migration to a country where there were no church establishments or church taxes.

Except for enacting naturalization laws and a few regulations of shipping, the United States government did little either to encourage or to discourage immigration. Immediately after the War of 1812 Irish, English, German, and Swiss groups pressed upon Congress a variety of projects for the establishment of colonies in the West on tracts either given free to immigrant groups or sold to them on long-term credit. Congress decided against such a policy on various grounds: it would create a precedent for a flood of similiar demands; it would discriminate against native-born citizens by granting special privileges to immigrants; it would encourage the growth of districts where the entire population was of a particular nationality, thus endangering national unity. Stated more positively by Secretary of State John Quincy Adams in 1818, the policy of the United States was this: it invited none to come; it would not keep out those who had the courage to cross the Atlantic; they would suffer no disabilities as aliens, but they could expect no special advantages; foreign-born and natives alike faced the same opportunities, and their success would depend upon their individual activity and good fortune.

While the Federal government was content with a hands-off policy, many local units were less cautious. Frontier communities, eager to increase their population, actively solicited immigration. In 1828 the Western Pennsylvania Emigrant Society appointed a committee of correspondence to provide information to prospective settlers. Europeans were told:

> The United States of America possess advantages which are not to be found in Europe, nor in any other quarter of the globe. Enjoying an almost total exemption from taxation, the whole earnings of the inhabitants ensure to their use and every emigrant who settles here can by industry and economy not only provide amply for the wants and comforts of himself and family, but render himself independent, provided he is careful in the first instance in choosing a proper situation.[1]

During the 1850's several Middle Western states maintained commissions for the purpose of encouraging immigrants to their respective states. Equally eager for large-scale immigration were shipping companies, speculators in land, and contractors seeking laborers for work on canals, railroads, and urban paving projects.

The eagerness of Europeans to learn about America resulted in the publication of scores of books and pamphlets. Travel books described American institutions and commented upon the opportunities offered by various parts of the country. Some condemned a society that they found unbearably crude; others—particularly those written by middle- and lower-class travelers—were lavish in their praise. Emigrant guides were available in almost every European language, advising the prospective migrant just what he should take with him, how he should secure passage, and where he should settle in America. Many of these were published to promote the interests of particular shipping or land companies.

Of great influence were the so-called "America letters." Thousands of immigrants wrote to relatives and friends in the old country, describing in careful detail just what they liked and disliked in their new homes. When such an epistle arrived, the whole neighborhood might congregate to hear it read. If it contained a long recital of disappointments, the villagers resigned themselves to enduring their present burdens a little longer. If the report was favorable, or, better still, if it was accompanied by a remittance of money as tangible proof of success, those who heard it were encouraged to undertake the great adventure

[1] Edith Abbott, ed., *Historical Aspects of the Immigration Problem: Select Documents* (University of Chicago Press, Chicago, 1926), 732–733.

themselves. Many of these letters circulated widely, either in manuscript or collected and published in books.

Although American political freedom received its due meed of praise, the real enthusiasm of the immigrants was usually for more prosaic things. From Paterson one wrote, "Now we get beef and pudding, tea and rum pretty regularly; to us who have long been half-starved in England, it appears like a continual feast." From Wheeling came the report: "The poorest families adorn the table three times a day like a wedding dinner—tea, coffee, beef, fowls, pies, eggs, pickles, good bread; and their favorite beverage is whiskey or peach brandy. Say is it so in England?" [1]

Two glittering prospects above all others determined Europeans to undertake the hardships of emigration—the low price of American land and the high price of American labor. Even though the United States government persisted in selling its land rather than in giving it away, it was a good bargain in European eyes. A German tenant learned with amazement that what he paid in one year's rent for a holding in Germany would buy a tract of land in America twice as large. Or, more tempting still, a German owner could count on selling his farm, using two-thirds of the proceeds for passage money, and still having enough money left to buy four times as much American land as he had originally owned. Although government land prices figured largely in these calculations, the wise immigrant learned to leave virgin tracts to the American pioneer. For the thrifty German there were better bargains to be had in purchasing the cleared acres of Americans who decided to move on. During the 1820's and 1830's immigrants bought the land of New York, Pennsylvania, and Ohio farmers who had caught the western fever; in the 1840's they had similar opportunities in Missouri, Illinois, and southern Wisconsin; in the 1850's, in eastern Iowa and Minnesota.

For immigrants too poor to buy land even at American prices, American wages were enticing. A traveler in 1835 reported:

> In a country where Nature is so bountiful and land so abundant and cheap, the wages of labour must necessarily be high. Accordingly, an ordinary mechanic obtains $1 per day, with board, including washing; and superior workmen, engineers, and millwrights, get from $2 to $3. Farm labourers are engaged at from $100 to $120 a year. Female house-servants obtain $1 in private families, and from $2 to $2.50 a week in hotels.[2]

Although such wages do not seem high by twentieth-century standards, by contemporary European standards they were very attractive. The same traveler calculated that whereas the American farm laborer's annual income would buy 222 bushels of wheat or 5,000 pounds of beef, the yearly pay of English laborers would buy only 70 bushels of wheat or 1,560 pounds of beef, that of Scotch laborers 62 bushels of wheat or 1,400 pounds of beef, and that of Irish laborers 30 bushels of wheat or 750 pounds of beef.

[1] *Ibid.*, 37, 40. [2] *Ibid.*, 269–270.

Hardship in Europe and opportunity in America could not result in large-scale immigration without the addition of another factor, cheap transportation. In 1817 steerage passage to America from the British Isles cost £10 to £12—a rate high enough to deter most poor Europeans. By 1832 rates had been halved. Passage on the swift packets could be had for £6; on the slower trading vessels the rate was about £4. This drastic reduction in rates was a consequence of the great expansion in American trade described in the preceding chapter. Since American exports to Europe consisted of bulky natural products and imports from Europe were mostly manufactured goods taking much less space, there was room aboard west-bound freight ships for many humble passengers.

The lines of trade determined the ports of embarkation for the emigrants. Since most of the cotton for English textile mills was shipped to Liverpool, this great northern port attracted thousands seeking cheap passage to America. Most of its vessels, carrying English manufactured goods as well as passengers, made New York their destination. An even cheaper passage to the New World could be had on ships returning to the Maritime Provinces and Quebec after carrying lumber to Irish ports. By this means many Irish emigrants reached Canada. Some settled there, and others either walked across Maine or took passage in some New England vessel engaged in the gypsum trade. In either case they were likely to end their journeys in Boston or some New England mill town.

The two greatest emigrant ports on the Continent were Le Havre and Bremen. The French port was the destination of many ships, carrying cotton for French textile mills. The freight wagons which transferred this commodity overland to Alsace often returned to Le Havre with loads of German emigrants from the Rhineland. Other Germans from this area began their long trip to America by driving their own heavily laden farm wagons to Paris, where they sold their horses and took passage on Seine steamboats to Le Havre. Most of the emigrants from this French port were carried to New Orleans, where they transferred to river boats and continued their journey to booming western cities like St. Louis and Cincinnati.

Bremen became a great port as a consequence of the extraordinary popularity of American tobacco in Germany and Central Europe. Concentrating their activities at Baltimore, the Bremen merchants handled half the tobacco exports of the United States. Since they needed cargoes for their westbound voyages, they offered attractive rates to emigrants. Thus was developed a route by which thousands of Germans secured passage to Baltimore, thence passing over the mountains to the Middle West. Hamburg merchants, eager to share in these profits, were handicapped by lack of an important direct trade with America. However, since Hamburg had close commercial relations with England, a favorite itinerary for German migrants became Hamburg to Hull by steamboat and thence by railway to Liverpool, where a passage to New York was readily obtained.

The old redemptioner system under which ship captains had transported penniless emigrants to America and then sold their services for a period of years persisted into the nineteenth century. But the speculators in servants were badly caught by the panic of 1819. Unable to obtain bids for the immigrant laborers, they lost a heavy investment in passage money and board. The organized trade in redemptioners never recovered from this disaster.

Even without this incentive passengers for the emigrant ships were eagerly solicited. At first captains handled this business directly, but eventually it became the custom for firms to contract for the entire steerage capacity of certain vessels and then to send their agents out to find emigrant customers. In an investigation of 1837 the methods of these agents were thus described:

> And this deponent further says, that there were hand bills placarded on every corner, tree, and pump and public place in the city of Dublin, and for forty or fifty miles in the surrounding country, stating, in substance, that the people were fools not to leave the country, where there was nothing but poverty staring them in the face. That laborers were so much wanted in America, that even women were employed to work at men's work—that work was plenty in America, and wages high, to wit, 9 or 10 shillings a day, British money, and his diet. And deponent further says that William Wiley of Dublin, the agent of Rawson and McMurray of New York, told this deponent that he, deponent, could get ten pounds of British money per month, and his diet as wages; that every one was on a perfect equality in America. . . .
>
> And this deponent further states, that there is one or more agent in every principal town in Ireland, who receives a commission for collecting and forwarding emigrants to Liverpool, where they take ship for America.[1]

In order to relieve taxpayers of the burden of supporting pauper families, English parishes occasionally raised the money to send the unfortunates overseas. German and Swiss governmental units sometimes followed a similar policy, as did Irish poor-law unions. Since this procedure often had its only result in transferring paupers from the almshouses of the Old World to those of the New, the United States government remonstrated with the foreign powers. New York and other states attempted to protect themselves against unwelcome arrivals by laws requiring shipmasters to give bond against their passengers becoming public charges, but the laws proved ineffective.

Most emigrants, however, paid their own passage. Those who owned land sold their property to raise the necessary money. Tenants and laborers used their petty savings or borrowed from relatives and friends. Often a family would transfer to America, one at a time. Placing his wife and children in the poorhouse, a husband would emigrate, find a job, and hoard his earnings until he could send for those he had left behind. Or a brother and sister, coming over first and both working, would send money back to the old country to pay the passage of father, mother, brothers, and sisters. Remittances from America to relatives in Europe rose to larger totals each year.

[1] Quoted in Robert G. Albion, *The Rise of New York Port, 1815–1860* (Scribner, New York, 1939), 341.

Under this combination of favoring circumstances immigration gradually increased in volume. An average of over 60,000 alien passengers a year arrived in American ports between 1832 and 1834. A check in American prosperity reduced the flow in 1835, but in 1836 and 1837 the annual arrivals were over 80,000. The panic of 1837 discouraged the movement only briefly. In the early forties the annual average was about 85,000. Then came the tidal wave. In 1846 the arrivals exceeded 150,000; in 1851 they were more than 400,000; in 1854 they reached their mid-century peak of 460,000. For the rest of the decade immigration was smaller, although still large by earlier standards. The panic of 1857 reduced the arrivals of 1858 to 144,000, the lowest since 1845.

To an extraordinary degree, European immigrants entered America through the funnel of New York. Of the 5,500,000 alien passengers arriving between 1820 and 1860, almost 3,750,000 entered at this port. New Orleans with 555,000 was second, followed by Boston, Philadelphia, and Baltimore in that order.

The Irish

The great mid-century migration from Ireland was the climax of many decades of tragic development. In the great nineteenth-century growth of population the Irish shared conspicuously. The number of inhabitants of the island, estimated to be 4,200,000 in 1791, reached 8,200,000 in the census of 1841. Since there was little industry except in Ulster, the teeming population derived its precarious living from the soil.

The old curse of absentee landlordism continued, resulting in a landlord-tenant relationship that was complex and often acrimonious. Tenants would sublet their land and subtenants would repeat the process, further complicating the web of agrarian relationships. Although many farmers rented 30 or more acres and made a decent living raising wheat and livestock for the English market, the number of petty holders increased dangerously. In 1841 over half the holdings were 5 acres or smaller; included in these were over 100,000 of 1 acre or less.

That families could subsist on such miserable little patches of soil was a tribute to the extraordinary nutritive values in the potato. About four million Irish were kept alive on a diet of potatoes supplemented only by an occasional bowl of milk or a few herring. To pay the rent, tenants with land enough—say 5 or 6 acres—depended on growing wheat for the English market. Poorer tenants dedicated to this purpose the annual proceeds from the sale of the family pig and such eggs as their few hens could be induced to contribute. An increasing number of poor Irish supplemented their income with a few weeks of migrant labor each year in the English grainfields.

Discouragement with economic and social conditions had been reflected in emigration ever since peace in 1815 had brought an end to one of Ireland's rare periods of agricultural prosperity. At first most of those who left were middle-class farmers disgusted with rising rents and taxes or artisans thrown out of work by the process of economic change. As late as the 1830's Protestants from northern Ireland contributed a large proportion of the emigrants.

Not until the late thirties was there any significant exodus of the poorer peasants. Up to this time Irish landlords sought to discourage emigration, believing that their income depended on a large tenant class. But landlord opinion shifted radically as English grain prices declined and the burden of poor relief became increasingly heavier. Logic seemed to demand a drastic reorganization of Irish agriculture to reduce tillage and to convert much of the acreage to pasture. Since such a process was impossible unless thousands of the petty holdings could be eliminated and the land consolidated, landlords were glad to have the poor leave the country. Evictions for nonpayment of rent mounted, and tenants who wanted to emigrate were sometimes assisted with advances of passage money. Not all the uprooted Irish went to the United States. Many became permanently established as agricultural laborers or industrial workers in England and Scotland; others migrated to Canada, Australia, and other British Empire countries.

Despite its growing volume the Irish exodus did not become a mass movement until 1846. So long as the potato remained a faithful friend, most of the peasants clung to their tiny holdings. But in 1845 the potato began its shocking betrayal of the poor. In common with other European countries Ireland suffered a disastrous invasion of the rot, losing from one-third to one-half the vital food crop. Serious blow though this was, the Irish peasantry might have recovered had not the curse returned the next year.

The "starving time," the blackest period of Irish history, prevailed in grim earnest during the following winter. With the successive failure of two potato crops the Irish economy collapsed almost completely. Pigs, cows, and chickens were ruthlessly slaughtered for food or died for lack of forage. Thousands of peasants, victims of slow starvation, died apathetically in their huts. Thousands more took to the roads, pathetically pleading for food in one village after another. Weakened by hunger, the famine victims were easy prey for an epidemic of typhus that ravaged the land. The British government undertook relief measures, but its program was too little and too late to prevent wholesale suffering.

Every American and Canadian ship that carried provisions to Ireland returned with all the emigrants who could crowd aboard. Emigration was no longer the result of deliberation and careful planning; it was panicky flight from a homeland that seemed doomed. To get funds, every resource was tapped. Money that had been hoarded for rent was diverted to this purpose; remittances from America were thankfully put to use; famine victims even begged along the highways to obtain the money for their escape.

The emigrants did not leave all heartbreak behind when the Irish shore line faded from sight. In the badly overcrowded ships plague was likely to break out at any moment. Disease harassed especially the ships bound for Quebec and

New Brunswick. Thousands died at sea; thousands more, mortally stricken, were carried from the ships to die in hospitals and rooming houses. The Emigrant Society of Montreal declared:

> From Grosse Island up to Port Sarnia, along the borders of our great river, on the shores of lakes Ontario and Erie, wherever the tide of emigration has extended, are to be found one unbroken chain of graves, where repose fathers and mothers, sisters and brothers, in a commingled heap, no stone marking the spot. Twenty thousand and upwards have gone down to their graves.[1]

When they arrived in their new homes, the survivors of the famine, penniless, emaciated, and demoralized, still had a painful period of adjustment ahead.

Ireland's plight remained pitiful. Not until 1853 were potatoes again a dependable crop, and many years were required for a recovery of the livestock. Unable to grow food or to pay rent, the small-tenant class was largely liquidated. Thousands emigrated; others gave up their holdings to become landless laborers or to take up their residence in the crowded poorhouses of the country. Those who were reluctant to leave the soil were often forcefully evicted for nonpayment of rent. To make sure that they would not return, the landlords ordered thousands of hovels to be leveled. The extraordinary extent of this agricultural revolution is shown by the census figures: between 1841 and 1851 holdings of less than 1 acre were reduced from 134,000 to 31,000; those of from 1 to 5 acres declined from 310,000 to 98,000.

Even more than the famine itself, this drastic reorganization of the agricultural system swelled the tide of emigration. In 1847 about 105,000 Irish immigrants entered the United States. The annual total rose each year thereafter until it reached a peak of 221,000 in 1851. Between 1841 and 1855 about 1,600,000 persons—almost one-fifth the entire population—migrated from Ireland to the United States. Although a large proportion of the newcomers were desperately poor, there were numerous representatives of other classes. Irish tradesmen and professional people, their status threatened by the misfortunes of the island, decided to make a new start in another country. Priests, ceasing to advise against emigration, themselves crossed the Atlantic to minister to the growing Catholic population of the United States.

The Irish tended to settle in the east-coast cities, where they entered the country. Of the 1,600,000 Irish-born in the country in 1860, more than one-half were living in the three states of New York, Pennsylvania, and Massachusetts. New York City alone had 203,000 Irish, Brooklyn had 56,000, Philadelphia 95,000, and Boston 46,000.

That immigrants from an agricultural country should huddle together in the slums of the new American cities seems paradoxical but is easily understood. During the great mid-century influx the majority of Irish arrived with few assets besides the ragged clothes on their backs. To buy canal and railroad tickets to

[1] Abbott, *op. cit.,* 120.

the interior would have been difficult, to purchase land impossible. Nor did the peasant from a 1-acre potato patch have the knowledge necessary to grow wheat and corn on a Middle Western farm. He occupied whatever shelter was available in the city and accepted the status of common laborer. Other factors holding the Irish in the cities were a tradition of gregariousness—of living near other Irishmen where weddings, wakes, and other convivial occasions were frequent—and the influence of the Roman Catholic Church, fearful of the spiritual danger of wide dispersion of the faithful among a non-Catholic population.

Despite this concentration in the cities a minority of the Irish found their way into the smaller towns and villages of the country. Wherever a large force of Irish were employed in the building of a canal or a railroad, many were likely to settle in towns along its route. Sometimes they were employed in local factories. Sometimes they used their earnings to purchase land and to become farmers. Particularly was this true in Illinois, where thousands established themselves on tracts purchased from the Illinois Central Railroad.

Many of the first-generation Irish lived in desperate poverty. In ramshackle tenements along dark and narrow alleys the new Americans carried on their struggle for existence. "The decay and dilapidation of the premises," reported a committee to examine New York tenement houses in 1857, "was only equalled by the filth of the inhabitants." The great migration created social problems of an alarming character. Of 131,000 paupers relieved or supported by the State of New York in 1852, over 70,000 were Irish. Of 20,000 persons convicted of crime in the state in 1858, over 11,000 were Irish. About 6,500 of the convictions were for drunkenness, and most of the others were for disorderly conduct, rioting, or assault and battery.

To many impatient Americans, drinking and brawling seemed inherent characteristics of the Irish race. Actually, intemperance was a bad habit that had fixed itself upon many poor peasants in the Old World, where whisky was cheap even when everything else was dear. The desperation bred by intolerable social conditions had also fostered the habit of violence—of occasional resorts to fists, sticks, and rocks against some opponent who could for the moment symbolize the whole hostile environment. That some of the Irish should have continued to drink and to brawl in America, where they still had to struggle against poverty, grasping landlords, and profiteering shopkeepers, was only natural.

More remarkable was it that the Irish should have adapted as rapidly as they did to their new environment. In elections and politics they participated enthusiastically from the beginning. When police and fire departments became professionalized during the fifties and the sixties, the Irish eagerly sought and obtained employment. Despite their distaste for abolitionism the Irish were heavily represented in the regiments of the Union armies during the Civil War. Economically their position improved. As later immigrants from other countries took up the tasks of common labor, the Irish contractor, superintendent, and foreman became common. The "shanty Irish" soon gave way to the "lace-curtain Irish."

The Germans

As Irish immigration began to fall off slowly after 1851, first place in arrivals passed to the Germans. For the entire decade of the fifties 951,000 German immigrants entered the country as compared with 914,000 Irish. Added to those who had arrived earlier, this gave the United States 1,300,000 German-born inhabitants in the census of 1860.

In the great German migration no single episode like the Irish famine dominates the story. Popular tradition emphasizes the abortive revolution of 1848 and portrays disappointed liberals by the thousand deserting autocratic Germany for democratic America. There is just enough truth in this to explain the coming of Carl Schurz and a number of other university-trained idealists, who became persons of influence in their new homes. Indeed, this type had been migrating since the period of reaction following the Napoleonic Wars, when America had gained such able intellectuals as Karl Follen and Francis Lieber. Another group of liberals found refuge in the United States after the political troubles of 1830. But such scholars and reformers were to be counted in the hundreds, while migrating peasants and artisans numbered hundreds of thousands.

Although every region and occupational group made some contribution, the bulk of emigrants were small farmers from Bavaria, the Rhineland, and other parts of southwestern Germany—an area where there were many unsettling economic and social developments during the first half of the nineteenth century.

As in Ireland, the pressure of rapidly increasing population was everywhere evident. Villagers eager to turn additional land under the plow divided up the common pastures and encroached upon the forests—thereby making life more difficult for poorer peasants who had to rent pasture land and to buy wood instead of enjoying customary rights. Through inheritance and sale land holdings became smaller and smaller. On their bits of precious soil the peasants carefully cultivated vineyards and grew potatoes. Although less precarious than the Irish, the south German agricultural system resulted in widespread suffering in years of bad crops.

Many shrewd German farmers, foreseeing serious trouble in the homeland, moved to America in the 1830's. Those who left were seldom desperately poor. Rather they were men who had made a decent living themselves in the old country, but feared that their children could not. Other German farmers elected to stay in their native villages and to increase their income by investments in drainage, better barns, more fertilizer, and more livestock. Overly optimistic, they were inclined to burden themselves with debts and mortgages that added to their difficulties.

Although most of the peasants were little interested in parliaments or elections, other problems of liberty were of intimate concern. Throughout much of Germany exasperating feudal obligations still survived. Peasants still had to answer the lord's summons for work; they still had to surrender a portion of their crops or contribute eggs, hens, calves, and piglets to their superiors. Similarly harassed by archaic restrictions were the artisans and tradespeople of the towns. Peasants and mechanics alike resented the obligation of military service. In the letters from America no passages made a stronger impression than those dealing with the lightness of American taxes and militia duty and the freedom Americans enjoyed to make a living without burdensome regulation by state or guild.

Favorable reports from Germans who had settled in America prepared the minds of the people for the activities of Bremen and Hamburg emigration agents who extended their field of operations throughout the country during the 1840's and 1850's.

As the machinery of emigration became more efficient, the urge to move to America became steadily stronger. During the 1840's the difficulties of the peasants multiplied. First too little rain and then too much injured the pastures and reduced the livestock, and the wine crop became scanty and poor in quality. The alarming potato blight visited Germany even earlier than Ireland. The winter of 1846–1847 was one of extreme hardship. Food was scarce throughout the country and prices were high. Government relief was better organized than in Ireland, but fear of starvation gripped many villages. A false report that the United States was about to ban immigration added to the panic. Determined to go to America while it was still possible, thousands of Germans crowded into Bremen and Hamburg, desperately trying to obtain transport. When they discovered that the facilities of these ports were overtaxed, many made their way to the ports of Holland and Belgium in search of passage.

On the peasants who remained behind, the weight of debt bore down with increasing oppressiveness. Many had to borrow to get through the hard times of the forties. Others mortgaged their land after 1848, when in many states the peasants were given an opportunity to purchase freedom from their feudal obligations. During the early fifties these debts proved the most persistent of all spurs to emigration. Poor crops meant defaults on interest and principal payments; defaults led to wholesale foreclosures. Many debtors avoided this final humiliation by liquidating their affairs and emigrating while a little could be salvaged from the wreck.

In the great exodus of the fifties both rich and poor participated. Some moved to America with a comfortable sum of capital to invest; some were so impoverished that their passage had to be paid by their communes. The majority fell between the two extremes. Records at New York showed that the average German immigrant of the middle fifties arrived in the United States with about $125 in cash.

Like the Irish many Germans settled in the coastal cities. In 1860 there were 120,000 German-born inhabitants in New York City, 43,000 in Philadelphia, 32,000 in Baltimore, and 19,000 in New Orleans. Sizable German elements were also to be found in the principal cities along the inland routes. By the Erie Canal and the Great Lakes the Germans made their way into cities like Albany, Buffalo,

Cleveland, Toledo, Chicago, and Milwaukee. Another line of German travel from Baltimore to the Ohio River left its mark on the population of Cincinnati and Louisville, and both this route and the Mississippi River one contributed to the 50,000 German-born in St. Louis. Many of the German town dwellers became established as workers in flour mills, breweries, tanneries, dye works, and the like, often rising to ownership of their own businesses. Others of the first generation were compelled like the Irish to live in the slums while they made a precarious living as laborers or petty artisans.

But the Germans to a much greater extent than the Irish became farmers. By careful management of the funds obtained from the sale of their property in Germany, they were able to pay ship passage and transportation charges from the coast to interior America and still have money enough to purchase modest-sized farms with enough equipment and stock to operate them. The German farmers were found in substantial numbers throughout a belt of territory that began in the East from New York to Maryland and extended west to Minnesota, Iowa, and Missouri. States with more than 100,000 German-born inhabitants in 1860 were New York, Ohio, Pennsylvania, Illinois, and Wisconsin. Distaste for slavery and inexperience with the staple crops of the region diverted the main stream of immigration from the South, but many Germans nevertheless found their way into this section. In several counties of western Texas German farmers composed almost the entire population.

"Latin farmers," who read the classics while they plowed, quoted Goethe as they ate, and played the violin for relaxation, were an object of curiosity to their neighbors, but they were less typical of the immigrant farmers than men of less refinement whose greatest interest was in tight barns, sturdy livestock, and well-manured fields. From the Old World the Germans brought habits and attitudes strikingly different from the careless indifference of native American farmers who assumed that there was always new land to be had when wasteful methods ruined the old. The Germans felt particularly at home in Wisconsin, where soil and climate resembled that of Germany. Settling in large numbers in the eastern and north-central counties, they practiced diversified agriculture and dairying. Milwaukee, the cultural center of these Wisconsin immigrants, became known as "the German Athens."

Although the charges of pauperism and crime, so often brought against the Irish, were seldom raised against the Germans, other characteristics occasioned criticism. Native Americans often accused the newcomers of atheism, socialism, and dangerous radicalism. This reflected the vigor with which a few of the intellectuals, usually political refugees, propagated their advanced ideas in the German-language newspapers. The radicals, however, exerted small influence. The majority of German immigrants were conservative—pious and orthodox in religion, patriarchal in family authority, and firmly devoted to private property and low taxes.

There was more truth in the allegation that the immigrants brought with them certain social customs that clashed with older American traditions. Sunday laws were circumvented by German theaters and restaurants, whose weekly "sacred concerts" consisted of comedies, Strauss waltzes, billiard games, yodeling, acrobatics, and tinkling beer glasses.

Whether beer and the German Sunday were to be considered improvements in American life depended on the point of view, but there could be little doubt that the example of people who enjoyed good food, good music, athletic contests, and the drama had a far-reaching influence, particularly in the cities. Also important were the progressive educational methods introduced by German intellectuals. Of the first ten kindergartens in the United States all but one were founded and directed by Germans.

Immigrants and Natives

The American magnet drew in many other groups besides the Irish and the Germans. From Norway, Sweden, and Denmark, a total of almost 73,000 persons entered the United States during the 1850's. The familiar combination of increased population, smaller holdings, and heavier taxes was at work, as was also the enticing propaganda of shipping firms and land companies. The largest Scandinavian immigration of this period was from Norway. The favorite route was by Norwegian ship to Quebec and thence by the St. Lawrence and the Great Lakes to Illinois and Wisconsin. From these earlier settlements secondary migration carried an increasing number into Minnesota and Iowa. While the Scandinavians were establishing themselves on the soil, many Jews were settling in the cities. Coming during this period usually from Germany, where they suffered from anti-Semitic laws and adverse economic conditions, Jewish immigrants were largely professional or tradespeople. A few brought sufficient capital to become large-scale merchants; more began as peddlers traveling through the country until they saved enough to establish a business in some town. The French element in the populataion—strengthened by the refugees of the French Revolutionary period and the colonists acquired with the Louisiana Purchase—received additional increments in later decades. Largely artisans and professional people, the French lived in the cities and larger towns. During the 1840's several thousand Dutch, hard hit by economic depression and scandalized by the growing liberalism of the state church, moved to America. Settling especially in Michigan and Iowa, these Hollanders were conspicuous for strict Calvinist piety, thrifty farming, and stubborn persistence in old customs.

One of the major immigrant streams—so dispersed and easily assimilated that it received little attention—flowed from England. The American Industrial Revolution provided opportunities for many English artisans with valuable knowhow. The decline of English agriculture, especially after the repeal of the corn laws in 1846, made a new start in the United States attractive to thousands of farmers. Mormon Utah received frequent additions from the converts won by

Mormon missionaries among the English lower classes. English capitalists, investing heavily in the Illinois Central Railroad, encouraged the settlement of English immigrants on the railroad lands. The number of English-born in the United States rose to a total of 433,000 in the census of 1860. The Scotch and the Welsh also continued to come, the latter showing a strong tendency to settle in the coal- and iron-mining districts of Pennsylvania and in the lead-mining regions of Wisconsin.

FIG. 22. *Landing from an Emigrant Ship.* From *Gleason's Pictorial Drawing Room Companion,* June 14, 1851. (*Courtesy of the Library of Congress.*)

So easily crossed was the long Canadian frontier that accurate immigration figures are lacking. The movement was not all in one direction. In addition to the exodus of American Loyalists into Canada during the Revolutionary War, there was a substantial movement of New Englanders and New Yorkers into Ontario and the eastern townships of Quebec between 1790 and 1812. During the 1840's and 1850's the stream was reversed, and thousands of Canadians took up land in Michigan and elsewhere across the border. Canadian sailors, lumberjacks, fishermen, trappers, and miners all participated in the opportunities provided in the rapid expansion of the American economy.

Immigrants from Europe suffered many hardships in their long journey. Sometimes they were victimized in their native villages by sharp operators who sold them tickets on nonexistent ships and railroads. On shipboard their lives were jeopardized by overcrowding, lack of sanitation, and poor food. The wise emigrant carried provisions with him, since the rations provided by the captain were seldom adequate. Steerage passengers had to do their own cooking on crude fireplaces or stoves on the open deck. Even in fair weather it was hard to get a turn at the fire, and during a nasty spell the unhappy passengers might have to eat uncooked food for days. Since the length of time required for the crossing was unpredictable, sailing ships often ran dangerously low on provisions and drinking water. Short rations and malnutrition increased the ever-present hazard of ship fever.

When the emigrant ship arrived at its American destination, it was met by a horde of runners, salesmen employed by lodginghouse keepers, and railroad companies. The system was thus described in the 1850's:

> Such a scene of confusion and violence, of cheating, and swearing, and noise, and plundering, I have never witnessed. The runners had invaded the ship when it was in the harbor; they almost forced the passengers to follow them; girls went off with suspicious-looking men—like thousands of poor creatures here who are forced every year into prostitution; men were selling tickets, were bargaining about luggage, and, of course, the strangers suffered; rowdies were threatening the peaceable, and it seemed as if the whole flock were delivered up to plunder. The whole tribe of runners, hackmen, and tavern-keepers were combined to fleece the immigrant and often to ruin or sell the virtue of the unprotected girls. The worst cheating was always with the luggage. Tickets would be sold at a fair rate, and then the luggage be charged by weight. Weight, of course, was an arbitrary matter with these strangers; so that the poor foreigner, what with his cart-hire, tavern-hire, and luggage expenses, would lose his whole little property before getting out of the city. . . . Frequently it would cost emigrants treble or quadruple what it should to get to their destination at the West.[1]

In 1855 the State of New York effected a major reform. Historic Castle Garden—first, a fort, and later, a concert hall—was now converted into an immigrant reception center. Despite their outraged protests runners were barred from the premises, and the incoming foreigners were given an opportunity to exchange their money at honest rates and to buy railroad, steamboat, and canal-boat tickets at fair prices. Castle Garden remained the place of entry for a majority of immigrants until 1890, when the Federal government took charge of the new arrivals at Ellis Island.

Many Americans were alarmed by the tide of immigration which rolled in upon their country. Some of the reasons for their anxiety have already been indicated. Ignorant and poor, the newcomers often became criminals or paupers dependent on public relief. Gangs of foreign laborers employed on the canals and railroads were involved in riotous feuds that had to be suppressed by the militia. The fact that foreign governments sometimes assisted paupers to emigrate or released convicts on condition that they leave the country caused excitable Americans to suspect that despotic foreign states were scheming to purge themselves and to weaken republican America by the same operation. "Have we not

[1] *New York Daily Tribune*, Nov. 10, 1853.

a right," protested a native orator, "to protect ourselves against the ravenous dregs of anarchy and crime, the tainted swarms of pauperism and vice Europe shakes on our shores from her diseased robes?"

Advocates of clean politics deplored the manipulation of the immigrant vote by corrupt politicians. Everywhere the foreigners were urged to complete naturalization as quickly as possible. Party workers from New York's Tammany Hall and similar organizations obtained citizenship papers in wholesale quantities from complaisant courts. One judge of extraordinary efficiency created 10,000 new citizens in two weeks. Through such fraudulent procedures immigrants might be herded to the polls within a few days of their arrival at the ports. Since the foreign vote was cast largely for the candidates of the Democratic party, the Whigs were particularly distressed by the election abuses. However, the Whigs were restrained from advocating drastic curbs by the hope that they could convert the new voters to their own party. Individuals with influence among the immigrants were able, therefore, to solicit bids from the rival politicians of both parties.

Also quick to take alarm at the growing influx of foreigners were the native wageworkers. In 1844 a newspaper writer argued:

> Our laboring men, native and naturalized, are met at every turn and every avenue of employment, with recently imported workmen from the low wages countries of the old world. Our public improvements, railroads, and canals are thronged with foreigners. They fill our large cities, reduce the wages of labor, and increase the hardships of the old settler.[1]

Nativist prejudice was multiplied many times by the circumstance that most of the incoming foreigners were Roman Catholics. Protestants were easily persuaded that the extraordinary volume of immigration proved the existence of what Samuel F. B. Morse described as a "Foreign Conspiracy Against the Liberties of the United States." The Jesuits, it was alleged, were artfully encouraging as many Catholics as possible to settle in the United States, especially in the Mississippi Valley. The alien horde was instructed to participate in politics and to extend Catholic influence in preparation for the day when the Pope himself might transfer his headquarters to the United States. The priest-dominated immigrants were thus portrayed:

> Rome's true minions chain them down,
> In ignorance from heel to crown;
> In hopes, perchance, that when the pope,
> Is forced from Europe to elope,
> He here may find a sovereign throne;
> And ready serfs to bend and groan.[2]

Anti-Catholic agitation brought about sporadic acts of violence and street fighting. Hostility both to the immigrants and to Catholicism motivated the sev-

[1] Quoted in Ray Allen Billington, *The Protestant Crusade, 1800–1860: A Study of the Origins of American Nativism* (Macmillan, New York, 1938), 200.

[2] *Ibid.*, 128.

eral "Native American" parties that sprang up during the late 1830's and early 1840's. Nativist political action quieted down, only to break out again in more virulent form when the Know Nothings captured control of several state legislatures in 1854 and 1855 and ran a candidate for the presidency in 1856.

Despite the sound and the fury little was achieved through legislation. A measure which would have barred all foreign paupers, criminals, idiots, lunatics, insane, and blind persons was debated by Congress in 1855 and 1856 but was rejected on the grounds that the Constitution did not delegate to the Federal government power to take such action. The problem was thus returned to the states, which had been struggling with it ineffectively for decades.

The Native Americans expended most of their energy in clamoring for more drastic measures. They wanted to require twenty-one years of residence before an alien could be naturalized and even then to bar naturalized citizens from public office. The Order of the Star-Spangled Banner, whose phenomenal growth in the early 1850's astounded politicians, dedicated itself to an effort "to place in all offices of honor, trust, or profit, in the gift of the people, or by appointment, none but native-born Protestant citizens."

"America for Americans" was a dangerously popular slogan. Nativism became a fad, as Know-Nothing candy, Know-Nothing tea, and Know-Nothing toothpicks enjoyed a lively sale. Fortunately, however, this narrow concept of Americanism was effectively challenged by spokesmen for a more liberal tradition. Foreigners who occupied almshouses, jails, and hospitals and foreigners who sold their votes for whisky were shown to be less representative of the immigrant majority than foreigners who improved the American soil, did backbreaking construction work, and took pride in their newly granted citizenship. "Laboring like slaves for us, they have built our cities and railroads; piercing the western wilds, they have caused them to blossom into gardens; taking part in our commerce and manufactures, they have helped to carry the triumphs of our arts to the remotest corners of the globe."

"Who are Americans?" asked the critics of nativism. Were the immigrants who disembarked at Plymouth and Jamestown in an earlier day not Americans? Americanism was defined as a character acquired, not by accident of birth, but by dedication of loyalties:

> The real American, then, is he . . . who, abandoning every other country and forswearing every other allegiance, gives his mind and heart to the grand constituent ideas of the Republic—to the impulses and ends in which and by which alone it subsists. If he have arrived at years of discretion—if he produces evidence of a capacity to understand the relations he undertakes—if he has resided in the atmosphere of freedom long enough to catch its genuine spirit—then is he an American, in the true and best sense of the term.[1]

[1] "America for Americans," *Putnam's Monthly,* V (May, 1855), 534.

Chapter 13. The Rise of Democracy and Nationalism

Between 1789 and 1861 the economic framework of American society was radically altered. The advance of the frontier and the growth of cities were twin forces working against continuance of aristocratic privilege and toward increase of political democracy. The revolution in transportation gave the country an economic unity that fostered a growing loyalty to the nation. Against these prevailing political tides, however, there were strong countercurrents running in the South, where economic developments had fostered the growth of a different social structure and different ideas of government.

The Federalists

Despite the strength of the party which had opposed ratification of the Constitution, the finality of the decision was generally accepted. Conservatives and liberals vied with each other in protestations of loyalty to the new instrument of government. Only rarely in subsequent American history have individuals or groups frankly avowed a desire to overthrow the Constitution and substitute some other form of government. However bitterly parties have contended for power and denounced the policies of their opponents, each has claimed to be the true supporter of the venerated document.

Nevertheless, the hope expressed by Washington, Madison, and other founders of the government that there would be no party strife under the new dispensation was soon dashed. Before the first President's term of office was over, a bitter political struggle was in progress. Old friends and colleagues were separated. Alexander Hamilton and James Madison, allies in the fight to secure the Constitution, parted company as did John Adams and Thomas Jefferson, friends since the days of the Continental Congress. In domestic affairs the new Federalist party supported the centralizing policies of Hamilton, which the Republican party [1] opposed. In foreign affairs the Federalists were anti-French Revolution and pro-English; the Republicans sympathized with the Revolution and were hostile to the English.

By birth and experience Alexander Hamilton was without those local loyalties which inclined so many Americans to suspicion of central authority. A native of

[1] Not to be confused with the present Republican party, founded in 1854.

the British West Indies, he began to make his own way in the world at the age of twelve, when he became a clerk in a mercantile house. Impressed by his precocity, friends sent him to the mainland colonies for schooling. While still a student at King's, he became immersed in the Revolutionary struggle. His extraordinary intelligence and executive ability brought steady advancement. At the age of twenty he was a lieutenant-colonel in the Continental army and the personal aide of General Washington. Three years later he married Elizabeth Schuyler, a member of one of the wealthiest and most influential New York families. After the war he became a successful lawyer with close ties to the conservative business community.

Becoming Secretary of the Treasury at the age of thirty-two, Alexander Hamilton at once made himself the most influential adviser to President Washington. In a series of brilliant reports he urged upon Congress the measures he considered necessary to set the national finances in order and to increase the country's prosperity. His *First Report on the Public Credit* (1790) argued that the issuance of new securities to the full amount of outstanding obligations would not only establish the credit of the new government but would aid the economic life of the country. "It is a well-known fact," he said, "that in countries in which the national debt is properly funded, and an object of established confidence, it answers most of the purposes of money." By making available a larger fund of capital, it would expand trade, agriculture, and manufacturing and lower interest rates. For a country where wealth would be increasingly represented by stocks and bonds, Hamilton's argument had prophetic importance. Similarly imaginative was the young Secretary's *Report on Manufactures* (1791), in which he argued that the government should encourage the growth of manufacturing through bounties and tariffs:

> Not only the wealth but the independence and security of a country appear to be materially connected with the prosperity of manufactures. Every nation with a view to those great objects, ought to endeavor to possess within itself, all the essentials of national supply. These comprise the means of subsistence, habitation, clothing, and defence.[1]

Countering Jefferson's objections that Congress had exceeded its powers in chartering a national bank, Hamilton formulated a persuasive argument for a broad interpretation of the Constitution. The national government, he conceded, was not sovereign in all respects but it was sovereign to the extent of the objects of its specified powers:

> It leaves, therefore, a criterion of what is constitutional and of what is not so. This criterion is the *end,* to which the measure relates as a *mean.* If the *end* be clearly comprehended within any of the specified powers, and if the measure have an obvious relation to that *end,* and is not forbidden by any particular provision of the Constitution, it may safely be deemed to come within the compass of the national authority.[2]

[1] *The Works of Alexander Hamilton,* ed. by H. C. Lodge (New York, 1903), IV, 135.
[2] *Ibid.,* III, 458.

The doctrine of implied powers thus laid down was Hamilton's most enduring contribution to the strong nationalism which he desired to promote.

Opposition to Hamilton was based less on dislike for his specific proposals than on fear of the general tendency of his policies. That the Secretary admired the monarchial and aristocratic institutions of England was notorious; that he had little faith in republicanism was equally well known. In the Philadelphia Convention he frankly acknowledged that he did not think favorably of republican government and appealed to those who did "to tone their Government as high as possible." His mistrust of the people was similarly frank:

> All communities divide themselves into the few and the many. The first are the rich and well born, the other the mass of the people. The voice of the people has been said to be the voice of God; and, however generally this maxim has been quoted and believed, it is not true in fact. The people are turbulent and changing; they seldom judge or determine right. Give, therefore, to the first class a distinct, permanent share in the government. They will check the unsteadiness of the second; and as they cannot receive any advantage by a change, they therefore will ever maintain good government. Can a democratic assembly, who annually revolve in the mass of the people, be supposed steadily to pursue the public good? Nothing but a permanent body can check the imprudence of democracy. Their turbulent disposition requires checks.[1]

Hamilton's political ideas were more indebted to the Tory philosophy of David Hume than to the Whig principles of John Locke. With Hume he believed that "in contriving any system of government, . . . *every man* ought to be supposed a *knave*; and to have no other end, in all his actions, but *private interest.* By this interest we must govern him; and, by means of it, *make him co-operate to public good,* notwithstanding his insatiable avarice and ambition." [2] This principle of self-interest helps explain both the full implications of Hamilton's financial policy and the bitterness of the opposition which resulted. By his funding operation Hamilton not only established the national credit but he secured for the new government the active support of wealthy bondholders who received interest payments. By the assumption of the state debts this material interest was transferred from the state governments to the central authority. Even more effective in giving wealthy investors a stake in the success of the Federal experiment was the National Bank.

In the popular mind John Adams, even more than Hamilton, represented the antidemocratic bias of Federalism. Pompous, vain, and tactless, the second President was accused of dangerous leanings toward monarchism. Yet Adams was in fact a more moderate Federalist than Hamilton. Despite his affection for the British Constitution the Massachusetts patriot was a sincere republican. To his cousin Samuel Adams he wrote, "It is a fixed principle with me, that all good government is and must be republican."

[1] Max Farrand, ed., *The Records of the Federal Convention of 1787* (Yale University Press, New Haven, Conn., 1911), I, 299.

[2] *Works of Alexander Hamilton,* I, 73.

Adams never pretended to believe in democracy. Such a basis for government required an optimistic faith in the essential goodness of human nature that offended his unsentimental intelligence. In their old age Adams and Jefferson carried on a delightful correspondence in which they compared their ideas. In one of these letters, Adams wrote:

> The first time that you and I differed in opinion on any material question was after your arrival from Europe; and that point was the French revolution. You was well persuaded in your own mind that the nation would succeed in establishing a free republican government. I was well persuaded in mine that a project of such a government, over five-and-twenty millions of people, when four-and-twenty millions and five hundred thousand of them could neither read nor write, was as unnatural, irrational, and impracticable as it would be over the elephants, lions, tigers, panthers, wolves, and bears, in the royal menagerie at Versailles.[1]

It was, indeed, the radicalism of the French philosophers and the anarchy of Shays's rebellion that impelled Adams to elaborate his conservative philosophy in the *Defence of the Constitutions.* When he saw that his name was often quoted in France as an advocate of simple democracy and that "the sympathies in America had caught the French flame," Adams, as he said, was determined to wash his own hands as clean as he could of "all this foulness." To Samuel Adams he wrote: "I think with you, that knowledge and benevolence ought to be promoted as much as possible; but despairing of ever seeing them sufficiently general for the security of society, I am for seeking institutions which may supply in some degree the defect." [2]

Fundamental to Adams's thought was his belief that every society develops a natural aristocracy which political realists must recognize and provide for in the institutions of government. In a letter to John Taylor of Caroline, one of his sharpest critics, Adams explained:

> Once for all, I give you notice, that whenever I use the word aristocrat, I mean a citizen who can command or govern two votes or more in society, whether by his virtues, his talents, his learning, his loquacity, his taciturnity, his frankness, his reserve, his face, figure, eloquence, grace, air, attitude, movements, wealth, birth, art, address, intrigue, good fellowship, drunkenness, debauchery, fraud, perjury, violence, treachery, pyrrhonism, deism, or atheism; for by every one of these instruments have votes been obtained and will be obtained.[3]

Viewing aristocracy in terms as unflattering as those in which he described democracy, Adams obviously did not wish to deliver the government to either. Hence his insistence on balancing one element in society against another. "The fundamental article of my political creed," he insisted, "is, that despotism, or unlimited sovereignty, or absolute power, is the same in a majority of a popular assembly, an aristocratical council, an oligarchial junto, and a single emperor. Equally arbitrary, cruel, bloody, and in every respect diabolical." [4]

[1] *The Works of John Adams,* ed. by C. F. Adams (Boston, 1850–1856), X, 52.
[2] *Ibid.,* VI, 415. [3] *Ibid.,* 457. [4] *Ibid.,* X, 174.

The last of the great Federalists was John Marshall. Appointed Chief Justice of the Supreme Court by John Adams in 1801, this Virginia lawyer dominated the highest court in the land until 1835. As a young judge he censured the Presidential conduct of Thomas Jefferson; as an old judge he combated the democratic tendencies of the age of Andrew Jackson. Of formal schooling in the law Marshall had only a modicum, but his forceful personality, keen intelligence, and flair for lucid expression made him the most influential of American jurists. Profoundly influenced by Hamilton, he had frequent opportunity to translate Hamiltonian principles into law.

Marshall, however, had no need to depend on other men's ideas. In his sturdy determination to uphold the authority of the national government and to protect property rights, he developed his own powerful arguments. Into the teeth of upholders of state sovereignty, Marshall hurled such ringing assertions of nationalism as this:

> That the United States form, for many, and for most important purposes, a single nation has not yet been denied. In war, we are one people. In making peace, we are one people. In all commercial regulations, we are one and the same people. In many other respects, the American people are one, and the government which is alone capable of controlling and managing their interests in all these respects, is the government of the Union. It is their government, and in that character they have no other. America has chosen to be, in many respects, and to many purposes, a nation; and for all these purposes her government is complete; to all these objects it is competent. The people have declared that in the exercise of all the powers given for these objects it is supreme. It can, then, in effecting these objects, legitimately control all individuals or governments within the American territory. The constitution and laws of a State, so far as they are repugnant to the constitution and laws of the United States, are absolutely void.[1]

Such Federalists as Hamilton, Adams, and Marshall served their country well. Although they had no faith in democracy, their aggressive nationalism helped to create a strong and stable government that could eventually be directed to democratic ends.

Jeffersonian Democracy

Since wealthy planters and small farmers alike feared Hamilton's favoritism for commerce, the Jeffersonian party gained support from all the agrarian classes. In view of the predominantly agricultural character of the country the Republican triumph of 1800 and the subsequent disintegration of the Federalists were almost inevitable.

Jefferson's election appeared to be a victory for narrow construction of the Constitution and states' rights. Arguing against the National Bank in 1791, Jefferson, then Washington's Secretary of State, had said:

> I consider the foundation of the Constitution as laid on this ground: "That all powers not delegated to the United States, by the Constitution, nor prohibited by it to the States, are

[1] *Cohens v. Virginia,* 6 Wheaton 414 (1821).

reserved to the States, or to the people." To take a single step beyond the boundaries thus specially drawn around the powers of Congress, is to take possession of a boundless field of power, no longer susceptible of any definition.[1]

Indignant at the passage of the oppressive Alien and Sedition Acts, Jefferson was the secret author of the famous Kentucky Resolutions of 1798 and 1799. In these he asserted that the Constitution was a compact entered into by sovereign states, that the Federal government could not be the final judge of the extent of its delegated powers, and that the states through their legislatures could declare null and void Federal laws that violated the Constitution.

As might have been expected, Republicans in power were less fearful of Federal authority than Republicans out of power. Although some of the more obnoxious Federalist laws were repealed, the Jeffersonian party itself resorted to implied powers in the purchase of Louisiana and in the enforcement of the embargo. The President's partial acceptance of a broad construction of the Constitution was seized upon by his critics as evidence of insincerity and inconsistency, but Jefferson's defense was persuasive:

To lose our country by a scrupulous adherence to written law, would be to lose the law itself, with life, liberty, and property and all those who are enjoying them with us; thus absurdly sacrificing the end to the means. . . . The line of discrimination between cases may be difficult, but the good officer is bound to draw it at his own peril, and throw himself on the justice of his country and the rectitude of his motives.[2]

Jefferson's greatness lay less in his statesmanship than in his fundamental attitudes toward government and society. He had that faith in the basic goodness of men which the Federalist leaders so notoriously lacked. "I am not among those who fear the people," he wrote in 1816. "They, and not the rich, are our dependence for continued freedom." To another correspondent he confided, "I believe with you that morality, compassion, generosity, are innate elements of the human constitution. . . ." But Jefferson's democracy was subject to some qualification. The ignorance and vice of the masses in Europe, he acknowledged, provided a poor basis for popular government; it was America's good fortune to have a society in which the people could be trusted with power. In one of his letters to John Adams, Jefferson explained:

With respect to aristocracy, we should further consider, that before the establishment of the American States, nothing was known to history but the man of the old world, crowded within limits either small or overcharged, and steeped in the vices which that situation generates. A government adapted to such men would be one thing; but a very different one, that for the man of these States. Here every one may have land to labor for himself, if he chooses; or, preferring the exercise of any other industry, may exact for it such compensation as not only to afford a comfortable subsistence, but wherewith to provide for a cessation from labor in old age. Every one, by his property, or by his satisfactory situation, is interested in the support of law and order. And such men may safely and advantageously

[1] *The Writings of Thomas Jefferson*, ed. by P. L. Ford (New York, 1892–1899), V, 285.
[2] *Ibid.*, IX, 279, 282.

reserve to themselves a wholesome control over their public affairs, and a degree of freedom, which, in the hands of the *canaille* of the cities of Europe, would be instantly perverted to the demolition and destruction of everything public and private.[1]

In his actual suggestions for broadening the franchise Jefferson did not advocate universal suffrage but favored giving the vote to all men who paid taxes or served in the militia. Besides this minimum stake in society he believed that the voters should have an elementary education. In *Notes on Virginia,* he wrote:

Every government degenerates when trusted to the rulers of the people alone. The people themselves, therefore, are its only safe depositories. And to render even them safe, their minds must be improved to a certain degree.[2]

Jefferson urged that Virginia establish a system of free public schools that would give all children an elementary education and a few of the "best geniuses" to be "raked from the rubbish annually" a grammar school and college education as well. "Enlighten the people generally," he wrote on another occasion, "and tyranny and oppressions of body and mind will vanish like evil spirits at the dawn of day."

Jefferson agreed with Adams that there was a natural aristocracy based on virtue and talents, but there was also, he said, an artificial aristocracy based on wealth and birth alone. "The natural aristocracy I consider as the most precious gift of nature, for the instruction, the trusts, and government of society. . . . The artificial aristocracy is a mischievous ingredient in government and provision should be made to prevent its ascendency." To put the aristocracy in a separate chamber of the legislature as Adams advocated seemed to Jefferson irrational. "I think that to give them power in order to prevent them from doing mischief, is arming them for it, and increasing instead of remedying the evil." Jefferson wanted the natural aristocracy of virtue and talents to govern, but he trusted democracy to bring this result:

I think the best remedy is exactly that provided by all our constitutions, to leave to the citizens the free election and separation of the aristoi from the pseudo-aristoi, of the wheat from the chaff. In general they will elect the really good and wise. In some instances, wealth may corrupt, and birth blind them; but not in sufficient degree to endanger the society.[3]

Jefferson's philosophy of government was one of extreme individualism. He wanted "a wise and frugal government, which shall restrain men from injuring one another, shall leave them otherwise free to regulate their own pursuits of industry and improvement, and shall not take from the mouth of labor the bread it has earned." Government should be as decentralized as possible: no function should be taken over by the Federal authority that could be safely left to the states; within the states as much responsibility as possible should be left to county and local units. Thus would every citizen become "an acting member of

[1] *Ibid.,* 428–429. [2] *Ibid.,* III, 254. [3] *Ibid.,* IX, 426.

the government" attached by the strongest feelings "to the independence of his country and its republican government."

The most inspiring aspect of Jefferson's thought was his resolute belief in progress and the possibility of human improvement. Institutions must not be static but must be modified in the light of widening knowledge. "Forty years of experience in government," he wrote in 1816, "is worth more than a century of bookreading."

I am certainly not an advocate for frequent and untried changes in laws and constitutions. I think moderate imperfections had better be borne with; because, when once known, we accommodate ourselves to them, and find practical means of correcting their ill effects. But I know also, that laws and institutions must go hand in hand with the progress of the human mind. As that becomes more developed, more enlightened, as new discoveries are made, new truths disclosed, and manners and opinions change with the change of circumstances, institutions must advance also, and keep pace with the times. We might as well require a man to wear still the coat which fitted him when a boy, as civilized society to remain ever under the regimen of their barbarous ancestors.[1]

The most systematic thinker among the Jeffersonian Republicans was John Taylor of Caroline—the same scholar-planter whom we met in an earlier chapter as a pioneer in the agricultural revolution. The deep love for the soil which Taylor demonstrated in *Arator* dominated his politics. No one was more disturbed than he at Hamilton's financial policies. In *A Definition of Parties; or the Political Effects of the Paper System Considered* (1794) Taylor contrasted the interests of the nation's 5,000,000 inhabitants with those of the 5,000 individuals who composed what he called "the paper interest."

Believing with the French Physiocrats that agriculture was the only truly productive economic activity, Taylor contended that property in bonds and stock stood on a different basis from property in land:

Political property is distinguishable from natural property. Land cannot be increased by law—paper money may. Land, being incapable of an artificial multiplication, cannot by increasing its quantity, strengthen its influence—with paper the case is different. Land cannot in interest be at enmity with the public good—paper money is often so. Land cannot be incorporated by law, or by an exclusive interest, into a political junto,—paper credit may. Land is permanent, paper fluctuating. . . . If the antithesis is just, the danger to be apprehended from the one, and the confidence which may safely be reposed in the other, evidently evinces that its legislative influence is an usurpation upon the constitution, respecting both the rights of numbers and the rights of property.[2]

Taylor's *An Inquiry Into the Principles and Policy of the Government of the United States* (1814) was a belated reply to Adams's *Defence of the Constitutions.* Taylor denied that aristocracies arose through natural causes; on the contrary, he believed that "aristocracies, both ancient and modern, have been variable and artificial, that they have all proceeded from moral, not from natural causes;

[1] *Ibid.*, X, 42–43.

[2] Benjamin F. Wright, Jr., *A Source Book of American Political Theory* (Macmillan, New York, 1929), 347.

and that they are evitable and not inevitable." Aristocracy in the earliest age had taken the form of a priestcraft created and supported by superstition; the aristocracy of the second age had been the feudal system based on conquest; the aristocracy of the present age derived its power from "paper and patronage." Each aristocracy had artfully shielded itself behind pious slogans:

The aristocracy of superstition defended itself by exclaiming, the Gods! the temples! the sacred oracles! divine vengeance! and Elysian fields!—and that of paper and patronage exclaims, national faith! sacred charters! disorganization! and security of property! [1]

Taking this view of aristocracy, Taylor naturally rejected Adams's system of a balance of three orders. To entrust national liberty to the exclusive care of three guardians, all composed of political power, said Taylor, would be as wise and prudent as to entrust a bag of money to three thieves on the assumption that they would never carry it off because they could not agree about its division. The true moral principle underlying the government of the United States was that of division of power between people and government and among the various levels of government:

The more power is condensed, the more pernicious it becomes. Divided only into three departments, such as king, lords and commons, it can easily coalesce, plunder and oppress. The more it is divided, the farther it recedes from the class of evil moral beings. By a vast number of divisions, applied to that portion of power, bestowed on their governments by the people of the United States; and by retaining in their own hands a great portion unbestowed, with a power of controlling the portion given; the coalescence of political power, always fatal to civil liberty, is obstructed. Small dividends are not as liable to ambition and avarice, as great dividends.[2]

Decline of Aristocratic Privilege

The extent to which an American aristocracy existed and should be recognized in the institutions of government—the issue so vigorously debated by John Adams, Thomas Jefferson, and John Taylor—was of more than academic interest. In the 1790's class distinctions of a most obvious character still persisted despite the exodus of the Tories and the breaking up of many pre-Revolutionary estates. The aristocrat wore a coat of fine scarlet or blue cloth and close-fitting doeskin or satin breeches. Instead of the sword which had once denoted superior rank, he now frequently carried a cane. Such a magnificent figure was in little danger of being confused with his social inferior who wore baggy pantaloons and a rough jacket. The gentleman's manners were finer, and his speech testified to the superior educational advantages which he enjoyed. He still occupied the best seats at church or at the theater and took for granted a due deference from lesser beings. In politics he still enjoyed primacy—both by custom and by constitutional provisions restricting the franchise to property holders.

[1] W. Thorp, M. Curti, and C. Baker, eds., *American Issues* (Lippincott, Philadelphia, 1944), I, 225.

[2] Wright, *op. cit.,* 353.

But the position of aristocrats became steadily less secure. The blurring of the old distinctions was reflected in men's styles. In the days of the sans-culottes French nobles learned the wisdom of wearing long trousers instead of the hated breeches. What began as a healthy discretion was eventually accepted as a style by English and American gentlemen. The new vogue was taken up early by those with democratic sympathies, slowly and reluctantly by the conservatives. The first president of the United States to dress in the new fashion was John Quincy Adams. Chief Justice John Marshall, stanch Federalist in this as in other things, wore breeches until he died in 1835.

Even more prophetic of future trends was the gradual change in suffrage and office-holding requirements. The frontier states of Vermont and Kentucky were the first to grant the franchise to all free, white adult males in 1791 and 1792 respectively. Thereafter the states of the West usually provided for manhood suffrage in their original constitutions. Of the older states New Hampshire adopted the democratic franchise in 1792, Maryland in 1809, and South Carolina in 1810. Elsewhere the conservatives delayed the blow for another generation—usually through timely compromise. In the Massachusetts constitutional convention of 1821, where John Adams, Daniel Webster, and Joseph Story opposed an extension of the franchise, the democratic forces had to be content with the substitution of a tax-paying requirement for the older property qualification.

Particularly brilliant, though doomed to failure, was the defense of aristocratic privilege at the New York constitutional convention of 1821. The issue was a proposed broadening of the franchise to include all male taxpayers, all who had served in the militia, and all who had worked on the public highways. Although the conservatives conceded the inevitability of the new requirements for most elections, they fought to preserve a $250 freehold qualification for electors to the state senate. Chancellor James Kent, one of the nation's most respected judges, warned:

> The apprehended danger from the experiment of universal suffrage applied to the whole legislative department is no dream of the imagination. It is too mighty an experiment for the moral condition of men to endure. The tendency of universal suffrage is to jeopardize the rights of property and the principles of liberty.

Chief Justice Spencer argued that the broadened franchise would give too much power to factory owners: "That man who holds in his hands the subsistence of another will always be able to control his will." Elisha Williams, one of the leading lawyers of the state, defended property qualifications as a stimulus to thrift:

> If you *bestow* on the idle and profligate, the privileges which should be purchased only by industry, frugality and character, will they ever be at the trouble and pains to *earn* those privileges? No, sir; and the prodigal waste of this incalculable privilege—this attribute of sovereignty—like indiscriminate and misguided charity, will multiply the evils which it professes to remedy.[1]

[1] *Reports of the Proceedings of the Convention of 1821, Assembled for the Purpose of Amending the Constitution of the State of New York* (Albany, 1821), 253–254.

Despite these arguments, the broadened franchise was adopted. Five years later the voters swept away the tax-paying qualification in favor of simple manhood suffrage.

Elsewhere the conservatives held out longer. In Rhode Island the property qualification for voting was still in force in 1841, when a faction led by Thomas Dorr attempted to secure manhood suffrage by extreme measures. The radicals convened a "People's Convention," drafted a "People's Constitution" which they submitted to the voters for ratification, and finally "elected" Dorr governor. The conservatives denounced all these proceedings as illegal and called out the militia. Dorr was captured and sentenced to life imprisonment for treason, only to be released the next year. In 1843 Rhode Island adopted a new constitution, which permitted native citizens to vote if they paid at least $1 annually in taxes but maintained a property qualification in the case of naturalized citizens.

Although the property qualification was retained until 1844 in New Jersey, 1850 in Virginia, and 1856 in North Carolina, the great victories had already been won. The narrow electorate of the old days had lost its monopoly and government had been placed on a democratic basis.

Jacksonian Democracy

When Andrew Jackson was inaugurated President on March 4, 1829, the event was regarded by both his supporters and his opponents as a significant victory for democracy. The capital city was jammed with enthusiastic visitors eager to see the popular hero assume his new honors. "The reign of King 'Mob' seems triumphant," wrote Justice Joseph Story. But to Amos Kendall, a Jacksonian editor from Kentucky, the demonstrations appeared natural enough. "It was a proud day for the people," he reported in his paper. "General Jackson is *their own* president."

Jackson was a puzzling figure both to his own generation and to history. John Quincy Adams described him as "a barbarian who could not write a sentence of grammar and hardly could spell his own name." This estimate revealed not only personal pique but a Harvard graduate's inability to appreciate the knowledge of one who had learned little from books but much from experience as frontier lawyer, judge, soldier, and planter. Jackson was no buckskin-clad cabin dweller. His Tennessee home was a stately mansion; his manners and bearing were those of a courtly old gentleman. The scholarly interest in political theory that had delighted John Adams and Thomas Jefferson was scarcely to be expected of Jackson. Nevertheless, the latter's state papers were often remarkably effective documents. Presumably their skillful phrasing should be credited to the able group of editors, lawyers, and politicians who composed the "kitchen cabinet," but the basic ideas bear the stamp of Jackson's own vigorous personality.

Much of the Jacksonian philosophy was borrowed directly from Jefferson. The latter might have written the following passage in Jackson's *Farewell Address* of 1837:

From the extent of our country, its diversified interests, different pursuits, and different habits, it is too obvious for argument that a single consolidated government would be wholly inadequate to watch over and protect its interests; and every friend of our free institutions should be always prepared to maintain unimpaired and in full vigor the rights and sovereignty of the States and to confine the action of the General Government strictly to the sphere of its appropriate duties.[1]

The Jacksonian argument against the National Bank echoed many of the ideas of John Taylor. In his *Farewell Address,* for example, Jackson said: "Recent events have proved that the paper-money system of this country may be used as an engine to undermine your free institutions, and that those who desire to engross all power in the hands of the few and to govern by corruption or force are aware of its power and prepared to employ it. . . ."[2]

But in its essence Jacksonian democracy was more thoroughgoing than Jeffersonian. The latter had pinned its hopes almost exclusively on the virtues of the farmer; the former broadened its faith to include the common people everywhere. Nor was it longer believed that the only function of the average voter was to use his ballot to entrust power to the natural aristocrat. Rejecting the idea that only a few men possessed the requisite ability for officeholding, Jackson said:

The duties of all public officers are, or at least admit of being made, so plain and simple that men of intelligence may readily qualify themselves for their performance; and I cannot but believe that more is lost by the long continuance of men in office than is generally to be gained by their experience. . . . In a country where offices are created solely for the benefit of the people no one man has any more intrinsic right to official station than another. Offices were not established to give support to particular men at the public expense.[3]

Jackson's respect for state sovereignty stopped short of the extremes to which Jeffersonian theorists had been carried. When South Carolina attempted to nullify the tariff in 1832, Jackson reacted in a spirit closer to that of Hamilton and Marshall than to that of Jefferson and Taylor. Warning the people of the recalcitrant state of his intention to use force, if necessary, to secure compliance with the law, Jackson said:

I consider, then, the power to annul a law of the United States, assumed by one State, *incompatible with the existence of the Union, contradicted expressly by the letter of the Constitution, unauthorized by its spirit, inconsistent with every principle on which it was founded, and destructive of the great object for which it was formed.*[4]

Similarly, while Jackson professed adherence to the old doctrine of the minimized state, the actual policies of his administration tended toward greater use of governmental power to protect the interests of the people. In attacking the

[1] J. D. Richardson, ed., *A Compilation of the Messages and Papers of the Presidents* (Washington, 1907), III, 299.

[2] *Ibid.,* 302. [3] *Ibid.,* II, 449. [4] *Ibid.,* 643.

National Bank as a citadel of privileged financial monopoly, Jackson stretched Presidential powers to their limit. Again and again he emphasized the Chief Executive's direct responsibility to the people. He disliked the Constitutional machinery for the election of the President, because it did not always allow the majority will to prevail. "To the people," he said, "belongs the right of electing their Chief Magistrate; it was never designed that their choice should in any case be defeated, either by the intervention of electoral colleges or by the agency confided, under certain contingencies, to the House of Representatives." [1]

FIG. 23. *Verdict of the People.* Painting by G. C. Bingham. Balloting was obviously far from secret in early nineteenth-century elections. (*Courtesy of the Boatmen's National Bank of St. Louis.*)

Jacksonian democracy impressed itself on sensitive observers less in the pronouncements of political leaders than in a certain electrical quality in the atmosphere. Foreign travelers found the issues of the day being energetically debated on railroad coaches and in the saloons of river steamboats. The national party convention made its first appearance during the campaign of 1832, and political speeches and parades aroused more popular interest and excitement than ever before.

To Michel Chevalier, a French traveler who watched a Jacksonian procession through the streets of New York in 1834, the event was curiously like a European religious festival. Instead of sacred standards the marchers carried portraits of Washington, Jefferson, and Jackson together with innumerable banners:

[1] *Ibid.,* 447.

Among these figured an eagle, not a painting, but a real live eagle, tied by the legs, surrounded by a wreath of leaves, and hoisted upon a pole, after the manner of the Roman standards. . . . The democratic procession, also like the Catholic procession, had its halting places; it stopped before the houses of the Jackson men to fill the air with cheers, and halted at the doors of the leaders of the Opposition, to give three, six, or nine groans. If these scenes were to find a painter, they would be admired at a distance, not less than the triumphs and sacrificial pomps, which the ancients have left delineated in marble and brass; for they are not mere grotesques after the manner of Rembrandt, they belong to history, they partake of the grand; they are the episodes of a wondrous epic which will bequeath a lasting memory to posterity; that of the coming of democracy.[1]

Paralleling the struggle of Jackson against the National Bank were many similar battles between local Democrats and monopolistic corporations specially chartered by the states. In the thick of the conflict was the *New York Evening Post,* edited by the poet-journalist William Cullen Bryant. Bryant's chief lieutenant, William Leggett, wrote editorials of wide influence, in which he vigorously espoused the rights of the workers and assailed the dangerous power exercised by the bankers through their issuance of bank notes.

More consistent in his democracy than many of the national leaders, Leggett risked excommunication from the party by criticizing Postmaster General Amos Kendall for permitting southern postmasters to remove abolitionist literature from the mails:

Neither the General Post Office, nor the General Government itself, possesses any power to prohibit the transportation by mail of abolitionist tracts. On the contrary, it is the bounden duty of the Government to protect the abolitionists in their constitutional right of free discussion; and opposed, sincerely and zealously as we are, to their doctrines and practise, we should be still more opposed to any infringement of their political or civil rights. If the Government once begins to discriminate as to what is orthodox and what heterodox in opinion, what is safe and what is unsafe in its tendency, farewell, a long farewell to our freedom.[2]

Out of the Jacksonian ferment sprang a variety of movements intended to improve the lot of the people. Workingmen's parties and trade-unions were one manifestation. Others were agitation for public schools, for free homesteads, for utopian socialism, and for the numerous humanitarian causes described elsewhere in this book.

State Sovereignty versus Nationalism

The philosophy of state sovereignty, whose excesses Jackson had rebuked in his Nullification Proclamation, grew stronger during the next generation. Originally the doctrine had not been peculiar to the South. Federalist New England, resenting the annexation of Louisiana, the embargo, and the War of 1812, had asserted

[1] Michel Chevalier, *Society, Manners and Politics in the United States* (Boston, 1839), 318–319.

[2] *A Collection of the Political Writings of William Leggett* (New York, 1840), II, 10–11.

states' rights as vigorously as had Kentucky and Virginia on the issue of the Alien and Sedition Acts. State sovereignty pronouncements were the instinctive defense for sections that found themselves in a minority on deeply felt issues.

First the tariff and then the slavery controversy transformed the South into the most persistent of these conscious minorities. Spokesman for the section was the great South Carolinian John C. Calhoun, the most skillful logician of his generation. A strong nationalist during his early political career, Calhoun abruptly shifted to an extreme states' rights position when he became convinced that the interests of South Carolina were threatened by the increasing power of protariff and antislavery men in the national government.

Calhoun elaborated his arguments over the course of twenty years until they took the final form of his *Disquisition on Government* (1850), published shortly after his death. Like Madison and Adams, Calhoun was acutely aware of conflicting economic interests, each striving to gain control of the government and use it for selfish ends. But the South Carolinian had no confidence in the conventional checks and balances. A dominant majority might capture all departments of the government and interpret the Constitution to suit its own purpose. This was the error in basing government upon the fallacious principle of the numerical majority. Against this method of taking the sense of the community, Calhoun elaborated his principle of the concurrent, or constitutional, majority. This, he said, "regards interests as well as numbers;—considering the community as made up of different and conflicting interests, as far as the action of the government is concerned; and takes the sense of each, through its majority or appropriate organ, and the united sense of all, as the sense of the entire community." [1]

As Calhoun clearly saw, the consequence of legislating in this way was to give to each interest or portion of the community a veto on the others. "It is this mutual negative among its various conflicting interests, which invests each with the power of protecting itself;—and places the rights and safety of each, where only they can be securely placed, under its own guardianship." [2] By this ingenious argument Calhoun was, of course, asserting the right of a state to nullify an act of Congress. This right, as he explained elsewhere in terms more comprehensible to the layman, was based on the principle that the Federal government was simply the agent for the states, which were the principals in the constitutional contract and had the power to repudiate the act of the agent whenever the latter exceeded its delegated powers. The South Carolinian denied that his principles would paralyze government and asserted that they would instead compel the conflicting factions to accept compromise—"the conservative principle of constitutional governments."

In their narrow sense Calhoun's theories have gone into oblivion with other defenses of state sovereignty, nullification, and secession. In a broader application, however, the idea of concurrent majorities is of interest to twentieth-century

[1] *The Works of John C. Calhoun* (New York, 1888), I, 28.
[2] *Ibid.*, 35.

political thinkers. American parties, struggling to formulate legislative programs that will command the support of enough different groups to secure enactment, have been interpreted as agencies for taking the sense of the community in concurrent majorities.

Calhoun's superior in forensic skill, if not in philosophical subtlety, was Daniel Webster of Massachusetts. Reversing the path of the Carolinian, Webster began his career as a defender of states' rights and ended it as the great champion of the Union. His most powerful rebuttal of the Calhoun doctrines of nullification and secession was delivered in a Senate debate of 1829. In the so-called *Reply to Hayne,* Webster thundered:

> This leads us to inquire into the origin of this government and the source of its power. Whose agent is it? Is it the creature of the State legislatures, or the creature of the people? . . . It is, Sir, the people's Constitution, the people's government, made for the people, and answerable to the people. The people of the United States have declared that this Constitution shall be the supreme law. We must either admit the proposition, or dispute their authority.[1]

The argument that the people rather than the states adopted the Constitution might be of questionable historical accuracy, but it had tremendous appeal to a democratic age. When the Civil War brought the rival theories of the Union to the supreme test, Abraham Lincoln rallied the North with such phrases as the following:

> This is essentially a people's contest. On the side of the Union it is a struggle for maintaining in the world that form and substance of government whose leading object is to elevate the condition of men—to lift artificial weights from all shoulders; to clear the paths of laudable pursuit for all; to afford all an unfettered start, and a fair chance in the race of life. Yielding to partial and temporary departures, from necessity, this is the leading object of the government for whose existence we contend.[2]

In Lincoln there was a happy blending of what was soundest in both the Jeffersonian and Hamiltonian traditions. The Illinois Republican venerated the great Virginian and placed the Declaration of Independence at the foundation of all his political ideas. Speaking of Jefferson and his coauthors, Lincoln said:

> They meant to set up a standard maxim for free society, which should be familiar to all, and revered by all; constantly looked to, constantly labored for, and even though never perfectly attained, constantly approximated, and thereby constantly spreading and deepening its influence and augmenting the happiness and value of life to all people of all colors everywhere.[3]

Yet because he believed so thoroughly in government by the people, Lincoln was prepared to use strong Hamiltonian measures to preserve the Union. He states admirably the problem with which he had to struggle:

[1] *The Works of Daniel Webster* (Boston, 1853), III, 321.

[2] Richardson, *op. cit.,* VI, 30.

[3] *Complete Works of Abraham Lincoln,* ed. by J. G. Nicolay and John Hay (New York, 1894), 331.

And this issue embraces more than the fate of these United States. It presents to the whole family of man the question whether a constitutional republic, or democracy—a government of the people by the same people—can or cannot maintain its territorial integrity against its own domestic foes. It presents the question whether discontented individuals, too few in number to control administration according to organic laws in any case, can always, upon the pretenses made in this case, or on any other pretenses, or arbitrarily without any pretense, break up their government, and thus practically put an end to free government upon the earth. It forces us to ask: Is there in all republics this inherent and fatal weakness? Must a government, of necessity, be too strong for the liberties of its own people, or too weak to maintain its own existence? [1]

Lincoln's reply is history. By vigorous exercise of the powers of the central government, he demonstrated that a republic could maintain its own existence and, in the long run, enlarge rather than contract the liberties of its people. Democracy and nationalism, which had often seemed opposing forces during the early days of the American nation, had at last been wedded.

[1] Richardson, *op. cit.*, 23.

Chapter 14. Religious Ferment

During the early national period the diversity of American religious life, already a matter of curiosity to Europeans, was intensified. American worship was influenced by the heady wine of political independence, by immigration, by the rise of the lower classes, and by the special circumstances of the frontier movement. In surveying the religious life of the period, we study almost every facet of thought. We learn not only how Americans responded to the ultimate mystery of the universe but what they thought of human personality, of principles of government, and of such institutions as private property, marriage, and slavery.

Impact of the Revolution

All the churches felt the lash of war. The Anglicans suffered particularly. The great exodus of Tories took most of the missionaries of the Venerable Society and three-quarters of the Virginia clergy. Even the clergymen who remained in America found themselves suspected of Loyalist sympathies, often unjustly, for the patriot cause had warm partisans among the Anglican clergy and laity. The Methodists—who still considered themselves Anglicans—shared in the unpopularity of the parent church and had to bear an additional burden in John Wesley's well-publicized opinions upholding the King and condemning colonial resistance. Quakers and other opponents of war like the Mennonites and the Moravians were compelled to endure the taunts of their neighbors. Presbyterian difficulties were of a different kind. Their energy in the American cause made them special targets for British wrath, and some fifty of their churches were destroyed during the war. The Congregationalists suffered in prestige. In an age when authority was being uprooted, the privileges of the established order in New England could not escape attack. Baptists and other dissenting groups began to agitate energetically for complete religious equality.

Although the Congregationalists clung to their special position for another generation, the Church of England establishments were too vulnerable to survive. In most cases they disappeared without a struggle during the early years of the Revolution. Although the Anglicans fought to preserve their privileges in Virginia, it was a rear-guard action doomed to failure. The earliest and most aggressive foes of the establishment were the Baptists, but they found active allies among the Presbyterians, the Methodists, and the German sects. Liberal Anglicans like Thomas Jefferson and James Madison accepted leadership in the movement. The first blow to the old order came in 1776, when dissenters were exempted from taxes for the support of the Church of England. Three years later the legislature repealed the laws providing for the support of the clergy out of public funds. Even with its purse strings cut, the old church clung to a few vestiges of power. Dissenting ministers were still forbidden to perform marriage ceremonies, and Anglican vestries retained certain public functions. Bills that would completely separate church and state ran into determined opposition. Patrick Henry and Richard Henry Lee, more conservative in religion than in politics, advocated a general assessment whose proceeds should be applied either to the denomination of the taxpayer's choice or to education. But Madison and Jefferson opposed this compromise, and finally in 1786 the great Virginia Statute for Religious Freedom was passed. Declaring in the ringing words of Thomas Jefferson that "Almighty God hath created the mind free" and that all attempts to influence it by temporal punishments or civil disabilities "are a departure from the plan of the Holy Author of our religion, who being Lord of both body and mind, yet chose not to propagate it by coercions on either," the law required that all men be "free to profess, and by argument to maintain, their opinions in matters of religion and that the same shall in no wise diminish, enlarge or affect their civil capacities."

At the national level the separation of church and state was written into the Federal Constitution without serious controversy. Indeed the diversity of religion among the original states made this policy an obvious necessity. Unobtrusively placed near the end of the original document were the words, "No religious Test shall ever be required as a Qualification to any Office or public Trust under the United States." In 1791 a more explicit guarantee was added in the First Amendment, which provided that "Congress shall make no law respecting an establishment of religion, or prohibiting the free exercise thereof. . . ."

In forbidding religious tests or church establishments, the Federal government went further than most of the states. Several of the original state constitutions contained provisions which denied the right to hold public office to such groups as Catholics, Jews, Unitarians, or atheists, and the Puritan clergy continued to enjoy support from taxation throughout most of New England. But one after another, these provisions were altered until the removal of public support from the Congregational Church in Massachusetts in 1834 signaled victory for the American principle of separation of church and state.

It was not to be expected that Americans, exulting in their political independence, would continue to defer to the rule of English bishops and spiritual leaders. First to demand new organization were the Methodists. Before the Revolutionary War authority over the movement had rested in the strong hands of John Wesley and trusted lieutenants whom he sent out from England. Although most of these left during hostilities, Francis Asbury remained, patiently guiding American Methodists during difficult days. With the return of peace Wesley sought to reestablish his authority, but his American followers were restless. They believed that a movement directed from England could never accommodate itself successfully to the new situation. They objected particularly to the Wesley policy which forbade Methodist lay preachers to administer the sacraments. Since all but a few of the Anglican clergy had adopted an attitude of hostility toward these stepchildren of the Church, few Methodists could secure baptism or communion.

To meet these problems, Wesley adopted a bold program. He sent Dr. Thomas Coke to America with directions that he and Asbury should serve as bishops. Wesley bestowed episcopal authority upon Coke, and Coke was authorized in turn to consecrate Asbury. The two were then to ordain other American preachers. This assumption of the power to ordain was the most radical step of Wesley's career, marking the long-delayed separation of the Methodist movement from the Church of England. The American preachers approved Wesley's general program, but they quietly rejected the idea that the English leader could choose bishops for them. Instead they met at Baltimore in the so-called Christmas Conference of 1784, where they organized the Methodist Episcopal Church and formally elected Coke and Asbury bishops.

For no group did separation from England involve greater problems than for the Anglicans. American bishops were now imperative, and the Connecticut clergy took the initiative in electing Samuel Seabury to the episcopal office. In 1784 the new bishop went abroad seeking consecration from the dignitaries of the Church of England. When the latter refused on the ground that existing statutes did not permit them to exercise this function for territory no longer under the British flag, Seabury turned to the so-called "nonjuring" bishops of Scotland, who willingly accommodated him. The American church gained two additional bishops when Samuel Provoost and William White were elected by the clergy of New York and Pennsylvania respectively. By this time Parliament had removed the obstacles to the recognition of American churchmen, and in 1787 Provoost and White were consecrated at London. With the purity of the apostolic succession thus insured, the American bishops were able to confirm children, to ordain clergymen, and to consecrate additional bishops without help from abroad. Through a series of conventions the church was nationally organized as the Protestant Episcopal Church in the United States of America.

The Roman Catholic Church also had to recognize the new political situation. Before the Revolution the American clergy had been under the rule of the Vicar Apostolic in London. In 1783 a group of priests met at Whitemarsh, Maryland, and drafted a petition to the Pope for the appointment of a superior to head the American missions. The Vatican responded by assigning Father John Carroll of Maryland to this post in 1784. In 1790 Carroll became the first American bishop of his church, and in 1808 he was elevated to the rank of archbishop.

Despite these organizational achievements the churches seemed to be losing ground during the last decades of the eighteenth century. Skepticism and Deism were powerfully stimulated by the Revolution. When Ethan Allen, the Vermont hero, attacked organized religion in his little book, *Reason, the Only Oracle of Man* (1784), New England clergymen were deeply shocked. But Allen's work had too small a circulation to exert much influence. Much more important was Thomas Paine's *The Age of Reason* (1794), a popularization of Deism that supplied many a college youth and village skeptic with arguments against orthodox faith. The blind ex-minister and lawyer Elihu Palmer familiarized hundreds with the Deist arguments through his lectures and his book *Principles of Nature* (1802). Particularly in New England the religious issue became unfortunately involved in politics. Since the Congregational ministers were usually enthusiastic Federalists, thundering against the French Revolution and Thomas Jefferson from their pulpits, the Republicans were likely to become defiant worshipers of reason.

Particularly distressing to the pious was the decay of religion in the colleges. In 1794 the students at Harvard were described as diseased in imagination on account of the French Revolution and generally skeptical. The Dartmouth students were unruly, lawless, and without the fear of God. Only three or four Princeton students made any profession of piety. William and Mary was "a hotbed of infidelity." Yale was "in a most ungodly state" with the college church almost extinct and the students addressing each other as Voltaire and Rousseau.

Even more striking than the vogue of Deism was the drift from orthodoxy within the churches. Congregationalists in eastern Massachusetts were quietly abandoning the old Calvinist tenets. Thinking back to the decade before the Revolution, John Adams could remember five ministers of Boston and its suburbs who had even then adopted Unitarian beliefs. "Among the laity," he added, "how many could I name, lawyers, physicians, tradesmen, farmers!" In 1785 King's Chapel, an Anglican church before the Revolution, revised its liturgy to omit all references to the Trinity.

Not only predestination but hell itself fell into disfavor. In 1784 a book by Charles Chauncy of Boston's historic First Church argued that since Christ had died for all, all would be saved. The idea that a good God would not doom any of his children to everlasting punishment appealed to the rising humanitarianism of the day, and universalist sentiments were widespread. In 1779 a Universalist church was organized at Gloucester, Massachusetts, by the English clergyman John Murray, and the greatest of American Universalists, Hosea Ballou, began his career in 1794.

The Second Awakening

The law of action and reaction works with startling effect in the field of religion. Late eighteenth-century Deism, skepticism, and heterodoxy so alarmed the pious that they were spurred to vigorous counteractivity. The New Divinity of Dr. Samuel Hopkins of Newport, Rhode Island, restored vigor to evangelical Calvinism in the Jonathan Edwards tradition. Hidden in theological abstractions like Hopkins's doctrines of general atonement and disinterested benevolence was moral dynamite. Since Christ had died not for a privileged few but for sinners everywhere, there was a strong new urge to Christian activity—to the preaching of salvation to Negroes, Indians, the heathen of other lands, and the underprivileged everywhere. During the 1790's many of the New England churches again reverberated with earnest evangelical sermons. The results were to be seen in new converts, new churches, and a new passion for the promotion of schools and missions. When Timothy Dwight became president of Yale in 1795, he began such an earnest ministry to his students that the campus became as renowned for piety as it had shortly before been for skepticism. Since similar efforts were made elsewhere, the college revival became an oft-repeated phenomenon of the early nineteenth century.

But even in New England the evangelical activities of the Congregationalists were overshadowed by those of other groups. The Baptists were everywhere active and grew with particular rapidity in the South. The Methodists had their initial success in Virginia and its neighboring states but soon extended their conquests to other sections. The great Methodist itinerant Jesse Lee preached his first New England sermon on Boston Common in 1790, and within six years the new denomination numbered 3,000 members in this area alone. No denomination exceeded the Presbyterians in zeal for converts. Like Log College in an earlier generation Virginia's Hampden-Sidney and Washington Colleges provided a supply of enthusiastic Presbyterian evangelists.

The Second Awakening revealed its true force only after it crossed the Appalachians. Its advance agent was the Presbyterian James McGready, who migrated from North Carolina to Logan County, Kentucky, in 1796. Since no building would hold the crowds attracted by his preaching, McGready had to hold meetings in clearings in the forest. The frontiersmen who drove in from miles around often remained several days, living in their wagons or in temporary shelters. Thus evolved the camp meeting—an evangelical institution eagerly adopted by Baptists and Methodists.

In August, 1801, at Cane Ridge, Kentucky, occurred the greatest of the frontier revivals. The meeting had been carefully planned by Barton W. Stone, a Presbyterian convert of McGready, who had also been drawn from North Carolina to Kentucky. A large tent had been erected in the center of a great clearing, around which regular streets had been laid out for the tents and lodges of the visitors. But the success of the meeting exceeded all expectations. Over a thousand wagons were counted on the grounds, and the crowd was equally remarkable for its size and its wild emotionalism. The impression made upon one participant is thus recorded:

> We arrived upon the ground and here a scene presented itself to my mind not only novel and unaccountable, but awful beyond description. A vast crowd, supposed by some to have amounted to 25,000 was collected together. The noise was like the roar of Niagara. The vast sea of human beings seemed to be agitated as if by a storm. I counted seven ministers, all preaching at one time, some on stumps, others in wagons, and one . . . was standing on a tree which had, in falling, lodged against another. Some of the people were singing,

others praying, some crying for mercy in the most piteous accents, while others were shouting most vociferously. While witnessing these scenes, a peculiarly strange sensation, such as I had never felt before, came over me. My heart beat tumultuously, my knees trembled, my lip quivered, and I felt as if I must fall to the ground. A strange supernatural power seemed to pervade the entire mass of mind there collected. I became so weak and powerless that I found it necessary to sit down. Soon after I left and went into the woods, and there I strove to rally and man up my courage.[1]

FIG. 24. *Camp Meeting at Eastham, Massachusetts.* From *Gleason's Pictorial Drawing Room Companion,* Sept. 13, 1851. Although originally characteristic of frontier religion, the camp meeting became highly popular in the East as well. (*Courtesy of the Library of Congress.*)

That 25,000 were actually present may be doubted, since other estimates range from 10,000 to 20,000, but the wide variance of the figures simply emphasizes the fact that the Kentucky revivals became legendary. Exaggerated stories spread through the country and encouraged similar, if smaller, revivals elsewhere.

Frontier evangelism was extraordinary for the visible symptoms with which many of the converts got religion. Contemporary specialists classified these, distinguishing the "falling exercise"—which was most common—from the jerking, rolling, running, dancing, and barking "exercises." Although the revivalists defended this emotionalism as a mighty work of God, more conservative clergymen condemned it as unhealthy hysteria and advocated quieter methods for the salvation of souls. They were likewise distressed by the tendency of the camp meet-

[1] *Autobiography of the Reverend James B. Finley,* ed. by W. P. Strickland (Cincinnati, 1855), 166–167.

ings to attract dissolute characters. Ironically, on the very occasions when so many souls were being noisily saved, others were being lost through intoxication and seduction.

The drama of the camp meetings overshadowed important religious work of a very different character. Hundreds of preachers of every denomination were at work organizing churches in every backwoods community. The influence of these men was almost wholly good. Life on the frontier was rough, and the churches provided a steadying influence. The early records well illustrate the function that was performed. Members were expelled or suspended for drunkenness and immorality; gossipers who slandered their neighbors were rebuked; men who quarreled with each other were induced to accept the mediation of their fellow churchmen. In a more settled society these activities would have been meddlesome and unnecessary, but in pioneer communities the disciplinary action of the churches had a healthy influence. Religion was a civilizing force, not only imposing minimum standards of personal conduct, but eventually dotting the new states with academies and colleges.

The degree of success with which the various denominations adjusted to the challenge of the West largely determined their future importance. Some groups operated under obvious handicaps. The Episcopalians attempted to plant missions on the frontier but usually with small results. As an observer in Arkansas reported: "There are but two or three ministers of this denomination in the State. These, I believe, are good men & are trying to do good. But their whole system of worship is incongruous to the genius of the people of Arkansas. They have too much of formalism ever to do much good or harm here." [1]

The Congregationalists entered the competition for souls with two great advantages. They were the most numerous denomination at the end of the colonial period, and New Englanders participated in the westward movement in numbers unsurpassed by any other group. But Congregationalism proved less successful on the frontier than might have been expected. The denomination was in some respects provincial, more intent on retaining its prerogatives in New England than in expansion. Its college-trained clergy preferred the comfortable pastorates of the East to the struggling posts of the West. Its traditional prejudice against central organization also hampered its expansion into new territory. Congregationalists in the West tended to accept Presbyterianism. Since the two denominations had always agreed closely in creed, many isolated Congregational ministers gladly associated themselves with the presbytery of their area. This tendency, apparent among New Jersey Congregationalists a century earlier, was intensified by the Plan of Union of 1801, an agreement between the Presbyterians and the Connecticut Congregationalists for cooperation in the new territories. While Congregational churches might call Presbyterian pastors to their pulpits or Presbyterian churches call Congregationalists, the right of local churches to keep their

[1] William Warren Sweet, ed., *Religion on the American Frontier, 1783–1840,* Vol. II, *The Presbyterians* (University of Chicago Press, Chicago, 1936), 698.

own form of government and the right of the ministers to associate with synods or ministerial associations of their own denomination were assured. Although fair in its stipulations, the Plan of Union worked out largely to the advantage of the Presbyterians.

The Presbyterians enjoyed a great initial success on the frontier. Not only had the denomination grown rapidly during the eighteenth century, but its growth was greatest in western Pennsylvania, Virginia, and North Carolina, areas strategically located for expansion into Kentucky and Ohio. Another great asset was the prominence of the Scotch-Irish in the frontier movement. Presbyterian clergymen migrating to new settlements were almost certain to find families whose background was Presbyterian, however far they might have strayed from the faith. These factors, together with the militancy of the church and the windfall gained from migrating Congregationalists, explain the rapid growth of the Presbyterian Church during the first third of the nineteenth century. In 1829 it had a membership of 173,329, organized in 19 synods and 98 presbyteries. But as a frontier religion Presbyterianism eventually displayed certain weaknesses. Its rigid educational standards resulted in a scarcity of ministers, and many of those available were too freighted with book learning to please frontier congregations. Nor did frontiersmen accept without question the old Calvinist doctrines. Human depravity and predestination became increasingly unpopular, and the tendency for Presbyterian revivalists to temper these doctrines to make them more palatable to the democratic West caused serious dissension within the church. Nor was the heavy Congregationalist influx into Presbyterian ranks an unmixed blessing, since the New Englanders displayed a preference for mild Calvinism over the older statements and were guilty of many irregularities in their local church government. Dissent and schism seriously embarrassed the Presbyterians after 1830.

The Baptists were not a numerous group at the time of the Revolution, but they were growing rapidly. They did not lack for preachers, since the only requirements were evidence of true conversion and a "gift" for expounding which was acceptable to fellow church members. Nor was expansion of the denomination dependent upon fund raising, since the typical Baptist preacher of the day supported himself through farming. Church members helped him with his planting and harvesting and occasionally gave him something for marriages and funerals, but regular salaries were infrequent. Most Baptist ministers preached a mild form of Calvinism, but individual churches were permitted to fix their own creeds. In any case, the strength of the church was in its complete democracy and in its appeal to the poorer classes. In an age of emotional religion the dramatic character of baptism by immersion was a great asset. An English traveler was fascinated to see this rite performed in a Rhode Island river in January when the thermometer stood at 10 below zero. The ice, a foot thick, was cut through but had to be kept open with sticks and staves while the minister and the converts stood in the icy water for about ten minutes. For the enthusiast this was a hard religion and a good one.

Most remarkable of all was the growth of the Methodists. This new denomination, which had only 15,000 members in 1785, became the largest Protestant body in pre-Civil War America. With 1,068,000 members in 1844 the Methodists outnumbered the Baptists, their nearest rivals, by over 400,000. In part, the church's success resulted from its democratic Arminian doctrine, promising salvation to all who would believe. More important was its ceaseless activity. During the forty-five years of Bishop Asbury's American ministry, his travels over rough trails and roads were scarcely interrupted. Typical Methodist preachers of the early nineteenth century were the circuit riders, who were responsible for twenty or thirty "preaching places" along routes that often extended over 100 miles. These rugged clergymen conducted services every day of the week. Since church buildings were rare on the frontier, they preached in schoolhouses, courthouses, and private homes. At night they accepted the hospitality of church members, often too poor to offer more than a supper of corn-meal mush and a bed of boughs on the cabin floor. Like Asbury most circuit riders were unmarried—not because the church required a celibate clergy, but because neither the salary nor the hard life of the preachers made marriage feasible.

Since the circuit rider often visited the church groups under his charge only once in four or five weeks, much responsibility had to be placed in the hands of local preachers and class leaders. These laymen not only conducted weekly services but maintained careful supervision over their fellow members—observing "not only how each person observes the outward rules, but how he grows in the knowledge and love of God." The extensive use of lay preachers permitted the Methodists, like the Baptists, to spread their activities over new territories as fast as they were opened up.

The religious revival found many expressions. All denominations attempted missionary work among the Indians, widening their activities until by the 1830's they extended across the continent into Oregon. But the aspiration to save the souls of the heathen could not be exhausted within continental America. News of English missionary efforts together with the expansion of commerce opened American eyes to unnumbered millions who had never heard the name of Christ. In 1806 five students at Williams College secretly dedicated themselves to the cause of foreign missions. After their graduation from Andover Theological Seminary they appealed to the Massachusetts Congregationalists for support in their resolve. In 1810 the American Board of Commissioners for Foreign Missions was formed, and two years later the first American missionaries took ship at Salem for India. In 1820 the American Board began a work in the Hawaiian Islands which was so remarkably effective that it played no small part in bringing this territory under the American flag seventy-eight years later. Since the Presbyterian and Dutch Reformed churches soon decided to support the work of the American Board, there appeared some hope that Protestant missionary work would be free from the denominational rivalry so apparent on the domestic front. But this phase was short-lived. Baptists, Methodists, and other groups soon organized their own programs, and in time the American Board even had to contend with a separate Presbyterian missionary organization.

Although this contact with America had a great effect upon the nations visited by the missionaries, it had perhaps even more influence on the Americans themselves. Locally organized bodies like the Congregationalists and the Baptists developed their first national organizations. Women, whose role had been a silent one in most religious groups, found a field for activity in the organization of "mite societies," through which each member contributed a cent a week to the good cause. These groups also devoted themselves to studying the countries where the missionaries were working. The number of books and magazines devoted to missions was extraordinary, providing thousands of Americans with information—broadening even though distorted—about the civilizations of distant lands.

Since all Protestant bodies placed great emphasis on individual study of the Scriptures, general support was available for the activities of the American Bible Society, organized in 1816. Also acceptable to most groups was the voluminous literature published by the American Tract Society, which was founded in 1825 along lines already familiar in England. Evangelical piety found additional outlets in crusades for various reforms like temperance and the abolition of slavery—activities so characteristic of these years that a separate chapter will be devoted to them.

Revivalism was a flame that blazed high, burned down to glowing embers, and then blazed again. One of the most effective later evangelists was Charles G. Finney, New England-born but brought up in western New York State—an area famous for religious emotionalism. Although never an orthodox Calvinist, Finney secured ordination from a lenient presbytery and began an extraordinary ministry in 1824. The fame of his Jefferson County, New York, revival brought him invitations to extend his work over an ever-widening area in New York, Ohio, and Pennsylvania. Despite initial misgivings Boston and other New England cities invited Finney to visit them. When he visited Scotland and England, his influence became international. In 1836 he was appointed professor of theology at Oberlin, and later, its president. Since neither Finney's pulpit methods nor his theology were acceptable to conservative Congregationalists and Presbyterians, Oberlin encountered much criticism. Indeed, a convention at Cleveland in 1842 considered ways and means to curb "this fountain of evil and protect the saints from its pestiferous malaria." But Oberlin and Finney were forces too dynamic to be narrowly contained.

New Sects

The nineteenth century was an age of religious particularism, when the older denominations were afflicted with schism and the founding of new sects was frequent. This should occasion little wonder, since each zealous Protestant studied the Bible and felt full liberty to interpret the sacred writings for himself. Moreover, in an emotional age when thousands were involved in soul-searing religious experiences, many heard God speak in the thunder or encountered angelic visitants bringing a revelation that would save mankind. Most of these created a brief local sensation and then disappeared, leaving no permanent following. Such was the case of Jemima Wilkinson, "the Universal Friend" who claimed to be Christ and founded a New Jerusalem near Seneca Lake; of Isaac Bullard, who, attired only in a bearskin girdle, led a company of "Pilgrims" from Vermont to Missouri; and of Joseph Dylkes, who convinced a number of his Ohio neighbors that he was God.

Other doctrinal disputes and special inspirations left more permanent results. The great denominations were frequently split. The Baptists, for example, spawned sects like the Regulars, the Separates, the Primitives, the Anti-Missions, and the Two-Seed-in-Spirit Predestinarians. There were frequent protests against the highly centralized government of the Methodist Episcopal Church, and such separate bodies as the Republican Methodists, the Methodist Protestants, and the Free Methodists appeared. The Presbyterians lost some of their more enthusiastic frontier elements in the Cumberland Presbyterian movement; and serious controversy between the old Scotch-Irish Presbyterianism and the more liberal Presbyterianism fed from New England springs resulted in a split between the Old School and the New School, which lasted from 1837 to 1870.[1]

Even protests against denominationalism resulted in new denominations. Such was the case with Barton W. Stone of Cane Ridge revival fame, who rebelled against Presbyterian narrowness. Calling for a return to primitive faith, he organized his followers into churches identified simply as "Christian." Stone's action was closely paralleled by that of Thomas Campbell, a Presbyterian from Ireland who became a revivalist in western Pennsylvania. Renouncing denominationalism, Campbell based his theology on the simple principle: "Where the Scriptures speak, we speak; where they are silent, we are silent." In 1809 Campbell's son, Alexander, joined his father in America and soon established himself as one of the most effective religious leaders of his generation. Since they believed in immersion, the Campbells affiliated for several years with the Baptists. But doctrinal differences developed, and the Campbellites evolved into a separate denomination known as the Disciples, which drew heavily from the Baptists and somewhat less from the Presbyterians, Methodists, and other groups. Campbell's Disciples and Stone's Christians agreed sufficiently to merge forces in many localities. The resulting churches, sometimes called by one name, sometimes by the other, grew rapidly, particularly in the states bordering on the Ohio River. They claimed some 250,000 members in 1850 and twice that number in 1865.

Protestants zealous to restore the primitive purity of their faith were fascinated by the description of the early church contained in the second chapter of Acts: "And all that believed were together, and had all things common; and sold their

[1] Further and more serious Protestant schisms resulted from the slavery controversy. These will be discussed in Chap. 15.

possessions and goods, and parted them to all men, as every man had need." During the colonial period experiments in religious communism had been carried on at Ephrata, Pennsylvania, and elsewhere. After the Revolution such communities multiplied.

Particular interest attached to the sect popularly known as Shakers. These were followers of "Mother" Ann Lee, who with eight disciples had arrived in America in 1774. Four years earlier Mother Ann, a married woman who had borne four children, claimed to have seen Christ in a vision and been told that the marriage relation was not merely sinful but the fountainhead from which all the rest of the world's evil proceeded. This revelation so impressed the little group of religious enthusiasts with which Ann was already affiliated that she became their leader. Having experienced mob violence and imprisonment in England, Mother Ann felt that she was directed by God to transfer her mission to America. After working for several months as a domestic in Albany, she finally established her small company on a farm in nearby Watervliet. Before she died in 1784, she had traveled through eastern New York and through Massachusetts, where she aroused ridicule and persecution but won enough converts to assure the survival of her cult.

The founding of Shaker communities, in which the believers might practice community of goods, began at New Lebanon, New York, in 1787 and was followed at 10 other places in New York and New England during the next five years. News of the frontier revival inspired the sect to send missionaries to the West in 1805. Union Village, Ohio, became the principal new Shaker community, but several other settlements were founded in Ohio, Kentucky, and Indiana. The Shakers attained their greatest prosperity from 1840 to 1860, when they numbered about six thousand members living in 19 different communities.

The Shakers were ridiculed because of their insistence upon celibacy and because of the strange rhythmic dancing and singing which constituted their worship. Despite their eccentricities, however, they eventually achieved a large measure of toleration and respect. They were hard-working farmers, and their cooperative communities prospered. Their gristmills were usually the best in the district, and their furniture, baskets, and boxes were so beautifully made as to have a ready sale. But increasing respectability dulled much of the fervor that had sustained the movement. After the Civil War the Shakers went into a slow decline, which was marked by the gradual liquidation of their communities. A celibate sect which failed to keep its ranks full from new conversions was obviously doomed to eventual extinction.

Similar in many respects was the movement led by "Father" George Rapp, who brought a company of followers from Germany to America in 1803. First at Harmony, Pennsylvania, then at Harmony, Indiana, and finally at Economy, Pennsylvania, the Rappites maintained celibate communities which attained great material prosperity but fell into decline after Rapp's death.

Religious communism found its boldest champion in John Humphrey Noyes.

Convinced that true Christians could live without sin, this Dartmouth graduate organized a group devoted to "perfectionism" at Putney, Vermont, in 1836. He believed that this required not only the communal sharing of property but a radical reform of the marriage relationship. The doctrine of "complex marriage" forbade conventional family life but permitted sexual relations between any of the men and women of the group. Since Noyes also aroused the hostility of his

FIG. 25. *Shakers near Lebanon, N. Y.* Dancing was a form of Shaker worship. (*Courtesy of The New-York Historical Society.*)

neighbors by advocating birth control and eugenics, he found it expedient to transfer his church to central New York in 1848. Known there as the Oneida Community, the group became wealthy through the manufacture of traps, hardware, embroidery silks, and silverware. In the long run complex marriage proved no more acceptable to moralists in New York than it had in Vermont. In 1879 the Community finally abandoned this practice, and two years later its cooperative industries were reorganized along conventional corporate lines.

The Church of Jesus Christ of Latter Day Saints dates from 1830, when the *Book of Mormon* was published at Palmyra, New York. Behind this event lay a curious story. Joseph Smith, whose parents had brought him as a boy from Vermont to western New York State, was known to his neighbors as a young man more interested in clairvoyance and treasure hunting than in working on the family farm. In 1823, according to his later account, the angel Moroni appeared to him and revealed the hiding place of a mysterious book written in a strange language on golden plates. In 1827 he was permitted to carry the plates home and to begin their translation—a miraculous work made possible by the discovery of a pair of magic spectacles. To his wife and other early disciples Smith dictated a long narrative relating the adventures of the lost tribes of Israel who had made their way to America. One group of these, the Lamanites, cursed with dark skins because of their wickedness and identified with the American Indians, had waged incessant war with a second group, the Nephites, God's chosen people. The latter had been nearly exterminated in A. D. 384, but the prophet Mormon, one of the few survivors, had written this sacred book and hidden it on the hillside where Joseph found it.

Despite the fantastic quality of Joseph Smith's story he won many converts. In an age when thousands of people were bewildered by the conflicting arguments of sectarian preachers, there was welcome security in the young prophet's air of assurance and repeated announcement of new revelations from God. From 1831 to 1837 Joseph Smith lived at Kirtland, Ohio, where his church gained many members, especially among former Baptists and Campbellites. But bad financial management resulted in disaster and in a flight of the prophet to Missouri, where the Mormons had for several years been attempting to found a new Zion. Here the Saints suffered a series of persecutions that finally drove them from the state. In 1840 the church's headquarters were established at Nauvoo, Illinois, where it enjoyed several years of great prosperity, even drawing thousands of converts from England. But the presumption of Joseph Smith, who announced himself a candidate for President of the United States in 1844, rumors that the Mormon leaders were practicing polygamy, and the jealousy of less prosperous neighbors resulted in new violence. Following serious disorders, Smith and his brother were arrested on charges of treason. On June 27, 1844, they suffered martyrdom, when the jail at Carthage, Illinois, was surrounded by an angry mob which shot the brothers to death.

Despite the confusion caused by the prophet's death and resulting schisms, the main Mormon ranks held firm under the resolute leadership of Brigham Young. In 1846 Young began the task of transferring thousands of Mormons and their possessions from Nauvoo across the Great Plains and the Rockies to the barren basin surrounding the Great Salt Lake. Believing that this inaccessible and unhospitable place would give his followers security from further molestation, the new leader achieved a miracle of colonization. Hard work and irrigation brought wealth to Mormon farmers, and Salt Lake City became a model of careful civic planning. But trouble with the Gentiles continued for many years. Friction between the Mormons and California-bound emigrant companies sometimes led to pitched battles, and efforts by the Federal government to outlaw polygamy resulted in the imprisonment of the Mormon elders. Not until after the church authorities finally renounced polygamy in 1890 was Utah admitted to the Union and the Mormon Church grudgingly accepted as a respectable denomination.

Much of the religious tension of these years arose from millennialism—a belief in the imminence of Christ's second coming, which was shared by leaders with as little else in common as Alexander Campbell and Joseph Smith. Particular interest centered in the preaching of William Miller, whose study of the Bible had convinced him that the great day would occur in 1843 or 1844. The Millerite movement attracted thousands of adherents, particularly in the Northeast. In great camp meetings and city tent meetings excitement rose until it often became hysteria. As the fateful hour approached, the heavens were watched for celestial signs, and rumors of supernatural phenomena circulated widely. Some of the emotionally unstable ended in insane asylums; others sold their businesses or gave up their jobs to prepare for the great event. When after all this nothing happened, most of the Millerites abandoned their leader, but remnants were organized in the Seventh Day Adventist Church and other Adventist sects.

Scarcely had the Millerite excitement subsided, when the news spread through the country that Margaret and Kate Fox, two young sisters of Hydesville, New York, were communicating with the spirit world through mysterious rappings. In 1850 the young mediums gave exhibitions in New York which aroused the interest of Horace Greeley and other sober citizens. By 1852 several hundred thousand Americans, including some of the most prominent personalities of the day, had become convinced that the living could communicate with the dead through table tippings, rappings, and automatic writing. Perhaps the most extraordinary conversion was that of Robert Dale Owen, long famous as an agnostic, who now wrote such books as *Footfalls on the Boundary of Another World* (1860) and *The Debatable Land between This World and the Next* (1872). The excitement persisted through the fifties but largely subsided with the outbreak of the Civil War. It left a substantial legacy not only in thousands of honest believers associated with spiritualist churches but in many charlatans who preyed upon the credulous.

Rational Religion

Meanwhile, religious developments of a very different character centered in Boston—an intellectual capital far removed from the world of Cane Ridge, Palmyra, and Hydesville.

The drift from orthodoxy in the Congregational churches first brought sharp protest from the conservatives in 1805, when Henry Ware was appointed professor of theology at Harvard. Reluctant to have its ministers trained in the classes of this well-known liberal, the Calvinist faction established Andover Theological Seminary in 1808. But the liberals continued to consider themselves Congregationalists until the militancy of the conservatives drove them to separation.

Such vigorous assaults on the anti-Calvinists as the Reverend Jedidiah Morse's *American Unitarianism* (1815) compelled them to reply with equal determination. Leadership of the liberals fell to William Ellery Channing of the Federal

Street Church in Boston. In 1819 Channing stated the position of his faction with great clarity in a sermon preached at the ordination of Jared Sparks in Baltimore. A further step toward separation was taken in the organization of the American Unitarian Association in 1825.

Although the name Unitarian reflected the new denomination's opposition to the doctrine of the Trinity, disbelief in the divinity of Christ was less characteristic of the liberal position than other attributes. The Unitarians rejected the old Calvinist belief in an angry God condemning most of sinful mankind to eternal punishment. They emphasized the benevolence of God and the essential goodness of human nature. Man's reason was exalted, and all dogma that affronted reason was opposed.

But Unitarianism in its emphasis on individualism encouraged revolt against itself. Although conservative Unitarians clung to such aspects of historic Christianity as the unique inspiration of Jesus Christ and the truth of his miracles, radical Unitarians like Theodore Parker renounced all belief in the supernatural. In 1832 Ralph Waldo Emerson resigned his Unitarian pastorate rather than serve the Lord's Supper—a ritual which he regarded with "indifference and dislike." Six years later he shocked a Unitarian audience by his Harvard Divinity School Address in which he asserted that there was nothing peculiar or distinctive about Christianity. Religion he defined as a matter of the inner imperative. The transcendentalists with their belief that God revealed himself in nature and in human intuition represented the extreme in religious individualism.

Unitarianism and transcendentalism, like Deism before them, were for the few rather than the many. Methodists in the early days of the century sang lustily:

> Stretch out thy arm, thou Triune God!
> The Unitarian fiend expel,
> And chase his doctrines back to Hell.[1]

But if Unitarianism appealed more to the wealthy and well-educated classes of eastern New England than to the rest of the country, its influence was nevertheless profound. Its emancipating spirit stimulated the literary renaissance and eventually softened the creed of other American Protestants.

Even New England Calvinism evolved toward greater emphasis on the goodness of God and the ability of man to secure salvation. Lyman Beecher, though a stanch foe of Unitarianism, was himself accused of heresy by Old School Presbyterians. His son Henry Ward Beecher, the most famous pulpit orator of the Civil War generation, was particularly responsive to the new intellectual currents, rejecting the unpopular tenets of Calvinism and appealing to his congregations to love God and their fellow man.

One of the greatest influences in liberalizing the creed of the older churches was Horace Bushnell, Congregational minister at Hartford, Connecticut. He retained doctrines like those concerning the Trinity and the atonement but gave

[1] J. Nightingale, "Portraiture of Methodism," *Monthly Repository,* III (1808), 103.

them an interpretation acceptable to the humane impulses of the nineteenth century. Particularly noteworthy were his essays on *Christian Nurture* (1847), which quietly undermined the basic assumptions of revivalism. Rejecting the idea that children must be considered sinners whose salvation depended upon dramatic conversions when they reached adulthood, he argued that "the child is to grow up a Christian, and never know himself as otherwise." [1] He rebuked the excesses of contemporary Protestantism and pointed the way to a more effective faith:

> We preach too much, and live Christ too little. We do many things which, in a cooler mood, are seen to hurt the dignity of religion, and which somewhat shame and sicken ourselves. Hence the present state of religion in our country. We have worked a vein until it has run out. The churches are exhausted. . . . No nation can long thrive by a spirit of conquest; no more can a church. There must be an internal growth, that is made by holy industry, in the common walks of life and duty.[2]

Rise of Catholicism

When John Carroll became bishop of Baltimore in 1790, his task was a discouraging one. Although a large proportion of the Catholic population was concentrated in Maryland and Pennsylvania, the remnant was widely dispersed. There were perhaps 30,000 Catholics in the country, and to minister to these Carroll had some thirty priests, many of them old men accustomed to administer the sacraments in a perfunctory fashion to Catholic families who had learned the wisdom of remaining inconspicuous in an aggressively Protestant country. The recruiting of new clergymen was difficult. Since there were no American seminaries, Carroll had to accept priests from abroad, many of them eccentrics or inebriates who had failed in the Old World.

But the situation was not without its brighter aspects. Catholic loyalty during the Revolution had served to dilute, if not entirely to remove, the prejudices of American Protestants. When Bishop Carroll visited Boston in 1791, he was gratified by his friendly reception. In communities where the Catholics had no churches, they were permitted to hold services in public buildings and even occasionally in Protestant meetinghouses. Particularly influential in winning respect for his church was the scholarly and eloquent John England, Bishop of Charleston from 1820 to 1842. In 1826 when President John Quincy Adams joined many senators and representatives in hearing Bishop England speak in the House Chamber at the national Capitol, the occasion represented an impressive recognition of the Catholics' new status.

As a result of the French Revolution the Church in America gained clergymen of outstanding character—French priests who crossed the Atlantic to escape the rising tide of anticlericalism. Particularly active were the French Sulpicians, who founded a seminary at Baltimore for the training of priests and carried on mis-

[1] Horace Bushnell, *Christian Nurture* (Scribner, New York, 1871), 10.

[2] *Ibid.*, 61.

sionary work among the Indians and among the scattered Catholic communities of the Northwest. When the American Church was reorganized in 1808, two of the four new bishoprics were entrusted to Frenchmen. French influence reached a high point after the death of Carroll. From 1817 to 1828 the leading dignitary of the American church was Archbishop Maréchal, while French bishops ruled dioceses at Boston, New York, New Orleans, and Bardstown, Kentucky.

The prominence of the French clergy was resented in many quarters. Pious and learned men though they were, they gave the Church a foreign tone which disturbed Catholics trying to establish its Americanism. In a day when preaching was esteemed almost as highly by Catholics as Protestants, the hesitant English of the French priests was resented, and the rolling eloquence of the Irish was correspondingly admired. To add to the confusion, German Catholics in Philadelphia and Baltimore disliked both the Irish and the French and demanded German priests and bishops. In these controversies laymen played a conspicuous part. Because of the American legal situation most of the Catholic property of the country was in the hands of elected trustees, who often tried to choose their own priests and even to dictate the appointment of bishops.

Internal friction reached a high point under the unhappy Maréchal. When Catholics in Virginia and South Carolina carried their protests to the point of intriguing for the establishment of an "Independent Catholic Church of America," the Vatican hastily intervened by establishing new bishoprics in the South and entrusting them to Irishmen. But even the Irish bishops encountered difficulties. In 1820 Bishop Conwell of Philadelphia became involved in an eight-year struggle with Father William Hogan that resulted in actual schism when the priest, supported by his trustees, continued to perform clerical functions in defiance of suspension and excommunication. Although Hogan gave up his fight after his conduct was condemned by the Pope, he remained unreconciled and in later life became a twice-married man, a lawyer, and a bitter anti-Catholic. Similar though less serious incidents occurred in many other places until the abuses of trusteeism were finally eradicated by strong administrators like Archbishop Hughes of New York.

Despite internal friction the Church grew steadily. Although the Catholics were strongest in the growing cities of the Northeast, the West was not neglected. Frontier conditions forced upon the Catholics expedients somewhat similar to those of the Protestants. There were itinerant bishops whose palaces were log cabins; there were priests who rode circuit; there were even laymen authorized to read prayers, to administer baptism, and to register marriages for communities that had no regular priest. The Catholic population was increased by the annexation of Louisiana, Florida, Texas, and California. Although there were no large-scale conversions of Protestants, there were a few notable ones in each generation. One of the first priests at Boston was the Reverend John Thayer, a former Congregational minister; the great Catholic educator Mother Elizabeth Seton was a convert from Episcopalianism; Orestes Brownson, successively Presbyterian, Universalist, and Unitarian, became the most aggressive of Catholic publicists following his conversion in 1844.

But the Church's greatest growth came through immigration. In 1840 it numbered 660,000 souls; in 1850, 1,600,000; in 1860, 3,100,000. The hierarchy expanded to keep pace, and by 1852 the American church had 6 archbishops, 26 bishops, and 1,385 priests. Catholic convents and schools were numerous, and Catholic churches were each year becoming larger and more imposing.

The more excitable Protestants took alarm. The Reverend Lyman Beecher wrote and preached of the Roman menace, and the artist-inventor Samuel F. B. Morse warned of a papal plot to capture America through immigration and to overthrow its republican institutions. More incendiary was the material contained in the *Awful Disclosures* of Maria Monk, who claimed to have escaped from a convent in Montreal where she had been forced to become the mistress of a priest. Even after these adventures were proved fictitious and the supposed authoress landed in jail for picking pockets in a brothel, the *Awful Disclosures* continued to circulate widely. Indeed the alleged confessions of ex-priests and nuns became a popular type of literature, and renegade Catholics were assured of a good income as lecturers.

Attacks on Catholics were not limited to the printed page and the platform. A rumor that the Ursuline Convent at Charlestown, Massachusetts, contained a nun held against her will so inflamed nearby Boston that on the night of August 11, 1834, a mob burned the building. Ten years later anti-Catholic mobs in Philadelphia attacked convents and churches, precipitating riots in which 13 persons were killed and 50 wounded. New disorders occurred in 1853, when Monsignor Bedini toured the country as a papal nuncio. On this occasion leadership was assumed by Italian and German revolutionary exiles who accused Bedini of responsibility for Austrian atrocities against Italian patriots. In several cities there were great anti-Catholic demonstrations. In Cincinnati Bedini narrowly escaped hanging at the hands of a mob which found partial compensation in destroying the church where he had preached. Anti-Catholicism had its counterpart in anti-Protestantism. Irish gangs, fortified with whisky, sometimes ranged the streets of eastern cities, demanding of passers-by, "Catholic or Protestant?" and beating up those whose answers they did not like.

Protestant-Catholic friction was carried into politics. Brawls between the Irish and the nativists multiplied on Election Day. Attempts were made to build political factions on the prevailing anti-Catholic and anti-immigrant prejudices. Nativist parties, appearing in various parts of the country, culminated in the formidable Know-Nothing movement of the fifties.

But these assaults simply solidified the Church. Immigration and Catholic organizing activities had permanently changed the American religious situation. Although Protestants still outnumbered Catholics, the Roman Church was now larger than any single Protestant denomination.

Chapter 15. Humanitarian Reform

The first half of the nineteenth century was unique not only for the intensity with which men struggled to save their own souls, but for the passion with which they sought to reform society. Some worked for this end through utopian socialism; others through Christian anarchism. The evils of slavery, intemperance, male domination, and capital punishment all had their determined enemies.

The spirit of reform grew lustily, because the entire intellectual climate seemed to favor it. Religion at its best shook men out of indifference to poverty and suffering; at its worst it created an obsession with sin that led to fanatical means and impractical ends. Deists and agnostics were often more devoted to reform than were Christians, since they insisted that all evil was caused by bad laws and environment. Change these, they said, and mankind would achieve peace, prosperity, and happiness. Utilitarianism, derived from the English thinker Jeremy Bentham, provided a standard by which many American rationalists judged institutions on the extent to which they contributed to the greatest happiness of the greatest number. American political philosophy was a constant spur to reform when conditions inconsistent with the familiar axioms of the Declaration of Independence fell under attack. And, finally, rising romanticism contributed to the reform movement faith in the natural goodness of man, sentimental fervor, a tendency to exaggerated statement, and a delight in martyrdom and persecution.

Criminals, Debtors, and Lunatics

In comparison with eighteenth-century England, where the death penalty was stipulated for over one hundred different crimes, the penal laws of the American colonies had been lenient. Even so, death by hanging might be imposed in either Pennsylvania or New York for any one of 16 different crimes, and lesser penalties included flogging, mutilation, branding, and exposure to public ridicule in stocks and pillory.

Such punishments offended the more humane impulses of the Revolutionary generation. Pennsylvania pioneered in reform, largely because of Quaker influence. In 1786, in 1790, and in 1794 drastic revisions of the penal code were made. Only murder and treason now carried the death penalty, and prison terms were substituted for public whippings and mutilations. New York took similar action in 1796, and the other states followed. Progress was uneven. Rhode Island pilloried criminals and clipped their ears well into the nineteenth century, and Delaware and Maryland still had the whipping post in 1950.

The substitution of prison terms for harsher penalties focused attention on the local jails, the only places for detention before 1790. Intended for debtors, petty offenders, and persons awaiting trial, they were schools of vice rather than places of reformation. Men and women, old and young, hardened criminals and first offenders, were all herded together in a single room. No food was provided, and the prisoners either had to purchase victuals from the extortionate jailer or beg them from people passing by on the streets outside. No work was provided for the inmates, and they passed the time instructing each other in the finer arts of crime or imbibing rum, which the jailer gladly sold to all who had the price.

Once again Pennsylvania took the lead in attempting a better system. The Walnut Street Prison in Philadelphia, rebuilt in 1790, provided three major reforms: male and female prisoners were segregated, the use of intoxicating beverages by the convicts was prohibited, and the prisoners were fed by the state but were compelled to work. During its early years the Philadelphia institution was so obviously superior to the older jails that it served as a model for other states. Best known of the new institutions was Newgate Prison in New York City, which was opened in 1797 under the direction of Thomas Eddy, a Quaker philanthropist and well-known advocate of penal reform.

Time soon proved that prisons of the Walnut Street or Newgate type had their own serious shortcomings. Individual cells were provided only for the most hardened criminals. Other prisoners were confined in large "night rooms," thus perpetuating the problem of the inmates' corrupting each other or conspiring against the keepers. Overcrowding became worse with each passing year. The night rooms sometimes had to house thirty or forty convicts instead of the seven or eight originally intended. Even so, room could be made for incoming prisoners only by pardoning a sufficient number of inmates—a practice that opened wide the door to corruption and special privilege.

By 1820 the penal problem was again causing great concern. Many conservatives believed that increasing crime and bad prison conditions demonstrated an error in the humanitarian philosophy. They demanded more hangings, a return of the whipping post, or an American penal colony in some distant area like Oregon. Prevailing opinion opposed such draconic measures as these but called for the building of better planned prisons and stricter discipline. This was the spirit underlying the administration of the new prison erected at Auburn, New York, between 1816 and 1821. At night each prisoner was confined in a small separate cell; during the day he worked with other convicts in the prison shops and ate in the large dining halls, but all communication between prisoners was forbidden. Contemporary observers, accustomed to the insolence and profanity of the older prisons, were much impressed to see the Auburn convicts march silently from one part of the prison to another, work in silence without turning their heads to look at visitors, and return to their cells to spend the nights in silence with no other reading matter than the Bible. The Auburn system was extravagantly praised—particularly in the literature of the Boston Prison Discipline Society—and was widely copied.

But Pennsylvania penal reformers condemned the Auburn system and boasted of their own new penitentiary at Philadelphia. The Pennsylvania system provided entirely separate quarters for each prisoner. With no common shops or dining rooms the possibility of prisoners communicating with each other was almost completely eliminated. At first, the Pennsylvania prisoners were given nothing to do but to pace their cells and to meditate on their own wickedness. When this proved to be both expensive to the state and dangerous to the prisoners' sanity, work to be done in the individual cells was provided.

American prison experiments were watched with keen interest by Europeans, but both the Auburn and Pennsylvania systems had defects that became apparent as time went on. The Pennsylvania system was excessively expensive and provided no relief from the unhealthy monotony of life in solitary cells. The Auburn system depended on harsh disciplinary measures against infractions of the rules. At Sing Sing, for example, as many as 3,000 lashes were inflicted upon recalcitrant prisoners in a single month of 1843. Prison reformers consequently directed their agitation to moderating the methods of the keepers. Solitary confinement, bread-and-water diet, and dousing in cold water were substituted for the excessive use of the whip. But in an age where flogging was taken for granted in the home, the schoolhouse, as well as on naval vessels, its total abolition in the prisons was not to be expected. One of the great abuses of the day, the incarceration of juvenile delinquents in the same institutions with older criminals, was attacked through the establishment of the New York House of Refuge in 1825 and similar reformatories in Boston and Philadelphia.

The delusion that public executions were healthy deterrents to crime persisted for many years. But such scenes as that in the summer of 1833, when a hanging at Mount Holly, New Jersey, drew a crowd of 10,000 persons, so disgusted the better elements that within the next few years the legislatures of Pennsylvania, New Jersey, New York, Massachusetts, and Maryland passed laws requiring executions to be carried out within prison walls. Capital punishment itself fell under criticism and was abolished in Maine in 1837 and in Vermont in 1842. Similar "anti-gallows" laws were proposed in Massachusetts, New York, Connecticut, and Pennsylvania but failed to pass.

Imprisonment for debt scarcely commended itself to a rational age. If a debtor could not pay his creditor as a free man, how could he pay in the enforced idleness of the debtors' prison? But creditors continued to make extensive use of this weapon. Sometimes the complainant suspected that the debtor or his family had hidden savings which would be used to ransom him; sometimes he sent the debtor to prison simply out of revenge. At all events, the victim was in an unhappy situation. Not only was he confined until he paid his debt or until his creditor relented, but in many states he went cold and hungry unless assisted by one of the humane societies. He might be fed by the keeper, but the bill was assessed against him, making it more and more difficult for him to secure release. Most of the prisoners owed only petty sums. From January 1, 1820, to April 1, 1822, there were 3,492 persons imprisoned for debt in Boston, and 2,000 of these owed less than $20.

The old system gave way a little at a time. In 1817 New York forbade imprisonment for debts of less than $25, and several other states set limits ranging from $5 to $30. The system was particularly unpopular in the West, and several of the new states practically abolished it between 1816 and 1821.

In the older states merchants and lawyers stubbornly opposed the demand of the workingmen's parties for complete abolition. The issue was vigorously agitated for several years and even reached Congress. In session after session Colonel Richard M. Johnson of Kentucky sponsored bills to abolish imprisonment for debt through Federal court actions, and with the support of President Andrew Jackson, Johnson's proposal was finally enacted in 1832. Although this affected only a small number of debtors, it represented a significant breach in the wall. The State of New York prohibited imprisonment for debt that same year, and most of the other states did so within the next decade.

Even more deserving of humanitarian pity were the insane. The general public loathed and feared these unfortunates as creatures whose affliction must somehow be their own fault. Since their malady was regarded as incurable, the interest of the community was limited to seeing that they were kept where they could do no harm. The most fortunate were those who had relatives able to care for them in private homes where they would be spared the stares of the curious and the molestations of the mischievous. But since the nature of their affliction impoverished most of the insane, their maintenance fell upon the local authorities who sought to relieve themselves of the responsibility as cheaply as possible. Some victims were auctioned off to whoever would accept their custody for the lowest fee, but most of them were confined in local jails or county almshouses. In such places humane treatment was impossible. Ignorant attendants confined their unwelcome charges in cages or in underground dungeons, burdened them with heavy chains, and cowed them with beatings.

The persistence of these conditions for the greater part of the nineteenth century represented an extraordinary cultural lag. Before 1800 enlightened experiments both in Europe and America had demonstrated that the insane could be restrained without cruelty and that their misfortune was an illness which often responded to kind and intelligent treatment. As early as 1752 Philadelphia had built an asylum for the insane, and similar institutions had later been erected elsewhere. But the newer methods were given their first important American trial in a hospital opened by the Philadelphia Quakers in 1817. Even more influential were the McLean Asylum at Somerville, Massachusetts, opened in 1818, the Retreat at Hartford in 1824, and the asylum at Worcester, Massachusetts, in 1830.

It might have been expected that humane treatment for all the insane would now be speedily provided. But appropriations were difficult to secure. The most active champion of reform was Dorothea Lynde Dix, mistress of a private girls' school in Boston, whose eyes were opened to the situation by a chance visit to the East Cambridge jail in 1841. After devoting two years to investigation in all parts of the state, she wrote the shocking indictment, *Memorial to the Legislature of Massachusetts* (1843). Succeeding in her campaign for increased appropriations, she carried out similar investigations in other states. In 1854 she induced Congress to grant 10 million acres of public land for care of the indigent insane, but the bill was vetoed by President Franklin Pierce. Despite the activity of Miss Dix and other humanitarians the confinement of the insane in almshouses was not finally abolished until long after the Civil War.

Utopian Communities

During the same decades in which Shakers, Perfectionists, and Rappites were practicing communism as an expression of primitive Christianity, other idealists engaged in similar experiments in an attempt to achieve a new social order based upon purely rational principles.

When Robert Owen arrived in America in 1824, he was already a famous person. In his cotton mills at New Lanark, Scotland, he had shortened the hours of his workers, raised their pay, remedied the worst abuses of the child-labor system, and provided schools and wholesome amusements for the town. Not content with his great success as a benevolent capitalist, he now hoped to rebuild society through the establishment of cooperative communities. The New World seemed a more auspicious place to begin this process than the Old, and in 1825 Owen purchased the Rappite property on the Wabash River in Indiana. Rechristened New Harmony, the community began the next phase of its history under seemingly ideal conditions, since it was already a going concern with vineyards, orchards, grainfields, flour and cotton mills, dwelling houses, and public buildings.

Almost a thousand persons flocked to this site in 1825, eager to participate in Owen's experiment. They were singularly diverse in background, having been drawn from most of the countries of northern Europe and from every part of the United States. Many were intellectuals of exceptional talent like William Maclure, America's ablest geologist, and Thomas Say, outstanding student of insect life. Others were mechanics from the eastern cities and western farmers, who were anxious to better their lot. Many were industrious and eager to cooperate, but others were lazy and looked to Owen to support them.

Intellectually and socially the community succeeded. Good talk abounded—particularly in weekly discussion meetings where subjects of every description were debated in complete freedom. The colonists had an opportunity to hear good music in the weekly concerts and to dance at the weekly balls. The community newspaper, *The New Harmony Gazette,* was a medium for expounding the ideals of the experiment and for discussing the social issues of the day, and the schools were far in advance of their contemporaries.

But economically the community foundered from the start, and in 1827 it failed completely. Serious mistakes of judgment, dissension among the leaders, and laziness and dishonesty among some of the colonists contributed to the disaster. Owen suffered also from the hostility of much of the American public, which resented not so much his socialism as his aggressive assaults upon religion. He returned to England, a much poorer man but by no means disillusioned, for he persisted until he died in his aspirations to rebuild society.

More influential on American thought than Owen was Charles Fourier, a French philosopher who had worked out elaborately detailed plans for a reorganization of society through the formation of "phalanxes," or associations. Fourier's ideas, transmitted to American readers in Albert Brisbane's *Social Destiny of Man* (1840), aroused great interest, partly because the panic of 1837 had emphasized the weaknesses of competitive economy. Horace Greeley was converted to the cause of association and invited Brisbane to write a regular column for his *New York Tribune.*

During the next decade experiments in Fourierism were attempted in almost every state of the Northeast and the Middle West. Most of the phalanxes were poorly organized and failed within a few months, but a few gained a temporary success that served to sustain the associationist cause. Longest lived was the North American Phalanx at Red Bank, New Jersey, established in 1843. Located on fertile soil only 40 miles from New York, the community made a comfortable living for almost thirteen years by raising vegetables and grain for the metropolitan market, but restlessness and a feeling on the part of the members that they would command a better livelihood in competitive society eventually brought about the association's dissolution.

The most famous experiment was at Brook Farm near Boston. When first organized in 1841 by a group of New England intellectuals, headed by George Ripley, Unitarian minister and transcendentalist friend of Emerson, the Brook Farm Institute of Agriculture and Industry was largely free of doctrinaire theory. The original members organized a joint-stock company and purchased a beautiful property in West Roxbury, Massachusetts, where they lived together, sharing the menial tasks of agriculture and operating an excellent school to which outsiders sent their children. During its earlier and happier years the society grew to about seventy members and included such eminent persons as Nathaniel Hawthorne, John S. Dwight, and Charles A. Dana. Some, like Hawthorne, soon wearied of their manual chores and left, but others retained their enthusiasm, sustained by a feeling of high comradeship and spiritual adventure. In 1844 Brook Farm was radically reorganized along lines that reflected the conversion of George Ripley and other leaders to the Fourier principles. This involved the imposition of an unwieldy organization, the recruitment of artisans, and the establishment of new enterprises. Financial difficulties multiplied, but the courage of the members remained high until given a crushing blow by the fire which destroyed the nearly completed "phalanstery," or main building, in 1846. The experiment was abandoned the next year.

Another series of communal experiments was associated with the French theorist Étienne Cabet, whose utopian novel, *Le Voyage en Icarie* (1840) had aroused the interest of thousands of Europeans, many of whom urged the author to put his ideas into operation. In 1848 an advance guard of Icarians crossed the Atlantic and attempted a settlement in the Red River valley of Texas, but the difficulties of prairie farming and of disease combined to defeat the project. Cabet himself and some four hundred followers arrived at New Orleans early in 1849. After a delay of some months they decided to make the next attempt at Nauvoo, Illinois—a favorable site left largely vacant by the exodus of the Mormons. For seven years the French colonists appeared to prosper, but in 1856 a tragic schism occurred. A majority, resentful at Cabet's dictatorial tendencies, expelled him and his faction. The minority removed to St. Louis, where their leader died, and the rest dispersed after an unsuccessful attempt to operate a new community. The Icarians who remained at Nauvoo also encountered difficulties which resulted in their removal to Iowa. There they suffered desertions and further schisms, but a remnant, loyal to the old ideals, persisted in communal life until 1895.

The continuance of the Icarian experiment for forty-seven years was exceptional. In general, the rationalist attempts at utopian socialism failed speedily and completely. Only the religious communities, where personal ambition had been subordinated to otherworldly aspirations, achieved stability, and they too disintegrated when the faith of the early enthusiasts ran thin among their successors. The wide interest in utopian socialism was typical of American idealism in a romantic age; the poor record of achievement indicated that the experiments ran counter to the fundamental trends of nineteenth-century American life. The march of the frontier and the rapid economic development of the nation made for ruthless individualism rather than selfless cooperation.

Visionary reform took other shapes as well. During the years in which Frances Wright lived in America, her name became synonomous with advanced and generally unpopular causes. In a day when female lecturers and editors were regarded with disfavor anyway, the Scotchwoman's advocacy of Negro-white equality and her assaults upon organized Christianity and conventional marriage provoked indignant rebuke. But she had her enthusiastic followers. Robert Owen's son Robert Dale Owen became her loyal lieutenant, and the two propagated their ideas through the columns of the *Free Enquirer* and public lectures at the "Hall of Science" in New York City—a former church building which Frances Wright purchased and devoted to the causes of free thought and worker education. Owen added another affront to conservatives by writing *Moral Physi-*

ology (1830), a pioneer treatise on birth control.[1] But the two reformers placed their greatest emphasis on the need for "republican education." In order to erase distinctions between rich and poor, they urged a system of "state guardianship," under which all children should be placed in boarding schools and should be trained in both literary arts and manual skills. The rise of the New York Working Men's party brought Miss Wright and Dale to a peak of influence in 1829 and 1830, but schisms in the movement and the unwillingness of many to accept the leadership of agnostics reduced their prestige in succeeding years.

The Jacksonian ferment threw up other leaders with pet panaceas. Thomas Skidmore believed that all ills of society could be cured by a redistribution of land and wrote *The Rights of Man to Property!* (1829) to prove his case. Although Skidmore's agrarianism was too extreme to win many disciples, the later agitation of George Henry Evans was more successful. In 1844 Evans organized the National Reform Association to work for a change in Federal land policy. Evans believed that instead of being sold, the national domain should be granted in free homesteads to actual settlers. The Association broke up after its founder's death in 1849, but it had paved the way for the more aggressive homestead movement of the fifties.

Temperance

The prevalence of heavy drinking in the early nineteenth century cannot be doubted. An investigation in 1818 revealed that there were 1,900 licensed grogshops in New York City and at least 600 unlicensed ones. A similar survey of Philadelphia in 1821 disclosed that children five years of age were buying liquor by the penny's worth at corner grocery stores. Nor was it an abuse peculiar to the cities. The farmer kept abundant supplies of rum and whisky on hand to quench not only his own thirst but also that of his hired help. Liquor was regarded as necessary for every social occasion from a christening to a funeral, and most of the business of the country, whether Congressional lawmaking or frontier fence building, was conducted in an alcoholic vapor. It was generally believed that rum and whisky not only lightened the spirit but sustained the body, giving it strength for heavy tasks and protection from chills and disease.

Even in colonial days men like Cotton Mather of Massachusetts and Anthony Benezet of Pennsylvania had warned against the evils of intemperance, but an organized movement did not develop for many decades. In 1784 Dr. Benjamin Rush of Philadelphia, probably the best known physician of the day, published a pamphlet setting forth the injuries to health which he believed resulted from the use of distilled spirits. This challenge to prevailing ideas aroused wide interest and was reprinted in a number of later editions. But still no concerted attack on

[1] Dr. Charles Knowlton of Massachusetts published a similar work entitled *Fruits of Philosophy* in 1832.

intemperance was attempted. The earliest temperance societies were local in character and modest in program.

A more aggressive foe of intemperance appeared in Lyman Beecher. Impressed by Dr. Rush's pamphlet, Beecher preached earnest sermons on the subject at East Hampton, Long Island, and later at Litchfield, Connecticut, where he transferred in 1811. He had first to convince his fellow clergymen, who had not yet abandoned the practice of frequent visits to the sideboard during their consociation meetings. But his arguments were sufficiently convincing to make Congregational ministers the most prominent members of the Connecticut Society for the Reformation of Morals, organized in 1813.

Although similar societies were organized in other states—particularly in those in which New England influence was strong—the temperance movement lacked real vigor so long as its chief dependence was on quiet appeals to the intellect. The fervent evangelism which lashed the country during the twenties and thirties favored more vigorous tactics. Intemperance was now attacked not merely as a bad habit, but as a sin—in the words of Lyman Beecher: "a river of fire . . . rolling through the land, destroying the vital air, and extending around an atmosphere of death." [1] The leading Protestant denominations condemned the sale of intoxicants as immoral, and the American Society for the Promotion of Temperance was organized in 1826 to coordinate the efforts of the reformers.

The real vitality of the movement was in local associations founded in all parts of the nation but particularly in the Northeast and the Middle West. By 1835 there were more than five thousand of these with a membership of approximately one million. All members had taken a pledge to abstain from the use of ardent spirits, and the effect of their example was becoming evident. Fewer employers now provided strong drink for their help; fewer hosts offered it to their guests. Many towns boasted a "temperance hotel," where abstainers could find lodging without fear that their rest would be disturbed by noisy tipplers.

The temperance movement was by no means free of the schisms that plagued other reform agitations. Moderates wished to condemn only hard liquors in the belief that the substitution of beer and wine for stronger beverages would serve the cause of temperance. Extremists argued that alcohol in any amount or form was a habit-forming poison and insisted upon total abstinence. There was also a significant rift between the "moral suasionists" and the "legal suasionists." The former placed reliance upon changing individual habits; the latter believed that the liquor evil could only be destroyed by cutting it away at the roots—by laws prohibiting the sale of intoxicating beverages.

Although weakened by these disputes in the late thirties, the temperance cause enjoyed a striking revival during the forties. Hitherto, the pledge takers had usually been good churchgoers, who were in scant danger of disgracing themselves through drink in any case. The temperance workers had assumed that confirmed drunkards were beyond help and were useful to the movement only as

[1] Quoted in John A. Krout, *The Origins of Prohibition* (Knopf, 1925), 107.

horrible examples. But in 1840 six former alcoholics of Baltimore, having proved by their own example that it was possible to break the liquor habit, formed the Washington Temperance Society to help other unfortunates. The meetings in which the reformed drunkards related their experiences—often in lurid detail—drew large crowds, and within a year the Baltimore organization numbered 1,000 members. Similar Washington societies were organized in other cities with the

Fig. 26. *Father Mathew Administering the Temperance Pledge.* Lithograph by N. Currier. "I promise, while I belong to the Teetotal Abstinence Society to abstain from all kinds of intoxicating drink unless used medically. . . ." (*Courtesy of The New-York Historical Society.*)

original Washingtonians in great demand as temperance orators. John W. Hawkins, the most famous of the Baltimore group, is estimated to have traveled more than 100,000 miles in ten years and to have delivered 2,500 temperance addresses. An even more famous reformed drunkard was John W. Gough, whose career as a lecturer began in 1842 and lasted for forty-four years.

The Washingtonians aroused enthusiasm for their cause by great temperance parades. Bands, floats, and banners abounded, and the marching societies included not only reformed drunkards but the older church-supported groups and units of the Cold Water Army—boys and girls who had taken the pledge in their Sunday schools. Although the Washington societies had no national organization and were usually short-lived, the Sons of Temperance, a new fraternal order founded in 1842, attempted a more permanent work in fortifying rehabilitated alcoholics in their new life.

The temperance movement received strong Catholic support. Many Catholic societies participated in the mass demonstrations of the forties. Great excitement attended the tour of Father Theobold Mathew, who had won fame by his temperance crusade in Ireland. Between 1849 and 1851 Father Mathew visited 25 states and administered the total-abstinence pledge to an estimated half million people.

Although Father Mathew and most Catholics opposed prohibitory laws, the Protestant reformers now emphasized the coercive approach. In 1838 the Massachusetts legislature attempted to end tavern and grogshop abuses by forbidding the sale of hard liquors in quantities of less than 15 gallons. The act aroused the strong opposition of the tavern keepers and also of many others who regarded it as class legislation depriving the poor man of his glass but allowing the rich man his barrel. In 1840 the law was repealed. Meanwhile in 1839 Rhode Island had empowered local communities to refuse liquor licenses if a majority of the voters so decided. Similar local-option laws were passed in many other states during the next decade. Since it was difficult to enforce prohibition on a town or county basis, the temperance forces continued to seek state-wide enactments. In 1851 the first such law was passed in Maine—largely due to the ceaseless activity of Neal Dow, a Quaker merchant of Portland.

This victory spurred the prohibitionists to major efforts in every section. Impressive gains were made—only to be followed by disheartening losses. By 1855 every northern state legislature except that of New Jersey had approved some form of prohibition. But a popular referendum reversed the decision in Illinois, and in New York and several other states the new laws were invalidated by the courts. Even where they were upheld, surreptitious dealers and thirsty customers showed great ingenuity in evading the law. These difficulties in enforcement tended to discredit the whole prohibition movement, and by 1868 all the laws of the fifties had been repealed except that of Maine.

Despite this setback the temperance agitation left its permanent result in thousands of families where the use of intoxicating beverages was now regarded as sinful. Total abstinence was, however, much more characteristic of the rural districts than the cities, where greater sophistication and the heavy influx of immigrants encouraged the use of intoxicants.

Antislavery

The institution of slavery was equally repugnant to the Christian doctrine of the brotherhood of man and to the rationalist theory of natural rights. From both quarters it fell under attack during the eighteenth century. The Quaker leaders

John Woolman and Anthony Benezet early became conspicuous opponents of slavery, and men of other faiths soon joined them—among them such eminent New England divines as Samuel Hopkins, Ezra Stiles, and Jeremy Belknap. Thomas Jefferson, although a slave owner himself, was convinced that slavery was wrong and hoped for its eventual extinction. Many other leaders of opinion in the Upper South agreed with him.

Organized activity against the institution began in 1775 when the Quakers organized the Pennsylvania Society for Promoting the Abolition of Slavery, and the Relief of Free Negroes Held in Bondage. Although inactive during the Revolution, this association was revived in 1787 with Benjamin Franklin as president. Similar steps were taken elsewhere, and by 1792 there were antislavery societies in all states from Massachusetts to Virginia. In 1794 the Annual Convention for Promoting the Abolition of Slavery and Improving the Condition of the African Race, a loose confederation of these local societies, began an existence that was to continue for thirty-five years.

Although these groups were small and their methods conservative, humanitarian sentiment was sufficiently widespread to bring about a general abandonment of slavery in the northern states. In 1783 the Massachusetts courts ruled that slavery was incompatible with the provisions of the state constitution of 1780, and the other New England states outlawed the institution within the next year or two. In the Middle Atlantic states slavery lasted but little longer. Pennsylvania enacted a gradual emancipation measure in 1780, New York in 1799, and New Jersey in 1804. There was agitation for similar action in Maryland, Kentucky, Virginia, and North Carolina, but here the movement failed and the boundary between free and slave states became stabilized at the Mason and Dixon's line.

The slavery issue was also debated at the national level. Although Congress was unwilling to go as far as Jefferson proposed in forbidding slavery in all the western territory, it was barred from the area north of the Ohio River by the famous Northwest Ordinance of 1787. The Philadelphia Convention of the same year reflected more conservative trends. The new Constitution recognized the existing institution by providing for the return of fugitive slaves, by forbidding Congress to pass any prohibitory laws against the foreign slave trade for twenty years, and by providing that three-fifths of the slaves should be counted in the apportionment of representatives and of direct taxes. The last great victory of the early antislavery movement was the act of Congress which prohibited the importation of slaves after January 1, 1808—the earliest date at which it was constitutionally possible.

After 1808 antislavery activities slackened perceptibly. Some reformers believed that prohibition of the slave trade was the crucial victory and that slavery would now gradually disappear. But this expectation took scant account of the continued growth of the slave population through natural increase and illegal importations, which were never effectively halted.

Economic trends, which during the eighteenth century had favored emancipation, now worked the other way. The great boom in cotton growing created a lively demand for slaves and increased their value as property. Ceasing their apologies for the institution, southern spokesmen now asserted that slavery was necessary to the national prosperity and beneficial to whites and blacks alike. Voluntary manumissions, which had been numerous in the late eighteenth century, were now discountenanced by public opinion and in many states prohibited by law.

For a time projects for the colonization of freedmen in Africa attracted great interest. In 1817 the American Society for the Colonization of Free People of Color was organized, and four years later the transportation of free Negroes to Liberia began. The movement was supported by grants of money from the Federal government and from various states as well as by the gifts of many private individuals. During the twenties the organization had the support both of southern slave owners like Judge Bushrod Washington, Henry Clay, and John Randolph of Roanoke and of future abolitionists like William Lloyd Garrison, Arthur and Lewis Tappan, and Gerrit Smith. But Negro colonists became disillusioned through poverty and disease, and northern philanthropists soon realized that the expense and difficulty of colonization were so great that it was hopeless as a solution to the slavery problem. They also became convinced that the southerners who dominated the society were more interested in getting rid of already free Negroes than they were in further emancipations.

During the twenties the most persistent antislavery agitator was Benjamin Lundy, a New Jersey Quaker, who began the publication of *The Genius of Universal Emancipation* in 1821. Lundy changed the base of his activities several times, but in 1829, when he enlisted the help of the young Massachusetts printer William Lloyd Garrison, he was making his headquarters at Baltimore, a slave-trading center. Garrison's rather academic earlier interest in the slavery question quickened to obsessive hatred when he saw the institution at first hand—a hatred no doubt deepened by the seven weeks which he spent in a Baltimore prison after conviction for libeling a slave trader. Disapproving Lundy's advocacy of gradual emancipation and colonization, Garrison returned to New England in 1830, determined to launch an agitation for immediate and unconditional emancipation.

On January 1, 1831, from an obscure Boston printing shop, Garrison issued the first number of *The Liberator*. Gradual abolition he condemned as a sentiment of "timidity, injustice, and absurdity." His contention was for "the immediate enfranchisement of our slave population." In stinging words he set the tone for the new agitation:

> I am aware, that many object to the severity of my language; but is there not cause for severity? I *will be* as harsh as truth, and as uncompromising as justice. On this subject I do not wish to think, or speak, or write, with moderation. No! No! Tell a man whose house is on fire to give a moderate alarum; tell him to moderately rescue his wife from the hands of the ravisher; tell the mother to gradually extricate her babe from the fire into which it

has fallen;—but urge me not to use moderation in a cause like the present. I am in earnest—I will not equivocate—I will not excuse—I will not retreat a single inch—AND I WILL BE HEARD. . . .

Although Garrison's agitation was distasteful to most of the prominent citizens of Boston, including the clergymen, he won a handful of followers, who organized themselves as the New England Anti-Slavery Society in 1832. The next year a convention at Philadelphia, dominated by Garrison, founded the American Anti-Slavery Society, whose announced aim was to convince all citizens that: "Slaveholding is a heinous crime in the sight of God, and that the duty, safety, and best interests of all concerned, require its *immediate abandonment* without expatriation."

The new society's most effective agent was Theodore Weld. As sincere as Garrison but much better balanced, Weld had decided to dedicate his life to the ministry after listening to the preaching of Charles G. Finney at Utica, New York. In 1830 he became aroused by the slavery issue, and within the next few years he had won a remarkable group of converts to this cause, including the wealthy Arthur and Lewis Tappan of New York, Beriah Green of Western Reserve College in Cleveland, and James G. Birney, a slaveholding lawyer and politician of Danville, Kentucky. Weld carried his abolitionist campaign into Lane Theological Seminary at Cincinnati, where he studied for the ministry. When the trustees, alarmed lest this exhibition of radicalism frighten wealthy benefactors of the institution, prohibited further agitation in 1834, most of the students withdrew. Many finished their training at newly founded Oberlin, making that institution, like Western Reserve, a center of abolitionism. The Lane Seminary rebels became evangelists for the antislavery cause, carrying the message throughout the Middle West. Weld became not only the ablest lecturer of the American Anti-Slavery Society but especially successful in the training of other agents in the arts of effective propaganda. One of his aptest pupils was Angelina Grimké, who presently became Mrs. Theodore Weld.

The reaction to abolitionism was sharp. Southern legislatures forbade antislavery agitation within their own states and demanded that similar steps be taken by public authorities in the North. Southern postmasters refused to deliver "incendiary" literature that passed through the mails and were upheld by the Postmaster General. By the so-called "gag rule," in force from 1836 to 1844 despite the protests of John Quincy Adams, antislavery petitions to Congress were neither read nor printed. Prominent citizens in the North led mobs that broke up antislavery meetings and threatened the lives of abolitionist leaders.

Persecution served only to strengthen the reformers' zeal. In 1835, when a well-dressed mob dragged Garrison with a rope through the streets of Boston, the disgraceful scene was witnessed by young Wendell Phillips, a member of one of the city's leading families. This began Phillips's conversion to the antislavery cause—a conversion that was made public two years later in his dramatic condemnation of the murder of the abolitionist editor, Elijah P. Lovejoy, at Alton,

Illinois. Similarly, Gerrit Smith's disgust with the breaking up of an abolitionist meeting in Utica, New York, resulted in his enlistment in the antislavery cause, and Salmon P. Chase became an abolitionist following the destruction of James G. Birney's press by a Cincinnati mob.

Although the antislavery movement withstood the assaults of its enemies, it could not avoid divisions within its own ranks. Garrison, a kind and gentle man in his personal relationships, had a public character that repelled even his fellow abolitionists. The ferocity of *The Liberator's* attacks upon all who disagreed with it antagonized not only slave owners but northern moderates. Since one of his favorite targets was the conservatism of the churches, Garrison made powerful enemies among the clergy. Many who were sympathetic with the antislavery cause were disturbed by Garrison's insistence that women should have a prominent place in the movement. Still more shocking was the New Englander's condemnation of all existing governments as anti-Christ and his plea that followers of Jesus refuse to vote or to hold public office. Thus to the cause of abolitionism, unpopular enough, Garrison was attaching the controversial issues of anticlericalism, feminism, and nonresistance.

Events came to a crisis in 1840. Although Garrison retained control of the American Anti-Slavery Society by packing its convention with his New England followers, the moderates organized a rival national society. The latter lasted only a few years, but henceforth the strength of the antislavery movement was to be found in local bodies. While Garrison continued to oppose political action and encouraged secession through his condemnation of the Constitution as "a covenant with death and an agreement with hell," only a minority of abolitionists now followed his leadership. The non-Garrisonians, headed by Weld, opposed disunion and attempted political action. Antislavery lobbyists encouraged the growth of a bloc in Congress committed to legislating against slavery in every way possible under the Constitution. A new and more influential antislavery periodical, *The National Era,* was founded at Washington. In the elections of 1840 and 1844 the political abolitionists ran James G. Birney for the presidency as the candidate of the so-called Liberty party.

Although Birney's vote was disappointingly small and the abolitionists remained few in numbers and plagued by schism, general northern sentiment on the slavery issue was strongly altered during the forties and the fifties. The Mexican War, the Fugitive Slave Act of 1850, the Kansas controversy, and the Dred Scott decision all served to strengthen antislavery feeling, paving the way for the Republican victory of 1860 and the Civil War.

Legal emancipation had to wait upon political events, but in the meantime northern abolitionists felt no scruples about helping as many Negroes as possible to escape from slavery. The Underground Railroad became steadily bolder in its operations. The Fugitive Slave Law of 1850, intended to help masters recover their runaways, was impossible to enforce in many sections of the North. On several occasions antislavery mobs rescued Negroes from the Federal officials, and in many states accused fugitives had the protection of state Personal Liberty acts which practically nullified the Federal law. This refusal to respect their property rights infuriated the slave owners even more than abolitionist propaganda. Proslavery radicalism was strengthened and secession hastened.

The abolitionists strove to break down racial prejudice, almost as great in the North as in the South. Despite bitter opposition the public schools of some states opened their doors to Negroes, and in others special charity schools were established. Few colleges would accept colored students, but there were exceptions like Bowdoin and Oberlin. Negroes won their first recognition as public speakers in antislavery meetings. The eloquence and vigorous writing of the ex-slave Frederick Douglass was an effective answer to those who doubted the intellectual capacities of his race. Also successful as abolitionist speakers were William Wells Brown, an author and playwright, and Sojourner Truth, an uneducated but shrewdly intelligent female ex-slave.

The slavery issue was a difficult one for the churches. Although many clergymen were radical abolitionists, others firmly opposed the movement. Samuel J. May, himself a Unitarian minister, recalled that "the most violent conflicts we had and the most outrageous mobs we encountered, were led on or instigated by persons professing to be religious." [1] This conservatism reflected the fear of influential church members that the agitation would disrupt the business of the country and destroy the Union. Abolitionists during the thirties frequently found the church buildings unavailable for their meetings, and ecclesiastical conferences and conventions refused to pass controversial resolutions. During the forties antislavery sentiment became too strong to be silenced. The Methodists suffered a minor schism in 1843, when a group, impatient with the church's conservatism on the slavery issue and with its aristocratic government, withdrew to organize the Wesleyan Methodist Connection. This sharpened the conflict within the parent body, and at the general conference of 1844 a majority of the delegates voted to request a Georgia bishop to desist from his episcopal duties until he could rid himself of a few household slaves whom he had lately acquired along with a new wife. This indirect condemnation of slavery led in 1845 to a separation from the national body and the organization of the Methodist Episcopal Church, South. That same year the Southern Baptist Convention was organized as a result of conflict over the slavery issue. The Old-School Presbyterians took a conservative position, which postponed a split until the Civil War, but the New-School Presbyterians lost their southern churches in 1857. The inability of the major Protestant bodies to maintain their national unity foreshadowed the political secession of 1861.

Women's Rights

In the early nineteenth century the status of American married women still depended on the old English common law, a product of medieval civilization. In

[1] Samuel J. May, *Some Recollections of Our Antislavery Conflict* (Boston, 1869), 331.

Blackstone's succinct summary, "The husband and wife are one, and that one is the husband." Both a wife's property and her earnings belonged to her husband. She had no right to make a deed, a contract, or a will nor to sue in the courts without his consent. The law even recognized his right to administer "moderate correction"—through whipping or locking her up. To a large extent, of course, these provisions suggested a harshness untrue to actual conditions. American husbands who whipped their wives were few, and those who treated them with love and respect were many. But the old system denied protection to those women who most needed it. In every community there were pathetic cases of wives who had inherited wealth from thrifty fathers only to be reduced to poverty by the reckless expenditures of their husbands or of women who were laboring twelve hours a day to support husbands in the intoxication to which they were accustomed. Divorce was rarely a way out, since custody of the children was usually given to the father—no matter how worthless—and the divorced woman was scorned by the community.

But leadership in the assertion of women's rights came not so much from unhappy wives as from women who rebelled against their exclusion from whole areas of political and social activity. Women were not permitted to vote or to hold public office. They were denied admission to the colleges and, because of this and other barriers, they could not become ministers, lawyers, or physicians. By an absurd convention it was permissible for women to make speeches to members of their own sex but not to audiences that included men. Moral standards were patently unfair. The woman known to have had sexual relations outside of marriage became an outcast from society, while the same act brought only mild rebuke to the man.

The inequality of women, based as it was upon tradition rather than reason, inevitably fell under attack. The crusading Frances Wright was a visible challenge to male monopoly of the lecture platform, but the Scotchwoman's horrendous reputation as an infidel and an advocate of free love made her an example to be shunned by most American women. Similarly unacceptable to the conventionally respectable was Ernestine L. Rose, a brilliant Polish Jewess who began her American career in 1836 as a lecturer on the evils of the social system.

The great American agitation derived not from exotic foreign radicalism but from the indignation of earnest female advocates of temperance and antislavery who found their activities circumscribed by the conventions of the day. The issue was sharply presented, for Quaker women, accustomed to speak freely in their own religious meetings, brought the practice into the reform agitation. In 1837 conservative opinion in Massachusetts was shocked by the antislavery lectures of Angelina and Sarah Grimké. Their unseemly performance was sternly rebuked by the Congregational clergy in a "pastoral letter" issued by the General Association of Massachusetts. In the view of the conservatives:

> The power of woman is in her dependence, flowing from the consciousness of that weakness which God has given her for her protection, and which keeps her in those departments of

life that form the characters of individuals and of the nation. . . . But, when she assumes the place and tone of man as a public reformer, our care and protection of her seem unnecessary; we put ourselves in self-defence against her; she yields the power which God has given her for protection, and her character becomes unnatural. If the vine, whose strength and beauty is to lean upon the trellis-work and half conceal its clusters, thinks to assume the independence and the overshading nature of the elm, it will not only cease to bear fruit, but will fall in shame and dishonor into the dust.[1]

Controversy over women's participation in the abolition movement came to a climax at the World's Anti-Slavery Convention at London in 1840. While female delegates from American societies sat as silent witnesses, the men engaged in debate on whether the women should be admitted to the floor of the convention. Despite the eloquent appeals of Wendell Phillips and other champions of their credentials, the women were in the end voted down by English and American conservatives. Compelled to watch the proceedings from the gallery, where they were shielded from view by a screen, the indignant ladies spent their time more in reflection upon their own grievances than upon those of the Negroes. William Lloyd Garrison arrived in England too late for the debate, but gave dramatic demonstration of his sympathies by sitting with the women in the gallery and refusing to participate in the proceedings.

During the early forties women became more and more active in the temperance and antislavery movements—partly because of devotion to these causes and partly as an assertion of their right to make speeches and to serve on committees. The great reform agitations proved to be schools in which Lucretia Mott, Elizabeth Cady Stanton, Susan B. Anthony, and Lucy Stone gained the experience eventually put to use in the women's rights movement. Although Margaret Fuller moved in far different circles, her example undoubtedly hastened the feminist revolt. Talk of the inferior mentality of women seemed foolish during the years when the fabulous Margaret shone as one of the brightest stars in the transcendentalist constellation. Deeply resenting the conventions by which her sex was shackled, Margaret gave expression to her protest in *Women in the Nineteenth Century* (1845).

In 1848, when Lucretia Mott happened to visit in the vicinity of Seneca Falls, New York, where Elizabeth Cady Stanton was then living, the two women decided to organize a convention "to discuss the social, civil, and religious condition and rights of women." Although called on the spur of the moment, the meeting was crowded and enthusiastic. Boldly and ingeniously the ladies appropriated the classic Declaration of Independence and reworked it as their manifesto. They held it to be a self-evident truth that all men and women were created equal and asserted that the history of mankind was "a history of repeated injuries and usurpations on the part of man toward woman, having in direct object the establishment of an absolute tyranny over her." Then followed a specific bill of grievances against man to parallel the famous indictment of George III:

[1] Quoted in May, *op. cit.,* 243–244.

He has never permitted her to exercise her inalienable right to the elective franchise. . . . He has made her, if married, in the eye of the law, civilly dead. . . .

He has monopolized nearly all the profitable employments, and from those she is permitted to follow, she receives but a scanty remuneration. He closes against her all the avenues to wealth and distinction which he considers most honorable to himself. As a teacher of theology, medicine, or law, she is not known. . . .

He has usurped the prerogative of Jehovah himself, claiming it as his right to assign for her a sphere of action, when that belongs to her conscience and to her God. . . .[1]

The women had no reason to complain that the Seneca Falls Convention went unnoticed. Accounts of the meeting were widely published and provided the occasion for much heavy-handed editorial wit.

Although the timid drew back from this hail of ridicule, the feminist leaders pushed ahead, organizing conventions, writing letters to the newspapers, and preparing memorials to legislatures. The movement gained its most important recruit in 1850, when Susan B. Anthony, a Quaker schoolmistress of Rochester, New York, already active in the temperance and antislavery agitations, added that of women's rights to the list. Miss Anthony and Mrs. Stanton became close friends and developed extraordinary powers of collaboration. In the words of one observer, "Mrs. Stanton forged the thunderbolts and Miss Anthony hurled them."

A picturesque chapter in the women's struggle was the dress-reform episode of the fifties. Convinced that heavy skirts trailing through the dust were symbolic of female servitude, Elizabeth Smith Miller, daughter of Gerrit Smith, took the initiative in designing and wearing a radically different costume consisting of a knee-length skirt and loose trousers gathered at the ankle. Mrs. Amelia Bloomer of Seneca Falls gained immortality by donning the new attire and campaigning for its general adoption in her periodical *The Lily*. The Bloomer costume was soon adopted by other feminist leaders. It was welcomed also by women who particularly needed freedom in their movements—farm wives, Lowell factory girls, and patients in sanitariums. But the rebels against the tyranny of convention suffered greatly through the gibes of the crowd. As they walked along the streets, they were likely to hear voices from behind fences and hedges calling in shrill sing-song:

Heigh! ho! in rain and snow,
The bloomer now is all the go.
Twenty tailors take the stitches,
Twenty women wear the breeches.
Heigh! ho! in rain or snow,
The bloomer now is all the go.[2]

Sometimes the tormentors did not remain hidden. In Boston so great a crowd was attracted by the appearance of two Bloomer girls that they were forced to

[1] Elizabeth Cady Stanton, Susan B. Anthony, and Mathilda Joslyn Gage, eds., *History of Woman Suffrage* (New York, 1881), I, 70–71.

[2] Elizabeth Cady Stanton, *Eighty Years and More* (New York, 1898), 202.

seek refuge in a carriage. Although the costume was exceedingly modest, however inartistic, some officious males felt called upon to denounce it as immoral. A minister at Easthampton, Massachusetts, threatened to excommunicate any of his lambs seen abroad in bloomers. Despite ridicule Mrs. Stanton stuck to the

FIG. 27. *The New Female Costume.* From *Gleason's Pictorial Drawing Room Companion,* June 14, 1851. A "Bloomer girl." (*Courtesy of the Library of Congress.*)

costume for two years and Mrs. Miller for seven. (The real hero of the movement appears to have been Colonel Miller, who, as Mrs. Stanton recalls, "never flinched" in escorting his wife through the staring crowds.) But in the end the struggle seemed harder than it was worth, and the Bloomer girls reverted to trailing skirts.

Although the feminists lost many battles, they were destined to win the war.

Their demands for the franchise were for the time being regarded as fantastic not only by men but by most women as well. But they made good their right to be heard in public halls. At teachers' conventions, antislavery meetings, and temperance rallies the issue was fought out. Sometimes the women were temporarily silenced, but in the end their persistence won them the right to speak. Before the Civil War the assault upon the legal status of married women was bringing far-reaching results. The right of wives to control their own property was recognized by Mississippi in 1839 and by such other states as Texas, Indiana, Pennsylvania, Vermont, California, Wisconsin, and New York during the next two decades. In New York, as elsewhere, the feminists had as their allies many rich landowners, eager to remedy a situation that subjected the property of female heiresses to the vagaries of improvident husbands. Limited control over their property was given to married women by the New York legislature in 1848, and a much more comprehensive measure granting them full control over their property and earnings and joint guardianship over their children became law in 1860.

Meanwhile, the popular conviction that women's delicate constitutions could not withstand the rigors of Greek, mathematics, and other branches of higher learning was being proved erroneous. A superior secondary school for women, the Troy Female Seminary, was opened by Emma Willard in 1821. Catherine Beecher, one of Lyman Beecher's talented children, was less successful in the schools which she conducted at Hartford, Connecticut, and Cincinnati, Ohio, but her lectures and writings helped to stimulate interest in the educational problem. Mary Lyon, most famous of all the woman educators, founded Mount Holyoke Seminary at South Hadley, Massachusetts, in 1837. Excellent though these institutions were, they did not satisfy the aspiration which many girls now felt to secure a bachelor of arts degree. In 1837 Oberlin inaugurated a coeducational policy by accepting four women as regular students, Antioch took the same step in 1853, and the University of Iowa in 1860. Colleges for women only were also founded: Wesleyan Methodist College in Macon, Georgia, in 1836, the Elmira Female College in 1855, and Vassar in 1865.

Determined women forced their way into the professions. One of the earliest woman physicians was Dr. Harriot K. Hunt of Boston. Without much formal training she began practice in 1835, gaining some success both as practitioner of hydropathy and other medical fads of the day and as a lecturer on temperance, phrenology, the evils of tobacco, and sex hygiene. Her remonstrances against paying taxes without representation were an annual Boston event. Much better prepared for her profession was Dr. Elizabeth Blackwell. Refused admission to medical schools in Philadelphia and New York City, she applied at the small medical college at Geneva, New York. The professors could find nothing in the regulations to bar her, and the students, when consulted, voted her in—not out of sympathy with feminism, but because they looked forward with relish to the intruder's failure and withdrawal. But Elizabeth graduated at the head of her class in 1849. After her sister Emily received a similar degree, the two went to Paris for further study. There perplexed male authorities suggested that they dress as men but finally admitted them in their usual attire. After their return to America they encountered further obstacles. Not admitted to any established clinic for charity patients, they built their own New York Dispensary. In 1869 Dr. Elizabeth went to England, where she was the first woman admitted to the medical register and taught gynecology in the London School of Medicine for Women. Dr. Emily remained in America and became dean of the Women's Medical College of New York. During the fifties a number of medical colleges for women were founded, and a few institutions admitted both sexes. But the better schools still closed their doors. When the indefatigable Dr. Hunt, who had already been practicing for fifteen years, sought admission to Harvard Medical School in 1850, the students voted:

> That no woman of true delicacy would be willing, in the presence of men, to listen to the discussion of the subjects that must necessarily come under the consideration of students of medicine.
>
> *Resolved,* that we are not opposed to allowing woman her rights but do protest against her appearing in places where her presence is calculated to destroy our respect for the modesty and delicacy of her sex.[1]

Male monopoly of the ministry was even more jealously guarded. Antoinette Brown was admitted to the theological seminary at Oberlin only after the authorities had tried to talk her out of such a foolish step. She graduated in 1850, but the Oberlin authorities discreetly left her name off the class list. At first she could obtain no license to preach, but in 1853 she was finally accepted and ordained by a Congregational church in South Butler, New York. In later life Antoinette became the wife of Dr. Samuel Blackwell, brother of Elizabeth and Emily. She continued as an active feminist, a social worker, and a preacher—eventually transferring to the Unitarian denomination.

The Blackwells, an English Quaker family who immigrated to America in 1832, were deeply involved in the women's revolt. Henry, another brother of the famous doctors, attracted wide interest when he married Lucy Stone in 1855. Lucy, who had worked her way through Oberlin in the forties, had become one of the most successful woman lecturers of the fifties, speaking with equal earnestness in the causes of antislavery, temperance, and feminism. The *Boston Post,* believing that a husband was just what she needed, saluted the marriage in verse:

> A name like Curtius' shall be his,
> On Fame's loud trumpet blown,
> Who with a wedding kiss shuts up
> The mouth of Lucy Stone! [2]

[1] Quoted in E. Douglas Branch, *The Sentimental Years, 1836–1860* (Appleton-Century-Crofts, New York, 1934), 269.

[2] Quoted in Alice Felt Tyler, *Freedom's Ferment: Phases of American Social History to 1860* (University of Minnesota Press, Minneapolis, Minn., 1944), 435.

But Henry sympathized with all his wife's crusades. He joined with her in signing a Protest against the laws of marriage that gave the husband "injurious and unnatural superiority, investing him with legal powers which no honorable man would exercise, and which no man should possess." With his approval she refused to take his name and was known as Mrs. Lucy Stone.

The women's movement continued to invite the ridicule of editors like James Gordon Bennett, who thought Lucy Stone should be committed to a lunatic asylum, "where medicine and soothing treatment will extract from her brain that maggot of desire to exhibit herself at the polls," and who insisted that "the rights of women, like her duties, are bounded by her household." But the bitterness of the conservatives was that of men who knew that they were losing the fight. By 1861 the women had won their first victories and were girding for battles to follow.

Peace

A generation that believed in the possibility of freeing the world from evil could scarcely be indifferent to the horrors of war. The Quakers, of course, had from the earliest days advocated pacifism. Nor had they been without practical suggestions as to how international disputes might be settled without resort to war. As early as 1693 William Penn had suggested an international tribunal with binding powers of arbitration. Even during the Revolutionary War the Quaker philanthropist Anthony Benezet had urged the Continental Congress to seek a peaceful solution to the quarrel with the mother country. Philadelphia's famous physician Benjamin Rush was not a Quaker, but he had an equal abhorrence of war and in 1793 suggested that the new Federal government should establish a peace office to match its War Office.

The long Napoleonic agony, finally involving the United States through the War of 1812, encouraged the growth of peace sentiment. In the writings of David Low Dodge of New York and Noah Worcester of Massachusetts war was condemned as unchristian and irrational. In 1815 peace societies were formed in both New York and Boston, and that same year Noah Worcester began the publication of the *Friend of Peace.* The Massachusetts Peace Society had the support of such influential men as William Ellery Channing and Josiah Quincy, the president of Harvard. It showed evidence of health in a growth of membership, in the organization of public meetings, and in the preparation and distribution of tracts. Nor was the movement confined to the Northeast. By 1819 there were 17 peace societies, scattered over the country as far south as Georgia and as far west as Indiana.

Despite this promising start the peace crusade dragged feet until it was strengthened with the quickening energy of William Ladd. Ladd, a retired merchant, contributed his first articles and speeches in his own state of Maine, but he soon decided that the local societies would be ineffective until they could be coordinated in a national organization. Through his efforts the American Peace Society was founded at New York in 1828. Until his death in 1842 Ladd devoted all his energies to the cause of peace. He traveled extensively, spoke often, and wrote much. He encouraged the organization of college peace societies and sponsored essay contests that would focus attention on the problem of international organization. He himself developed a plan for a "congress of nations for the prevention of war," that would include a congress of ambassadors and an international court.

Despite these efforts the peace movement never attained the passion and drive of the antislavery and temperance crusades. Active peace workers were few and divided in their objectives. Sharp controversy arose between those who believed that only offensive wars should be condemned and those who believed that all war was wrong. Nor was that the end of the matter. The argument that all war was wrong pushed to an extreme led to the doctrine of absolute nonresistance. Christian perfectionism as developed by John Humphrey Noyes renounced earthly government and acknowledged Jesus Christ as rightful President of the United States. Such were the doctrines of radical nonresistance and nonparticipation in government to which William Lloyd Garrison, the Reverend Henry C. Wright, and other zealots became converted in the late thirties. The extremists seceded from the American Peace Society and organized the New England Non-Resistance Society in 1838. Members pledged themselves not to accept public office, not to vote, and not to resort to the courts.

Although the nonresistance doctrine added to Garrison's reputation as a visionary radical, it had little influence on the main trend of events. Most peace advocates continued to work through the American Peace Society. The rise of similar movements in England and on the Continent gave some ground for optimism, and in 1843 the first international peace congress convened at London. The American declaration of war on Mexico in 1846 was a great disappointment, but the conflict was sufficiently unpopular in antislavery circles to lead to bold protests like Thoreau's refusal to pay his poll tax and James Russell Lowell's sweeping indictment in the *Biglow Papers:*

> Ez fer war, I call it murder,—
> There you hev it plain an' flat.

During the forties the most effective peace orator was Elihu Burritt, already famous on lecture platforms as "the learned blacksmith." In 1846 he became dissatisfied with the conservatism of the American Peace Society and joined with Joseph Sturge of England in organizing the League of Universal Brotherhood, whose members signed the following pledge:

> Believing all war to be inconsistent with the spirit of Christianity, and destructive to the best interests of mankind, I do hereby pledge myself never to enlist or enter into any army

or navy, or to yield my voluntary support or sanction to the preparation for or prosecution of any war, by whomsoever or for whatsoever proposed, declared, or waged.[1]

Thirty thousand accepted this position in England, but the movement was much less successful in America.

Renunciation of war under all conditions proved hard doctrine for a generation passionately conscious of other evils. Hatred of slavery reconciled many to the use of force. For William Lloyd Garrison to defend the activities of John Brown was shockingly inconsistent, but he did it. And with the onset of the Civil War the New England radical at last gave to the Federal government the allegiance which he had long refused. After five decades of agitation for peace the bloody conflict between the states was bitter irony. Nevertheless, William Ladd and his fellow workers had planted ideas that were still growing a century later after they had been fed by the blood of two world wars.

Balance Sheet of Reform

Often the desire to perfect humanity seemed a sort of madness that would stop at no extreme. Tobacco was condemned by one reformer as "this nerve-prostrating, mind-benumbing, soul-paralyzing drug, this fleshly, ungodly lust!" Coffee fell under attack because of its alleged tendency to excite the baser passions; tea drinking was blamed for cold feet and hands, loss of appetite, and female disorders. The popular health lecturer Dr. Sylvester Graham converted thousands to a belief that the road to happiness lay in total abstinence from alcohol, eating coarse bread, fruits, and vegetables, wearing light clothes, sleeping on hard mattresses, taking daily exercise, and bathing three times weekly. Graham boardinghouses were established, and in innumerable households Dr. Graham's principles were religiously followed. When Margaret Fuller went to live with the Greeleys in New York, she was disconcerted to find that at the editor's table no meat, spices, liquors, tea, coffee, or pickles were served and that she was expected to subsist on beans, potatoes, boiled rice, bread, and milk. Other health addicts were hydropaths imbibing copious quantities of water "to cleanse, renovate, and rejuvenate the disease-worn and dilapidated system." Towns that boasted of particularly pure and healthful water drew visitors from hundreds of miles away, and a few like Saratoga and Ballston Spa in New York and Hot Springs in Virginia became fashionable vacation spots.

The age was not so remarkable for fads—for which Americans have always had an amiable weakness—as for the messianic claims made for each of them. Orson Fowler, the country's leading phrenologist, was not content to make a good living interpreting the bumps on his contemporaries' craniums, but had to assert that the truths of his science were antecedent to the Bible itself:

Its goal is eternal right. . . . Its roots run deep into the nature of man. Its branches yield all manner of delicious fruits, for the healing of the nations, and the renovation of man-

[1] Quoted in Tyler, *op. cit.,* 421.

kind. Its moral truths are food to the hungry, a cooling beverage to the thirsty soul, a foundation to those whom the tides of error are sweeping onward to destruction, and a feast of reason, with a flow of soul—sight to the blind, feet to the lame, health to the invalid, vitality to the dying, and life to the dead.[1]

But the exuberance of the period expressed itself in many admirable forms. Deep love for humanity led Thomas Hopkins Gallaudet to devote himself to the education of deaf-mutes at the American Asylum, opened in Connecticut in 1817, and a similar passion motivated Dr. Samuel Gridley Howe to become a teacher of the blind and to found the famous Perkins Institution for the Blind at Boston in 1832. Dr. Howe's success in opening the world to Laura Bridgman, who was blind, deaf, and dumb, aroused the interest of the country and encouraged the establishment of new schools for the handicapped.

With all its excesses this was an age of progress. The common man had attained to a new dignity and sense of participation in political affairs. Women had pushed open many doors that had hitherto been shut to them. Criminals, debtors, and lunatics no longer shared the same prisons but were treated in accordance with their separate deserts. Gross intemperance had become less frequent. The mind of the North had been prepared for the abolition of human slavery—although unfortunately no formula for a peaceful consummation of this great social revolution had been discovered.

[1] Quoted in Branch, *op. cit.*, 285.

Chapter 16. The Passion for Learning

If fair words could have built schools for American children, the young nation would have been well provided. The importance of education was affirmed in seven of the original state constitutions, and Congress proclaimed that in the Northwest Territory "schools and the means of education shall forever be encouraged." George Washington, John Adams, and Thomas Jefferson all used the prestige of the presidency to stress the educational responsibilities of the nation. But many decades passed before the actual situation gained any recognizable similarity to the generous phrases of the constitution makers and statesmen.

Education as Philanthropy

Except in New England the idea persisted that the education of children was primarily the responsibility of their parents. At the beginning of the nineteenth century practically all schools in the middle Atlantic and southern states were private institutions, controlled either by some religious denomination or by an individual schoolmaster. These schools often admitted children who were too poor to pay tuition. Indeed, the *Philadelphia Directory* of 1791 asserted that there was "no individual whose parents or guardians, masters or mistresses, will take the trouble to apply, but will be admitted into some one of these schools, and if they are unable to pay, will be taught gratis." [1] Unfortunately, relatively few parents "took the trouble to apply." And if they had, many would have been refused, since the number of nonpaying pupils that private schools could afford to accept was limited. With the growth of cities and the breakdown of apprenticeship the educational problem became more acute. The child who went to work in a factory at the age of eight learned neither his letters nor a trade.

American response to the situation was influenced by events in England, where the problem had arisen earlier. One line of attack had been initiated by Robert Raikes in 1781, when he organized the first Sunday school where child factory workers were taught reading and the catechism. Similar schools were soon to be found all over England. Sunday schools are known to have existed in Virginia by 1786 and, shortly after, in Philadelphia, Charleston, New York, Paterson, and the New England mill towns. But the American Sunday school

[1] Quoted in Paul Monroe, *Founding of the American Public School System* (Macmillan, New York, 1940), I, 208.

soon evolved into a pattern different from its English prototype. Instead of providing child workers with general schooling, it gave religious training to Protestant children of all classes. Instruction in reading and writing was soon relinquished to other agencies.

Provision of schools for poor children without religious affiliations became a favorite charity for public-spirited citizens. The Benevolent Society of the City of Baltimore for the Education of the Female Poor was founded in 1799 and the Male Free Society of Baltimore a little later. The Philadelphia Society for the Free Instruction of Indigent Boys was organized in 1800, and four years later a similar project took shape in Washington with President Jefferson as one of the first subscribers. The most famous of these organizations, the New York Free School Society opened its subscription list in 1805 with a gift of $200 from De Witt Clinton. Reorganized in 1826 as the Public School Society, it maintained schools in the great metropolis for many years with funds raised in part by private subscriptions and in part by grants from the city and state.

FIG. 28. *Plate of School When in Draughts.* From *New York Free School Manual,* 1820. Monitors instructing their fellow pupils under the Lancasterian system. (*Courtesy of The New-York Historical Society.*)

Philanthropists who wanted maximum results from their gifts were much excited by news from England, where Joseph Lancaster, a Quaker schoolmaster, was demonstrating that the poor could be educated at an annual expense of only 5*s.* a head. Lancasterian methods were introduced by the New York Free School Society in 1806 and soon became as popular in America as in England. In 1818 Lancaster himself came to America, where he spent much of the remaining twenty years of his life lecturing and demonstrating his methods.

Visitors were fascinated by the organization and efficient functioning of a good Lancasterian school where several hundred children were taught in a single room. The army of learners was divided into squads of 10, each of which was placed under the direction of a clever child known as the "monitor." The essence of the system was simple: the teacher taught the monitors and the monitors taught the other children. All was done with military precision. The monitors were summoned to the front of the room to receive their instructions. Then they returned to their groups and marched them to fixed stations facing the walls.

Each squad stood with its toes touching a semicircle drawn on the floor while the monitor drilled it on the day's lesson, which was printed on a card suspended from the wall. Other monitors kept attendance, handed out supplies, tested the scholars, and promoted them from group to group. Over the busy scene the teacher presided like the general of an army—or the superintendent of a factory.

In comparison with contemporary ungraded schools the Lancasterian schools were efficient. Pupils were carefully graded and subject matter was systematically organized. Many of the usual disciplinary problems disappeared in a system where pupils were kept constantly busy and competition was keen. The formula was believed capable of unlimited extension. Monitorial high schools were attempted, and there were even proposals for monitorial colleges. But the system proved ill adapted for subject matter that depended on thought and analysis rather than on drill and memory. Teaching by monitors was highly successful while the system was new, because the youngsters made up in energy and enthusiasm for what they lacked in learning. As time went on, however, the weakness of a system dependent on children teaching other children became steadily more apparent.

Despite their limitations the Lancasterian schools served a useful function. In making education appear cheap, not only did they appeal to thrifty philanthropists, but they won the support of state legislatures unwilling to erect complete systems of public schools.

Public Schools

The New England idea of public schools was gradually extended. In part, this reflected the actual migration to other sections of Yankees who had grown up with the institution. But it also represented a conviction everywhere that republican institutions and universal manhood suffrage demanded an enlightened citizenry. In New York, progress was rapid after 1812. In Ohio the idea of public support for education was as old as the state, having been incorporated in the Northwest Ordinance, the state constitution, and the Federal land grants, but effective legislation to implement the idea was not forthcoming until 1825. Frontier poverty retarded the establishment of a public-school system even longer in the other trans-Appalachian states.

In Pennsylvania, agitation for public schools met stubborn opposition. Conservatives were convinced that government provision for education should be limited to the children of parents unable to pay tuition at private schools. Parents who declared themselves paupers might have their children's tuition paid out of the poor rates. But pride prevented many parents from taking advantage of the law, while indolence or the desire to have their children work deterred others. The children who did attend private schools as charity pupils were often made unhappy by the snobbery of their schoolmates. In 1818 the legislature authorized the city of Philadelphia to build public Lancasterian schools for the education of the poor. Similar permission was later given to other urban areas, but neither this limited type of public school nor the provisions of the pauper law met the needs of the day. In 1829 it was reported that not more than 150,000 of an estimated 400,000 children between the ages of five and fifteen were attending schools of any kind.

In Pennsylvania, as in other laggard states, the demand for genuine public schools became more insistent with the rise of Jacksonian Democracy. The reformers gained an important victory in 1834, when a so-called "free-school" law was passed, providing for a division of the state into 987 districts, each of which might decide for itself whether it wished to continue under the old pauper-school system or to establish a public school. Despite its optional character the new law aroused the bitter opposition of private and denominational schools and of conservative German farmers, who disliked school taxes and objected to having their children educated in English. The foes of the law almost secured its repeal, but the free-school faction rallied its forces in the legislature, where Thaddeus Stevens delivered a speech long remembered in legislative history. In the end, the law was not only saved but strengthened. Although three-quarters of the districts established public schools by 1836, it was not until 1873 that the last district in the state accepted the new system.

A similar struggle occurred in New Jersey. There the free-school forces won a temporary victory in the school law of 1829, but the next year private and denominational school interests exercised such pressure that the law was repealed. The democratic movement finally carried the day, and a public-school system was established in 1838.

In the South, education continued largely in private hands. Several of the states accumulated a school fund from which they either granted aid to private institutions or established public charity schools. Although no general public-school system took shape until after the Civil War, the South was not as far behind the rest of the country as is often asserted. In 1860 there were 425,600 children attending school in the Lower South. This was about one white child out of every seven as compared with one out of six receiving education elsewhere.

Even where schools were public, education was by no means universal. One deterrent was the rate bill, a special tax assessed against parents who had children in the public schools. To avoid paying this, parents often kept their children out of school completely or sent them for only a few terms. This they could do without penalty, since there were no compulsory-attendance laws before the pioneer Massachusetts act of 1852. Provision was often made for the payment of the rates by the overseers of the poor, but the stigma involved deterred many parents from sending their children, and in some districts the authorities took no steps to implement the law. In 1851 nearly 50,000 children were prevented from attending the public schools of the State of New York by inability to pay the rates. Since farmers were particularly conservative in accepting the principle that the school taxes should be borne by the whole community, the rural districts clung to the rate bill long after the cities had made their schools entirely free. Although the rate bill was eliminated in Massachusetts as early as 1827, it persisted much longer elsewhere. In New York it was not entirely abolished until 1867, and it lasted until 1868 in Connecticut and until 1870 in New Jersey.

The Religious Issue

Whether the state supported education through the establishment of public schools or through granting aid to private charity schools, the religious issue could scarcely be avoided.

Considering the diversity of religious beliefs in the country, the elimination of sectarian instruction in the public schools was inevitable. The textbooks used in Massachusetts during the early national period—books like Noah Webster's famous *American Spelling Book* (1783), Lindley Murray's *Grammar* (1795), and Jedidiah Morse's *Geography* (1784)—differed from their colonial predecessors in their emphasis on general morality and patriotism rather than on the tenets of Calvinism. In many of the Massachusetts districts the teaching of the catechism and similar material was dropped even before 1827, when sectarian instruction in the public schools was forbidden by state law. Conservatives lamented the trend and, as late as 1840, tried unsuccessfully to restore the old system. The religious indoctrination which had once been so characteristic of Massachusetts public education left as its sole vestige the custom of opening the daily session by reading a passage of the Bible without comment. In other states where public schools developed, a similar policy was usually adopted.

The rapid growth of the Catholic Church during the thirties and forties brought to a crisis an issue which had long been agitated without decision. In demanding government grants for the support of their parochial schools, the Catholics were echoing demands made from time to time by Presbyterians, Episcopalians, and other Protestant groups. The problem had been particularly troublesome in New York City. Exempt from the general school law of 1812, the city's educational needs were met by the Public School Society, by certain similar but smaller charitable organizations, and by the various denominations. For a time all of these received state aid, apportioned according to the enrollment in their schools. But this practice led to such serious abuses that in 1824 the state adopted the policy of assisting only the Public School Society and a few other nonsectarian organizations. Although there were occasional eruptions during the thirties, the real fight on the issue did not come until the early forties, when the Catholics raised a violent protest against the Public School Society, which they regarded as a Protestant enterprise despite its avowed nonsectarianism. They demanded that the school funds be so divided as to permit the expansion of their own parochial-school system. Harassed by wrangling Catholic and Protestant partisans, the New York legislature finally cut the knot with commendable decision. The principle of refusing grants of public funds to sectarian schools was reaffirmed, but the virtual monopoly of the Public School Society was broken through the establishment of a city board of education with adequate powers to erect and to maintain a genuine public-school system. Although the Society continued to operate its own schools for another decade, it finally surrendered its property to the city and disbanded.

Other states where the legislators had occasionally yielded to the importunities of the denominational schools learned the dangers of the practice. Eventually the principle of refusing all such aid became generally established. Between 1840 and 1861 nine states wrote into their constitutions provisions forbidding public support of religious schools.

Educational Reform

The public school of the nineteenth century was almost always a district school. The district idea had originated in Massachusetts during the eighteenth century, when the dispersion of population had gradually made it impossible to teach all the children of the town in one central school. Outlying areas had been permitted to build their own schoolhouses, and the evolution of the new system had been formally recognized in the school law of 1789. Later laws added more powers to the districts until they received an almost complete charter of independence in the law of 1827. In Connecticut the evolution and legal recognition of the district system paralleled that in Massachusetts, and its establishment in the other New England states and in New York followed soon after. The free schools provided by Pennsylvania and New Jersey laws in the thirties were organized on a district basis, and the same system soon became firmly established in the West.

For the adult population the district provided an excellent school of politics. The embryo politician found a field for his energies in soliciting the votes of his neighbors for school trustee; the fledgling orator developed his talents by urging the merits of one crossroads over another for the school site. District issues often aroused far greater interest and excitement than the controversies of state or nation. School politics were a lively expression of grass-roots democracy.

In providing education for the children, the district system was less successful. Disliking heavy school taxes, the district voters often provided a shabby schoolhouse without adequate sanitary facilities. The school term was frequently reduced beyond the minimum prescribed by law, and teachers were offered less than a decent wage and usually had to "board around" in various households for part of their compensation. These teachers often knew little more than their charges. The principal requirement was that they be able to keep order. Most districts contained husky youths who delighted in attending school just long enough to try out each new teacher. If the educator could "lick" the troublemakers, he was a success no matter how deficient his training; but if his tormentors were too much for him—if they threw him out the window or barred him from the building—he had to retire in disgrace, and the school trustees looked for a bigger and more brutal man. During the 1830's between three and four hundred Massachusetts schools were broken up each year. The disciplinary problem was particularly difficult because the schools were ungraded and contained children ranging all the way from beginners to well-advanced pupils. The master would call two or three children to his desk to recite their lessons while the others were left at their benches, supposedly to study, but more frequently—like Tom Sawyer—to play with ticks or to show off before the opposite sex.

Under the district system teachers were always underpaid and often incompetent, supervision was negligible, uniformity in standards nonexistent, and attendance irregular. But with all its faults the crossroads schoolhouse was dearly loved. Although it was a place where the indolent need do little, it spelled opportunity for the ambitious. Reading, writing, arithmetic, grammar, spelling, and geography were rungs to be climbed toward some desired goal. The graduates of the district school were to be found in banks and factories, in courtrooms and hospitals, in statehouses and gubernatorial mansions, in the national Capitol and the White House. So deeply enshrined in American affection was the one-room school that attempts to reform it were usually resented.

Despite this sentimental attachment to the old order thoughtful citizens began to insist upon the necessity of change. In many areas the decay of the public schools was obvious. The poor kept their children out of school to work; the rich, disgusted with public-school conditions, patronized private institutions of learning. In Massachusetts in 1824 James G. Carter began a prolonged campaign. In newspaper articles, pamphlets, and books he emphasized the need for better trained teachers, better textbooks, and adequate supervision. As a member of the Massachusetts House of Representatives, he drafted the bill which created the state board of education in 1837.

The post of secretary of the new board was given to Horace Mann, an able lawyer and politician who had risen to the rank of president of the state senate. Mann's friends regarded his acceptance of this thankless $1,500 job as an inexplicable folly, but he knew the deficiencies of the existing system from personal experience and threw himself into the cause of reform with remarkable energy. It was a crusading generation, and Mann preached better schools with the same passionate intensity with which other men demanded prohibition or the abolition of slavery. During the twelve years in which he held the new office, public-school appropriations were doubled, 2 million dollars was spent to improve schoolhouses, teachers' salaries were increased by more than half, a month was added to the ordinary length of the school year, and three normal schools were established.

Mann's influence went far beyond the borders of the state: his annual reports were manifestoes which inspired educational reformers throughout the country, and the *Common School Journal,* which he edited for ten years, brought knowledge of better methods to ordinary teachers. In his famous *Seventh Report* of

1843 the secretary provoked controversy by pointing out that the schools of Prussia were in many particulars better than those of Massachusetts. Attendance was compulsory and rigidly enforced. Schools were carefully graded and supervised. Teachers sought to awaken their pupils' interest and controlled them without corporal punishment. In a document drafted by 31 Boston schoolmasters, Mann's observations were denounced as both unpatriotic and impractical. The educational value of flogging was asserted, and the principle that teachers should keep their children interested in their studies was branded as bad since "mental discipline" required that the child learn to work at dull and distasteful tasks.

Mann's controversy with the Boston schoolmasters well illustrates the deeper implications of educational reform. The conservatives, knowingly or not, were basing their case on the old Calvinist doctrine of human depravity. Children were by nature bad; only by stern discipline could their wicked willfulness be broken. Since the aim of life was not the achievement of happiness but the performance of duty, the young should be taught to do what was required of them without irrelevant considerations. The reformers were proceeding on radically different assumptions. They believed that human nature was essentially good and that children had instincts for truth and virtue which needed only to be encouraged by understanding teachers. Mann, a Unitarian, believed that better education was the key to a better society. This optimistic philosophy was one of the finest fruits of romanticism.

American educators, stirred by these generous impulses, found much to interest them in Europe. There a new philosophy of education had sprung from Rousseau's *Émile* (1762) and the experiments of Pestalozzi in Switzerland. The Prussian schools which Mann so much admired were permeated with the idealism of Pestalozzi and his disciples. The Massachusetts leader was neither the first nor the last American to be deeply influenced by contact with this line of European thought. The first account of Pestalozzian methods to be published in this country was written by William Maclure of Pennsylvania in 1806, but a much more influential description was contained in *A Year in Europe* (1819), written by John Griscom, a retired Quaker from New York.

Scarcely less influential than the work of Horace Mann in Massachusetts was that of Henry Barnard in Connecticut. In many ways the careers of the two were similar. Like Mann, Barnard was a lawyer-politician who worked for new educational laws in the state legislature. As secretary of the new Board of Commissioners for Common Schools, Barnard urged better schoolhouses, better teaching methods, and the organization of school libraries and evening schools. Although his career in Connecticut was interrupted when the legislature voted to discontinue the board as a "useless expense," Rhode Island, long negligent in school matters, made use of Barnard's services as state commissioner of education from 1845 to 1849. By 1851 the cause of educational reform was again in the ascendancy in Connecticut, and Barnard became principal of the state's first normal school and ex officio secretary of the state board of education. Barnard later served as president of the University of Wisconsin and as the first United States Commissioner of Education. But the Connecticut reformer's greatest contributions were in the field of scholarship. In the 31 volumes of the *American Journal of Education,* which Barnard began to edit in 1855, were assembled vast stores of information about educational history and the school systems of foreign countries.

Less well remembered than Mann and Barnard are the leaders who fought for educational reform in other states. Calvin Wiley, superintendent of common schools in North Carolina from 1853 to 1865, organized a system of public education that was unique for the South. Caleb Mills, shocked by Indiana's reputation of having a higher illiteracy rate than any other free state, led the agitation for reform and became the most influential figure in the great reorganization of that state's public schools during the fifties. Similar work was performed by Calvin Stowe in Ohio, Robert J. Breckinridge in Kentucky, and John D. Pierce in Michigan.

The Academies

The Latin grammar schools of colonial days had served the few boys who needed the classical languages for admission to college. Their narrow curriculum had little appeal for youths who wanted to become merchants, clerks, navigators, surveyors, or to follow some other middle-class calling. Except in the larger New England cities the Latin grammar schools languished, and the state laws requiring their maintenance were relaxed. Secondary schools of a different type developed in their place.

Many of these were fashionable finishing schools maintained by private masters. For most of these President Dwight of Yale had a hearty contempt, saying:

> To enable children to appear with such fashionable advantages, as to gain admiration and applause, is the sole concern. To enable them to be what they ought to be, wise, virtuous, and useful, is left out of the system. The mind, instead of being educated, is left to the care of accident and fashion. Dress, manners, and accomplishments are placed under expensive masters, and regulated with extreme solicitude. With this education, what can a son or a daughter become? Not a man nor a woman; but a well-dressed bundle of accomplishments. Not a blessing nor an heir of immortality; but a fribble or a doll.[1]

Much sounder education was provided by the academies. A few of these had been founded during the late colonial period, but their greatest expansion was during the early nineteenth century. There were 17 incorporated academies in Massachusetts in 1800, 68 in 1830, and 154 in 1860. Elsewhere a similar development occurred. Most of the income of the academies came from tuition fees but this was supplemented by endowments, gifts, and occasional state and local

[1] Timothy Dwight, *Travels in New-England and New-York* (New Haven, 1821-1822), I, 478.

aid. Control rested in boards of trustees, often self-perpetuating—a system well adapted to keep the academies under the control of particular religious denominations.

Largely independent of both public-school laws and the curricular traditions that inhibited the colleges, the academies experimented with many lines of training. Priding themselves on being "poor men's colleges," they taught any subject for which there was demand. New York regents' reports reveal that in 1837 the academies of that state were offering more than sixty different subjects including architecture, Biblical antiquities, embroidery, extemporaneous speaking, nautical astronomy, Hebrew, Italian, and physiology. However exotic many of these course offerings may seem, the general pattern is clear. To the Latin, Greek, and mathematics inherited from the old Latin grammar schools, the academies invariably added courses in English composition and literature, the modern languages, natural science, and practical business subjects.

Although many of the academies were for boys only, this exclusiveness was by no means universal. Before the end of the eighteenth century, at least two Massachusetts academies admitted both sexes, and after 1800 such coeducational institutions became more and more common. In addition, there were an increasing number of "female seminaries," serving a useful function in providing higher education for women in a day when the doors of most colleges were closed against them.

The academies showed great vitality. Their graduation exercises were local holidays, when relatives and friends drove to town from miles around, tying their buggies to every available hitching post and tree. The students revealed their erudition in orations, debates, and dialogues, and the presentation of Shakespearean plays provided an opportunity for them to demonstrate histrionic abilities developed in elocution classes. The exercises often continued all day with intermissions long enough for family parties to eat their basket lunches on neighboring lawns or to purchase lemonade and candy from temporary stands.

Although the tuition rates of the academies were low by present-day standards, they were high enough to exclude a majority of the population. In states where public elementary schools had become thoroughly established, the next democratic demand was for tax-supported secondary schools. The pioneer institution of this type was founded at Boston in 1821. First called the English Classical School and later the English High School, this admitted boys twelve years of age or over to study English, declamation, science, mathematics, history, and logic. Similar public high schools were organized at Portland, Maine, in 1821 and Worcester, Massachusetts, in 1824. The new trend was recognized in a Massachusetts law of 1827 requiring that each town of 500 families or over maintain a high school in which should be taught United States history, bookkeeping, algebra, geometry, and surveying and that in every town having 4,000 inhabitants or over, Latin, Greek, and other college-preparatory subjects were to be offered. But the law did not immediately secure the institution. Taxpayers in many places rebelled against the idea of paying for education beyond the elementary level and obtained changes making the high-school requirement optional. Not until 1857 was legislation passed to make the provisions of the earlier act fully operative. Despite legislative meanderings and local evasions, however, there were over one hundred high schools in Massachusetts by 1860.

A demand for free instruction at the secondary level swept New York during the forties and fifties. Since the academies received substantial aid from the state and sometimes local public aid as well, there was pressure, oftentimes successful, to secure free tuition for scholars from the towns where the institutions were located. Meanwhile, new "free academies" were established at New York City and elsewhere in the state. At first these were under the direction of special trustees rather than the local school boards, but eventually they were brought under exclusively public control. By 1860 there were 22 free, tax-supported, publicly controlled secondary schools in the state. But so indirect had been their evolution that only one of them bore the name of high school; the others were variously designated free academies, institutes, and classical schools.

Despite the rise of the public high school in Massachusetts, New York, Ohio, and a number of other states, there were only some three hundred such institutions in the United States in 1860. Secondary education was still dominated by some six thousand private schools and academies.

Colleges: Private and Public

At the level of higher education private institutions were equally well entrenched. The nine colleges founded before the Revolution were incorporated under charters which gave almost unlimited power to their trustees. Since these boards were self-perpetuating bodies in which all vacancies caused by death or resignation were filled by the surviving members, control could be tightly held by the denominations which had promoted the enterprises originally.

This monopoly of higher education fell under attack during the early national period. Rationalists demanded colleges where greater freedom of inquiry would prevail, and democrats urged the establishment of institutions less aristocratic and conservative in their policies. Such considerations were strong in the establishment of the first state universities. Georgia chartered such an institution in 1785, North Carolina in 1789, Vermont in 1791, Ohio in 1804, and South Carolina in 1805. But these institutions proved to be only quasi-public in character. In most of them the state's control was indirect, exercised through boards of overseers or visitors, while large powers were vested in the trustees. The states' financial support was fickle, leaving the infant institutions to support themselves largely through private endowments, gifts, and tuition fees.

Even less successful were attempts to enlarge state control over already established institutions. In Virginia, where Thomas Jefferson struggled for years to reorganize William and Mary, conservative opposition proved too strong, and the college continued under Episcopal control—a Pyrrhic victory since it resulted eventually in the establishment of the University of Virginia. Harvard and Yale preserved their independence by timely compromise. Before the Revolution both institutions had had close relations with the governments of their respective colonies, receiving financial grants and other privileges. Since the Harvard Board of Overseers already provided ex officio membership for certain government dignitaries, the post-Revolutionary agitation simply resulted in an increase in this representation. At Yale there was no similar precedent, but the corporation was enlarged in 1792 to include eight high officials of the state. At neither college did these changes result in any effective public control, but they quieted agitation and prevented the foundation of rival state institutions. In the middle states similar contests had similar results. The College of Philadelphia underwent various vicissitudes before it evolved into the University of Pennsylvania in 1791, but control was eventually vested in a board of trustees of which the governor was the only ex officio member; and King's College in New York, renamed Columbia, retained the status of a private institution under the nominal control of the newly created Regents of the University of the State of New York.

The proponents of increased public control suffered their most disastrous defeat at the hands of the Supreme Court in the Dartmouth College case of 1819. This litigation arose out of a controversy between the trustees of the college and its second president, John Wheelock, son of the founder. When the trustees dismissed Wheelock in 1815, the Democrats of the state took up his cause with enthusiasm, since it gave them full opportunity to denounce the Federalists and Congregationalists for perpetuating a selfish monopoly of higher education. Upon the issue of reform of the college the popular party rode to power in the election of 1816. The new legislature promptly passed a law amending the college charter to provide a new name, Dartmouth University, an enlarged board of trustees, and a new state-appointed board of overseers. Since the old trustees refused to recognize the legality of these changes, the village of Hanover was for two years the seat of rival institutions—Dartmouth College with 3 professors and 95 students and Dartmouth University with 4 professors and 14 students. In the ensuing court battles the University won the first round when the New Hampshire Superior Court ruled that the institution was a public corporation subject to legislative control. But Daniel Webster's arguments were more successful before the Federal Supreme Court, and in February, 1819, John Marshall read a strongly worded decision completely upholding the rights of the old trustees. The college, said the Chief Justice, was not a civil institution but a private "eleemosynary" one, "incorporated for the purpose of perpetuating the application of the bounty of the donors to the specified objects of that bounty." Its charter was a contract the obligation of which might not be impaired by subsequent action of the state.

The decision which killed Dartmouth University was hailed with enthusiasm by private-college interests throughout the country. It strengthened the position of existing institutions and encouraged the establishment of new ones. To the nine colleges of 1780 there were added during the next eighty years 173 colleges which survived and perhaps four times that number which failed. Only a few of these were public institutions; the rest were founded in the interest of some particular denomination. The Presbyterians with their emphasis on a well-educated clergy were particularly active. Forty-nine Presbyterian colleges dotted the country from Princeton in the East to Pacific University in the West. The Congregationalists with similar traditions supported 21 colleges, mostly located in New England and the Middle West. The Methodists and Baptists at first manifested some prejudice against higher education, but this phase was short-lived. Thirty-four Methodist and 25 Baptist colleges were founded by 1860. Active also were the Catholics, who founded 14 institutions, and the Episcopalians, who founded 11.

To many the situation seemed absurd. In 1860 Ohio had 17 colleges, Pennsylvania 16, New York 15, and Illinois 12. The supply of colleges was obviously far in excess of the demand for higher education. The largest institutions like Yale and Harvard had only four or five hundred students; the smaller ones had two hundred or less. Largely dependent on student fees, none of these institutions could afford a really adequate faculty or proper equipment. All of them were poor, struggling institutions, whose presidents spent much of their time begging for funds to save them from disaster.

Meanwhile, the rival ideal of the state university had at last achieved a measure of success. Defeated in his attempt to extend public control over William and Mary, Thomas Jefferson secured legislative support for the creation of the University of Virginia in 1819. Although assisted in his work by other men, the philosopher-statesman was allowed unusual freedom in planning the campus, organizing the curriculum, and selecting the faculty. In all these things the new institution was given a character unique in the America of its day, reflecting both Jefferson's admiration for French education and his independent thought on the purposes and methods of higher learning. The university buildings, attractively designed in classical style, were grouped to form "an academical village," connected by corridors and surrounding a lawn. The curriculum differed from that of contemporary American colleges in its emphasis on modern languages, government, political economy, and science, and its omission of theological subjects. The first faculty was an able one, recruited in England by an emissary whom Jefferson sent abroad for the purpose. The new institution began operations in 1825 amidst the applause of liberals and the condemnation of conservatives. After Jefferson's death in 1826 his great experiment was somewhat modified, particularly through the admission of more religious influence.

The most successful of the pre-Civil War state institutions was the University of Michigan. As early as 1817 plans were laid for a system of public education which should extend from the lowest to the highest level of learning. For a generation frontier poverty delayed the project. But in 1837, when Michigan was admitted to statehood, the legislature granted a charter for a university, completely under public control, in which the admission fee should not exceed $10 and tuition should be free for residents of the state. The financial basis of the new institution was uncommonly strong because of shrewd management of the land grants which Michigan, like other trans-Appalachian states, had received from the Federal government for the support of higher education.[1] Despite these favoring circumstances the university was a small, struggling institution until Henry P. Tappan became its president in 1851. Tappan greatly admired contemporary German universities with their extensive course offerings, their advanced instructional methods, and their freedom of election. His aggressive efforts to give a similar character to the University of Michigan aroused criticism and led eventually to his dismissal in 1863, but he held office long enough to transform the institution from a small provincial college to a true university, attracting students from all over the country. By 1860 it had over five hundred students, and there were more than twice that number in 1865.

The Curriculum

Since a fixed curriculum was followed almost everywhere, students destined for careers in business or law studied the same subjects as those preparing for the ministry. The list of studies was usually an impressive one, but only Latin, Greek, mathematics, and philosophy received much serious attention. A smattering of science—without laboratory work and with only a few demonstrations—was provided in the course in natural philosophy, and a little economics and political science might be included in moral philosophy. Almost completely neglected were English literature, modern languages, and modern history. Since the purpose of higher education was held to be mental and moral discipline, the irrelevance of most of the subject matter to early nineteenth-century life disturbed only a few critics.

The curriculum was not, however, entirely invulnerable to change. Between 1780 and 1860 it was cautiously modified to include natural science, English literature, and modern languages. The new subjects often had to be studied as extras, not counting toward the venerable A.B. degree. Even when they finally won adoption into the regular course, their status was a lowly one. At Dartmouth, for example, the professor of modern languages, appointed in 1859, was compelled to give his courses during the winter term, when most of the students were absent teaching school. Consigned to the same poorly attended session were such other exotics as modern history and international law.

[1] These grants—usually two townships—began with one to the Ohio Associates in 1787. All 21 states admitted to the Union before the Civil War, with the exception of Vermont, Kentucky, Maine, and Texas, received grants, but the results were for a long time disappointing. Land brought no income unless it could be sold or rented, and even then the funds so raised were often mismanaged, misappropriated, or dispersed among several institutions.

As long as the colleges attempted to teach their entire curriculum to all their students, the introduction of new subjects simply diluted the course. European universities had met this problem by allowing students to choose for themselves what they wished to study, but the efforts of American reformers to introduce the elective system met determined resistance. Thomas Jefferson strongly urged the change, but even at the University of Virginia there were rather strict requirements for the bachelor of arts diploma, and only students who were not candidates for a degree enjoyed full freedom of election. George Ticknor, agitating for change at Harvard, succeeded only in securing a few new nondegree courses and a few options in the regular curriculum. Nondegree courses in which literature and modern languages might be substituted for the classics were introduced at Union, Amherst, and the University of Vermont but attracted few students. The bachelor of science degree, granted first in 1850 by the Lawrence Scientific School at Harvard and soon after by the University of Michigan, helped the cause of reform by providing a distinction which might be earned without taking the ancient languages.

Professional training increased in importance. To the pioneer medical schools at the College of Philadelphia (1765) and King's (1767) were added Harvard Medical School (1782), Dartmouth Medical School (1798), and several others during the first decades of the nineteenth century. Law schools came somewhat later. Professorships of law were instituted at William and Mary in 1779, at Pennsylvania in 1790, and at Columbia in 1797. But the best legal training of the period was offered at the private law school of Tapping Reeve in Litchfield, Connecticut, where such well-known figures as John C. Calhoun and Horace Mann received their training. The Harvard Law School was organized in 1817 but did not achieve distinction until Joseph Story joined its faculty in 1829. Even the best of these schools depended on the part-time teaching of active practitioners and maintained few standards either for admission or graduation. The majority of American doctors and lawyers still gained their training through the old system of apprenticeship.

The rapid growth of the country and the building of turnpikes, canals, railroads, and factories demanded trained engineers, but the supply was small. For the first decades of the nineteenth century the Military Academy at West Point, opened in 1802, was the only institution where such training could be had. Nor was the need adequately supplied by the founding of Norwich University at Northfield, Vermont, in 1820, Rensselaer Polytechnic Institute at Troy, New York, in 1825, and the Franklin Institute in Philadelphia the same year. Not until after the Civil War did professional engineering schools gain a status commensurate with their importance in American society.

A curious phase of collegiate history was the establishment of numerous "manual-training institutes," deriving their inspiration from the famous institution conducted by Emanuel von Fellenberg in Switzerland. Typically romantic was the thought that the ideal education might be provided by combining intellectual studies with training in trades and agriculture. By 1835 manual-training schools had been attempted in 12 states and were particularly popular in New York and in the Middle West. Such colleges as Oberlin, Wabash, and Knox all began in this fashion. In its American trial the manual-training idea proved less an experiment in education than a way in which poor colleges and poor students could help each other through the operation of college farms. Having served this function, the manual-training feature was almost everywhere abandoned.

But a demand for genuine agricultural education took its place. The first state agricultural college was founded at Lansing, Michigan, in 1857, and in 1859 a bill providing land grants to each state for the establishment of similar institutions passed Congress only to be killed by President Buchanan's veto.

College Life

It was still common for students to enter college at the age of fourteen or fifteen and to graduate at eighteen or nineteen. Even when they were older, the faculty treated them as boys rather than men. Their days were carefully planned from five o'clock in the morning when they were awakened until nine at night when they were sent back to bed again. In unheated chapels the students shivered through morning and evening prayers. On Sundays there might be as many as four religious services to fortify the college community for the week to follow. Not satisfied with these regular exercises, conscientious college presidents frequently conducted revivals during which all other activities were suspended so that the students might be guided through soul-saving experiences.

As if to confirm Calvinist educators in their doctrine of human depravity, the students responded to all this moral guidance by throwing food in the college commons, shuffling their feet noisily during recitations, tethering livestock in the chapel, and cutting the bell rope. Such evidences of youthful high spirits were accepted as normal tribulations by the long-suffering faculty. More serious were the incidents which involved the use of explosives. In 1814 pranksters at Princeton cracked the walls and broke most of the windows of Nassau Hall by setting off the famous "big cracker"—a hollow log charged with 2 pounds of gunpowder. A few months later a boy playfully shot a pistol through the door of one of the tutors. In 1817 the students, deciding that their assignments were too long, nailed up the doors of the college buildings, broke the windows, rang the bell incessantly, shouted "Fire!" at the top of their lungs, and hurled firewood and decanters at the faculty. Such episodes were by no means peculiar to Princeton. In 1824 a resident of Hanover, New Hampshire, wrote:

> It is now almost commencement. Three days more will bring us to that day when the devil reigns predominant; he has come this year a week beforehand; already have the students burnt one barn, stoned Prof. Chamberlain, burnt him & tutor Perley & hung the President in effigy.[1]

[1] Leon Burr Richardson, *History of Dartmouth College* (Hanover, N. H., 1932), I, 382.

It is little wonder that the minutes of faculty meetings were largely concerned with the imposition of fines, suspensions, and expulsions.

The disciplinary problems of the colleges arose largely out of the rebellion to be expected from young human males subjected to too many rules and sermons. A contributing factor was the absence of any organized program of athletics. Instead of the overemphasis on sports often criticized in the twentieth century, foreign visitors of this period commented on the absence of any attempt by the colleges to provide exercise for their students.

Lyceums and Libraries

The passion for learning was not exhausted by the establishment of schools and colleges. Busy adults, conscious of the rapid expansion of knowledge, attempted to extend their education through study clubs and library societies. In the cities mechanics' institutes began to develop along the lines of similar institutions in England, and a lending library was often accumulated for the benefit of the group.

The cult of self-improvement was best exemplified by the lyceum movement. Acting along the lines of an article which he had written for the *American Journal of Education,* Josiah Holbrook organized the first branch of The American Lyceum at Millbury, Massachusetts, in 1826. Similar groups were formed in several nearby towns and promptly federated into a county lyceum. The movement spread rapidly, and in 1831 the national lyceum held the first of its annual conventions. By 1835 Holbrook estimated that there were some fifteen state lyceums, over one hundred county groups, and about three thousand town and village organizations.

At the local level the movement was exceedingly simple. As Holbrook outlined it:

> The first step to form a Lyceum is for a few neighbors or citizens to agree to hold meetings for their mutual improvement. The second is to agree upon the place where they will meet. The third to procure a book, a periodical, or a tract, from which they can read. The fourth is to procure a few articles of apparatus to illustrate what is stated in the book. These steps seldom fail to lead to others, and to secure success. . . .[1]

The early lyceums studied many different subjects, but were particularly interested in elementary science. They conducted simple experiments in chemistry and physics, collected rocks and plants, and sometimes compiled local maps and histories. They agitated for better public schools and sought to stimulate both teachers and pupils by allowing them to attend lyceum meetings without charge.

With an enthusiasm characteristic of the period the lyceum leaders believed that their movement would transform society. State lyceums would act as boards of education, and the national lyceum would coordinate the educational activities

[1] *American Lyceum, or Society for the Improvement of Schools, and Diffusion of Useful Knowledge* (Boston, 1829), 16–17.

of the whole nation. It was even proposed to establish special academies in every part of the country:

> These seminaries are to be upon the manual labor, or self-supporting plan, and especially designed for the *qualification of teachers*. It is supposed that one of these institutions may eventually be established in nearly every county, and be the centre and moving spring of the county and town lyceums in the several districts where they are established.[1]

Such an institution was actually founded at Berea, Ohio, "the first lyceum village."

No national conventions were held after 1839, and other overambitious aspects of the movement soon died out. But as local institutions the lyceums became firmly rooted. A principal activity was the sponsorship of public lectures. Lyceum audiences were introduced to the wonders of science by college professors like Benjamin Silliman of Yale and Louis Agassiz of Harvard; they were warned of the evils of slavery, intemperance, and the unequal status of women by reformers like William Lloyd Garrison, Wendell Phillips, John B. Gough, and Susan B. Anthony; they were given a sense of personal contact with the literary world by hearing famed foreign authors like Charles Dickens and William Makepeace Thackeray. A favorite lecturer was Elihu Burritt, "the learned blacksmith," whose ability to read nearly fifty languages was rightly regarded as an extraordinary demonstration of the possibilities of self-culture. But the lyceum platform's greatest ornament was Ralph Waldo Emerson, whose moral earnestness and gift for vivid phrase made his lectures unforgettable experiences.

Adult education was also fostered by the establishment of libraries. Excellent collections of books were assembled by the athenaeums of cities like New York, Boston, and Providence, but since these were open only to their aristocratic members, they were of little help to the classes which most needed cheap access to books. More democratic were the facilities provided by the Mercantile Library Association and by the Apprentices' Library Association, established in New York in 1820, and by similar institutions in Boston, Philadelphia, and Portland. In smaller communities modest collections of books were provided in district-school and Sunday-school libraries. Small public libraries were established at Castine, Maine (1827), Peterborough, New Hampshire (1831), and Orange, Massachusetts (1846), and much larger and more influential institutions were founded at Boston (1854), New York (1854), and Baltimore (1857).

Newspapers and Magazines

Contributing also to popular education was the new journalism. Earlier newspapers had been expensive and dull. The most influential had been published at the successive seats of the Federal government—at New York, Philadelphia, and Washington. Heavily subsidized through contributions by political

[1] *American Lyceum, With the Proceedings of the Convention Held in New York, May 4, 1831* (Boston, 1831), 10.

leaders and the allotment of government printing, their principal content had been official documents and ponderous attacks on the men and policies of the opposing camp. This tradition of journalism began with the establishment of John Fenno's *Gazette of the United States* as a Federalist organ in 1789 and Philip Freneau's *National Gazette* as its Republican rival in 1791. It was carried on by the *National Intelligencer,* established in 1800, and by Duff Green's *United States Telegraph* and Francis P. Blair's *Globe,* both products of the Jackson administration. But although the Washington papers were sent into every part of the country, they did not prevent the growth of a local press. Every sizable town had its journal. Most of these were weeklies, but a growing number, following a precedent established by the *Pennsylvania Packet* in 1784, appeared daily. Their circulation was still largely confined to the mercantile and professional classes, since neither in content nor price did they attract the ordinary citizen.

The possibilities of a different kind of paper, priced at 1 penny and printing news of general interest was first demonstrated by *The New York Sun,* which was established by Benjamin H. Day in 1833. When the *Sun* described astonishing details of life on the moon as lately revealed by a new telescope, its readers were delighted, nor was their pleasure diminished by the editor's subsequent confession that the moon story was a hoax. Increased advertising revenues and more economical printing methods made possible the paper's low price. Bolder still were the methods of James Gordon Bennett, who founded the *New York Herald* in 1835. He disdained, he frankly asserted, "all principle, as it is called, all party, all politics." His business was selling news, which he gathered with ingenuity and presented with skill. Nor would he change his methods, no matter how the fastidious might condemn the publication of scandal or the unscrupulous lengths to which Bennett would go to scoop his competitors.

When Horace Greeley founded the *New York Tribune* in 1841, he created not merely another popular newspaper but a mid-century institution. Greeley was an earnest party man—first a Whig and later a Republican. But his party affiliations did not destroy his independence. The *Tribune* told the unpleasant truth about the growing slums of the city and the heartless exploitation of labor. It championed a miscellaneous list of causes ranging all the way from the protective tariff to Fourier socialism. Particularly in its weekly edition the *Tribune* found its way to every part of the North and West. In many households it was regarded as scarcely less infallible than the Bible.

More conservative than Greeley was Henry J. Raymond, who founded the *New York Times* in 1851. "There are few things in this world which it is worth while to get angry about," wrote Raymond in the first issue, "and these are just the things anger will not improve." Despite its distaste for crusades the *Times* gained an early reputation for accuracy and honesty—a solid foundation for the building of one of the world's truly great journals.

Throughout the nineteenth century magazines were born and died with bewildering rapidity. Of the periodicals founded before 1850, only the *North American Review* (1815–1940) was still alive at the end of the century. But influential in their day were: the *Dial* (1840–1844), the vehicle of the New England transcendentalists; the *Knickerbocker Magazine* (1833–1865), to which the leading writers of the country contributed, especially in the forties; the *Western Messenger* (1835–1841), a cultural force in the Old Northwest; and the *Southern Literary Messenger* (1834–1864), edited for a time by Edgar Allan Poe. Achieving a circulation greatly in excess of all of these was *Godey's Lady's Book* (1830–1898). Its colored fashion plates and sentimental verse and stories won thousands of feminine readers and made the name of its editor Sarah J. Hale a household word for forty years. Of particular importance were two magazines founded during the fifties. *Harper's Monthly Magazine,* founded in New York in 1850, and the *Atlantic Monthly,* founded in Boston in 1857, were excellent periodicals, destined to achieve their full influence after the Civil War.

Science Becomes a Profession

In the early nineteenth century scientific investigation was still the avocation of gentlemen. Thomas Jefferson loved to throw off the cares of the presidency by withdrawing to an unfinished room in the Executive Mansion to study his collection of fossils. With equal eagerness he collected data on the comparative weights of European and American animals, the fertility of the Indians, and the various species of American plant life. A similar catholic interest in the world of nature was to be found among many other gentlemen. In Philadelphia the painter Charles Willson Peale operated a natural-history museum which was one of the city's famous show places. Bird lovers were delighted with the patient study and exquisite draftsmanship displayed in John James Audubon's *Birds of America* (1827–1838).

American intellectual life was stimulated by exiles from Europe. Joseph Priestley, the discoverer of oxygen, came to America in 1794 to escape the hostility which his liberal opinions had provoked in England during the period of the French Revolution. Until his death in 1804 Priestley lived in the frontier village of Northumberland, Pennsylvania, carrying on his studies and corresponding with his many friends. Sharing the Priestley home was another English chemist and political exile, Dr. Thomas Cooper, who survived his friend by thirty-five years. Cooper had a notable teaching career at Dickinson College, at the University of Pennsylvania, and at the College of South Carolina, where he was president for thirteen years. His unorthodox religious and political views involved him in a sequence of troubles, which extended from a six-month jail sentence in 1798 for criticizing President John Adams to dismissal from his college presidency in 1834 for challenging the Biblical story of creation. Even more brilliant and decidedly more eccentric was Constantine Rafinesque, who came to America from Italy in 1815. Ridiculed for his grandiose ideas, Rafinesque died in abject poverty in Philadelphia in 1840; but later scientists have testified to the importance of his botanical studies and astute generalizations, which anticipated Darwin's theory of evolution.

Since the chief incentive to scientific study was individual curiosity, notable achievements were not confined to any particular discipline or center of study. Nathaniel Bowditch of Salem passed from the practical problems of navigation into the field of advanced mathematics, where he distinguished himself. William

FIG. 29. *Exhuming the Mastodon.* Painting by C. W. Peale. Peale, an enthusiastic scientist, depicts himself on the right directing the collection of fossil remains. (*Courtesy of the Peale Museum, Baltimore; photograph by the Metropolitan Museum of Art, New York.*)

Maclure, a Scotch merchant who immigrated to America in 1796, became an enthusiastic student of geology. Maria Mitchell of Nantucket studied astronomy with her father and confounded those who doubted the intellectual capacities of women by discovering a telescopic comet in 1847—an achievement that gained international notice.

The discovery of anesthesia was in many ways America's most valuable contribution to scientific knowledge during this period. Before this event surgery could make little progress. Although operations were often performed, the terrible pain that accompanied them made the operating room a place of horror, and the need for the surgeon to work as rapidly as possible prevented the development of careful technique. Apparently the first man to use ether as a surgical anesthesia was Dr. Crawford W. Long of Georgia in 1842, but his failure to publish his findings until 1849 resulted in other men's receiving credit for the discovery. Likewise unfortunate was Dr. Horace Wells, a Hartford dentist, who used nitrous oxide during tooth extractions in 1844 but failed when invited to demonstrate his technique before a group of physicians. The fame which these men narrowly missed was won by Dr. W. T. G. Morton, a Boston dentist who had the assistance of C. T. Jackson, a local chemist, in his experiments with ether. In 1846 Dr. Morton administered ether to a surgical patient in the Massachusetts General Hospital with complete success. A distinguished group of witnesses accepted the verdict of Boston's leading surgeon, "Gentlemen, this is no humbug!"

But research was not exclusively dependent on individual initiative. Government sponsorship played an increasingly important role. Even before the purchase of Louisiana Jefferson had seen the value of an exploration of the trans-Mississippi West and had commissioned Meriwether Lewis and William Clark for the task. Leaving St. Louis in 1804, the exploring party followed the Missouri River for over 2,000 miles, struck a trail across the Continental Divide, and followed the Columbia River to the Pacific, returning to St. Louis by a similar route two years later. Data of every kind—geographical, geological, zoological, botanical, ethnological—were collected and made available through the publication of the journals of the explorers. Additional information about the West resulted from the exploration of Captain Zebulon M. Pike and the later exploits of Captain John C. Frémont.

Despite delays caused by provincial Congressmen who could not appreciate the need for such projects, the United States Coast Survey was organized in 1832. At first under the direction of Ferdinand Hassler, a Swiss engineer, and then under that of Alexander Dallas Bache, the talented great-grandson of Benjamin Franklin, the survey was pushed forward over a period of more than thirty years. A similar study of the Great Lakes began in 1841. A project better adapted to capture the popular imagination was that of the United States Exploring Expedition under the command of Lieutenant Charles Wilkes. Between 1838 and 1842 it surveyed 800 miles of the western coastline of North and South America and some 280 islands in the South Atlantic and the South Pacific. The existence of an antarctic continent was demonstrated, and data were collected of great importance not only to geography and navigation, but to geology, biology, and ethnology. Some twenty-five volumes eventually resulted from these four years of adventure and study.

The possible results of government support for a talented scholar were well illustrated by the career of Lieutenant Matthew Fontaine Maury of Virginia, a naval officer who first won notice in 1836 by the publication of a standard treatise on navigation. Five years later he was made director of the United States

Naval Observatory and Hydrographic Office. Maury undertook to organize an extensive study of the winds, currents, and seasonal temperature changes affecting navigation. Through the cooperation of hundreds of sea captains who kept special log books, Maury assembled voluminous data and wrote his great book, *The Physical Geography of the Sea* (1855). The practical result of his research was the establishment of new routes, whereby ships were able to save days of sailing time and to diminish the risk of losses through storm.

The scientific activities of the Federal government were further expanded by the establishment of the Smithsonian Institution in 1846. Behind this event lay a curious story. James Smithson was the illegitimate son of a British nobleman. Although he had inherited wealth through his mother's family and achieved some success as a chemist, Smithson carried through life a feeling of deep resentment against his father and English society generally. Obsessed with the ambition that his name should "live in the memory of man when the titles of the Northumberlands and the Percys are extinct and forgotten," he bequeathed his fortune to the United States "to found at Washington, under the name of Smithsonian Institution, an Establishment for the increase and diffusion of knowledge among men." In 1838 the bequest was brought to America in the form of 105 bags containing gold sovereigns of a total value of some $500,000.

The use to which this windfall should be put was debated in Congress at intervals over the course of the next eight years. John C. Calhoun advocated the rejection of the gift, since the acceptance of money from a private foreigner was beneath the dignity of the nation. Jefferson Davis suggested a perpetual series of popular lectures, Andrew Johnson the establishment of a national normal school, and Rufus Choate the building of a great library. At last the issue was resolved through the incorporation of an institution which should encourage research and maintain museums of art and science.

To direct the new enterprise, Joseph Henry was selected—an excellent choice since Henry's scientific achievements were unsurpassed by any other American scholar of his generation. While teaching at Albany Academy and later at Princeton, he had discovered principles important in the construction of electromagnets and demonstrated how electromagnets might be used for telegraphic communication—thus laying the scientific basis for Morse's famous achievement. The principle of electromagnetic induction, which is basic for the construction of dynamos and the practical harnessing of electricity, was discovered by Henry in 1831. This discovery probably antedated the demonstration of the same principle by Faraday in London, but the American unfortunately delayed publication of his results. During his thirty-two years at the Smithsonian Henry contributed greatly to the organization of scientific research, developing a type of administration that was to be increasingly important as science moved toward cooperative activity. Characteristic of Henry's initiative were the Smithsonian's researches into such practical subjects as meteorology, foghorn acoustics, ballistics, and the strength of building materials.

Although science's place in the college curriculum was still a minor one, it gave employment to an increasing number of scholars. In 1802 President Timothy Dwight of Yale appointed Benjamin Silliman professor of chemistry and mineralogy—not because Silliman then knew anything of those subjects, but because he was an intelligent young man not likely to be seduced from Calvinist orthodoxy by his scientific studies. Silliman prepared himself for his post by study in England and then returned to teach at Yale for fifty years. His contributions to research were not important, but he served a vital function in transmitting to America new knowledge from Europe. His influence extended far beyond Yale, first, through the *American Journal of Science and Art,* which he founded in 1818 and edited for many years, and second, through his many appearances on the popular lecture platform, where he had singular success. Benjamin Silliman, Jr., developed interests strikingly similar to those of his father, with whom he was associated for many years. The elder Silliman's pupil and son-in-law, James Dwight Dana, was an even more remarkable scholar. Specializing in geology and profiting greatly from his employment on the United States Exploring Expedition of 1838–1842, Dana became the leading American authority in the field, teaching for many years at Yale and publishing over two hundred papers and books.

Louis Agassiz, a Swiss, had already established a great reputation for his studies of fishes and the movement of glaciers before he came to America in 1846 to speak at Lowell Institute and decided to remain as professor of zoology and geology at Harvard. Although he continued to do important research, Agassiz' fame was based in equal measure on his success as a teacher and lecturer. He had the gift of making science seem exciting, and he emphasized the importance of studying nature from direct observation rather than from textbooks.

At Harvard also was Asa Gray, who, despite a very inadequate formal education, became America's leading botanist. He built up the largest herbarium in the country, and his studies of plant distribution were so significant that they won the attention of Charles Darwin. Gray and Darwin entered upon an intimate correspondence, which was of material assistance to the English scholar in the formulation of his evolutionary theory. When the *Origin of Species* finally appeared in 1859, Gray became its leading champion among American scientists.

The achievement of American men of science during the first six decades of the nineteenth century was a modest one, but the broadening base of education and the wider interests of American scholars gave promise of greater things to come.

Chapter 17. Literary Nationalism

Travelers rarely failed to comment on the assurance with which Americans discussed their political institutions. That these were the freest and best in the world appeared to be taken for granted. But national pride was scarcely content with this area of supremacy. Americans longed for a similar confidence that American books were more interesting, American art more majestic, and American music more stirring than European. It was not easy for the patriotic to understand why ambition and energy would not produce masterpieces of literature and art with the same certainty that they built canals and railroads. Yet two generations after the Declaration of Independence the United States was notable not for the richness of its cultural production but for its relative poverty. In 1835 Alexis de Tocqueville wrote:

> It must be acknowledged that in few of the civilized nations of our time have the higher sciences made less progress than in the United States; and in few have great artists, distinguished poets, or celebrated writers, been more rare. Many Europeans, struck by this fact, have looked upon it as a natural and inevitable result of equality; and they have thought that, if a democratic state of society and democratic institutions were ever to prevail over the whole earth, the human mind would gradually find its beacon-lights grow dim, and men would relapse into a period of darkness.[1]

During the next twenty-five years, fortunately, such beacon lights as the essays of Emerson and Thoreau, the novels of Hawthorne and Melville, and the poetry of Walt Whitman gave assurance that literature would not be lost in the democratic night.

Birth of a National Literature

If maturity in literature was slowly and painfully achieved, it was not because of lack of ambition. Five years before the Battle of Lexington, young John Trumbull at Yale wrote:

> This land her Steele and Addison shall view,
> The former glories equall'd by the new;
> Some future Shakespeare charm the rising age,
> And hold in magic charm the listening stage.

The anticipated arrival of an American Addison or Shakespeare was delayed, however, both by the unpredictability of genius and through inhibiting circum-

[1] Alexis de Tocqueville, *Democracy in America,* translated by Henry Reeve, revised and edited by Francis Bowen (Cambridge, 1864), II, 40.

stances peculiar to a young nation. The country certainly did not lack for vigorous minds, but these were more likely to be engaged in pamphleteering and political organization than in the writing of imaginative literature. Good poems and novels, like good woolens, were assumed to be products of English origin; homespuns in literature were regarded with suspicion. Even the machinery of publication was discouraging to native efforts. Not until the 1820's were there American publishers who would assume the risks of publication and pay authors a royalty. Even then the copyright situation was such that publishers found it more profitable to market pirated editions of English authors than to publish the work of Americans. Since magazines and newspapers offered a better market than the book trade, more Americans experimented with the essay, sketch, short story, and lyric poetry than with the longer forms.

Despite these handicaps many literary flights were attempted, and although only a modest altitude was achieved, generous applause rewarded some of the adventurers. Particularly admired by their own generation was a group of Connecticut writers known as the Hartford Wits. Closely imitating the themes and literary forms of English eighteenth-century poetry, they produced such works as John Trumbull's Revolutionary mock epic *M'Fingal* (1776), Timothy Dwight's allegorical epic *The Conquest of Canaan* (1785) and his pastoral *Greenfield Hill* (1794), and Joel Barlow's humorous *Hasty Pudding* (1796) and epic *The Columbiad* (1807). The Hartford Wits were enthusiastic patriots, but they had no love for the radical impulses released by the Revolution. In the party battles of the 1780's and 1790's the Connecticut writers employed their pens in works like *The Anarchiad* (1786–1787), vigorously condemning paper money, Deism, and Jeffersonian Republicanism. In their ardent espousal of Federalism the Hartford Wits suffered one notable desertion. During a long residence abroad Joel Barlow became an enthusiastic convert to all the radical political and religious ideas which were anathema to Connecticut Federalism. Falling to the ultimate depths, he spent his later years in Washington as the close friend and adviser of Jefferson and Madison.

Sharing Barlow's democratic enthusiasm and much more gifted as a poet was Philip Freneau. During the rare intervals when this New Jersey writer was not in the thick of some political battle, he wrote simple lyrics of great beauty. Less bound by the conventions of eighteenth-century English poetry than the Connecticut group, he struck a note that anticipated the newer moods and interests of the romanticists. Freneau was a man of passionate convictions who devoted most of his energies to attacking men and ideas that aroused his hatred. Turning journalist with the assistance of Jefferson and Madison, he sounded the alarm against Hamilton and Adams in the *National Gazette*. So bitterly resented were these invectives against the heroes of Federalism that conservative literary historians were reluctant to concede Freneau his rightful rank as the finest poet of the Revolutionary generation.

The reading of novels—a diversion that had become very popular during the eighteenth century in England—was soon taken up in America. Their rising vogue was viewed with much concern by the moralists. It was alleged that young ladies who read novels were transferred to a world of fancy that spoiled them for the hard world of reality, that they lost their taste for republican simplicity by learning of more sophisticated foreign fashions and customs, and, worst of all, that they wasted their time.

Until 1790 Americans with the novel-reading vice had to depend on the work of English authors, but American writers began to pander to their tastes during the next decade. Probably the first American novel to be published was William Hill Brown's *The Power of Sympathy* (1789), but this story of seduction and suicide had so obvious a basis in an actual event in Boston that the author was prevailed upon to suppress it. Susannah Rowson's *Charlotte Temple,* on the other hand, was widely read. This novel, also based on a true story, related the sad experience of an English girl induced by an offer of marriage to come to New York, where she died in childbirth after being deserted by her lover. *Charlotte Temple* was first published in London in 1791, but its extraordinary success dated from 1794, when it was brought out in America by the energetic Matthew Carey of Philadelphia. Eventually *Charlotte Temple* went through two hundred editions and drew sentimental tears from many generations of readers. Similar in theme was Mrs. Hannah Foster's *The Coquette; or The History of Eliza Wharton* (1797), based upon a famous Hartford scandal of the day. To moralists who deplored these portrayals of seduction, their defenders replied that the melancholy fate which invariably befell the fallen heroines offered a solemn warning to feminine readers.

Quite different lessons were to be learned from Hugh Henry Brackenridge's *Modern Chivalry,* published in parts between 1792 and 1805. This related the adventures of Captain Farrago and his Irish servant Teague O'Regan, American Don Quixote and Sancho Panza. Although Teague was an ignorant rascal, the backwoods communities would gladly have accepted him as legislator, preacher, philosopher, and diplomat. Through this satiric device Brackenridge, himself a Pennsylvania judge, rebuked the tendency of frontier America to elevate incompetent men, but in depicting pompous Federalists, he was even more severe.

The most ambitious of the early novelists was Charles Brockden Brown of Philadelphia. Having no taste for the legal career which his family had planned for him, Brown moved to New York, determined to support himself by writing—and thus became the first American bold enough to attempt to make literature his profession. Just as English sentimental and satirical novels had been imitated by other Americans, the so-called "Gothic novel" in vogue abroad served as a model for Brown. In order to hold its readers in fascinated suspense, this type of fiction resorted to gloomy, isolated houses or castles, lovely heroines in mortal fear of supernatural terrors or crazed villains, and frequent murders and suicides. Despite his resort to such mechanical horrors Brown achieved an interesting psychological study of religious obsession in his best novel, *Wieland* (1798).

Also redeeming his work from mere sensationalism was Brown's humanitarianism and aspiration for social justice.

European criticism of American literary efforts reflected the political sympathies of the critic. "In the four quarters of the globe," jibed the English Tory, Sydney Smith, "who ever reads an American book?" Europeans with republican and democratic leanings, on the other hand, not only read American works but often praised them beyond their merit.

The first American to obtain international recognition on a more substantial basis was the genial Washington Irving of New York. His first notable success was won with a humorous *History of New York* (1809), which he pretended was the work of an eccentric antiquarian named Diedrich Knickerbocker. Although certain prominent members of New York society were believed to be offended by his flippant treatment of their Dutch ancestors, the *History* was intended not to make fun of the dead but, as Irving later said,

> . . . to embody the traditions of the city in an amusing form . . . to clothe home scenes and places and familiar names with those imaginative and whimsical associations so seldom met with in our new country, but which live like charms and spells about the cities of the old world, binding the heart of the native inhabitant to his new home.

This affectionate interest in the past was to color all the most effective of Irving's literary work. Part of his material he drew from the old Dutch country along the Hudson, part from protracted residences abroad. Irving thus recorded what travel in the Old World meant to him:

> My native country was full of youthful promise: Europe was rich in the accumulated treasures of age. Her very ruins told the history of times gone by, and every moldering stone was a chronicle. I longed to wander over the scenes of renowned achievement—to tread, as it were, in the footsteps of antiquity—to loiter about the ruined castle—to meditate on the falling tower—to escape, in short, from the commonplace realities of the present, and lose myself among the shadowy grandeurs of the past.[1]

Combining these romantic tastes with a graceful, easy style, Irving gained fame with *The Sketch Book* (1819–1820), *Bracebridge Hall* (1822), and *Tales of a Traveller* (1824). Three years' residence in Spain provided him with material for *The Life and Voyages of Columbus* (1828), *The Conquest of Granada* (1829), and *The Alhambra* (1832). After he returned to America, he discovered a new vein of material in the West. Although *A Tour on the Prairie* (1835), *Astoria* (1836), and *The Adventures of Captain Bonneville* (1837) dealt with authentically American themes, Irving's treatment was characteristically romantic. The author's final effort was a ponderous five-volume *Life of George Washington* (1855–1859). The most enduring part of Irving's large output was to be found in such well-told stories as "Rip Van Winkle" and "The Legend of Sleepy Hollow," both contained in *The Sketch Book.*

For his career as a romantic novelist James Fenimore Cooper was well pre-

[1] Washington Irving, *The Sketch Book of Geoffrey Crayon, Gent.* (Dutton, New York, 1906), 2.

pared. His boyhood was spent in the beautiful frontier village of Cooperstown, New York; his father, Judge Cooper, was an excellent example of the eighteenth-century gentleman. After two years at Yale young Fenimore Cooper spent several exciting years as sailor, midshipman, and naval officer. Upon marrying, he settled down to life as a country gentleman in Westchester County, New York, a region rich in Revolutionary traditions. Later he traveled extensively in Europe and returned to Cooperstown to live in the baronial fashion of his father.

When Cooper began writing novels in 1820, he needed only one unhappy experiment with borrowed English materials to convince him that he should exploit distinctly American themes. His first success was with *The Spy* (1821), an exciting story of the Revolutionary War laid in the Westchester region which he knew so well. Next he turned to the Otsego Lake region of his boyhood. Writing of American frontier experience in a vein half realistic, half romantic, Cooper began mining the lode from which he was to take his richest ore. Americans and Europeans alike found fascination in *The Pioneers* (1823), *The Last of the Mohicans* (1826), *The Prairie* (1827), *The Pathfinder* (1840), and *The Deerslayer* (1841). To the critical eye of Mark Twain and other realists of a later generation, Cooper's Leatherstocking tales were full of absurdities—Indians and white hunters who were nature's noblemen, impossible feats of marksmanship, stock characterizations, and stilted conversations. But contemporaries gladly overlooked these faults as their imaginations were stirred by the romantic wilderness settings and by the exciting pursuits and narrow escapes which Cooper provided in generous measure.

During the course of thirty years Cooper, who was a persistent and rapid worker, produced a total of more than thirty novels, several travel books and collections of essays, and a history of the United States Navy. Just as his frontier novels had opened up one great field of fiction, his stories of the sea like *The Pilot* (1823) and *The Red Rover* (1828) revealed another.

Despite Cooper's success as a storyteller he aspired to the more serious role of social critic. He was unsparing in his condemnation of American types which he disliked—the acquisitive Yankee who made money through speculation and sharp dealing, the political demagogue who manipulated the democratic machinery, and the frontier squatter who defied the law by settling on land to which he had no title and for which he refused to pay rent. He praised the American gentleman of an older school who invested in the land, lived a life of culture and refinement, and exerted his political influence neither to further his personal fortunes nor to court popularity with the mob but to assure sound government. Cooper's truculent comments aroused wide resentment and lost for the author much of his earlier popularity.

Romanticism, which inspired Irving's evocations of the past and Cooper's narratives of the forest and the sea, also found expression in William Cullen Bryant's lyrical meditations on nature and human destiny. When Bryant's noble "Thanatopsis" appeared anonymously in the *North American Review* in 1817, the poet was a twenty-four-year-old country lawyer in Great Barrington, Massachusetts. Quietly and unsensationally Bryant's reputation grew during the 1820's. In 1821 a volume containing eight of his early poems was published; his work appeared regularly in the *United States Literary Gazette* in 1824 and 1825. In 1825 he gave up his legal practice and moved to New York, where for fifty years he made the *New York Evening Post* a powerful influence for reform and good government. A second edition of Bryant's *Poems,* published in 1832, assured him for the time being first place among American poets.

New England's Golden Age

The extraordinary flowering of talent in eastern Massachusetts during the 1840's and 1850's is not easily explained. The contemporary Unitarian and transcendentalist movements were both cause and symptom. In the revolt against Calvinism the New England mind was emancipated from the shackles of a narrow orthodoxy. But in discarding the old answers, the Yankees did not lose interest in the old questions. With a seriousness of purpose and intensity inherited from Puritanism, they struggled anew with fundamental problems: the nature of the universe and the nature of man, the essence of good and evil, man's duty to himself and to society. If the speculations were often metaphysical in origin, they rarely remained at that level. Yankee practicality instinctively demanded that ideas be put to work; this generation's thought found its natural outlet in earnest struggle with moral issues.

More than in most sections of the country the irritant of change—sometimes productive of literary pearls—was at work in New England. Whatever of provincialism and complacency had once characterized the section was shaken as the old commercial aristocrcy had to make way for new captains of industry and as fishermen and farmers became a minority compared to industrial workers. On Thoreau's tramps through the countryside he encountered not only animals, birds, and rustic human beings, but Irish laborers earning 60 cents a day laying track for a new railroad. These also were worth thinking about.

The New England renaissance was also stimulated by the region's scholarly tradition. Voracious readers found an abundance of exciting ideas in books and periodicals from abroad. German idealism, embodied in the works of philosophers like Kant, Fichte, and Schelling, and literary masters like Goethe and Schiller, intrigued young intellectuals. Although some went to Germany to study or read extensively in the German classics, a larger number came under the influence of German ideas at second hand through reading English authors like Coleridge and Carlyle. English literature itself was alive with new impulses. The poetry of Wordsworth and Keats and the novels of Scott were emancipating forces, encouraging aspiring authors to cut loose from the pseudoclassic rules of the eighteenth century. Still other foreign influences were provided by the humanitarianism of French romantic thought and the mysticism of Oriental literature. But New England writers by no means depended on a slavish borrowing of foreign materials. In typically American fashion immigrant ideas mingled with native and resulted in a product distinctly Yankee in flavor.

The central figure in the New England literary scene was Ralph Waldo Emerson. After giving up his career in the Unitarian ministry, Emerson spent an influential year in foreign travel and then, at the age of thirty-one, took up his residence at Concord, where he found his true vocation as lecturer, essayist, and poet. In 1836 his literary career was quietly launched with the publication of *Nature,* an early statement of the transcendentalist philosophy. These same ideas provided material for lively discussion in the talented group that was beginning to form around Emerson—the group that would eventually be known as the Transcendental Club. In 1837 the Concord thinker made a deep impression on a Harvard Phi Beta Kappa audience with his lecture, "The American Scholar," in which he hailed the day "when the sluggard intellect of this continent will look from under its iron lids, and fill the postponed expectation of the world with something better than the exertions of mechanical skill." Emerson's fame now spread rapidly. He was in great demand as a lecturer; the first series of his *Essays* appeared in 1841; his first volume of *Poems* in 1846. In 1847 and and 1848 he traveled in England and Europe, lecturing and visiting with the celebrities of the day.

Emerson's faith in the essential divinity of human nature gave his work the buoyancy of high optimism. "Nothing shall warp me from the belief," he declared, "that every man is a lover of truth." And in another place: "Things refuse to be mismanaged long. . . . Nothing arbitrary, nothing artificial can endure."

Yet belief in the ultimate goodness of the universe did not blind the Concord thinker to the existence of mundane evil. Under the impact of the Mexican War and the slavery controversy Emerson became an increasingly outspoken critic of contemporary abuses. Complacency was sharply rebuked:

But who is he that prates
Of the culture of mankind,
Of better arts and life?
Go, blindworm, go,
Behold the famous States
Harrying Mexico
With rifle and with knife! [1]

His idealism recoiled not only from the evils of imperialism and slavery but from materialism in any form:

'Tis the day of the chattel
Web to weave, and corn to grind;
Things are in the saddle,
And ride mankind.[2]

[1] "Ode Inscribed to W. H. Channing," *The Complete Works of Ralph Waldo Emerson* (Century ed., Boston, n. d.), IX, 76.

[2] *Ibid.*, 78.

Emerson's sovereign remedy for these ills of society was an inspired individualism:

Hence, the less government we have, the better,—the fewer laws, and the less confided power. The antidote to this abuse of formal government, is, the influence of private character, the growth of the Individual; the reappearance of the principal to supersede the proxy; the appearance of the wise man, of whom the existing government, is, it must be owned, but a shabby imitation. . . . The appearance of character makes the State unnecessary. The wise man is the State. . . .[1]

Emerson's friends of the Transcendental Club were a remarkable group. There was Margaret Fuller, whose wide reading, flow of talk, and exuberant enthusiasm were a little terrifying to most males. There was George Ripley, whose passion for a better society found expression in the Brook Farm experiment. There was Theodore Parker, radical Unitarian minister, social reformer, and scholar. There was Bronson Alcott, visionary and eccentric but one of the finest teachers of his generation. Scarcely less interesting were Orestes Brownson, Frederic Henry Hedge, and William Henry Channing. From 1840 to 1844 the transcendentalist group published many essays and poems in its struggling magazine *The Dial,* edited first by Margaret Fuller and later by Emerson.

In his extreme individualism and in his love for nature Henry David Thoreau translated transcendentalist thought into a mode of life. Though graduated from Harvard, his real education was derived from his extraordinarily wide reading and from his close relationship with Emerson, in whose home he lived for extended periods. From 1845 to 1847 Thoreau lived alone in a rude shack which he built in Emerson's wood lot by the side of Walden Pond. Eating wild berries and vegetables grown in his garden patch, he largely freed himself from the need of money and devoted his hours to reading, writing, walking, conversing with frequent visitors, and thinking. "I went to the woods," he later declared, "because I wished to live deliberately, to front only the essential facts of life, and see if I could not learn what it had to teach, and not, when I came to die, discover that I had not lived."

If Thoreau's two years in the woods were a rebuke to men who reckoned wealth and progress in material terms, the young author's imprisonment for one night in 1846 was a protest against slavery and imperialism. By going to jail rather than pay his poll tax, Thoreau refused allegiance to the State for reasons that seemed compelling to his sturdy conscience:

Under a government which imprisons any unjustly, the true place for a just man is also a prison. . . . It is there that the fugitive slave, and the Mexican prisoner on parole, and the Indian come to plead the wrongs of his race should find them; on that separate, but more free and honorable ground, where the State places those who are not *with* her, but *against* her,—the only house in a slave-state in which a free man can abide with honor. . . . Cast your whole vote, not a strip of paper merely, but your whole influence. . . . If the

[1] "Politics," *The Complete Works of Ralph Waldo Emerson* (Century ed., Boston, n. d.), III, 215–216.

alternative is to keep all just men in prison, or give up war and slavery, the State will not hesitate which to choose.[1]

Although two years in the woods and one night in jail provided Thoreau's most dramatic demonstrations of individualism, his whole life was punctuated with minor gestures of protest. Never marrying, he supported himself by occasional work as pencilmaker, surveyor, and handyman.

Thoreau's literary achievement received scant recognition during his lifetime. His first book, *A Week on the Concord and Merrimack Rivers* (1849), sold so poorly that *Walden*—one of the finest books of the nineteenth century—remained unpublished for five years. Finally appearing in 1854, this account of Thoreau's famous experiment in living enjoyed only a modest success. Still little known except in his own section, Thoreau died, a victim of tuberculosis, in 1862, when he was only forty-four years old. But later generations placed a different value on his work. *Walden* grew steadily in prestige, and Thoreau's ability as essayist and poet gained recognition with the collection and republication of his magazine pieces. In the end, his influence became international: English socialists, somewhat paradoxically, found inspiration in the great individualist as did Russian and Indian revolutionaries.

Although he lived several years in Concord as the neighbor of Emerson, Thoreau, and Alcott and frequently listened to their discussions, Nathaniel Hawthorne never disguised his skepticism about the transcendentalist movement. While these friends asserted their faith in the divinity of human nature, he adhered to the less optimistic point of view of New England tradition. His best novels and short stories depicted with sharp insight the impact of guilt upon human character.

Before Hawthorne moved to the optimistic air of Concord, he had spent many years in Salem, where memories of somber Puritan ancestors still persisted despite the bustle of a busy port. Following his graduation from Bowdoin College in 1825, Hawthorne lived twelve years as a virtual recluse in a strange household composed of his mother and two sisters, also recluses. From his solitary study came an increasing flow of essays, short stories, and sketches that found publication in the magazines and gift-book annuals of the day. Some of the best of these Hawthorne republished as *Twice-Told Tales* (1837). The young author's personality was more normal than his solitary habits would suggest. In 1842 he began a happy married life with the charming Sophia Peabody, sister of Mrs. Horace Mann and Elizabeth Peabody of kindergarten fame. Through his friends in the Democratic party he was able to supplement his precarious literary earnings with his income from positions in the Boston and Salem customhouses and as United States consul at Liverpool.

But despite wife and children, public offices and travel, and the interesting

[1] "Civil Disobedience," *Henry David Thoreau: Representative Selections,* ed. by B. V. Crawford (American Book, New York, 1934), 255–256.

experience of a few months at Brook Farm in 1841, Hawthorne was not diverted from his preoccupation with somber problems of character. After the publication of several collections of short stories he enjoyed his first great success with *The Scarlet Letter* in 1850. This masterly study of seventeenth-century Puritanism was followed by *The House of the Seven Gables* in 1851, *The Blithedale Romance* in 1852, and *The Marble Faun* in 1860. Hawthorne's literary skill and psychological insight left their influence on American fiction and were particularly admired by Henry James.

Although in the judgment of later generations Emerson, Thoreau, and Hawthorne held first place among New England authors, contemporary opinion paid equal or greater respect to such figures as Henry Wadsworth Longfellow, Oliver Wendell Holmes, James Russell Lowell, and John Greenleaf Whittier.

From the first Longfellow's poetry received an enthusiastic reception. His *Voices of the Night* (1839) and *Ballads and Other Poems* (1841) were filled with simple verses that appealed to American sentiment—poems that praised the sturdy virtues of the village blacksmith, that dramatized the familiar New England tragedy of shipwreck, and that assured an ambitious generation:

> Life is real! Life is earnest!
> And the grave is not its goal;
> Dust thou art, to dust returnest,
> Was not spoken of the soul.

The nation's pride in the Cambridge poet was confirmed by his later success in composing long narrative poems on themes from the American past—works like *Evangeline* (1847), *The Song of Hiawatha* (1855), *The Courtship of Miles Standish* (1858), and *Tales of a Wayside Inn* (1863). For those who had read little, Longfellow's clear and musical verse opened the door to new experience; more sophisticated readers were less impressed but had reason to admire him for his technical competence and for his wide knowledge of European literature, which he made available through translations and rewritings.

Born in a Cambridge parsonage, graduated from Harvard, and teaching many years in the Harvard Medical School, Oliver Wendell Holmes was a well-known figure both in Cambridge and Boston. Holmes was a highly competent doctor and teacher, struggling to free medicine from quackery and to establish it as a science. But Holmes the physician was not too busy to restrict the activities of Holmes the diner-out and wit, the author of light verse, sparkling essays, and didactic novels. The versatile writer found a particularly appropriate form for his thought in *The Autocrat of the Breakfast Table* (1858), a series which proved one of the most popular features in the newly founded *Atlantic Monthly*. These witty monologues had the quality of Holmes's own effervescent conversation. He was a man of sturdy prejudices who defended Boston as the hub of the universe and believed that the rich and the wellborn should be secure from the assaults of the levelers. Despite this conservatism he hated all restrictions on freedom of thought and was a spirited assailant of surviving Calvinism.

Equally a product of Cambridge and Boston was James Russell Lowell. Son of a Congregational minister, nephew of Francis Cabot Lowell, the textile manufacturer, and graduate of Harvard College, Lowell as a young man wrote poetry, traveled in Europe, and worked for Boston and Philadelphia magazines. This apprenticeship was excellent preparation for his later career as Longfellow's successor at Harvard, editor of the *Atlantic Monthly,* and American minister to Spain and to England. In the *Biglow Papers* (1846) and other works the young Lowell was a vigorous spokesman for Northern radicalism on the slavery issue, but as he grew older assaults upon the established order became less frequent. The dignified James Russell Lowell of post-Civil War days confined his liberal impulses to such safe causes as civil-service reform and frowned upon labor unions and eight-hour laws. Lowell's work as poet, essayist, and literary critic gave frequent evidence of his broad culture and technical skill but lacked the unity of purpose and deep feeling that characterized the efforts of his great contemporaries.

Quite without the cultural advantages of either the Concord or the Cambridge groups was John Greenleaf Whittier, who was brought up on a farm in Haverhill, Massachusetts. Contributing poems and sketches to country newspapers and becoming himself a small-town editor, Whittier began his literary career in modest fashion. The abolitionist cause captured him completely, and for thirty years he was one of the most aggressive fighters in the movement, condemning in prose and verse both the slaveholders and their northern apologists. When this issue had been settled by the Civil War, Whittier had more time to write on the quieter themes that had always attracted him. His *Snow-bound* (1866) had great appeal for farm-bred readers who had experienced such winter captivities themselves. Widely popular also were his ballads of the simple life and his hymns and religious poems, which were sincerely expressive of Quaker serenity.

Not least among the New England greats were the historians. Over the course of half a century George Bancroft published 10 volumes of a famous *History of the United States* (1834–1882). Bancroft's enthusiasm for American liberty and democracy earned him the ardent applause of contemporary readers, but his reputation suffered a serious drop when history written in the florid manner of Fourth-of-July orations went out of fashion. More enduring fame was won by the New Englanders who wrote colorful narratives of Spanish imperial conquest, of the Dutch struggle for religious and political liberty, and of the forest conflict between England and France for control of a continent. William H. Prescott, John Lothrop Motley, and Francis Parkman, who explored these romantic themes, came from the same background. All three belonged to wealthy Boston families and inherited sufficient money to live the lives of gentlemen-scholars. All three graduated from Harvard and rounded out their educations by European travel. All three aspired to literary fame and regarded the writing of history as a means to this end. The remarkable thing is that all three escaped dilettantism and contributed works that were sound in scholarship and brilliant in style.

Outside New England

Although New England boasted more authors and readers to the square mile than any other section, the rest of the country was by no means the cultural desert that the Yankees sometimes assumed.

In the South, to be sure, writers worked under handicaps. Gentlemen who threw themselves energetically into politics or hunting were more numerous than those who developed a passion for books. And even those who were readers had a tendency to prefer English or even northern authors to southern. The latter complained bitterly that they were neglected in their own section and belittled elsewhere. The South was little touched by the intellectual currents that had stirred New England. Religious orthodoxy being only weakly challenged, there was infrequent occasion for the wrestling with moral problems that toughened the mind of the North. Romanticism dominated both sections, but in southern romanticism there was less of humanitarian earnestness and more of escape from reality to idealizations of the past, wishful thinking about the present, and pleasant dreams for the future.

Yet these retarding influences did not prevent the appearance of talented authors. Center of a Baltimore literary circle was John Pendleton Kennedy, who wrote urbane sketches of Virginia plantation life, historical romances, and satires upon Jacksonian democracy. Less suspicious of the North than other southern writers, he remained loyal to the Union during the Civil War. Very different were the loyalties of the Virginian Nathaniel Beverly Tucker, whose novel *The Partisan Leader* (1836) exulted in an imagined War of Secession that should emancipate the South from the rabble democracy of the North. William Gilmore Simms of Charleston was the most capable novelist of the South, dealing with themes reminiscent of Cooper, although somewhat differently handled. Novels like *The Partisan* (1835) and *Woodcraft* (1854) were exciting stories of the activities of the southern guerrillas during the Revolutionary War. Simms's most popular work, *The Yemassee* (1835), was a tale of pioneers and Indians during the early days of South Carolina.

Edgar Allan Poe was a southerner by affirmation, although he was born in Boston and spent many of his adult years in Philadelphia and New York. After the disappearance of his father and the death of his mother—both traveling actors—Poe was brought up by John Allan, a prosperous merchant of Richmond, Virginia. Relations between the high-strung youth and his foster father were far from harmonious. Thrown on his own resources after a series of quarrels, Poe made a precarious living from his writing. His first book of poems was published in 1827; his first short stories appeared in Philadelphia and Baltimore newspapers during the early 1830's.

Through the influence of John Pendleton Kennedy, who had been impressed by one of his stories, Poe became editor of the *Southern Quarterly Review* in 1835. In this post he first attracted wide attention. His book reviews displayed a keenness of judgment and brilliance of expression hitherto unknown in American literary criticism. Poe's work made the magazine famous, yet the young editor held his job little more than a year. The pattern of most of Poe's subsequent career here established itself: an interval of prodigiously hard work and steady habits was followed by melancholia, bouts of heavy drinking, illness, and loss of job. With variations the story was repeated in Philadelphia and New York, where he held later editorial posts. The final chapter of the tragedy opened with his wife's death in 1847 and closed with his own in Baltimore in 1849.

Despite his instability of character Poe accomplished many things. His tales, although often obsessed with the macabre, were excellent examples of short-story writing—a craft for which he laid down rules of great value for later practitioners. Particularly influential were his tales of crime and detection in which he prepared the way for the later vogue of the mystery story. As a poet Poe practiced an equally conscious art. Believing with Coleridge that the primary purpose of the poet was not to proclaim a truth or to teach but to give pleasure through the rhythmical creation of beauty, he fashioned work so haunting in mood, so musical in meter and language that readers were fascinated. With the general public such showpieces as "The Raven" and "The Bells" attained great popularity; with discriminating readers works like "The City in the Sea" and "The Haunted Palace" had priority. Emerson dismissed Poe as a mere "jingle man," but his influence was great—particularly in France and England.

The strangest literary career of the period was that of Herman Melville. In early books like *Typee* (1846) and *White-Jacket* (1850) based upon his own unusual experiences as a sailor and adventurer in the South Sea Islands, Melville strongly appealed to the tastes of a romantic generation. But this early popularity suffered total eclipse when Melville elected to produce works so philosophic in mood and symbolic in utterance that his contemporaries were both perplexed and irritated.

Despite the poor reception accorded *Mardi* (1849), his first venture in this new direction, Melville poured all his energies into the writing of *Moby Dick* (1851). This unforgettable narrative of the monomaniac Captain Ahab and his suicidal pursuit of the great white whale Moby Dick was at its most obvious level an exciting narrative of the whaling industry in its greatest days. But it was much more than this. Through symbols, sometimes explicit, sometimes subtle, Melville wrestled with the problem of evil. Evil, he appeared to say, exists in the very nature of the universe; for man to hope to destroy it is madness certain to end in disaster; yet this madness possesses a fascinating element of the heroic. The philosophical implications of *Moby Dick* ran against the grain of nineteenth-century optimism. Significantly, Melville's masterpiece first gained recognition as one of the world's greatest books during the troubled decades that followed World War I.

In Walt Whitman cultural nationalism reached its apogee. He believed that by poets alone could "the States be fused into the compact organism of a Nation."

Of all races and eras, These States, with veins full of poetical stuff, most need poets, and are to have the greatest, and use them the greatest,
Their Presidents shall not be their common referee so much as their poets shall.[1]

FIG. 30. Walt Whitman, about 1866. Photograph by Matthew Brady. (*Courtesy of the National Archives.*)

For his career as poet of American democracy Whitman was well prepared. His father, a farmer and carpenter, was a disciple of Fanny Wright and an enthusiastic Jacksonian Democrat; his Quaker mother familiarized Walt with the idea that God might speak directly to the humblest soul. During boyhood and youth Walt had opportunity to taste the flavor of both city and country life. When he was four or five years old, his family moved from a Long Island village to Brooklyn, where he attended public school and played in the streets. But long visits to the country taught him to love the song of birds, the murmur of brooks, and the thunder of the ocean. Leaving school at about the age of eleven, Whitman went from one job to another. As office boy, apprentice printer, village

[1] *The Complete Poetry and Prose of Walt Whitman* (Pelligrini & Cudahy, New York, 1948), I, 312.

schoolteacher, country editor, and newspaperman in New York, Brooklyn, and New Orleans, he mingled with Americans of every type.

Although Whitman had shown competence and liberalism as a roving journalist, he had given little evidence of possessing a powerful and original mind. Yet the inner man had been growing steadily during these years of apparent drift. Reading Emerson and hearing him lecture was a great experience for Whitman, confirming his faith in intuition and in the divinity of human personality, but transcendentalism, like Quakerism, was too pallid a philosophy to satisfy this vigorous man, who exulted in his body no less than in his soul.

Walt Whitman's new poetry, gestating many years in his notebooks, came to birth with the publication of *Leaves of Grass* in 1855. For a work so unorthodox there was at first practically no public sale. But Walt gained some attention by sending the slender volume to the leading literary celebrities and editors of the day. The reviews thus invited were for the most part hostile: Whitman was conceded to have power and originality, but his flouting of traditional rules of meter and rhyme was deplored, and his treatment of sex was condemned as indecent. From the great Emerson, however, Whitman received a most gratifying letter: "I give you joy for your free and brave thoughts. I find the courage of treatment that so delights us, and which large perception only can inspire. I greet you at the beginning of a great career."

For the rest of his life Whitman continued to write poetry and occasional prose. With the years he learned to bring somewhat more discipline to his art, and his thought became more mellow and reflective in response to his later experiences as Civil War nurse, Washington clerk, and sufferer from paralysis.

Despite his numerous rewritings Whitman never recanted from the fundamental tenets of the faith he had announced in 1855. The hundreds of lines which he devoted to his own experiences and aspirations revealed not brash egotism but a mystic belief that he shared the life of every person who ever had lived or ever would live.

> I celebrate myself, and sing myself,
> And what I assume you shall assume,
> For every atom belonging to me as good belongs to you.[1]

He particularly identified himself with the American en masse—the men and women he had seen in his wanderings—carpenters and butchers, church soloists and opera singers, even slaves, lunatics, and prostitutes. America, he believed, was heir to the culture of the ages, destined to build its own great civilization. Whitman again and again reaffirmed his faith in democracy—which he identified with maximum of opportunity for the individual.

> I was looking a long while for Intentions,
> For a clue to the history of the past for myself, and for these chants—and now I have found it,

[1] *Ibid.,* 62.

It is not in those paged fables in the libraries, (them I neither accept nor reject,)
It is no more in the legends than in all else,
It is in the present—it is this earth to-day,
It is in Democracy—(the purport and aim of all the past,)
It is the life of one man or one woman to-day—the average man of to-day,
It is in languages, social customs, literatures, arts,
It is in the broad show of artificial things, ships, machinery, politics, creeds, modern improvements, and the interchange of nations,
All for the average man of to-day.[1]

In the prose pamphlet *Democratic Vistas* (1871) and in many poems Whitman showed that he was not blind to the faults of American democracy. He thought:

Of the President with pale face, asking secretly of himself,
What will the people say at last?
Of the frivolous Judge—of the corrupt Congressman, Governor, Mayor—of such as these, standing helpless and exposed.[2]

But he grounded his faith in the people—in the soundess of ultimate public opinion and "the rising forever taller and stronger and broader of the intuitions of men and women, and of self-esteem, and of personality."

Whitman remained a controversial figure. At worst he could be bombastic and tedious—even Emerson became impatient with his interminable "inventories." But Whitman gained a large company of admirers who were ready to judge him by his best work. In this they found a boldness of style and a sensitivity of feeling unsurpassed by any other American poet. Whitman's influence was far-reaching, encouraging later writers to experiment freely and to explore without fear whatever aspects of life aroused their interest.

The People's Choice

The growth of population and the rise of literacy created an expanding market for newspapers and books. When Mrs. Trollope revealed her annoyance at the amount of time her rustic Cincinnati neighbors spent in reading the newspapers, the rejoinder that she received was quite in the spirit of Jacksonian Democracy:

> And I'd like you to tell me how we can spend it better. How should freemen spend their time, but looking after their government, and watching that them fellers as we gives offices to, does their duty, and gives themselves no airs? [3]

But affairs of state did not exhaust American interest in the printed page. Not only did the newspapers devote an increasing proportion of their space to reporting crime and other sensational happenings, but they frequently set aside columns for homely poems and sentimental stories. Indeed, such weekly periodi-

[1] *Ibid.*, 345. [2] *Ibid.*, 413.

[3] Frances Trollope, *Domestic Manners of the Americans*, ed. by Donald Smalley (Knopf, New York, 1949), 102.

cals as *Brother Jonathan,* founded in 1839, and *New World,* founded in 1840, were printed in newspaper format only to qualify for special postal rates; their contents were almost entirely fictional—stories and serialized novels, mostly pirated from English authors. Presently these "newspapers" began to print complete books in "extras" or "supplements," selling for 50, 25, or 12½ cents. Other publishers entered the field so that by 1843 the country was flooded with cheap books. English authors were highly indignant at this wholesale piracy, but it helped to create a mass market for books from which both English and American authors eventually benefited.

In the popular field Home and God were the themes most likely to be profitable. This was demonstrated by the success of the Reverend Jacob Abbott of Boston, author of *The Young Christian* (1832) and 28 "Rollo Books"—highly popular vehicles for teaching children facts of travel, history, science, and morals. Similar to these were the "Peter Parley" books, written in astonishing quantity by S. G. Goodrich. Pious and sentimental novels of family life were highly successful during the 1850's. Susan Warner's tearful *The Wide, Wide World* (1850) retained its popularity for decades and eventually sold over half a million copies. Equally popular was Maria Susanna Cummins's *The Lamplighter* (1854), and successes almost as great were won by the novels of Mary Jane Holmes and Augusta J. Evans. Timothy Shay Arthur's *Ten Nights in a Bar-room and What I Saw There* (1854) was a melodramatic appeal for temperance that enjoyed a large sale.

The most sensationally successful of all pre-Civil War best sellers was Harriet Beecher Stowe's *Uncle Tom's Cabin* (1852). Daughter of Lyman Beecher, famous clergyman and temperance crusader, Mrs. Stowe was brought up in an atmosphere of moral earnestness and zeal for good works. Her sister was Catherine Beecher, one of the pioneers in women's education; one of her brothers was the great preacher Henry Ward Beecher; several other brothers were well-known clergymen. She herself was the wife of the Reverend Calvin E. Stowe, professor first at Lane Theological Seminary and later at Bowdoin College.

The Beechers, although opposed to slavery, had disapproved the radicalism of the abolitionists. Like many people of conscience, however, they were deeply disturbed by the Fugitive Slave Law of 1850 with its shocking denial of fair trial to accused fugitives. This was the spur that prodded Mrs. Stowe to write the long serial which began publication in the *National Era,* a leading antislavery weekly, in the spring of 1851. The completed novel made its first appearance in book form in March, 1852. Presses had to run day and night to keep up with the demand. The first year's sales were more than 300,000; the sales of succeeding years totaled almost 3,000,000 in the United States alone. Abroad *Uncle Tom's Cabin* was equally popular. During the first year some forty pirated editions were issued in Great Britain and her colonies; a million and a half copies were estimated to have been sold. In France, Germany, and Italy the record was similar; eventually Mrs. Stowe's novel was translated into 40 languages.

This success involved more than mere timeliness of publication. With all its preaching the story had wide appeal—pathos, humor, excitement, and generous humanitarianism. It was by no means so slanderous of the South as popular legend now supposes. Indeed, Mrs. Stowe disappointed abolitionists by conceding that southern planters often treated their slaves with kindness and by assigning the villains' roles to renegade northerners. But this attempt to practice tact and charity did not save the author from the indignant condemnation of southerners, who regarded her as a meddlesome Yankee writing out of prejudice and ignorance.

On the stage *Uncle Tom's Cabin* had a career even more remarkable. Thousands of Americans who had regarded the theater as sinful overrode their scruples to witness the dramatization of so powerful a moral lesson. Thousands more who had no particular desire for edification delighted in the play's absorbing melodrama. Long after the book was gathering dust on library shelves, itinerant companies were still drawing laughter and tears from village audiences with their portrayal of the saintly Uncle Tom, the angelic Little Eva, the mischievous Topsy, and the utterly villainous Simon Legree.

By 1861 American literature was vigorously alive. At its best it dealt with great themes in a style worthy of the thought. At its worst it was conventional in subject matter, excessively sentimental, and awkwardly written. As a whole it served the democratic function of providing reading material for Americans of every level of taste.

Chapter 18. The American Spirit in Arts and Amusements

Cultural nationalism sought outlet through many channels. While some Americans struggled to write operas and symphonies, others sought to execute monumental buildings that would symbolize the nation's faith in its glorious future or huge paintings that would capture the grandeur of its scenery. American achievement in the arts rarely equaled American ambition. In their more pretentious efforts native composers and artists often succeeded only in producing imitations of Old World masterpieces that lacked the power of the originals. Closest perhaps to capturing the elusive quality of American life were works never intended as national epics. There was much of America in the songs of Stephen Foster, in the paintings of William Sidney Mount, and in the circus of Phineas T. Barnum.

Music Hath Charms

In 1853 the *Pittsburgh Evening Chronicle* complained that society was "music-mad." The town buzzed with the advent of one "Signor Pound-the-keys" after another, each billed as the greatest.

> And Signor Pound-the-keys for having rattled and splurged and hammered and tinkled and growled through three or four musical compositions with long-line names, fills his pockets for one night's work with as many dollars as three-fourths of the community earn in a year, while the mustached gentleman who assists him by quavering, quivering and shouting through three or four songs in as many different European languages, which is all gibberish to all of the audience with perhaps the exception of some dozen, pockets one-half as much more.[1]

One of the first European musicians to exploit the American passion for gaping at celebrities was Ole Bull. The great Norwegian violinist gave some two hundred concerts on a tour of the eastern states from 1843 to 1845 and returned to other triumphs in later years. The unsophisticated audiences of the New World were fascinated by his showy technique—his ability to draw exquisite music from a single string or, by contrast, to play on all four strings at once. But the Norwegian's great success was completely overshadowed by the sensational tour of Jenny Lind, "the Swedish Nightingale," under the management of P. T.

[1] Quoted in John Tasker Howard, *Our American Music: Three Hundred Years of It* (Crowell, New York, 1939), 203.

Barnum. On this occasion the famous showman outdid himself in advance publicity. The American public—most of it scarcely aware of Jenny Lind's existence—suddenly discovered that she was not only "the greatest musical wonder in the world" but a paragon of beauty, goodness, and generosity. An audience of 7,000 crowded Castle Garden for her first concert on September 11, 1850. When the demure figure in white appeared, she was greeted by such a tempest of clapping, cheering, and handkerchief waving that it seemed that the performance would never be permitted to begin. The same excitement prevailed in every other city visited by Jenny Lind in this memorable tour of almost two years.

FIG. 31. *Grand Vocal and Instrumental Morning Concert at the Music Hall, Boston. Given in Honor of the Prince of Wales, Oct. 18, 1860.* (*Courtesy of the Massachusetts Historical Society.*)

There was only one Jenny Lind, but other well-known artists of the day made profitable American visits. During the 1850's Adelina Patti, then a child prodigy, toured with Ole Bull while Henriette Sontag was a sensation in opera and concert. The American-born Louis Moreau Gottschalk returned to his native country in 1853, after winning fame as a virtuoso pianist in Europe. Women found the handsome Gottschalk irresistible as with studied grace he played "The Last Hope," "The Dying Poet," and other romantic works of his own composition.

A magnificent figure also was Louis Antoine Jullien, who brought his great orchestra "complete in every department" and including "many of the most distinguished Professors, selected from the Royal Opera Houses of London, Paris,

Vienna, Berlin, St. Petersburg, Brussels, etc." to America in 1853. A showman from whom Barnum could have taken pointers, Jullien delighted his audiences with his "ambrosial whiskers and moustaches," his "immaculate waistcoat," "transcendant shirt front," and "unutterable cravat." Waving a jeweled baton in white-gloved hands, the French conductor exerted marvelous discipline over his orchestra. "He obtains from fifty strings a pianissimo which is scarcely audible and he makes one hundred instruments stop in the midst of a fortissimo which

FIG. 32. *Music Hath Charms.* Painting by W. S. Mount. The folk tradition in American music. (*Courtesy of the Century Association; photograph by the Metropolitan Museum of Art, New York.*)

seems to lift the roof, as if a hundred men dropped dead at the movement of his hand." Such playing was a revelation to Americans, who had heard only the poorly rehearsed efforts of the New York Philharmonic Society, founded in 1842, and other native orchestras.

A few ambitious Americans aspired to be the Beethovens and Verdis of the New World. Anton Philip Heinrich, an immigrant from Bohemia, composed a whole trunkful of symphonies and oratorios on themes derived from Indian lore and American tradition. Pioneer American operas were William Henry Frye's "Leonora" (1845) and George F. Bristow's "Rip Van Winkle" (1855).

But American music made its soundest progress in less ambitious forms. Healthiest of all was the unstudied tradition of country fiddlers who played with gaiety and humor for rural dances, of dwellers in remote mountain cabins who accompanied themselves on archaic instruments while they sang ballads transmitted from the Old World or composed new ones of their own. To the treasure of American folk music—not to be properly valued for many years—men and women in scores of different walks of life contributed. There were sea chanteys and whaling songs, lumberjack songs and canalboat songs, steamboat songs and railroad songs, Negro work songs and Negro spirituals.

The patriotic songs which American nationalism required were largely sung to tunes borrowed from the English. "Yankee Doodle" appears to have been first sung by British soldiers in ridicule of the colonials during the French and Indian War and later appropriated by the Americans. The words of "Hail, Columbia" were written by Joseph Hopkinson to promote patriotism during the war scare of 1798; the music was that of "The President's March," probably composed by Philip Phile, an obscure Philadelphian. Francis Scott Key's patriotic "Star-Spangled Banner," written during the War of 1812, was set to the music of a popular English drinking song. The Reverend Samuel F. Smith wrote the words of "America" (1831) to fit a tune easily recognized as that of the English national anthem, "God Save the King," but familiar under different names in several other countries.

New England, musically backward during the colonial period, compensated by unusual activity in hymn writing during the late eighteenth and early nineteenth centuries. Greatest of these New England musicians was Lowell Mason, composer of "Nearer, My God, to Thee," "My Faith Looks Up to Thee," and "From Greenland's Icy Mountains." Even more important than his compositions were Mason's earnest efforts to introduce music into the public schools. In 1832 he cooperated with others to found the Boston Academy of Music, where children were given free instruction; four years later he began teaching without pay in the public schools of Boston; in 1838 the school board began to appropriate funds to support the project. Meanwhile, in 1834 Mason began the organization of annual music conventions to train teachers in his methods. Twelve persons attended his 1834 convention; 134 came to the 1838 meeting; by 1849 the annual attendance had grown to 1,000.

Stephen Foster, son of a prosperous merchant of western Pennsylvania, gave evidence of unusual talent at an early age, but his attempts to write music received no encouragement from his family. When he was twenty, he gave a number of his early works including "Uncle Ned" and "O Susanna" to a publisher who promptly published *Songs of the Sable Harmonists* at a profit of $10,000 to himself—but without credit or compensation to the composer. Discovering that there was money in the popular-music field, Foster gave up his uncongenial Cincinnati bookkeeping job and moved to New York to earn a precarious living selling his songs to publishers of sheet music. "Old Folks at Home" appeared in 1851, and a year later, according to the *Albany State Register,* the tune was on everyone's lips:

> Pianos and guitars groan with it, night and day; sentimental young ladies sing it; sentimental young men warble it in midnight serenades; . . . all the bands play it; amateur flute players agonize over it at every spare moment; the street organs grind it out at every hour. . . .

Popular also were "My Old Kentucky Home," "Old Dog Tray," "Come Where My Love Lies Dreaming," and a dozen others. Despite such apparent success Foster's life was haunted by tragedy. Much of his output was miserable hack stuff sold for a pittance; his marriage was unhappy; he became an increasingly heavy drinker. Health ruined, he died at the age of thirty-eight in a New York lodging house.

Republican Architecture

American architecture continued to draw its ideas from European tradition. Charles Bulfinch of Boston, traveling during the 1780's, studied the buildings of England, France, and Italy but was most impressed by the beautiful London residences designed by Robert Adam and his brothers. Escaping the domination of Palladio, Adam had studied Greek and Roman survivals at first hand and had drawn from them the inspiration for a light and graceful style of his own. He and his brothers had executed buildings that charmed by the harmony of design between exterior and interior, by the tasteful use of ornamental detail—Greek honeysuckle leaves, wreaths, fans, and toothlike moldings—and by the appropriateness of the Adam-designed furniture. Returning to America, Bulfinch practiced the profession of architecture for many years and did much to encourage "Adamesque" architecture in his native land. Adamesque—often called Late Georgian or Federal—was represented in Bulfinch's fine Boston residences, many of them built in blocks, in Homewood, the Baltimore mansion of Charles Carroll of Carrollton, and in the White House at Washington, designed by the Irish architect James Hoban. During the days of Salem's great prosperity her streets were lined with fine examples of Adamesque—the best of them designed and ornamented by Samuel McIntire.

American nationalism naturally demanded public buildings grand enough to inspire the pride of natives and to command the respect of foreigners. For such monumental edifices colonial architecture provided few precedents. Thomas Jefferson, serving as American minister to France during the 1780's, was tremendously impressed by the Roman survivals that he saw. At the Maison Carrée, beautiful Roman temple at Nîmes, he gazed for hours "like a lover at his mistress." This, he was resolved, should serve as a model for a stately capitol at Richmond, Virginia. Aided by a professional French architect, Jefferson drew the plans from which the Virginia statehouse was built in 1789. Although Jefferson's design had far-reaching influence, American notions of how a state capitol should appear were more powerfully shaped by the high-domed Massachusetts statehouse at Boston, designed by Bulfinch in 1798.

Both George Washington and Thomas Jefferson took keen interest in planning the new Federal city of Washington. Major Pierre Charles L'Enfant, who had served as an engineer during the Revolution, provided a noble conception of streets and avenues that was followed in spirit, although L'Enfant himself was soon involved in quarrels that brought about his dismissal. The designing and construction of the Capitol was punctuated by a succession of similar disputes.

FIG. 33. Gardner-White-Pingree House, Salem, Massachusetts. Designed by Samuel McIntire in the Federal, or Adamesque, style. (*Courtesy of the Library of Congress.*)

First Stephen Hallett directed construction, then William Thornton; their conflicting ideas were not resolved until Benjamin Henry Latrobe took charge during the Jefferson administration. The half-finished building was gutted by fire during the British capture of Washington in 1814. Latrobe began the rebuilding but was succeeded by Bulfinch in 1818. Still further changes came during the fifties and sixties when the present dome and House and Senate wings were added. Despite these vicissitudes of construction the Capitol was an impressive achievement. Mrs. Trollope's party, visiting Washington in 1830, was "struck with admiration and surprise. None of us . . . expected to see so imposing a structure on that side the Atlantic."

Latrobe, an English-born engineer who moved to America in 1796, left his mark on cities other than Washington. In Philadelphia he designed the waterworks with its attractive Center Square Pump House and fine buildings for the Bank of Pennsylvania and the Bank of the United States. In Baltimore he planned the Catholic Cathedral. Latrobe's skill in adapting Greek and Roman forms to new American uses was transmitted to his pupils William Strickland and Robert

FIG. 34. Magnolia Grove, Greensboro, Alabama. Southern mansion, built about 1830 in the Greek revival style. (*Courtesy of the Library of Congress.*)

Mills. Strickland employed Greek-temple-style architecture in his Philadelphia Exchange and Tennessee State House; Robert Mills used Greek columns and Roman vaulting in the Treasury Building at Washington and in many other monumental structures.

Thomas Jefferson watched with delight the growth of this crop of domes, rotundas, pediments, and columns, inspired by the classical architecture which he so much admired. In his old age he contributed one more fine example of his own—the "academical village" of the University of Virginia at Charlottesville with its rotunda based on the Roman Pantheon and its professors' houses—each in its details an illustration of some famous classical structure "to serve as specimens for the architectural lecturer."

Greek Revival architecture reached a peak of popularity during the generation 1825–1850. Behind colonnades and pediments Americans made laws, decided cases, worshiped God, engaged in banking and trade, and raised families. The Athenian Parthenon, reproduced in New Haven, served as the Connecticut capitol; in New York it did duty as customhouse; in Philadelphia it gave shelter to Girard College. The smaller temples in which Americans lived were to be found from New York to Michigan and from Maine to Georgia.

The Greek style appealed to many tastes. To conservatives it was a symbol of order and stability. To intellectual rebels it represented the Athenian passion for beauty and love of truth. The Greek War of Liberation, followed during the twenties with eager interest, contributed further to its popularity. Most important of all, perhaps, was the fact that local carpenters dressing their frame houses with columns and pediments could provide homes that gave an appearance of stately grandeur but were not too expensive. To obtain the necessary instructions the local builders had only to consult such popular manuals as Asher Benjamin's *Practical House Carpenter* (1830), Minard Lafever's *Beauties of Modern Architecture* (1835), or Edward Shaw's *Civil Architecture* (1830).

Although the absurdity of practical Yankees eating and sleeping in Greek temples was occasionally pointed out, the Revival style had in its favor an appealing simplicity and restraint. Talbot Hamlin, eminent historian of architecture, has written:

> Never before or since, I believe, has there been a period when the general level of excellence was so high in American architecture, when the ideal was so constant and its varying expressions so harmonious, when the towns and villages, large and small, had in them so much of unostentatious unity and loveliness as during the forty years from 1820 to the Civil War.[1]

The Greek Revival style never held the field alone. It was not to be expected that a generation with a passion for the novels of Sir Walter Scott and romantic literature in general would fail to experiment with Gothic architecture, then enjoying a revival in England. For churches the medieval style naturally suggested itself early. Latrobe used pseudo-Gothic details on churches that he designed in Washington and Alexandria; Ithiel Town contributed an early example of the medieval style in Trinity Church at New Haven. Churches built later by Richard Upjohn and James Renwick better captured the Gothic spirit. Upjohn's finest work was Trinity Church in New York, built in 1846; Renwick's was St. Patrick's Cathedral in the same city, begun in 1853 but not finished until 1887. Meanwhile, buildings erected at New York University, Yale, and the University

[1] Talbot Hamlin, *Greek Revival Architecture in America* (Oxford, New York, 1944), 319.

of Michigan marked the beginning of a Gothic invasion of American campuses. Gothic town houses and country cottages—many of them designed by Alexander J. Davis—now appeared in increasing numbers. Although in skillful hands the style might possess a quiet charm, its frequent abuse cluttered the landscape with eyesores—ostentatious castles whose forbidding grimness suggested the terrors of romantic melodrama.

During the 1850's the confusion of tongues in architecture rivaled the babel of languages to be heard on the docks of New York. The newly rich could choose the style of their homes from architects' suggestions that included the manor-house style, the French-suburban, the Swiss-cottage, the Lombard-Italian, the ancient-Etruscan, the Oriental, the Moorish, and the castellated. Or they could mix them. P. T. Barnum dwelt at Bridgeport, Connecticut, in a domed and minareted palace appropriately named "Iranistan." After Orson S. Fowler, famous phrenologist, published his popular book, *A Home for All* (1854), a rash of octagonal houses dotted the country.

Painting and Sculpture

For the painter's work there was a sizable, although uncertain, market. Wealthy merchants like Philip Hone of New York and Robert Gilmor of Baltimore collected painting and helped young artists to obtain instruction. Congress, state legislatures, and city councils appropriated funds for the purchase of historical scenes and portraits of statesmen. Even the general public occasionally provided patronage for the artist by paying admission to view famous paintings on exhibition. In the 1840's several thousand Americans belonged to the Art Union: for $5 annual dues each member received an engraving and a lottery ticket on one of the original paintings on display at the Art Union's galleries in New York. Although the ambition of most young artists was to study in Europe, increasingly competent training was provided at institutions like the Pennsylvania Academy of Fine Arts, founded by Charles Willson Peale in 1806, and the National Academy of the Arts of Design, founded at New York by Samuel F. B. Morse twenty years later.

The Peales were an extraordinary family. Charles Willson Peale,[1] Revolutionary soldier, amateur naturalist, and ingenious mechanic, learned something of painting techniques from brief contacts with Copley and West. Developing a large measure of skill himself, he painted portraits of many prominent men, George Washington among them. To his children he gave such illustrious names as Raphaelle, Rembrandt, Rubens, Titian, Angelica Kauffman, Franklin, and Linnaeus. Several of them became able painters. Rembrandt and Rubens Peale, both artists, founded the Museum and Gallery of the Fine Arts in Baltimore, which like the older institution founded by their father in Philadelphia, exhibited both works of art, stuffed animals, and other curiosities.

[1] See Fig. 29.

American portrait painting attained a high level of excellence. The most famous artist of the young republic was Gilbert Stuart. Born in Rhode Island twenty years before the Revolution, Stuart studied for some time in the London studio of Benjamin West but was more deeply influenced by the contemporary portrait painting of Gainsborough, Reynolds, and Romney. After achieving a great success in England and Ireland, Stuart returned to America in 1792, where he painted most of the leading personalities of the day. Particularly admired were his several portraits of George Washington, which preserved for the future an impressive record of the first President's dignity and nobility of character. Portraits done by Chester Harding, a native of western Massachusetts, had little of Stuart's eighteenth-century elegance but were excellent expressions of a simpler, more democratic age. In contrast to this blunt realism the work of the English-born Thomas Sully reflected the age's sentimentalism in his appealing portraits of women and children. John Neagle, who married Sully's stepdaughter, combined sentimentalism with good-natured vigor in works like his well-known *Pat Lyon at the Forge.*[1] Samuel F. B. Morse was a successful painter before he turned nativist author and inventor. His striking portrait of Lafayette in the New York City Hall was a magnificent commemoration of the French hero's American visit of 1824–1825.

An ambition to paint heroic themes on canvases of huge size was widespread among a generation still impressed by the grandiose projects of Benjamin West. John Trumbull of Connecticut with varying degrees of success painted Revolutionary battle scenes and other great episodes of national history. Four large Trumbull paintings were commissioned for the rotunda of the national Capitol, but Congressmen—not without reason—expressed disappointment at the results. Rembrandt Peale's *Court of Death* was a huge canvas depicting Death as a grim monarch attended by Want, Dread, Desolation, Gout, Dropsy, Hypochondria, and Intemperance. Exhibited first at the Baltimore Museum and later sent from one seaboard city to another, this lugubrious work was viewed by 30,000 Americans and provided a theme for many sermons. Less successful was the attempt of John Vanderlyn to induce the public to pay admission to see three of his famous paintings housed in a specially built rotunda in New York's City Hall Park. The works were dramatic enough—a panorama of the palaces and gardens of Versailles, 3,000 square feet in size, a melancholy *Marius Amid the Ruins of Carthage,* and a voluptuous *Ariadne*. But Vanderlyn after a long residence in France misunderstood American opinion, which was suspicious of French luxury in general and particularly shocked by Ariadne's nudity. An ambitious work never completed was Washington Allston's *Belshazzar's Feast.* Allston, native of South Carolina and traveler in Europe, eventually settled in Boston, where he enjoyed the reputation of being a great artist although his output was disappointingly small.

Nationalism and romanticism found their most adequate expression in paint-

[1] See Fig. 18.

ings of the American landscape. Among the earliest artists to make this their specialty were Thomas Doughty of Philadelphia and Thomas Cole of frontier Ohio. In the works of Cole, the poet Bryant took particular delight, declaring that they "carried the eye over scenes of wild grandeur peculiar to our country, over our aerial mountain tops with their mighty growth of forests never touched by the axe, along the bank of streams never deformed by culture and into the depth of skies bright with the hues of our climate."

Although the landscapists early discovered the beauties of the White Mountains of New Hampshire and the unspoiled scenery of other eastern regions, they devoted so many of their works to the Hudson River and the Catskills that the name "Hudson River school" became attached to the group. Asher Durand entered the field in the mid-thirties, transferring to canvas the talent for meticulous detail that he had developed as an engraver. Later still came the work of John Kensett, Albert Bierstadt, Frederick E. Church, and many others. During the 1850's and 1860's the landscapists were exploiting the dramatic scenery of the Rockies. As in music the public often applauded the wrong things. Many of the landscapes were admired for their huge size and minuteness of detail while less spectacular products of the painter's art went unappreciated.

For the student of American life particular interest attaches to the genre painting of these years. William Sidney Mount [1] portrayed the life of his Long Island neighbors, showing with affectionate skill their barn dances, their eel spearing, their whittling, and their tavern sports. George Caleb Bingham [2] was meanwhile compiling a record of life in Missouri ranging from scenes of fur traders and rivermen moving along the river to the raucous excitement of village elections. Although Richard Caton Woodville of Baltimore died at the age of thirty-one and spent most of his working years in Germany, he also contributed several interesting paintings of small-town American life. A whole regiment of artists was kept busy by Currier and Ives and other lithographers recording scenes that would appeal to their customers. Famous horses and ships, fires and explosions, hunters and fishers, idyllic farm scenes, and political cartoons all found a record in the work of the print makers.

Visitors to Italy during the 1840's and 1850's were amazed at the number of American sculptors whom they found practicing their art in Rome, where they worked among congenial surroundings and found models and materials cheaper than at home. Many of these did a good business supplying their wealthy countrymen with portrait statues and classical figures for their drawing rooms and gardens. Most successful was Hiram Powers, shrewd Vermonter, who learned his art making wax figures for a Cincinnati museum. Powers's *Greek Slave* was a sensation of the 1840's: thousands crowded the halls where it was placed on exhibit; other thousands bought miniature copies for their homes. Shipped from Italy to America in 1841 was Horatio Greenough's huge statue of George Washington, executed on commission for the national Capitol. First placed in the

[1] See Fig. 32. [2] See Figs. 13 and 23.

rotunda, later moved outside to the eastern front, Greenough's statue was the subject of lively controversy. To lovers of the classical the first President's seated posture, upraised arm, bare chest, draped legs, and sandaled feet suggested the majesty of Zeus; to the irreverent he looked more like an old gentlemen preparing to take a bath. After half a century of snickers the statue was finally banished to an obscure corner of the Smithsonian Institution. Much better conceived and executed were the statues of John Quincy Adams Ward and William Rimmer. The equivalent of genre paintings was meanwhile being achieved by John Rogers,[1] whose plaster groups, depicting village checkers players, wedding scenes, the weighing of babies, and other simple aspects of life, found their way into thousands of American homes.

America Seeks Amusement

The theater needed whatever aura of respectability it could gather to itself by presenting *Uncle Tom's Cabin* or temperance dramas like *The Drunkard* and *Ten Nights in a Bar-room.* During the first half of the nineteenth century the playhouses became exceedingly popular, but they made little progress in combating the hostility of the righteous. Evidence of Satan's influence was all too abundant. The actors of the day were often as famous for their prowess as heavy drinkers as for their histrionic abilities, and in many theaters the third balcony and adjoining bar were frankly set aside for toughs and prostitutes. Scarcely more genteel was the pit, where row after row of men shifted noisily on hard benches, attempting to stretch out and make themselves comfortable. With hats on and coats off, chewing tobacco, and spitting incessantly, they were an unedifying spectacle for the few ladies who ventured to the theater and sat with their escorts in the boxes. When displeased with the performance, rough customers shouted their sentiments or threw eggs and vegetables. Sufficiently provoked, the actors would sometimes step out of character, advance to the edge of the stage, and hurl insults back at their tormentors.

Such abuses had not prevented a rapidly growing interest in the theater. Companies of English actors like those who had toured the colonies before the Revolution gradually reappeared after hostilities ceased. The most famous of these, the Old American Company managed by Lewis Hallam, Jr., presently established itself as a resident company in New York, first at the John Street Theater and after 1798 at the Park Theater. After some resistance by the municipal authorities the famous Chestnut Street Theater was opened in Philadelphia in 1794. In Boston the struggle was sharper; but in 1793 the old prohibitory law was repealed, and the next year the new Federal Street Theater, designed by Charles Bulfinch, was ready. These victories were facilitated by the patronage extended to the playhouses by President Washington and many aristocratic Federalists. In the hinterland, theaters and resident companies established themselves more slowly, but by

[1] See Fig. 47.

1850 they were to be found in all the larger towns as far west as Iowa. Many of the theaters were built on a huge scale: the second Park Theater in New York, opened in 1821, held an audience of 2,500; the Broadway, built during the next decade, advertised seats for 4,000. To attract the masses admission prices were reduced until the usual range of the 1840's was from 12½ to 50 cents.

Polished performances were hardly to be expected of stock companies that presented a different work every three or four days. Despite this situation Americans had an opportunity to see the most famous actors of the day. There were now enough theaters in the country to make it profitable for English stars to cross the Atlantic and to tour the principal cities, drawing their supporting casts from the resident companies. George Frederick Cooke made the first such venture in 1811; he was followed by such English celebrities as Edmund Kean, Fanny Kemble, and William Charles Macready. Since the preeminence of foreign actors grated upon nationalistic sensibilities, native stars received vociferous encouragement. James H. Hackett became a popular favorite in comic Yankee parts, while Edwin Forrest won extravagant praise in Shakespearean roles. So intense were nationalistic rivalries that in 1849 a Bowery mob—champions of Forrest—stormed the theater on Astor Place, where Macready was playing. Troops were called out, but before the riot could be quelled, 22 persons were killed and a large number wounded. During the 1850's Americans took justifiable pride in the great Edwin Booth and Charlotte Cushman.

Cultural nationalism demanded not only American actors but American dramatists. As a promising first step in 1787 came the popular comedy, *The Contrast,* by Judge Royall Tyler. The proper note was struck in the prologue:

> Exult each patriot heart—tonight is shown
> A piece which we may fairly call our own.

Native audiences were delighted to watch a pure American girl saved from an English cad by a resolute American hero, Colonel Manly. Highly popular also was the character of Jonathan—prototype of hundreds of later stage Yankees, strangely compounded of shrewdness and gullibility.

Other American plays soon followed. A prolific, if seldom inspired, dramatist was William Dunlap of New York, an enthusiastic promoter of all the arts during the early national period. John Howard Payne, famous for his song "Home, Sweet Home," was both actor and author of plays. James Kirk Paulding defended American virtues from the condescension of the British in patriotic plays, and the novelist Robert Montgomery Bird wrote several dramas for Edwin Forrest. But American writing for the stage never approached the level achieved in other forms of literature. Perhaps the best work by a native dramatist was George Henry Boker's *Francesca da Rimini* (1855), but this had only a few performances and was not appraised at its true worth until it was revived many years later.

The taste of theater audiences appeared to deteriorate rather than to improve.

Shakespearean drama retained its popularity as the perfect medium for the florid elocution of old-school actors, but standard theatrical fare was high-flown melodrama and trivial farce. Ingenious stage effects—visions and transfigurations—especially pleased the public. *Mazeppa, or the Wild Horse* was a hit of 1837, offering, as it did, the attraction of 50 fiery steeds in addition to its human actors. Equestrian drama rose in popularity until even Shakespeare's *Henry IV* and *Richard III* were played on horseback.

The public's appetite for novel spectacles was catered to in a variety of theatrical fare. When French ballet was introduced during the 1820's, the theaters were crowded with customers eager to be shocked. Other ingenious mediums for exhibiting the feminine figure were soon contrived. In 1848 the "Living Models," featuring such acts as "Psyche Going to the Bath" and "Venus Rising from the Sea," were the sensation of New York until the show was closed by the police.

In the growing market for mass amusement Phineas T. Barnum found his great opportunity. Son of a Connecticut innkeeper and merchant, Barnum tried storekeeping and country journalism before finding his true vocation as showman. The first group of exhibits which he collected and took on tour in 1835 featured Joyce Heth, whom Barnum blandly advertised as 160 years in age and the one-time nurse of the infant George Washington. In 1841 Barnum purchased Scudder's American Museum in New York, which he soon developed into the most famous amusement center in the country. Here were to be seen General Tom Thumb and other midgets, as well as tall men, fat men, bearded ladies, mermaids, trained fleas, panoramas of the Holy Land, a knitting machine run by a dog, and thousands of other curiosities. In his "Lecture Room" Barnum presented "chaste scenic entertainments" designed to please "all those who disapprove of the dissipations, debaucheries, profanity, vulgarity, and other abominations which characterize our modern theatres." Many of Barnum's shrewdly exploited attractions were genuine curiosities, assembled from the four quarters of the globe; many were "humbugs," as he cheerfully admitted.

In the circus business, evolving during these decades, Barnum found another field for exploitation. Since colonial days showmen had often traveled about the country exhibiting camels, elephants, and other curious animals. More ambitious menageries soon took to the road—invariably emphasizing their educational and highly moral character. Separate at first were the troupes of acrobats who traveled from village to village giving nightly performances on outdoor stages lit by flaring pine torches. Menageries and acrobatic troupes eventually joined forces to provide more ambitious traveling tent shows. Rings and riding acts had meanwhile come to characterize the indoor circuses staged in urban amphitheaters. When these features were added to the traveling tent shows of the 1840's, all the elements of the American circus had been finally assembled. To the several circuses of the 1850's Barnum added his Grand Colossal Museum and Menagerie.

Peculiarly American was the minstrel show, at a height of popularity during the 1840's and 1850's. White performers had long before discovered how to please audiences by appearing in blackface while they plucked banjos, sang pseudo-plantation songs, and performed shuffling dances. As early as 1829 Thomas D. Rice was presenting a highly popular "Jim Crow act." From such performances evolved the standardized minstrel show with interlocutor, endmen, jokes, songs, and dances. In 1843 New York was delighted by Dan Emmett's "novel, grotesque, original and surpassingly melodious Ethiopian band, entitled the Virginia Minstrels." Barnum offered the Ethiopian Serenaders, with "six performers, each one of whom is a professor of music." Particular favorites were Christy's Minstrels, who played in New York for years. Numerous traveling companies carried the minstrel show to every corner of the country. Many favorite American songs like Dan Emmett's "Dixie" and Stephen Foster's "Old Folks at Home" owed their initial popularity to the minstrels.

The growing American appetite for spectacles found outlet in numerous sporting contests. In the absence of professional promoters ferryboat operators and tavern keepers sometimes put up the prizes for races or contests of strength in order to profit by selling transportation and refreshment to the crowds. Races between famous horses attracted thousands of spectators. Between 50,000 and 100,000 persons from every rank of society thronged to the Union Course on Long Island in 1823 to watch Eclipse, champion of the North, beat Sir Henry, the pride of the South. The excitement of this event was rivaled by many other races at New York, Washington, Louisville, Cincinnati, and New Orleans. Because of the heavy betting that always accompanied these running races, they were not permitted in New England, but the more respectable trotting matches were popular features of county fairs everywhere.

Races of any kind attracted enthusiastic crowds. Professional foot races sometimes took place through city streets and sometimes were run over horse-race tracks. In 1835 thousands of New Yorkers turned out to watch nine runners compete for a prize of $1,000 offered to anyone who could complete a 10-mile course in less than sixty minutes. Many spectators were also attracted to rowing matches on the rivers. During the 1850's college crew races began to be popular. Yachting had its devotees, and great interest attended sailing races along the Atlantic Coast or on the Great Lakes.

Although prohibited by law, prize fights were frequently arranged to take place on the outskirts of cities or on islands, where the police were unlikely to interfere. Gamblers put up the purses and were the principal spectators of these brutal contests in which bare-fisted bruisers pummeled each other until one was unable to continue. Despite the limited attendance possible at events so conducted, the general public eagerly followed the sports through the newspapers. Particularly great was the excitement aroused by John C. Heenan's trip to England in 1860 to meet the British champion Tom Sayers. Although the fight was broken up by the crowd in the forty-third round before either man could win, thousands of Americans turned out to witness the "exhibitions" staged by the popular Heenan after his return.

On city lots and village fields boys played a variety of games with bat, ball, and bases—four-old-cat, rounders, town ball, and cricket. Out of these evolved the American game of baseball. Just how is uncertain. The story that the game was invented in 1839 by Abner Doubleday of Cooperstown, New York, has little satisfactory evidence to confirm it. By 1845, however, baseball was sufficiently established for the publication of a code of rules—the work of a group of New York business and professional men, calling themselves the Knickerbocker Club, who played regularly on the Elysian Fields in Hoboken. Other clubs were soon organized in the New York area. At first the game was played only by the white-collar classes, but during the fifties teams made up of workingmen began to appear. By 1860 baseball was becoming popular in cities as remote as Chicago and New Orleans.

Despite the apparent interest in sports much of the population still believed that play was only for children. When the Englishwoman Sophie Jex-Blake visited Oberlin College during the 1860's, she found no gymnasium for either sex. The utmost effort at physical recreation appeared to be a walk in the country, and that was not frequent. "This absence of desire for physical sport seems more or less common throughout America, and is very strange in the eyes of those accustomed to the exhibition of animal spirits in the English youth of both sexes. . . . There seems an absolute deficiency of vitality in Americans in this respect. . . ." [1]

The wealthy, eager for a change of scene, often spent their summers at such fashionable health resorts as Saratoga Springs or Ballston Spa in New York. Life in the great hotels was leisurely in the extreme. Visitors walked on the grounds, drank water from the fountain, and sat long hours on the porches. Young people flirted discreetly and danced at the balls. The principal benefits to be sought were social: to be able to afford a long stay at a fashionable resort was impressive evidence of worldly success. At first the northern spas attracted thousands of southerners each summer. When relations between the sections deteriorated during the 1850's, southern patronage was largely transferred to such resorts as Virginia's White Sulphur Springs.

The seashore also attracted fashionable vacationers. The elite of Boston favored the rocky coastline of nearby Nahant. Wealthy New Yorkers and southerners met in the hotels and fine summer residences of Newport, Rhode Island. Somewhat less pretentious was the society that patronized Long Branch and other shore resorts along the coast of New Jersey. Bathing in the ocean was a recreation at first largely monopolized by males. At certain hours of the day when stern convention dictated that the ladies take their naps or at least stay off the beaches, the men would sport in the breakers unencumbered by clothing. Women who donned old clothes and ventured into the ocean had to depend on female attendants. Gallantry at length, however, seemed to require that the lady bathers

[1] Sophie Jex-Blake, *A Visit to Some American Schools and Colleges* (London, 1867), 33–34.

should be protected from the perils of the ocean by gentlemen escorts. Despite the fact that both sexes were swathed in bulky bathing costumes, mixed bathing was regarded as deliciously daring. Newspaper reports of the 1850's described the popularity of bathing at resorts like Newport, where ladies and gentlemen—sometimes 40 in a group—would join hands and dash into the surf or where men "handed about their pretty partners as if they were dancing water quadrilles."

The rich were learning to play, and the sports that they developed soon attracted participants from the less fortunate classes.

III. Triumph of the Businessman, 1861-1914

Chapter 19. Upheaval in the South

All major wars leave their deep marks on social history. Lives rich in promise are cut short; other lives are handicapped by burdensome disabilities. Ships, railroads, bridges, barns, growing crops, and hundreds of other products of men's labor are destroyed. Religion and morals suffer as the spirit of violence and strife gains ascendancy for the moment. Yet against these debit items in the grim profit and loss statement must be placed such social gains as the increased productiveness forced upon industry and agriculture, the spur to medical and scientific progress, and the sense of solidarity shared by a generation who pour their energies into a common cause.

In the American Civil War all these usual consequences of war were magnified. The losses of life and property were staggering, the brutalizing and corrupting effects were far-reaching, and the stimulus to change was sharply felt. In the South the results of conflict were catastrophic: the economic and social structure of ante-bellum days was almost completely destroyed, and the establishment of a new pattern was a painful process. If war's impact on the North was less immediately dramatic, it was not less important in the long run. All the forces that worked toward increased reliance on the machine, the growth of cities, the interdependence of one section upon another, and the promotion of science—in short all forces that were to characterize later American civilization—were powerfully accelerated by the great intersectional conflict.

The Clash of Interests and Ideals

Why did North and South lock grips in four years of desperate warfare? To this apparently simple question historians have given a dozen different answers. It was a war of rival theories of government, state sovereignty against national supremacy. It was a war of rival economic interests, agrarian South against commercial and industrial North. It was a war of rival nationalisms, loyalty to the South against loyalty to the United States as a whole. It was a war of different social ideals, aristocratic South against democratic North. All these elements, and others as well, were present, and a complete account of the causes of the Civil War would be a review of most of American history prior to 1861.

Yet however other issues complicated the quarrel, the basic difference between North and South was in their attitudes toward slavery. Lincoln said, "One section of our country believes slavery is right, and ought to be extended, while the other believes it is wrong, and ought not to be extended. This is the only substantial dispute." Jefferson Davis blamed the situation on the antislavery bias of the Republican party:

> Finally a great party was organized for the purpose of obtaining the administration of the Government, with the avowed object of using its power for the total exclusion of the slave States from all participation in the benefits of the public domain acquired by all the States in common, whether by conquest or purchase; of surrounding them entirely by States in which slavery should be prohibited; of thus rendering the property in slaves so insecure as to be comparatively worthless, and thereby annihilating in effect property worth thousands of millions of dollars.[1]

The Republican victory in the election of 1860 brought to power a party that based its platform on the assumption that slavery was wrong. Under the Constitution slavery in the states could not be touched by Federal action; but slavery might be prohibited in the territories, and Negroes accused of being fugitive slaves might be assured fair trial. From the Republican point of view this was a moderate, not a radical, program. It was essentially defensive, aimed at preventing the Federal government from continuing to be the tool of the slave power—as, from the antislavery point of view, it had been in the cases of the Mexican War, the Fugitive Slave Act of 1850, the Kansas issue, and attempts to annex Cuba.

But Republican opposition to the extension of slavery and to the Fugitive Slave Act were—from the southern point of view—aggressively hostile to the South. If slaves were a perfectly legitimate form of property, it was a violation of the slave owner's rights to deny him the privilege of taking his property with him into the territories, and it was equally wrong to place obstacles in the way of recapturing fugitive slaves. Even if the Republicans respected the constitutional bars to legislating against slavery in the states, southerners feared that their peculiar institution would have a short life if no new lands were opened to plantation agriculture, if agitation and assistance from outside the South made it ever easier for slaves to escape, and if, through the admission of new free states to the Union, the political climate became increasingly hostile to slaveholding. The South never forgot that Lincoln had said:

> I believe this government cannot endure permanently half slave and half free. . . . Either the opponents of slavery will arrest the further spread of it, and place it where the public mind shall rest in the belief that it is in the course of ultimate extinction, or its advocates will push it forward till it shall become alike lawful in all the States, old as well as new, North as well as South.

It was to preserve the institution of slavery that the South seceded from the Union, established a new government, and fought to maintain its independence. But this still leaves much to be explained. Why, for example, did the nonslaveholding majority support such a course of action? If slaves had been merely property, the attitude of those who had no such property to lose would be in-

[1] J. D. Richardson, comp., *Messages and Papers of the Confederacy* (Nashville, 1906), 67–68.

explicable. But the issue involved much more than dollars and cents. Slavery was a social institution, rigidly fixing the status of some four million Negroes. Convinced of the racial inferiority of the blacks, southern whites almost universally believed that wholesale emancipation would bring chaos. Even more than plantation aristocrats poor whites were horrified by the prospect of a social revolution in which Negroes would become free laborers competing with whites for jobs, mingling on terms of equality in churches, theaters, and railroad coaches, and—horror of horrors—voting and being elected to office.

To believe that Lincoln and the moderate wing of the Republican party had any such revolutionary immediate objective was fantastic, as southern conservatives who urged postponement of secession and a policy of wait-and-see pointed out. Why then did the people of the cotton states act so precipitately? Their haste in severing the bonds of Union reflected a hatred of the Yankees that had been growing for decades. The Yankee devil had long been blamed for every southern difficulty. If manufactured goods were expensive, it was because of the Yankee tariff. If cotton growers made no profit, it was because of the Yankee middleman. The conviction had grown that the South had lost more than it gained from the Federal Union. "Then why," demanded the Charleston *Mercury*, "should we any longer submit to the galling yoke of our tyrant brother—the usurping, domineering, abolition North?"

Southern romanticism was stirred by the idea of founding a new nation purified of corrupting contact with the North and dedicated to chivalric ideals. In justification of their action secession leaders could cite from the Declaration of Independence its assertion that governments rested on the consent of the governed and that it was the right of the people to alter or to abolish them whenever they became destructive of the ends for which they were established. From the southern point of view, moreover, the secessionists were not destroying the old Constitution but restoring it to its original meaning. "We have changed the constituent parts," said Jefferson Davis, "but not the system of government. The Constitution framed by our fathers is that of these Confederate States." Repeatedly the southern leaders insisted that they were fighting for the ideal of constitutional liberty as opposed to what Davis called "the tyranny of an unbridled majority, the most odious and least responsible form of despotism."

Although the impulse to preserve the institution of slavery, to gain freedom from northern commercial domination, and to preserve a cherished concept of constitutional liberty gave a strong sense of solidarity to the South in the early months of the war, a troublesome conflict of loyalties developed over the course of time. To some southerners state sovereignty was a fetish, causing them to view the central government of Jefferson Davis with scarcely less suspicion than that of Abraham Lincoln; for others southern nationalism became a living faith subordinating all local interests; for still a third group secession and war had as their ultimate objective reunion with the North on terms that would adequately protect southern interests. Together with personal rivalries this conflict of loyalties eventually hampered the southern war effort and contributed to the northern victory.

If the Lincoln administration had been willing to let the seceding states go, there would have been no Civil War. Hostilities began when Lincoln held to the symbols of Federal authority represented in the southern forts and the Confederates challenged those symbols by attacking and capturing Fort Sumter in Charleston harbor.

When the South fired upon the flag, it resolved the doubts that had been paralyzing northern policy. Lincoln's call for troops met enthusiastic response, and the nation steeled itself for a conflict that most men up to that moment had hoped to avoid. The summons was not to a crusade against slavery but to a war to uphold the authority of the national government, to suppress "rebellion," and to preserve the Union. Only through such a statement of objectives could Lincoln hope to hold the support of the slave-owning border states, of large sections of the Northwest where migration from the South was reflected in a public opinion violently opposed to abolitionism, and of cities like New York where tolerance of slavery was strong both among cotton-dealing merchants and Irish laborers who disliked the Negroes as competitors for jobs.

The fact that the ideal of Union was an expedient standard did not detract from its potency. However much southerners might protest that they were the true defenders of the principles of the Declaration of Independence and the Constitution, it was the northerners who possessed all the beloved symbols of nationhood. The flag carried by the Union forces was the flag that had flown over American troops in the War of 1812 and the Mexican War; Lincoln lived in the White House, where Jefferson and Jackson had lived; the laws for the Union were made in the Capitol, where Webster, Clay—and Calhoun too—had won their fame.

To Lincoln maintenance of the Union meant more than the continuance of a political state with its historic boundaries. He insisted that it was a test of democracy itself—of whether a nation "conceived in Liberty, and dedicated to the proposition that all men are created equal" could long endure.

Impact of War

National authority was significantly strengthened during the long struggle. Never before had the Presidential powers been so vigorously exerted. To save the Union, Lincoln proclaimed a blockade of the southern ports, enlarged the army, and authorized the arrest and imprisonment of many northerners engaged in disloyal activities. All telegraph lines in the country fell under government control, and the newspapers were told what they might and might not print.

Congress also established new precedents. It issued legal-tender currency, levied an income tax, and passed a conscription law. Even more important than this emergency legislation was the extension of national authority into areas where military needs were involved only indirectly if at all. Taking advantage of the absence of representatives from the narrow-constructionist South, the Republican Congress passed a high protective tariff, a homestead law, a Pacific railroad act, a national-bank act, and a law providing Federal land grants in support of higher education in agriculture and the mechanical arts.

Paradoxically, the nationalizing influence of war manifested itself almost as strongly in the Confederacy. Despite the dogma of state sovereignty the Confederate Congress enacted a conscription law a year earlier than did the northerners, and by other laws it authorized the impressment of food stocks and slaves for military purposes, taxed incomes, and required the payment in kind of one-tenth of various crops. Military authorities in the South made arbitrary arrests, disciplined the newspapers, and required traveling civilians to carry passports. The concept of total war in which every conflicting interest must yield to paramount national needs developed strongly in both sections.

War also made its imperative demands upon northern business and agriculture. Although cotton textile factories were hard hit by the scarcity of raw material, the manufacture of woolens for uniforms and blankets boomed as did also the ready-made clothing and the shoe industry. Government arsenals and private companies worked day and night filling orders for arms and ammunition. Coal mining and the making of iron and steel expanded with the demands of war industry. The enormous productivity of the North permitted not only the filling of immediate military requirements but a continuance of railroad building both east and west. Agriculture, although for a time injured by the loss of southern markets and a shortage of labor, soon expanded production through an increased use of machinery to meet the needs of the army and the increased demands for American foodstuffs abroad.

Heavy government purchasing, the issuance of paper money, the suspension of gold payments, and general prosperity inevitably resulted in a spiral of inflation. Prices for food, clothing, and rent soared; people with fixed incomes or inflexible salaries and wages suffered; speculators found golden opportunities. Shrewd capitalists began an accumulation of stocks and key properties that was to lead to an unparalleled concentration of economic control during the postwar generation.

In the South the war's economic consequences were different. Only in rudimentary form was there an industry capable of weaving cloth, making uniforms and shoes, and manufacturing arms and ammunition. In North and South Carolina, Georgia, and Virginia there were cotton-textile factories. In Virginia, Georgia, and Alabama were ironworks that could be converted to the making of guns. Around this nucleus southern nationalists hoped to expand manufacturing to a degree that would forever free them from dependence on the hated Yankees. Newspapers were full of ambitious projects for establishing factories in every section of the Confederacy. Out of all this talk a considerable expansion of industry actually resulted. The niter needed for gunpowder was collected by ingenious methods; window weights, roofs, and cistern linings were melted down for lead; even North Carolina's numerous stills were sacrificed for the copper they contained. Through increased production, blockade running, and goods illicitly purchased in the North, the South supplied its most imperative needs. Its soldiers were provided with weapons for battle and were clothed and shod, although far from adequately.

Despite these heroic measures southern industrial production fell far short of meeting the total needs of the section. Civilians to an increasing degree were reduced to dependence on homespun textiles and the crude tools hammered out on the forge of the village blacksmith. The Confederacy never found any adequate solution for the shortages of certain raw materials like wool and leather. Any large-scale building of factories was precluded by the difficulty of securing machinery. Even existing factories were hard pressed to maintain production, cut off as they were from the machine shops of the North and of England.

Perhaps the most vulnerable spot in the southern economy was transportation. As against the North's 22,000 miles of railroads, the South had only 9,000 miles. Texas and Florida had no rail connections with the rest of the Confederacy; most of Louisiana and Arkansas were similarly isolated; elsewhere in the South through routes were circuitous and involved many transshipments. The importance of further construction was recognized, and the Confederate Congress provided for substantial subsidies. But only two or three new lines were actually constructed. The most serious obstacle was the difficulty in obtaining rails. Since southern ironworks were working to capacity on armament orders and since rails were too bulky to be run through the blockade, track could only be secured by confiscating the roadbeds of lines that had been abandoned or deemed unessential to the war effort. Equally serious in hampering the equipment of new lines and lessening the efficiency of old ones was the impossibility of purchasing locomotives and cars. Even the repair of existing equipment was handicapped by a shortage of trained mechanics. Transportation difficulties hampered the movement of troops and supplies and accentuated civilian shortages.

Food and other goods often glutted the warehouses of one section of the Confederacy while inhabitants in other sections were in dire need. These shortages were further intensified by the flood of paper money. Facing runaway inflation, speculators hoarded goods and fattened on the exorbitant prices they exacted from frantic consumers.

Southern agriculture required drastic reorientation. The customary markets for cotton were largely disrupted by war. The northern blockade was not at first very effective, but the Confederate government itself laid an embargo on cotton exports—hoping to bring about European intervention. Later this policy was reversed, and large amounts of cotton were run through the blockade to pay for importations of munitions and other supplies. But Confederate soldiers could not eat cotton, and the South's desperate need for food led to an extraordinary conversion of acreage to grain crops. Most of the states limited the production of cotton by law, and newspapers and local committees of safety through patriotic appeals and threats of violence worked to achieve the same end. The success of these measures is to be seen in the reduction of the annual cotton crop from 4,500,000 bales in 1861 to 300,000 bales in 1864.

The South's precarious war economy was eventually ruined by enemy invasion. Wool and meat became even scarcer when Yankee control of the Mississippi cut off Texas from the rest of the Confederacy, and northern occupation of Louisiana deprived the South of desperately needed salt and sugar. Military operations in the Upper South ruined wheat production and made corn bread almost the universal diet. Finally came the crippling blow of General Sherman's march across Georgia and South Carolina. Cutting a swath of destruction 60 miles wide, the army of vengeance blew up bridges and warehouses, heated and twisted railroad track beyond possibility of repair, burned factories, barns, and mansions, ruined crops, and slaughtered livestock. This devastation of one of the richest areas of the South together with similar events elsewhere hastened the collapse of the Confederacy.

The excesses of Sherman's "bummers" were only one manifestation of the demoralizing effect of four years of conflict. Public opinion both North and South was inflamed by stories of the atrocities committed by the opposing armies. The Confederates were accused of starving and maltreating prisoners of war, of torturing southern Unionists, and even of drinking from Yankee skulls. Union soldiers, on the other hand, were portrayed in the southern press as "fiends and demons, not men"; they destroyed property, abused women and children, and murdered unoffending civilians.

Although most such stories represented the exaggerations and untruths of wartime propaganda, evidence was not lacking that morals had deteriorated to a shocking extent. Northern cities struggled with outbreaks of rowdiness, drunken brawls, and increased prostitution. On a different level unscrupulous operators grew rich selling "shoddy" woolens or spoiled provisions to the army. Dishonest contractors often found their accomplices in dishonest public officials. Many of the newly rich indulged in a conspicuous luxury that aroused natural resentment on the part of those to whom the war had brought not money but bereavement and sacrifice. Nor was the South free from similar scandals. Indeed, it was notorious that the blockade runners favored trade in luxuries and fine liquors over the less profitable carrying of needed military supplies. Trading with the enemy was widespread, as unscrupulous northerners conspired with their southern counterparts to exchange manufactured goods for cotton. In both Union and Confederate armies there were many abuses arising out of recruitment and conscription: men volunteered to secure the bounty, deserted, and claimed another bounty when they enlisted again; rich men escaped conscription by hiring substitutes; exemptions were secured through political influence, false medical certificates, and other subterfuges.

But the war had its heroic side. If some soldiers deserted, many more gave the last full measure of devotion. If some women complained querulously of war's inconveniences, more gave generously of their energy to sew and to knit for the soldiers or to make bandages for the wounded. In the North Dorothea Dix, famous for her work on behalf of the insane, organized a corps of women nurses to serve in the military hospitals; in the South courageous women like Sally L. Tompkins of Richmond volunteered for similar work. Great fairs were organized to raise funds for the United States Sanitary Commission, a northern organization that did excellent work in collecting medical supplies, improving hospital facilities, and providing wholesome recreation for the soldiers.

"Let My People Go"

Throughout the first year of the war Lincoln handled the slavery issue with extreme caution, believing that it was imperative for him to preserve unity in the North, avoid offense to the border states, and leave the door open for reconciliation with the South. No incitement of the slaves to rebel against their masters was countenanced. Even in areas where Congress had the constitutional power to act, as in the District of Columbia or the territories, it took no step. Negroes attempting to enlist in the Union army were rejected. Southern slaves seeking refuge behind the northern lines usually met a cool reception. Sometimes they were turned back at the outposts; sometimes slave owners were permitted to cross the lines and claim their property.

This policy brought down upon Lincoln's head a deluge of criticism from disappointed abolitionists. Partially in response to this pressure, partially in recognition of new elements in the situation, the Lincoln administration step by step changed its policy. One important consideration was the diplomatic advantage to be gained by identifying the cause of the Union with that of human freedom—particularly important in our relations with England, where the sympathies of the governing class had tended strongly toward the South. Another major objective was to weaken the military strength that the Confederacy enjoyed through its exploitation of slave labor and to strengthen the Union armies by the addition of Negro workers and soldiers.

Lincoln's program for terminating slavery was characteristicly moderate. He advocated that the Federal government give financial assistance to the states in carrying out a program of gradual, compensated emancipation with extensive colonization of the freedmen outside the United States. Such a policy, he believed, might best begin with the loyal border states and then be extended to the states in rebellion as part of a program of reconciliation.

But such moderate counsels found little support either with abolitionists or proslavery men. Even the border states failed to read the signs of the times and to cooperate with the President in working out a program of gradual emancipation. In the hurricane of war the house of slavery was destroyed—at first, one timber at a time, in the end, through complete collapse. The rising gale was signaled by the action of Congress in abolishing slavery in the District of Columbia in April, 1862, and in the Federal territories in June of the same year.

Meanwhile, attention was increasingly focused on the 3½ million slaves of the Confederacy. Although slave owners had feared trouble when hostilities began, the blacks were at first extraordinarily quiet. For the most part unable to read and isolated on the plantations, the slaves had only vague information about the great conflict that was to determine their destiny. Sometimes all the white males in the planter's household went off to war, and the slaves loyally worked the plantation under the direction of women. Slaves were used to support the Confederate war effort in a score of ways. They labored in the arms factories and served as wheelwrights, blacksmiths, harness makers, and carpenters. They traveled with the army as cooks, teamsters, hospital attendants, and servants. They did particularly vital heavy labor on Confederate fortifications.

Obviously, quite apart from considerations of social justice, military expediency demanded that the North encourage the southern Negroes to desert their posts and to accept employment that would help the Union cause. First of the northern generals to adopt such a policy was General Benjamin F. Butler, who began as early as the summer of 1861 to treat southern slaves who came within his lines as "contraband-of-war." Through the Confiscation Acts of 1861 and 1862 Congress encouraged the military to recognize the freedom of the runaway or abandoned slaves of rebel masters.

The boldest step in the new policy was taken by President Lincoln himself. On September 22, 1862, he issued the Preliminary Emancipation Proclamation, stating that on January 1, 1863, "all persons held as slaves within any State or designated part of a State the people whereof shall then be in rebellion against the United States shall be then, thenceforward, and forever free." This step he took as Commander-in-Chief "as a fit and necessary war measure" for suppressing the rebellion. Although applauded abroad, the Emancipation Proclamation had no very substantial support at home, either in its preliminary form or in the definitive document of January 1, 1863. Abolitionists were disappointed because it applied only to the slaves within the unconquered parts of the Confederacy; anti-abolitionists condemned it as unconstitutional and disruptive of northern unity. Within the Confederacy the document was denounced as a wicked incitement to slave insurrection.

From the legal point of view the Emancipation Proclamation was indeed an extraordinary document, since by its very terms it applied only to those slaves whose location within the Confederacy made it impossible for them to enjoy their freedom. Yet far from being a futile gesture, the famous proclamation actually marked a turning point in the war. All confusion of military policy was now ended. As the Union armies fought their way through the South, more and more slaves sought protection in claiming their rights as freedmen. Emancipation had been fixed as an objective of the war, and the peculiar institution disintegrated rapidly during the next two years. The border states at last abolished slavery, and in December, 1865, the Thirteenth Amendment to the Constitution, prohibiting slavery or involuntary servitude except as a punishment for crime, went into effect throughout the United States.

Meanwhile, Negroes were making a large contribution to the Union war effort. In 1862 the northern army began accepting Negro enlistments. By 1865 some 186,000 had enrolled: 53,000 from the free states, 40,000 from the border slave states, 93,000—or half—from the seceded states. At first the Negro soldiers

FIG. 35. Effects of the Proclamation. From *Harper's Weekly*, Feb. 21, 1863. Negroes claiming their freedom under the Emancipation Proclamation coming into the Union lines at New Bern, North Carolina. (*Courtesy of the Library of Congress.*)

were subject to discrimination. They were paid less than whites and were used mostly as labor battalions, but in time they obtained equal pay and won distinction in combat. Although some northern officers refused to command Negro troops, others like Colonel Thomas Wentworth Higginson and Colonel Robert Gould Shaw became famous through their leadership of black soldiers.

Confederate authorities watched these developments with dismay. At first they greeted the news that the North planned to use Negro troops with assertions that members of "the inferior race" would never fight and that if they did, they would, when captured, not be treated as prisoners of war but as slave insurrectionists. But even the South was compelled to acknowledge that the balance of military power might hinge on the Negro soldiers. A growing demand was heard that the Confederacy itself use black troops. To die-hards this was an intolerable thought. Howell Cobb argued, "If slaves will make good soldiers our whole theory of slavery is wrong." But General Robert E. Lee urged that Negroes be recruited with a promise of freedom at the end of the war, and, in addition, he advocated "a well digested plan of gradual and general emancipation." In March, 1865, the desperate Confederacy gave official sanction to the conscription and recruitment of Negro troops. As the world turned upside down, an enthusiastic crowd watched a unit of black soldiers clad in Confederate gray parade through the streets of Richmond just a week before the capital was captured by Grant.

Reconstruction and the Freedmen

Long before the war was over, the growing multitude of Negroes freed by the advancing Union army constituted a displaced-persons problem not unlike that of World War II. Destitute Negroes uprooted by the conflict attached themselves to the Union armies, begging piteously for food and clothing. With no general policy to guide them, officers on the spot were left to deal with the problem as best they could. The unimaginative kept the freedmen alive with doles and provided occasional labor on fortifications or road building. More intelligent administrators endeavored to make the Negroes self-supporting by settling them on abandoned farms or obtaining work for them as agricultural laborers and artisans.

The energetic measures of a few army officers, however, could not save the majority of freedmen from terrible hardships. Weakened by insufficient food, clothing, and shelter, the Negroes were so vulnerable to disease that 25 per cent of those in camps were estimated to have died between 1862 and 1864. Since government relief measures were inadequate, numerous private organizations in the North solicited funds and collected food and clothing to be sent to the South. Several of these societies were combined in 1865 to form the American Freedmen's Aid Commission. Northern bodies like the American Missionary Association began educational work. As early as 1864 some three thousand Negroes were attending schools conducted by teachers from the North.

As the war approached its end, the problem of aiding the freedmen became increasingly acute. In March, 1865, Congress belatedly established in the War Department the Bureau of Refugees, Freedmen, and Abandoned Lands. Usually known as the Freedmen's Bureau, the new branch of government undertook a multiplicity of tasks. As a relief agency it gave out about 22 million rations to desperately needy people in the devastated South—about 15½ million to former slaves and the rest to whites. As an employment agency it helped the Negroes to secure work, provided transportation to places where they were needed, and supervised the writing of contracts between the freedmen and their employers. As a settlement agency it administered certain abandoned properties, which it leased to Negro cultivators for a term of years. As a health agency it employed doctors, maintained hospitals, and did much to reduce the shocking Negro mortality of the early days of freedom. As an educational agency it encouraged the establishment of Negro schools and granted them financial aid. In addition to all this it maintained special courts in which both civil and criminal cases involving the ex-slaves were dealt with through an informal procedure.

The Freedmen's Bureau was involved in a storm of controversy from its establishment to its final liquidation in 1872. Originally authorized for the duration of the war and one year thereafter, the bureau secured an extension of its life only after a bitter struggle between Congress and President Johnson. Some southern criticisms of the agency were justified; others were based principally on resentment against any attempt by northerners to interfere in the explosive area of race relationships. Although General Oliver O. Howard, the commissioner of the bureau, and many of his subordinates were conceded to be honest men, sincerely devoted to their mission, many local agents did not enjoy the same reputation. Some were corrupt; others were arbitrary. A favorite allegation was that certain agents were responsible for widespread indolence and vagrancy by encouraging the Negroes to believe that the government was about to present them with "forty acres and a mule." Others were accused of being more interested in transforming the Negroes into Republican voters than in anything else.

Even more disliked, perhaps, than the personnel of the Freedmen's Bureau were the army of northern teachers who came south to serve in Negro schools. Some southern whites opposed the whole idea of Negro education; others conceded education to be necessary but insisted that the blacks should be taught by native whites who understood the southern point of view. At best the Yankee schoolmarm was believed to purvey an impractical type of book learning more likely to spoil a Negro worker than to improve him. At worst she was accused of indoctrinating the Negroes with dangerous ideas of racial equality.

Behind the controversy over Negro education and other activities of the Freedmen's Bureau were the fundamentally different points of view that had developed during the slavery controversy. Northern idealists believed that whites and blacks were equal in the eyes of God and should be recognized as equal in all human laws and institutions. Southern whites almost universally persisted in the conviction that the Negroes were an inferior race. Although willing to concede the finality of the abolition of slavery and the right of the blacks to earn wages, to possess property, and to enjoy security of person, they were entirely opposed to extending full rights of citizenship.

The difference in viewpoint was well illustrated by the "Black Codes," enacted by most of the southern states after the close of the war. These laws, which applied only to Negroes, dealt with the making and enforcement of labor contracts, the apprenticeship of minors, and the punishment of vagrancy and crime. Excited northerners, learning that the South Carolina code provided that Negro children between the ages of two and twenty-one might be apprenticed to masters who had authority to "inflict moderate chastisement" and to "recapture" those who ran away or that the Mississippi code authorized the hiring out of "vagrants" by the sheriff, accused the South of attempting to revive slavery. The Chicago *Tribune* warned Mississippi that "the men of the North will convert the State of Mississippi into a frog pond before they will allow any such law to disgrace one foot of soil in which the bones of our soldiers sleep and over which the flag of freedom waves." Actually, what the South was attempting was not to restore slavery but to provide the freedmen with a new status, similar to that of free Negroes before the Civil War. The codes were based upon the premise that the Negro's natural improvidence, proclivity to vagrancy and crime, and lower intelligence required careful enumeration of his rights and duties. Consistent with this point of view were laws forbidding Negroes to serve on juries or to testify in any case where a white person was the defendant.

The Black Codes confirmed Radical Republicans in their suspicion that the southern leopard had not changed his spots—that the governments established under the lenient reconstruction policy inaugurated by Lincoln and continued by Johnson could not be relied upon to deal justly with the Negro. To protect the freedmen against discriminatory legislation, Congress passed the Civil Rights Act of 1866, which bestowed United States citizenship on all persons born in the United States and granted to citizens "of every race and color" the same rights to make and to enforce contracts, to sue and to testify in courts, to convey property, and to be subject to the same punishments and penalties. Doubts as to the constitutionality of this measure were silenced by the embodying of its essence in the Fourteenth Amendment to the Constitution, which became effective in 1868. This great extension of the Federal Bill of Rights defined United States citizenship and prohibited the states from passing laws that abridged any of the privileges or immunities of citizens, that deprived any person of life, liberty, or property without due process of law, or that denied to any person the equal protection of the laws.

The controversy over the status of the Negroes reached its climax in the struggle over the franchise. Lincoln's position had been characteristically moderate. He believed that the issue should be decided by the individual states, but his personal desire seems to have been that Negro soldiers and Negroes of superior intelligence should receive the vote promptly and other Negroes when they proved their capacity. This position satisfied neither southern whites nor northern radicals. All but a few of the former were opposed to any Negro suffrage at all; most of the latter were convinced that immediate enfranchisement was essential to protect Negro rights.

The growing determination of Congress to force Negro suffrage upon the South represented much more, however, than humanitarian concern for the oppressed race. The Republicans believed that their party's control of the national government depended on extending the vote to Negroes and taking it away from whites who had been prominent in the Confederacy. Important economic consequences were believed to hinge on the issue. It was feared that if the Republicans were to lose control of the government, Federal bondholders might suffer a reduction of income, manufacturers might be deprived of tariff protection, and bankers, railroads, and western homesteaders might lose the special benefits they had gained.

In this atmosphere of conflicting prejudices and struggling interests there was little opportunity to debate the Negro suffrage question on its merits. Despite the fact that only six northern states permitted Negroes to vote, the Reconstruction Acts of 1867 declared existing state governments in the South illegal, restored military rule over the region, and laid down as essential steps for readmission to the Union the drafting of new state constitutions based upon Negro suffrage and the adoption of the Fourteenth Amendment. Forced upon the South in this form, Negro suffrage was of course triply damned. Southerners burned with rage, not only because they believed that the blacks were too ignorant and irresponsible to vote, but because their vote was associated with Federal bayonets and with the exploitation of carpetbaggers or northern adventurers.

During the years of Radical Reconstruction the Negroes not only voted but held many public offices. In South Carolina the constitution of 1868 was drafted by a convention containing 76 black and 48 white delegates; in Louisiana Negro members composed 50 per cent of the constitutional convention; in Florida they were 40 per cent. In the governments organized under the new constitutions, Negro lieutenant governors were elected in South Carolina, Louisiana, and Mississippi, and Negro secretaries of state, state treasurers, judges, and legislators were common. A score of Negroes appeared in Washington as senators and representatives from the reconstructed states.

Although hatred of carpetbag rule had its roots in racial prejudice, the Reconstruction governments fell under heavy criticism on other and more legitimate grounds. The graft and corruption that had invaded all levels of American politics during the postwar period attached themselves to the governments of the South in particularly virulent form. The scandals of the Grant regime in Washington, the Conkling machine in Albany, and the Tweed gang in New York City had their counterparts in all the southern capitals. In the disordered state of Reconstruction society there were opportunities for plunder that drew scoundrels from every direction. Governors grew wealthy through selling their influence; treasurers and tax collectors helped themselves to public funds; legislators padded their expense accounts and accepted bribes. Taxes mounted and state debts multiplied while government units bonded themselves recklessly to aid railroads and other businesses promoted by northern financiers and southern speculators. The major offenders in this orgy of fraud were whites—northern carpetbaggers and southern scalawags who had thrown in their lot with the Republican machines. Such Negro officeholders as shared in the plunder were usually involved only on the level of petty graft. Despite the greater guilt of the whites the corruption of carpetbag government afforded southern conservatives their most persuasive argument against Negro suffrage. Even in the North a growing body of opinion supported the contention that honest government could not be restored in the South until ignorant and inexperienced blacks were dissuaded from using their ballots to keep the carpetbaggers in power.

Despite these grave abuses the Reconstruction governments accomplished a number of worthwhile things. The constitutions of 1868 were, for the most part, excellent documents. They democratized government, abolishing both racial and property qualifications for voting and officeholding and providing for the election of judges. They reapportioned representation on a more equitable basis and reorganized the system of local government. Imprisonment for debt and seizure of homesteads were forbidden. A great deal of progress was made in the establishment of public schools. There were also erected many penitentiaries, insane asylums, orphans' homes, and other welfare institutions. Indeed, a substantial proportion of the increased taxes so much complained of by the planters was made necessary by the expansion of state services in directions long familiar in the North but new and resented in the South.

White Supremacy

Intimidation and violence played an increasingly prominent part in the southern situation. Whites condemned northern troublemakers for organizing thousands of Negroes in the Union League of America, often called the Loyal League. This society, replete with mysterious oaths, rituals, and passwords, was accused of regimenting the Negro vote for the Republican party, preaching hatred of the whites, and encouraging the blacks to carry arms. The Leaguers were accused of burning barns and ginhouses and of shooting the livestock of white planters. Finding justification for their action in this situation and in the general disorder, southern whites had begun to join various "protective societies" even before the inaugurataion of carpetbag government. During the period of Radical Republican rule this rash of secret societies grew with prodigious speed.

Most famous was the Ku Klux Klan, first established in 1865 but little known until 1868. Superstitious Negroes were terrified to see white-hooded horsemen—supposedly ghosts of Confederate soldiers—ride wildly through the night. In its earliest days the Klan engaged in such activities largely in the spirit of horseplay, but it—and similar organizations like the Knights of the White Camelia and the White Brotherhood—soon passed to serious acts of violence against Negroes, carpetbaggers, and scalawags. Night riders whipped, tortured, and killed. Southerners justified these acts as the necessary resort of a people who had been wickedly wronged and who had no other remedy. Victims of the Klan were described as evil persons whom the law had left unpunished. Northerners asserted that the Klan was instituting a reign of terror to drive the Negro from the polls and to deprive him of his gains under Reconstruction. Whatever the intentions of the leaders of the order, it is certain that many Negroes were punished for no other crime than exercising their rights of citizenship. Negro schoolhouses were sometimes burned down and white teachers run out of town by white mobs that resented the school taxes. The excesses committed in the name of the Klan became so notorious that its more respectable members tried to disband the order in 1869, but the dragon seed had been so widely sown that night-riding violence increased rather than diminished during the early seventies.

Since terrorism threatened Republican success at the polls, efforts were made to strengthen carpetbag rule through new legislation. State laws against masked secret societies were passed. The Fifteenth Amendment to the Constitution, adopted in 1870, provided that the right of citizens to vote should not be denied on account of race, color, or previous condition of servitude. To protect the Negro in his rights under the Fourteenth and Fifteenth Amendments, Congress passed drastic enforcement laws, authorizing Federal policing of southern elections and the use of martial law to break up combinations like the Klan, which were attempting to deprive the Negro of his right to vote. Under this authority President Grant sent additional troops to the South, and the carpetbag regimes were given a brief new lease on life.

But southern Republicanism suffered a succession of defeats during the middle seventies. Disgust for carpetbag corruption caused many honest whites and blacks to disassociate themselves from the ruling machines. Sometimes the dissidents organized third parties dedicated to reform; sometimes they allied with the Democrats. In any case this defection together with personal feuds among the carpetbag leaders led to a weakening of Republican ranks at just the time when the Democrats were regaining strength. Pardons and amnesty laws restored the right to vote and to hold office to many prominent white Democrats who had been disenfranchised by earlier legislation. As the rival parties began to approach each other in strength, elections became more and more disorderly. Democrats resorted to violence to keep black voters from the polls; Republicans shamelessly manipulated the election machinery. But the trend of events was clear. The Democrats won back control of Virginia and North Carolina in 1870 and of Georgia in 1871. By 1876 they had regained supremacy in all the South except South Carolina, Florida, and Louisiana. By desperate means the Republicans were able to use the electoral votes of these three states to elect Hayes to the presidency in the famous disputed election, but this was Reconstruction's final victory. The next year the last Federal troops were removed, and the last of the carpetbag governments disappeared.

Developments in the North had contributed to the collapse of Radical Reconstruction almost as effectively as events in the South. Northern public opinion was weary of the issue. A new generation of Republican leaders was more interested in tariff schedules, rivers-and-harbors bills, and railroad subsidies than in protection of the Negroes. Indeed, many of the best Republicans, distressed by political corruption, favored the restoration of home rule to the South as a necessary first step toward reform. Conservative also was the trend of Supreme Court decisions, defining narrowly Negro rights under the Reconstruction amendments and laws.

Conservative southern whites now had a practically free hand to do what they had wanted to do since 1865—to fix the status of the Negro in southern society without interference from the North. The events of the Reconstruction period had deepened their determination to exclude the freedmen entirely from politics. Not yet daring to violate the Fifteenth Amendment by depriving the Negro of the right to vote by law, the dominant whites reduced his vote to manageable dimensions by a dozen devices. Some were crude, as when whites simply patrolled the streets on election day to keep Negroes from the polls. Others were more subtle, as when white planters gave their fatherly advice to their Negro tenants and employees or when the election procedure was made so bafflingly complex that the Negro gave up his ballot in despair.

For twenty years there was still a substantial Negro vote that might be maneuvered for by rival white factions. In the heated politics of Populist days the Negroes for a brief time again heard energetic pleas for their support. This development so alarmed the zealots of white supremacy that drastic steps to disenfranchise the blacks were taken in new state constitutions adopted during the 1890's and early 1900's. The Fifteenth Amendment was circumvented by literacy clauses, poll-tax and residence requirements, and disqualifications for petty crime. Race or color was never mentioned as one of the tests for the franchise, yet white election officials could find some grounds for denying enrollment to almost any Negro bold enough to appear before them. In Louisiana, for example, where 130,344 colored voters had been registered under the old laws in 1896, only 5,320 remained on the books after a new state constitution was adopted.

But "keeping the Negro in his place" involved much more than depriving him of the ballot. Negroes in court had a difficult time. Negroes were systematically passed over in compiling panels of jurors, Negro defendants accused of crimes against whites were usually convicted, and white defendants accused of crimes against Negroes usually went free. Even this unequal brand of justice did not, however, satisfy the white demand for vengeance against alleged wrongdoers. Lynchings continued to be a national disgrace: 106 Negroes were thus killed in 1900, 105 in 1901, and never less than 50 in any year thereafter until 1914. Meanwhile, beginning with the reestablishment of white supremacy in the 1870's, stringent segregation laws had been enacted in every southern state: marriages between blacks and whites were prohibited; Negroes were restricted to separate sections in trains, in depots, and on wharves; Negroes were barred from white hotels, barbershops, restaurants, and theaters.

Segregation extended early to the field of education. From primary school to university the Negro was barred from white institutions. Appropriations for the Negro public schools were pathetically low. Fortunately, funds from other sources became available. The American Missionary Association and various religious denominations, both white and black, contributed to the support of Negro schools and colleges. Larger amounts became available when wealthy northern philanthropists gave high priority to Negro needs in their gifts. Massachusetts-born George Peabody, who had made a fortune in commerce and banking in England, pointed the way when he set up his Educational Fund in 1867 for the advancement of both white and Negro education in the South. John F. Slater, Connecticut textile manufacturer, followed with a million-dollar gift for the training of Negro teachers, and Negro education also benefited through other foundations. Happily for Negro colleges, both northern and European audiences discovered the beauty of Negro folk music. Following the successful tour of the Jubilee Singers of Fisk University in 1875, several other institutions sent student choruses and quartets on concert tours through which thousands of dollars were added to their funds.

Significantly, the best-known Negro of this generation was an educator, Booker T. Washington. Strongly influenced by the emphasis given to industrial training at Hampton Institute in Virginia, where he received his education, Washington founded his own famous industrial school at Tuskegee, Alabama, in 1881. Overcoming the prejudices of the whites in the section, Washington won good will through the courteous behavior and industrious habits that he inculcated in his students. Washington believed that Negroes could win a secure place in society by learning to be good farmers and artisans and so earning the respect of their white neighbors. This philosophy was highly acceptable to the white South, and Washington was widely commended for a speech at the Atlanta Exposition in 1895 in which he said: "In all things that are purely social we can be as separate as the five fingers, yet one as the hand in all things essential to mutual progress."

Although Washington was not indifferent to the ultimate objective of equality of opportunity, his concentration on immediate economic objectives brought protests from a minority of Negro intellectuals. In *Souls of Black Folk* (1903), W. E. B. Du Bois, a Negro with a doctor of philosophy degree from Harvard University, criticized Washington for deprecating classical education for Negroes, for preaching a gospel of work and money to the exclusion of "the higher aims of life," and for acquiescing in the South's imposition of an inferior status for the Negro. Du Bois was a leading figure in the so-called "Niagara movement"—an aggressive demand for Negro rights first organized in 1905—and in the much broader National Association for the Advancement of Colored People, founded in 1910.

Negroes in the North were subject to discriminations almost as galling as those they faced in the South. In seeking jobs, admission to colleges and professional schools, and entrance to hotels, restaurants, and bathing beaches, colored residents of every section of the country met frequent rebuffs. Some of the worst race riots occurred in northern cities.

The New South

Quite apart from the shifting fortunes of the Negro, the Civil War and the Reconstruction period brought changes in the South so sweeping that they amounted to a social revolution. The ante-bellum plantation aristocracy suffered a shattering blow. In the end the northern confiscation policy was much less drastic than that which the passions of wartime had threatened. Title to most of the land remained in the same hands as before the war. But large estates were worthless without capital and labor to work them. Many large planters, ruined by the destruction of war, heavy taxation, and the worthlessness of Confederate money and bonds, sold their land for whatever it would bring. Some, romantics to the end, went off to Brazil or to Mexico in search of adventure and new fortunes; others more realistically made a new life for themselves in Texas or Arkansas, in the North, or in southern cities. As men with proud family names became merchants, bankers, factory superintendents, and clerks, much of the old distinction between gentlemanly and ungentlemanly vocations disappeared.

Despite the difficulties of the moment southern land was still fertile, and the world still needed its products. Many of the old planters weathered the crisis and held on to their property, and new large landholders appeared. Some were wealthy northerners like Whitelaw Reid and Henry Lee Higginson; others were southern businessmen who had made fortunes in the war. Most of the northerners, finding postwar agriculture unprofitable, soon retired from the scene. Southerners, who had a better understanding of the ups and downs of the cotton market and handled their Negro laborers more skillfully, had a better chance for success.

Several alternatives were open to owners of large properties. If they could manage to pay wages to Negro laborers, they could maintain much of the organization and discipline of the old-time plantation. More generally, however, they parceled out their land to tenants. This tendency was strengthened both by the scarcity of money and by the reluctance of many Negroes to perform gang labor in the fields—a regimentation that reminded them unpleasantly of slavery. Although black or white tenants who could pay money rents were sometimes available, most tenants were far too poor to do so. Hence the rapid extension of sharecropping—a system whereby the landlord provided land, house, seed, and tools and received in return a fixed portion, usually one-half, of the crop.

One of the most significant trends in the postwar South was the large increase in the number of family-sized farms. Many of the old plantations were broken up for sale, and large tracts that had not been cultivated before the war were now made available—some of them under the Federal Homestead Act. In one way or another the total number of farms in the South doubled between 1860 and 1880. Among the new landowners were both whites and Negroes. Particularly in the Lower South thousands of poor whites obtained farms, thereby rising in social status and becoming a more important element in southern politics.

Every group of agriculturists—landlords, yeomen, tenants, sharecroppers—was in desperate need of credit. Banks were scarce and rates of interest usurious. Out of this situation grew the crop-lien system, an old arrangement now radically extended. The cultivator of the soil who needed food and other goods that he could not pay for received these on credit from his landlord or from the crossroads merchant, mortgaging his crop as security. Since the landlord rarely had capital enough to finance these transactions, he frequently gave a crop lien to the merchant also. The ultimate creditor was often a bank which had advanced funds to the merchant.

Although the crop-lien system solved the immediate needs of the farmer, its long-range tendency was to impoverish him still further. He had to pay exorbitant prices for his necessities, often twice their cash value. Required to deliver his crop promptly to the merchant, he lost the opportunity to sell to the highest bidder or to withhold his product when the market was glutted. Furthermore, the much-needed diversification of southern agriculture was retarded by the crop-lien system. Banks, merchants, and landlords all insisted that the established staples like tobacco and cotton be grown as the only reliable security for their loans.

During this period manufacturing gained a new prestige. "With the emancipation of the slaves, agriculture ceases to be the all absorbing pursuit," declared a Georgia editor in 1865. "Manufacturers must take their proper position, and, this fact once thoroughly comprehended, let the grand Anvil Chorus of a thousand sturdy hammers awaken the highway and the by-way with resounding clamor."

Local enthusiasts promoted cotton mills with evangelical fervor. They pointed out the advantages of the South—abundance of water power, proximity to raw material, and suitable climate. Cotton mills, they declared, would give employment to Confederate widows and orphans and other self-respecting poor. Since northern capital was not interested in creating an industry to compete with the factories of New England, the southern mills were built on funds subscribed by hundreds of small investors. Usually the stockholders were well rewarded, for despite some failures most of the new mills proved highly profitable. Although the wages they paid were low by northern standards, they were attractive to the poor whites of the Upper South.

Meanwhile, the tobacco industry was expanding rapidly. During the Civil War, soldiers of both sides smoked and chewed more than ever before. Many of them became particularly fond of a light smoking tobacco grown in the vicinity of Durham, North Carolina. On this preference John Ruffin Green laid the foundation for a great business. Choosing a Durham bull for his trademark, he began to bag and sell a product whose dependable quality commanded a rapidly expanding market. After Green's death in 1869 the firm of Blackwell and Carr made "Bull Durham" a familiar name everywhere. In the first great campaign of tobacco advertising, the famous bull adorned signs to be seen in every part of the United States and even on the pyramids of Egypt.

The pre-Civil War assumption that cigarettes were only for hussies and sissies was gradually broken down. At first, addicts had to roll their own, but enterprising dealers soon supplied cigarettes manufactured in quantity by hand workers from Europe or by native artisans to whom they taught their craft. Entering the cigarette business in the early 1880's were old Washington Duke, one of the most successful tobacco dealers of the day, and his aggressive son James Buchanan Duke. In 1884 the Duke firm introduced the use of cigarette machines. Now able to manufacture and to sell cheaply, they and their competitors used every device of advertising to popularize the product. Youthful cigarette smokers eagerly collected the pictures of flags, boats, and actresses enclosed in each package.

A third important industry of the new South was the manufacture of iron and steel. Large deposits of iron ore and coal were discovered in Alabama, Georgia, Tennessee, and Virginia. Chattanooga, Tennessee, enjoyed a rapid growth, but the most sensational boom town was Birmingham, Alabama. Founded by a land company in 1871 at a point where two railroads met in a cotton field, Birmingham contained 3,000 inhabitants in 1880, 38,000 in 1900, and 132,000 in 1910.

By the standards of the East and the Middle West the South was still agricultural in 1914. The great majority of the population still lived in small communities, drawing a livelihood from the old staples and a few other commercial crops like fruits, vegetables, and peanuts. But industry had developed sufficiently to alter significantly the structure of southern society. Besides landlords, yeoman farmers, tenants, and sharecroppers there were now a powerful group of industrialists, bankers, and merchants and a growing number of industrial workers.

Chapter 20. Last Frontier

In 1912 when New Mexico and Arizona became the forty-seventh and forty-eighth states of the Union, the event provided the final chapter in an American story that had started at Jamestown three hundred years before. Although the Americans continued to be a rootless people, moving frequently from one section of their country to another, the frontier movement in the form which it had hitherto taken was over. The last great wave of settlement and state building after 1860 had created 14 commonwealths west of the Mississippi River. The lure of precious metals, vast grazing lands, and fertile soil had brought thousands of settlers into the great region between the Missouri River and the Sierras—an area ignorantly designated "the great American desert" by earlier generations.

The new West was a land of paradoxes. Through the miracle of railroads it was more accessible to the urban East than any previous frontier had been. Yet the contrast between West and East had never been so striking. To easterners, pale from work in urban offices and factories, the deeply tanned westerners—prospectors, cowboys, bad men, vigilantes, and homesteaders—seemed like characters from another planet. The America of mass industry and mechanized agriculture delighted in vicarious adventure. For every Billy the Kid or Wild Bill Hickok there were a thousand American boys and men who identified themselves with the violent westerners. Dime novels, stage shows, movies, radio, and television were destined to keep alive a legendary West of hard-riding heroes and villains long after the real West had settled down to dull respectability.

The Miners

On January 24, 1848, employees of John A. Sutter found traces of gold in a millrace that they were digging for the Swiss adventurer on the south fork of the American River. Despite efforts to keep the discovery secret, the exciting news soon leaked out in San Francisco. Almost the entire population of that village port, together with most of the other inhabitants of California, deserted all other occupations to hunt for gold. From San Francisco the news was carried to Hawaii, to Australia, to China, to Europe, and to the eastern United States. The story also spread across the overland trails to the Mississippi Valley. Many emigrants who had left Missouri for Oregon in 1848 ended up in California instead.

But the great migration came the next year. Although the "forty-niners" converged on California from every corner of the globe, the majority of the fortune seekers were Americans from the East and Middle West. The long trip was made by all possible routes. Thousands took passage on ships sailing from eastern ports to California around Cape Horn. This tedious six-month journey could be substantially shortened by sailing to Colon, crossing the Isthmus on foot—at the risk of cholera, dysentery, and yellow fever—and then taking passage from Panama to San Francisco. Other thousands pushed their weary way across the various overland trails—through South Pass, Santa Fe, or El Paso.

In California the gold hunters met with varying success. A few struck it rich, extracting gold in quantities as great as a thousand dollars a day. But the great majority either found no precious metal at all or worked hard to make a dollar or two a day. More likely to become wealthy were those who supplied the miners with necessities or luxuries. Farmers, merchants, boardinghouse keepers, saloonkeepers, gamblers, and prostitutes followed their respective trades with more than the usual profit.

Miners working as individuals or as small groups used crude methods. They searched the rocks for nuggets of pure gold, or they engaged in placer mining, washing small particles of gold out of panfuls of mud and sand scooped up from the beds of streams. But the amount of gold that could be thus collected was relatively limited. In 1852 California's gold production exceeded 80 million dollars but thereafter it began to decline. Many more prospectors had been drawn to the Far West than could make a living. Some returned to their homes, some settled down to agriculture or merchandising, but many remained perennial treasure seekers ready to hurry off to any remote spot where strikes of gold had been rumored.

Just ten years after the California mania gold was reported in the vicinity of Pikes Peak. In 1859 an estimated 100,000 adventurers crossed Nebraska, many with wagons bearing the defiant motto, "Pikes Peak or Bust." A substantial proportion were soon to be seen making their way east again, their disillusionment blazoned to the world in the new slogan, "Busted by God!" The amount of gold accessible enough to be taken out by individual miners was soon exhausted. But Colorado contained abundant quantities of gold, silver, and lead which might be extracted by machinery. Promoters able to finance the exploitation of these deposits made millions, and Leadville, Colorado, became one of the boom towns of the seventies.

More kaleidoscopic still was the history of Nevada. In the spring of 1859 prospectors in the eastern Sierras, attempting to dig a reservoir for placer operations, discovered a vein of dark rock thickly flecked with gold. For some weeks the miners chipped out the chunks of gold and threw away the encasing black substance. Then it occurred to someone to send a sample of the waste to California to be assayed. Presently the exciting news came back that each ton of the "black stuff" contained $1,595 in gold and $4,791 in silver. Thus were revealed the startling potentialities of the Comstock Lode, so named for an old prospector who staked out one of the early claims and sold it before its real value was known.

Four thousand prospectors rushed to the scene from California before winter snows blocked the trails over the mountains; 10,000 more came in 1860.

The miners who swarmed into the district could do little real mining. Most of the gold and silver was locked in quartz from which it could be extracted only by expensive machinery. The individual prospectors could only hunt for evidence of the metals, stake out claims, and wait for the appearance of companies with sufficient capital to exploit them. Miners bought and sold shares in each other's claims—talking in millions while their pockets were actually empty. And penniless most of them remained. Companies were organized and stamp mills erected, but out of 3,000 claims staked out in the area less than a dozen proved profitable. For the lucky ones who held shares in these the rewards were fabulous.

In the early seventies, when pessimists were already saying that the Lode was running out, the richest strikes of all were made by drilling deep into the flinty rock. In 1873 the Big Bonanza was discovered 1,167 feet below the surface in a shaft sunk by the Consolidated Virginia Company, a partnership of two prospectors and two San Francisco saloonkeepers. This strike—the richest in mining history—brought a fortune of 200 million dollars to the partners and raised a new fever of excitement.

At the heart of the Nevada mining district was Virginia City, supposedly christened with a bottle of whisky by a drunken prospector known as "old Virginney." In its brief span of glory Virginia City boasted a stock exchange, five newspapers, an opera house, and many luxurious homes—together with a bizarre concentration of saloons, dance halls, gambling dens, and bawdyhouses. But Nevada's decline was almost as rapid as its rise had been. Not even the bold engineering feats of the seventies could halt the diminishing profitableness of its mines. Stocks in the Comstock properties which had been valued at 293 million dollars in 1875 were worth less than 7 million dollars in 1880. By the end of another decade the Lode was exhausted, and Virginia City had become one of the "ghost towns" of the West.

Meanwhile, the Comstock prospectors, like the California tribe before them, had dispersed to other areas reputed to hold treasure. Within Nevada itself reports of gold in districts both north and south of Virginia City created so much excitement that the mining capital from time to time lost almost all its population. El Dorado was also reported in Arizona. An early rush to this area in 1858 soon dwindled out, but more promising discoveries in 1862 brought thousands of adventurers from California. Tucson became a typical boom mining town of the sixties. A decade later the prospectors moved farther east where the town appropriately named Tombstone achieved notoriety through the exploits of Billy the Kid and other bad men.

While some prospectors were searching for gold and silver in the Southwest, more were exploring the Northwest. In 1858, 35,000 left California for the Frazer River district in British Columbia. Most of this army returned empty-handed, but some persisted. A few pushed farther north into Canada; others moved south across the border into present-day Idaho, where they discovered gold in the early sixties along the Clearwater, Salmon, and Snake Rivers. Thousands of California prospectors rushed to this area and then on to Montana, encouraged by reports of strikes near the headwaters of the Missouri. Luckiest of the Montana prospectors were those who discovered the rich treasures of Alder Gulch and the almost equally fabulous deposits in Last Chance Gulch. Earlier mining history was repeated in Idaho and Montana, where the gold to be collected by individual effort was soon exhausted but rich deposits of silver, lead, and copper remained to be extracted by mining companies with adequate capital.

As the western mines passed increasingly under the control of eastern capitalists, the incorrigibly optimistic prospectors transferred their activities to new areas. Persistent reports of gold in the Black Hills of South Dakota fired their imaginations and led to increasing impatience with the efforts of the army to keep the miners out of the area reserved for the Sioux Indians. Unable to induce the Indians to move, the army at length accepted the inevitable and threw the Black Hills open to all comers in October, 1875. The miners' hunch had been a sound one. For the lucky, fortunes in gold and silver were at hand. To the list of roaring mining towns were now added Custer City and Deadwood.

All the boom towns of the mining frontier—San Francisco and Sacramento during the fifties, Denver, Virginia City, Tucson, and Helena during the sixties, Leadville, Tombstone, and Deadwood during the seventies—exhibited the same characteristics. From uninhabited spots on the map or sleepy villages they jumped to bustling communities within a few months. Their new population was singularly mixed. Adventuresome young men of good families mingled with rum-soaked and ignorant old men who had passed their entire lives in search of sudden wealth. Northerners, southerners, middle westerners, and westerners rubbed elbows with fortune hunters from foreign countries. Many were hard-working and orderly; others were dangerous outlaws, who followed the frontier not so much because they expected to find gold as because they were marked men in their former habitats. Much of the miner's life was prosaic in the extreme—living in a tent or a shack and eating a monotonous diet of flapjacks, beans, and bacon while he labored long hours to pan out a few dollars in gold dust each day. But when his luck was good, the miner was likely to spend his money as fast as he made it. His taste in entertainment was not invariably wicked. Itinerant lecturers and Shakespearean companies had a better reception in frontier opera houses than might have been expected, and preachers were able to raise the funds for church buildings and to find occupants for their pews on Sundays. But although the men of God were not absent from the mining towns, they usually waged an uneven contest with the agents of the devil. Family life was almost nonexistent, and most miners spent their spare time in saloons and gambling dens. Although good women were scarce, bad ones were not. Quarrels over the favors of these light ladies combined with poker disputes and raw whisky to precipitate the fights and shootings which enlivened mining society.

Such minor wickedness as this was amiably tolerated, but the mining towns soon rebelled against more vicious characters. Desperadoes who gathered in gangs to hold up stages and to rob the gold in transport across the wilderness or who shot prospectors and "jumped" their claims sometimes rendered the more law-abiding element helpless for a time. Much of the trouble derived from the fact that the new communities were likely to grow up in territories for which Congress had provided no legal government. To the sober element this was no great handicap under ordinary circumstances; they met in mass meetings, enacted laws and regulations regarding the staking out of claims and other matters, and elected officials. But these *de facto* governments found it difficult to deal with persistent troublemakers. To handle these, self-constituted vigilance committees sprang up. These captured the most notorious malefactors, subjected them to summary trial, and strung them up on the nearest trees. After a few such executions the surviving bad men usually decided to move on.

Although the day of the prospectors was soon over, the results of their activities were not ephemeral. Decades after the individual miners had disappeared from the scene, large mining companies owned by eastern capitalists were still extracting gold, silver, lead, and copper worth millions of dollars from the mountain states. The mining boom had brought to these areas thousands of men who were not miners—preachers, lawyers, editors, doctors, storekeepers, farmers, and cattle-raisers—and many of these remained when the boom was over. The migrations of the miners opened up new territories, speeded the subjection of the Indians, and had its political effects in the admission to the Union of Nevada in 1864, Colorado in 1876, Montana, South Dakota, and Washington in 1889, and Idaho in 1890.

Stage Lines and Railroads

The conquest of California and its rapid settlement during the gold rush centered attention on the problem of communications between the West Coast and the rest of the country. So obvious was the need that the government from the beginning encouraged regular service through mail subsidies. The first contracts went to steamship lines. Mail, freight, and passengers traveled from New York to Colon by the United States Mail Steamship Company, were transferred across the Isthmus, and then carried from Panama to San Francisco by the Pacific Mail Steamship Company. Rates were high, and the trip was long and slow—even after the opening of the Panama Railroad in 1855.

Westerners were clamorous in their insistence that a more direct and rapid route should be provided. Contracts were given to overland mule pack trains during the early fifties, but mail and news still traveled with frustrating slowness. Railroads, it was acknowledged, would be ideal; indeed, Asa Whitney, a retired New York merchant, had been energetically demanding a transcontinental railroad since 1845. But sectional jealousies made the project for the time being impossible. Legislators from the South blocked all efforts to provide government assistance to any northern or central route; northern Congressmen were opposed to a southern route.

In 1857 the Post Office Appropriation Act authorized the Postmaster General to call for bids for carrying mail from any point on the Mississippi River to San Francisco. The contractor was to receive an annual subsidy of $600,000 but must guarantee delivery within twenty-five days. The contract was eventually granted to a company of experienced eastern expressmen, headed by John Butterfield of New York, who proposed to use a southern route beginning at St. Louis and passing through Fort Smith, El Paso, and Los Angeles to San Francisco. This involved a circuitous journey of 2,795 miles, but it was a politically expedient route since the Postmaster General was a southerner.

Careful preparations, costing about a million dollars, occupied the next year. The route had to be marked out and stations of wood or adobe built at intervals of 8 to 25 miles. Here were kept spare horses and mules, fodder for the animals, and bacon, beans, bread, and coffee for the passengers. Coaches suitable for this heavy work were purchased from the Abbott-Downing Company of Concord, New Hampshire. Their wheels had broad iron tires which would not sink into the sand and which were widely spaced to prevent the coach from tipping over. Nine passengers could ride inside, and, if necessary, one or two more could sit with the driver on the high box in front. Luggage and mail were carried on a boot at the rear. Although the brightly painted red or green Concord coaches, pulled rapidly along by four horses or six mules, were better adapted for western travel than any previous vehicle, the stagecoach journey was only for the hardy. Jolting over primitive roads day and night for three weeks, passengers could get their sleep only in snatches. Food was atrocious, water was scarce, and toilet facilities were nonexistent. The Butterfield drivers and station agents were always profane, usually alcoholic, and not infrequently criminal. It was little wonder that travelers arrived at their destination stiff-limbed, unshaved, and a little crazy from whisky. In spite of all its crudeness the overland express fired the nation's imagination. Service began on September 15, 1858, when a westbound coach dashed out of Tipton, Missouri, and an eastbound coach left San Francisco. The first trip to the West was completed in twenty-four days; the eastbound coach did even better, arriving in St. Louis in twenty days, eighteen hours, and sixteen minutes.

Less spectacular methods sufficed for heavy freighting. Along Butterfield's long southern route plodded heavily loaded wagons drawn by mules and oxen while similar wagon trains under different management carried provisions for the Mormons and the California miners across the central route.

Most ambitious of the freighting companies was Russell, Majors, and Waddell, a partnership formed in 1855. Three years later it was employing 4,000 men, 3,500 covered wagons, and 40,000 oxen in its operations along the Platte River route. Having made a conspicuous success of this venture, the firm attempted to capture the transcontinental mail contract through a dramatic demonstration of the superiority of the central route. Thus was born the idea of the pony express. Between St. Joseph, Missouri, and San Francisco 190 way stations were built; speedy horses were purchased and distributed along the route; riders were carefully chosen for lightness and courage.

On April 3, 1860, service began with riders leaving St. Joseph and San Francisco. Each galloped 10 miles to the first relay station, where a fresh mount was saddled and waiting. It was the matter of a moment for the rider to transfer himself and his mail pouch from one horse to another and then to dash off again at top speed. Transfers were made every 10 miles until the rider had traveled from 75 to 100 miles. Then the pouches were handed on to another horseman. The first relay to the coast was completed in 10½ days—ten days faster than the speediest stagecoach crossings. Over plains and mountains, through summer heat and winter snow, the pony express was kept in operation, giving ample proof of the advantages of the central route. But it was an expensive operation. Even though the rates were high—$5 a half-ounce at first, later reduced to $1—the mail was carried at a heavy loss and no government subsidies were forthcoming. When the transcontinental telegraph was completed in October, 1861, providing instantaneous communications across the nation, the pony express abandoned operations.

To add to its misfortunes, Russell, Majors, and Waddell had been sustaining heavy losses in stagecoach operations. The firm went into bankruptcy in 1862, and its assets were purchased by Ben Holladay, who dominated western transportation for the next four years. Holladay was uneducated and crude, but he had an extraordinary genius for business. He gathered up the tangled affairs of the bankrupt company and soon had the enterprise in vigorous operation. In addition to his long stage route across South Pass, he developed a network of connecting lines to mining towns in Montana and Idaho. By 1866 Holladay had over 3,000 miles of stagecoach lines under his control. He also carried on an extensive freighting business and owned steamships that plied between California, Oregon, Panama, and Japan. In 1866 Holladay sold out his overland interests for 2½ million dollars to Wells, Fargo, and Company.

Holladay's decision to sell was as shrewd as his earlier decision to buy. Energetic construction of a transcontinental railroad now gave clear warning that the days of the stagecoach were numbered. But the great vehicles did not disappear all at once. Long after California-bound travelers were able to use the railroad, coaches carrying mail and passengers were still lurching over the roads to out-of-the-way places like Deadwood, South Dakota.

When secession and Civil War removed southern politicians from Congress, the principal obstacle to a transcontinental railroad was removed with them. A key figure in bringing the long-talked-of project to successful accomplishment was Theodore D. Judah, a young California engineer who had had railroad experience in the East. Judah made extensive surveys for building a railroad eastward across California as one link in a transcontinental line. He gained the support of four prosperous Sacramento businessmen—Leland Stanford, Collis P. Huntington, Mark Hopkins, and Charles Crocker—who proceeded to organize the Central Pacific Railroad Company of California. Late in 1861 the enthusiastic Judah arrived in Washington, ready to press his plans upon Congress. Judah's efforts together with those of other lobbyists resulted in the Pacific Railroad Act of July 1, 1862. This legislation chartered the Union Pacific Railroad and authorized it to build a line from Nebraska along the route of the old California trail to the west, while the Central Pacific was to build east across California and Nevada until the two lines should meet and connect. Each road was to receive an extensive land grant including not only a 400-foot right of way and adjacent stone, timber, and earth for construction purposes but also five alternate sections of public land per mile on each side of the line. In addition, the railroads received loans from the Federal government of $16,000 for each mile of track laid down over the greater part of the route, $48,000 for each mile of difficult construction across the Sierras and the Rockies, and $32,000 for each mile of the stretch that lay between.

Generous though these terms appeared, the profits to be expected from operating a railroad across unpeopled plains and mountains were so dubious that investors hesitated to put their money into the Union Pacific. The necessary capital was not forthcoming until Congress passed a second Pacific Railroad Act in 1864, doubling the land grant and giving the Federal government only a second mortgage on the railroad instead of the first mortgage provided by the earlier law.

Money alone would not build the transcontinental system. The problem of laying ties across the treeless prairies was only one of many involving shortages of material, and the recruitment of an adequate labor force was even more troublesome. Although the Union Pacific began construction at Omaha in December, 1863, it had completed only 40 miles two years later. The Central Pacific had meanwhile completed about 60 miles despite the frustrating delays encountered in securing iron, machinery, and rolling stock from the East by sea. For laborers the California company had turned to the Orient: 3,000 of its 4,000 construction workers in 1864 were Chinese; 9,000 out of 10,000 were Chinese in 1869.

Construction of the Union Pacific finally gathered speed. After the Civil War thousands of eastern laborers—most of them Irish—were available for the great project. Many were veterans of the Union Army and their military experience proved useful when they had to drop their shovels and grab rifles to repel the attacks of the Indians. General G. M. Dodge became chief engineer, and the work was organized with great ingenuity. Advance parties surveyed the route, graded it, and built bridges for a 100-mile stretch. Then the track was laid with military precision. A car loaded with rails was drawn forward, one gang of men lifted off the right hand rail, another the left, and the two were carefully dropped in their proper places, for the gaugers, spikers, and bolters to fasten down. Meanwhile, other gangs were duplicating this operation so speedily that four rails were placed in position each minute. At the peak of operations 12,000 laborers were employed, and the plains and mountains rang with the clamor of sledge hammers and shouting men. The Union Pacific laid down 266 miles of track in 1866, 240 in 1867, and 425 in 1868. The Central Pacific's mileage was less sensational—30 in 1866, 46 in 1867, and 360 in 1868. For the first two of these years the comparison is misleading, since the Central Pacific was building with great ingenuity across the precipitous Sierras while the Union Pacific was rushing its construction across the level plains.

Moving across Nebraska and Wyoming with the lengthening Union Pacific was the strange town appropriately known to posterity as Hell on Wheels. For a few months or for an entire winter thousands of construction workers made their homes in a temporary city, going out to work each morning and returning each evening on "track trains." At the center of the settlement stood the "big tent"—a canvas structure, 100 feet by 40, which housed a great bar, a dance floor, and gambling machines. The rest of the town consisted of shacks and tents sufficient to provide 22 more saloons, 5 dance halls, sleeping quarters for the men, and rooms for the painted ladies who followed this rough army. When construction was completed on one section of track, the town could be dismantled in a few hours. Tents, houses, bars, bottled goods, and gambling wheels were loaded onto flat cars and moved 60 to 100 miles farther west, where the raucous night life was soon resumed with full vigor.

Throughout 1868 and the early months of 1869 fierce competition raged between the two railroads. Since land grants and loans depended on the amount of track laid down, each sought to outdo its rival. Indeed, in 1869 both lines seemed reluctant to complete their labors. To the bewilderment of the nation the advance parties of the two railroads pushed past each other along parallel routes that would never meet. Congress put an end to this nonsense by specifying that the junction should be made at Promontory Point, 53 miles west of Ogden, Utah. Here on May 10, 1869, with impressive ceremonies, the last spike was driven, and two locomotives—one representing the Central Pacific, the other the Union Pacific—moved slowly forward until their pilots touched. The entire country participated in the festivities. Over the telegraph wires came three impulses representing the final blows of the construction hammers. New York City, gaily bedecked in bunting, heard a hundred guns salute the event; Philadelphia listened to the pealing of the old Liberty Bell; Chicago celebrated with a parade 7 miles in length.

The building of the first transcontinental railroad epitomized the post-Civil War Gilded Age. From the engineering point of view it was a notable achievement. Neither mountains nor desert had been allowed to halt the great project. When the difficulties of raising capital, securing materials, and recruiting labor are remembered, it was no less extraordinary from the business point of view. Yet pervading the whole transaction was the stench of political corruption, financial chicanery, and irresponsible waste. Both government money and that of private investors made its way into the pockets of insiders who organized dummy construction companies and paid themselves handsome profits. Congress itself was badly besmirched in the so-called Crédit Mobilier scandal. When the Union Pacific was completed, its promoters gave eloquent evidence of their estimate of its future prospects by promptly selling their own stock. The unfortunate railroad began its career with depleted treasury, heavy debts, and a roadbed so badly constructed that within a generation it had to be rebuilt.

FIG. 36. *The First Transcontinental Train Leaving Sacramento.* Painting by Joseph Becker. Note the Chinese laborers in the foreground. (*Courtesy of the Thomas Gilcrease Foundation; photograph by the Metropolitan Museum of Art, New York.*)

The Union Pacific and Central Pacific did not long maintain a monopoly of transcontinental transportation. Other roads—most of them beneficiaries of government land grants—were pushing their way across the country during the late sixties and early seventies. The panic of 1873 halted or slowed down all these ambitious projects, but most of them were revived in the great railroad boom of the late seventies and early eighties. Stanford, Huntington, Hopkins, and Crocker, the masterful team which had promoted the Central Pacific, aspired to dominate the transportation system of all California. Organizing the Southern Pacific Railroad, they built a long line south from San Francisco, finally reaching Yuma and Needles on the southeastern border of the state. This achievement gave them a tremendous advantage, since they now controlled the only two points at which the Colorado River could be crossed by any transcontinental line using the southern route. The roads pushing westward across New Mexico and Arizona had to come to terms with the California magnates. The first to do so was the great Atchison, Topeka, & Santa Fe, which had been building steadily through Kansas, Colorado, New Mexico, and Arizona. In 1881 it made connections with the Southern Pacific at Deming, New Mexico, and another junction was made in 1883 at Needles. But the Santa Fe was not content to be dependent on the western line. By threatening to build a rival system across Mexico to the Gulf of California, it forced the Southern Pacific to let it extend its lines to San Francisco. Meanwhile, the Southern Pacific had made a connection with the Texas and Pacific at El Paso in 1882. A year later the California giant purchased lines of its own across Texas and was able to send its trains all the way from San Francisco to New Orleans.

The fourth of the transcontinental lines was the Northern Pacific Railroad, chartered by Congress in 1864 to build from Lake Superior to Portland, Oregon. Construction did not begin until 1870, when Jay Cooke of Philadelphia—accounted a financial genius because of his financial services to the government during the Civil War—threw his energies into the railroad's promotion. Great enthusiasm sustained the project over the next few years, but Cooke had plunged too deeply, and the failure of his banking house in 1873 signaled the beginning of a nation-wide depression. The Northern Pacific was forced into bankruptcy and did not resume construction until 1879. In 1881 Henry Villard, a German immigrant and former newspaper man who had become deeply involved in the transportation affairs of the Columbia River area, gained control of the Northern Pacific through the famous "blind pool"—one of the most spectacular *coups* of Wall Street history. Under Villard's promotion the transcontinental line was completed in 1883.

Another great system appeared in 1893, when the Great Northern Railroad was completed across Minnesota, North Dakota, Montana, and Washington. Building without government land grants or loans, James J. Hill provided his railroad with a financial structure strong enough to withstand the panics that drove other systems into receivership. Keenly aware of the need for prosperous customers, the Minnesota promoter encouraged immigration and sponsored many projects to promote agriculture and to provide banks, schools, and churches for the new communities which sprang up along the route of the Great Northern.

The rapid building of the transcontinentals together with the construction of connecting lines gave the last frontier a character different from that of any earlier frontier. Throughout most of the West the railroad preceded, rather than followed, settlement. Pioneers, moving out to new homes, made journeys in two or three days which would have taken them months in an earlier period. Nor were they cut off from civilization when they arrived. In this generation the frontiersman was more likely to be clad in Montgomery Ward overalls than in a buckskin jacket. Nor was his primary concern merely the growing of enough corn or the killing of enough venison to feed his family. From the first he was a producer of staples, shipping out over the railroads large quantities of wheat, corn, wool, cattle, and hogs.

Buffaloes and Indians

Early travelers in the West had been fascinated by the great buffalo herds. One wrote of traveling past a herd for a hundred miles; another of riding through milling buffaloes for three days. Trains might be halted for hours while a herd crossed the track. In 1865 the buffaloes of the West were estimated to number some fifteen million.

To the Indians of the Great Plains the buffalo meant life itself. They ate the flesh, used the hides for clothing, shoes, tents, and blankets, made knives from the bones and glue from the hoofs, and burned the dried "chips," or excrement, as fuel. Long before the Civil War white hunters had discovered a uniquely exhilarating sport in shooting buffaloes while riding at full speed along the flanks of the thundering herds. But neither Indian nor white killing seriously reduced the number of buffaloes until the railroads were driven deep into the western plains.

The Union Pacific split the great animals into northern and southern herds and restricted their grazing area; the Santa Fe, the Kansas Pacific, and the Northern Pacific brought thousands of white men into the heart of the buffalo country. Professional hunters like Buffalo Bill Cody killed thousands of animals to provide meat for construction workers and emigrants; thousands more fell before the guns of eastern sportsmen visiting the West in special expeditions. Buffalo robes became a fad in the East, and the market for skins was given a further boost when eastern tanneries discovered means of transforming them into leather. The buffaloes were now hunted by parties of professional hunters, employed by companies. They killed the animals by the thousand, packed the skins into bales, sent them to the railheads in wagons, and shipped them east by the carload. Meat enough to feed armies was left to rot on the plains. The carnage reached a peak after 1872 when two or three million buffaloes were killed each year. By 1878 the southern herd was practically extinct; the northern herd survived only until the Northern Pacific Railroad pierced its ranges in the early eighties. By 1885 few buffaloes were to be found in the entire West. All that remained were tons of whitened bones, which were presently collected and sent east as fertilizer.

The slaughter of the buffaloes speeded the conquest of the Indians. The depredations of the white hunters combined with other grievances to provoke the Indians to warfare. Throughout the sixties and the seventies there were serious clashes. The red men, naturally indignant as the whites demanded more and more of their territory, attacked stagecoaches and stations, mining camps, railroad construction gangs, and isolated army posts. Again and again the frontier was aroused by the massacre of some party of whites.

Indians on the warpath provided the United States Army with a succession of hard problems. Officers like Sherman, Sheridan, and Miles, who had fought for the Union during the Civil War, found themselves involved in campaigns for which their previous experience gave them little preparation. Not only were they fighting an elusive and unorthodox foe, but they were vulnerable to criticism no matter what they did. If they failed to protect the western settlements, they were damned by the frontiersmen. If they killed the savages with ruthless efficiency, they were condemned by eastern humanitarians. To add to the confusion of policy, there was divided responsibility between the Indian agents of the Interior Department, whose duty it was to keep the Indians happy with gifts, and the War Department, which often seemed to assume that its mission was to exterminate them.

The Indian wars could have but one result. The red men might sometimes avoid defeat by masterly retreats; they might even win victories like the Battle of the Little Big Horn of 1876, when the colorful Colonel Custer brought death upon himself and 225 cavalrymen by leading them against the Sioux in reckless disregard of orders. But such Indian triumphs were few, and defeats were many. The most defiant chiefs perished in battle; those who were more prudent surrendered to their white conquerors. Indeed, after the extinction of the buffalo the Indians of the Plains could avoid starvation only by remaining on the reservations, where they grew a few crops and took whatever they could get in rations from the government.

The plight of the Indians brought them numerous expressions of sympathy. Many Americans were shocked by the record of broken faith set down in Helen Hunt Jackson's *A Century of Dishonor* (1881), and the Indians Rights Association and other organizations appealed for justice to the red men. Prodded by changing public opinion, Congress struggled to frame a more rational policy. In 1871 the troublesome fiction that the Indian tribes were sovereign nations with which treaties could be made was abandoned. Through the Dawes Act of 1887 Congress sought to transform the Indian from hunter to farmer by providing for the gradual breaking up of tribal lands and the substitution of individual allotments. Indians receiving such grants became United States citizens. Although hailed as a great reform, the law had disappointing results. Many of the new citizens accounted the right to buy whisky as their most valuable privilege. They scorned farming, which had always been accounted squaw's work, and raised too little to support their families. They got into debt, mortgaged their land, and often lost it as soon as the grant became final. In 1934 the Wheeler-Howard Act sought to undo the damage by encouraging a revival of communal ownership.

Reformers who depended on education to solve the Indian problem encountered similar obstacles. In 1880 only one Indian child in twelve was in school. Those who went to school on the reservation, moreover, were likely to be more influenced by the customs of their family and village than they were by the admonitions of their teachers. Many who struggled with the problem believed that young Indians could be given a white man's education only by placing them in an entirely new environment. So strongly of this opinion was Captain Richard H. Pratt that he organized a movement which resulted in over one thousand Indian boys and girls attending Hampton Institute, a Negro school in Virginia. In 1879 Pratt founded a new institution in some old army barracks at Carlisle, Pennsylvania. The Carlisle Indian School was in successful operation until World War I, and a number of similar schools were founded elsewhere. But the bulk of Indian youth attended reservation schools, which were greatly improved after 1890.

Cowboys and Ranchers

Raising cattle on unclaimed grazing lands and driving the stock hundreds of miles to established markets had been a feature of American frontier life since colonial days. But in this as in other things the scale of operations achieved on the last frontier dwarfed all earlier efforts. Herds were larger, drives were longer and more hazardous, rewards were more tempting, and the life of the cattlemen was more vigorous and colorful.

Texas, with its mild climate and vast expanses of grassy plain, was ideal grazing country. This fact had been noted by the early Spanish colonists who had brought over lean, long-horned cattle of the type raised by the Moors in Andalusia. These had multiplied so prodigiously that by the time American settlement began the Texas plains were already inhabited by vast herds of these wild and hardy beasts. The Americans brought with them domestic cattle of the breeds then common in the eastern United States. Allowed to run at large over the range, the new stock soon interbred with the old and brought into existence the Texas longhorns, a hardy type ideally equipped to fend for itself and to provide beef that was palatable, if somewhat tough. Hundreds of thousands of these animals roamed the ranges unmarked by the brand of any owner. Hundreds of thousands more were appropriated by ranchers, but the market for them was limited. Some were driven to New Orleans or other Mississippi River towns; others to Gulf ports like Galveston, whence they were shipped to Cuba and the East Coast. A few went to California; others were driven through Arkansas and Missouri to Illinois.

The infant Texas cattle industry was disrupted by the Civil War. All intercourse with northern markets was cut off, and Union conquest of the Mississippi interrupted sales to the rest of the Confederacy. By the end of the war there were some five million cattle grazing the Texas ranges. This vast oversupply was matched by an acute postwar shortage in the North. Good prices obviously awaited Texas owners who could get their cattle to railheads in Missouri and Kansas.

The first postwar attempts to drive cattle north had discouraging results. Heavy rains made the trails across northern Texas almost impassable. Red men in the Indian Territory demanded payment for the grass which the herds consumed, stampeded the animals at night, and collected rewards for rounding them up in the morning. The cattle, used to the treeless plains of their native state, were so terrified by the wooded Ozarks that they became almost unmanageable. And to complete this chapter of woes, the Texas cattle drivers were met on the boundaries of Kansas and Missouri by armed farmers determined to bar the passage of animals that might be carriers of the dread Texas fever. Of the 260,000 cattle driven north from Texas in 1866, only a small portion were actually sold to northern buyers.

After this disastrous experience only the hardiest Texans attempted to drive cattle north in the next year. Many of those who did were met in the Indian Territory by a rider sent out by Joseph G. McCoy, a prominent Illinois cattle dealer, who had spent the previous winter building stock pens, loading chutes, and a hotel for the cattlemen at Abilene, Kansas, on the new Kansas Pacific Railroad. By following McCoy's advice and taking a route farther west through the middle of the Indian Territory and across south-central Kansas, the Texans succeeded in driving about 35,000 cattle to Abilene in 1867 without serious trouble from Indians, homesteaders, hills, or woods.

This success encouraged imitation. Abilene received 75,000 cattle in 1868 and a total of nearly 1,500,000 between 1868 and 1871. By that time the westward movement of the small farmers encroached upon the cattle trail, and Abilene's business passed to Ellsworth, farther west along the Kansas Pacific, and to Newton, south of Abilene on the newly built Atchison, Topeka, & Santa Fe. When the irresistible pressure of the homesteaders forced the cattle trail farther west again, other Kansas towns had their brief day of glory. Most famous of all was Dodge City on the Santa Fe in southwestern Kansas, the destination of most Texas cattle after 1875.

Through trial and error the Texans developed the methods best adopted for the long drive. About twenty-five hundred cattle proved the ideal herd for the trip. To drive these, about a dozen men were required. The commander of the expedition was the trail boss, who usually rode ahead of the herd to survey the route and to locate watering places. Riding at the head of the mile-long column of cattle were two cowboys, called the "point," since their duty was to keep the cattle moving in the right direction. A third of a mile behind them rode two more, called the "swing"; another pair, called the "flank," guarded the column a third of a mile farther back. Behind the herd rode three cowboys composing the "drag," whose responsibility was to prod on the stragglers. The rest of the gang was composed of the "wrangler," a boy of fourteen or fifteen who cared for the fifty or more horses required for the cowboys, and the cook, an important personage who drove the chuck wagon loaded with provisions and cooking equipment.

Cattle driving was hard work. Since a herd moved only 10 or 12 miles a day, the 1,000-mile drive required several months. The cattle had to be carefully handled, because they took fright easily and were pacified only with great difficulty. Particularly hard to curb were stampedes that began at night, when any unexpected noise might set the herd into headlong flight. Stampeding cattle were brought under control by heading off the leaders and diverting their course until the whole mass of animals began moving in a great circle, or "mill." The cattle might move about for hours before they finally quieted down and gave the exhausted cowboys a chance to rest. The Indians rarely attacked the cattle drives, but they paid frequent visits to the trail bosses, demanding and receiving tribute in choice animals. In normal weather the cattle could ford the rivers, but in rainy weather they were compelled to swim. This the stubborn animals sometimes refused to do, and the exasperated cowboys had to make camp until the swollen stream subsided or the animals changed their minds.

Small wonder that the cattlemen arrived in Abilene or Dodge City tired, thirsty, and eager for excitement. Relieved of their responsibilities and paid off, the cowboys made for the nearest saloon. As fancy spenders they gained a reputation that held its own even against such western competitors as miners and railroad laborers. Inevitably the cattle towns attracted whisky dealers, gamblers, and prostitutes from every direction. Celebrating cowboys were particularly addicted to gunplay, and the town's few sober citizens prudently took to cover when the shooting began. "Boot Hill" was the Dodge City cemetery reserved for the victims of these affrays.

Kansas farmers continued to regard the Texas cattlemen as their enemies. Fearing that their stock might contract Texas fever or that their growing crops might be damaged by the trampling herds, the Kansans took up guns, when necessary, to keep the great drives away from the agricultural settlements. Presently the farmers carried their prejudices into legislation. Early Kansas quarantine laws prohibiting the entrance of cattle during the summer and fall seasons were subject to wholesale evasion, but the drastic law of 1884 forbidding Texas cattle to be driven into the state except in December, January, and February proved an insuperable obstacle. The cattle route was diverted to Colorado, but here also difficulties were encountered. Although Texans proposed that Congress should set aside a national cattle trail extending from Texas to the Canadian border, the idea was never carried out. The long drive was really no longer necessary, since the railroad building of the late seventies now provided rail connections between Texas and such important markets as St. Louis, Kansas City, and New Orleans.

Meanwhile, the cattle business had entered a new phase. Even before the Civil War experience had shown that livestock thrived the year around on the northern and central plains. So long as the range was open, most healthy animals could survive severe winter weather, drifting before the storm winds and scraping away the snow to find forage. A few disappointed participants in the Pikes Peak gold rush had discovered that there was more money to be made in selling meat to emigrants than in searching for minerals. They accumulated their earliest herds by bargain purchases of cattle that had become too weak or too lame to continue the trip across the continent with migrating families. Indian agents and railroad construction gangs provided an increasing number of customers, and Kansas City and Chicago packers were eager to buy as soon as the western plains were linked to the packing centers by rail. The development of the refrigerator car in the middle seventies opened the whole eastern market to western beef.

Under these favoring circumstances the cattle industry expanded with astonishing rapidity. Between 1860 and 1880 the number of cattle in Kansas rose from 93,000 to 1,500,000; those in Nebraska from 37,000 to 1,100,000; those in Colorado from practically none to 791,000; those in Wyoming from none to 521,000. Texas continued to be a state of great ranches, and the cattle belt also extended to New Mexico, Oklahoma, the Dakotas, Montana, California, and Oregon. Most of the cattle driven north from Texas in the later days of the long drive went to stock the northern ranches; many of the Texas cattlemen themselves moved to the central and northern plains. Texas longhorns were still esteemed for their hardy independence, but they were crossed with Hereford and Angus bulls from the East to produce a much finer grade of beef.

The cattlemen helped themselves to large areas of the public domain. Since water was no less essential than grass, a rancher first laid claim to a spring or to a lengthy stretch along the bank of some stream. Then he extended his domain over the entire back country to the crest of the watershed. Sometimes he went to the trouble of gaining legal title to a portion of this land under the homestead or preemption laws. But the Federal land laws were not designed to permit the acquisition of ranches of 30 or 40 square miles such as became common on the Great Plains. Most of the land was held without legal warrant. This did not greatly matter so long as the population of these areas was predominantly made up of cattlemen. The ranchers respected each other's claims and formed great livestock associations to protect their mutual interests.

The cowboy, employed by the rancher to do the hard work of the industry, seemed a curious and romantic figure to easterners. Yet his distinctive costume was adopted, not because it was picturesque, but because it was practical. The ten-gallon hat shielded the cowboy's head from the fierce summer sun and winter sleet; the handkerchief knotted about his neck was there to be pulled over his face in dust storms; the leather boots were designed to fit comfortably into stirrups; the leather chaps to protect the cowboy's legs from the brush; the fine buckskin gloves to save his hands from rope burns. The glaring sun tanned the cowboy's skin and gave his eyes their characteristic squint; long hours in the saddle bowed his legs. Often garrulous with his fellow ranch hands, the cowboy was moody and taciturn in contacts with strangers and painfully self-conscious in the presence of ladies.

Much of the cowboy's work was monotonous. Alone or with a single companion, he might be stationed for months in a lonely camp to "ride the line," that is, to patrol the imaginary line bounding his employer's ranch, turning back

FIG. 37. *Heading a Steer on the Foothills.* Drawn by Frederic Remington for *Harper's Weekly*, Apr. 16, 1892. Remington's drawings and paintings contributed much to making the cowboy a favorite American character. (*Courtesy of the Library of Congress.*)

cattle that wandered over from some neighboring property, preventing his employer's herd from straying away, and watching out for "rustlers," or cattle thieves. More exciting was the spring or fall roundup. Despite the best efforts of the line riders, one rancher's cattle were likely to become mixed with those of another. So the roundup was often a cooperative affair in which the cowboys of several ranches participated. The cattle were driven to some central place and those of one owner separated from the others. The hardest work was to locate the calves, to rope, to throw, and to tie them up, and to drag them to the fire and to brand them. Another task was to locate the creatures who were ready for the market and to separate them from the herd, preparatory to driving them to some cattle shipping point on the railroad. Even after the long drive was a thing of the past, innumerable small drives occurred each year. These rare visits to town gave the cowboys an opportunity to drink and to gamble in a few hours of noisy relaxation that were likely to give outsiders an extremely distorted idea of the cowboys' normal life.

During the early eighties cattle prices were so high that a get-rich-quick fever swept over the plains. Westerners borrowed recklessly to purchase breeding stock, and easterners invested heavily. The craze crossed the Atlantic and invaded England, Scotland, and the Continent. Wealthy men thousands of miles from the Great Plains bought shares in large corporations owning thousands of cattle in ranches of fantastic size. This vast expansion of ranching brought fierce competition. Access to water became a right of great value, and ranchers began to protect their interests by stringing mile upon mile of barbed-wire fence—despite Federal laws forbidding this practice on the public domain.

The cattle boom collapsed in a series of disasters during the late eighties. Supply had overtaken demand and prices fell to unprofitable levels. The ranges were grossly overstocked and the cattle no longer thrived. Finally, nature itself turned against the men who had squandered its bounty. The hard winter of 1885–1886 was followed by a summer so hot and dry that the grass shriveled and the streams dried up over large areas. Then came the killing blow, the terrible winter of 1886–1887. Cattle perished by the thousand when they piled up against the fences which prevented their drifting before the storms as in earlier years.

This sobering experience forced a drastic reorganization of the ranching business. Many of the corporations failed and smaller ranches took their places. The number of stock was reduced to bring about a better balance with the amount of forage available. Prudent ranch management now required wells and windmills to augment the water supply and haymaking to assure ample food for the winter. Fencing, hitherto the exceptional practice, became universal. Much of the stock was now sold while it was still young to Middle Western corngrowers who fattened it for the market.

Not least among the vexations besetting the cattlemen was an influx of sheep raisers. Land in the Middle West was now too valuable to make wool-growing profitable, but the grazing lands of the West were ideally suited for it. To the cowboys the sheep were foul-smelling "woolies," that ruined the grass by their close cropping, and the sheepherders an outlandish lot who performed their duties on foot instead of riding like men. The cattlemen expressed their sentiments by driving sheep over cliffs and by shooting herders. But the sheepmen persisted and their rivals learned to tolerate them. Moreover, since wool brought better profits than beef with less exertion, many of the cattlemen themselves invested in the despised "woolies." By 1900 sheep outnumbered cattle in Wyoming, Montana, Colorado, Utah, California, New Mexico—and even in Texas.

The Farmers

Again and again during the seventies and eighties the ranchers had been compelled to transfer their activities farther west as the farmers pushed steadily into new territory. The same railroads that had made the cattle business profitable brought out thousands of pioneers determined to acquire land and to plow under the grass that had provided cheap forage for the ranchers. Like earlier wars the Civil War had shaken men out of their normal patterns of activity and paved the way for a great forward thrust of the agricultural frontier. The booming industries and growing cities of the East gave promise of a constantly expanding market for food, and beyond the Atlantic industrial Europe was buying more and more from America.

Adventurous farmers were encouraged to seek more fertile lands in the West by the seemingly bright promise contained in the Homestead Act of 1862. Anyone who could read could see that this assured a farm of 160 acres free except for registry fees to any pioneer who would improve the land for five years. But the free land which the Homestead Act promised was usually not the land which the migrating farmer actually acquired. The free land was all too often far from the railroads, away from the river valleys, or lacking in fertility. The better land was usually in the hands of individuals or corporations eager to sell it at a profit. The railroads were tremendous landowners, having received over 180 million acres in grants from Federal and state governments—an area larger than Texas. This land was obviously the most desirable in the West because of its easy access to transportation. Other large owners purchased directly from the Federal government or from the states that had received grants under the Morrill Act for the support of agricultural and engineering colleges. Many monopolists acquired tremendous holdings through illegal means. They hired bogus homesteaders to enter claims, or they took advantage of special Federal laws to appropriate large areas of land without planting the trees or constructing the irrigation works on which the grants were conditional. Instead of getting his land free, therefore, the typical western farmer purchased it from some railroad or speculator at a price which varied widely but was often about $5 an acre.

Whether the pioneer bought his farm or secured it under the provisions of the Homestead Act, he needed money to work it. Western agriculture was profitable only when a sizable acreage was producing crops. The farmer needed to purchase machinery and fencing material. Sometimes the necessary water was secured only after the expenditure of several hundred dollars on professional well borers. To stock the farm with cattle, hogs, and work animals also required money. The wage earners of eastern cities possessed neither the resources nor the knowledge to become homesteaders on the western prairies. The opportunities of the frontier beckoned to men who were already farmers rather than to discontented factory workers. And even among farmers the most successful frontiersmen were not those from distant sections but those who moved to new homes within the same or neighboring states. The frontier movement of the seventies and eighties flowed principally from the states bordering on the Mississippi Valley. To this main stream, immigration from Sweden, Norway, and Germany—energetically promoted by the railroads—provided a sizable tributary.

Firstcomers made their homes along the river valleys, where they found not only water but wood for houses, barns, fences, and fuel. But later arrivals had to settle on land covered only with grass. No longer could the frontiersman house his family in the traditional log cabin. Sometimes he built a dugout—a room enclosed on three sides by the hillside or ravine into which he burrowed and on the fourth by a wall of square-cut turf.

More ambitious were the sod houses in which all four walls were built of bricks cut from the tough prairie turf. Such dwellings, warm in the winter and cool in the summer, provided adequate shelter for the pioneer families during their first few years. But they were far from comfortable. Housewives despaired of keeping their homes clean when dirt and straw from the walls and roof were perpetually dropping over dishes and furniture. During a heavy rain the water poured through the roof in rivulets. The desperate wife used every available pot or pan to catch it, but even so all the bedding and clothing of the family had to be hung out to dry after the rain was over. To protract the discomfort, the sod-covered roof was usually so thoroughly soaked that water continued to drip into the house for several days. Little wonder that one of the first ambitions of the moderately successful frontier family was to replace the sod house with one of frame construction. Lumber merchants were soon doing an excellent business.

The scarcity of trees created other problems. In the earliest days buffalo chips provided a satisfactory fuel. When these were gone, the farmers sometimes found a substitute in the droppings left by the Texas cattle herds. This too was a temporary expedient. Sunflower stalks, cut green and seasoned, made good firewood, and this fact contributed to the popularity of these rank plants in the prairie states. Grass was even cheaper, and hay-burning stoves, most of them more ingenious than practical, were widely used; but hay burned with a sudden intensity that was the despair of good cooks trying to bake. Nor were corncobs and cornstalks much better. The best fuels were still wood and coal. Farmers often drove many miles to secure a wagonload of firewood from trees growing along the banks of a stream. Those who could afford to buy coal provided good business for the merchants of the towns.

Much of the controversy between farmers and cattlemen was over who should build fences. The farmers contended that it was up to the ranchers to keep their livestock out of the growing crops; the ranchers believed that the cattle should be allowed to range at will and that the farmers should fence in their fields. The truth was that neither cattleman nor homesteader could afford to build a long fence from wood that had to be transported for many miles. The imperative need for a cheaper fencing material led to the invention of barbed wire during the seventies. At $20 a hundred pounds, the price at which it appeared on the market in 1874, barbed wire was too costly for extensive use, but large-scale production soon brought the price down. In 1880 a hundred pounds of barbed wire could be bought for $10; in 1890 for $3.45; in 1897 for $1.80.

Shortage of water was a problem even more serious than scarcity of timber. The farther west the frontier farmer ventured, the less likely he was to be able to depend on some neighboring stream or spring. Wells had to be dug deeper and deeper. Sometimes courageous pioneers shoveled their way 200 or 300 feet into the earth, but the most satisfactory way to tap these subterranean water supplies was to have a well sunk by professional drillers. Since it was a back-breaking chore to pump water from these great depths, thousands of windmills were purchased to harness the cheapest and most abundant source of power on the western prairies and plains. But artesian wells, windmills, and tanks were too expensive for most of the pioneer farmers. The first extensive use of such equipment was by the railroads; the second by the ranchers. Not until almost the end of the century did many of the farmers feel prosperous enough to invest their money in this way.

The most ambitious wells could provide water only for men and animals. For growing crops the farmer had to develop new methods of cultivation which would make the most efficient use of the scanty moisture provided by nature or he had to irrigate. So-called "dry farming" required deep plowing, harrowing after every fall of rain, and deep and scanty planting of seed. Such methods were introduced in California before the Civil War, but in the area of the Great Plains they were not extensively used until after 1900. Dry farming permitted the cultivation of thousands of acres previously considered suitable only for grazing, but it brought many heartaches. In seasons of unusually dry weather the most careful methods could not prevent catastrophic crop failures. Irrigation was more dependable, but only rarely was an individual farmer able to provide for his own needs. Despite the early success of the Mormons in Utah, irrigation did not become a major factor in western agriculture until the Federal government began to build projects under the Newlands Act of 1902. Even then the states most benefited were mountain states like California, Colorado, Idaho, Montana, and Wyoming rather than the states of the Great Plains.

Through painful trial and error the pioneer farmer discovered which parts of the West would grow crops and which would not. Despite many failures the cultivators made an extraordinary record. In the thirty years after 1870 the farmers brought under cultivation 225,000,000 acres of land—considerably more than had been improved in the preceding 263 years since the settlement of Jamestown. During these three eventful decades the population of Minnesota jumped from 439,000 to 1,751,000; that of Kansas from 364,000 to 1,470,000; that of Nebraska from 123,000 to 1,012,000. Most extraordinary of all was the history of Oklahoma. Not opened for white settlement until 1889—despite frequent incursions of "boomers" from Kansas—Oklahoma had a population of 258,000 in 1890 and 790,000 in 1900.

The Frontier Tradition

In 1890 the Superintendent of the United States Census wrote: "Up to and including 1880 the country had a frontier of settlement, but at present the unsettled area has been so broken into by isolated bodies of settlement that there can hardly be said to be a frontier line." These prosaic words seemed to mark the end of an epoch, to declare the American frontier—open for nearly three centuries—now closed. In a sense this statement was misleading, for there were still millions of acres of land in the West that had never been broken by the plow, and, although much of this was mountain or desert, a substantial portion was arable. Indeed, as late as 1939 over 1,000,000 acres of the public domain were still being granted annually in homesteads. Four times as much land was homesteaded after 1890 as had been previously.

Yet if the frontier did not disappear abruptly, it ceased to be a major historical force. Like a military campaign in which the main front of the enemy has been broken but hundreds of isolated pockets of resistance are yet to be mopped up, the American conquest of the continent had overcome all major obstacles and could now proceed to humdrum completion. As a distinct section of the country with unique characteristics, the frontier no longer existed.

But if gone, the frontier was far from forgotten. Indeed, the last frontier had captured the American imagination as no earlier frontier had done. Dime novels, originating about 1860 and exceedingly popular during the seventies and eighties, discovered in western cowboys and bad men stock characters certain to delight their juvenile readers. Edward Zane Carroll Judson, who ground out dime novels under the name of Ned Buntline, transferred his talents to writing for the popular stage. As early as 1872 New York audiences were applauding a Judson thriller entitled *Buffalo Bill, the King of the Border Men.*

Although theatergoers might be happy with simulated Buffalo Bills, their enthusiasm was unbounded when the real Buffalo Bill, William F. Cody, appeared on the stage in 1873 in another Judson play, *The Scout of the Plains.* Cody embodied all the romance of the West. In his youth, he had been one of the daring riders of the pony express. As a professional hunter he had shot thousands of buffaloes. As scout and guide for the United States Army he had participated in numerous campaigns against the Indians. Best of all, he looked the part.

Buffalo Bill proved an even greater showman than scout. In 1883 he organized an outdoor Wild West Show, in which he assembled as many authentic western characters as possible. Real cowboys rode real cowboy ponies. Real Indians—even the famous Sitting Bull who had led the Sioux against Custer—grimaced and danced. There were pony races, bronco-bucking contests, astounding feats of skill with the lariat, and phenomenal exhibitions of pistol shooting. The performance came to a crashing climax with an exciting attack upon the Deadwood stage. For many years the Wild West Show was a popular form of entertainment. In 1887 Buffalo Bill's unique circus netted $700,000 on a tour of England. Gladstone witnessed the performance six times; the Prince of Wales rode in the Deadwood stage; Buffalo Bill was presented to Queen Victoria herself.

Although the outdoor Wild West Show eventually declined in popularity, the frontier tradition found an even more indulgent patron in the motion-picture industry. Cowboys and Indians were characters well adapted for exploitation on the screen. Buffalo Bill himself appeared before the movie camera in 1910, but a man of sixty-four hardly fitted the popular conception of a western hero. It was a group of younger men who gained fame and fortune as the favorite stars of millions of juvenile movie-goers. Broncho Billy, William S. Hart, Tom Mix, Hoot Gibson, and Roy Rogers personified the glamorous West for successive generations of hero-worshipers. Although the western movie showed little evidence of diminished popularity after World War II, juveniles could now thrill to the adventures of the Lone Ranger, Hopalong Cassidy, and other hard-riding heroes and villains through radio and television. Needless to say, the Wild West of movies and radio had scarcely greater resemblance to the West of history than King Arthur and his knights had to the real world of feudalism. Both were creations of the imagination of earth-bound mortals dreaming of supermen and stirring feats of valor.

Meanwhile, the frontier legend was perpetuated in a variety of literary forms. Exploiting with greater skill the field that had been opened up by the dime novelists came a group of highly popular writers like Owen Wister, Emerson Hough, Harold Bell Wright, and Zane Grey. Appealing to an audience of lower intelligence were the innumerable writers who ground out stereotyped stories for pulp magazines. For people too lazy to read even these, cowboy adventures could be followed in comics on sale at every newsstand during the 1950's.

While millions of movie-goers and magazine readers experienced vicarious adventure in the West of imagination, serious scholars pondered the extent and nature of the frontier's influence on American civilization. The problem was first clearly stated by Frederick Jackson Turner, professor of history at the University of Wisconsin. In 1893 Turner prepared an important paper entitled "The Significance of the Frontier in American History." Rebuking the prevailing school of scholarship which largely concentrated its energies on tracing the Germanic roots of American institutions or on following political developments through the debates of Congress, Turner called for a new approach to the study of United States history. At one point he asserted:

American social development has been continually beginning over again on the frontier. This perennial rebirth, this fluidity of American life, this expansion westward with its new opportunities, its continuous touch with the simplicity of primitive society, furnish the forces dominating American character. The true point of view in the history of this nation is not the Atlantic coast, it is the Great West.[1]

Developing the point further, he wrote:

Moving westward, the frontier became more and more American. . . . Thus the advance of the frontier has meant a steady movement away from the influence of Europe, a steady growth of independence on American lines. And to study this advance, the men who grew up under these conditions, and the political, economic, and social results of it, is to study the really American part of our history.[2]

To the influence of the frontier Turner attributed the rise of American nationalism, the promotion of democracy, and the growth of ruthless individualism. He suggested that America's relative freedom from serious class conflict might have resulted from the existence of the frontier as a "safety valve of discontent."

The reorientation of scholarship which Turner had wanted was largely achieved. Inspired by his brilliant writings and by his magnetic teaching at Wisconsin and Harvard, a new generation of scholars explored the frontier movement in every aspect. Sometimes Turner's disciples out-Turnered the master. There was danger that out of the thread of Turner's striking generalizations would be woven an historical tapestry almost as unrealistic as the West of the movies. This West of unlimited opportunity beckoning to the weary wage earner of the East, this West where inequalities of class and wealth did not exist and all men were democrats, this West of bold and original political thought was a West largely imaginary.

Critical scholarship eventually retouched the picture. A study of land policy soon demonstrated the romanticism involved in the assumption that most public land was free after 1862. Throughout the history of the West the land speculator was shown to have been as omnipresent as the squatter. The idea that eastern industrial workers had any significant part in the westward movement was soon demolished, and the impulse to democratic and humanitarian reform was traced as frequently to eastern or European sources as to western.

The attack on the Turner thesis demonstrates only that American civilization has been the product of many forces rather than one. Immigration, the interplay of European and American ideas, changing technology, the growth of capitalism, sectionalism, the rise of cities, the aspirations of preachers and idealists—all had

[1] Frederick Jackson Turner, *The Frontier in American History* (Holt, New York, 1920), 2–3.

[2] *Ibid.*, 4.

their impact on American social development. Along with these the existence of the frontier must be given prominent place. Much of history is concerned with the adaptation of old institutions to new conditions, and great emphasis is rightly placed on the impact of the unusual conditions of the frontier on American political practices, on American religious life, on American education, and on American thought.

Chapter 21. Rise of Big Business

The victory of the North in the Civil War insured more than the preservation of the Federal Union. While the conflict was in progress, the national government gave strong encouragement to the investing classes through enactment of high tariffs, establishment of national banks, and grant of generous subsidies for building railroads. The Republican party, which had enacted these policies, remained dominant in national politics for all but eight of the next fifty years. Nor was the Democratic party when led by Grover Cleveland much less sympathetic to the demands of the capitalists.

In this favoring political atmosphere masterful men built larger and larger business units. By 1914 many sectors of the economy were dominated by huge corporations, each representing an accumulation of millions of dollars in capital, employing thousands of workers, and selling its products throughout the country —and sometimes throughout the world.

High Finance and the Railroads

Although railroads had played a vital part in the Civil War, there were in 1865 only 35,000 miles of track to serve the needs of a nation of continental size. The lines, financed mostly with local capital, were short and poorly built. Since some had wide gauge, some narrow, and some assorted medium gauges, the cars of one company would not go over the rails of another. Collisions and derailments occurred with sickening frequency, and wooden cars, wooden trestles, light-iron rails, inadequate brakes, and poor couplings all added to the horror of the accidents.

The progress of the next fifty years was remarkable. Not only was the nation's railway mileage multiplied by seven, but travel was made far safer and more comfortable. Standard gauge was adopted by nearly all lines—making it possible to transfer coaches and freight cars from one line to another across the entire continent. Use of the air brake, invented by George Westinghouse in 1869, contributed much to safety, as did also the introduction of steel rails, improved couplings, and electrical signaling devices. Improved roadbeds and more powerful engines greatly speeded service. Passengers traveled in greater comfort because of the general improvement of coaches and the development of sleeping and dining-cars specially designed by George M. Pullman.

Despite this impressive record of achievement the railroads had by no means endeared themselves to the general public. Reckless financing and erratic management antagonized stockholders and shippers.

The building of the railroads was not a steady and well-planned procedure but a cyclical process of intense speculation, feverish construction, financial collapse, and slow recovery. The first great wave of building from 1868 to 1872 was halted by the panic of 1873. A new speculative fever gripped the country in the early eighties. Although briefly interrupted by the depression of 1884–1885, the decade as a whole was the most remarkable in American railroad history. Total mileage increased from 93,262 in 1880 to 156,414 in 1890. Once again, however, construction had proceeded more rapidly than the country could support it. Railroad inflation played its part in bringing on the great depression of 1893. By 1895 there were 169 railroads—one-fifth the mileage of the country—in the hands of receivers.

The fits and starts of railroad building had much to do with the railroads' loss of public esteem. New lines were launched on waves of local enthusiasm. The projected railroads, it was argued, would assure the region's prosperity. Country storekeepers, professional men, and farmers used their savings to buy stock. Towns and counties issued bonds to help the project. The funds thus entrusted to the promoters were in many cases rashly used. Insiders enriched themselves through construction contracts or sold property to the company at absurd prices. With their original capital squandered, their stock watered, and their assets mortgaged, these railroads could scarcely meet their fixed charges in good times and inevitably went into receivership during periods of depression. Through reorganizations the original investors were squeezed out, and control of the roads passed into the hands of shrewd men able to turn the situation to their own advantage. Long after municipalities and counties had lost their investment in such lines, they might be paying interest and principal on the bonds which they had issued to raise the initial funds.

While small investors suffered through the vagaries of railroad finance, great wealth was achieved by capitalists endowed with the proper combination of judgment, imagination, boldness, and luck. Thus did Commodore Cornelius Vanderbilt create over a period of twenty years a railroad empire that included 4,500 miles of track and a quarter billion dollars in capital. The Commodore began selling his ships and investing his money in railroads in 1857, when he was sixty-three years old. Gaining control of the short but strategically located New York and Harlem Railroad, he extended it into the center of the great metropolis. By 1865 he owned a controlling interest in the Hudson River Railroad. Four years later, having purchased control of the New York Central, he was able to consolidate the two lines as the New York Central and Hudson River Railroad. The system was extended to Chicago in 1873, when the old Commodore added the Lake Shore and Michigan Southern to his trophies. Rough and profane, Vanderbilt was adept at stock manipulation and political bribery. But he gave his railroads sound management. He double-tracked his main lines, purchased good equipment, and built excellent terminals. Following the Commodore's death in 1877, his son William H. and grandson Cornelius extended the family's stock holdings still further in railroads of the northeast and north-central states.

Commodore Vanderbilt met one of his few defeats when he tried to add the Erie Railroad to his system. In 1868 the Erie was controlled by Daniel Drew, an elderly speculator as slippery as he was sanctimonious, and his two young lieutenants, James Fisk, Jr., and Jay Gould. Fisk was a flamboyant character notorious for fast living and stock gambling, and Gould was a singularly shrewd and cold-blooded manipulator. Into this unholy alliance had also been drawn William M. Tweed, Tammany boss of New York City. While Vanderbilt bought more and more Erie stock in an attempt to secure control, Drew and his accomplices flooded the market with a new issue of dubious legality. To escape the net of injunctions and suits in which the angry Commodore sought to ensnare them, the Erie gang fled across the Hudson River and set up headquarters in Jersey City. The struggle was carried to Albany, where Gould bribed enough legislators to secure an act validating the disputed stock issue. In the end Vanderbilt sold back most of the stock he had purchased, Drew retired with large profits, and Fisk and Gould were left in control of the unfortunate Erie.

Jim Fisk came to an appropriate end in 1872, when he was shot by a jealous rival for the affections of a lady. But Gould, as correct in his personal life as he was unscrupulous in his business dealings, had a much longer career. Although his attempt to corner the gold market in 1869 ruined scores of brokers and petty speculators, Gould himself escaped unscathed—except in reputation. In 1872 the security holders of the Erie rebelled against his stock-jobbing operations and drove him from the management, but he had already fixed his attention on the western field. Until 1883 he played a cat-and-mouse game with the Union Pacific, almost ruining the railroad while enriching himself. During the final decades of his life he built up a great system based upon the Missouri Pacific and the railroads of the Southwest. When he died in 1892, he controlled some 8,000 miles of railroad, the New York elevated transit system, and the great Western Union Telegraph Company.

Although there were lesser Drews and Goulds living as parasites upon transportation, the railroad kings were not all of this type. J. Edgar Thomson and Thomas A. Scott, displaying boldness and skill, built the Pennsylvania Railroad into a system which surpassed all others in the volume of its freight. Although Thomson and Scott were often accused of undue influence with the Pennsylvania legislature and high-handed treatment of shippers, no one could charge that they were ruining the railroad for their own benefit. With the general public, however, the most respected transportation magnate was James J. Hill, who built the Great Northern on the foundations of sound financing and good engineering and had the intelligence to see that the railroad's success depended upon the prosperity of the regions through which it passed.

By 1900 the most powerful figure in the railroad world was J. Pierpont Morgan. Yet the nature of his power is not easily explained. During the seventies Drexel, Morgan & Co. had established a reputation as a sound private-banking house, specializing in the sale of government bonds and corporate securities to English investors. To Morgan, accordingly, William H. Vanderbilt went in 1879, when he wished to sell quietly a substantial portion of his shares in the New York Central in order to relieve himself of the reproach attached to holding 87 per cent of its stock. Morgan found English purchasers and was elected to the Central's board of directors to protect the interests of the new holders. His prestige in the railroad world was further enhanced in 1885, when he intervened to make peace between the warring New York Central and Pennsylvania. Control over the bankrupt West Shore line, which the Pennsylvania had been attempting to gain in order to divert traffic from the Central, was now abandoned to the Vanderbilt system. Similarly, the new Southern Pennsylvania, projected by the Central group to injure its rival, was sold to the Pennsylvania, which promptly abandoned it. By such arrangements Morgan sought to convince railroad executives that they should desist from raids on each other's spheres of influence. Less successful were the meetings of rail presidents from all sections of the country in 1888 and 1889 through which Morgan sought to halt ruinous rate cutting.

Within a decade Morgan had abundant opportunity to impose his ideas of proper railroad policy. In the eighties he achieved his first success in reorganizing insolvent railroads, thus developing a talent which made him a key figure after 1893 when some of the leading lines of the country were in receivership. Unable to straighten out their own affairs, the railroads had to accept plans contrived in the Morgan offices. Bondholders had to accept a scaling down of their claims, old stockholders had to pay assessments, and large issues of new stock were sold. For its services the Morgan firm demanded generous compensation. More important, it insisted that the interests of the new investors should be protected by the presence of Morgan-designated directors on the boards of the reorganized companies and by the employment of managers whom Morgan approved. In one form or another Morgan's influence was powerful in the New York Central, the Erie, the New Haven, the Reading, the Norfolk and Western, the Lehigh Valley, and the Southern Railway System. In alliance with James J. Hill he extended control over the Great Northern, the Northern Pacific, and the Baltimore and Ohio. Although Morgan's influence was generally conservative, he was occasionally guilty of reckless action that he would have condemned in others. The most notorious example of this was his support of the disastrous efforts of Charles S. Mellen, Morgan-designated president of the New Haven Railroad, to build up a transportation monopoly in New England—efforts that inflated the capitalization of the New Haven from 93 million dollars in 1903 to 417 million dollars in 1913.

Morgan's most celebrated battle was with Edward H. Harriman, who sought to wrest control of the Northern Pacific from Morgan and Hill in 1901. Harriman, originally a New York broker, developed an extraordinary talent for both railroad finance and practical railroad management. He first displayed his gifts as vice-president of the Illinois Central. But his more spectacular achievements were in his management of the Union Pacific—an opportunity he gained through alliance with the powerful banking house of Kuhn, Loeb & Co. Harriman practically rebuilt the line, placing it at long last in a position to compete effectively with its rivals. Steadily extending the scope of his interests, Harriman purchased control of the great Southern Pacific–Central Pacific system, which dominated transportation in California. Looking toward Chicago, he aspired also to grasp the strategically located Chicago, Burlington, & Quincy. But in this field he moved too late. Hill and Morgan had already purchased the Burlington for the Northern Pacific.

Checked for the moment, Harriman retaliated with a maneuver of astounding boldness. Through huge but well-concealed stock purchases he attempted to gain control of the Northern Pacific itself. Learning belatedly what was happening, Hill and Morgan began an aggressive buying campaign of their own. The results were dramatic—but inconclusive. The rivals bought more stock than existed, and the shorts, driven desperate by efforts to cover, drove the price of the stock to 1,000 before the leading figures mercifully saved them from disaster. But who had control? The legal issues involved were so difficult that only the courts could have decided. Faced with this situation, the titans decided to compromise. The Northern Securities Company, a gigantic holding corporation in which Hill, Morgan, and Harriman all participated, was organized to take over the control of both the Great Northern and the Northern Pacific. This was the trust challenged by Theodore Roosevelt during the first year of his presidency and dissolved by the Supreme Court in 1904.

Although Harriman failed to conquer any part of the Hill-Morgan empire of the Northwest, he pressed on to other Napoleonic ventures. He secured control over two lines connecting the Union Pacific with the Atlantic seaboard; he became the dominant influence in the Baltimore and Ohio and in the Central of Georgia; he intrigued in the railroad politics of far-off Manchuria. When Harriman died in 1909, he was reputed to dominate 60,000 miles of rails—about one-quarter of the national total. But his empire was a personal one, and only a portion of it was retained by his heirs.

Of more interest to ordinary shippers were railroad rate policies. In the decades immediately following the Civil War, *laissez faire* enjoyed its widest acceptance. Railroading was regarded as a purely private business in which traffic managers and shippers had a right to strike any bargain that they could agree to. The nature of the terms depended on many factors. From Chicago to the East was a competitive haul in which several railroads bid not only against each other but against lake and canal carriers. The result was a wildly fluctuating rate policy. When the waterways were frozen, the railroads raised their rates sharply. When they were open, the rates came down again. At one time the railroads would almost ruin themselves with rate wars such as that of 1876, when passengers were being carried from Chicago to New York for $7 a head and cattle for $1 a carload. Then there would be periods of truce during which the railroads would maintain a pool, keeping the rates high while they divided the profits—to the vast indignation of the shippers. Pittsburgh, largely at the mercy of the Pennsylvania for transportation to the Atlantic Coast, received different treatment. Shippers there complained that rates were so outrageously high that it was sometimes cheaper to send a ton of steel from Chicago to New York than from Pittsburgh to New York.

Discriminations between places were bad enough, but discriminations between shippers had consequences far more serious. Small shippers paid high rates; large shippers received a variety of special rates, rebates, and drawbacks, which gave them crushing advantages over their competitors. The great monopoly achieved by the Standard Oil Company was based in large part upon the special terms which it was able to extract from the railroads. A rash of "Granger laws" attempted to halt these abuses during the seventies, but state action proved inadequate. The Federal government made its first move with the Interstate Commerce Act of 1887. But inadequate powers were given to the new Interstate Commerce Commission, and unreasonable rates and rebating continued to harass shippers until stronger legislation was passed during the Roosevelt and Taft administrations.

Electricity, the New Servant

When Abraham Lincoln wanted to know how the battles of the Civil War were going, he crossed the street from the White House to the War Department building, where telegraph reports were received from the front. There he would remain for hours, eagerly studying each message that came in. The same great invention that brought the President into instantaneous communication with battlefields a thousand miles away revolutionized the gathering of news and the transaction of business. The successful laying of a transatlantic cable in 1866 extended these benefits to the international field.

The telegraph was especially vital to railroading. The orders that moved the trains and prevented accidents were flashed along wires from station to station. The interdependence of railroad and telegraph was reflected in a vast network of contracts between the Western Union Telegraph Company and most of the nation's railroad corporations. The railroads permitted Western Union to erect poles and wires along their rights of way; they provided free transportation for telegraph workers and materials; they supplied in their stations about 9,000 of the 12,000 telegraph offices of the country. In return for all this the railroads received the wire services which were so important to them free.

Western Union's near-monopoly and its highhanded business practices made it unpopular. Demands that the government should take over the entire system or at least compete with it by providing telegraph services through the Post Office were heard from farmers' organizations, labor unions, and boards of trade. Even John Wanamaker, Postmaster General under the Republican Harrison and himself a great merchant, strongly urged government intervention in 1892. But

FIG. 38. *Awaiting the Reply.* Painting by Robert Dudley. Cyrus W. Field and others testing the Atlantic cable. (*Courtesy of the Metropolitan Museum of Art, New York.*)

although 75 bills for the establishment of a government telegraph service were introduced into Congress and 17 different investigating committees before 1900 recommended the step, no legislation was passed. Congress's acquiescence in the private monopoly was perhaps not unrelated to the thoughtful courtesy of Western Union in allowing the legislators to send their telegrams free.

Western Union was less successful in controlling a rival method of electrical communication which developed during the seventies. Regarding the telephone, patented by Alexander Graham Bell of Boston in 1876, as little more than a toy, the Western Union executives passed up an opportunity to purchase Bell's rights at the bargain price of $100,000. When they at length awoke to the telephone's real importance, they organized the American Speaking Telephone Company in 1877. Backed by Western Union's great economic and political power, the new company threatened the Bell interests with disaster. The Western Union puppet installed 56,000 telephones in 56 cities and created innumerable difficulties for the Bell Company. But the Bell corporation, then under the vigorous management of Theodore N. Vail, brought suit against its competitor for infringement of patents and presented such a damning array of evidence that in 1879 the Western Union group gladly accepted a settlement under which the American Speaking Telephone Company sold out to the Bell Telephone Company.

Thereafter, the telephone business grew rapidly. Development of the underground cable gave relief from the ugly jungle of poles and wires growing up in the business districts. Copper wire was substituted for iron, greatly improving transmission and making long-distance lines feasible. New York and Boston were connected by telephone in 1884 and New York and San Francisco in 1915.

After the basic Bell patents expired in 1893, the telephone business provided more opportunities for competition than the telegraph had done. Numerous local companies were founded, and telephones organized in independent exchanges perhaps equaled the number in the Bell system in 1900. But Bell's control of long-distance connections gave it a great advantage. The dominant influence in the industry was the American Telephone and Telegraph Company, a great holding corporation organized around the Bell system in 1900.

In 1901, when the Italian inventor Guglielmo Marconi successfully received by wireless a message sent from Cornwall, England, to St. John's, Newfoundland, the exciting possibilities of a third system of electrical communications was demonstrated. The Marconi Wireless Telegraph Company of America was established in 1902, and within the next few years wireless became standard equipment on all large ships.

Meanwhile, electricity had been put to work lighting city streets and homes. Although arc lights had been used on the boulevards of Paris as early as 1876, Charles F. Brush of Ohio developed a much superior system. In 1877 the Franklin Institute of Philadelphia pronounced Brush's dynamo to be the best in the field, and in 1879 Brush arc lights were installed in the parks of Cleveland and along the streets of San Francisco. Another type of arc light, developed by Elihu Thomson of Philadelphia, also proved successful. During the early eighties more and more cities began to light their streets with electricity.

Arc lights were poorly adapted to most interiors. The problem of developing an electric lamp that would compete with gas in home lighting was attacked with great patience and ingenuity by Thomas A. Edison—already well-known as the inventor of the stock ticker and the phonograph. In January, 1880, Edison patented the incandescent lamp. With the backing of the Morgan banking firm the Edison Illuminating Company was organized, and in 1882 the famous Pearl Street Station began supplying electricity to offices and homes in lower Manhattan. Edison's success in New York stimulated the establishment of similar systems elsewhere.

At first the new business was decentralized. Direct current, the only type in use, could be profitably distributed only to a distance of 1 or 2 miles. This meant that to serve a city as large as New York some sixty generating systems would be required. George Westinghouse, the inventor of the air brake and other railroad devices, began a study of the problems of long-distance electric transmission. In 1886 he purchased the Gaulard-Gibbs patents which had been developed in France and began an aggressive campaign to convert the country to alternating current, which could be sent long distances at high voltage and then reduced by transformers for domestic use. Edison stubbornly refused to admit the advantages of alternating current, and his arguments were echoed by capitalists who had invested heavily in direct-current equipment. Alternating current was depicted as so dangerous as to require prohibitory legislation.

Despite this propaganda alternating current made steady progress. The Westinghouse Company won the contract to light the Chicago World's Fair in 1893. Visitors were enormously impressed by the great dynamos, weighing 75 tons each, and by the marble switchboard 1,000 feet square. At night when the great white buildings were bathed in the light of 5,000 arc lamps and over 100,000 incandescent bulbs, the fair grounds seemed a fairyland. Even more important was the contract awarded to the Westinghouse Company in 1893 to build dynamos for a great hydroelectric development at Niagara Falls. In 1895 when Niagara-generated electricity went on sale in Buffalo, 25 miles away, the age of long-distance transmission by alternating current really began.

Electricity also entered the field of transportation. Although attempts to propel cars by electricity had begun as early as 1835, the first notable success was achieved in Germany in 1879. American inventors like Leo Daft and Charles J. Van Depoele built reasonably satisfactory streetcars during the middle eighties, but the first electric transportation system to arouse genuine enthusiasm was that built in 1888 by Frank J. Sprague in Richmond, Virginia. Thereafter, streetcar lines multiplied rapidly. In 1890 there were 51 such lines and in 1895 about 850. Surburban and interurban lines became so extensive that in 1914 a traveler could go from New York City to Portland, Maine, or from New York City to Sheboygan, Wisconsin, entirely by electric roads.

The electrical industry, dependent on dynamos, transformers, motors, light bulbs, and the like, was particularly well adapted for control by large corporations owning key patents. During the eighties three such companies were organized. The Thomson-Houston Company manufactured dynamos and arc lights; the Westinghouse Electric and Manufacturing Company pioneered in the development of alternating-current equipment; the Edison General Electric Company of New York owned the basic incandescent-light patents and various streetcar inventions of Frank J. Sprague. These three giants were reduced to two in 1892, when the Thomson-Houston Company and the Edison General Electric Company of New York merged to form the great General Electric Company under the presidency of Charles A. Coffin.

Wealth in Oil

Before the Civil War tallow candles and whale-oil lamps had lighted most American homes. Both had been so expensive that only the well-to-do used them freely. Various new illuminants derived from animal fat or turpentine were tried with only limited success. During the fifties Americans began to use kerosene—at first in the form of coal oil, distilled from soft coal and shale by processes developed in Canada and England.

Meanwhile, petroleum, or rock oil, was attracting desultory attention. Such oil was sometimes to be seen on the surface of American streams and springs as it was also in certain areas of the Old World. Prospectors sinking salt wells occasionally struck oil instead—to the disgust of most of them. The more ingenious developed a market for the stuff. Since the Indians had used it for a liniment, it was not difficult to convince white men that "Seneca oil" had important therapeutic qualities. Particularly successful was Samuel M. Kier of Pittsburgh, who about 1849 began to sell "Kier's Petroleum or Rock Oil, Celebrated for its Wonderful Curative Power. A Natural Remedy." At 50 cents for an 8-ounce bottle this was a profitable business; presently Kier developed an additional market by distilling petroleum and selling "carbon oil" as an illuminant. Other men entered the business, and kerosene manufacturers now began to use crude oil as well as coal.

But the real possibilities of the situation were yet to be realized. Petroleum was still being collected in small quantities from springs or from wells that had been originally intended for salt. Not yet had it occurred to anyone that millions of gallons of black gold lay beneath the surface of the earth awaiting only the searching drill of the prospector. In 1854 on a visit to Dartmouth College, his alma mater, George H. Bissell, a New York lawyer, examined a bottle of petroleum and heard one of the professors discuss its possibilities as an illuminant. Much impressed, Bissell and his law partner bought a tract of land containing surface oil in Titusville, Pennsylvania, and submitted a sample of the oil to Professor Benjamin Silliman, Jr., of Yale, one of the country's best known chemists. Silliman's report was enthusiastic: through fractional distillation about one-half of the crude oil could be transformed into an excellent illuminant and lubricants, paraffin, and other valuable products could also be secured. This report resulted in the investment of substantial capital by New Haven bankers and businessmen—so much, in fact, that Bissell, who had more ideas than money, lost control of the enterprise.

But Bissell had one more pregnant suggestion to offer. Learning through Kier's advertising that oil had been found 400 feet under the surface of the earth in a salt well, Bissell convinced his business associates that large quantities might be secured through drilling wells specifically for that purpose. Going out to Titusville in 1858, "Colonel" Edwin L. Drake secured the services of an experienced salt-well driller, and on August 28, 1859, oil was struck—to the amazement of the natives who had regarded Drake as crazy.

News of the incident spread rapidly, and soon the district swarmed with drillers and speculators. Within two years 800 wells were in production and many more were sunk each month. The rush to the oil fields duplicated the strange scenes of the gold and silver rushes.

Although the first shipments from the new wells were sent to the established manufacturers of kerosene, the extraordinary expansion of production inevitably brought scores of new refiners into the business. At first the margin of profit was wide, and a small investment and crude equipment were all that was needed. Refineries were numerous in New York, Philadelphia, Pittsburgh, the oil regions themselves, and Cleveland. In the bitter competition among these cities Cleveland gradually pushed into the lead—largely because of the advantageous transportation rates which she secured through the three-way competition of the New York Central, the Erie, and the water carriers compared with the high charges imposed upon cities dependent on the Pennsylvania Railroad.

Chaotic conditions characterized the early industry. Each year more Americans adopted kerosene as cheaper and better than any rival illuminant, and rising exports testified to the great foreign demand for both kerosene and lubricants. But even with this rapid expansion of the market, supply tended to overrun demand. The wells were owned by hundreds of independent producers, who poured oil into the market as fast as they could take it out of the earth. Prices fluctuated wildly but tended strongly downward. Refiners were in similar difficulties. Fierce competition reduced the price of kerosene until it was hard to make a profit.

Conditions that ruined some men enriched others. John D. Rockefeller, who had come with his family to Cleveland when he was a boy of fourteen, became a bookkeeper two years later. By investing $2,000—partly his own savings, partly money borrowed from his father, a patent-medicine vendor—Rockefeller became a partner in a produce commission business at the age of nineteen. In 1863 this precocious businessman, now twenty-three, made his first investment in oil refining. Two years later Rockefeller and Andrews was the biggest of Cleveland's 30 refineries. Another partner was presently added, and by 1868 Rockefeller, Andrews, and Flagler was the largest oil manufactory in the world. In 1870, when Rockefeller was thirty years old, he became president of the newly organized Standard Oil Company of Ohio, capitalized at 1 million dollars and doing about one-tenth of the nation's refining.

This rapid rise reflected Rockefeller's extraordinary talent for business. Believing strongly in the superior efficiency of large units, he expanded boldly, plowing most of his profits into the business and borrowing as much as the Cleveland banks would lend him. He cut his costs at every possible point. By owning his own cooperage works, he halved the expense of barrels. By careful management most of the by-products of kerosene manufacture were saved and sold. But Rockefeller's most telling advantage was his ability to exact preferential rates from the railroads. He was by no means the only refiner to receive rebates, but he drove the hardest bargains and gained thereby an advantage which made competition with his firms increasingly difficult.

Restraint of competition was indeed Rockefeller's scarcely concealed objective. In 1871 he cooperated with the Pennsylvania Railroad in organizing the so-called South Improvement Company, whereby a combination of the leading refiners proposed to control production, to maintain prices, and to divide oil shipments among the three leading railroads according to an agreed schedule. In return for this the railroads were to raise their rates sharply and then to give the favored refiners not only a substantial rebate on their own shipments but a drawback on the business of all their competitors. If the plan had gone into operation, all independent refiners would have had to enter the organization or to face swift destruction, and producers and consumers would have had to accept whatever terms the combination offered. But news of the secret negotiations leaked out and created such indignation that the whole project collapsed. Although Standard Oil was only one of the parties to the conspiracy, public wrath largely centered around Rockefeller's head.

The collapse of the South Improvement Company only steeled Rockefeller in his determination to force order upon the industry. Of 26 refineries in Cleveland all but 5 merged with Standard between December, 1871, and March, 1872. Conditions in the industry were bad, and many of the independents willingly sold out to escape their losses. Others decided to sell after trips to the railroad offices and the banks had convinced them that Standard would continue to enjoy preferential rates and that bank credit would not be forthcoming to fight the dominant company.

By a similar process Rockefeller and his associates eliminated competition elsewhere. Concealing their hand as much as possible, they negotiated deals whereby the principal refineries of New York, Philadelphia, Pittsburgh, and the oil regions came one after another under their control. Nor were they long content to dominate only the refining business. More and more of the local pipelines connecting the oil wells with the railroad terminals came into their possession—thus strengthening the combination's hand in dealing with both producers and carriers. Standard's victories continued to be based on the triple foundations of abundant capital, superior efficiency, and special railroad rates.

In an attempt to circumvent railroad favoritism, producers and independent refiners invested heavily in the Tidewater Pipe Line, which in 1879 began to pump oil 110 miles over the Allegheny Mountains to a railhead on the Reading Railroad. This was an engineering achievement of prime importance—demonstrating the practicability of long-distance pipelines and presaging the end of oil transportation by rail. But it did not for long challenge Rockefeller's control of the industry. Standard speedily built long lines of its own and entered into an agreement whereby it divided the pipeline business with its rival on the basis of 88½ per cent for Standard and 11½ for Tidewater. Thus defending itself against every threat, Standard continued to grow until by 1882 it controlled over 90 per cent of the refining capacity of the country.

The Trusts

Although the reality of Standard's power could not be doubted, the actual mechanism of control posed a difficult problem for Rockefeller and his allies. The Standard Oil Company of Ohio was authorized by its charter only to manufacture, to ship, and to sell petroleum products. Its legal right to hold plants in states other than Ohio or to own stock in other companies was dubious, to say the least. During the seventies various makeshifts of control had been tried—particularly that of requiring subsidiary companies to turn over all their stock certificates to individual Standard executives to hold as trustees. This device was clumsy, however, and Rockefeller welcomed a new formula, devised in 1882 by Samuel C. T. Dodd, his astute legal adviser. The stockholders of the Standard Oil Company and its satellites surrendered their stock to nine trustees and received instead trust certificates entitling them to share in the profits of the combined operations but not in their management. The nine trustees, headed by John D. Rockefeller, controlled some forty companies from their new headquarters in New York City. They named the subordinate officers and directors and dictated policy.

As in all his dealings Rockefeller tried to keep this agreement as nearly secret as possible. But Dodd's creation was too well adapted to the needs of other industrialists to remain unpublicized. In order to escape ruinous competition, manufacturers had often resorted to pools whereby they agreed to maintain prices and to divide business according to some acceptable ratio. But pool agreements could not be enforced in the courts and inevitably broke down. Consequently, the trust form of organization was taken up with enthusiasm. Following the organization of the Standard Oil Trust in 1882, there appeared a cottonseed-oil trust in 1884, a linseed-oil trust in 1885, and lead, sugar, whisky, and cordage trusts in 1887.

Some Americans accepted the new trusts as inevitable. Their position was that of Rockefeller, who later said, "The day of combinations is here to stay. Individualism has gone, never to return." But the general public opposed the new giants. They hated to see small businessmen driven to the wall; they took alarm at the control over prices and supplies now held by small groups of men; they feared that through campaign gifts and lobbying the trusts would dominate the government itself. Blows against the trusts were struck at both the state and Federal levels during the nineties. In 1890 the New York courts voided the charter of a corporation which had surrendered its management to the sugar trust, and in 1892 the Ohio courts ruled that since the object of the Standard

Oil trust agreement was "to establish a virtual monopoly," it was "contrary to the policy of our state and void." Meanwhile, in language vague but portentous, Congress had in 1890 enacted the Sherman Antitrust Act declaring illegal "every contract, combination in the form of trust or otherwise, or conspiracy, in restraint of trade. . . ."

Although the Sherman Antitrust Act was not vigorously enforced until after 1900, events in the early nineties demonstrated the need for new forms of corporate organization. Some combinations resorted to mergers; others to holding companies. The organization of the latter was made possible by a series of New Jersey laws passed between 1888 and 1896 to permit one corporation to hold the stock of another—a procedure generally considered illegal before this time. The device was ideally adapted for building huge economic empires. Instead of purchasing all the assets of the subsidiary company, it was necessary only to secure a controlling interest in its stock. Often this could be done with very little new capital through the exchange of the stock of the holding company for that of the subsidiary. Between 1899 and 1902 there appeared such giant holding companies as the Standard Oil Company of New Jersey, the American Telephone and Telegraph Company, the United States Steel Corporation, and the Northern Securities Company, together with many smaller ones.

A trust by another name was no less a trust to the general public. Although in the technical sense the trust form of organization had been abandoned, the word was retained in the language to describe any large industrial combination that sought to control prices or production. A generation of vigorous publicists attacked the great corporations and made trust busting popular. The wicked deeds of the Standard Oil Company were related in lurid detail by Henry Demarest Lloyd in *Wealth Against Commonwealth* (1894) and more soberly by Ida M. Tarbell in *The History of the Standard Oil Company* (1904), while other muckrakers laid bare conditions in the meat industry, the railroads, and the bizarre world of patent medicines.

The actual line between legal and illegal corporate behavior was drawn with difficulty. The Northern Securities Company was ordered dissolved in 1904 and the American Tobacco Company and the Standard Oil Company of New Jersey in 1911. But the Supreme Court adopted a "rule of reason," which served to protect the large corporations unless they had clearly attempted to manipulate prices or to stifle competition.

Iron and Steel

The iron industry, at last linked to bituminous coal, expanded greatly to meet the needs of post-Civil War railroad and factory building. During the seventies the ore deposits of northern Wisconsin and Michigan supplied the needs of ironworks in western Pennsylvania and newer ones in Michigan, Illinois, and Ohio. During the eighties the industry was carried into sections of the West and the

South, where the necessary combination of iron, coal, and limestone was also to be found.

But iron in its usual forms no longer served all needs. For high speeds and heavy traffic better railroad rails were imperative. Steel would serve the purpose admirably, but it had hitherto been made by hand processes too costly to permit its use for anything but fine tools and weapons. In 1857 William Kelly, an American ironmaster, had patented a process for making steel cheaply by blowing air through molten pig iron to burn out the excess carbon. Manufacture of steel under the Kelly process began at Wyandotte, Michigan, in 1864. Meanwhile, in England Henry Bessemer had developed the famous converter which bears his name. Alexander M. Holley of Troy, New York, began making steel under rights acquired from Bessemer in 1865. A bitter patent war threatened, but this was avoided when Holley purchased the Kelly patents and combined the two processes. Large-scale production of steel by the new methods was extended during the early seventies to such Pennsylvania plants as the Bethlehem Works and the Cambria Works.

Andrew Carnegie, whose success in steelmaking matched that of Rockefeller in oil refining, was born in Scotland and came to America with his family as a boy of twelve. The next year he got his first job—that of bobbin boy in a textile factory at $1.50 a week. Positions as messenger boy, telegraph operator, and railroad clerk followed. In 1859, when he was twenty-four, Carnegie became a division superintendent on the Pennsylvania Railroad and a favorite of J. Edgar Thomson and Thomas A. Scott, the heads of the company. But his real talents were for business organization. He had a sound instinct for coming developments, a flair for making timely investments, and a genius for inducing others to back him. Carnegie's experience as a railroad man led him to specialize in the iron industry. During the sixties he became a partner in a rail mill, a locomotive works, and a smelting plant. He had particular success with the Keystone Bridge Company, which profited greatly by the post-Civil War railroad boom.

Carnegie watched the foundation of the early steel industry with open skepticism, but a trip to England in 1872 brought a dramatic conversion. At last convinced that the manufacture of steel offered almost limitless possibilities for profit, he secured partners and in 1873 began the construction of the Edgar Thomson Steel Works at Pittsburgh. The name was a characteristic bit of Carnegie shrewdness, since he counted upon the Pennsylvania Railroad to be his best customer for steel rails.

Carnegie was a pioneer in the vertical integration of industry. His steel-rail mill needed blast furnaces to supply it with a dependable quantity of pig iron, and Carnegie saw that these were purchased. Since the blast furnaces in turn required good coke, the steelmaker allied himself in 1882 with Henry C. Frick, who controlled the finest and largest bed of coking coal in the world. By getting coke both better and cheaper than his competitors, Carnegie secured an advantage of supreme importance. Partnership with Frick also gave him the services of an associate who ran the business with ruthless efficiency while the loquacious Carnegie spent more and more of his time traveling or entertaining notables in his castle in Scotland.

In 1892 the Carnegie Steel Company, Limited, was organized to consolidate the numerous Carnegie interests. The great profits of the enterprise were testimony to the sound financing and efficient operation which had created it. In accordance with his practice of using the best equipment and methods, Carnegie invested heavily in the basic open-hearth process, recently developed in Europe.

The most important development of the nineties, however, was the opening of the great Mesabi range in Minnesota. Here ore of unparalleled richness and softness lay so near the surface that it could be dug with steam shovels. John D. Rockefeller, with characteristic vision, had perceived the value of these properties earlier than most men and had purchased the best of them. From Rockefeller, therefore, Carnegie secured a long-term lease of the best ore land in the world in return for moderate royalties. Other Minnesota ore properties passed under direct Carnegie control.

Despite Carnegie's old-time friendship with the men who ran the Pennsylvania Railroad, the great transportation system bled him unmercifully, taking advantage of his dependence on it for carrying ore from Lake Erie ports, bringing in coke from Connellsville, and shipping finished products. Rebelling during the nineties, Carnegie bought and rebuilt an independent line from Conneaut Harbor on Lake Erie to Pittsburgh. By threatening to extend this so-called "Bessemer line" to Connellsville, he won important rate reductions for all his other business with the Pennsylvania Railroad. Two other steps completed his integration of the industry: he built a splendid fleet of lake steamers to transport his ore, and he purchased for the Bessemer Railroad practically all the shore front of the port of Conneaut.

For the year 1900 the profits of the Carnegie Steel Company were 40 million dollars, and Carnegie's personal share was about 25 million dollars. His company produced about 4 million tons of steel—compared with a total English production of about 5 million tons and a total American production of 10 million tons. Although the Carnegie Company had to compete with great rivals like Bethlehem, Cambria, Jones and Laughlin, and Federal, its enormous size, sound financial structure, and progressive technology gave it a position of dominating power. Price-fixing agreements were as common in steel as in railroading and refining, but the Carnegie Company would repudiate such arrangements during periods of depression and capture the reduced market by drastic price cuts. During boom periods it raised prices to levy heavy tribute on the manufacturers of wire, nails, tubing, tin plate, and the like, who had to purchase bulk steel.

American businessmen loved Andrew Carnegie for his geniality and personal charm, but they feared him for his ruthlessly competitive tactics. They concluded that his ambition to retire and to spend the balance of his days in good deeds ought to be encouraged at all costs. But who had the money to buy him out?

Probably the only person with sufficient prestige to mobilize the necessary funds was J. Pierpont Morgan.

By 1900 Morgan was deeply involved in the steel business. His specialty was the marketing of large new issues of securities, and the steel industry—except for Carnegie—was prolific of such issues during the last years of the nineteenth century. Making use of the new holding company device, great consolidations had been effected in the manufacture of finished steel products. Some of these were promoted by speculators in whom Morgan had little confidence like John W. ("Bet-a-Million") Gates and the Moore brothers of Chicago. But other great ventures had been financed with Morgan's active participation. The Federal Steel Company, a vertical combination making basic steel in competition with Carnegie, was a Morgan company, as were the National Tube Company and the American Bridge Company.

Most of the great new companies were customers of Carnegie rather than competitors, but they were exceedingly restive customers, complaining bitterly of their dependence on the capricious Scotchman. During the summer of 1900 the Carnegie Company received a cluster of contract cancellations—clear warning that the manufacturers of finished products were going to make their own basic steel. Carnegie reacted with characteristic vigor. He began to build his own mills for the manufacture of finished products. Morgan was threatened with a rival tube company; Gates with wire and nail mills; the Moore brothers with hoop and rod plants. As though this were not enough to upset Wall Street, Carnegie renewed his feud with the Pennsylvania Railroad and began negotiating for the construction of an independent line between Pittsburgh and the seaboard.

In American economic history such open preparations for war are more often the prelude to truce than to suicidal strife. At a New York dinner given in his honor, Charles M. Schwab, Carnegie's youthful chief lieutenant, made an impressive speech, dilating upon the advantages to be secured by a steel corporation which would integrate basic steel production with the manufacture of finished products. Hearing the speech, J. P. Morgan was inspired to plan the United States Steel Corporation, greatest of the holding companies. Using Schwab as an intermediary, Morgan invited Carnegie to set a price. Word came back that it would require $400,000,000 in the stocks and bonds of the new holding company to gain complete control of the Carnegie empire. The ex-bobbin boy's personal share would be $225,639,000, to be paid entirely in bonds—a testimony both to Carnegie's desire to escape all responsibility for the management of the new venture and his skepticism regarding the earning power of a corporation likely to be heavily overcapitalized.

Even after accepting Carnegie's terms, Morgan had much work to do. Control over nine other great corporations had to be acquired, and some of the bargaining was hard. But terms were at last arranged, and in March, 1901, the United States Steel Corporation was organized under the laws of New Jersey. By consolidating Carnegie Steel, Federal Steel, National Steel, National Tube, American

Steel and Wire, American Tin Plate, American Steel Hoop, American Sheet Steel, American Bridge, and the Lake Superior Consolidated Iron Mines, the new corporation controlled three-fifths of the steel business of the country. The par value of its stocks and bonds totaled $1,400,000,000, making it the nation's first billion dollar corporation. This vast sum was more representative of things hoped for than of visible assets. Despite the estimated 50 per cent of water in the new securities, however, they were successfully marketed. Still more marvelous to relate, the company's great earnings made it possible to pay dividends on the huge mass of stock with few interruptions.

Finance Capitalism

In the preceding sections of this chapter all roads may seem to lead to J. Pierpont Morgan, but they did not all do so. Some led to Lee, Higginson & Co. and Kidder, Peabody & Co. of Boston; some to Kuhn, Loeb & Co., the First National Bank, and the National City Bank of New York. The basic trend, however, was toward an increasing power in the hands of the bankers.

The reason for this was obvious. The consolidation of American industry and transportation required tremendous amounts of capital, and the bankers were the essential middlemen between those who had funds to invest and those who needed them. When several million dollars' worth of new securities had to be marketed, a corporation availed itself of the services of a syndicate of bankers. Similarly, an insurance company, a university, or a wealthy individual seeking suitable investments turned to the banker for securities. For his services the financier demanded a princely tribute. The Morgan firm's profit in the transactions connected with the organization of the United States Steel Corporation amounted to 12 million dollars. More significant, however, was the banker's expanding power over management. Morgan named the officers of the new steel corporation: Charles Schwab became president; Judge Elbert Gary, who had proved himself as head of the Morgan-dominated Federal Steel Company, became chairman of the board of directors; Robert Bacon, a Morgan partner, became head of the finance committee. But "Bet-a-Million" Gates was denied even a directorship. Thus did Morgan assure himself that the management of a corporation in which millions of dollars had been invested on his advice would be in the hands of men whom he trusted.

Some of the great industrial empires had been built without dependence on the bankers. Standard Oil largely lifted itself by its own bootstraps, expanding steadily by investing its profits in the business and by inducing competitors to merge interests with the dominant group. The Carnegie Company also prided itself on independence from Wall Street: all of its stock was owned by a small group of partners; it could not be bought on the exchange and had to be sold back to the company when a partner died or retired. The Ford Motor Company, just beginning its sensational growth in 1914, secured most of its capital from its own earnings.

These cases, however, were exceptional. Most corporations, old and new, found it possible to expand only through the sale of stocks and bonds. More and more the reins of control fell into the hands of Wall Street. Indeed, some of the great industrial fortunes became themselves agencies of finance capitalism. John D. Rockefeller's purchase and lease of the Mesabi ore lands have already been mentioned, and he invested also in the Colorado Fuel and Iron Company and in railroads.

To the general public the situation was alarming. Men talked of a "money trust"—an octopus extending long tentacles out of Wall Street to entrap more and more of the nation's business. In 1912 and 1913 the Pujo Committee, a subcommittee of the House Committee on Banking and Currency, held extensive hearings and drew up a report of their findings. They depicted the core of the money trust as an informal alliance among J. P. Morgan & Co., the First National Bank of New York, and the National City Bank. These three institutions had combined resources of over $600,000,000 and control of seven other New York banks and the Equitable Life Assurance Company. Direction over the investment of over $2,000,000,000 thus lay in the hands of a few individuals. The power of the group was represented by 341 directorships in 112 corporations having aggregate capitalization of $22,245,000,000. These conclusions were perhaps misleading. Many of these directorships were probably little more than honorary, and the elderly gentlemen who occupied the center of the web would have had to be Argus-eyed to direct actively all that they were reputed to control. But that the bankers exercised vast power no one could deny.

The Capitalist Defense

Despite growls of protest most Americans seemed content with the passage of a few regulatory laws and the prosecution of a few conspicuous culprits. Demand for more fundamental remedies lacked vigor. Even after the highhanded tactics of the Vanderbilts, Drews, and Goulds, the Populists and Socialists could win no mass support for proposals that the government take over the railroads. While condemning big business for its methods, the general public obviously admired it for its accomplishments. It was true that speculators had made millions, but the nation had secured the world's greatest transportation system. The annual value of products manufactured in American factories had risen from less than $2,000,000,000 in 1860 to more than $24,000,000,000 in 1914. Among the industrial nations of the world the United States had risen from fourth in 1860 to first in 1894. By 1914 she was producing as much as her three nearest competitors—Great Britain, France, and Germany—combined.

Price-fixing agreements, trusts, and monopolies notwithstanding, Americans had greatly improved their standard of living. Whatever the sins of John D. Rockefeller, he had provided millions of his countrymen with an illuminant of reliable quality at a price low enough to effect a cultural revolution. Carnegie, more articulate than most of the captains of industry, described his own accomplishment thus:

> To make a ton of steel one and a half tons of iron stone has to be mined, transported by rail a hundred miles to the Lakes, carried by boat hundreds of miles, transferred to cars, transported by rail one hundred and fifty miles to Pittsburgh; one and a half tons of coal must be mined and manufactured into coke and carried fifty-odd miles by rail; and one ton of limestone mined and carried one hundred and fifty miles to Pittsburgh. How then could steel be manufactured and sold without loss at three pounds for two cents? This, I confess, seemed to me incredible, and little less than miraculous, but it was so.[1]

Since the canny Scotchman sold steel by the ton rather than in three-pound units, this statement was somewhat disingenuous, but the unvarnished truth was impressive enough. In 1875, when Carnegie began to manufacture steel rails, the price was $160 a ton; in 1898 it was $17 a ton.

The economies possible in large-scale production were often striking. By requiring the use of 39 drops of solder instead of 40 in sealing each can of kerosene, John D. Rockefeller saved the Standard Oil Company $2,500 a year. When Schwab assured Carnegie that steel could be made 50 cents a ton cheaper in a new mill, Carnegie ordered it erected. When two months' experience with this plant showed ways in which savings of a dollar a ton would be possible, Carnegie ordered the new plant torn down and another erected in its place.

In the long run economies based on trial and error or flashes of intuition were less important than savings made possible through intelligent planning and scientific method. Carnegie pioneered in substituting the exact knowledge of the chemist for the vague know-how of the artisan. Particularly significant were the techniques of scientific management developed by Frederick W. Taylor. As a young engineer for the Midvale Steel Company of Philadelphia, Taylor had been exasperated by management-labor disputes over what constituted a fair day's work and a fair day's pay. This led him to analyze each job in the Midvale machine shop. Equipped with stop watch and chart, he recorded the time required to perform each essential part of the task. These time studies led to the retraining of workers to eliminate waste motions, to the clear definition of the tasks to be performed by each, and to standardization of the conditions under which the work was done. "Scientific management," as Taylor described his system, soon involved more and more factors—cost accounting, special personnel officers to hire and to fire workers, and a new philosophy of wages that would reward rather than penalize workers for increases in productivity. These ideas, first formulated in the eighties and later tried out in other industries, gained a slowly widening circle of influence. Such papers as Taylor's *A Piece Rate System* (1895), *On the Art of Cutting Metals* (1906), and *The Principles of Scientific Manage-*

[1] *Autobiography of Andrew Carnegie* (Houghton Mifflin, Boston, 1920), 227.

ment (1911) were translated into many languages. In 1908 the Harvard Graduate School of Business Administration began teaching the Taylor system.

To the general public, however, Henry Ford's name was more familiar than that of Taylor. Nor was this necessarily an injustice to the older man. Ford proved that the automobile—prior to 1908 the plaything of the rich—could be manufactured at a price that would make it the servant of the farmer and the worker. The essence of mass production was neither standard interchangeable parts, in use since Eli Whitney's day, nor the conveyer belt, already common in meat packing and elsewhere. Mass production in the new sense depended less upon technology than upon organization—careful planning to break down manufacture into thousands of special tasks and then to integrate the performance of these tasks so that they resulted in a steady stream of completed products. A recent writer has thus described the importance of this development:

> The world revolution of our time is not communism, fascism, the new nationalism of the non-Western people, or any of the other "isms" that appear in the headlines; they are reactions to the basic disturbance, secondary rather than primary. The true world revolution is "made in U. S. A.," and its principle is the mass-production principle. Nothing ever before recorded in the history of man equals in speed, universality, and impact the transformation that modern industrial organization has wrought in the foundations of society in the forty years since Henry Ford developed the mass-production principle to turn out the Model T.[1]

"The millionaires," said William Graham Sumner of Yale in 1902, "are a product of natural selection, acting on the whole body of men, to pick out those who can meet the requirement of certain work to be done. . . . They get high wages and live in luxury, but the bargain is a good one for society." [2]

Only through the incentive of unstinted rewards, it was believed, could these men of genius be spurred on to the performance of economic miracles. Vast sums of money in the hands of the rich were judged to be of more use to society than the same money thinly dispersed among the masses. The wealthy gave employment to the poor—directly, in building their Fifth Avenue mansions and Newport villas and, indirectly, through their investments. The more enlightened millionaires felt also a compulsion to donate vast sums to worthy causes. Andrew Carnegie gave away nine-tenths of his fortune in accordance with a philosophy which he never tired of publicizing. In 1889 he wrote:

> This, then, is held to be the duty of the man of Wealth: First, to set an example of modest, unostentatious living, shunning display or extravagance; to provide moderately for the legitimate wants of those dependent upon him; and after doing so to consider all surplus revenues which come to him simply as trust funds, which he is called upon to administer, and strictly bound as a matter of duty to administer in the manner which, in his judgment, is best calculated to produce the most beneficial results for the community—

[1] Peter F. Drucker, "The New Society," *Harper's Magazine,* CXCIX (September, 1949), 21.

[2] W. G. Sumner, "Consolidation of Wealth: Economic Aspects," *The Independent,* LIV (May 1, 1902), 1040.

the man of wealth thus becoming the mere agent and trustee for his poorer brethren, bringing to their service his superior wisdom, experience, and ability to administer, doing for them better than they would or could do for themselves. . . .[1]

Although less given to writing articles and books, John D. Rockefeller was no less conscientious in making carefully planned gifts in the fields of religion, education, medicine, and science. Many other rich men were more notable for conspicuous consumption than for philanthropy, but there were enough generous donations to colleges and civic purposes to blunt popular resentment against the rise of great wealth.

The defenders of capitalism did not rest their case merely on the social benefits of large-scale business and the benevolence of the wealthy. Able speakers and writers praised the existing economic system in persuasive terms. The most popular lecture of the day was "Acres of Diamonds," delivered over six thousand times by its author, the Reverend Russell H. Conwell of Philadelphia's Baptist Temple. "Money is power," the clergyman declared, "and you ought to be reasonably ambitious to have it. You ought because you can do more good with it than you could without it." Employers distributed to their employees millions of copies of *A Message to Garcia* (1899) in which the publisher Elbert Hubbard denounced "the imbecility of the average man" and praised exceptional young men with stiff vertebrae who would do what they were told. Expressing impatience with "maudlin sympathy" for the sweatshop workers and the unemployed, Hubbard reserved his pity for "the employer who grows old before his time in a vain attempt to get frowsy ne'er-do-wells to do intelligent work."

University professors and distinguished judges united in preaching a philosophy of *laissez faire,* which would permit businessmen a maximum of freedom from government regulation. Yale's Professor Sumner wrote: "The truth is that the social order is fixed by laws of nature precisely analogous to those of the physical order. The most that man can do is by his ignorance and conceit to mar the operation of the social laws."

Business and Politics

Businessmen believed themselves to be upholders of *laissez faire.* All they wanted of government, they were fond of asserting, was that it should be an umpire, enforcing the rules of the game but keeping out of the play. And of rules they wanted only the most necessary—those required to punish theft and embezzlement and to enforce the obligations of contract. Laws that would fix rates or prices, limit profits, or set minimum wages or maximum hours of labor were opposed as hampering the operation of economic forces. Yet businessmen rarely allowed their love for *laissez faire* to inhibit their demands for government protection and encouragement. High protective tariffs that would reduce

[1] Andrew Carnegie, "Wealth," *North American Review*, CXLVIII (June, 1889), 661–662.

competition with foreign goods, generous subsidies for railroads, exclusive franchises, and lucrative contracts were positive measures of assistance which businessmen urged upon government.

In order to obtain the right kind of government—one that would abstain from measures that would hamper business and would enact measures that would promote it—businessmen participated increasingly in politics. The Senate of the United States, elected by the state legislatures rather than by the people, was sometimes called the "millionaires' club" because of the large number of wealthy men who sat in it. Another view might have held the Senate to be a feudal council composed of political barons who ruled their separate states—Conkling and Platt of New York, Cameron and Quay of Pennsylvania, Sawyer of Wisconsin, Dorsey of Indiana, and Hanna of Ohio. The great state bosses were political middlemen who collected campaign contributions from businessmen and saw to it that only "safe" men were elected to office and only "safe" measures became law. Much of the lubrication needed to keep the political machine running smoothly was forthcoming through the patronage whereby faithful party workers received appointments to government jobs.

As a matter of insurance many businessmen contributed to both the Republican and Democratic parties. Yet the Republican party was regarded as the safer investment. With more money for campaigning, with the support of farmers grateful for Federal aid to agriculture and of many workers convinced that the protective tariff assured a "full dinner pail," and, above all, because of the prestige of having saved the Union during the Civil War, the Republican party enjoyed a generation of unusual power. The vetoes of the uncooperative President Johnson were monotonously overridden, and in President Grant, popular with the voters and deferential toward men of wealth, the machine politicians found an ideal puppet. Hayes, Garfield, Arthur, and Harrison, made occasional gestures toward independence but lacked the capacity for leadership necessary to challenge the bosses effectively. Cleveland, the only Democrat to hold the Presidential office between Buchanan and Wilson, was a man of stubborn courage. His attempt to reduce the tariff threw terror into the businessmen and resulted in doubled contributions to the Republican war chest; but in dealing with the demands of western inflationists and striking wage earners, Cleveland protected business interests most effectively.

The alliance between business and the political bosses resulted in increasing protest. Many respectable easterners had no desire to alter fundamental economic policy but were heartsick at widespread evidence of political manipulation and corruption. These "mugwumps," emphasizing the need for civil-service reform, gained occasional victories like the enactment of the Pendleton Act in 1882 and the election of Cleveland in 1884 and 1892. Strongly impressed by contemporary English Liberalism, many of the mugwumps became advocates of tariff reduction.

To a growing element, however, civil-service reform and tariff reduction seemed superficial remedies. Farmers and industrial workers rebelled against important features of the existing order. They demanded the issuance of more money to raise prices and wages; they demanded laws to regulate business and to protect labor; they demanded an income tax to compel the wealthy to pay their fair share of government expenses.

The contest between the businessmen and their rivals for control of government was fought out in many states during the generation after the Civil War. At the national level the struggle came to a climax in the election of 1896. The victory of William McKinley in that contest seemed to leave the businessman in secure possession of the field, but the victory was short-lived. A new period began when Theodore Roosevelt moved into the White House in 1901. Although big business had come to stay, big agriculture, big labor, and big government soon followed, bringing some prospect of a new balance of power.

Chapter 22. Protests from Labor

In an age of big business the highly trained artisan played a role of steadily diminishing importance. More and more of the nation's work was done by men who were useful to their employers as groups rather than as individuals. Labor became an impersonal factor in production, to be purchased as cheaply as possible. Nevertheless, the fiction persisted that employer-employee relations were fixed by individual contract. The employer offered a certain wage for a certain number of hours; the employee accepted these terms or sold his services elsewhere. Actually, of course, the advantages in bargaining were all with the employer. If a particular individual refused his terms, there were usually many others who would accept them, but for the worker it was often this job or no job at all.

In dealing with the new industrial order the wage earners turned first to one program of action and then to another. Sometimes they sought better working conditions through legislation; sometimes they tried to escape from the wage system by organizing cooperatives. Henry George's single tax promised salvation to one group; Edward Bellamy's utopian socialism to another. From Europe came such explosive ideas as Marxian socialism, anarchism, and syndicalism—each appealing to a segment of the American working class. Such radical doctrines were repudiated by most labor spokesmen, who urged the workers to organize unions and to seek better working conditions through peaceful negotiations with employers. But the principle of collective bargaining secured no wide acceptance. Management's obstinacy and labor's desperation involved the country in the bloodiest and most destructive strikes in its history.

Aspirations of the Sixties

In 1861 American labor was largely unorganized. Most of the unions of the early fifties had broken up during the depression of 1857. In only a few trades like the printers', the molders', and the machinists', did the workers attempt to maintain national unions—and these were struggling bodies. The first effect of the Civil War was to disrupt business and to create unemployment, thus increasing the difficulties of the workers.

As the war progressed, however, conditions were radically altered. The wartime boom and the government's issuance of legal-tender currency, or greenbacks, sent prices rocketing upward. Although employment was good and wages were rising, the cost of living rose faster than the workers' income and invited labor-union activity. Employees were eager to unite in pressing their demands; employers confronted with a labor shortage were inclined to make concessions. In

December, 1863, there were in the entire country only 79 local unions representing 20 different trades; two years later there were about 300 unions representing 61 different trades. During the same period every important industrial city saw the development of a trades' assembly—a central labor organization composed of the leaders of the various local unions.

The spread of unionism, although temporarily checked by the depression of 1867, was soon resumed and continued until the panic of 1873. Besides local unions and trades' assemblies there were a growing number of national unions, reflecting the realization that local groups could not long succeed in improving working conditions unless they were affiliated with similar groups in other cities. In 1872 there were about 300,000 workers enrolled in unions and about thirty-two national organizations.

Particularly influential was the Iron Molders' International Union, founded in 1859. William H. Sylvis, its president, became the best-known labor leader of his day. Like an itinerant evangelist he traveled continuously, visiting almost every American and Canadian city where stoves were manufactured. The personal sacrifice that this involved is suggested in his brother's description: "He wore clothes until they became quite threadbare and he could wear them no longer. . . . The shawl he wore to the day of his death . . . was filled with little holes burned there by the splashing of molten iron from the ladles of molders in strange cities, whom he was beseeching to organize."

During the war the molders pressed their demands with great success, gaining wage raises, a closed shop, and limitation of apprentices. The national union was strongly organized. Although locals were warned to avoid striking whenever possible and not to strike without the authorization of the national officers, contests once begun were carried through vigorously. The union's success brought countermeasures from the employers. In 1866 the American National Stove Manufacturers' and Iron Founders' Association was organized, and two years later this combination of employers confronted the workers with a 60 per cent wage cut. The ensuing nine months' struggle came at a bad time for the union. Business was poor, many of the molders were unemployed, and repeated strike assessments aroused resentment. The workers finally straggled back to their jobs on the employers' terms.

Confronted with the problem of reorganizing the shattered remnants of his union, Sylvis repudiated traditional trade-union tactics, asserting:

> Combination as we have been using or applying it, makes war upon the effects, leaving the cause undisturbed, to produce, continually, like effects. . . . The cause of all these evils is the WAGES SYSTEM. . . . We must adopt a system which will divide the profits of labor among those who produce them. . . .[1]

Changing its name to Iron Molders' International Co-operative and Protective Union, the national organization devoted itself to promoting cooperative stove

[1] Quoted in John R. Commons *et al., History of Labour in the United States* (Macmillan, New York, 1918), II, 53.

founderies. The first of these had already been established at Troy in 1866, and its initial success encouraged the organization of ten more, including the International Foundry at Pittsburgh—a pet project of the enthusiastic Sylvis.

The molders' experiments in producer cooperation were paralleled by similar ventures of machinists, shoemakers, coopers, and other worker groups. But the difficulties which had defeated earlier cooperatives doomed most of these. Inexperienced management ruined some; union poverty and inability to secure capital hopelessly handicapped others. Even when a temporary success was achieved, the interests of the workers were often sacrificed in the effort to compete with capitalist rivals.

The search for a magic formula which would dispel all the evils of industrialism still continued. Ira Steward, a self-educated machinist of Massachusetts, zealously advocated the eight-hour workday. Not content with earlier arguments that shorter hours had their principal benefit in spreading available work among the laborers and providing them with more leisure for relaxation and self-improvement, Steward elaborated a more subtle theory. If work in excess of eight hours were prohibited by law, he argued, laborers would universally demand as much for the shorter hours as they had for ten or more hours before. As a couplet of the day had it:

> Whether you work by the piece or work by the day
> Decreasing the hours increases the pay.

More important, shorter hours and more leisure would stimulate new demands for goods. Manufacturers, enjoying an ever-expanding market for their products, would invest more capital and install more machinery. This mechanization should not be resisted by the workers. Instead, they should demand higher and higher wages—thus winning for themselves the major share in the wealth created by technological progress.

Thoroughly convinced by his own argument, Steward had scant patience with the limited demands of traditional trade-unionism. He urged the workers to employ political action, casting their ballots only for candidates pledged to vote for eight-hour laws. This philosophy gained thousands of supporters, who organized themselves in local and state eight-hour leagues. Politicians recognized the strength of the new demands by passing eight-hour bills in several state legislatures; but since the new acts did not prohibit working additional hours under special contract and made no adequate provision for enforcement, their results were disappointing.

In 1866 a National Labor Congress at Baltimore attracted 77 delegates from various parts of the country, and from this meeting the National Labor Union resulted. The new organization's membership was drawn not only from trade unions and eight-hour leagues but from middle-class reform associations and farmers' societies as well. Its program was equally diffuse. In 1866 principal emphasis was placed on the demand for eight-hour laws, but strong support was also given to producers' and consumers' cooperatives, to trade-unions and collective bargaining with employers, and to the principle that the public domain should be reserved for actual cultivators. In 1867 the platform gave central place to a new panacea—repeal of the National Bank Act of 1864 and the substitution of legal-tender treasury notes as the exclusive currency of the nation. From this great reform all other blessings would flow:

> . . . money, the medium of distribution to capital and labor, must be instituted upon such a wise and just principle that instead of being a power to centralize the wealth in the hands of a few bankers, usurers, middlemen and non-producers generally, it shall be a power that will distribute products to producers in accordance with the labor or service performed in their production—the servant and not the master of labor. This done the natural rights of labor will be secured, and co-operation in production and in the distribution of products will follow as a natural consequence. The weight will be lifted from the back of the laborer, and the wealth producing classes will have the time and the means necessary for social enjoyment, intellectual culture and moral improvement, and the non-producing classes compelled to earn a living by honest industry.[1]

The National Labor Union reached the height of its prestige in 1868. Responding to pressure from businessmen and farmers as well as from the workers, Congress passed a law prohibiting further contraction of the currency—a concession to Greenbackism. By another prudent election-year gesture the legislators prescribed the eight-hour day for all Federal employees. Encouraged by these victories, the National Labor Union elected the energetic William H. Sylvis president and greatly expanded its activities. But returning prosperity raised issues that split and eventually destroyed the movement. The sudden death of Sylvis in 1869 was a serious loss, and the leaders who succeeded him were badly divided over tactics.

The blow that finally killed the National Labor Union was its disastrous attempt to launch a third party in 1872. A national convention at Columbus adopted a platform and nominated Supreme Court Justice David Davis of Illinois for the presidency. But Judge Davis, after giving a qualified acceptance, finally declined the nomination—too late for the labor politicians to make a substitution. Although the National Labor Union disappeared, the greenback issue continued to agitate middle-class reformers and farmers. A third party dedicated to currency reform nominated Peter Cooper, the New York philanthropist, for the presidency in 1876, but it secured most of its votes from farmers rather than from industrial workers.

The Desperate Seventies

The panic of 1873 liquidated the labor gains of the sixties almost as completely as earlier depression periods had done. Of the 30 national unions of 1872 all but eight or nine succumbed during the next five years. Total union member-

[1] J. R. Commons *et al.*, eds., *A Documentary History of American Industrial Society* (Arthur H. Clark Co., Cleveland, 1910–1911), IX, 179–180.

ship declined from 300,000 to 50,000. When workers attempted to resist drastic wage cuts, they often lost not only the strikes but their jobs as well.

Among the unions to suffer disaster was the Miners' and Laborers' Benevolent Association, to which most of the Pennsylvania anthracite miners belonged. This organization met an implacable enemy in Franklin B. Gowen, president of the Philadelphia and Reading Railroad, which controlled many coal mines. Gaining the support of other operators, Gowen challenged the union with a drastic wage cut in December, 1874. After a bitterly fought strike lasting seven months, the union was completely defeated, and the miners returned to work on the operators' terms.

Gowen's most crushing blow was still to fall. Since 1873 James McParlan, a Pinkerton detective, had been living in the anthracite district, gaining the confidence of the miners and accumulating evidence of terroristic activities. In the fall of 1875 numerous arrests were made, and a fantastic story of conspiracy and crime was released to the press. According to McParlan, a secret society called the Molly Maguires had been responsible for a long list of murders running back to 1862. The Mollies had committed their acts of vengeance against owners, foremen, and fellow workers who attempted to oppose them. After a sensational trial 24 of the alleged conspirators were convicted; 10 were hanged and the rest received prison sentences.

Students of American labor history have long been puzzled by the lurid episode of the Molly Maguires. Actually, there was no such American organization. The term was loosely applied to the Ancient Order of Hibernians, an Irish nationalist and fraternal order, which had many local chapters in the mining districts. The extent to which desperate men gained control of these chapters and used them to plot acts of violence is impossible to measure. Gowen and the operators may themselves have instigated some of the crimes to lay the basis for their smashing blows against the union. At all events, the organized labor movement suffered a serious setback. The disorganized miners were left at the mercy of their employers, and other laborers who protested against working conditions exposed themselves to accusations of criminal conspiracy.

The most serious labor conflicts that the nation had yet experienced broke out in July, 1877. Railroad workers, already desperate because of reductions in pay and irregular employment, rebelled against another 10 per cent wage cut announced by several of the largest companies. On July 17, the day after the cut became effective on the Baltimore and Ohio, the men seized control of the line at Martinsburg, West Virginia, and stopped all freight trains. When the mayor attempted to have the strike leaders arrested, a crowd composed not only of railroad employees but of other workers and miners gathered to secure their release. From the beginning it was obvious that local opinion usually sided with the workers against the railroads, whose highhanded business methods had made them enemies among every class. This situation was further clarified when the West Virginia militia, called out by the governor, fraternized with the strikers.

Not until President Hayes responded to the governor's request by dispatching Federal troops to Martinsburg was the railroad able to move its trains freely in and out of the city. Meanwhile, the strike had spread to other points on the Baltimore and Ohio. When strikers seized control of the terminal at Cumberland, the governor of Maryland ordered out two Baltimore militia regiments. A Baltimore crowd attempted to halt the troops but were answered by a volley of gunfire that killed 12 and wounded 18. That night a mob assailed the depot, where the troops were awaiting trains to take them to Cumberland, set fire to the building, and threatened the lives of the firemen. The police finally restored order, and the next day Federal troops arrived at Baltimore and at other trouble points in the state. The strike was completely broken, and the railroad employees had to accept the hated wage cut. Workers everywhere protested against the policy of the authorities in this first important instance of Federal intervention during a peacetime strike.

The labor disturbances of the year were far from over. On the Pennsylvania Railroad the workers took a pay cut on June 1 without striking, but their patience suddenly snapped when the management announced that double-header freight trains would be introduced. This threatened to throw many trainmen out of work and to increase the burden of the train crews. On July 19 rebellious employees at Pittsburgh took possession of the switches and refused to allow the freight trains to move. In their defiance the railroad workers had the sympathy of most of the inhabitants of the city. The Pennsylvania Railroad had so systematically discriminated against Pittsburgh that it was thoroughly hated. Although the railroad officials received only a half-hearted response when they appealed to the local authorities for protection of their property, the governor was more responsive and ordered 650 Philadelphia militiamen to the trouble spot. These troops met the first display of hostility by firing upon the crowd, killing some twenty-five persons and wounding as many more. This act aroused the whole countryside, drawing to the scene not only railroad men but several thousand factory hands, miners, and unemployed laborers. The mob broke into gunshops, secured arms, and laid siege to the roundhouse where the soldiers were quartered. During the ensuing all-night battle the rioters set fire to scores of freight cars and pushed them into the roundhouse until that too was ablaze. In the morning the soldiers retreated from the city under a hail of bullets. The city was left to the mob, which celebrated its victory in an orgy of destruction. Roundhouses, machine shops, a grain elevator, and the Union Depot itself went up in flames; 2,000 cars and 25 locomotives were destroyed; many sections of track were pulled up. Hoodlums and criminals took advantage of the situation to break into liquor stores, to guzzle their stock, and to loot warehouses and shops indiscriminately.

The great Pittsburgh riot largely subsided of itself, although aid in restoring order was obtained from the local police, hastily organized citizens' committees, and reinforcements of militia. Detachments of Federal troops finally arrived to patrol the city, and all United States forces in the Atlantic Department were ordered to keep in readiness to repress any renewal of the disturbance.

News of the Pittsburgh uprising spread rapidly to other cities along the Pennsylvania Railroad and resulted in similar, though less serious, demonstrations. Erie Railroad wage cuts precipitated strikes in New York, Hornellsville, and Buffalo. Similar demonstrations broke out in cities as far removed as Cincinnati, Toledo, St. Louis, and San Francisco. In Chicago the railroad situation threatened to develop into a general strike. Police, militia, Federal troops, and vigilante groups took drastic measures to break up the labor demonstrations. Scores were killed and wounded in street fighting before the strike was finally broken on July 28.

The judgment expressed by the St. Louis *Republican*—"It is wrong to call this a strike; it is a labor revolution"—might have been repeated in a score of cities throughout the nation. The railroad pay cut touched off an explosion of all the pent-up resentment of the depression-harassed workers. The protest failed miserably, but its results were far-reaching. Middle-class opinion, somewhat sympathetic with the railroad men at first, was soon frightened by the violence of the strike. Employers demanded more efficient police and militia forces and set their faces sternly against the trade unions. They imposed on their employees the ironclad oath, a pledge not to join a labor union while they were employed by the company. They hired detectives to spy on their workers and used professional strikebreakers when trouble arose. Men discharged for union activity often found themselves black-listed and unable to follow their trade.

For different workers the great defeat spelled different lessons. To some the alliance between government and the employers proved the need for political action. New workingmen's parties sprang up in various parts of the country, and Greenbackism was revived in the National Greenback-Labor party. Socialism, hitherto a movement largely confined to recent immigrants and plagued with doctrinal disputes, showed a sudden burst of energy. Local socialist groups showed strength in Chicago, St. Louis, New York, and other cities, and the Socialist Labor party was organized on a national basis in December, 1877. But the socialists continued to bicker over tactics and failed to build up any mass support.

The Knights of Labor

The hazards of open union activity—painfully obvious during the depression of the seventies—favored the growth of secret workers' societies like the Sovereigns of Industry, the Industrial Brotherhood, and the Junior Sons of '76. Eclipsing all these in its rapid growth during the late seventies and early eighties was the Knights of Labor.

Organized in 1869 by Uriah S. Stephens, a Philadelphia garment cutter, the

Knights slowly grew behind their veil of secrecy. Assembly No. 1 in Philadelphia was composed of garmentworkers, but provision was soon made for "sojourners" —members of other crafts who might belong until there were enough of them to "swarm," or to establish an assembly of their own. By the end of 1873 there were 80 assemblies, all in or near Philadelphia. In 1874 branches were organized in New York, Trenton, and other cities. Meanwhile, the various assemblies of Philadelphia had been brought together in a so-called "district assembly"—a step that was duplicated elsewhere as soon as there were enough locals.

In 1878 the Knights of Labor held their first national or general assembly at Reading, Pennsylvania. In a lengthy constitution the Knights dedicated themselves to general virtues like the promotion of knowledge and morality, the equitable distribution of wealth, and the maintenance of good government. They endorsed such specific reforms as producers' and consumers' cooperatives, the reservation of public land for actual settlers, laws to compel corporations to pay their employees weekly, the substitution of arbitration for strikes, the prohibition of child labor, the right of women workers to equal pay for equal work, the eight-hour day, and a national legal-tender currency.

Following its reorganization on a national basis, the Knights of Labor developed along lines somewhat different from those first laid down by the Philadelphia founders. By this time the excessive secrecy in which the order had tried to clothe itself was proving a handicap. In 1879 the rules were partially relaxed, and in 1881 the ritual was amended to remove the oath and other features which were displeasing to the Roman Catholic Church. The Knights hereafter conducted much of their business publicly, although they still retained the secret ceremonies peculiar to a fraternal order.

In 1879 Uriah Stephens, plagued by ill-health and preoccupied with politics, declined reelection as Grand Master Workman of the order and Terence V. Powderly of Scranton, Pennsylvania, was elected in his place. Powderly was an expert machinist, who knew from personal experience the hardships of trying to maintain trade-unions in defiance of black-listing employers. He was active in the Greenback-Labor movement and was elected mayor of Scranton in 1878. Despite the misgivings of the city's property owners he proved to be a conscientious public official and was twice reelected.

As head of the Knights of Labor, Powderly displayed both virtues and defects. He was thoroughly honest, refusing to sell his power or influence. He handled with tact and skill difficult negotiations with Cardinal Gibbons, which prevented a condemnation of the order by the Vatican. He was a vigorous and inspiring speaker. Despite his sincerity and good intentions, however, he was essentially a talker rather than a man of action. It was Powderly's misfortune that while genuinely opposed to the strike as a labor weapon, he found himself again and again forced to support strikes begun by the local assemblies. In such situations he was inept; he could neither exercise effective generalship himself nor delegate responsibility to others.

The difficulties encountered by the Knights arose in part from uncertain leadership and in part from weaknesses in organization. In theory the order was highly centralized with large powers vested in the national officers. In practice the local and district assemblies enjoyed so much autonomy that the national officers were repeatedly embarrassed by action taken by some branch of the great, sprawling organization.

The Knights, however, emphasized the solidarity of labor. Although local assemblies usually consisted of the members of a single trade with a few sojourners, the district assemblies represented the interests of many different trades. Moreover, the mixed local assembly, a unit particularly adapted to the growth of the Knights in small communities, became common during the eighties. The mixed assembly might be mixed indeed, since members did not even have to be wage earners. Farmers, merchants, ministers, and manufacturers might join the order; indeed, the only occupations of such dubious honesty that their practitioners were excluded were liquor dealers, gamblers, lawyers, and bankers. In 1880 the general assembly voted to admit women to membership on the same terms as men; by 1886 there were 192 women's locals and such outstanding feminists as Susan B. Anthony and Frances E. Willard had become Knights. In 1886 there were about 60,000 Negro members—some in locals of their own, others in the same locals as whites.

The Knights of Labor differed from the trade-unions in accepting the membership of workers who had no skilled craft—a rapidly growing class under the new industrial conditions. This policy was never entirely acceptable to the skilled workmen, who were as much interested in protecting their jobs from invasion by the unskilled as in pressing their demands upon employers. The Knights attempted to recognize these trade interests by permitting the organization of special district assemblies, composed entirely of members of a single craft.

But this policy did not satisfy the more aggressive trade-unionists, who believed that craft interests and practical wage-and-hour issues could never be efficiently handled by the Knights with their heterogeneous membership and their multiple objectives. Samuel Gompers of the Cigarmakers' Union was the leader of a trade-union element that attempted to found a Federation of Organized Trades and Labor Unions in 1881. The new organization, a weak and struggling body, was no rival for the fast-growing Knights during the next five years. But renamed and reorganized as the American Federation of Labor in 1886, it was in a position to grow steadily during the years in which the Knights were disintegrating.

Powderly and other national officers, who had seen labor's costly defeats during the seventies, hated strikes. They accepted their inevitability under certain circumstances and set up machinery for collecting funds to fight them, but their real hope was that American society could be so reformed that these conflicts would be unnecessary. Their program was exceedingly vague. They talked much of the need for settling wage issues by peaceful conference between labor representatives and employers or by arbitration, but they found few industrialists who were ready to deal with them on this basis. They talked also of escaping entirely from the wage system through the organization of cooperatives. Local assemblies often operated cooperative stores, and a number of small producers' cooperatives were attempted—with the usual discouraging results. Actual experiments with cooperation were less common than earnest discussion of the principles involved. Indeed, yeasty debate was probably the most characteristic activity of the Knights.

However, the almost universal demand for the eight-hour day and for higher wages—or at least resistance to wage cuts—often required the Knights to turn from talk to action. When local or district assemblies proclaimed boycotts against employers accused of oppressing their workers, the weapon proved extremely effective. In 1885 boycotting reached the epidemic stage: a survey of that year revealed that 196 boycotts had been instituted—mostly by the Knights of Labor—and that a large proportion of them had been successful in forcing concessions from the employers under attack. But the boycott was a two-edged sword, injuring the workers as well as the capitalists. It was, moreover, an activity likely to bring arrest and punishment to organizers whom unsympathetic courts found guilty of conspiracy in restraint of trade.

The Knights became increasingly involved in strikes. In 1883 the telegraphers organized themselves as National District Assembly No. 45 and rushed into a strike against Jay Gould's Western Union. The telegraphers were completely defeated and had to submit to the ironclad pledge in order to get their jobs back. This was a serious setback for the Knights, but their stock went up in 1884 and 1885 when workers affiliated with the order were victorious in several well-publicized strikes.

Although these gains resulted more from fortuitous circumstances than good generalship, the Knights gained an extraordinary degree of prestige from them. So many workers joined the order and so many local assemblies were organized that—in Powderly's words—"our general office was too small to hold the force necessary to open the envelopes and take care of the money sent in as charter fees." [1] Orders went out to suspend organizing activities, but the snowballing growth of the Knights could hardly be halted. From July 1, 1885, to July 1, 1886, membership jumped from 100,000 to 700,000.

The Debacle

The Knights' sudden prosperity was their undoing. The thousands who joined the order in the middle eighties had little interest in its long-term objectives. Local and district assemblies rushed into strikes and then appealed to their brother Knights for assistance. Poorly organized and poorly financed, most of these contests had disastrous results. Employers—no less impressed than the

[1] *The Path I Trod, The Autobiography of Terence V. Powderly* (Columbia University Press, New York, 1940), 143.

workers with the growth of the Knights—were determined to break the power of the movement.

The first great defeat was suffered by the employees of Gould's Southwestern Railroad System. In March, 1886, District Assembly No. 101 ordered a strike to protest alleged discriminations against workers who had joined the Knights of Labor. The work stoppage spread rapidly, halting the movement of freight trains over 5,000 miles of track in Missouri, Kansas, Arkansas, Indian Territory, and Nebraska. The strikers—largely shopmen, yardmen, and section gangs—resorted to desperate tactics, sabotaging engines, wrecking trains, and threatening engineers and conductors who opposed them. But Gould's lieutenants had expected trouble—perhaps had provoked it—and were prepared to fight back. Through the vigorous use of strikebreakers, Pinkerton guards, and militia the strike was decisively broken.

The middle class's growing fear of the labor movement was much increased by simultaneous strikes for the eight-hour day which swept the country in May, 1886. Since the earlier campaign to secure the shorter workday through legislation had been so disappointing in its results, a school of thought had for years advocated a national general strike to achieve the goal. In 1884 the Federation of Organized Trades and Labor Unions had passed the following resolution: "Resolved . . . that eight hours shall constitute a legal day's labor from and after May 1, 1886, and that we recommend to labor organizations through this jurisdiction that they so direct their laws as to conform to this resolution by the time named." How the eight-hour day was to be secured was not specified, and the resolution at first brought little response. But during the labor excitement of the early months of 1886 the idea of a mass movement to achieve the shorter working day suddenly took vigorous root.

Powderly watched the rise of the new eight-hour movement with serious misgivings. He did not believe that the workers had achieved sufficient organization for the simultaneous strikes to succeed. If the national officers identified themselves with the movement and it failed, the Knights would suffer a damaging blow to their prestige. Moreover, they would be undertaking these risks in support of a project that had originated with a rival organization. On March 13, 1886, Powderly sent out the following secret circular:

> The executive officers of the Knights of Labor have never fixed upon the first of May for a strike of any kind, and they will not do so until the proper time arrives and the word goes forth from the General Assembly. No assembly of the Knights of Labor must strike for the eight-hour system on May first under the impression that they are obeying orders from headquarters, for such an order was not, and will not, be given. Neither employer or employee are educated to the needs and necessities for the short hour plan.[1]

Discipline being what it was among the Knights, Powderly's order did not stop many local assemblies from continuing to plan a May Day demonstration, but it prevented the national officers from exercising any kind of leadership of the

[1] T. V. Powderly, *Thirty Years of Labor, 1859–1889* (Columbus, Ohio, 1890), 476.

movement. Nor was generalship forthcoming from the faltering Federation of Organized Trades and Labor Unions.

Neither businessmen nor labor leaders knew quite what to expect on May 1, 1886. In many ways the day proved to be an anticlimax. There were parades, speeches, and work stoppages but no general action. In the whole country about 190,000 workers went out on strike; of these only 42,000 secured the eight-hour day by their action. About 150,000 other workers secured a promise of shorter hours without striking, but most of these gains proved temporary. Many employers conceded the shorter hours only on condition that others took like action. This left the way open for them to reimpose the longer hours when, as was usually the case, their competitors continued on the old basis.

The greatest eight-hour demonstrations occurred in Chicago, where 80,000 workers participated in the strikes and demonstrations. Although May Day itself passed without serious clashes, the excitement exacerbated the already bad relations between local capital and labor. Since the railroad strikes of 1877 the workers of Chicago had regarded the police as their enemies. A minority faction among the city's socialists had lost faith both in the ballot box and in the trade-unions as solutions for the grievances of labor. Through radical newspapers and street speeches they urged the workers to secure arms to defend themselves against the assaults of their enemies and to hasten the millennial day of revolution. Condemned by the leaders of the Socialist Labor party, these extremists—sometimes called "social-revolutionaries," sometimes "anarchists"—were loosely linked with similar groups in other American cities and in Europe. The revolutionaries were not numerous, but their ceaseless activity had given them some influence in Chicago labor circles. This well-known circumstance increased the uneasiness with which the Chicago business community regarded the eight-hour demonstrations.

Serious trouble, so obviously brewing, actually erupted out of a situation only remotely related to the eight-hour demonstrations. On May 3 a clash occurred near the McCormick reaper factory between McCormick workers who had been on strike for two months and "scabs" whom the company had hired. The police, summoned to the scene, used guns and clubs with such vigor that one striker was killed and many others were injured. To protest against this brutality, a mass meeting was held near Haymarket Square on the night of May 4. A crowd of only twelve or thirteen hundred turned out, and three-quarters of these deserted the meeting when a drizzle of rain began to fall. Although the gathering was addressed by some of the city's best known anarchists, their speeches were comparatively mild. The meeting continued for over two hours without incident and was almost over when it was suddenly interrupted by the arrival of a company of 180 policemen. The crowd, or what was left of it, was beginning to disperse at the order of the officers when suddenly a bomb was hurled at the policemen. Exploding with a frightful blast, it killed one officer instantly and injured six others so badly that they died later. Over sixty more policemen received lesser injuries, and one member of the crowd was killed and many others were injured in the ensuing charge of the officers.

The Haymarket affair shocked Chicago and the entire nation. The police, determined to avenge their fellow officers, raided the homes and meeting places of all known radicals. Many arrests were made and eight anarchists were eventually brought to trial for murder. There was no evidence that any of them had actually thrown the bomb, but the state charged that their revolutionary propaganda inciting the workers to use force had made them accessories before the fact. Seven of the defendants were condemned to death; one was sentenced to prison for fifteen years. One of the doomed men committed suicide in his cell; two others had their sentences commuted to life imprisonment; the remaining four were hanged on November 11, 1887.

The last chapter in the grim Haymarket affair was written in 1893, when Governor John P. Altgeld pardoned the three surviving anarchists. He was bitterly condemned both for the pardons and for an accompanying message in which he criticized the original trial as unfair. The *New York Sun* spoke for millions of Americans, when it said:

> O wild Chicago, when the time
> Is ripe for ruin's deeds,
> When constitutions, courts, and laws
> Go down midst crashing creeds,
> Lift up your weak and guilty hands
> From out of the wreck of States,
> And as the crumbling towers fall down
> Write ALTGELD on your gates! [1]

Although the anarchists of the country were only a handful, the entire labor movement suffered through the Haymarket affair. Despite the timidity of Powderly and his fellow officers in the Knights of Labor, the great order was feared by businessmen as the most conspicuous embodiment of the labor threat. Employers fought the Knights vigorously over the next several months. Supporting each other through local or county employers' associations, they locked out employees who joined labor organizations and subjected them to the ironclad oath. Strike after strike was lost, and these defeats soon undermined the popularity of the Knights of Labor. Membership began to fall off after May, 1886, and declined at an accelerated pace thereafter. The order, which had had 700,000 members in 1886, had only 100,000 members in 1890. Speeding this disintegration were the growing bitterness of the struggle between the Knights and the new American Federation of Labor and internal squabbles among the Knights themselves. When Powderly was ousted as General Master Workman in 1893 and James R. Sovereign of Iowa was elected in his place, the Knights

[1] Quoted in Henry David, *The History of the Haymarket Affair: A Study in the American Social-Revolutionary and Labor Movements* (Farrar & Rinehart, Inc., New York, 1936), 497.

entered their last phase. They now disclaimed any program for advancing wages and devoted themselves exclusively to politics and to the promotion of the cooperative ideal in alliance with farmers' organizations.

Even the trade-unions found themselves weak when strongly opposed by the giant corporations of the day. During the early nineties the strongest union in the country was reputed to be the Amalgamated Association of Iron and Steel

FIG. 39. *The Homestead Riot.* Drawn by W. P. Snyder for *Harper's Weekly*, July 16, 1892. The Pinkerton guards leaving the barges after their surrender. (*Courtesy of Library of Congress.*)

Workers with over 24,000 members. The Amalgamated had for years represented its members in negotiating contracts with the Carnegie Steel Company, but in 1892 the labor spokesmen found themselves in a precarious situation. The genial Carnegie had taken himself off to Scotland and left negotiations for a new contract in the hands of the inflexible Henry Clay Frick, who proposed to reduce the pay scale. When the union leaders rejected his terms, Frick broke off negotiations and closed down the plant. In obvious preparation for the wholesale use of strikebreakers, he hired 300 Pinkerton guards. On July 6, 1892, this private army, equipped with rifles, was towed up the Monongahela River to the Carnegie mills at Homestead. Its landing was contested by the strikers, who barricaded themselves behind railroad ties and steel billets and fired upon the hated "Pinks." An all-day battle followed. Three of the guards were killed and many were wounded, and seven of the strikers lost their lives. The Pinkertons had to surrender and received rough handling from the angry mob before they finally made their retreat.

The strikers' victory was short-lived. On July 12 strong units of the state militia were moved into Homestead and martial law was proclaimed. The plant was reopened and thousands of strikebreakers took the jobs of the unionists. The Carnegie workers might have gained more sympathy had not their cause been further compromised by the violent act of an outsider. On July 23 Alexander Berkman, a Russian-born anarchist, gained admittance to Frick's office and attempted to assassinate the hated capitalist. Although shot and stabbed, Frick survived the attack. Berkman was captured and sentenced to prison for twenty-one years. The strike was called off on November 20, but only a portion of the men secured reinstatement. The Amalgamated lost its recognition not only at the Carnegie plant but in many other steel companies.

In 1894 occurred the bitter Pullman strike. Most of the Pullman Company's repair and manufacturing activity was concentrated at Pullman, Illinois, a suburb of Chicago. This town was entirely owned by the company, which built tenements and provided public buildings, parks, and playgrounds. Carefully landscaped and scrupulously maintained, Pullman enjoyed an international reputation as a model town. But the Pullman workers were increasingly irked by the excessive paternalism of the experiment. As early as 1888, the Chicago *Tribune* had warned:

> There are variety and freedom on the outside. There are monotony and surveillance on the inside. None of the "superior," or "scientific" advantages of the model city will compensate for the restrictions on the freedom of the workmen, the denial of opportunities of ownership, the heedless and vexatious parade of authority, and the sense of injustice arising from the well founded belief that the charges of the company for rent, heat, gas, water, etc. are excessive—if not extortionate. . . . Pullman may appear to be all glitter and glow, all gladness and glory to the casual visitor, but there is the deep, dark background of discontent which it would be idle to deny.[1]

During the depression of 1893 the Pullman workers suffered seriously through wage cuts and irregular employment. The company contended that the cuts were necessary in order to meet competition and to secure contracts. The workers complained that the company refused to reduce their rents, that it did not cut the salaries of its executives, and that it continued to pay 8 per cent dividends to its stockholders. Early in May, 1894, representatives of the workers presented

[1] Quoted in Almont Lindsey, *The Pullman Strike: The Story of a Unique Experiment and of a Great Labor Upheaval* (University of Chicago Press, Chicago, 1942), 91.

their grievances to the Pullman executives. The management rejected these demands and laid off three members of the grievance committee—ostensibly because of economic conditions. On May 10 about three thousand workers quit work, leaving so few hands in the shops that the company had to suspend operations.

The situation of the strikers soon became hopeless. Most of them were already in debt to the company for arrears on rent. The loss of their wages brought them to a pitiful state of destitution only partially alleviated by public and private charity. Unless they could get support, it was obvious that they would have to surrender. This was the situation when the problem was taken up by the American Railway Union, which most of the Pullman workers had joined shortly before the strike. The American Railway Union was a new organization, founded in 1893 to advance the interests of all railroad employees through one big union. Its leader was Eugene V. Debs, whose experience in the railroad brotherhoods had convinced him of the need for an organization that would include the unskilled as well as the skilled. When the Pullman Company rebuffed its proposal that the dispute should be submitted to arbitration, the American Railway Union announced that unless the Pullman workers' grievances were adjusted before noon of June 26, the union members would refuse to handle Pullman cars and equipment on any railroad.

But the railroad men found themselves opposed by a most formidable combination. Twenty-four railroads entering Chicago were linked by a General Managers' Association, which resolved to support the Pullman Company by instantly discharging any employee who refused to handle its equipment. Trouble began when switchmen refused to throw switches for trains containing Pullman cars. When the defiant workers were discharged, most other railroad employees left their jobs in protest. By June 28 almost 18,000 Chicago railroad workers were on strike. Although the great Illinois transportation hub remained the center of the struggle, attempts to carry out the boycott precipitated parallel events in many other parts of the country. On June 29 the *New York Times* asserted that the strike had "assumed the proportions of the greatest battle between labor and capital that has ever been inaugurated in the United States."

The Railway Union showed great strength during the earlier rounds of the conflict. By July 5, 13 railroads had been compelled to suspend all service in and out of Chicago, and 10 others were operating passenger trains only. Although disturbances in the early days of the strike were few and well within the ability of the police to handle, the managers did their best to make it appear that Federal intervention was necessary. They found a willing ally in the Attorney General of the United States, Richard Olney. On July 2 the Federal courts in Chicago issued an omnibus injunction forbidding Eugene V. Debs and other officers and members of the American Railway Union to interfere with trains engaged in carrying mail or interstate commerce or to attempt to induce employees of the railroads to refuse to perform their duties. When the Federal marshals reported the gathering of mobs who refused to disperse at the reading of the injunction, President Grover Cleveland ordered Federal troops to Chicago—a step bitterly criticized by the Illinois governor, John P. Altgeld, since he had made no request for Federal help and considered the state militia entirely capable of dealing with the situation. The greatest disorders followed rather than preceded the soldiers' appearance upon the scene. On July 6, mobs—composed mostly of boys and hoodlums—set the torch to hundreds of railroad cars and destroyed railroad property valued at $340,000.

The railroad workers were unable to continue their resistance to the forces now mobilized against them. Debs and many other strike leaders were arrested, and the trains began to move under the protection of the soldiers. By July 13, schedules were almost back to normal, and on August 2 the Pullman Company began to resume work in its shops. The great strike had failed completely. Not only did the Pullman workers have to accept the wage scale which had precipitated the rebellion, but several hundred were refused reinstatement and replaced with new men. Those who were taken back had to surrender their membership cards in the American Railway Union and to sign a contract stipulating that they would have nothing to do with this or any other union. Many of the railroad strikers were also denied reemployment. Completely demoralized, the American Railway Union finally dissolved in 1897. Debs was sentenced to six months imprisonment for contempt of court in failing to observe the omnibus injunction.

Henry George and Edward Bellamy

While the wage earners struggled to improve their lot through organized bargaining, the new industrial order was twice confronted with effective challenges on the intellectual front.

Henry George, son of middle-class Philadelphia parents, received only a scanty formal education, but he had rich opportunities to observe the rapid growth of the American economy. At the age of nineteen—after he had already visited Australia and India as a sailor and had learned the printing trade in a Philadelphia shop—George worked his passage to California, where he spent the next twenty years as a gold hunter, laborer, printer, and struggling journalist. Knowing well both the East Coast with its festering slums and the West with its buoyant frontier spirit, Henry George became obsessed with the paradox of the country's increasing want which seemed to accompany increasing wealth. In 1879 the California journalist published his famous book, *Progress and Poverty.* Developing the problem in his introduction, he wrote:

> . . . In the United States it is clear that squalor and misery, and the vice and crimes that spring from them, everywhere increase as the village grows to the city, and the march of development brings the advantages of the improved methods of production and exchange. It is in the older and richer sections of the Union that pauperism and distress among the working classes are becoming most painfully apparent. If there is less deep poverty in San

Francisco than in New York, is it not because San Francisco is yet behind New York in all that both cities are striving for? When San Francisco reaches the point where New York now is, who can doubt that there will also be ragged and bare-footed children on her streets?

This association of poverty with progress is the great enigma of our times. . . . It is the riddle which the Sphinx of Fate puts to our civilization, and which not to answer is to be destroyed. So long as all the increased wealth which modern progress brings goes but to build up great fortunes, to increase luxury and make sharper the contrast between the House of Have and the House of Want, progress is not real and cannot be permanent.[1]

Henry George found the answer to the riddle in the private ownership of land. Like sunlight, air, and water, land is, he believed, a natural resource to which all men should have equal access. Men who improve the land through their labor have a right to property in those improvements, but the land itself belongs to society. Poverty is caused by monopolists, who gain control of the land and grow rich, not through any effort of their own, but through the nation's expanding population and the increasing need for soil, timber, and minerals. As he simplified the situation:

Poverty deepens as wealth increases, and wages are forced down while productive power grows, because land, which is the source of all wealth and the field of all labor, is monopolized. To extirpate poverty, to make wages what justice commands they should be, the full earnings of the laborer, we must therefore substitute for the individual ownership of land a common ownership.[2]

Wholesale expropriation of land could be avoided by the simple expedient of having the government appropriate through taxation the entire economic rent of the land, that is, tax away all land value created by the growth of population and not by the expenditure of labor in improvements. Not only would this policy compel monopolists to make available to small holders millions of acres of unimproved land held as a speculation, but it would permit the abandonment of all other forms of taxation, freeing the productive efforts of both manufacturers and workers. Thus was launched the idea of the "single tax" as the panacea for all the evils of the new industrial order.

Both Henry George's diagnosis and his prescription were too simple. But *Progress and Poverty* was a bold indictment of the monopoly of natural resources during a generation of wholesale grab. Moving to New York in the early eighties, George secured a wide following both in the United States and abroad. In 1886 a new party composed of labor leaders and middle-class reformers nominated him for mayor of New York. He was defeated, but his vigorous campaign threw a genuine scare into the dominant Democratic machine. During the nineties his influence continued to grow, and many "single tax" or "land and labor" clubs were organized to promote his ideas. He died suddenly

[1] Henry George, *Progress and Poverty: An Inquiry Into the Cause of Industrial Depressions and of Increase of Want with Increase of Wealth: The Remedy* (Robert Schalkenbach Foundation, New York, 1940), 9–10.

[2] *Ibid.*, 328.

in 1897 in the midst of another energetic campaign for the New York mayoralty.

The passion for social justice which Henry George had inspired was given further stimulus by Edward Bellamy. Born in a Baptist parsonage in rural Massachusetts, Bellamy turned to literature after earlier experience as a lawyer and journalist. His first novels and short stories gained little notice, but *Looking Backward, 2000–1887* (1888) proved fascinating to several hundred thousand readers. It was the story of Julian West, a wealthy Bostonian who was so thoroughly put to sleep by a hypnotist in 1887 that he did not awake until the year 2000. For the romantic reader Bellamy related Julian's strange experience in falling in love with the great-granddaughter of his nineteenth century fiancee. For the curious he predicted some of the inventions of the twentieth century. But for the serious reader *Looking Backward's* unique fascination lay in the contrast between the America of 1887 and the possible America of 2000. The latter was a far happier society without poverty, crime, or cutthroat competition. Youth was reserved for education, middle age and old age for pleasant cultural activities. All necessary work was done by men between the ages of twenty-one and forty-five who served in the industrial army. Each man did what he could do best. Those who performed the heaviest labor were compensated by working the shortest hours. No wages were paid, and each person received an equal share in the total production of the nation.

Bellamy's type of socialism appealed to thousands of Americans who would have been repelled by the class struggle, the violent revolution, and the proletarian dictatorship postulated by Karl Marx. The socialized state of *Looking Backward* had been achieved through peaceful social evolution and the application of social intelligence. In Bellamy's words:

> . . . The movement toward the conduct of business by larger and larger aggregations of capital, the tendency toward monopolies, which had been so desperately and vainly resisted, was recognized at last, in its true significance, as a process which only needed to complete its logical evolution to open a golden future to humanity.
>
> Early in the last century the evolution was completed by the final consolidation of the entire capital of the nation. The industry and commerce of the country, ceasing to be conducted by a set of irresponsible corporations and syndicates of private persons at their caprice and for their profit, were intrusted to a single syndicate representing the people, to be conducted in the common interest for the common profit.[1]

Inspired by *Looking Backward,* hundreds of local Bellamy or Nationalist clubs were organized. Bellamy himself devoted all his efforts to the movement. For several years he published a magazine called *The New Nation,* and in 1897 he wrote *Equality,* a sequel to his famous novel. A year later Bellamy died, but his ideas continued to enjoy great popularity, particularly with idealistic youth. Like *Progress and Poverty, Looking Backward* had challenged the idea that all

[1] Edward Bellamy, *Looking Backward, 2000–1887* (World Publishing, Cleveland, Ohio, 1945), 61.

was well with American society during the seventies and eighties. While faith in the specific programs of George and Bellamy did not become widespread, the two men had helped to inspire a zeal for reform that was to flower in the progressive movement during the first two decades of the twentieth century.

Unionism: Conservative and Radical

The growth and decline of the trade-unions continued to follow the ups and downs of the economic cycle. Following a period of defeats and losses during the depression of 1893, the labor movement displayed new vigor during the business boom that began in 1897. The American Federation of Labor, organized in 1886, had only 278,000 members in 1898, but its membership doubled in the next two years and then trebled in the next four. In 1904 the AFL had 1,676,200 members, organized in 114 international unions,[1] 828 directly affiliated locals, 549 city centrals, and 29 state federations.

President of the American Federation of Labor in 1904—as he had been every year but one since its organization—was Samuel Gompers. This hard-headed labor executive was born in London in 1850, the son of an East End cigarmaker. The family emigrated to America in 1863, and young Samuel followed his father's trade in the tenements of New York. He joined a union as early as 1864 and took a prominent part in the reorganization of the seventies which made the International Cigarmakers' Union a model for the new unionism. Hitherto weak and shifting in membership, the new unions achieved stability through high initiation fees and dues, sickness and death benefits, strong disciplinary powers of the international officers, and conservatively administered strike funds.

Brought up in this tradition of unionism, Gompers had little patience with the visionary projects that had captured the enthusiasms of Sylvis and Powderly. He believed, so he said, in "pure and simple unionism." In his youth he had toyed with the ideas of Marx and other socialists, but he perceived that these doctrines had so little appeal for the majority of Americans that it would be suicidal for the organized labor movement to commit itself to a socialist program. He was equally opposed to the formation of an independent labor party, believing that the workers' best interests lay in keeping the labor vote independent so that it could be cast for or against individual candidates. Since Gompers believed that the government was as likely to be controlled by the enemies of labor as by its friends, he opposed measures that would make the status of labor dependent on legislation. He opposed laws that would compel corporations to deal with unions or impose compulsory arbitration. This hostility to legislative remedies was far from complete, and the AFL eventually made many demands upon Congress and the state legislatures.

[1] An international union was composed of all the various local unions of a particular craft in the United States and Canada.

But the AFL placed its highest priority on objectives that could be secured directly from employers—higher wages, shorter hours, and job security. The various unions endeavored to gain recognition as bargaining agents for their members and were eager to enter upon contracts that would guarantee working conditions. The AFL urged a conservative strike policy, but left its constituent unions complete autonomy in this as in most other matters. The boycott was retained as a labor weapon but an attempt was made to control its use.

Unionism seemed to be gaining a new respectability by 1900. Governors and congressmen accepted invitations to address union conventions; state legislatures enacted many of the measures which the AFL endorsed. The Civic Federation, started in Chicago in 1896, was organized on a national basis in 1900. In this organization capitalists, like Mark Hanna, John D. Rockefeller, Jr., and Charles M. Schwab, civic leaders, like Grover Cleveland, Archbishop Ireland, and President Eliot of Harvard, and labor leaders, like Samuel Gompers and John Mitchell of the United Mine Workers, attempted to promote industrial peace by recognition of labor's right to organize, by promotion of trade agreements, and by the settlement of disputes through conciliation and mediation. When a great coal strike in 1902 threatened to develop into a national emergency, President Theodore Roosevelt set a new precedent for Federal intervention by compelling the unwilling operators to accept arbitration.

But many employers continued to follow a strong antiunion policy. Strikes against the new United States Steel Corporation were unsuccessful, and most of the other large corporations followed a policy of refusal to bargain collectively. The smaller manufacturers combated the unions through local employers' associations, trade associations, and the National Association of Manufacturers. A particularly effective weapon against strikers and boycotters had been developed in the injunction. Some state or Federal judge could usually be found to issue an order forbidding the strike leaders to interfere with the trade or business of the employer. If the union men violated the injunction, they could be fined or imprisoned for contempt of court without jury trial by the same judge who had issued the injunction. Federal judges were generous with such injunctions, usually basing their orders on the Sherman Act, which prohibited conspiracies in restraint of trade.

Spokesmen for labor were particularly bitter that the antitrust law which had been singularly ineffective in controlling the activities of big business should be thus used to hamstring the unions. In the Danbury Hatters' case not only the officers but the individual members of a striking union were held liable for triple damages for losses sustained by the company through a nationwide boycott. In the Buck's Stove case Gompers was sentenced to prison for contempt of court in ignoring an injunction against listing the Buck's Stove and Range Company of St. Louis in the "We Don't Patronize" list of the *American Federationist.* Labor secured some protection from these judicial attacks by the Clayton Act of 1914, which declared that "the labor of a human being is not a commodity or article of commerce," that labor organizations should not be held conspiracies in restraint of trade, and that injunctions should not be issued in labor disputes unless necessary to prevent irreparable damage to property.

While conservative unionism in the AFL pattern struggled to secure recognition, a radical minority attempted to launch a movement dedicated to far different ends. In 1897 the Western Federation of Miners, already notorious for the violence of its tactics, seceded from the American Federation of Labor and sought to organize a new national movement that would be frankly revolutionary in its objectives. At first these efforts had little success, but in 1905 the leaders of the Western Federation met in a secret meeting with other radicals like Daniel De Leon, the "socialist pope" who dominated the Socialist Labor party, and Eugene V. Debs, who led the more moderate Socialist party, organized in 1900. These men and a number of others organized the Industrial Workers of the World. The most aggressive leader in the new movement was "Big Bill" Haywood, a one-eyed giant who had been a cowboy, a miner, and a fighting organizer for the Western Federation of Miners and for the Socialist party. In the preamble to its constitution the I.W.W. proclaimed both its revolutionary purpose and its hostility to the AFL:

> The working class and the employing class have nothing in common. . . . Between these two classes a struggle must go on, until all the toilers come together on the political as well as on the industrial field, and take and hold that which they produce by their labor through an economic organization of the working class without affiliation to any political party. . . . The rapid gathering of wealth and the centering of the management of industries into fewer and fewer hands make the trade unions unable to cope with the ever-growing power of the employing class, because the trade unions foster a state of things which allows one set of workers to be pitted against another set of workers in the same industry, thereby helping defeat one another in wage wars. The trade unions aid the employing class to mislead the workers into the belief that the working class has interests in common with their employers. . . .

The attempt of the I.W.W. to weld all workers, skilled and unskilled, into one big union had only limited success. Membership in the organization probably never exceeded 60,000 and the movement soon lost the support of Debs and other socialists who opposed the tendency to embrace syndicalism and to reject political action. Despite its numerical weakness the I.W.W. possessed a militancy that brought wide publicity to its activities. Its greatest strength was achieved in the West among miners, construction workers, lumberjacks, and migratory harvest hands—laborers so poorly paid and so badly treated that they were ready for desperate tactics. The I.W.W. also invaded the East and won its most striking victory in 1912, when the unorganized textile workers of Lawrence, Massachusetts, rebelled against intolerable conditions and gladly accepted the leadership of the I.W.W.

But the majority of American workers feared the taint of association with the hated "wobblies." By 1914 the movement had already passed its peak of power.

Its disintegration was speeded by the draconic penalties imposed on its leaders for their antiwar activities during World War I.

After futile earlier protests most American workers now accepted the finality of the industrial revolution. The machine and the corporation had come to stay and the workers demanded not control of the system but a just share in the wealth that it was creating. Wages, hours, and job security were the things that mattered. The most dangerous element in the situation had been labor exasperation at the apparent alliance between employers and the governments which controlled city police, state militia, and Federal troops. But the feeling that the state was an alien and hostile force was considerably reduced by the progressive movement. In governors like Altgeld of Illinois and La Follette of Wisconsin, in presidents like Roosevelt and Wilson, the workers could see executives attempting to deal justly with both capital and labor, and some of the worst abuses of the old order were remedied by workmen's compensation and factory regulatory laws. American laborers in 1914 were far from content with their status, but most of them wanted to carry on their struggle for advancement within the framework of the American system.

Chapter 23. Protests from the Farmer

The industrialization of the country profoundly altered rural life. Each decade found city and country more closely bound. The great centers of population depended for all of their food and many of their raw materials on the work of the farmer. He, in turn, became steadily less self-sufficient. He clothed his family in factory-made garments and worked his farm with factory-made tools. Producing constantly larger crops through the miracles of mechanization, he looked not only to American cities but to those of Europe for his markets. Railroads and steamships linked farmers with consumers thousands of miles away.

Growing crops for distant markets involved many hazards. To the whims of nature, which had always made the farmer's lot an uncertain one, were now added a score of other factors over which he had little control. His success or failure might depend on transportation charges, margins of profit, speculation on the exchanges, foreign tariffs or embargoes, or crop conditions on other continents. When prices rose, the ambitious farmer borrowed money to buy more land and machinery. When prices fell, he often lost his property through inability to pay his taxes and interest charges. An individualist in an economy in which more and more activity was corporate, the farmer felt the full brunt of hard times. He sought desperately to fix the responsibility for his misfortunes and focused his wrath at one time on railroads and middlemen and at another on politicians and the gold standard.

Commercial Agriculture

In the decade before the Civil War the Middle West and the East had been firmly linked by rail. Illinois had become the greatest producer of both wheat and corn. Throughout the new agricultural heartland large and progressive farms were now harvesting and threshing by machine.

The Civil War accentuated these trends. The army stripped the rural districts of their best workers, leaving behind the old, the very young, the weak, and the women. Yet the demand for food was greater than ever. Through its wasteful purchasing methods the Union Army bought so much that the loss of southern markets was hardly felt. Moreover, crop failures in England and on the Continent resulted in the export of American wheat and flour in unprecedented quantities. To the spur of large demand was added that of sharply rising prices resulting from the issuance of greenbacks and general wartime inflation.

The need to expand production at a time when labor was extremely scarce brought a flood of orders for farm machinery.

After the war manufacturers had little to fear from the farmers' traditional hostility to new methods. The agriculturists were eager to buy as many machines as they could afford—and sometimes more. Inventors patented hundreds of improvements, and farmers thronged state and county fairs, studying the new machinery exhibited each year.

Plow design was radically altered to meet new soil conditions and the larger acreage of western farms. In 1877 James Oliver perfected the chilled-iron plow, whose hardened surface scoured the prairie soil with an efficiency rivaling that of the earlier steel plows of John Deere. The development of sulky plows made it possible for farmers to ride rather than to plod all day through the furrows. New gang plows turned several furrows at once. In the great wheat fields of the West these moved across the countryside like an army. The scene is thus described by the novelist Frank Norris:

> The plows, thirty-five in number, each drawn by its team of ten, stretched in an interminable line, nearly a quarter of a mile in length. . . . They were arranged, as it were, *en echelon,* not in file—not one directly behind the other, but each succeeding plow its own width further in the field than the one in front of it. Each of these plows held five shears, so that when the entire company was in motion, one hundred and seventy-five burrows were made at the same instant. At a distance, the plows resembled a great column of field artillery. Each driver was in his place, his glance alternating between his horses and the foreman nearest at hand. Other foremen, in their buggies or buckboards, were at intervals along the line, like battery lieutenants.[1]

Despite the invention of seed drills, broadcast sowing dominated prairie agriculture until the seventies. Thereafter, drills and other automatic planters came rapidly into use. Plows, harrows, and drills were sometimes ingeniously combined. Before 1900 steam tractors pulled through California wheat fields machines that plowed and planted 13-foot strips in a single operation. Such gargantuas proved of limited utility, however, and most of the country's plowing and planting equipment continued to be drawn by horses.

Harvesting was still a critical operation. When wheat was ready, it had to be cut and gathered within a few days or be ruined. Before the Civil War, reaping machines could cut as fast as horses could move across the field, but it required many hands to gather and to bind the grain. The Marsh harvester, patented in 1868, speeded the operation because it deposited the grain on a platform where the binders could ride and do their work. But it was still a hand process, requiring two or three men on each machine. Inventors struggled with the problem of developing a harvester that would do its binding automatically. A wire binder, patented in 1873, was unpopular, because the pieces of wire were likely to dam-

[1] Frank Norris, *The Octopus, a Story of California* (Doubleday, Page, New York, 1901), 95–96.

age threshing machines or cattle eating the straw. The much more satisfactory twine binder was invented by John F. Appleby in 1878.

Threshing machinery was steadily improved. The combine that harvested, threshed, and bagged the grain as it was drawn across the field by a steam tractor was developed in California about 1880. It was a fascinating machine capable of filling a 150-pound bag with wheat in only twenty seconds, but the combine was too heavy and expensive for general use. Not until 1910 was it employed east of the Rocky Mountains and then only in smaller machines pulled by horses or gasoline tractors.

Each crop presented its peculiar problems. Corn was well adapted for mechanical planting and cultivating, but corn-harvesting equipment was crude and ineffective until a number of useful machines were developed in the nineties. Before the Civil War, haymaking had been speeded by mowing machines and horse-drawn rakes; later progress consisted of the development of mechanical loaders and conveyers to transfer the hay from windrow to wagon and from wagon to loft. The dairy industry was greatly assisted by the invention of centrifugal cream separators and testers and the improvement of churns. But some agricultural tasks defied all efforts at mechanization. The great southern staples continued to demand many hours of backbreaking manual labor. To produce an acre of tobacco required almost 253 hours of human labor in 1896, and an acre of cotton took 78¾ hours. This contrasted with 15 hours per acre for corn and 4 hours per acre for hay. Wheat continued to be the most spectacular example of the new age. By the old methods an acre of wheat had demanded over 61 hours of labor from plowing to threshing; by the new methods 3⅓ hours sufficed.

Mechanization encouraged attempts to farm on a scale comparable to the great factories of the day. The famous "bonanzas" were wheat farms opened up during the seventies and eighties in the fertile Red River Valley of the Dakotas and Minnesota. The area was too far north for winter wheat but ideal for spring wheat, from which good flour could now be made by important new milling methods developed at Minneapolis. Estates of fabulous size developed: those owned by the Grandin brothers totaled 61,000 acres—nearly five times the area of Manhattan Island; the even larger holdings of Oliver Dalrymple amounted to about 100,000 acres. Scores of others ranged from 5,000 to 40,000 acres. Like the great industries of the day these gigantic enterprises increased their profits by wholesale purchasing and special railroad rates.

But bonanza farming prospered only under favoring circumstances. During the late eighties and nineties the great farms were hard hit by a succession of bad harvests and poor prices. Many of the Dakota bonanzas disintegrated, although large-scale and highly mechanized wheat growing continued in California.

Much more typical of Middle Western agriculture were the farms of 160 to 320 acres that abounded throughout the prairie states. Although a more diversified agriculture was practiced on these family farms than on the great wheat or livestock ranches, they depended heavily on producing staples for distant markets. Under their influence the wheat and corn belts continued to move west. Illinois's preeminence in wheat continued until the eighties, when Minnesota took the lead. By 1914 Kansas and North Dakota were the greatest wheat-producing states. In corn Illinois led all other states for almost half a century but was eventually passed by Iowa and Kansas.

For the states of the Northeast, competition with the fertile prairie states was almost impossible. The eastern farmers had to concentrate on products in which proximity to the great cities gave them a decisive advantage. Their most obvious opportunity was in providing milk. Typical was the case of Connecticut, whose milk production jumped from 6 million gallons in 1870 to 33 million in 1900—a fivefold increase in a generation. The growing of vegetables and fruits—particularly potatoes and apples—was also greatly expanded. The farmers of New York were particularly successful in readjusting to the new conditions. At the end of the nineteenth century there were more dairy cattle in New York than in any other state of the Union; New York also led all rivals in growing hay and potatoes and was second only to California in the production of fruit. Pennsylvania made a similar adjustment, but New England with its less fertile soil had a more difficult time. There the abandonment of farms and the drift of the rural population to the cities was so pronounced as to arouse wide comment. A song of the day counseled youth thus:

Come, boys, I have something to tell you,
Come near, I would whisper it low;
You are thinking of leaving the homestead.
Don't be in a hurry to go.
The city has many attractions,
But think of the vices and sins,
When once in the vortex of fashion,
How soon the course downward begins.

Chorus:
Stay on the farm, stay on the farm,
Though profits come in rather slow.
Stay on the farm, stay on the farm;
Don't be in a hurry to go.[1]

But the trend was too strong to be halted by appeals to sentiment.

Grievances of the Farmers

Despite the problems with which the eastern farmer wrestled, the loudest agrarian protest came from the West and the South. On the prairies life tended to extremes. Summers were hotter than elsewhere, and winters were colder;

[1] Quoted in Fred A. Shannon, *The Farmer's Last Frontier: Agriculture, 1860–1897* (Farrar & Rinehart, Inc., New York, 1945), 249.

droughts were drier and grasshoppers more voracious. The psychological climate seemed equally uneven. Upsweeps of the economic cycle were greeted with an excess of optimism; depressions brought unparalleled despair.

The major cycles were clear: the Civil War and European shortages combined to bring an agricultural boom during the sixties; this broke in the early seventies and was followed by several years of agricultural depression; the late seventies and early eighties brought another inflationary rise, only to be followed from 1887 to 1897 by a decade of disaster. But the situation was complicated by other factors. The general trend was toward great expansion of acreage and production. In 1866 the devastated South produced only 2,000,000 bales of cotton on 6,300,-000 acres; in 1898 over 11,000,000 bales were grown and almost 25,000,000 acres devoted to the crop. Wheat production expanded almost as much. In 1866 152,000,000 bushels were grown on 15,000,000 acres; in 1898 675,000,000 bushels were raised on 44,000,000 acres. Much of this increase was normal. The population of the United States doubled during this period, and that of industrial Europe was also growing rapidly. But American agriculture, nevertheless, tended to expand more rapidly than the markets on which it depended. Particularly was this true after Russian, Argentine, and Australian wheat began to enter the world market. These circumstances were reflected in a downward drift in prices. Wheat fluctuated from year to year, but the general trend was clear. In 1866 a bushel of wheat brought its producer $1.53; in 1898 it brought only 58 cents.

Farmers, being human, were not given to dispassionate analysis of sagging agricultural prices. They sought to place the blame not on invisible factors but on visible devils—land monopolists, railroad magnates, wholesalers, speculators, bankers, and politicians. Nor was their indictment without justice. All of the accused had taken more than a legitimate profit in dealing with rural customers.

In an earlier chapter the circumstances that rendered the Homestead Act so largely illusory have been discussed. The farmers were bitterly critical of the abuses which left them at the mercy of speculators, who had acquired large sections of the public domain either free or at bargain prices and had then profited at the expense of the real homemakers. Particularly subject to attack were foreigners, who had acquired tremendous holdings of American land, and the railroads, which were accused not only of holding their own land off the market in order to get better prices but of preventing the disposal of the government land lying within their sphere of influence.

The ill will created by the railroads' land policies was magnified by their arbitrary rate charges. The farmer rarely had any alternative to shipping his produce by a particular line. Unable to bargain or to demand rebates, it was his unhappy lot to pay the high rates which the railroads needed to make up for the losses sustained on competitive business. The farmers were also embittered by the influence which the railroads exercised over politicians and by the financial skulduggery which resulted in large losses to rural investors in railroad securities.

The small return which the farmer's labor brought him was also attributable to abuses in marketing. The wheat elevators were great storehouses for the grain awaiting shipment. Some of the elevators were owned by the railroads; others were operated by powerful firms. Some were in the great market cities like Chicago; others were in the growing areas. Everywhere the farmers protested against the elevators' excessive charges and arbitrary methods of grading. Farmers complained also of the reckless speculation that sometimes characterized trading in the Chicago Grain Exchange and of the close alliance of the great packers, which controlled the prices they received for their cattle and hogs.

While one combination of factors reduced to a minimum the farmer's cash return for his crops, another resulted in his paying maximum prices for all he had to buy. Selling his surpluses in a world market, the farmer received no real help from the tariff, yet he paid heavily in higher prices for the protection enjoyed by the manufacturers. Farm machinery was sold at extortionate prices. Manufacturers' agents collected high commissions and arranged credit terms which bled rural customers in interest charges.

The farmer's need for loans and his inadequate facilities for securing them were at the root of many of his troubles. Since the $50,000 capital necessary for establishing a national bank under the Act of 1863 was available only in the larger towns, many farmers were miles away from such an institution. Moreover, even when the rural citizen could get to a national bank, he was likely to have difficulty in borrowing as much as he needed on terms that he could afford to pay. The Middle Western states tried to meet the situation by permitting the establishment of state banks with as little as $5,000 capital, but these institutions were too poor to make enough loans to serve the needs of the agricultural districts, particularly at crop-moving time. One result was that the farmer, finding it impossible to hold his produce off the market, had to sell it as soon as it was harvested for whatever it would bring from the nearest elevator or buyer. Another was that the farmer had to accept the hard credit terms offered him by merchants, commission men, or implement dealers.

The high interest rates of the West appealed to thousands who had money to invest. Private loan companies opened little offices in the East to gather in the savings of the thrifty, and in the Middle West solicitors sought out the farmers who wanted to borrow. By 1889 there were about two hundred of these mortgage companies doing business in Kansas and Nebraska. The result was unfortunate. In the belief that such mortgages on fertile prairie farms offered a particularly safe investment, the loan agents encouraged the farmers to borrow freely. But these debts proved much easier to contract than to carry. In addition to 6 or 7 per cent interest on the principal, the farmer had to pay commissions and fees that brought the actual charges to 10 per cent or more on real-estate mortgages and as high as 18 per cent on chattel mortgages. The inflationary bubble burst during 1886–1887. Thousands of farmers were unable to meet their interest and principal payments. Mortgages were foreclosed, often with severe loss to the loan companies. Some of the dispossessed farmers remained as tenants on land which they had once owned; more of them moved out of the section. The disaster fell particularly on western districts in Kansas, Nebraska, and South Dakota—a semiarid region into which thousands of optimists had moved during the early eighties when unusual rainfall encouraged a belief that a permanent change of weather conditions had occurred. Badly burned, the loan companies reversed their policies or went out of business. Throughout the nineties the farmers found it hard to borrow money on any terms.

Struggling to meet fixed charges with declining income, the farmers took intense interest in the money problem. Remembering the high agricultural prices of Civil War days, when the country was flooded with greenbacks, they believed that new issues of money would solve their problems. For thirty years the struggle between inflationists and deflationists was a central issue in national politics. The continued domination of the government by the conservative, hard-money faction added greatly to the farmer's sense of grievance.

The Granger Movement

As individuals the farmers could do no more than grumble; in cooperation they might exercise tremendous power. The lesson was plain for all to read. Yet many years were to elapse before the isolation and suspicion of the agriculturists could be sufficiently curbed to make them an effective force. In the interim they learned to combine for temporary purposes, but their organizations lacked staying power.

A long stride toward joint action was taken during the early seventies, when farmers by the thousand joined a fraternal order popularly known as the Grange. During a period of service in the United States Department of Agriculture, the founder of the movement, Oliver Hudson Kelley of Minnesota, became deeply conscious of the farmers' need for social contacts and intellectual stimulus. In December, 1867, Kelley induced six other men—all but one of them government clerks—to join with him in organizing the National Grange of the Patrons of Husbandry. Shortly thereafter, Kelley resigned his government position and devoted all his energies to promoting the new order. For several years, progress was extremely slow. Of the first four branches that Kelley planted, only one—that in Fredonia, New York—took firm root. He had better luck in his home state, and by the end of 1869 there were 37 active granges in Minnesota. During the next two years the movement gradually spread. There were local granges as far east as Vermont and New Jersey and as far south as Mississippi and South Carolina, and branches were numerous in Minnesota, Iowa, Wisconsin, Illinois, and Indiana.

In 1872 the Grange began three years of phenomenal expansion. Although the boom in railroad building and manufacturing was still in full swing, the farmers were already experiencing hard times. Falling agricultural prices made high railroad rates and high prices on agricultural machinery increasingly burdensome. Grange organizers enjoyed their greatest success when they resorted to the slogans "Cooperation" and "Down with Monopoly." The movement reached its peak early in 1875, when some 1½ million members were enrolled in the order, mostly in the Middle West.

So strong was the impulse to combine that the Grange had many rivals in the form of independent farmers' clubs and farmers' political parties. Such organizations had been multiplying in Illinois in the late sixties, and by 1870 they were strong enough to force into the new state constitution mandatory provisions directing the legislature to pass laws to prevent extortion and unjust discrimination in railway charges. The legislature passed such a law in 1871, but it was declared unconstitutional by the Illinois supreme court in January, 1873.

This setback brought the Illinois farmers into determined action. The following April they timed a convention in the capital city to coincide with a session of the legislature and secured from the politicians new and more stringent regulatory laws. In June they went to the polls and elected two of their own candidates for the state supreme court while defeating the judge who had written the hated decision. On Independence Day, 1873, they demonstrated their strength in meetings and picnics so well attended and so enthusiastic that the day has passed into history as the "Farmers' Fourth of July." In the November election that followed, an independent farmers' party was successful in local contests in 53 out of 66 Illinois counties.

Events in other Middle Western states followed a parallel course. Disgusted with the politicians, the farmers threw their support to a mushroom crop of so-called "Granger parties." The situation was somewhat curious, since the Patrons of Husbandry professed itself to be devoted to social and intellectual ends and stressed its nonpolitical character. But the Grange's organizing campaign fanned the farmers' sense of grievance; grange meetings brought them together and made it possible to reassemble to plan political action as soon as the formal lodge meetings were adjourned. The independent farmers' clubs, meanwhile, went directly into politics without the need for subterfuge. By 1874 there were new parties—variously named Independent, Reform, Anti-Monopoly, or Farmers' parties—operating in 11 states. For two or three years the organized farmers were an effective force. In 1873 a Reform-Democrat coalition elected William R. Taylor governor of Wisconsin. In several other states third-party representatives secured a balance of power in the legislatures. The most conspicuous result was the passage of "Granger laws" regulating the railroads in Illinois, Minnesota, Iowa, and Wisconsin. The Illinois legislature also passed an act fixing the maximum rates that might be charged for storing grain in the warehouses of the state.

To combat the high prices charged by merchants and manufacturers, the granges resorted to other tactics. Sometimes they tried to find a local dealer who would offer special prices in return for a pledge by grange members to buy only from him. Or members of a local or county grange would pool their orders and try to cut out the middleman by dealing directly with the manufacturer or some large wholesaler. Montgomery Ward and Company of Chicago, founded in 1872, did most of its early business with the granges. Some of the granges opened their own cooperative stores. By similar means the farmers undertook to market their products without resort to the usual channels. Cooperative creameries and elevators were established in several states, and in others exclusive contracts were made with private firms that promised fair treatment.

In their enthusiasm the farm leaders plunged into more and more hazardous adventures. Angry with the harvester manufacturers who had refused to sell to the granges at wholesale prices, the Iowa state grange bought a harvester patent and began manufacturing its own machines. In 1874 it turned out about 250 machines, which it sold for $140 each—about one-half the price charged by the established companies. This apparent success so intoxicated the executive committee of the national Grange that they determined on an extensive program of manufacturing. Patents were purchased and plans were formulated for manufacturing cultivators, seeders, hay rakes, wagons and sewing machines. The grange members also organized a number of mutual fire- and life-insurance companies.

These varied activities were launched far too rapidly for safety. In 1875 a series of disastrous setbacks began. Manufacturing was a more complicated business than the grangers realized. When their factories suffered delays in production and harvesters were delivered too late for the harvest, the farmers were of course indignant. Some of the machines proved defective and it was difficult to get them repaired. The factories were hard up for working capital and were harassed by patent suits and price cutting. The Iowa harvester factory failed in 1875, bringing the state grange into bankruptcy with it. When other failures followed, the manufacturing activities of the Grange were largely abandoned. Many local granges disbanded out of fear that they might be held responsible for the debts of these enterprises. Grange merchandising experiments met similar disaster. Established firms engaged the cooperatives in price-cutting wars that ruined the new enterprises.

The business failures of the Grange estranged many of its followers. By the fall of 1875 the order appeared to be disintegrating rapidly. Membership was only about half what it had been a few months earlier. The Grange's decline continued until it reached a low point in 1880. In five years the number of granges had dropped from 21,000 to about 4,000 while total membership fell from an estimated 1,500,000 to 150,000. Thereafter a slow recovery began. The Patrons of Husbandry attained a secure position as a rural fraternal order, but its eventual stronghold proved to be in the North Atlantic states, where its growth had been slower but sounder. The Grange never really flourished again in the states where it had suffered its most severe financial reverses.

The Granger movement's collapse was hastened by the assaults of the railroads. The carriers fought attempts to regulate their rates on two fronts. In some states they refused to obey the new laws and appealed to the courts to declare them void as a deprivation of property without due process of law. In other states they carried out the regulations but did so in a way calculated to make the measures unpopular with the voters. In the courts the cause of the farmers enjoyed initial victories of great importance. In the "Granger cases" of 1876 the United States Supreme Court ruled that businesses like grain elevators or railroads in which the public had an interest were subject to regulation by the state legislatures. On this fundamental point the Court never reversed itself, but state regulation of railroads was made more difficult during the eighties by decisions providing that the *reasonableness* of rates fixed by the states might be challenged before the courts and exempting from state regulation all traffic crossing state lines. Effective control of the railroads demanded Federal action. The Interstate Commerce Act of 1887 promised such control but proved ineffective until later amendments provided the Interstate Commerce Commission with adequate powers.

Meanwhile, the railroads fought to get the offending laws repealed. In Iowa, legislators who had voted for regulation were left out in the usual distribution of passes. Laws requiring uniformity in rates were carried out by raising the low rates instead of reducing the high ones. Where maximum rates had been prescribed, the railroads reduced the service. Individual shippers feared to complain of railroad practices lest they suffer retaliation. Their grain might be delivered to the wrong elevators or it might be allowed to spoil in damp freight cars. Eastern periodicals—even supposedly liberal journals like the *Nation*—denounced the laws as an unwarranted interference with the rights of private business. Railroads published pamphlets depicting the folly of such regulations. The campaign against the laws gained strength by certain deficiencies in the regulations themselves, which made them difficult to administer. At all events, the anti-Granger campaign was largely successful. Conservative elements regained control of the legislatures of Minnesota, Iowa, and Wisconsin, and the drastic regulatory laws were repealed. Like the failure of the cooperatives this political reverse was a painful disillusionment to thousands of farmers who had looked to the Grange for speedy deliverance from their troubles.

The failure of the Granger movement was by no means complete. The Illinois regulatory laws of 1873 remained in effect, and their constitutionality was upheld. This pioneer legislation was destined to serve as precedent for many later laws. Some of the mutual insurance companies and cooperative creameries and elevators likewise survived, pointing the way for subsequent programs of self-help. The farmers became more discriminating buyers, and railroads, manufacturers, and merchants learned the importance of dealing more fairly with rural customers.

Meanwhile, the social and educational program of the Patrons of Husbandry—all-important to the founders but largely obscured by the excitement of the seventies—proved its value. Farmers learned the pleasure of meeting in village grange halls, there to participate in an inspiring ritual, to sing Grange songs, and to listen to lectures and entertainments. This opportunity to escape the dull daily routine was particularly welcome to the farmers' wives. Women were admitted to membership on the same terms as men and took a prominent part in the ritual. Books and periodicals were circulated through the local granges, and farmers were encouraged to become readers. National conventions brought together representatives of the different sections and helped to heal the wounds left by the Civil War.

The Farmers' Alliances

As Grange membership and influence declined, other attempts to organize the farmers gained ground. Up to 1873 interest in the Greenback movement was found largely among eastern wage earners, but the great panic convinced many of the farmers that expansion of the currency was the most promising remedy for falling prices. Several thousand secret Greenback Clubs were organized. Although Peter Cooper, candidate of the Greenback faction for President in 1876, received only 80,000 votes in the entire country, he made a fair showing in Illinois and in several other Middle Western states. Two years later about one million votes—two-thirds of them from the West—were cast for Greenback candidates, and 15 of these were elected to Congress. But thereafter the movement lost ground. General James B. Weaver, Greenback candidate for President in 1880, received about 300,000 votes; General Benjamin F. Butler, the candidate in 1884, received only 175,000. Better times killed the Greenback agitation after internal dissension had already weakened it. The eighties saw a number of good crop years, and agrarian discontent momentarily subsided. But the worst was still to come. After 1886 bad crops and prices impelled the farmers to protest more vigorously than ever.

In great numbers the rural population now allied itself with the Farmers' Alliances. In the South this new movement first centered in Texas. As early as 1874 a farmers' alliance, devoted to such good works as catching horse thieves and rounding up stray cattle, had been organized in Lampasas County. This body had developed a secret ritual, broadened its purpose to the protection of the general interests of the farmers, and expanded into other counties. A Grand State Alliance was organized in 1878. For the next several years the Texas Alliance followed an uneven course. One year it would attain a high degree of success; the next it would be threatened with extinction because of some internal dispute or an unsuccessful foray into politics.

In 1886 leadership of this stumbling organization fell into the hands of C. W. Macune, an able promoter who had lived in several northern states before settling in Texas, where he dabbled in law and medicine as well as in agriculture. Macune believed that the time was ripe for a bold policy which would "organize the cotton belt of America so that the whole world of cotton raisers might be united for self-protection." By the end of 1887 the National Farmers' Alliance and Co-operative Union of America, chartered in the District of Columbia, had branches in practically all the southern states.

Like the Standard Oil Company the Alliance met competition by merger. In 1887 it united with the Farmers' Union, an organization of similar purpose which had existed in Louisiana since 1880. In 1889 a similar consolidation merged the Alliance with the Agricultural Wheel, a rival organization strong in Arkansas and neighboring states. Although Negroes were not admitted to membership, a separate Colored Alliance was organized in 1886. By 1890 membership in the white body was estimated at 3 million and in its Negro appendage at over 1 million.

Meanwhile, in the North a parallel movement was in progress. The northern movement originated in Illinois, where a Cook County alliance was founded in 1880. The chief promoter in the early years was Milton George of Chicago, editor of a farm paper called the *Western Rural.* Similar bodies were founded in other Middle Western areas, and the infant movement was given a loose central organization at the Farmers' Transportation Convention held at Chicago in 1880. The name there adopted was the National Farmers' Alliance, but the organization was usually called the Northwestern or the Northern Alliance to distinguish it from the southern movement. After several years of indifferent success the Northwestern Alliance grew rapidly during the hard times of the late eighties. It was strong throughout the upper Mississippi Valley and particularly active in Kansas, Nebraska, Minnesota, and the Dakotas.

In 1889 an attempt was made to create a united front of the agricultural and labor forces of the country. At St. Louis simultaneous national conventions were held for the Southern Alliance, the Colored Alliance, and the Northwestern Alliance. Also present in the city were representatives from certain independent farm organizations and from the Knights of Labor. In an effort to absorb the other bodies, the Southern Alliance amended its constitution and changed its name once again to the National Farmers' Alliance and Industrial Union. But the proposals for a merger were wrecked on stubborn obstacles. The Northwestern Alliance admitted Negroes to membership, and the Southern excluded them; the Northwestern Alliance was an open movement, and the Southern Alliance attributed much of its success to its organization as a secret society. More important, perhaps, was the persistence of sectionalism. Civil War veterans were prominent in the Northwestern Alliance, and it went against their grain to merge their smaller body in a movement directed by southerners.

Although union was not achieved, the two Alliances adopted platforms so similar that their essential solidarity was obvious. Both called for more money, for government ownership of the railroads, and for new laws to reserve the public land for actual settlers. The Knights of Labor kept its independent organization but endorsed the demands of the Southern Alliance.

Like the earlier Grange the Alliances undertook to fight monopoly by a variety of business ventures. In the Northwest a new crop of cooperative grain elevators, creameries, and retail stores appeared. Many of the elevators and creameries survived, but the cooperative stores were less successful. Inexperienced management, the price-cutting attacks of their rivals, and inability to extend credit contributed to the failure of most of these efforts.

In the South cooperative stores and marketing agencies were particularly handicapped by the crop-lien system through which most of the farmers were shackled to the local merchants. Nevertheless, some of the most ambitious Alliance projects were attempted in the cotton states. In Texas a huge Farmers' Alliance Exchange was organized under the promotion of C. W. Macune. Cotton and grain from all over the state were to be marketed through Exchange headquarters at Dallas, and farmers were to purchase most of their implements and supplies through the same agency. The experiment was launched with high hopes in 1887, only to fail amid bitter recriminations two years later. The managers had attempted to operate on too narrow a margin of profit; they had accepted a huge volume of business with inadequate capital; they had sold goods on an unwise credit scheme. The Georgia Exchange, more conservatively managed, survived for several years, and local cooperative gin associations were often quite successful.

The Populists

More and more the farmers staked their hopes on political action. During the eighties the Farm Alliance vote had been big enough for the politicians to bid for it. Pledges of reform and regulation had been frequent, but the farmers were far from satisfied with the record of performance of either the Republicans or the Democrats. In 1890 the Alliances went into action with a vigor that caught the professional politicians by surprise. Early in the summer William Allen White, then a young Kansas newspaper man, heard that the country schoolhouses were all lit up once or twice a week—a sure sign of seething rural politics. Furthermore, as White recalled:

> And right square in mid-July, almost without notice, certainly without any clamor in the Republican papers, a procession two miles long moved down Main Street in Eldorado. It was made up of protesting farmers, their wives, and their children. There were floats on hayracks filled with singers crying political protest to gospel tunes. There were mottoes: "Special Privileges for None; Equal Rights for All," "Down with Wall Street," "Kill the Great Dragon of Lombard Street," "Let Us Pay the Kind of Dollar We Borrowed." [1]

These demonstrations were in support of the People's party, an independent faction which had nominated a complete slate of candidates and was waging an exciting campaign. Enthusiastic meetings were held not only in country schools and courthouses, but at picnics and barbecues all over the state.

The Populist movement threw up a colorful group of leaders, ridiculed by supercilious easterners but idolized by rural voters. William A. Peffer, whom the

[1] *The Autobiography of William Allen White* (Macmillan, New York, 1946), 186.

Kansas Populists sent to the United States Senate, invited caricature by his extraordinarily long beard, but he was an able rural editor. Shrewder still was Jerry Simpson; "Sockless Jerry" the reporters dubbed him, but his rusticity was largely a pose. In the estimate of William Allen White:

He had read more widely than I, and often quoted Carlyle in our conversations, and the poets and essayists of the seventeenth century. . . . He accepted the portrait which the Republicans made of him as an ignorant fool because it helped him to talk to the crowds that gathered to hear him. . . . He was opposed in this first victorious campaign for Congress by a Wichita railroad lawyer who went around campaigning in a private car and was known as "Prince Hal." In a contest wherein the bidding was for the farmer staggering under his mortgage, it is not strange that "Sockless Jerry" defeated "Prince Hal" in the race for Congress in the seventh Kansas District. "Sockless Jerry" became a national figure. The real Jerry Simpson profited by the fame of his own effigy.[1]

Women took a prominent part in the campaign. Mary Elizabeth Lease—who became famous for advising Kansas farmers to raise less corn and more hell—struck the youthful White as utterly lacking in feminine appeal, "like a kangaroo pyramided up from the hips to a comparatively small head" and wearing "the most ungodly hats" he ever beheld. But she was an exceedingly effective speaker with a golden, hypnotic quality in her voice. Said she:

The great common people of this country are slaves, and monopoly is the master. The West and South are bound and prostrate before the manufacturing East. . . . Kansas suffers from two great robbers, the Santa Fe Railroad and the loan companies. . . . We will stand by our homes and stay by our firesides by force if necessary, and we will not pay our debts to the loan-shark companies until the Government pays its debts to us. The people are at bay, let the blood-hounds of money who have dogged us thus far beware.[2]

Irish blood ran in the veins of Mary E. Lease, and the same vigorous strain was conspicuous in the red-headed Minnesota Populist Ignatius Donnelly. To his neighbors he was known as the "sage of Nininger," since he interspersed sallies into politics with the writing of novels and books on popular science. He was, moreover, the author of an erudite volume demonstrating, to his own satisfaction at least, that Francis Bacon wrote the plays commonly attributed to William Shakespeare.

When the votes were counted in 1890, the organized farmers made an impressive showing. In Kansas the People's party secured a majority in the lower house of the state legislature, elected five candidates to the national House of Representatives, and secured the choice of "Whiskers" Peffer as Senator. In Nebraska an Independent party secured a majority in both houses of the legislature and sent two representatives to Congress. Alliance parties also made a strong showing in South Dakota, Minnesota, and several other western states.

In the South the Farmers' Alliance did not attempt to launch a third party at this time. But it demonstrated its political strength no less effectively through

[1] *Ibid.*, 217–218.

[2] Quoted in John D. Hicks, *The Populist Revolt: A History of the Farmers' Alliance and the People's Party* (University of Minnesota Press, Minneapolis, Minn., 1931), 160.

action within the Democratic party. In South Carolina a convention of farmers endorsed the radical Benjamin R. Tillman for governor and men of similar views for other posts. They overawed the regular Democratic convention, secured the nomination of their candidates, and saw them elected in the fall of 1890. Tillman was as colorful as any of the northwestern Populists. A one-eyed back-country farmer, he hated the "Bourbon" element which had hitherto dominated the Democratic party of his state. He gained a large following among the poorer farmers through his effective stump oratory—especially rich in rough epithets to describe his opponents. Another conspicuous figure was Thomas E. Watson, who secured election to Congress in Georgia. A fiery young country lawyer and editor, he enjoyed rough-and-tumble politics and waged a campaign described as "hot as Nebuchadnezzar's furnace." As a result of the great upheaval three newly elected governors were Alliance men; the legislatures of eight states were dominated by the Alliance; thirty or forty Congressmen and two or three Senators professed themselves to be friends of the Alliance.

Having tasted blood in 1890, the farm leaders of the North were eager to organize a national party for the election of 1892. In the South third party sentiment was slower to develop. Any weakening of the dominant Democratic party, it was feared, might bring the Negroes into politics and threaten white supremacy. It seemed safer to continue the effort to convert the Democrats to the agrarian platform. This argument, however, lost much of its force when it became evident that the national Democratic organization was no more sympathetic to the farmers' demands than was the Republican.

After several preliminary meetings the People's party was finally launched on a national basis in a great convention at Omaha, Nebraska, in July, 1892. The platform was a stirring document embodying demands developed over several years by the farmers' organizations and the Knights of Labor. The preamble was in the rolling rhetoric of Ignatius Donnelly:

> The conditions which surround us best justify our co-operation; we meet in the midst of a nation brought to the verge of moral, political, and material ruin. Corruption dominates the ballot-box, the Legislatures, the Congress, and touches even the ermine of the bench. . . . The newspapers are largely subsidized or muzzled, public opinion silenced, business prostrated, homes covered with mortgages, labor impoverished, and the land concentrating in the hands of capitalists. The urban workmen are denied the right to organize for self-protection, imported pauperized labor beats down their wages, a hireling standing army, unrecognized by our laws, is established to shoot them down, and they are rapidly degenerating into European conditions. The fruits of the toil of millions are boldly stolen to build up colossal fortunes for a few, unprecedented in the history of mankind; and the possessors of these, in turn despise the Republic and endanger liberty. From the same prolific womb of governmental injustice we breed the two great classes—tramps and millionaires. . . .

The specific demands were for a safe, sound, and flexible national currency to be issued by the government rather than the banks, for the free coinage of silver, for an increase in the circulating medium until it reached at least $50 per capita, for a graduated income tax, for government ownership of railroads, telegraph, and telephone, and for the reservation of public land for actual settlers. After nominating the Union veteran General James B. Weaver of Iowa for President, the ticket was adroitly balanced by adding the name of General James B. Field of Virginia, who had lost a leg fighting for the Confederacy, for Vice-President.

The campaign of 1892 repeated in many particulars that of 1890. In the Middle West outdoor meetings, picnics, and long parades attracted great crowds. The atmosphere was reminiscent of the old-fashioned camp meetings. General Weaver traveled widely and spoke often, and Mrs. Lease was indefatigable in her oratorical labors. The Populist speakers gained an enthusiastic hearing in the western states, but their invasion of the South was a failure. Former Union generals and crusading Amazons were ideal targets for howling mobs, brass bands, and egg-throwing hoodlums.

The misgivings of many Southern Alliance leaders regarding third party activity proved well founded. Even the radical Ben Tillman was unwilling to abandon the Democratic party. Tom Watson ran for reelection to Congress as an out-and-out Populist but was counted out by the Democratic machine. In Georgia and Alabama, where the Populist threat seemed most serious, the Bourbons herded their employees and tenants to the polls to beat it down. With cynical craft the dominant faction used the Negro vote to defeat what they considered a challenge to white supremacy.

In the November balloting Weaver received over a million popular votes and 22 electoral votes. Populist governors were chosen in Kansas, North Dakota, and Colorado, and Populist legislators were numerous in the legislatures of Kansas, Nebraska, North Dakota, Minnesota, and Colorado. General Weaver proclaimed that the election marked the death of the Republican party and a bright future for the party of the people.

But the Populist position was not as strong as it seemed to the optimistic general. The attempt to mobilize the agricultural and labor interests of the country in a single party had, in fact, failed. The farmers of the South would have little to do with the new party; the farmers of the Northeast even less. The Knights of Labor, who supported the movement, were losing strength rapidly. The new American Federation of Labor opposed alliance with the farmers, who were an employing rather than a wage earning class. Even in the trans-Mississippi states Populist success was largely made possible by the strategy of western Democrats in throwing their votes to the Populists to embarrass the Republicans. Paradoxically, one of the casualties of the campaign was the Farmers' Alliance movement itself. Members opposed to political action deserted the organization when it abandoned nonpartisanship; members who approved political action lost interest in the older movement in their enthusiasm for the new.

The Battle for Silver

The agrarian movement had developed a broad program of demands, centering around more popular control of government, railroad regulation, land reform, and more equitable taxation. But during the nineties all other issues became subordinated to that of "free silver." The farmers attributed the fall in agricultural prices, which made it so difficult for them to pay their debts, to a shortage of money. From the Civil War to the Spanish-American War gold was scarce and gold coinage by no means met the needs of expanding population and business. Silver became plentiful through the opening of new mines, but the conservative statesmen of the day attempted to restrict silver coinage and to make all the country's money redeemable in gold. Paper currency was likewise scarce: the volume of greenbacks in circulation was restricted by law; the volume of national bank notes was controlled by factors that had little relation to the country's actual need for money.

In the seventies many of the farmers had been interested in the program of the Greenback party, which called for suppression of the national bank notes and the issuance of ample quantities of legal-tender currency by the government. In the eighties the Southern Alliance developed an ingenious proposal of its own—the so-called "subtreasury plan." At convenient points throughout the country the government was to establish great warehouses to which the farmers could bring their nonperishable staples for storage. It was then to loan the farmers up to 80 per cent of the market value of the stored crops, thus putting into circulation legal-tender currency that varied in amount with agricultural needs. The promoters of the plan believed that it would raise prices, not only by increasing the volume of money, but by making it possible for the farmer to hold his produce off the market when prices were at a seasonal low.

The subtreasury scheme was subjected to unmerciful ridicule by easterners. It was a proposal for "potato banks" dreamed up by "hayseed socialists." Why not, asked one scoffer, establish also a literary warehouse where poets could borrow 80 per cent on unsold poetry and then "set down an' wait for poetry to go up?" Actually, the idea was not so crazy as its opponents made it seem. In the twentieth century the Federal Reserve System has supplanted the unsatisfactory national bank notes with a more flexible currency, and the government has used commodity loans to farmers as a device for supporting agricultural prices.

Besides the subtreasury plan the Omaha Platform of 1892 endorsed the "free and unlimited coinage of silver at the present legal ratio of sixteen to one." Thus did the Populists recognize an issue which was rapidly eclipsing all others in popular interest. "Free silver" proved to have an emotional appeal which the "greenback" or "subtreasury" demands could not hope to match.

The demand for free silver had first been heard in the middle seventies, when a flood of white metal from the West swept into the market and brought a sharp drop in the price. If the miners could have had their silver coined into money at the old standard, they would have avoided the consequences of this price drop, but a revision of the monetary laws in 1873 had omitted the silver dollar from the list of standard coins. To make matters worse, silver had been demonetized in most European countries at about this time. Small wonder that the mining interests complained bitterly of an "international conspiracy" and the "crime of 1873." Actually, the Congressional law had been passed not through intrigue but because silver had for many years been so scarce and so high priced that the question of whether it should be coined into money seemed largely academic.

When silver prices dropped, the producers demanded an immediate return to the old system of free coinage. But easterners, convinced that a return to free silver would rob creditors and upset business, insisted that the standard of values should continue to be gold. Squirming at this clash of interests, the politicians attempted to compromise. The Bland-Allison Act of 1878 required the government to purchase between 2 million and 4 million dollars' worth of silver each month and to coin it into dollars. But the government never purchased more than the minimum amount, and the price of silver continued to drop. In 1890 another attempt at appeasement was made. Under the Sherman Silver Purchase Act the government was committed to purchase 4½ million ounces of silver each month—practically the entire output of the American mines—and to issue treasury certificates against the metal. But this was not free coinage. Silver was purchased at the market price rather than at the old mint price, and very little of it was actually coined into money.

The mining interests had as their enthusiastic allies millions of debt-harassed farmers in the South and the West. The free and unlimited coinage of silver, they were convinced, would result in a rise in agricultural prices that would solve their most pressing problems. In the election of 1892 many votes went to the People's party because it had taken a forthright stand for silver while the older parties were straddling this issue and debating the tariff, in which the farmers had much less interest.

The second administration of Grover Cleveland presented the money problem in a form that could no longer be avoided. In 1893 the country plunged into a frightening depression. Corporations failed; unemployed men walked the streets in search of jobs; farmers lost their land through foreclosures. Conservatives and radicals differed completely on both the causes and the remedy for the disaster. Cleveland believed that the panic had been caused by uncertainty as to whether the gold standard would be maintained. With stubborn courage he forced through Congress a repeal of the Silver Purchase Act and saved the Federal gold reserve, even though it meant appealing for help to J. P. Morgan and the bankers.

Cleveland's policies aroused the West and South to explosive rage. "I haven't got words," Ben Tillman shouted to a South Carolina audience, "to say what I think of that old bag of beef." In the opinion of the agrarians the economic distress of the country was caused by the wicked resistance of eastern capitalists to the free coinage of silver—the people's money.

Such was the background for the election of 1896. The Republicans committed themselves to the gold standard and nominated William McKinley—the protégé of Mark Hanna, millionaire Ohio industrialist. The Democrats pledged themselves to free silver and nominated William Jennings Bryan, a youthful and eloquent Nebraska congressman. Although a lifelong Democrat, Bryan had grown up in western territory and his oratory was cast in the Populist mold. In his famous "Cross of Gold" speech at the Democratic convention, he said:

> We say to you that you have made the definition of a business man too limited in its application. The man who is employed for wages is as much a business man as the corporation counsel in a great metropolis; the merchant at the cross-roads store is as much a business man as the merchant of New York; the farmer who goes forth in the morning and toils all day, who begins in the spring and toils all summer, and who by the application of brain and muscle to the natural resources of the country creates wealth, is as much a business man as the man who goes upon the Board of Trade and bets upon the price of grain; the miners who go down a thousand feet into the earth or climb two thousand feet upon the cliffs, and bring forth from their hiding places the precious metals to be poured into the channels of trade are as much business men as the few financial magnates who, in a back room, corner the money of the world. We come to speak of this broader class of business men. . . . We do not come as aggressors. Our war is not a war of conquest; we are fighting in the defense of our homes, our families, and posterity. We have petitioned, and our petitions have been scorned; we have entreated, and our entreaties have been disregarded; we have begged, and they have mocked when calamity came. We beg no longer; we entreat no more; we petition no more. We defy them!

The Democratic platform borrowed other issues than that of silver from the Populists. It demanded an income tax; it urged stricter railroad regulation; it condemned the bond-selling policy of the Cleveland administration and the system of national bank notes. The Populists recognized the situation by naming Bryan as their candidate for President, but they refused to endorse the Democratic candidate for Vice-President and named Tom Watson of Georgia instead.

The lines were thus drawn for a political contest unique in American history. Twenty years of agrarian protest culminated in the crusade for Bryan and free silver. Bryan's campaign took him all over the country, and immense crowds thronged the places where the suddenly famous orator spoke. But the western challenge was met by a shrewd counteroffensive. The Republicans had the use of a huge campaign fund collected by Mark Hanna from frightened industrialists and bankers. Tons of literature poured out to "educate" the voters on the need for an "honest dollar." The middle class was solid for McKinley, and most of the industrial workers were frightened into believing that wholesale factory shutdowns would follow a Bryan victory. The election returns proved the effectiveness of these tactics. Bryan swept the South and the West, but McKinley carried the heavily populated East and the north-central sections that meant victory.

After 1896 the farm agitation subsided. New discoveries of gold and new processes for extracting it increased the supply until much of the larger volume of money for which the agrarians had been contending was actually provided. Since agricultural prices went up more than the prices of manufactured goods, the lot of the farmers was substantially improved between 1900 and 1920. Like the Grange and the Farmers' Alliances before it, the People's party ceased to be an important force. But the long agitation had left its mark on American politics. The older parties took up and made respectable many of the demands first voiced by the farmers.

The Literature of Rural Protest

The farmers' crusade had been fought with newspapers, pamphlets, and books as well as with conventions and elections. Almost every one of the agrarian leaders had his own farm periodical. C. W. Macune, leading figure in the Southern Alliance until he fell from grace in 1892, edited the *National Economist* of Washington, D. C. This journal was recognized as the official organ of the Southern Alliance and had a wide circulation among farmers of all sections. Through this medium Macune gave wide publicity to such pet projects of his as the farmers' exchanges and the subtreasury plan. Colonel Leonidas L. Polk, for several years president of the Southern Aliance, edited the influential *Progressive Farmer* of Raleigh, North Carolina. Georgia's fiery Tom Watson edited the *People's Party Paper,* and Minnesota's irrepressible Ignatius Donnelly edited the *Anti-Monopolist* during the seventies and the *Representative* during the nineties. In all, the Farmers' Alliance movement spawned perhaps a thousand separate papers, which were eventually organized in a National Reform Press Association. Through these periodicals thousands of farmers followed the issues of the day.

The Alliances and the People's party also promoted the distribution of books. Circulating libraries were established in many districts, widening the influence of reform novels like Edward Bellamy's *Looking Backward* (1888) and Ignatius Donnelly's *Caesar's Column* (1890) and of Populist tracts like Senator Peffer's *The Farmer's Side* (1891) and General Weaver's *A Call to Action* (1892).

The silver cause brought forth a particularly provocative literature. Mrs. S. E. V. Emery, one of the Kansas Populists, wrote a widely circulated book entitled *Seven Financial Conspiracies Which Have Enslaved the American People,* (1895). The demonetization of silver, Mrs. Emery charged, was put through with $500,000 as the result of the efforts of one Ernest Seyd of London after silver had been demonetized in France, England, and Holland. She wrote:

> God of our fathers! A British capitalist sent here to make laws for the American people. England failed to subjugate us by the bullet, but she stole into our Congressional halls and by the crafty use of gold, obtained possession of the ballot, and to-day, American industry pays tribute to England despite our blood-bought seal of independence.

Ignatius Donnelly in *The American People's Money* (1895) also identified the gold standard with the imperialist designs of Great Britain. With characteristic exaggeration he wrote:

> The nation that forced opium and missionaries—in the same treaty—upon the Chinese, at the point of the bayonet . . . would shed no tears if the people of these United States, from ocean to ocean, were starving, or were swimming in a sea of fraternal blood.[1]

By far the most effective of the free-silver appeals was *Coin's Financial School,* published in 1894 by William H. Harvey of Chicago. "Professor Coin" was depicted as a precocious juvenile who enlightened the simple and confounded the wise by his elucidation of the mysteries of economics. In his Chicago school appeared all the leading gold supporters of the country, but Coin refuted their arguments and sent them away convinced against their will. The book was so adroitly written that many readers believed that such a school actually existed. Much of the book's popularity derived from the sprightly drawings which drove home the argument of almost every page.

The sensational success of *Coin's Financial School* encouraged Harvey to write two sequels. The publicist turned to fiction in *A Tale of Two Nations* (1894), in which the chief villain of a gigantic international conspiracy to destroy the United States was depicted as a British banker, the hero as a Nebraska congressman.

The literature of protest obviously did far more than to popularize the grievances of the farmers and the agrarian demands. It encouraged the growth of Middle Western isolationism. Great Britain was stereotyped as a selfish imperialist power, attempting to enslave other nations through its control over the world's money. All proposals for international cooperation were attacked as intrigues of British capitalists and their Wall Street hirelings. This trend in American thinking was destined to have a great influence on world history during the twentieth century.

[1] Ignatius Donnelly, *The American People's Money* (Chicago, 1895), 137.

Chapter 24. Problems of the City

The rise of the great American cities, clearly foreshadowed before the Civil War, was accelerated by every trend of the postwar period. Through mechanization agriculture greatly increased the national food supply at the same time that it released workers for urban industry. Manufacturing for a national market was encouraged by tariff protection and technological advance. Great railroads fed food, fuel, and raw materials into the cities and carried away their vast production. Because of the consolidation of business the cities attracted a growing army of financiers, produce dealers, wholesalers, clerks, and salesmen.

America was proud of its cities—proud of New York, the rival of London and Paris in size, and proud of Chicago, which had grown from frontier fort to second city in the nation within the memory of living men. But America also feared its cities. Frederic C. Howe, energetic crusader for reform, warned:

> The city has replaced simplicity, industrial freedom, and equality of fortune with complexity, dependence, poverty and misery close beside a barbaric luxury like unto that of ancient Rome. Vice, crime, and disease have come in. The death-rate has increased, while infectious diseases and infant mortality ravage the crowded quarters. The city has destroyed the home and substituted for it the hotel, flat, tenement, boarding-house, and cheap lodging-house. Our politics have suffered, and corruption has so allied itself with our institutions that many despair of democracy. The city exacts an awful price for the gain it has given us, a price that is being paid in human life, suffering, and the decay of virtue and the family.[1]

Urban Growth

The immense growth of cities was not peculiar to America. During the second half of the nineteenth century London and Paris doubled in population, and Berlin more than quadrupled. Rural districts in England, Wales, France, and Prussia all suffered either absolute or relative declines in population while urban districts were growing rapidly. The rise of American cities reflected the play of similar economic forces, accentuated by such peculiarly American factors as large-scale immigration.

The older seaports held their rank fairly well. The New York area, brought together under one government in 1898, grew from a population of 1,174,779 in 1860 to 4,766,883 in 1910—a fourfold increase. Philadelphia, now third largest American city, attained a population of 1,549,008 in 1910—three times its population of 1860. Baltimore, growing less rapidly, fell from third place in

[1] Frederic C. Howe, *The City: The Hope of Democracy* (Scribner, New York, 1905), 32.

1860 to seventh in 1910. Boston with a threefold increase slipped only one rank —fourth in 1860, fifth in 1910. The greatest drop in relative importance was suffered by New Orleans, victim of the diversion of river traffic to the railroads. Fifth in rank in 1860, New Orleans had fallen to fifteenth by 1910.

The most dramatic population increases were those of the Middle Western cities. All the world was fascinated by the growth of Chicago. Eighth among American cities with 109,260 inhabitants in 1860, it forged steadily ahead. In 1890 its population passed the million mark, and it supplanted Philadelphia as the second largest city in the country. In 1910 its population reached 2,185,283—a twentyfold increase since 1860. Also growing rapidly were St. Louis, Cleveland, and Detroit, ranking by 1910 fourth, sixth, and ninth among the nation's cities. No less significant than the growth of the large cities was the great increase in the number of small cities and towns. In 1860 there had been 141 places with 8,000 or more inhabitants; in 1910 there were 778 such communities. During this period the proportion of the entire population living in places of 8,000 inhabitants or more rose from 16 to 38 per cent.

Even at the level of the smaller towns various sections of the country showed very different degrees of urbanization. Although almost 46 per cent of the entire population lived in places of 2,500 inhabitants or more, there were seven states—North and South Dakota, North and South Carolina, Mississippi, Arkansas, and New Mexico—where less than 15 per cent of the population lived in such towns or cities. At the other end of the scale in eight states—Rhode Island, Massachusetts, Connecticut, New York, New Jersey, Pennsylvania, Illinois, and California—over 60 per cent of the population lived in urban communities.

The Immigration Problem

Although America would have had cities in any case, their rise was much accelerated by immigration. In the eight largest cities of the country—all places of 500,000 inhabitants or more in 1910—more than one-third of the population was foreign-born, and considerably more than another third was of second-generation immigrant stock. On the other hand, less than 8 per cent of the rural population was born outside the United States.

The large-scale immigration of the early 1850's was sharply reduced by the depression of 1857 and by the Civil War. With the return of peace the volume of arrivals again increased. Except for four years during the hard times of the 1870's, more than 200,000 immigrants entered the country each year between 1866 and 1917. The flow followed with rough fidelity the ups and downs of the American economic cycle. During the prosperous decade of the 1880's over 5,000,000 foreigners arrived; during the first ten years of the twentieth century 8,795,000 came.

For a generation after the Civil War most of the immigrants came from the same countries from which they had come before the war. Of the more than

10,000,000 entering the United States between 1860 and 1890, almost 85 per cent came from northern and western Europe and from Canada: from Germany almost 3,000,000, from England 1,600,000, from Ireland 1,500,000, from the Scandinavian countries 1,000,000, and from Canada 930,000.

German immigration changed somewhat in character. After the construction of railroads eastern and central Germany contributed much more heavily to the emigrant stream than formerly. Although the rural population continued to leave, they were joined by more artisans and town dwellers. The German industrial revolution, retarded by adverse political conditions during the first half of the century, proceeded all the more rapidly thereafter. Handicraft workers, particularly hard hit by the transition, made their way to America in increasing numbers. Frequent wars, the obligation to perform military service, and heavy taxes all helped to swell the emigrant total. The great exodus fell off sharply after 1890 with the improvement of political and economic conditions in the homeland. In America the German immigrants continued to concentrate in the old German belt lying between New York and New Jersey on the east and Iowa and Missouri on the west. Although a substantial proportion continued to take up farming, an increasing number settled in the cities. In 1910 New York City had 278,000 German-born inhabitants, Chicago had 182,000, and Milwaukee 64,000.

The large number of English emigrating to the United States reflected many forces. The population of mid-Victorian Britain was increasing rapidly, and despite the apparent prosperity many persons found it difficult to make a living. The rural laborer had a diminishing demand for his services after the repeal of the Corn Laws; the industrial worker complained of periods of unemployment and low wages. It was, however, not so much discontent with England as enthusiasm for America that led to large-scale migration. In the rapidly expanding American economy the English worker saw an opportunity to sell his services for more than they would bring in the mother country. In America the English were widely scattered. A considerable number found employment in the New England textile mills, some became engineers and machinists in other industrial states, many became farmers and ranchers in the West, and others entered the professions. This wide dispersal together with common language and similar customs resulted in an assimilation so rapid that most Americans were unaware of the size of the English influx. Nevertheless, this strengthening of the English stock during a period of large immigration was of obvious importance.

The Irish never again came in the volume of the early fifties. Famine and emigration had so reduced the population that those who remained had a better chance to make a living. Yet the number of Irish who migrated was still large. Economic opportunities at home were limited, and America constantly beckoned through the letters of relatives or acquaintances. The end result was extraordinary. Although in 1910 the population of Ireland was only 4,381,000, there were 4,500,000 persons in the United States of immediate Irish stock—1,350,000 born in Ireland, 3,150,000 born in the United States of parents one or both of whom had been Irish-born. Over 58 per cent of this immediate Irish stock lived in four states—Massachusetts, New York, Pennsylvania, and Illinois—and by adding four other states—Connecticut, New Jersey, Ohio, and California—no less than 75 per cent of the Irish stock is accounted for. Over 81 per cent of the Irish lived in places of 2,500 inhabitants or more, with particularly large concentrations in New York, Philadelphia, Chicago, and Boston.

Scandinavian immigration reached a peak during the 1880's. The great attracting force was still the rich agricultural country along the upper Mississippi Valley. Of 665,000 Swedish-born Americans in 1910, over one-third were living in Minnesota and Illinois; a large part of the rest were in nearby states like Michigan, Wisconsin, and Iowa, although sizable Swedish groups were to be found as far east as Massachusetts and as far west as Washington. Of 403,000 Norwegian-born Americans almost two-thirds were living in Minnesota, Wisconsin, North Dakota, Illinois, and Iowa. A larger proportion of the Scandinavians than of any other immigrant group took up agriculture. Yet even on them the urban magnet was at work. The census of 1910 enumerated 87,000 Scandinavian-born inhabitants in Chicago and 42,000 in Minneapolis.

In addition to these immigrant streams to which Americans had become well accustomed, new ones began to flow during the post-Civil War generation. The needs of California's mining camps and railroads led to a small but controversial influx of Chinese: during the decade of the 1850's, 41,000 entered the country; during the 1860's, 74,000; during the 1870's, 123,000. Although most of them were employed as laborers on the West Coast, a few were brought to the East. A shoe factory in North Adams, Massachusetts, experimented with Chinese workers, and one or two southern railroads used the "Celestials" for construction jobs. American workers became highly alarmed at this threat, which was soon magnified out of all proportion by agitators like Denis Kearney of California. In the West mobs, largely Irish in composition, assaulted and killed Chinese and destroyed their property. In 1882 Congress passed an act excluding Chinese laborers for ten years; by later laws the exclusion was renewed and made more drastic. Although this legislation reduced Chinese immigration to small dimensions, enough were here to provide San Francisco and New York with picturesque Chinatowns and hundreds of American cities with hard-working laundrymen and restaurant keepers.

Also resented by American workers, although not to the same degree, was the immigration of French Canadians. Allowed by the English to retain their own language, religion, and customs, the French population of Canada, which was largely concentrated in the province of Quebec, had grown prodigiously. Since they were hampered by lack of opportunity in their native villages, the French Canadians crossed the border to work in American factories. After 1870 an increasingly large number of them settled permanently in the New England mill towns. Their coming was encouraged by employers who found them industrious, willing to work for low wages, and indifferent to the appeals of labor-union organizers. In 1910 there were 134,000 first-generation French Canadians in Massachusetts and about 130,000 more in the other New England states. French Canadians also settled in substantial numbers in Michigan, Illinois, and Wisconsin.

FIG. 40. *In the Land of Promise.* Painting by Charles F. Ulrich. Recently arrived immigrants at Castle Garden, New York, in 1884. (*Courtesy of the Corcoran Gallery of Art, Washington.*)

The immigrant wave that was to tower over all earlier ones began to mount during the 1880's. Between 1880 and 1910 over 3,000,000 persons born in Italy, over 3,000,000 born in Austria-Hungary, almost 2,500,000 born in Russia, and smaller numbers from the Balkans and the Near East entered the country. This so-called "new immigration" was so huge in volume and so different in language and custom that protesting voices were soon demanding a radical change in American immigration policy.

Before the large-scale movement of Italians to America began, there had already been a sizable exodus from the overpopulated peninsula into other European countries, northern Africa, and South America. This earlier movement had been largely from northern Italy, the most progressive section of the country. The much larger emigration from southern Italy, which developed during the nineties, was mostly directed toward the United States. Conditions in southern Italy were notoriously bad. The population was increasing rapidly; the arable land was largely held in great estates. Tenants paid extortionate rents, and agricultural laborers received miserable wages. Taxes on such necessities as flour, bread, macaroni, sugar, and salt imposed a crushing burden on the poor.

Italian peasants, thus chained to poverty, eagerly undertook the hazards of emigration. Thousands availed themselves of the services of "bankers"—unscrupulous fellow countrymen in America who solicited immigrants through agents in Italian villages, arranged for the sale of whatever property their clients had in the old country, obtained steerage passage for them across the Atlantic, housed them in the tenements of the great cities, and sold their services as laborers. On all these transactions the bankers collected a handsome profit, while their ignorant victims were little better than slaves. Italian workers built railroads, dug sewers and subways, and provided cheap labor for New England textile mills, New Jersey silk mills, Pennsylvania mines, and the New York garment industry. In 1910 almost 60 per cent of the Italian-born were living in New York, Pennsylvania, and New Jersey; they were also to be found in large numbers in Massachusetts, Illinois, and California. Over 64 per cent lived in cities of 25,000 inhabitants or more.

The statistics of the new immigration are at first somewhat puzzling. That the Italians came to America in large numbers is obvious, but where are the Austrians, the Hungarians, and the Russians? The answer is simple. All but a small proportion of the immigration from Austria-Hungary and Russia was not from the dominant elements of those polyglot empires but from the subject peoples—Jews, Poles, Czechs, Slovaks, Croats, Slovenes, and Ukrainians.

Long subject to burdensome residence and occupational laws, the Jews became the victims of active persecution after 1880. Russian peasants, ignorant and desperately poor, found an outlet for their resentment in killing Jews, whom they hated as moneylenders and traders. Particularly brutal massacres occurred in 1881 and 1906. Far from attempting to repress these pogroms, the Russian government welcomed them. After the assassination of Alexander II in 1881, reactionary officials followed a policy of terrorizing the Jews and forcing them out of the country. Residence laws were ruthlessly enforced, and Cossack soldiers brutally expelled Jewish families from Russian villages. Elsewhere in eastern Europe mistreatment of the Jews was less active, but they suffered both from prejudice and poverty. Often forbidden to own land, so many crowded into trade and industry that it was difficult to make a living.

Under these tragic circumstances thousands of families sacrificed all that they had to reach the promised land across the Atlantic. Between 1881 and 1910 about 1½ million Jews entered the United States. Over 71 per cent came from Russia, 18 per cent from Austria-Hungary, and 4 per cent from Rumania. Already strongly urbanized through historical circumstances, their tendency to gather in cities was even more pronounced in America. An extraordinarily large percentage settled in New York, but large communities were also to be found in each of the other major cities. The Jew who fitted the American stereotype was one who began as a peddler or junk dealer and ended as a millionaire merchant, banker, or Hollywood executive. But the spectacular success of a few obscured the sober truth that the great majority of Jewish immigrants passed their days as exploited garmentworkers or petty tradesmen.

For the Slavic peasants of eastern Europe life became more and more difficult at this period. Rapidly increasing population resulted in smaller holdings, and the region was too economically backward to offer many opportunities in industry. Exploitation by taxgatherers, landlords, moneylenders, and merchants added to their burdens. In America they were welcomed by many employers. Operators of Pennsylvania coal mines, alarmed by the vigor of unionism among the older miners, began to employ an increasing number of Slavs. By 1900 about 54 per cent of the miners were from the new immigrant groups. By temperament and physique the Slavs proved particularly well adapted to heavy work in the steel mills and in the meat-packing industry. America's urban growth was also aided by the arrival of numerous Greeks, Syrians, Armenians, and Portuguese.

The arrival of 26,000 Japanese in the United States during the 1890's and 129,000 during the next decade alarmed Californians in much the same way as had the earlier influx of Chinese. The "gentleman's agreement" of 1907, under which the Japanese government promised not to issue passports to laborers seeking to emigrate to the United States, eased the tension, but nativists continued to demand more effective barriers. Despite hostile legislation the Japanese were extraordinarily successful in the California truck-farming industry.

Between 1861 and 1914 American attitudes toward immigration changed drastically. In earlier days nativists had attempted to place obstacles in the way of the naturalization of foreigners and to ban paupers but had rarely opposed the free entry of aliens willing and able to work. Under pressure from American employers Congress in 1864 even went so far as to pass a law under which the courts were authorized to enforce contracts made in foreign countries whereby emigrants pledged their wages for a term not exceeding twelve months to repay the expenses of emigration. Taking advantage of this protection, emigrant companies recruited laborers abroad, paid their passage across the Atlantic, and placed them in American jobs. Meanwhile, steamship companies and western railroads continued their active solicitation.

All organizations claiming to speak for American labor protested vigorously against these practices. Labor's growing political influence was marked by laws restricting the admission of contract laborers in 1868 and 1885. In 1891 transport companies were prohibited from advertising for immigrants. Meanwhile, Congress had been erecting barriers against certain undesirables: prostitutes were excluded in 1875; lunatics, idiots, convicts, persons likely to become public charges, and Chinese laborers in 1882; polygamists and sufferers from loathsome and dangerous diseases in 1891.

Although the Federalists of the 1790's had complained of the radicalism of French immigrants and the Know-Nothings of the 1850's had made similar charges against German socialists and freethinkers, widespread concern over alien radicalism did not develop until the 1880's and the 1890's. But the Haymarket affair of 1886, the assault on Frick during the Homestead strike of 1892, and the assassination of McKinley in 1901 all tended to magnify the menace of the foreign agitator. Anarchists and persons advocating the forceful overthrow of the government were added to the excluded classes in 1903.

In the opinion of many Americans these restrictive laws were not enough. They met the problem of an immigrant flood by skimming a little scum off the surface. What was needed, it was asserted, was a dam of adequate bulk to hold back the rushing waters. The first such dam proposed was a literacy test which would exclude all immigrants who could not read or write either their own or some other language. The true purpose of this innocent-sounding proposal was frankly revealed by Senator Henry Cabot Lodge of Massachusetts, one of its principal supporters:

> It is found . . . that the illiteracy test will bear most heavily upon Italians, Russians, Poles, Hungarians, Greeks, and Asiatics, and very lightly, or not at all, upon English-speaking emigrants or Germans, Scandinavians, and French. In other words, the races most affected . . . are those whose emigration to this country has begun within the last twenty years and swelled rapidly to enormous proportions, races with which the English-speaking people have never hitherto assimilated, and who are the most alien to the great body of the people of the United States. . . . The races which would suffer most seriously by exclusion under the proposed bill furnish the immigrants who do not go to the West or South, where immigration is needed, but who remain on the Atlantic Seaboard, where immigration is not needed and where their presence is most injurious and undesirable.[1]

Congress passed a literacy test in 1897, but the measure was vetoed by President Cleveland, who said:

> In my opinion, it is infinitely more safe to admit a hundred thousand immigrants who though unable to read and write, seek among us only a home and opportunity to work, than to admit one of those unruly agitators and enemies of governmental control, who can not only read and write but delights in arousing by inflammatory speech the illiterate and peacefully inclined to discontent and tumult.

Presidential opposition did not kill the agitation for the literacy test. Demand for some such barrier increased as immigration swelled to unprecedented volume early in the twentieth century. The all-time peak came in 1907, when 1,285,349 foreigners entered the country, and in each of five other years—1905, 1906, 1910, 1913, and 1914—arrivals exceeded 1,000,000. Over 70 per cent of the newcomers were from southern and eastern Europe.

Criticism of the new immigration rested on grounds of varying validity. It was unscientific and mischievous to assume, as Lodge and others did, that Jews, Italians, Poles, and other peoples of eastern and southern Europe were racially

[1] *Congressional Record,* 54th Cong., 1st Sess., XXVIII, 2817.

inferior to the northwestern Europeans. Time was to prove that most of the newcomers made excellent Americans. On the other hand, American workers had reason to complain of the effect on wages of admitting an unlimited number of immigrants willing to accept almost any pay. Particularly unfair was it for them to have to compete with "birds of passage"—immigrants without families who had no intention of becoming citizens and who stayed only a few years before returning to the old country to spend their hoarded earnings. The sheer bulk of immigration after 1900 also created serious problems of assimilation.

Although many students of the problem were willing to concede that some further regulation of immigration was necessary, they doubted that the highly discriminatory literacy test was the answer. Taft vetoed a literacy-test bill in 1911; Wilson disapproved a similar measure in 1915 with the following comment:

> Hitherto we have generously kept our doors open to all who were not unfitted by reason of disease or incapacity for self-support or such personal records and antecedents as were likely to make them a menace to our peace and order or to the wholesome and essential relationships of life. In this bill it is proposed to turn away from tests of character and of equality and impose tests which exclude and restrict; for the new tests here embodied are not tests of quality or of character or of personal fitness, but tests of opportunity. Those who come seeking opportunity are not to be admitted unless they have already had one of the chief opportunities they seek, the opportunity of education. The object of such provisions is restriction, not selection.[1]

But the restrictionists finally won their battle. Over another Wilson veto the literacy test was enacted in 1917—a forerunner of more drastic legislation to follow.

Poverty and Crime

Advocates of drastic immigration restriction often drew their arguments from the statistics of crime and pauperism. As in the 1840's and 1850's it was easy to prove that a large proportion of the inmates of the prisons and poorhouses were of foreign birth or parentage. Yet there was reason to question whether this condition represented something that the immigrant had done to America or something that America had done to the immigrant. Jacob Riis, journalist-crusader for housing reform, declared:

> New York's tough represents the essence of reaction against the old and the new oppression, nursed in the rank soil of its slums. Its gangs are made up of the American-born sons of English, Irish, and German parents. They reflect exactly the conditions of the tenements from which they sprang. Murder is as congenial to Cherry Street or to Battle Row, as quiet and order to Murray Hill. The "assimilation" of Europe's oppressed hordes, upon which our Fourth of July orators are fond of dwelling, is perfect. The product is our own.[2]

[1] *Congressional Record,* 63d Cong., 3d Sess., LII, 2482.

[2] Jacob A. Riis, *How the Other Half Lives: Studies among the Tenements of New York* (Scribner, New York, 1890), 218.

New York's rocketing population confined within the narrow limits of Manhattan Island created a housing problem that was already desperate by the time of the Civil War. When the municipal board of health, endowed with wide powers in 1866, investigated its Augean stable, it discovered that nearly 20,000 persons were living in cellars and 400,000 more in tenements. Some of the tenements were old houses, once occupied by wealthy owners and now converted into living quarters for several families by the simple expedient of partitioning each large room into several smaller ones without regard for light or ventilation. Others were new buildings—rear tenements built in the back yards of older houses or vast barracks fronting on the street but covering the whole lot so that light and fresh air had no access to most of the rooms. As an initial reform the board of health ordered the cutting of more than 46,000 windows to ventilate stifling bedrooms. As a second step it closed the dank cellars, many of them below tidewater, where so many unfortunates had been living.

This campaign—and other reforms like driving the pigs from the streets, cleaning up the accumulated garbage of many years, and prohibiting slaughterhouses in the heart of the city—touched only the most blatant evils. Owners of old properties continued to collect high rents from their dark and filthy houses; builders of new tenements made as few concessions to the demands of health as the law would allow—and law enforcement under Tammany was rarely rigorous against landlords and contractors who knew the right people. Periodically, the public conscience would be stirred through the revelations of charity workers, home missionaries, and newspaper reporters. Official investigations and enforcement campaigns would result, and the general public would hope that the problem had been solved.

But as more and more inhabitants crowded onto Manhattan Island, discouraged reformers wondered whether any real progress had been made. An investigating commission in 1900 concluded that conditions were worse than they had been fifty years before and that the city had "the most serious tenement house problem in the world." The "dumbbell type" tenement then prevalent pretended to provide light and ventilation through air shafts, but these narrow crevices between buildings were so malodorous from accumulated refuse that disgusted tenants often nailed down the windows.

Life in the tenements, which would have been drab and uncomfortable at best, was made worse by overcrowding. Within the two or three rooms which composed each dwelling unit, there often lived a household composed not only of man, wife, and several children but of other relatives or lodgers as well. Discussing an East Side Jewish district in 1890, Riis said:

> It is said that nowhere in the world are so many people crowded together on a square mile as here. The average five-story tenement adds a story or two to its stature in Ludlow Street and an extra building on the rear lot. . . . Here is one seven stories high. The sanitary policeman whose beat this is will tell you that it contains thirty-six families, but

the term has a widely different meaning here and on the avenues. In this house . . . there were fifty-eight babies and thirty-eight children that were over five years of age. In Essex Street two small rooms in a six-story tenement were made to hold a "family" of father and mother, twelve children and six boarders. . . . These are samples of the packing of the population that has run up the record here to the rate of three hundred and thirty thousand per square mile. The densest crowding of Old London . . . never got beyond a hundred and seventy-five thousand.[1]

Sanitary facilities were rudimentary. Several families used a common sink and a common toilet, rarely cleaned by anyone. Bathtubs were luxuries enjoyed only by the well-to-do; tenement dwellers performed their infrequent ablutions in bowls or patronized commercial bathhouses. Even water to drink was scarce, since during the heat of summer the city pressure was usually too low to lift it above the first floor of the tenements.

Ancient plagues like smallpox, cholera, and typhus threw the city into a state of terror from time to time, and less sensational but scarcely less deadly killers like tuberculosis, diphtheria, and scarlet fever were ceaselessly at work. Even measles slew undernourished and feeble children by the hundreds. During the 1880's, when the general death rate of the country was probably less than 20 per thousand inhabitants, that of New York City averaged over 25. In the notorious slums of Mulberry Bend the general death rate for 1888 was 38 per thousand, and that for children under five years of age was 136.

A large proportion of the tenement dwellers were decent people, trying to make an honest living. When the wage earner was a man, the struggle was desperate enough. When it was a woman, the problem was still more difficult. Thousands of exploited women workers slaved in the tenements, sewing garments or making cigars at piece rates so low that they could earn only $2 or $3 a week. Despite laws to the contrary thousands of children under fourteen years of age worked long hours in stores and factories.

Below the level of these honest, if underpaid wage earners were thousands of slum dwellers who had no regular employment. Some were unemployable, blind, crippled, or senile. Some were alcoholics, dismissed from one job after another. Some were marginal workers, last to be employed in good times, first to be laid off in bad. Not a few, discouraged and demoralized by slum life, had given up trying to support themselves and were chronic applicants for charity, sometimes from organizations, sometimes from individuals whom they accosted on the streets. The lowest ranks of this pauper army had no regular domicile. Riis estimated that some 14,000 homeless men, women, and children were roaming New York streets in 1890, drinking stale beer and eating rolls at 2-cent restaurants, sleeping in 10- or 15-cent lodginghouses when they had the price, or in alleys, hallways, or police stations when they were penniless. Despite the pathetic desire of the poor to be buried in style, one person in ten dying in New York between 1883 and 1888 was placed in a nameless grave in the pauper

[1] *Ibid.*, 105.

cemetery. Many of these had ended their days on the islands in the East River where stood the municipal almshouse, workhouse, and insane asylum.

If the pauper was one product of the slums, another—more dangerous to the community—was the criminal. Boys whose only playground was the streets easily learned to steal from sidewalk stands or unconscious drunks. To graduate to more serious crimes was easy, since youths fell under the influence of hardened

FIG. 41. *The Cliff Dwellers.* Painting by G. W. Bellows. Realistic portrayal of street scene in the slums. (*Courtesy of the Los Angeles County Museum; photograph by the Metropolitan Museum of Art, New York.*)

criminals in saloons, in lodginghouses, and on street corners. The lawless elements organized in gangs with their headquarters in the Five Points, Mulberry Bend, Poverty Gap, Hell's Kitchen, and other slum sections. Armed with brass knuckles, sandbags, knives, and revolvers, rival gangs fought each other, held up pedestrians, looted stores and warehouses, robbed banks, and wrecked the premises of storekeepers who refused to "contribute" to their picnic or ball funds. The murder rate rose alarmingly. For honest law agencies the situation would have been difficult to handle. In a city where both police officers and courts were often corrupt, criminals were treated with alternating tolerance and brutality.

The conditions that had developed in New York were largely duplicated in other great cities. Describing slum districts in Chicago, a journalist wrote in 1907:

> In the center of Chicago are now two small cities of savages—self-regulating and self-protecting. In one of these there are thirty-two thousand people; in the other, thirty thousand. . . . The adults neither labor regularly nor marry. Half of the men are beggars, criminals, or floating laborers; a quarter are engaged in the sale of dissipation; and a third of the women are prostitutes. . . . Society here has lapsed back into a condition more primitive than the jungle.[1]

Urban Reform Movements

The humanitarian impulse, always strong in America, prompted a great variety of efforts to ease the lot of the poor. Cities maintained hospitals and almshouses. Private organizations established clinics, orphanages, children's aid societies, settlement houses, and stations where food, clothing, and emergency funds were available to prevent suffering. A thousand babies a year, most of them born out of wedlock, were cared for in the Foundling Asylum, maintained by the Sisters of Charity in New York; and numerous other Catholic, Protestant, and Jewish agencies were at work.[2]

Although the total amount expended for public and private relief was great, much of it was wasted through graft, poor administration, and lack of coordination between various agencies. Some families became highly skillful in milking several charitable funds at the same time, while others through ignorance or false pride never applied for the help that they desperately needed. A first step toward more scientific administration came with the establishment of state boards of charities to supervise the work of public institutions; Massachusetts took this step in 1864, and 18 other states followed before 1893. A second step was to set up clearinghouses where public and private organizations could exchange information about cases and avoid duplication of effort; a Charity Organization Society was founded at Buffalo in 1877, and similar bodies were soon to be found in many other cities.

Reformers believed that a substantial proportion of the nation's growing prison population could be salvaged. Despite earlier reform movements most of the penal institutions of the country were filthy, overcrowded dungeons which confirmed convicts in their hatred of society. First offenders and habitual criminals were thrown together in the same institutions. The most important movement of the period was that toward segregating and reclaiming youthful first offenders. At the state reformatory at Elmira, New York, which was opened in 1877, men between the ages of fifteen and thirty convicted of their first crime served inde-

[1] George Kibbe Turner, "The City of Chicago—A Study of the Great Immoralities," *McClure's Magazine,* XXVIII (April, 1907), 587.

[2] See the discussion of the "Church and the City" in Chap. 25.

terminate sentences. By fair treatment and industrial training, an earnest effort was made to prepare them for useful lives. Earning release by good conduct, the inmates were placed in jobs and supervised by parole officers until their discharges were made final. Stimulated by the success of the Elmira experiment, similar reformatories were opened in Massachusetts, Pennsylvania, and a number of other states. New York opened a special institution for young female first offenders in 1893. New penal methods for older criminals were tried more cautiously, but important precedents were established when Massachusetts began to experiment with placing reformable offenders on probation and Ohio developed the parole system.

On every hand, the importance of keeping children out of trouble was emphasized. Public playgrounds, first financed by charitable societies and later by municipalities, were begun in Boston in 1885. By 1898 they were to be found in 13 eastern cities; by 1915 in 432 cities in all parts of the country. Charitable organizations and newspapers raised "fresh-air funds" to provide summer vacations in the country for slum children. Wholesome recreational activities were provided by numerous youth clubs and societies. The most important were the Boy Scouts of America, chartered in 1910, and the Girl Scouts and Camp Fire Girls, both organized in 1912.

In the cities evidence of indifference to the sufferings of animals was everywhere to be seen. Overloaded omnibuses were dragged along the streets by bruised and faltering horses; hackmen and draymen used the whip without mercy; unfed and unwatered cattle bellowed in the stockyards; cockfights and other survivals of animal baiting still amused slum audiences. Against all this brutality Henry Bergh, a wealthy merchant of New York City, led a determined crusade. Organizing the Society for the Prevention of Cruelty to Animals in 1864 on the model of a well-known English society, Bergh induced the New York legislature to pass laws against the maltreatment of animals and personally intervened between hundreds of dumb beasts and their tormentors. Bergh won an able group of disciples, who carried the humane campaign into other cities throughout the country. Soon discovering that children were often treated worse than animals, many of the same individuals joined in organizing the Society for the Prevention of Cruelty to Children in 1874.

Since bad housing caused so much crime, disease, and pauperism, a few philanthropists experimented with model tenements. Describing the famous Riverside Buildings erected by Alfred T. White in Brooklyn, Riis wrote:

> Its chief merit is that it gathers three hundred real homes, not simply three hundred families, under one roof. Three tenants . . . use each entrance hall. . . . Each has its private front-door. The common hall, with all that it stands for, has disappeared. The fireproof stairs are outside the house, a perfect fire-escape. . . . There are no air-shafts, for they are not needed. Every room, under the admirable arrangement of the plan, looks out either upon the street or the yard, that is nothing less than a great park with a playground set apart for the children. Weekly concerts are given in the park by a brass band.[1]

[1] Riis, *op. cit.,* 295.

After paying himself a reasonable return on his investment, White shared the profits with his tenants. But "philanthropy plus five per cent" had few practitioners. Providing poor tenants with facilities that they might misuse was regarded as risky business, and the vast majority of landlords stuck to time-honored methods of charging a maximum rent and holding expenses for improvements or repairs to a minimum.

Without the prod of state intervention private enterprise had no real remedy for the housing problem. After 1900 the prod was applied more vigorously than ever before. In 1901 the New York legislature passed a special tenement-house law for cities of 250,000 or over. All rooms and hallways had to be lighted and ventilated, and the size of rooms, provisions for water supply and sewage disposal, and the adequacy of fire escapes were matters of strict regulation. New Jersey passed a similar law for all cities of the state in 1905, and Pennsylvania and Connecticut also enacted state-wide codes. Between 1905 and 1908 Chicago, Boston, Cleveland, and San Francisco all adopted strict municipal building ordinances.

Laws, of course, were no better than the men who enforced them. In the minds of many citizens the most needed reform was a cleansing of municipal government. Corrupt politicians conspired with businessmen to defraud the taxpayers in the construction of buildings, the paving of streets, the laying of sewers, and the purchase of supplies. Transit companies bribed aldermen to secure their franchises, then continued the bribes to prevent investigation of their profits. Gambling resorts, houses of prostitution, and other illegal establishments remained open by paying regular tribute to the police. Fundamental to the continued plundering of these political machines was success at the polls. In part, this success depended on stuffing ballot boxes, buying votes, using repeaters, and other fraudulent practices. But corruption alone would not have carried so many elections for Tammany and other big city organizations. Thousands of poor immigrant voters regarded the ward heeler as one of their few friends in a cold world. To him they appealed when some member of the family got in trouble with the law; it was to him that they looked for occasional picnics and outings to brighten their drab lives; to him, accordingly, went control of their votes on election day.

To defeat these machines required great outbursts of public indignation. *Harper's Weekly* through the cartoons of Thomas Nast and the *New York Times* through fearless reporting helped to overthrow New York's Tweed Ring in 1871. Soon back in power, Tammany was somewhat more discreet in its operations but fell again under serious attack during the 1890's when Dr. Charles H. Parkhurst, a prominent Presbyterian minister, shocked the city with revelations of police-protected vice. The Lexow investigation, authorized by the state legislature in 1894, further discredited Tammany and resulted in a reform administration. But in New York, as in other cities, machine government was the rule, and occasional upsets provided only temporary housecleanings.

Although corrupt municipal government continued to disgrace the nation, the cities of 1914 were in many respects cleaner and safer than they had been in 1861. Efficient fire departments with paid, full-time firemen began to replace the volunteer companies soon after the Civil War; New York's department was organized in 1865, Philadelphia's in 1871. The movement was hastened by the Chicago fire of 1871, which destroyed 17,450 buildings and left over one-third of the population homeless. The importance of pure water and adequate facilities for disposing of sewage and garbage was emphasized by advancing medical knowledge. Municipal practice still lagged, but progress was made in these basic conditions of public health. Since incessant traffic over city streets required more attention to paving, there were experiments with every kind of material—wooden blocks, granite blocks, bricks, asphalt, and macadam. Other aids to urban transportation were great bridges like the famous Brooklyn structure, completed in 1883, and rapid-transit systems. The first elevated railroad, utilizing diminutive steam locomotives, began to operate along New York's Ninth Avenue in 1870; the first American subway was opened in Boston in 1897.

Urban Influence

The city had many faces. Slums, criminals, beggars, and grafters displayed one side of urban life. Beautiful parks, broad avenues lined with smart stores and fine mansions, great churches, theaters, museums, and libraries showed another. The best hospitals and the best schools were to be found in the cities, as were also the intellectual nerve centers of the country—the offices of the leading magazines, newspapers, and book publishers. It was part of the centralization of American life that the more sophisticated manners and morals of the city should exert a steadily widening influence over the country as a whole.

The city was the home of the rich no less than of the poor, and the rich were enjoying their golden hour. With taxes on incomes, estates, and corporate profits still nightmares of the future, the wealthy could expend huge sums on Fifth Avenue mansions, summer houses at Newport and Bar Harbor, fine horses and carriages, sumptuous dinners, and fancy-dress balls.

The city gave women new opportunities for independence. The narrow alternatives of earlier days—school teaching, domestic service, factory work—now broadened to offer employment to women doctors, lawyers, and typists, telephone girls, librarians, journalists, and social workers. The number of women gainfully employed rose from 2½ million in 1880 to 8 million in 1910.

Particularly interesting were the opportunities in nursing. Except for a few Catholic and other religious orders female nurses before the Civil War were an untrained and little-respected group. But public attitudes were radically altered after the famous exploits of Florence Nightingale in the Crimean War and of Dorothea Dix and Clara Barton in the American Civil War. The systematic training of nurses began about 1872 in the New England Hospital for Women at Boston and at the Bellevue Hospital in New York soon after. By 1883 there were 22 training schools in the country. Meanwhile, the energetic Clara Barton had provided the principal impetus in the organization of the American Red Cross in 1882 and in mobilizing its resources to deal with such disasters as the Johnstown flood of 1889.

Urban conditions, the growing independence of women, and many other economic and social factors were having their influence on American family life. Between 1860 and 1910 the birth rate declined from about 41 per thousand to about 27. Smaller families were particularly characteristic of the urban professional and business classes, who found it increasingly expensive to give children the education and other advantages that were considered necessary. Although delayed marriage and sedentary occupations contributed to the declining fertility of this group, conscious planning appeared to be the major factor. President Theodore Roosevelt denounced what he called "race suicide," but neither his preaching nor that of various religious leaders could halt the trend toward smaller families.

Even more alarming to many moralists was the steady increase in divorce. In 1867 fewer than 10,000 divorces were granted in the whole country—27 divorces for each 100,000 population. In 1914 there were over 100,000 divorces and the rate had risen to 100 per 100,000 inhabitants—the highest for any civilized country except Japan.

The lack of uniformity in state divorce laws invited many abuses. In states like New York, where the law was strict, grounds were often established through collusion of the parties. On the other hand, states where the law was notoriously lax had a steady stream of out-of-state visitors remaining just long enough to fulfill the residence requirements. First Indiana, then South Dakota, and finally Nevada were famous for their divorce colonies. The National Divorce Reform League, founded in 1881, agitated unsuccessfully for uniform divorce laws to be achieved either through common action of the states or by amendment to the Federal Constitution.

Despite feminine progress in other lines men held to their monopoly of voting and office holding with surprising tenacity. Since Susan B. Anthony, Elizabeth Cady Stanton, and other feminist leaders had given valuable support to the Republicans during the Civil War, they had hoped to secure woman suffrage as their reward. But they had a bitter disappointment. Evidently believing that it was difficult enough to force through Negro suffrage, the Radical Republicans declined to take up the highly controversial woman-suffrage issue. A number of feminists attempted to vote during the 1870's claiming that the franchise was one of the privileges and immunities of citizenship guaranteed by the Fourteenth Amendment. With firm male logic the United States Supreme Court rejected this ingenious proposition in 1875.

The cause was hardly strengthened by the spectacular career of Victoria Woodhull. After an apprenticeship in the business of fortunetelling, spiritualism, and patent medicine, Mrs. Woodhull and her sister Tennessee Claflin opened a stockbrokerage office in New York, where with the patronage of Commodore Vanderbilt they made good profits. Adopting the suffrage cause in 1871, Victoria bore down on Washington, where she received from admiring congressmen an audience much more attentive than any that had ever been accorded less glamorous feminists. Meanwhile, *Woodhull and Claflin's Weekly,* founded in 1870, had become an energetic promoter of radical causes. Equal rights for women was disturbing enough; Victoria Woodhull for President of the United States was still more startling; free love most shocking of all. Serious trouble began when Victoria's journal undertook provocative discussions of the prostitution problem and published lurid allegations regarding the private life of the great Henry Ward Beecher. In righteous wrath the public turned on the beautiful broker-politician-journalist. Although acquitted on a charge of publishing obscene material, Victoria became involved in more and more difficulties until she finally moved to England.

Although Miss Anthony had sought to preserve the respectability of the women's rights movement by disavowing Mrs. Woodhull before her final disgrace, the suffrage cause encountered increased hostility. Another unfortunate circumstance of these years was a disagreement among the feminists over basic strategy. Miss Anthony and Mrs. Stanton concentrated their heaviest guns on Congress, endeavoring to secure a constitutional amendment that would do for women what the Fifteenth had done for Negroes. Lucy Stone, Julia Ward Howe, Henry Ward Beecher, and William Lloyd Garrison advocated a campaign to secure the ballot by action of the individual states. From 1869 to 1889 rival organizations were at work: the National Woman Suffrage Association followed Miss Anthony's leadership; the American Woman Suffrage Association adopted the more conservative tactics of Lucy Stone. After twenty years the schism was finally healed through a merger of the two organizations.

The suffrage cause won a few significant victories. The territorial legislature of Wyoming voted to give equal franchise to men and women in 1869, and that of Utah took the same step in 1870. In 1893 Colorado women received the vote after a popular referendum on the issue; in 1896 the same thing happened in Idaho. Meanwhile, women had been given the right to vote in school elections and on other municipal issues in 13 other states. Offsetting these gains, however, were a series of discouraging defeats.

One of the most powerful groups opposed to woman suffrage was the liquor trade, which feared that women voters would support the rising prohibition movement. Indeed the Prohibition party, organized on a national basis in 1869, had endorsed woman suffrage in its first platform. The party failed to make an impressive showing in national elections, but in many local contests it showed effective strength. Through local option many towns and villages voted against granting licenses to liquor dealers, and by 1898 Kansas, North Dakota, New

Hampshire, and Vermont had followed the example of Maine in establishing state-wide prohibition.

The crusade against rum gained a new militancy with the birth of the Woman's Christian Temperance Union in 1873. The first permanent chapter was founded at Hillsboro, Ohio, where a group of 70 women prayed and pleaded with saloon-keepers so effectively that several gave up their business and poured their fiery stock into the gutters. Even more dramatic was the campaign in Washington

FIG. 42. *Woman's Crusade against Intemperance.* Drawn by C. S. Reinhart for *Harper's Weekly*, March 14, 1874. A saloonkeeper's wife orders praying members of the W.C.T.U. from the premises. (*Courtesy of the Library of Congress.*)

Court House, Ohio, where a barrage of prayer closed all the town's 14 saloons. Newspapers across the nation gave wide publicity to the "Washington Court House movement," and women were inspired to institute hundreds of similar local crusades. The Woman's Christian Temperance Union was organized on a national basis in November, 1874. Under the shrewd leadership of Frances E. Willard, formerly dean of women at Northwestern University, the new society exerted a wide influence. Working through Sunday schools, it induced thousands of children to pledge themselves never to use intoxicating beverages. Even more important, it induced one state after another to teach temperance in the public schools. Millions of children were told that alcohol was a habit-forming poison highly injurious to the human body.

The women were by no means without powerful allies in their condemnation of the liquor business. The Methodist Episcopal Church set up a temperance bureau during the 1890's, and most other Protestant bodies were aggressive in the cause. A Catholic Total Abstinence Society was active, and the third plenary council of Catholic bishops at Baltimore in 1884–1885 instructed priests to induce all Catholic liquor dealers to "choose a more honorable way of making a living." Many employers refused to hire any but teetotalers, and the Knights of Labor under Powderly vigorously condemned the rum business. Finally, in 1895 the most militant of all the temperance organizations, the Anti-Saloon League of America, was organized. Through its many branches the League quickly became a political force—rewarding with dry votes politicians who voted for prohibition laws and punishing those who opposed.

Despite all this activity the total consumption of intoxicating beverages went, not down, but sharply up. In 1860 the American population imbibed some 200,000,000 gallons, or 6.43 gallons per capita; in 1910 they drank 2,250,000,000 gallons, or 22.66 gallons per capita. The rise was not quite as startling as these figures suggest, since most of the increased consumption was in beer. Per capita consumption of distilled spirits actually fell from 2.86 in 1860 to 1.44 in 1914 while that for malt beverages was climbing from 3.22 to 20.69.

The rise of the city had obviously provided a widely expanded market for the liquor business. Most of the immigrants came from countries where W.C.T.U. societies and Anti-Saloon Leagues were unknown. They drank beer or wine with their meals as a matter of course and celebrated every wedding, birth, funeral, and holiday with extra potations. Drinking at home was supplemented by drinking at the corner saloon. The poor thronged these establishments not merely because of thirst but because they offered warmth, companionship, and free lunches to thousands of slum dwellers who hated to go back to their dark, dirty, overcrowded quarters. The reputation of being the poor man's club, however, did not save the saloon from condemnation as a den of iniquity where men squandered their pay, ruined their health, and were enticed into vice and crime. Municipal reformers everywhere regarded the saloonkeeper as the most powerful ally of the corrupt political machine. Nor was the drink habit peculiar to the urban poor. At the other end of the social ladder, the rich enjoyed their cocktails before dinner, drank the appropriate wine with each of many courses, and finished with a little brandy. Then when the ladies had excused themselves, the men settled down to their cigars and more serious drinking. The divergent attitudes of city and country, sharply outlined between 1861 and 1914, had their dramatic climax in the struggle over national prohibition after World War I.

Nor was the saloon the only challenge to the traditions of rural Protestant America. Despite nonconformance by the Germans and the Irish, the old-fashioned Sunday still imposed a somber outward decorum on most American communities during the generation of the American Civil War. All theaters and places of amusement were closed by law, and only the most necessary business establishments were allowed to remain open. Where the laws left off, community opinion took up the matter. Swimming, fishing, driving for pleasure, and even sewing for the poor were desecrations of the Sabbath in the eyes of millions of Americans. But in this matter also the city was synonymous with change. In their new homes, as in their old, most immigrants looked upon the first day of the week as a time for relaxation and amusement once the obligation to attend church had been fulfilled. Factory workers were particularly resentful of attempts to restrict their activities on their one free day. With increasing boldness city saloon-keepers and theater managers ignored the closing laws. In 1883 highly urbanized New York, Massachusetts, and California began liberalizing their so-called "blue laws." After 1900 Sunday baseball and Sunday movies became increasingly common.

Thus in many ways did the sophisticated manners and morals of the city first diverge from the older patterns of rural society and then proceed to impose themselves on the smaller communities as well.

Chapter 25. Religion's Response to the Industrial Age

In 1861 American religion was peculiarly the product of rural frontier society. From the village it derived both its virtues—sincerity, simplicity, enthusiasm—and its vices—narrowness and excessive individualism. America's rapid transition to an urban, industrialized nation, looking to science for its miracles, challenged the old religion at many points. Although the churches lost some of their prestige and authority, their wounds were by no means mortal. In membership and wealth they continued to grow. More important, in the maladjustments of the new society they found a stimulus to new forms of activity.

Growth of the Churches

In the area of the last frontier the old agencies of religious expansion went vigorously to work. Circuit-riding parsons again ministered to crossroads congregations; local preachers, uneducated but earnest, labored without pay in hundreds of isolated hamlets. Behind these efforts there was now more institutionalized support. Each of the leading denominations had its church-extension society or board of home missions. Large sums of money were contributed in the East for the support of missionaries and for the building of churches in the newer sections. Exulting in the growth which seemed to them the perfect answer to the activities of Colonel Bob Ingersoll and other agnostics of the day, the Methodists sang:

> The infidels, a motley band,
> In council met and said:
> "The churches die all through the land,
> The last will soon be dead."
> When suddenly a message came,
> It filled them with dismay:
> "All hail the power of Jesus's name!
> We're building two a day." [1]

Nor were the Methodists alone in expanding at a rate that confounded those who predicted their demise; so rapidly did the Baptists grow, especially among

[1] Quoted in W. W. Sweet, *The Story of Religion in America* (Harper, New York, 1939), 484.

the Negroes, that they overcame the lead which the Methodists had held at the mid-century mark. According to the religious census of 1916 each of the two leading Protestant denominations had about seven million adherents in its various branches. The Presbyterians numbered a little over two million members. The growth of the Lutherans to a membership of over 1½ million in 1916 reflected several decades of heavy German and Scandinavian immigration. The Disciples of Christ, youngest among the major American denominations, was fifth in size in 1916, while the Episcopal and Congregational churches, the two oldest, were sixth and seventh respectively.

Interest in foreign missions remained high. The Student Volunteer Movement, organized at Northfield, Massachusetts, in 1886, became a potent agency in inducing college students to devote their lives to missionary work. The buoyant optimism of the enterprise was well illustrated by the title of a book written by John R. Mott in 1900, *The Evangelization of the World in This Generation.* Although this goal was by no means achieved, the Student Volunteer Movement had recruited 5,000 missionaries by 1915.

Many American Protestants saw God's hand in the disintegration of the independent nations of Asia and Africa. They regarded the extension of the British Empire as a providential expansion of Christian civilization and gave their blessing to rising American imperialism. In a book written for the American Home Missionary Society, Josiah Strong contrasted the virile strength of American Protestantism with the decaying institutions of other continents and asserted:

> Thus, while on this continent God is training the Anglo-Saxon race for its mission, a complemental work has been in progress in the great world beyond. God has two hands. Not only is he preparing in our civilization the die with which to stamp the nations but, by what Southey called the "timing of Providence," he is preparing mankind to receive our impress.[1]

Although the jingoism of Hearst and Pulitzer was occasionally rebuked from the pulpit, the Spanish-American War was supported by most Protestants as a necessary crusade to rescue tortured Cuba from the corrupt rule of Catholic Spain. The acquisition of the Philippine Islands was regarded as a further opportunity provided by God for extending His kingdom. Considering the spirit of the times, there is no reason to suspect President McKinley of hypocrisy in telling a group of Methodists:

> . . . I am not ashamed to tell you, gentlemen, that I went down on my knees and prayed Almighty God for light and guidance more than one night. And one night late it came to me this way . . . there was nothing left for us to do but to take . . . and to educate the Filipinos and uplift and civilize and Christianize them and by God's grace do the very best we could by them, as our fellow men for whom Christ also died.[2]

[1] Josiah Strong, *Our Country: Its Possible Future and Its Present Crisis* (American Home Missionary Society, New York, 1891), 225.

[2] Charles S. Olcott, *The Life of William McKinley* (Houghton Mifflin, Boston, 1916), II, 110–111.

Impact of Immigration

The religious situation was significantly altered by the large-scale immigration of these years. Among Protestant denominations the Lutherans profited enormously despite the fact that many Scandinavians failed to affiliate with the old church in their new homes. But the majority of the newcomers were not Protestants. To the great stream of Irish and German Catholics entering the country were added after 1880 large numbers of Italian, Polish, Czech, and Slovak Catholics. Equally remarkable was the great influx of Jews.

Estimates of the number of Catholics in the United States vary widely, but those made by Gerald Shaughnessy, a careful student of the problem, indicate that the Catholic population for some time doubled every twenty years. In 1860 there were about three million American Catholics; in 1880 about six million; in 1900 about twelve million; in 1910 about sixteen million. Naturally, Catholic spokesmen ascribed their church's growth to the miraculous providence of God. In the words of Dr. Shaughnessy:

> . . . Not another instance in history is recorded, where millions of different races and nationalities, of varied natural prejudices and leanings, made their way to a strange country, not *en masse* but individually, there to build up what they found practically non-existent, a flourishing, closely knit, firmly welded Church in what was, and even today may be truthfully described as, otherwise a religious wilderness.
>
> Only the miraculous work of a St. Peter, a St. Paul, or a St. Patrick, in ancient history is comparable to this phenomenon, and even this is comparable only in its wonderful character, and not in the particular circumstances. In modern history there is nothing even remotely to be compared with it.[1]

The rapid expansion of Catholicism, accompanied as it was by the establishment of thousands of Catholic convents and parochial schools, resulted in anti-Catholic protests, similar in spirit though less serious than those of the generation before the Civil War. In 1887 H. F. Bowers, a lawyer in Clinton, Iowa, organized the American Protective Association. Members of the A.P.A. took a secret oath to use all possible power to "strike the shackles and chains of blind obedience to the Roman Catholic Church from the hampered and bound consciences of a priest-ridden and church-oppressed people," and promised never to aid in the building and maintaining of any Catholic church or institution and never to countenance the nomination or election of any Roman Catholic to public office. In addition to alleged revelations by ex-priests and ex-nuns, the A.P.A. circulated spurious documents intended to prove an imminent Catholic plot to take over the country and to exterminate the heretics. The arrival of Archbishop Satolli as papal representative at the Chicago World's Fair in 1893 played into the hands of the anti-Catholics, and the A.P.A. gained an extensive membership

[1] Gerald Shaughnessy, *Has the Immigrant Kept the Faith?* (Macmillan, New York, 1925), 268.

in states like Iowa, Nebraska, Kansas, Missouri, Illinois, and Ohio, even securing a balance of political power in some districts. But the movement collapsed as rapidly as it had risen and was of little importance after 1896.

The success of the Church in achieving its great expansion without more serious opposition was a tribute to the popularity of Cardinal Gibbons, the most important figure in the American hierarchy for many years. Born in 1834 of Irish-immigrant parents in Baltimore, Gibbons understood well the peculiar problems of Catholicism in the American environment. As a young bishop ministering to the needs of the small and scattered Catholic population of North Carolina, he had learned to value the good will of non-Catholics. Often in these years he had had to borrow a Protestant church building for his services; sometimes he had had to use a Protestant Bible and a Protestant choir as well. Without deviating from stanch loyalty to Catholicism, Gibbons developed a gift for explaining the Church's tenets in ways unlikely to irritate Protestants.

Gibbons's intelligence, simplicity, and winning personality brought him rapid elevation in the Church. He became archbishop of Baltimore in 1877 and a cardinal in 1886—the second American to receive this distinction. Although not a profound or original thinker, Gibbons had a sound instinct to guide him in dealing with fundamental issues. Intensely proud of his American citizenship, the cardinal stressed the compatibility of the Roman Catholic Church and American institutions. Perceiving the danger implicit in the antirepublican and ultraconservative philosophy of many European clericals, he took every opportunity to praise democratic government and to assert that the Church was the friend of the workingman. Acknowledging that the separation of church and state was not ideal from the point of view of Catholic philosophy, he nevertheless defended it as highly advantageous to the Church under American conditions.

Agreeing with Gibbons that American institutions offered a particularly favorable environment for Catholic growth were other prominent churchmen like Archbishop Ireland of St. Paul, Bishop Keane, first rector of Catholic University, and Father Isaac Hecker, founder of the Paulist order. Archbishop Ireland's popularity in Republican political circles was so great that President Theodore Roosevelt attempted to engineer his elevation to the rank of cardinal and was indignant when his wirepulling failed.

Father Hecker's career was a curious one. Brought into the Catholic fold by his friend Orestes Brownson, this former transcendentalist and Brook Farmer aspired to convert as many other Protestants as possible. Hecker's deep piety, persuasive preaching, and emphasis on individual responsibility made a deep impression on Catholics and non-Catholics alike. After his death in 1888 a fellow Paulist, Father Elliott, wrote a warmly sympathetic biography, to which Archbishop Ireland contributed an introduction, lauding Hecker as the ideal American priest. Translated into French, this work was eagerly read by a group of French Catholics distressed at the Church's unpopularity in the Third Republic. They concluded that Father Hecker's career exemplified a new and superior kind of Catholicism, which placed less emphasis on religious rules and observances and more on the individual conscience and social work among the people. This development greatly distressed clerical conservatives, who besought the Pope to intervene. With some show of reluctance Leo XIII issued an apostolic letter in 1899 condemning "false Americanism." The censured tendencies were undue insistence on interior initiative in the spiritual life, attacks on religious vows, the minimizing of Catholic doctrine, and the minimizing of the importance of spiritual direction. The Pope did not assert that these unsound doctrines had actually been held by Father Hecker, and Cardinal Gibbons assured the Vatican that they had no existence among American Catholics.

Even though the papal action had more reference to the French situation than to the American, it seems likely that it was to some extent intended as a timely warning to Gibbons and other American clerics. Catholic conservatives had become concerned with the extent to which Gibbons and Ireland were fraternizing with non-Catholics. Criticism was particularly severe in 1893, when the two appeared at the World's Congress of Religions at Chicago, where the Cardinal made the opening prayer. The Pope, famous for his diplomatic skill, upheld Gibbons and Ireland on a number of issues that arose in the early nineties but pacified the conservatives by removing Bishop Keane from the rectorship of Catholic University, by condemning "false Americanism," and by forbidding Catholics to take part in mixed religious congresses.

Another problem concerned the proper treatment of foreign-speaking American Catholics. A demand not only for German priests but for German bishops had been heard as early as Archbishop Carroll's day. The Church had responded by assigning German-speaking priests to German parishes when possible but had steadfastly refused to set the German Catholics apart as a special group with their own bishops. The issue continued to be agitated and became serious in 1890, when the Archangel Raphael Society in Germany, a group interested in American missionary work, presented a memorial to the Pope, alleging that the failure to provide immigrant groups with priests and bishops of their own nationality had resulted in a loss of 16 million adherents to the faith. The memorial urged that each of the various nationality groups should have its own churches and priests, its own foreign-language schools, and a number of bishops proportionate to its strength in the Catholic population. These demands, known as Cahenslyism after Peter Cahensly, secretary of the German society, encountered determined opposition from Cardinal Gibbons. Any such policy, he believed, would not only destroy the unity of the American church but make it a vehicle for perpetuating foreign-culture groups within the American population. The Pope upheld the cardinal. Ecclesiastics of German origin became bishops, but their elevation was based on individual merit rather than on the principle that each national group should have its own prelates.

Although Cahenslyism gradually subsided, flare-ups of jealousy recurred from time to time. Usually they took a form no more serious than German, Italian, Polish, or French grumbling at the predominance of Irish in the American hierarchy. In extreme cases this friction led to schism. Influenced by the Old Catholic movement in Europe, small bodies of American Catholics rejected the authority of the pope and established independent communions. Largest of these was the Polish National Church of America, which claimed some 28,000 members in 1916.

Jews, even more than Catholics, were divided as to whether they should cling to all their Old World observances or should accommodate themselves to the new American environment. To the distress of conservatives many synagogues introduced innovations like the use of organs, mixed choirs, family pews, bared heads, and the substitution of prayers in English for the traditional ones in Hebrew. Rabbi Isaac Wise, who came to America from Germany in 1846, was for fifty years a resolute champion of "reform." He was instrumental in establishing the Union of American Hebrew Congregations in 1873 and the Hebrew Union College at Cincinnati in 1875. More radical than Wise was Rabbi Kaufmann Kohler of New York, who asserted:

> Judaism must drop its orientalism, and become truly American in spirit and form. . . . It will not do to offer our prayers in a tongue which only few scholars nowadays understand. We cannot afford any longer to pray for a return to Jerusalem. It is a blasphemy and lie upon the lips of every American Jew. . . .[1]

A conference of rabbis at Pittsburgh in 1885 renounced the Mosaic code:

> We accept as binding only its moral laws, and maintain only such ceremonies as elevate and sanctify our lives, but reject all such as are not adapted to the views and habits of modern civilization. . . . We hold that all such Mosaic and rabbinical laws as regulate diet, priestly purity and dress originated in ages and under the influence of ideas entirely foreign to our present mental and spiritual state.[2]

Against these trends there was strong reaction. The radical Pittsburgh platform resulted in the establishment of the conservative Jewish Theological Seminary of America, dedicated to the preservation of "historical Judaism, as ordained in the Law of Moses and expounded by the Prophets and Sages of Israel in Biblical and Talmudical writings." In the twentieth century there were three federations of synagogues: the reformed federation was composed of Jews most influenced by modern trends; the orthodox federation followed traditional law and custom most strictly; the conservative federation adopted a middle course between these extremes. Largest by far was the orthodox group, which was strongly reinforced by Polish and Russian immigration.

[1] Quoted in Ismar Elbogen, *A Century of Jewish Life* (Jewish Publication Society of America, Philadelphia, 1945), 344.

[2] *Ibid.*, 345.

Darwinism and Higher Criticism

For men of simple faith who cherished each verse of the Bible as divinely inspired and literally true, the theories of Charles Darwin had shocking implications. Genesis said that the earth and all living things were created in six days; Darwin described a process extending over millions of years. Genesis said that each species of animal life was separately created; Darwin undertook to prove that the more complex species evolved from the simpler through a process of natural selection. Most important of all, Genesis said that God's culminating miracle was the creation of man in His own image, but Darwin demoted man to a place in the animal world and traced his descent from other species.

The publication of Darwin's most famous book, *Origin of Species,* in 1859 provoked relatively little discussion in America—probably because of the overpowering political crisis of the time. Not until the seventies was controversy over evolution pushed to the fore by a number of events. In 1871 Darwin published his *Descent of Man,* which was much more specific in applying the evolutionary theory to the human species than the earlier book had been. The ponderous volumes of Herbert Spencer's *Synthetic Philosophy,* then being widely read in America, not only assumed Darwinism to be true but extended the evolutionary theory far beyond the biological field. John Fiske began his career as the great American popularizer of the new thesis with lectures at Harvard in 1869 and 1870. English science was directly presented to American audiences when John Tyndall made a lecture tour in 1872 and 1873; Thomas Huxley, "Darwin's bulldog," followed in 1876, and Herbert Spencer arrived in 1882. President Andrew D. White of Cornell defended the evolutionary hypothesis in a well-publicized lecture at Cooper Union in New York, and the new learning's impatience with narrow orthodoxy found expression in John W. Draper's *Warfare of Science and Religion* (1874). Most disturbing of all was the aggressive agnosticism contained in "The Mistakes of Moses" and other popular lectures being delivered during the seventies by Colonel Bob Ingersoll.

Against the propagation of the evolutionary theory, religious conservatives set up hastily constructed defenses. In a book entitled *What Is Darwinism?* (1874), Charles Hodge, an esteemed theologian of the day, asserted that "a more absolutely incredible theory was never propounded for acceptance among men." In a lecture before Princeton theological students Mark Hopkins, the famous former president of Williams College, attacked Darwinism as "essentially atheistic." President Eliot of Harvard was denounced for arranging the John Fiske lectures, and Fiske himself was for years denied an invitation to deliver the Lowell lectures—one of Boston's most esteemed honors. In most of the denominational colleges the theory of evolution was condemned without a hearing.

Although uncompromising opponents of the theory were for many years a militant majority, a few outstanding spokesmen not only accepted the new hypothesis but gave it a religious interpretation. John Fiske proved to be far from the agnostic whom his critics painted. In books like *Outlines of a Cosmic Philosophy* (1874), *The Destiny of Man* (1884), and *The Idea of God as Affected by Modern Knowledge* (1886), Fiske identified God with the great creative force behind the whole evolutionary process. Evolution he defined as "God's way of doing things."

The evolutionary theory's most sensational convert was Henry Ward Beecher. In a magazine article published in 1882, Beecher rejoiced at the gradual substitution of a "theory of evolutionism" for Calvinism. When his statements brought sharp criticism from fellow Congregationalists, Beecher resigned from his local Congregational association. In 1883 he described himself as a "cordial Christian evolutionist," and in 1885 he expanded his views in a book entitled *Evolution and Religion*.

Even more influential than Beecher in winning support for the new ideas was Lyman Abbott, editor of the independent religious periodical *Christian Union* and later Beecher's successor at Plymouth Church, Brooklyn. Accepting John Fiske's theistic definition of evolution, Abbott explained that man's method of doing things was the method of manufacture and that God's method was the method of growth. He kept the old concepts—sin, revelation, redemption, miracles, and immortality—but he redefined them to conform with his belief in evolution.

Some of the Christian evolutionists made elaborate efforts to harmonize the new theory with the familiar story in Genesis, interpreting each verse to describe a phase in the evolutionary process. But bolder spirits dismissed this effort as futile. Genesis they now regarded as a magnificent poem of creation, rich in spiritual meaning but not to be taken literally.

This attitude toward Genesis gained support from a radically new type of Biblical scholarship then gaining attention in America. Theological students, going to German universities for graduate work, came back with disturbing ideas—ideas that were also transmitted to America through the works of English and Scotch Biblical scholars. The new theories denied that the first five books of the Old Testament had been written by Moses or by any other one man. Internal evidence was held to prove that the Pentateuch was a composite of passages written by different authors at widely different times—usually many centuries after the events which they related. The story of the flood and Noah's ark was explained as a borrowing from Mesopotamian literature, and Abraham, Isaac, and Jacob became folk heroes standing for certain collective experiences of the Hebrew tribes. Other parts of the Bible came under similarly radical scrutiny. "Higher criticism," as the new scholarship was called, caused controversy fully as acrimonious as that about evolution.

The clerical thinkers were divided on other important issues as well. Conservatives still preached frequently and enthusiastically on the subject of hell, but liberals tended to emphasize divine love rather than the wrath to come. The radicals no longer believed in future punishment; the moderates ingeniously softened the doctrine. Many refused to believe that a loving God would condemn unbaptized infants or heathen who had never heard the gospel. Miracles were another stumbling block; conservatives accepted them as the principal proof of the power of God and the divinity of Christ; liberals doubted that the God revealed in evolution and the orderly processes of nature suspended His laws to raise the dead or to cause virgins to conceive.

The new and the old in Protestantism came to grips in a number of heresy trials. The most significant of these involved the Reverend Charles A. Briggs, whose book *Biblical Study: Its Principles, Methods, and History* (1883) had done much to familiarize Americans with higher criticism. Controversy over Briggs's teaching came to a crisis with his appointment to a professorial chair at Union Theological Seminary in 1890. Expertly dissected by his critics, Briggs's inaugural address provided the basis for no fewer than eight charges of heresy and ten specifications. The alleged errors were a representative cross section of the new teachings. Briggs had asserted that divine authority was based on the church and on the Reason as well as on the Bible; he had taught "that errors may have existed in the original text of the Holy Scripture, as it came from the author," "that Moses did not write the Pentateuch," "that Isaiah is not the author of half the book which bears his name," and "that the processes of redemption extend to the world to come." The New York presbytery voted for Briggs's acquittal on the ground that he had not transgressed the limits of liberty permitted within the Presbyterian denomination. But the case was appealed to the General Assembly, and in 1893 this body convicted the professor and suspended him from the ministry "until he could give satisfactory evidence of repentance." Briggs transferred to the Episcopal Church and continued to teach at Union. Professor Henry Preserved Smith of Lane Theological Seminary was similarly disciplined the same year.

Although the Episcopal Church was sufficiently liberal to receive Briggs, there were limits to its tolerance. In 1906 the Reverend Algernon Sidney Crapsey, rector of an Episcopal church in Rochester, New York, was convicted by an ecclesiastical court of denying the virgin birth, the divinity of Christ, and other points in the historic creeds. Crapsey refused to recant and resigned from the ministry.

Although the majority of Protestants remained conservative on these issues, the liberals won strategic ground of great importance. A controversy so bitter that it was taken into the civil courts of Massachusetts resulted in a victory for academic freedom at Andover Theological Seminary—the historic citadel of Congregational orthodoxy. Union Theological Seminary upheld not only its "heretical" Professor Briggs but also A. C. McGiffert when criticism of the latter's teaching drove him from the Presbyterian Church. Identified with the new liberalism still more closely was the University of Chicago Theological Seminary, and a similar trend was obvious in other northern institutions.

The liberals' capture of the principal ministerial training schools greatly alarmed the conservatives, who organized a vigorous counteroffensive. For a generation after 1876 the sessions of the Niagara Bible Conference, where the orthodox consolidated their forces for assaults on the new teachings, were annual events. In 1895 the Niagara Conference formulated five points of sound doctrine, which later became famous as the charter of "fundamentalism." The tests of orthodoxy were belief in the inerrancy of the Scriptures, the deity of Christ, the virgin birth, substitutionary atonement, and the coming bodily return of Christ to earth. New institutions like the Moody Bible Institute of Chicago and the Los Angeles Bible Institute educated preachers untainted by contact with either evolutionary theory or the higher criticism. In 1909 two California oil millionaires financed the publication and distribution of a series of little books entitled *The Fundamentals: A Testimony to the Truth.* Three million copies of this work together with other propaganda were sent to preachers and leading laymen in every part of the country and to missionaries abroad. The alarm against modernism had been sounded, and militant recruits were secured for a war destined to have its bitterest battles during the 1920's.

In Europe the Roman Catholic Church had to deal with problems similar to those disturbing American Protestants. In 1907 Pius X issued an encyclical condemning "modernism," and the leading Catholic practitioners of higher criticism were either silenced or excommunicated. But the American church, preoccupied with practical problems of organization, was largely untouched by these issues.

The Church and the City

In the pulpits of the large and wealthy churches of the great cities were to be found the most popular preachers of the day. The prototype of the urban minister was the popular idol Henry Ward Beecher. Called to the newly organized Plymouth (Congregational) Church of Brooklyn in 1847, Beecher enjoyed a sensational success. His impressive presence, his mastery of language, and his dramatic eloquence drew congregations of two and three thousand that filled Plymouth Church every Sunday and made it the most famous Protestant church in the country. So great was Beecher's hold on his admirers that they remained loyal despite accusations of unorthodoxy and sensational adultery charges that would have ruined any other man's career.

More substantial was the nationwide respect gained by Phillips Brooks, pastor of Trinity (Episcopal) Church of Boston from 1869 to 1891. Brooks's huge physical size—6 feet 4 inches in height, 300 pounds in weight—seemed to be matched by a largeness of spirit which overrode the controversies of the day. Neither attacking nor defending the new religious ideas, he had a warm spiritual message, the transparent sincerity of which profoundly impressed his generation.

But the cities were full of human needs that could not be met by preaching, however eloquent. A recognition of the problems peculiar to young men who had been drawn away from their home environment to jobs in the city had led to the organization of the Young Men's Christian Association in England in 1844. The first American Y.M.C.A. was established in Boston in 1851. There were 200 local associations in 1861 and 2,000 in 1914. A parallel if smaller growth was experienced by the Young Women's Christian Association, which was founded in England in 1855 and gained its first American branch in 1866.

Also originating in England, the Salvation Army began its work among the urban poor of America in 1880. Within a decade the blue-uniformed street-corner preacher and his accompanying brass band became a familiar sight in every large city of the country. Not long confining itself to the spiritual needs of its clients, the Salvation Army provided temporary shelter and food for the homeless, collected castoff clothing and distributed it to the poor, and sought to rehabilitate those who had been defeated in the hard competition of urban life.

Still another English precedent destined to have great influence in America was the establishment of Toynbee Hall in London. Many American social workers visited this pioneer settlement house and used it as a model for similar efforts in the great American cities. In 1886 the Neighborhood Guild, organized by Dr. Stanton Coit, began its work in New York. Three years later Jane Addams and Ellen G. Starr founded the famous Hull House in Chicago. The settlement movement made great progress during the nineties. Houses were established in many cities, and college students eagerly accepted service in them.

More peculiarly American was the institutional church. Catholic churches had always been cores around which a variety of charitable and social activities had taken shape. But American Protestant churches had been open only for Sunday and midweek services. First to develop a broad program of weekday activities were some of the Episcopal churches of New York. The Church of the Holy Communion organized such a program during the pastorate of Henry M. Mühlenberg from 1846 to 1858, and Grace Church took similar steps in 1868.

The institutional church produced a new type of ecclesiastical architecture. One of the first examples of this was the Congregational church erected at Elmira, New York, in 1872 under the direction of the Reverend Thomas K. Beecher, brother of Henry Ward Beecher and Harriet Beecher Stowe. Beecher's church, an object of amazement to Mark Twain, contained a library, lecture halls, and a gymnasium.

One of the boldest experiments was that carried out at St. George's Episcopal Church in New York. When D. W. S. Rainsford became its rector in 1882, he faced a discouraging situation typical of the problems created by the shifting population of the cities. The neighborhood in which the church stood had lost its wealthy residents and become a densely inhabited tenement district. The membership of the church had dwindled to 87, and Dr. Rainsford had either to preach to empty pews or to develop a program that would fit the vital needs of the area. Under his vigorous leadership vocational classes were organized, a cooperative grocery established, sickly mothers and children sent to the seashore on vacations, and wholesome recreational activities provided for every age group. In fifteen years the membership of the church grew to 4,000.

From other cities came similar stories. From the night school for workers at Russell Conwell's Baptist Temple in Philadelphia, Temple University evolved. In Boston the Morgan Memorial Methodist Church organized the Goodwill Industries—a highly successful project for enabling the aged poor and other unemployed persons to make a living. Castoff clothing, shoes, and furniture were collected from the well to do, carefully repaired, and then sold at low prices to the poor.

Most churches were content with less ambitious projects, but they at least recognized a need to provide wholesome recreational activities for their own membership. They were now open seven days a week instead of one or two. Nursery groups, Boy Scouts and Girl Scouts, young people's societies, men's clubs, and women's organizations all had their weekday activities. Either in separate parish houses or in wings of the church buildings there were card parties, dances, and basketball games—often to the dismay of the older generation, who feared desecration of the Lord's house.

The Social Gospel

The best churches and the best Christians did much to ease the lot of the poor, but the very urgency of these charitable needs raised questions for the thoughtful. Why was there so much poverty and suffering? The old answer had been simple. America was "a land of opportunity," but the poor had wasted that opportunity through laziness or intemperance. This assumption no longer completely satisfied. Much of the grinding poverty of the cities seemed to arise from conditions for which the individual poor could not be blamed. Was it the needleworker's fault that she was paid only a pittance for hours of confining work? When the factory worker's wages hardly sustained his family in good times, was it his fault that he had no savings to support the household when he became ill, or was injured at his work, or was thrown out of employment during an economic depression?

The idea that Christians should address themselves to the reform of society conflicted with the traditions of historic Protestantism, which had been preoccupied with the salvation of individual souls. How men made their living had been considered a secular question to be left alone by the preachers—except in notorious cases where money was made by robbery, prostitution, slaveholding, or rum selling. Wealth achieved through hard work, thrift, savings, and wise investment had been regarded as wholly meritorious. This reflected, of course, the predominantly middle-class composition of most Protestant churches.

Two considerations weighed heavily in a modification of the old attitudes. One was the loss of membership which the churches must suffer if the growing class of industrial workers became convinced that the churches had no sympathy with their problems. The other was the obvious connection between social injustice and the kind of personal sin with which the churches had always been concerned. Unemployed or poorly paid men, desperate to provide for their families, often turned to crime. Unemployed or poorly paid women were often forced into lives of immorality.

The growing concern of American Protestants with social conditions was fed by both foreign and domestic springs of thought. In England Christian Socialism was stirring the religious world under the leadership of such figures as John Ruskin, Charles Kingsley, and Frederick D. Maurice. In America some of the early Unitarians like William Ellery Channing and Theodore Parker had directed attention to the evils of society, and the liberal Congregationalist Horace Bushnell had placed great emphasis on the importance of bringing up young people in the environment of a Christian home and a Christian community. Bushnell had not followed the social implications of this line of thought to their logical conclusion, but men influenced by his teachings did so.

Washington Gladden, pastor of a Congregational church in Cleveland from 1882 to 1918, was a bold critic of contemporary American society. He believed that a wage system based solely on competition was "anti-social and anti-Christian." He asserted the right of workers to organize and to strike: "If war is to be the order of the day we must grant to labor belligerent rights." Nevertheless, such warfare was "a senseless, brutal, barbarous business." He believed that the churches should work for a better economic order, that moral force could essentially modify the economic process, and that Christianity should supply that moral force. When the Congregational Foreign Missionary Board received a large gift from John D. Rockefeller, Gladden condemned the transaction vigorously, declaring that the Rockefeller money was "tainted" and that the church entered into a "partnership with plunderers" by accepting it. Needless to say, Gladden's scruples in this matter never became popular. Most churches—and colleges—continued to receive all gifts gratefully without scrutinizing too closely the processes by which the donors had made their fortunes.

Most energetic in promoting the social gospel was Walter Rauschenbusch. As pastor of a small German Baptist church in the New York slums during the eighties and nineties, Rauschenbusch saw at first hand the desperate poverty of the urban masses. He sympathized strongly with Henry George, who was then at the climax of his New York career. The young minister, pondering the issues of the day, came to believe that the Kingdom of God was not something for the next world but that it was to be worked for here and now through the ideals of human brotherhood and social justice. From 1897 to 1918 Rauschenbusch taught at Rochester Theological Seminary, where he exerted a steadily widening influence both in the classroom and through such widely read books as *Christianity and the Social Order* (1907) and *Prayers of the Social Awakening* (1916).

Rauschenbusch and a number of other clergymen of the period like George

D. Herron of Grinnell College and W. P. D. Bliss, founder of the Church of the Carpenter in Boston, were socialists. Believing that an economic order based on competition was fundamentally un-Christian, they called for a co-operative society inspired by Christian ideals. The Christian Socialists condemned the Marxian Socialists for their materialism and were in turn scorned by the Marxists for their rejection of the class struggle and for their adherence to supernaturalism.

Although the Christian Socialists assumed a position too advanced and vulnerable to win a large following, many ministers found courage to preach the social gospel in less radical form. Both unregulated capitalism and socialism were condemned. America could be saved, they asserted, through social meliorism—through the regulation of business, the passage of laws to protect the workers, and the achievement of higher standards of conduct in business.

Within the Episcopal denomination the impact of English Christian Socialism had its greatest force. Bishop F. D. Huntington became a member of the Knights of Labor and took a prominent part in organizing the Church Association for the Advancement of the Interests of Labor in 1887. Five years later the Christian Social Union was organized with Bishop Huntington as its president and Richard T. Ely, professor of economics at the University of Wisconsin, as its secretary. Although these early organizations had no official connection with the Episcopal Church, the denomination recognized the new trends by establishing a commission on the relations of capital and labor in 1901.

The Methodist Episcopal Church showed the impact of change very clearly. As late as 1888 the bishops had appeared more concerned with the dangerous power of the labor leaders than with the grievances of the workers. But in 1908 the General Conference adopted a social creed of striking boldness, calling for "a living wage in every industry," "the highest wage that each industry can afford, and . . . the most equitable division of the products in industry that can ultimately be devised," the abolition of child labor, regulation of the conditions of labor for women, the suppression of the "sweating system," and the reduction of the hours of labor to the lowest practical point with "work for all." The Methodist statement was taken over almost word for word in the social creed of the newly organized Federal Council of Churches.

Other denominations took similar steps. Commissions to study social problems were established, and the most obvious injustices were condemned. Theological seminaries introduced new courses in sociology and social ethics. The social gospel had a particular appeal for the younger ministers. Acceptance of the teachings of science and higher criticism had weakened the old creeds and outmoded many of the old sermon topics. The social gospel gave themes for warmly idealistic preaching and a field for useful activity. The new emphasis was less acceptable to laymen, who often grumbled that their ministers had abandoned religion for sociology and socialism. The extent to which businessmen consciously carried the new teachings into daily practice was probably not great, but the preaching of the social gospel contributed to the new climate of opinion in which political progressivism flourished. It was entirely appropriate that in 1912 Theodore Roosevelt's admirers launched the Progressive party at Chicago to the stirring accompaniment of "Onward, Christian soldiers, marching as to war."

The Roman Catholic Church also felt the challenge of new problems. Conservative churchmen like Archbishop Corrigan of New York and Bishop McQuaid of Rochester opposed the agitations of the eighties, but a more liberal group represented by Cardinal Gibbons, Archbishop Ireland, and Bishop Keane showed sympathy with them. Without subscribing to the specific programs of the reformers, they felt that the workers had real grievances and that the Church should appear as the friend and champion of the workers rather than, as so often in Europe, the ally of the privileged classes. Although Archbishop Corrigan excommunicated Father Edward McGlynn, pastor of the largest Catholic parish in New York City, for persistently advocating the doctrines of Henry George, this decision was overruled, and McGlynn was reinstated by the apostolic delegate in 1893. Cardinal Gibbons cooperated with Cardinal Manning of England to defeat the attempt of the conservatives to have *Progress and Poverty* condemned.

Even more delicate was the issue presented by the rapid growth of the Knights of Labor. The Canadian bishops secured a condemnation of the order, but Gibbons, after questioning Terence V. Powderly, who was both head of the Knights and a Catholic, satisfied himself that the principles of the organization did not conflict with Catholic teachings. On his visit to Rome to receive the cardinal's hat in 1887, Gibbons secured a removal of the condemnation. The extent to which conservative and liberal factions were contending within the Church is reflected in the Cardinal's later comment:

> Ah, what a struggle it was on both sides of the water! I had so many difficulties that I wonder I got through them. Bishops are so hard to persuade! They have fixed and positive opinions and I can scarcely imagine a class of men less easy to deal with on a subject of that kind.[1]

Obviously the attitude of the Roman Church toward social problems was a matter of great importance both in America and in Europe. In this situation Pope Leo XIII issued the famous encyclical *Rerum Novarum* in 1891. As in earlier pronouncements socialism was condemned as a denial of the right of private property, which the Church recognized as based in natural law. But the evils of the existing industrial system were also condemned as "laying upon the shoulders of the working classes a yoke little better than slavery itself." The obligations of Christian employers toward their employees were stressed equally with the obligations of the workers. Leo was acclaimed as "the workingman's pope," and Catholic scholars had moral support for studying the maladjustments of society.

[1] Allen S. Will, *Life of Cardinal Gibbons, Archbishop of Baltimore* (Dutton, New York, 1922), I, 360.

Dr. John A. Ryan became the best known Catholic authority on American economic problems through such books as *A Living Wage* (1906) and *Distributive Justice* (1916).

Evangelism in a New Age

The new Protestantism with its social creeds and church gymnasiums seemed far removed from the old Protestantism of George Whitefield and Charles G. Finney. But revivalism still remained a potent force.

Greatest of the post-Civil War evangelists was Dwight L. Moody. Born in Northfield, Massachusetts, in 1837, Moody moved to Chicago as a young man and soon became a highly successful shoe salesman. An eager Congregational layman, Moody early made it a practice to buttonhole strangers on the street and to induce them to accompany him to church, where they sat in four pews which he had rented for the purpose. His zeal for saving souls soon led him to other activities. He became an early leader in Y.M.C.A. work in Chicago. A class which he organized for street urchins expanded until it became a great Sunday school, and the Sunday school in turn grew until it developed into a nonsectarian mission church. Moody gave up his business and became a full-time preacher. Visiting England to study city-mission work, he established contacts that led to his first great evangelistic tour. Accompanied by his chorister, Ira D. Sankey, Moody conducted highly successful meetings from 1873 to 1875 in England, Scotland, and Ireland.

When Moody and Sankey returned to America, they were famous. Their first great meetings in this country were held in Brooklyn and attracted crowds of from 15,000 to 20,000 persons daily. Similar success followed in Philadelphia, New York, and other cities throughout the country. Twice they returned to England, the scene of their earliest triumphs.

Moody's great success puzzled his own generation. Never ordained, poorly educated, and entirely lacking in the polish of conventional oratory, he seemed to be seriously handicapped. But straightforwardness, simplicity, and earnestness gave his preaching an appeal unmatched by that of any of his contemporaries. His theology was old-fashioned, but he avoided the hysterical emotionalism that had marred earlier revivals. He placed a high value on Christian education, and his most enduring monuments were the excellent Northfield School for Girls and the Mount Hermon School for Boys, which he founded in his native village.

Many other evangelists accompanied by sweet-voiced singers attempted to duplicate Moody's success. Most ingenious in capturing public attention was Billy Sunday—a former baseball player turned revivalist. Sunday's picturesque use of slang and acrobatic gestures fascinated huge audiences in the special "tabernacles" built for his meetings. Thousands professed conversion, or "hit the sawdust trail," as Sunday said.

But Sunday's excesses deeply pained more thoughtful Christians and helped to discredit revivalism. By 1914 more Protestants than ever before preferred the quiet methods of Christian nurture to the noisy dramatics of the popular evangelists.

Union and Disunion

The notoriously divided state of American Protestantism distressed many Christians, who yearned to fit together the broken pieces. Sentiment for unification was promoted by the declining emphasis placed upon creed and the rising interest in social problems.

Within the various denominations a slow mending process was evident. The schism between Old School and New School Presbyterians, which had existed since 1837, was healed in the South during the Civil War and in the North in 1870. In 1906 a part of the Cumberland Presbyterians accepted union with the Northern Presbyterians, and in 1909 the Free Will Baptists of the North merged with the Northern Baptists. But sectional differences proved more difficult to overcome than doctrinal. Fifty years after the Civil War the schism between the northern and southern branches of the Methodist, Baptist, and Presbyterian churches was still unrepaired.

In some of the rural villages progress toward Protestant union was more evident than elsewhere. The old-time rivalry proved too expensive to maintain. Common sense asserted itself, and in many small towns community churches were established to take the place of struggling rival sects.

Although denominational labels were more jealously guarded in the cities, the various churches achieved a measure of cooperation through the establishment of city and state federations. In 1908 this movement culminated in the establishment of the Federal Council of Churches of Christ in America. Through this agency some thirty Protestant denominations, although maintaining their full autonomy, found it possible to speak with a single voice on important issues of the day.

But while the larger denominations discussed mergers and achieved measures of cooperation, the founding of new sects continued unabated. Indeed, the same forces that had minimized doctrinal differences among the older religious groups tended to alienate thousands of Christians who hated the new tendencies. Denouncing the theory of evolution, higher criticism, the social gospel, the institutional church, and all other innovations, many determined souls sought by separating from the major bodies to keep the old-time religion pure and undefiled.

Within the Methodist denomination there were thousands who deplored the new trends. In the orderly worship of the new middle-class congregations they missed the loud "Amens" and vigorous personal "testimony" that had been so prominent a feature of early Methodism. Especially resented was the neglect of the doctrine of "entire sanctification"—that mystical freedom from sin described by John Wesley. A mushroom crop of "holiness" sects, largely fed by dissident Methodists, sprang up after 1880. One of these, the Church of the Nazarene, achieved considerable size.

Much of the fervor of the minor sects still derived from the eagerly awaited second coming of Christ. Charles Taze Russell, a successful businessman of Allegheny, Pennsylvania, wrote so extensively on the millennial theme that it was claimed that his "explanatory writings on the Bible are far more extensive than the combined writings of St. Paul, St. John, Arius, Waldo, Wycliffe, and Martin Luther—the six messengers of the Church who preceded him." At the time of his death in 1916 it was estimated that twelve million copies of his books had passed into circulation. "Pastor" Russell's study of the scriptures led him to some remarkable conclusions. Christ had returned to the "upper air" in 1874; in 1878 the dead had been raised to meet the Lord and were thereafter floating in space. Further catastrophic events occurred in 1914 and in 1918. Despite the apparent delay in the end of the world the Russellites continued to assert that "millions now living will never die." Eventually known as the International Bible Students' Association or Jehovah's Witnesses, they distributed—or sold—their propaganda with fanatical zeal.

The new sects made their principal appeal to the poor. Men and women who had been unsuccessful in the material world found emotional satisfaction in cults that promised a superior brand of holiness for the faithful or that depicted with lurid detail the fate soon to befall the world of sinners. Prophets and miracle workers found a particularly fertile field among the exploited Negro population.

Christian Science was unique among the new religious movements in winning thousands of converts from the comfortable middle class. Mary Baker Eddy, its creator, found no comfort for her restless spirit in the Calvinist orthodoxy of her native New Hampshire village. Misfortune tagged her footsteps. Her first husband died a few months after her marriage. Her second husband, an itinerant dentist, deserted her. She herself was sickly and subject to fits of hysteria. She dabbled in the fads of the fifties and sixties—spiritualism, mesmerism, clairvoyance, and hydrotherapy. Twice during the early sixties she traveled to Portland, Maine, to receive treatment from Dr. Phineas P. Quimby, a remarkably successful mental healer. Moving to Lynn, Massachusetts, in 1864, she made a precarious living treating the sick and teaching students to treat them in accordance with principles which she was now formulating. In 1875 her famous book, *Science and Health,* was published in the first of its numerous editions. Critics charged that her work was largely borrowed from the unpublished writings of Dr. Quimby, embellished with additional ideas that Mrs. Eddy had picked up from the Shakers and transcendentalists. Mrs. Eddy and her disciples denied this vigorously, insisting that the principles of Christian Science constituted a unique discovery.

Christian Science identified God with mind and the good. It denied the reality of matter, evil, and disease. Christ had come to redeem men not merely from sin but also from sickness and death. Through correct understanding of these principles men could heal both themselves and others.

The publication of *Science and Health* did not immediately bring success to its author. In 1877 she married her third husband, Asa G. Eddy; in 1879 she secured a state charter for the establishment of The Church of Christ (Scientist). But the real turning point of her career came in 1881, when at the age of sixty-one she moved from Lynn to Boston. Within the next few years Mrs. Eddy achieved fame, power, and great wealth. At the Massachusetts Metaphysical College she instructed hundreds of healers who carried Christian Science to every section of the country.

Christian Science met with bitter opposition. Preachers of the older denominations denounced it in unsparing terms. Doctors, seriously troubled, warned of the danger and tragedy which might result from denying the reality of disease. Mark Twain aimed the big guns of his ridicule at Mrs. Eddy, and the *New York World* devoted much space to hostile accounts of her strange career. But these attacks appear to have advertised the movement more than they injured it. The new church passed successfully through various crises, including that created by Mrs. Eddy's death in 1910. Christian Science's success testified to the appeal of its teachings for thousands of middle-class people who found security in denying the reality of sickness and evil. Its converts were drawn not only from the various Protestant denominations but from Jewish congregations as well.

Whatever might be said in criticism of American spiritual life, it could scarcely be denied that there was a church to serve the needs of almost every type of mind. For many the inevitable result of the intellectual trends of the day had been a loss of faith in all religion. But even for these there were churches! The Society for Ethical Culture was established in New York in 1876 by Felix Adler, and similar societies were founded in several other cities.

Chapter 26. The New Age of Science

By the time of the Civil War the transformation of American life through science was already well begun. The completion of a telegraph line across the continent to San Francisco in 1861 permitted Californians to hear almost instantaneously the results of battles fought in Virginia 3,000 miles away. Another triumph of science was the use of ether to mitigate the horrors of emergency surgery for the wounded.

Telegraphy and anesthesia illustrated the limitations as well as the achievements of pre-Civil War American science. When the experimentation was motivated by an urgent practical need and when the problem required chiefly mechanical skill, native ingenuity, or physical courage, Americans more than held their own with Europeans. But in the fields of pure science, in which scholars devoted years of patient investigation to the search for knowledge for its own sake, the Americans were far behind. In 1876 a writer in the *Popular Science Monthly* pointed out that for every piece of research of this kind published in the United States, at least fifty appeared in Europe.

During the next half century the situation was radically altered. Americans began to show an aptitude for research equal to their skill in practical mechanics. The extraordinary esteem now enjoyed by the scientists caused philosophers and students of society to change radically their own approaches to knowledge, and both taxpayers and philanthropists invested more money in education.

Medicine Becomes a Science

To the layman the achievements of science were most obvious in the field of medicine. Mid-nineteenth-century doctors practiced what was partly an art and partly a craft. The dexterity of the experienced physician often saved mother and child in difficult deliveries. With similar skill the doctor set broken bones, probed out bullets, sewed up wounds, cut out tumors, and amputated limbs. Through the trial-and-error methods of many decades, he had learned to administer drugs which would deaden pain, stimulate or depress the heart action, reduce fever, or allay malaria. He had even learned to prevent smallpox through vaccination. But for most illnesses he could treat only the symptoms; in the end, nature, functioning in still mysterious ways, either killed or cured the patient. The actual causes of diseases were almost unknown, and doctors were helpless to halt the ravages of typhus, cholera, typhoid fever, diphtheria, and tuberculosis, which killed thousands of Americans every year.

The unscientific character of the profession was clearly evident in medical education. The student usually gained his practical knowledge through a three-year apprenticeship to some physician, and his theoretical training by two years' attendance at a medical school. The school was generally organized on a proprietary basis by a group of practicing physicians who arranged to give an annual series of lectures on their craft. The medical student bought tickets and attended when he pleased. There were no entrance requirements and few or no examinations. The course lasted only four months each year, and the same lectures were given the second year as the first. The student had some opportunity to learn anatomy from actual dissection and to observe the treatment of patients in clinics. But with these exceptions his training was exclusively verbal. The professor told what to do for each disease; the student wrote the information in his notebook and memorized it. There was no laboratory work and no supervised internship. The results were those which might have been expected. To the hazards of uncontrolled disease were added the often fatal mistakes of ignorant doctors.

A few physicians, intelligent enough to realize the inadequacy of their American training, went to Europe to complete their education. Here they found a different world—a world of laboratories and carefully controlled experiments. They learned to use the microscope to distinguish between normal and abnormal tissue and to identify the conditions which accompanied certain diseases. The study of pathology and physiology, hardly recognized in American medical schools, was here well advanced. Bacteriology—the science more than any other destined to revolutionize medicine—was in a stage of vigorous youth. Louis Pasteur, a French chemist, and Robert Koch, a German country doctor, following their separate lines of research, had conclusively demonstrated not only that diseases were caused by germs but that they could be cured or prevented through inoculation. European scientists turned to hundreds of projects relating to the cause and prevention of disease, and American graduate students crossed the Atlantic to learn the new techniques.

The greatest germ discoveries continued to be made in Europe, but American investigators soon began to play their own part. In 1893 Theobald Smith, employed by the United States Bureau of Animal Industry, completed an invaluable piece of research on the cause and prevention of Texas fever—a plague then killing western cattle by the thousand. American military occupation of Cuba after the Spanish-American War gave a fatal urgency to the study of yellow fever, long a curse to the island. A special medical commission, headed by Dr. Walter Reed, was frustrated in its efforts to discover the enemy germ, but it successfully demonstrated how the disease was transmitted and how it might be controlled. Testing a theory long held by Carlos J. Finlay, a Cuban doctor, Reed proved that yellow fever was carried by a certain species of mosquito. The experiments cost the life of Dr. Jesse W. Lazear and the health of Dr. James Carroll, two of Reed's associates. Since earlier European research had proved that malaria was also transmitted by mosquitoes, the importance of controlling these pests in semitropical areas was now obvious. Major William Crawford Gorgas of the Army Medical Corps fought so brilliant a battle against disease during the building of the Panama Canal that not a single case of yellow fever was reported between 1906 and 1914, and malaria was well controlled. The role of other insects in the transmission of disease was clarified by Dr. Howard T. Ricketts of the University of Chicago, who proved that Rocky Mountain spotted fever was transmitted by ticks and Mexican typhus by fleas. Ricketts died of the latter disease in 1910, a victim of his own experiments.

Particularly fruitful were the efforts of Major Bailey K. Ashford to discover the cause of the anemia prevalent in Puerto Rico when that island was acquired by the United States. The enemy was discovered to be the hookworm, which in its larval state penetrated the skin of the barefooted native and journeyed by a circuitous route to the intestines. There it laid eggs by the hundred and fed on the blood corpuscles of its unhappy host, sapping vital energies until the victim lost all ambition and zest for life. Relentless war on the hookworm showed good results in Puerto Rico and pointed the way for a similar campaign in the South where many persons showed the same symptoms. The initiative in this area was taken by Dr. Charles W. Stiles, a zoologist and public health official, who in 1909 won the support of the Rockefeller family for the organization of a great cooperative effort of southern newspapers, schools, boards of health, and medical organizations. It was a dramatic demonstration of the possibility of rehabilitating entire communities through the application of scientific medical knowledge.

Fortunately, science was not bound by narrow nationalism. American doctors quickly appropriated whatever was valuable in the discoveries of foreign investigators. As early as 1894 American doctors were beginning to treat diphtheria with the antitoxin serum developed in German laboratories. Accurate diagnosis of syphilis was made possible through the Wassermann test developed in Germany in 1907, and in 1909 an efficient specific for its treatment was provided in Salvarsan, which was developed by the great German scientist Paul Ehrlich.

Man's complete conquest of disease seemed imminent, but there were many disappointments for the overoptimistic. Although tuberculosis was a subject for concentrated research and the tuberculosis bacillus was discovered by Koch himself, the serum or drug which would provide the patient with a speedy cure could not be found. But intelligent observers discovered how to help nature do its own curative work. Techniques of early diagnosis were developed along with sanitarium treatment of fresh air, rest, and good diet. The efficacy of these measures was demonstrated by the patient work of Edward L. Trudeau at Saranac Lake, New York. A nationwide campaign against the disease began with the organization of the National Tuberculosis Association in 1904. Raising funds in part through the sale of Christmas seals, the Association did extraordinary work. The death rate from tuberculosis fell from 202 per 100,000 inhabitants in 1900 to 114 in 1920. The fight against typhoid fever was even more effective when boards of health, at last fortified with adequate powers, began to insist upon pure milk and drinking water.

The new discoveries obviously demanded a new type of doctor. The inadequately trained practitioner of the 1860's had no place in this world of laboratories, microscopes, serums, and X rays. Step by step with the revolution in medical science came a revolution in medical education. As soon as he became president of Harvard University in 1869, Charles W. Eliot proposed drastic changes in the

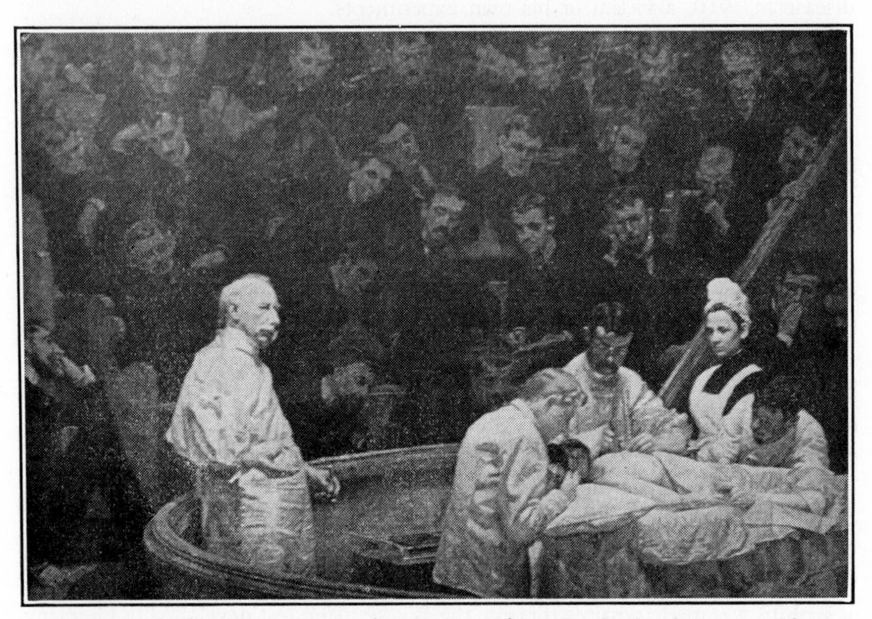

FIG. 43. *The Agnew Clinic.* Painting by Thomas Eakins. Dr. D. H. Agnew, well-known professor of surgery at the University of Pennsylvania, talks to his class about an operation that he has just performed. (*Courtesy of the University of Pennsylvania.*)

medical school. He wanted stiff entrance examinations, a graded course, better teachers, adequate laboratories, and the transfer of control from the participating doctors to the university itself. These proposals were strenuously opposed by a faction of conservatives who were convinced that medicine was essentially an art, not a science; but Eliot and his allies persisted, and the school was steadily improved. Similar reforms were effected at Pennsylvania, Columbia, and other established universities. Perhaps the most active institution in advancing medical knowledge was the new university at Baltimore, Johns Hopkins, where graduate instruction in medicine was begun in 1886 and a regular medical school was opened in 1893. Under the leadership of Dr. William Henry Welch the Johns Hopkins medical faculty attracted brilliant students from all over the country.

American Science Comes of Age

When scientific investigation served obviously useful purposes, it was generously supported. The United States Weather Bureau, established in 1870, became the largest and best equipped agency of its kind in the world. In 1879 the United States Geological Survey was organized as a permanent bureau within the Department of the Interior. Its director during its first two years was Clarence King, already well known for the youthful energy with which he had carried through a great Federal survey along the route of the Union Pacific Railroad. When King resigned to go into the mining business, he was succeeded by Major John W. Powell, a one-armed Civil War veteran who had led a famous exploration of Grand Canyon in 1869. Powell's brilliant work ranged all the way from studying the languages and customs of the Indians to farsighted projects for the reclamation of western lands through irrigation. Geologists also secured employment from state governments, railroad builders, and mine operators. But they did not confine themselves to problems of immediate dollars-and-cents value. They studied the abundant American evidence on earth history, particularly the influence of glaciers, and made important contributions on the subject.

The rocks contained many other fascinating clues to the remote past. For generations curious Americans had collected fossils which abounded in sections like the Big Bone Lick of Kentucky. Othniel C. Marsh, the first American professor of paleontology, took up his duties at Yale in 1865. Having secured funds from his uncle, the wealthy George Peabody, for the construction of the Peabody Museum of Natural History, Marsh worked energetically—even ruthlessly—to make the Yale collection the greatest in the world. He found an almost virgin field for his investigations in the regions just opened up by the western railroads. His first great collecting expeditions were adventuresome affairs in which Marsh and other young Yale men rode the prairies together, hunting both buffaloes and ancient bones. Marsh was well known to the general public, not only through his reconstructions of giant creatures of earlier ages, but through his bitter and well-publicized rivalry with another great collector of fossils, Professor Edward D. Cope of the University of Pennsylvania.

The sound scholarly instinct which led King, Powell, Marsh, and Cope to investigate data in which America was particularly rich impelled Lewis Henry Morgan to study Indian social organization. As a lawyer in Rochester, New York, Morgan won the confidence of the Senecas by championing their rights in Washington. He was adopted into the tribe and used this opportunity to accumulate a vast fund of information. In 1851 he published his first important study, *The League of the Ho-de-no-sau-ne or Iroquois.* This was followed in 1868 by *Consanguinity and Affinity* and in 1877 by *Ancient Society.* Morgan's generalizations, in which he described social evolution as falling everywhere into an identical pattern of progress from savagery through barbarism to civilization, are now regarded as oversimple and misleading, but his bold pioneering assured his reputation as the first great American anthropologist.

The stimulus that some scientists found in exploring the West and studying the Indians others discovered within their own offices and laboratories. Benjamin Peirce of Harvard was the country's best known mathematician of the seventies, and Peirce's pupil, Simon Newcomb of the Washington Observatory, gained an international reputation both in mathematics and astronomy. Another capable astronomer, Samuel P. Langley of the Smithsonian Institution was familiar to the general public for his attempts at building a flying machine.

Less known to his own generation was Yale's Willard Gibbs, who in 1871 became the first American professor of mathematical physics. In 1876 he submitted to the Connecticut Academy of Arts and Sciences a lengthy paper entitled *On the Equilibrium of Heterogeneous Substances.* Both in title and content the work was a forbidding one, and the academy had difficulty in securing the funds to publish it. At first only a few powerful minds like that of Clerk Maxwell in England grasped the study's real significance, but a generation later the practical applications of Gibbs's difficult mathematical abstractions began to be made. The chemical industry discovered in Gibbs's "rule of phase" the important principle that made it possible to organize processes without wasteful trial-and-error techniques. Metallurgy was transformed from an art to a science by the establishment of the temperature conditions necessary for the production of various alloys. "Mathematics is a language," said Gibbs, and he displayed unique genius in developing that language for the use of future scientists.

Other great American physicists were Henry A. Rowland and Albert A. Michelson. Rowland was a brilliant experimenter who greatly advanced the techniques of spectrum analysis and became the world's leading authority on magnetism. Michelson's achievements were still more remarkable. In 1879 at the age of twenty-seven he published the results of his first ingenious measurements of the speed of light. In 1931, when he died at the age of seventy-nine, he was engaged in research on the same problem. Since the speed of light is probably the most important constant in physics, its measurement was enough to assure Michelson's place in the history of science. Of almost equal significance, however, were the ether-drift experiments of Michelson and Professor Edward W. Morley of Western Reserve University. With an ingenious piece of equipment called the "interferometer," they measured the speed of light both in the direction of the earth's motion and at right angles to that direction. When the experiment demonstrated that the speed of light was the same in either direction, the hypothesis of a stationary ether was given a mortal blow. Nothing could be of less immediate consequence to the man in the street than this research in the field of pure science. Yet the incompatibility of the results of the ether-drift experiment with the principles of classical physics was one of the challenges that led to Einstein's theory of relativity, to the intensive study of nuclear physics, and ultimately to the atomic bomb.

While the physicists probed the mysteries of the inanimate universe, other scientists explored various aspects of the world of living things. All such studies had been revolutionized by the publication of Charles Darwin's *Origin of Species.* If the theory of evolution through natural selection was strenuously opposed by many clergymen and even by reputable scientists like Louis Agassiz of Harvard, it was warmly defended by others. Asa Gray, also of Harvard, was a leader on the intellectual front, and John Fiske and Edward A. Youmans introduced the Darwinian thesis to a much wider public through their lectures and writings.

The new conception of the human mind implicit in the evolutionary theory led to the gradual divorce of psychology from philosophy. The former now became an experimental science. The pioneer psychological laboratory was that of Wilhelm Wundt in Leipzig, but in America William James, G. Stanley Hall, John Dewey, and Edward L. Thorndike introduced new methods for the study of human behavior.

With a different approach Jacques Loeb studied the reactions of living matter to various stimuli. By his theory of tropisms he attributed all the activity of lower forms of animal life to physical or chemical stimuli. Loeb's most startling experiments were those in which he fertilized the eggs of sea urchins and frogs by treating them with chemicals or pricking them with needles. Loeb became the leading champion of the "mechanists," who believed that all life processes might ultimately be explained in physical and chemical terms—a school vigorously opposed by the "vitalists," who taught that the essence of life was a mystic force which scientists could never hope to understand.

In a long career of research first at Columbia and then at the California Institute of Technology, Thomas Hunt Morgan discovered many of the mechanisms involved in heredity. Morgan experimented with *Drosophila,* or fruit flies, which were ideally suited for the purpose, since they developed from egg to fly in ten days or less and might breed as many as thirty generations in a year. Morgan demonstrated that physical characteristics were transmitted by units which he called "genes." The close connection between pure and applied science was once more demonstrated in this new field of genetics. Intensive breeding of flies in the laboratory—an activity certainly open to the ridicule of the layman—led to the discovery of laws of inheritance which have already made possible improved breeds of livestock and plants and may some time lead to the birth of better babies.

Morgan's experiments along with those of the Dutch biologist Hugo de Vries led to important modifications in the theory of evolution. Instead of Darwin's gradual modification of species through the inheritance of minute differences, science now had to recognize mutations—the sudden appearance of new species or variations due to disturbance of the normal arrangement of the genes. Mutations, as Hermann J. Muller demonstrated at the University of Texas, could be artificially induced by X rays or radium. Darwinian evolution was as radically altered by the principles of genetics as was Newtonian physics by the theories of

Einstein. Ironically enough, the American public in 1914 was adjusting itself to the uncomplicated materialism of nineteenth-century science just when intellectual pioneers were opening up new and vastly more complex frontiers.

The Social Sciences

The achievements of the physical scientists suggested the possibility of applying scientific methods to the study of society. The French thinker Auguste Comte had called for such an approach, as had John Stuart Mill and Henry Thomas Buckle in England. The works of Herbert Spencer, however, had greater prestige in American eyes. Indeed, the publication of the English writer's monumental *Synthetic Philosophy* had been greatly aided by donations collected in the United States by Edward L. Youmans. All these thinkers emphasized the importance of objectivity and of inductive reasoning—patient fact finding and cautious generalization. They were fundamentally materialistic, either denying or minimizing divine intervention in human affairs and seeking the universal laws which they believed controlled all social activity. While discarding older preconceptions, the new intellectuals accepted rather blindly some preconceptions of their own. Spencer and his American admirers were so ardent in their admiration for Darwin that they attempted to transfer his theory from the field of biology to that of human institutions. The family, government, religion, and business were all to be studied not merely as the results of evolutionary growth but as subject to the identical struggle for existence and survival of the fittest which Darwin had seen at work within his much more limited field.

The evolutionary theory was used to fortify the arguments of both conservatives and reformers. Captains of industry who were literate enough to desire a rational justification for their wealth and power accepted Social Darwinism with enthusiasm. All life was struggle and competition. It was the essential condition for progress that the strong should survive and that the weak should perish. The existing social order was good because it was the product of evolutionary processes; advance could only be made by gradual change; attempts to better social conditions through legislation ran counter to natural law and thus hampered rather than aided mankind. All the reformers' demands from factory regulation to socialism fell equally under condemnation. William Graham Sumner of Yale was the ablest spokesman for this school of thought. But other students of society, equally impressed with the evolutionary concept, stressed different aspects of it. They emphasized the inevitability of change. Present society was obviously imperfect, and must be altered. Intelligent men could speed and direct institutional evolution by conscious planning. There was in nature not merely ruthless individual conflict but a principle of mutual aid whereby men could improve their lot through cooperative effort. Lester Frank Ward's *Dynamic Society* (1883) gradually gained acceptance as the bible of this more liberal approach.

The scientific study of society was hastened by the hard realities of American life. Industrialization, immigration, and urban growth had, as we have seen, brought in their train pauperism, disease, insanity, and crime. However grudgingly, the state had to intervene, and officeholders struggling with these problems found themselves without the knowledge that they needed for effective action. Thus it was that in 1865 the Massachusetts board of state charities issued the call which resulted in the organization of the American Association for the Promotion of Social Science. The association held annual meetings for many years and was influential in introducing courses in social science in the colleges.

Many scholars hoped for the establishment of a single unified study of society, but the breadth of the field encouraged the growth of separate disciplines. The emergence of these may be roughly followed in the establishment of the American Historical Association in 1884, the American Economic Association in 1885, the American Academy of Political and Social Science in 1889, the American Political Science Association in 1903, and the American Sociological Society in 1905.

History was an old rather than a new area of learning, but its teaching and writing underwent great changes between 1860 and 1914. Such history as had been taught in colleges before the Civil War had been thin in content with no pretense at relevance to contemporary problems. In very few institutions were there professors of history; elsewhere, the courses were taught by professors of classical languages, theology, or philosophy. Although the German universities had for several decades been giving rigorous training in the methods of historical research, few Americans had received such instruction. But these conditions soon changed. History gained its own important place in the college curriculum, and historians were prepared for their profession through a rigorous course of graduate study.

Although most historians continued to follow the well-worn path of political history, a few pioneers ventured into new fields. Attempts at the portrayal of American social and intellectual life were contained in the writings of John Bach McMaster and Henry Adams. Adams soon tired of pedestrian research, but he pondered years over the underlying forces operative in history. With a mind too subtle to be satisfied with the easy optimism of a simple evolutionary theory, Adams—half in earnest, half in fun—constructed a philosophy of history based on the second law of thermodynamics and Willard Gibbs's law of phase. Less exotic but more influential was the thesis contained in Frederick Jackson Turner's essay, "The Influence of the Frontier on American History" (1893). Scarcely less stimulating were Charles A. Beard's writings, which stressed the importance of the struggle for power of economic classes.

In most colleges history and political science were now taught in the same department. This resulted in a generation of scholars whose interests embraced both fields. Many of these like Woodrow Wilson were trained in the seminars of Herbert Baxter Adams at Johns Hopkins. Adams, a firm believer in Darwinian principles, taught his students to look for the roots of every American institution in England and of every English institution in the folk laws of the Germans. At Columbia John W. Burgess indoctrinated his students with a similar point of view. The marriage of history and political science had both good and bad consequences. To see political institutions in the perspective of time was illuminating, but it carried with it the danger of making history too legalistic and of divorcing political science from adequate reference to the contemporary situation. Charles A. Beard's *An Economic Interpretation of the Constitution* (1913) probably overstated its thesis, but it served as a healthy corrective to a generation of scholars who had paid insufficient attention to group pressures in the shaping of institutions.

The rapid industrialization of the country led to increased interest in economics. Laissez-faire principles held ascendancy and businessmen were for the most part well satisfied. They echoed eagerly the scholarly doctrine that there should be a minimum of intervention by the state because government regulation interfered with the beneficent workings of natural economic laws. But when economists were consistent enough to point out that the same principle required the abandonment of tariff protection, industrialists and Republican party leaders became suddenly deaf. William Graham Sumner, whose teachings were in general so acceptable to the established order, condemned the fetish of protectionism in forthright fashion, as did also influential publicists like Daniel A. Wells and Edward Atkinson.

Most nineteenth-century economists showed little sympathy with the demands of organized labor, but there were conspicuous exceptions. At the University of Wisconsin Richard T. Ely instituted studies of the American trade-union movement, and Ely's student John R. Commons exploited the new field with great success. The liberal economists combated the narrow teachings of the strict laissez-faire school and taught that the power of the state should be actively directed toward the elimination of poverty and injustice.

Belief in evolution which led many social thinkers to complacency induced others to subject the existing order to critical appraisal. In several brilliant studies the economist Thorstein Veblen distinguished between true industry, whereby goods were produced through uniting the workers' labor and the engineers' skill, and business, which was merely the predatory activity of financiers—the latest form of the role once played by the robber-barons.

Late in the nineteenth century, sociology, the youngest of the social sciences, was securing recognition as a separate branch of learning. William Graham Sumner of Yale and Lester Frank Ward of Brown were the best known of the older generation of sociologists; the second generation was marked by the preeminence of Albion W. Small of the University of Chicago, Franklin Giddings of Columbia, and Edward A. Ross of the University of Wisconsin. Both sociologists and economists came to rely increasingly on the intelligent study of statistics. College courses in this technique began to be organized as early as 1882. The responsibility of the government to gather statistical information had been recognized since the first Federal census of 1790, but much remained to be done in the handling of this information. The greatest statistical administrator of the period was Carroll D. Wright, successively director of the Massachusetts Bureau of Labor Statistics, of the Federal Bureau of Statistics, and of the United States census of 1890.

Philosophy and the Rise of Pragmatism

The search for knowledge in the physical and social sciences stimulated American philosophers to struggle anew with the age-old question, What is Truth?

Charles S. Peirce gave the discussion a new turn by the development of what he called "pragmatism." In an article entitled "How to Make Our Ideas Clear" (1878), he reasoned that the purpose of thought was to arrive at belief. But beliefs were important only because they were "rules for action." Different beliefs were distinguished by the different modes of action to which they gave rise. If beliefs did not differ in this respect, they were not different beliefs any more than tunes played in different keys were different tunes. Peirce believed that valid general ideas or habits of looking at things developed from the testing process which he had described.

Peirce's life was an unhappy one. A son of the great Harvard mathematician Benjamin Peirce, he had been endowed with an extraordinary mind and received an excellent education. Although thoroughly trained in mathematics and physics, he was not content merely to emulate his father but devoted himself to intensive search for the philosophical concepts on which mathematics and physics were based. His personality was so difficult and his language so abstruse that he was unable to teach for more than a few years at any university. His major projects were too grandiose to secure a publisher, and although he wrote incessantly, little of his work appeared in print during his lifetime. Despite these failures a later generation has recognized him as one of the major figures in the history of American thought.

Peirce greatly influenced two other men, who had in liberal measure the flair for communication which he so conspicuously lacked. The first of these was Josiah Royce, a Californian, who began teaching philosophy at Harvard in 1882. Royce had great learning, an impressive presence, and a beautifully eloquent style. He restated the philosophy of idealism in singularly persuasive terms, fortifying his position with arguments from the logic of mathematics which he borrowed from Peirce.

Very different was the line of thought developed at Harvard by William James, whose first teaching had been in the fields of physiology and psychology. His *Principles of Psychology* (1890), developed from a biological approach, enjoyed a great success, and in his later work in philosophy James never forgot what he believed he had learned about the human mind. He described his philosophical system as "radical empiricism"—a theory that attributed all knowledge to particular experiences.

In a lecture at the University of California entitled "Philosophical Conceptions and Practical Results" (1898), James called attention to Peirce's hitherto neglected principle of pragmatism—a principle which James considered to be "the most likely direction in which to start upon the trail of truth." For example, James argued, most of the definitions of God given by the theologians have no real meaning because they awaken no responsive feelings in mankind and call for no particular conduct. What the word "God" really means is summed up in practical religious experiences—"conversations with the unseen, voices and visions, responses to prayer, changes of heart, deliverances from fear, inflowing of help, assurances of support." This application of pragmatism was characteristic of James's lifelong interest in the phenomena of religious experience, but he extended his principle to many different areas. He insisted that the "cash-value" of ideas must be extracted. "Pragmatism unstiffens all our theories, limbers them up and sets each one at work."

Pragmatism involved not only a new method in the search for truth. It pointed toward a new definition of truth itself. Truth was not an absolute and final thing but the quality that ideas had for individuals if they worked for those individuals. By the first decade of the twentieth century James could see that science itself was moving away from the belief that its "laws" were "a transcript of reality." They were instead only "approximations"—"a man-made language, a conceptual short-hand, as someone calls them, in which we write our reports of nature."

Pragmatism, developed by James as a philosophy of extreme individualism, was given a very different emphasis by John Dewey and his fellow philosophers at the University of Chicago. In a system called "instrumentalism," they defined ideas as plans for solving problems. Arguing from biological evolution, they taught that human intelligence had developed not merely to register the environment but to grapple more effectively with it. Men's thoughts were themselves important factors in directing the course of social evolution. This point of view forbade dogmatism about the customs and ideals of society. All such ideas were ideas on trial to be retained or rejected according to their effectiveness in promoting the well-being of mankind. Dewey laid primary emphasis on the need for educational reform to prepare children to think intelligently, that is, purposively, about human problems.

Education for the New Age

The pre-Civil War public-school movement had been closely related to the extension of the franchise. Political democracy required that the masses of the population receive at least the rudiments of education. After the Civil War the need was all the more obvious. The problems of government, particularly in the new great cities, were growing annually more complex, and the ignorance and apathy of the citizens encouraged political corruption and the rule of bosses.

The need for better informed voters was not the only one to be met. American industrialization created an insistent demand for men and women with sufficient education to write letters, to keep books, and to serve as foremen, superintendents, and executives as well as lawyers, chemists, and engineers. Farmers needed education, not only to raise crops and livestock more efficiently, but to understand better the political and economic forces that were affecting agricultural prices in markets thousands of miles away.

There were many evidences of educational progress. In 1870, 20 per cent of the population ten years of age or over were unable to write; by 1910 the percentage had fallen to 7.7—a good record considering the large number of unschooled immigrants in the country. Not only was education reaching more of the children, but its content was being steadily enriched. Between 1860 and 1890 literature, geography, history, civics, and nature study made their way into the elementary school curriculum; after 1890 drawing, domestic science, and manual training became increasingly popular. The kindergarten idea, which had originated in Germany, found its earliest American adoption among the Germans of the Middle West. The first English-speaking kindergarten was that of Elizabeth Peabody, opened at Boston in 1860. Private kindergartens spread rapidly thereafter, and the first public-school kindergarten was organized in St. Louis in 1873.

In 1860 secondary education was still largely in the hands of private academies. In the whole country there were probably fewer than 350 public high schools, and these were mostly in New England and the Middle West. Following the Civil War the opening of new high schools progressed steadily and became particularly rapid after 1890. In 1915 there were almost 12,000 high schools with a student enrollment of 1,300,000 in contrast with 2,500 high schools with 200,000 pupils twenty-five years before. The rising popularity of the high school was closely related to its broadened curriculum. Bookkeeping, typing, shorthand, woodworking, metalwork, printing, agriculture, mechanical drawing, cooking, and dressmaking all appeared in the offerings. Purists might throw up their hands in horror, but the innovation was not actually great. The practical work of the high schools took the place of the vocational training once provided by apprenticeship. With the same school providing for the needs of both the future lawyer and the future typesetter, American secondary education had departed far from the European class system of education which segregated the intellectual elite from the masses who would follow the common trades.

It was an age in which close attention was paid to educational experts and to the innovations of particular school systems. The United States Bureau of Education, established in 1867, gathered statistics and other information on school conditions in various parts of the country. Particularly outstanding was the work of William T. Harris, who became United States Commissioner of Education in 1889 and served for seventeen years. Harris, formerly superintendent of schools in St. Louis, was a man of broad culture and one of the leading exponents of Hegelian idealism in the country. He did much to extend and to enrich public-school education along essentially conservative lines. More radical were the ideas developed by Colonel Francis W. Parker at Quincy, Massachusetts, and William A. Wirt at Gary, Indiana. By 1914 John Dewey had become the country's most influential writer on educational matters. As a professor both at the University of Chicago and at Columbia and as the guiding spirit behind several experimental schools, Dewey laid insistent stress on the function of the schools in prompting social progress—a stress closely related to the instrumentalist philosophy. The problem of the teacher was not to suppress the child's lively instincts but to direct them into useful channels. In the classroom the pupil was to have experience in democratic adjustment to his fellows, and he was to be guided step by step into knowledge of the wider world in which he lived. The merits of the progressive-school approach were hotly debated, but Dewey's ideas, at least in attenuated form, were widespread in educational circles by 1914.

Educational progress was notoriously uneven. While the schools of the cities were being transformed by the introduction of new courses and new methods, poor rural districts were finding it desperately hard to teach even the simplest subjects. Poverty led to frequent abbreviation of the school year. In the North Atlantic states, where conditions were best, the average school year was 152 days in 1870 and 180 days in 1910; in the south-central states, where they were worst, the year averaged only 91 days in 1870 and 126 days in 1910.

The temptation was great for parents to keep children out of school to work in factories or on the farm. The first modern compulsory attendance law, enacted in Massachusetts in 1852, provided merely that children between the ages of eight and fourteen must attend school for twelve weeks each year, six weeks of which must be consecutive. Similar legislation was enacted for the District of Columbia in 1864 and for Vermont in 1867. Thereafter, the compulsory principle spread rapidly, reaching 17 states and territories by 1880 and 15 more by 1900. But with few exceptions these laws were lenient in their requirements and scanted in their enforcement. The average attendance in public schools in 1880 was only 41 per cent of the children of school age, that is, between five and seventeen; by 1910 the percentage had risen to 53 per cent. Most Americans remained in school only a few years. As late as 1907 only one out of three who entered the elementary schools graduated, and less than one out of ten continued through high school.

Teachers were poorly paid everywhere, and especially so in the rural districts. In 1883 teachers in the ungraded schools of Iowa averaged less than $150 a year at a time when ordinary farm hands were receiving $200 with board. Conditions had improved somewhat by 1914 but not enough to make schoolteaching an attractive career. There were fewer men teachers in the public schools in 1910 than there had been in 1880; in the earlier year men teachers had constituted 43 per cent of the total, in 1910 they were only 21 per cent. Even for women schoolteaching had little to offer as a lifetime profession, and the teacher who married the village's most eligible bachelor and retired after a few years in the classroom was considered fortunate.

Poorly trained and poorly paid teachers, short school years, and ungraded and badly equipped buildings characterized the age of the little red schoolhouse. Massachusetts sought to meet the problem in 1882 by abolishing the district system and restoring school authority to the townships. In other states less drastic

FIG. 44. *Country School.* Painting by E. L. Henry. Three boys have been called before the teacher to recite, while the other pupils study at their benches. One of the latter is reaching for an ink bottle, which he has just dropped on the floor. (*Courtesy of the Mabel Brady Garvan Collection, Yale University Art Gallery.*)

steps were taken, but it became at least permissive for school districts to consolidate and to build central graded schools to which children might be brought in wagons. It was a development which held promise for the future but one whose possibilities could not be fully exploited until the advent of the school bus.

All these educational problems were encountered in exaggerated form in the South, where the public-school system had made little progress prior to the Civil War. During the Reconstruction period the need for schools was desperately felt, but the section's poverty raised formidable obstacles. White opposition to mixed schools made necessary a dual system of education for Negroes and whites despite the heavy expense involved. During the 1880's there were proposals for Federal aid, but Congress refused to take action. Some assistance was forthcoming from private philanthropy, particularly from the Peabody Fund. For the most part, however, the South was thrown upon its own resources, and progress was necessarily slow. Each decade, however, saw more and more children provided with schools, and the advance between 1898 and 1914 was particularly impressive. But the funds appropriated for Negro education remained pitifully inadequate. In 1900, 44.5 per cent of the Negroes were illiterate; in 1910 the percentage was 30.4.

Colleges and Universities

Science's rapidly expanding frontiers and the urgent needs of industrial civilization called for a radical reform of higher education. But the colleges of 1865 showed little awareness of these new responsibilities. The core of instruction was still Latin, Greek, mathematics, and philosophy—the cluster of subjects considered essential for the polished gentleman of an earlier generation. To these traditional courses there had been added a haphazard collection of new subjects. In most institutions all students were required to take the same sequence of courses—a sequence that laid emphasis on introducing the student to many subjects rather than on making him proficient in a few. Professors as well as students suffered from this system, since almost all their teaching was on an elementary level and might be spread over several different fields. One Columbia savant, for example, taught moral and mental philosophy, English literature, history, political economy, and logic.

Despite the expansion of the curriculum there were serious deficiencies. Usually the only scientific experiments the students ever saw were a few classroom demonstrations by the professor. Although tremendously important contributions to knowledge were being made by French and German scholars, some colleges offered no work at all in the modern languages and others very little. Both English and American literature were neglected, and very little instruction was offered that would enable the student to understand the political, economic, and social forces at work in post-Civil War America.

But better days were near at hand. The reform movement was led by a generation of astute college presidents, who secured the often reluctant support of their faculties and induced men of wealth to finance their new departures.

When Charles W. Eliot became president of Harvard in 1869, the country's oldest institution for higher learning began a generation of important change. Eliot's reforms were numerous. Entrance requirements were raised, the faculty was enlarged, many new courses were introduced, graduate work was organized on a respectable basis, the professional schools were strengthened, and the students were treated as men rather than as boys. But none of Eliot's other reforms aroused so much interest as his extension of the elective system. The system was not Eliot's invention. German universities had long operated on this basis; so had such American institutions as William and Mary, the University of Virginia, and the University of Michigan, and even at Harvard the older narrowly prescribed course of studies had gradually been modified to allow certain options for upperclassmen. But Eliot gave the students more choice than they had ever before enjoyed in any American institution. First the senior year was made completely elective, then the junior, then the sophomore. In the end, even freshmen received a large measure of freedom. The only required subjects were English composition, a modern language, and a few lectures in chemistry and physics.

The experiment at Harvard became a subject for lively debate. President Noah Porter of Yale was as conservative on the issue as Eliot was radical. Porter argued that college undergraduates were too immature to know what courses they ought to take or even what courses they would like. Taking a middle ground, President James McCosh of Princeton developed a curriculum which would compel freshmen and sophomores to take mostly prescribed courses but allow a large measure of freedom in the last two years. Most other institutions arrived at some similar compromise.

Vocational education was given great impetus by the Morrill Act of 1862, which provided a Federal land grant equal to 30,000 acres for each senator and representative to which each state was entitled under the 1860 census. The income on the funds secured from the sale of these lands was to be used for "the endowment, support, and maintenance of at least one college where the leading object shall be, without excluding other scientific and classical studies, and including military tactics, to teach such branches of learning as are related to agriculture and mechanic arts . . . in order to promote the liberal and practical education of the industrial classes in the several pursuits and professions in life." Hastening to avail themselves of this gift, the states either assigned the funds to established institutions which could be made to qualify or founded new ones. Among the latter were the state universities of Kansas (1864), Illinois (1867), Minnesota (1868), and California (1868), as well as institutions more narrowly directed to agricultural or mechanical education.

In 1868 Cornell University was established at Ithaca, New York, with the assistance of land-grant funds and an endowment from Ezra Cornell, who had accumulated a fortune in the Western Union Telegraph Company. The new institution's first president, Andrew D. White, defied criticism by establishing the university on a strictly nonsectarian basis and by permitting women as well as men to enroll. In the spirit of the Morrill Act he organized excellent agricultural and engineering schools, but he also built up a strong liberal-arts college with more offerings in history and the social sciences than were to be found in most contemporary institutions.

Cornell's successful experiment in coeducation was a novelty only in the East. In the Middle West, Oberlin had been coeducational since its opening in 1833, and women as well as men had been allowed to enroll at Antioch and at other colleges founded during the fifties. The first of the state universities to accept the principle was Iowa in 1858, but it was followed during the next fifteen years by Kansas, Minnesota, Michigan, Illinois, and Wisconsin. Although coeducation came to be taken for granted in this region, resistance to it continued in the older sections of the country. One result was the establishment of such separate women's colleges as Vassar (1865), Smith (1875), and Wellesley (1875). Another was the organization of affiliated women's colleges at some of the institutions hitherto exclusively masculine. Harvard Annex, later Radcliffe, was opened in 1879, and Columbia took a similar step in the establishment of Barnard in 1889.

Prior to the Civil War American colleges gave no graduate instruction worthy of the name. Although the master-of-arts degree was liberally bestowed upon students who remained in residence a stipulated period of time, for systematic advanced study Americans were compelled to go to Germany. Yale and Harvard began to respond to the situation in the postwar years. The first American doctor-of-philosophy degree was granted by Yale in 1861, and both Yale and Harvard organized special graduate divisions in the early seventies. But it remained for a new institution to assemble a faculty specially chosen to give advanced instruction. Founded in 1876 at Baltimore, Johns Hopkins University differed from any other of the day in being primarily for graduate study. Greatly influenced by German practice, President Daniel Coit Gilman laid heavy stress on the research training provided by laboratories and seminars. Clark University, established in 1887 at Worcester, Massachusetts, under the presidency of G. Stanley Hall, attempted a similar program. But the emergence of special institutions for graduate instruction was a short-lived trend. The country's great universities—Harvard, Yale, Columbia, the University of Pennsylvania, and the state universities of the Middle West—steadily improved their graduate schools.

Important new institutions were Stanford University, established in 1885, and the University of Chicago, 1892. The former was liberally endowed by Leland Stanford, the California railroad magnate; the latter was the recipient of princely gifts from John D. Rockefeller. The expansion of the University of Chicago under President William Rainey Harper was particularly rapid. It soon boasted one of the best faculties in the country and enjoyed a prestige rivaling that of institutions founded two centuries earlier.

University administrators found a great field for reform in the professional schools. Paralleling the change in medical education already described was a stiffening of the standards of the law schools. A reform destined to have wide influence was the introduction of the case system by C. C. Langdell, whom Eliot made dean of Harvard Law School in 1870. Besides the reorganization of the older schools there was a strong trend toward the establishment of new schools. Dentistry, business administration, education, and journalism all gained a place.

Narrow denominationalism, although it persisted in the small colleges, had a rapidly diminishing influence on the universities. But there was some danger that higher education might be emancipated from one strait jacket only to be bound in another. Dependence for funds upon either politicians or millionaires had its disadvantages. It became dangerous for professors to be too outspoken on political issues or too critical of American business methods. Even so conservative a figure as William Graham Sumner laid himself open to attack when he opposed the protective tariff, and bolder individuals who defended labor's right to strike or condemned monopolies sometimes found themselves among the professorial unemployed. Issues of academic freedom and security of tenure contributed to the organization of the American Association of University Professors in 1914.

Adult Education

The American passion for self-improvement continued to be evident. The lyceum movement was revived under the promotion of James Redpath, who opened a central booking agency in 1868. Lecturers as diverse in background as James B. Gough, the reformed drunkard, Henry Ward Beecher, the country's leading clergyman, and Thomas Nast, the cartoonist, earned thousands of dollars annually through lecture engagements. Russell H. Conwell, a Philadelphia minister, delivered one lecture, "Acres of Diamonds," five thousand times between 1868 and 1913, and the travel talks of John L. Stoddard, illustrated with colored lantern slides, had an almost equal popularity. But the evolution of the lecture series was more in the direction of entertainment than of instruction. Humorists and readers were highly esteemed, but elevating discourses on the older Emersonian model no longer attracted audiences.

A new educational force had meanwhile been released. In 1874 the Reverend John H. Vincent, later a Methodist bishop, joined with Lewis Miller, an Ohio manufacturer, in organizing a summer assembly for the training of Sunday-school teachers at Lake Chautauqua, New York. The sponsors believed in the spiritual value of all knowledge, both religious and secular, and their programs were so interesting that they attracted thousands of earnest adults to the lectures of leading scholars like William James, Josiah Royce, Herbert Baxter Adams, and Richard T. Ely. The summer assemblies had many offshoots. In 1878 a Literary and Scientific Circle was organized to make it possible for Chautauqua enthusiasts to carry on directed reading within their own homes. Many books were specially written for the purpose, and a monthly magazine, the *Chautauquan,* was founded. Meanwhile, several independent summer assemblies on the Chautauqua model were established elsewhere. In 1903 the Redpath Lyceum Bureau organized a traveling Chautauqua, which was so successful that rival circuits were soon organized. By 1914 millions of Americans who had never heard of Lake Chautauqua associated the Chautauqua name with a week or two of culture and entertainment that was brought to their home towns each summer. Protected from the sun and rain by great canvas tents, the Chautauqua audiences sat patiently through programs which ranged from Hawaiian bands and dramatic readers to lectures on popular science or on contemporary problems. Such early twentieth-century personalities as Theodore Roosevelt, Robert M. La Follette, Jane Addams, and Samuel Gompers made occasional appearances in the Chautauqua tents, and William Jennings Bryan was a regular attraction. Adult education of a more formal character was offered by the universities through summer schools, extension schools, and correspondence courses.

Especially important in the popularization of knowledge were the public libraries. Only a few tax-supported libraries were in existence prior to the Civil War, but they were established by the hundreds thereafter. The donation of funds for library purposes now became a favorite form of philanthropy. Chicago received 4 million dollars from William Newberry, New York 2 million dollars from Samuel J. Tilden, and Baltimore 1 million from Enoch Pratt. The public library's greatest impetus came when Andrew Carnegie began his gifts in 1881. The Carnegie plan was to pay for the erection of library buildings in cities or towns which would acquire a site and provide for the maintenance of the library by taxation. By the time of his death in 1919 Carnegie had helped in the establishment of over twenty-five hundred such institutions.

Millions of Americans who seldom read books and never attended a summer assembly gained most of their information from magazines and newspapers. The circulation of all types of periodicals expanded greatly with the growing population and the rising literacy rate.

Although the discriminating still clung to magazines like the *Atlantic Monthly* and *Harper's* or the newer *Scribner's Magazine,* established in 1871, the magazines of widest circulation were more popular in tone and cheaper in price. The existence of this wider public had been revealed by the great success of the *Ladies' Home Journal*, established in 1883 by Cyrus H. K. Curtis and brilliantly edited from 1889 to 1919 by Edward Bok. Advertising revenue and new manufacturing methods made it possible to sell the *Journal* for 10 cents. Other publishers quickly entered the field. *McClure's*, established in 1893, sold for 15 cents; *Munsey's* and *Cosmopolitan*, established a few months later, were priced at 10 cents; the *Saturday Evening Post*—revived from decrepitude by Curtis who purchased it for a thousand dollars in 1897—cost only a nickel.

Some of the magazines were notable for their aggressive treatment of contemporary political and social problems. A pioneer journal of opinion was the *Nation,* founded by E. L. Godkin in 1865. The *Forum* (1886) and the *Arena* (1889) also devoted themselves to issues of the day. But the exposure of corruption both in politics and in business did not become a major influence in the the magazine field until *McClure's* began to publish the work of Ida M. Tarbell and Lincoln Steffens in 1902. For the next several years muckraker articles in the popular magazines had an enormous vogue.

Newspapers, both city dailies and country weeklies, increased in number and circulation. A revolutionary force was Joseph Pulitzer, an immigrant from Hungary, who gained control of the St. Louis *Post-Dispatch* in 1878. His success in St. Louis made it possible for him to purchase the struggling New York *World* in 1883. Within a year Pulitzer raised the *World's* circulation from 15,000 to 60,000. By 1898 it had passed the million mark. Many factors contributed to this result. Naturally a crusader, Pulitzer had an extraordinary skill in organizing a campaign to reform some civic abuse or to raise money for some worthy cause. In this way the *World* created much of its own news and gave it a treatment which thousands of readers found exciting. But Pulitzer knew how to capitalize on public curiosity in less admirable ways. Murders, robberies, assaults, and divorces were exploited to the full. Popular features were introduced, including the first colored comic, "The Yellow Kid" by R. F. Outcault.

Pulitzer's success invited competition. After beginning a turbulent newspaper career in San Francisco, William Randolph Hearst purchased the New York *Journal* in 1895 and sought to beat the *World* at its own game. Since both papers now published comics under the title of "The Yellow Kid," the phrase, "yellow journalism," caught the public fancy as descriptive of the sensationalism of the two giants. Pulitzer had a basic honesty that made the *World* a great paper despite its sins against good taste, but Hearst had no comparable redeeming qualities.

The competition of Pulitzer and Hearst tended to obscure more fundamental trends. The day of personal journalism was in reality passing, and newspaper publishing was taking on more and more of the aspects of big business. Linotype machines and improved presses speeded immeasurably the process of getting out an edition, but such mechanical improvements demanded an increasingly large amount of capital. Small newspapers found it harder to compete; many went to the wall or were purchased by larger ones. By 1914 the activities of Hearst, of the Scripps-McRae interests, and of Frank A. Munsey had already resulted in the creation of great newspaper chains. Papers everywhere became more dependent on the Associated Press and other great news services. Syndicates were organized from which newspapers all over the country could purchase the same comic strips, advice to the lovelorn, household hints, and other features. There were frequent charges that the dependence of the newspapers on advertising revenue influenced their editorial positions and even their handling of the news.

With all their faults the newspapers gave millions of Americans their only knowledge of a wider world than their own communities. They served as one more educational force in an age when education was vital. Modern industry and modern science were changing the world so rapidly that the democratic destiny of the country was dependent upon sharpening the intelligence, not only of the leaders, but of the rank and file of American society.

Chapter 27. From Romanticism to Realism

Between the Civil War and World War I the United States witnessed herculean achievements—huge railroad systems spanning the country, gigantic corporations organizing the country's production and distribution, and large-scale mechanized agriculture. The wealth and power of the nation were tremendously increased. But the heroic age of free enterprise was also an age of political corruption, financial manipulation, ugly and overcrowded cities, ostentatious wealth, exploited workers, and impoverished farmers.

The effect of these paradoxes on American culture was both good and bad. Although increasing wealth meant greater patronage, many authors and artists were tempted to cling to romanticism, to search for beauty and truth in ancient societies or imaginary kingdoms, in the world of nature, or in the emotional impulses of the individual—anywhere except in the real world of contemporary society. Yet cultural health required that literature and art come to some sort of terms with reality, that they begin to tell the truth about American life. A revolt against romanticism was inevitable, and by 1914 the impact of realism was evident in every sphere of artistic activity.

Literature under Handicaps

Between the extraordinary literary output of the 1850's and the flourishing 1880's, when Mark Twain, William Dean Howells, and Henry James were developing their full powers, lay the comparatively barren stretches of the sixties and the seventies. One after another, the older voices became quiet. By 1865 Thoreau and Hawthorne were dead. Emerson lived until 1882, but the pronouncements of his old age lacked the originality and force of those of his youth. Lowell and Longfellow, much shallower vessels than Emerson, were even sooner emptied. Melville, repudiated by the general public, now wrote but little. Of the old giants Whitman alone had important things to say in the beautiful lyrics of *Drum Taps* (1865) and the vigorous prose of *Democratic Vistas* (1871).

That the older men should become silent or repetitious was to be expected. More disquieting was the scarcity of talent in the new literary generation. For this many explanations may be offered. Many young men of promise had been killed during the Civil War. The spiritual exhaustion that followed the great conflict was a temporary factor, and another, more lasting in its effects, was the concentration of national energy in the settling of the West and the building of the great business empires. Not only did these activities attract many of the most vigorous and original minds, but they involved a new set of values. The captains of industry enjoyed a prestige that in another age might have gone to novelists and poets.

Since most men considered themselves too busy to read more than the daily newspapers, the reading of books and literary magazines was a largely feminine activity. Much of the writing was done by women; that done by men was more or less consciously addressed to a feminine audience. Although this situation had long existed, its consequences were particularly in evidence after the Civil War. Women's great emancipation had only begun; their world was still a sheltered one, and a literature written largely for their eyes was inevitably lacking in frankness and force.

Literary activity was still under the handicap of bad copyright laws. Publishers hesitated to commit themselves to the payment of royalties to unknown American authors when they could pirate without fear of penalty the work of established English favorites. Not until 1891 did Congress finally pass an international copyright law, which, by assuring American royalties for foreign authors, protected native writers from unfair competition.

The literary desert was not, however, without its pleasant oases. Poets like Edmund Clarence Stedman, Bayard Taylor, and Thomas Bailey Aldrich applied themselves conscientiously to their craft, attempting to express ideals of beauty and truth within the conventional forms of the day. Bolder to experiment was Sidney Lanier. A native of Georgia and a Confederate veteran, Lanier spent the immediate postwar years traveling from job to job, struggling with poverty and broken health. Settling at last in Baltimore, he played the flute in a local orchestra, wrote poetry, and lectured on literature at Johns Hopkins until death struck him down at the age of thirty-nine. Lanier was fascinated by the affinity of music and poetry. His *Science of English Verse* (1880) was an interesting statement of his theories; his lyrics—thin in ideas but rich in cadence and imagery—demonstrated them effectively.

The most important New England author of the period was a woman unknown to her own generation. Emily Dickinson passed her days in the quiet college town of Amherst, Massachusetts. Not only did she never marry, but she spent the last three decades of her life as a recluse, scarcely seen by her neighbors except as a tiny figure in white flitting through her garden in the evening or speaking to them from the shadows at the head of the stairs while they stood in the hall below. But Emily Dickinson's timidity and eccentricity did not prevent her from living in a vivid world of her own. She phrased her intuitions about life and nature in hundreds of little poems. Although she made no attempt to have these published, she did send some of them to Colonel Thomas Wentworth Higginson of Worcester. This kindly patron of the arts scarcely knew what to make of the strange friend with whom he exchanged letters for eight years before he met her for the first time in 1870. But fortunately he sensed her genius and encouraged her to continue writing. In 1890, four years after Emily Dickinson's death, the first selection of her poetry, compiled by Higginson and Mabel Loomis Todd, her former schoolmate, was published. Later collections followed, and the Amherst poet gradually gained recognition as one of the major figures of American literature.

Samuel Langhorne Clemens, universally known as Mark Twain, experienced American life in all its fascinating variety. He passed his boyhood in a sleepy Missouri village; he worked as an itinerant printer in Middle Western and eastern cities; he spent four years as a Mississippi river pilot during the golden age of steamboating; he crossed the plains to Nevada, where he prospected for gold and served as a reporter for the Virginia City *Enterprise.* In 1865, while he was doing newspaper work in San Francisco, he first gained notice in the East through a preposterous story about a jumping frog accepted for publication in a New York paper. The next year he convulsed a San Francisco audience with a drawling account of a trip to the Hawaiian Islands. Outstandingly successful on the lecture platform in a day when humorous lecturers were at the height of their popularity, Mark Twain soon earned the funds for a visit to Europe and the Holy Land. *Innocents Abroad* (1869), in which he recounted his experiences, delighted Americans and shocked Europeans with its breezy irreverence toward the historic shrines and art treasures of the Old World.

A succession of remarkable books now followed. *Roughing It* (1872) and *Life on the Mississippi* (1883) caught the color and raw vigor of the mining boom and the steamboat age. *The Gilded Age* (1873), Mark Twain's first novel, written in collaboration with Charles Dudley Warner, was uneven in quality but effectively satirized political and business corruption in post-Civil War Washington. *Tom Sawyer* (1876) was an imperishable story based upon Mark Twain's own boyhood in Hannibal, Missouri. *Huckleberry Finn* (1885)—one of the few truly great novels of American literature and a treasure of social history—derived its appeal from memorable characters, robust humor, the recapture of the mystery and beauty of the Mississippi, and sharply drawn pictures of revivalists, patent-medicine vendors, rural gentry, and white trash.

With the completion of *Huckleberry Finn* Mark Twain exhausted his richest vein of material. His attempts to write about medieval Europe were less successful but resulted in such memorable works as *A Connecticut Yankee in King Arthur's Court* (1889) and *Personal Recollections of Joan of Arc* (1896). For medieval civilization, built, so he believed, on ignorance and cruelty, Mark Twain had scant respect, but he idealized Joan as the epitome of feminine purity.

Long applauded as a humorist and storyteller, Mark Twain aspired in his later years to a different kind of fame. Bereavement and financial reverses accentuated a vein of disillusionment and bitterness that had long run through his work but had usually been regarded as merely a facet of his mordant wit. In his late writing, some of it unpublished until after his death in 1910, he gave expression to a determinist philosophy as pessimistic as that of Melville.

The Rise of Realism

Writers were beginning to rebel against literary conventions that divorced the settings and actions of fiction from those of life itself. Some applied what they called "local color." In *The Hoosier Schoolmaster* (1871) Edward Eggleston portrayed a region of the Middle West which, as a Methodist circuit rider, he knew intimately. Local customs and dialect were used with similar success by Bret Harte in his stories of western mining camps, by George W. Cable in stories of New Orleans, and by Mary Noailles Murfree, writing under the pseudonym of Charles Egbert Craddock, in stories of the Tennessee mountains. The somber charm of old New England villages was captured in the work of Thomas Bailey Aldrich, Sarah Orne Jewett, and Mary E. Wilkins. John William De Forest, a Connecticut Yankee who had lived for extended periods in the prewar South, utilized his close observation to write the realistic novels *Miss Ravenel's Conversion from Secession to Loyalty* (1867) and *Kate Beaumont* (1872).

Realism gained its most important champion in William Dean Howells. Howells knew small-town life in the Middle West from his Ohio boyhood and from his youthful experiences as printer and newspaperman. He observed urban society in the East through long residences in Boston and New York. First as an editor of the *Atlantic Monthly* and later as a member of the staff of *Harper's Magazine,* he exerted important influence. A close friend of Mark Twain, he encouraged that moody genius to carry through some of his best work. With Henry James he maintained a long friendship, and he was one of the first to recognize the talents of such younger authors as Stephen Crane, Hamlin Garland, and Frank Norris. He used his editorial posts to expound his conviction that "fidelity to experience" and "probability of motive" were essential conditions of great imaginative literature.

More important than precepts were the examples Howells provided in his own 38 novels, published between 1871 and 1920. Outstanding among these were *A Modern Instance* (1882), *The Rise of Silas Lapham* (1885), *Indian Summer* (1886), and *A Hazard of New Fortunes* (1890). Readers who liked sentimentality and excitement found Howells dull, but the more discriminating delighted in his faithful treatment of themes typical of contemporary American life—businessmen struggling with problems of business ethics, newly rich families embarrassed and blundering in their social life, self-indulgent and unscrupulous newspapermen, women trapped by love and disillusioned in marriage, immigrant socialists dreaming of a better world, and the gossipy society of summer hotels.

Lustful love, crimes of violence, and scenes of degeneracy found no place in Howells's writings, since he frankly acknowledged that he thought American authors should write only what it would be proper for young girls to read. He denied that this qualified his realism. Chaste love and not guilty passion, he said, was faithfully representative of the tone of American life. Howells's reserve in these matters did not extend to issues of social justice. He sympathized with the workers in the labor difficulties of the 1880's and spoke out bravely against the execution of the Chicago anarchists. His novels contained vigorous criticism of the existing economic order and contrasted contemporary inequalities with the ideal conditions of a socialist utopia.

Howells's friend Henry James lived a very different life. Born in New York City, he was educated in Europe and America under the somewhat erratic guidance of his talented father, the senior Henry James, a wealthy man with a passion for unorthodox theology and philosophy. After attempting to study painting and law, young Henry James found that his natural aptitude was for literature just as that of his older brother William was for psychology and philosophy. His first efforts at writing were not notably successful, but he eventually gained an appreciative public with works of fiction like *The American* (1877), *Daisy Miller* (1879), and *The Portrait of a Lady* (1881).

The setting which Henry James usually portrayed was that of English and European high society. This world, so remote from that of most Americans, was one that James knew intimately. As a youth he had traveled widely; as a writer he found it much more congenial to live and to work in England than in his native land. From 1876 until his death in 1916 he returned to America only for a few brief visits. But James's voluntary exile did not deprive him of a lively interest in his fellow countrymen. Again and again he introduced American characters into his novels, seemingly fascinated by the situations created through the contacts of rude but innocent Yankees with sophisticated Europeans.

James agreed with Howells in sternly excluding from his novels weak sentimentality and improbable motivation, but in other respects the two friends practiced very different crafts. Although his earlier books were simple and direct in style, James came to prefer a more subtle artistry. His later works achieved their characterizations and told their stories by weaving together innumerable details and impressions. Their leisurely pace, their involved structure, and their difficult literary style discouraged many readers. James's final public, although small, was enthusiastic, since it was composed of those who appreciated exquisite craftsmanship—intricately constructed novels with every well-polished part in its proper place. His last major achievements, particularly esteemed by those who admired his fully elaborated style, were *The Wings of the Dove* (1902), *The Ambassadors* (1903), and *The Golden Bowl* (1904).

Realism of the Howells and James variety had its disciples in such fine later novelists as Edith Wharton, Willa Cather, and Ellen Glasgow. But other writers presented harsher truths—truths often distasteful to their contemporaries. Long perpetuated in literature had been the myth that village life was invariably innocent and happy and that cruelty and crime were peculiar to the city. The poverty, harshness, and narrow bigotry often characteristic of rural life now received realistic treatment in such books as E. W. Howe's *The Story of a Country Town* (1883) and Hamlin Garland's *Main-Travelled Roads* (1891).

Naturalism

As writers sought to tell the truth about life, their work necessarily reflected their basic philosophy. Earlier novelists had assumed that their characters were free agents choosing between right and wrong and suffering the consequences of their choice. But Darwin's theory of evolution emphasized the brute origins of human nature and the struggle for survival whereby the strong conquered and the weak were destroyed. Individual strength and weakness were the result of heredity and environment; man's destiny seemed to be shaped by blind forces which he could not control. European fiction had shown a growing awareness of the new philosophy, and naturalism had found its most uncompromising exponent in the French novelist Emile Zola.

A pioneer effort at American naturalism was Stephen Crane's *Maggie: A Girl of the Streets* (1892). This story of an unfortunate Irish girl, brought up in a degenerate family, victimized by a bartender, and driven to streetwalking and eventual suicide, violated all the taboos of the day and secured few readers. But Crane's next novel, *The Red Badge of Courage* (1895), brought him sudden fame. It was a story of the Civil War told without any of the conventional trappings of historical romance. War was depicted in all its brutality and horror, and the confusion and terror of the young soldier in his first battle were conveyed with graphic realism—a realism all the more remarkable because the youthful Crane knew war only through the reminiscences of other men. Before his tragic death in 1900 at the age of twenty-nine, Crane had further demonstrated his versatility in excellent short stories and poems.

After achieving a modest success with earlier fiction, Frank Norris clearly revealed his naturalism in the brutal novel *McTeague* (1899). Norris's most ambitious plan was to write three novels around the theme of wheat. This epic trilogy was to portray the production of wheat on the great farms of California, the trade in wheat in the Chicago grain market, and the distribution of wheat in Europe. When Norris died in 1902 at the age of thirty-two, he had written only two of the projected three novels. The first of these, *The Octopus* (1901), was an arresting account of the struggle between the wheatgrowers and the railroad trust. It dealt with the grim realities of the misuse of economic power, the evils of political corruption, and the general ruthlessness of the universe. *The Pit* (1903) contained memorable pictures of the mad clamor of the grain exchange, the conspicuous consumption of the wealthy, and the swift changes of fortune of those who lived by speculation.

Admirers of naturalism, shocked at the early deaths of Crane and Norris, hoped for a while that Jack London would carry on in the tradition that they had established. But even though London knew the seamy side of life from personal experience and had a flair for writing, he soon found it more profitable to publish popular adventure stories than to write novels dealing in grim truths.

The greatest exponent of naturalism proved to be the clumsy but powerful novelist Theodore Dreiser. Born in 1871 in Terre Haute, Indiana, Dreiser had varied experiences in many different occupations and in many cities before he wrote his first novel, *Sister Carrie* (1900). Even more than Crane's *Maggie* did Dreiser's book violate the conventions of the day. The earlier novelist had his heroine, a lady of easy virtue, commit suicide, but Dreiser—truer to life perhaps—allowed his to achieve success on Broadway. So disturbed was his publisher's wife that the first edition was suppressed, and the book did not go on sale until seven years later when another company accepted the risk. Subsequent novels involved Dreiser in similar difficulties extending over many years. His persistence and eventual victory opened the way to greater liberty for later authors.

Although perhaps excessively preoccupied with problems of sex, Dreiser pioneered in the realistic treatment of other aspects of life. The dreariness and low wages of labor in a shoe factory contributed to Sister Carrie's downfall, and the bigotry of a narrowly religious father helped to push *Jennie Gerhardt* (1911) along a similar path. Dreiser's characterization of Frank Cowperwood in *The Financier* (1912) and *The Titan* (1914)—based upon the actual career of Charles T. Yerkes, the Chicago traction magnate—provided a shocking revelation of contemporary business morals.

The Strange Case of Henry Adams

Of all writers who felt compelled to describe late nineteenth-century American civilization, none came to more pessimistic conclusions than Henry Adams. Adams belonged to one of the most famous American families. His great-grandfather and grandfather had been Presidents, and his father was a distinguished diplomat and a leading citizen. He aspired to comparable distinction but suffered many disappointments. His attempts at studying law were frustrated by his own lack of interest; his efforts in journalism received no serious recognition. Despite apparent success as a professor of history at Harvard he was not satisfied with this career and gave it up to write. In his *History of the United States of America during the Administrations of Jefferson and Madison* (9 vols., 1884–1889), he produced a magnificent account of early national politics and society. But neither this masterpiece nor his other efforts at writing biographies and historical essays gave him the sense of achievement for which he yearned.

For many years Adams lived in Washington as an amused and cynical spectator of the political scene. Traveling frequently in Europe and other parts of the world, he had unusual opportunities to compare American civilization with earlier ones which survived in works of art and literature. Out of his reflections Adams wrote two extraordinary books. The first of these, *Mont-Saint-Michel and Chartres* (privately printed, 1904; published, 1913), was at its most obvious level a fascinating study in Romanesque and Gothic architecture. In its wider implications it was one of the most sympathetic and sensitive appreciations of medieval civilization ever written. Deeply philosophical, it wrestled with the problem of explaining the historical force which made such triumphs as the cathedrals possible. In his intellectual autobiography, *The Education of Henry Adams* (privately printed, 1906; published, 1918), Adams returned to the same problem and stated his arresting conclusion: "Symbol or energy, the Virgin had acted as the greatest force the Western world ever felt, and had drawn man's activities to herself more strongly than any other power, natural or supernatural, had ever done. . . ." But the Virgin whom Adams extolled was not the Virgin Mary of Catholic theology; she was a much older object of veneration, the female element in nature, "reproduction—the greatest and most mysterious of all energies."

This curious terminal point in the thought of a blue-blooded Yankee reflected his pessimistic conclusion that the civilization of his own day was doomed because it had lost the unifying faith which gave vitality to earlier ages. The *Education of Henry Adams* was a chronicle of disillusionment. It recorded Adams's conviction that his own life had been a failure and that the times were hopelessly out of joint. It represented also Adams's attempt to formulate a philosophy of history on the basis of the latest findings of science. He rejected the easy optimism of the Social Darwinists for a pessimistic determinism grounded upon the physicists' law of the dissipation of energy. Energy, according to this statement, was constantly being expended without being replaced. Adams believed that human society was controlled by the same law. In the unity of the thirteenth century and the multiplicity of the twentieth there was evidence of disintegrating force. Since the process was one of constant acceleration, Adams took a gloomy view of the immediate future. The honest historian, he asserted, must "treat the history of modern Europe and America as a typical example of energies indicating degradation with headlong rapidity toward inevitable death." Fortunately, American civilization had an underlying soundness that Adams failed to detect. Moreover, by his own brilliant criticism of the shoddy aspects of American life he helped to combat the conditions which he portrayed.

Popular Literature

As in earlier generations, most of the authors who had a lasting influence on American thought never enjoyed the luxury of large royalty checks. The best sellers of the period were written by authors whose contribution to enduring literature was small.

A generation that took religion seriously, but loved melodramatic adventure at the same time, found General Lew Wallace's *Ben Hur* (1880) an ideal book. This story of early Christianity with its exciting chariot-race climax had at first only a modest success, but its popularity grew with the years until it eventually sold some 2,600,000 copies. Widely read also was the Reverend Charles M. Sheldon's *In His Steps* (1897), narrating the attempt of nineteenth-century Americans to apply literal Christianity to the problems of a Middle-Western city. Sheldon's novel sold perhaps 2,000,000 copies and was as popular in the British dominions as in the United States. Other clergymen discovered that sermons in fictional form might reach an audience greater than that drawn by the most famous pulpit orators of the day. The Reverend E. P. Roe had a spectacular success with *Barriers Burned Away* (1872), which moralized upon the great Chicago fire. A generation later Harold Bell Wright left the ministry to devote himself to writing for the vast public which liked to have a good story and a good lesson bound together in the same cover. Between 1903 and 1942 Wright wrote 19 novels, which achieved a total sale of some ten million copies. His greatest successes were *The Shepherd of the Hills* (1907), *The Calling of Dan Matthews* (1909), and *The Winning of Barbara Worth* (1911).

There was no single formula for popular success. Young ladies, eager to sigh and weep with the joys and sorrows of lovely heroines, read with eagerness as many as possible of the fifty or more sentimental novels which poured from the pen of Mrs. E. D. E. N. Southworth. The verse of Will Carleton, James Whitcomb Riley, and Eugene Field enjoyed a great popularity with readers who delighted in folksy philosophy and idealizations of childhood and rural life. Equally successful were engaging portrayals of shrewd rustic characters like Opie Read's *The Jucklins* (1896) and Edward Noyes Westcott's *David Harum* (1898). The great city found its most sympathetic portrayal in the skillful short stories of William S. Porter (O. Henry). Detective fiction's coming popularity was foreshadowed in the large sales of Anna Katharine Green's *The Leavenworth Case* (1878) and Mary Roberts Rinehart's *The Circular Staircase* (1908).

With the mass reading public, novels of pure romance were clearly more popular than attempts at realism. F. Marion Crawford delighted readers with melodramatic stories that had their settings in Italy, India, England, and Germany. Historical novels ranged in time and space from Tudor England, the scene of Charles Major's *When Knighthood Was in Flower* (1898), to Civil War Kentucky, where John Fox, Jr.'s *The Little Shepherd of Kingdom Come* (1903) had its setting. This type of fiction reached a high point of excellence in such novels as Winston Churchill's *Richard Carvel* (1899) and *The Crisis* (1900), Paul Leicester Ford's *Janice Meredith* (1899), and S. Weir Mitchell's *Hugh Wynne, Free Quaker* (1898).

After 1900 historical romance shared popularity with red-blooded stories of the western plains or the frozen North. Owen Wister's *The Virginian* (1902) achieved a success that encouraged other writers to exploit the field. Among those to do so very profitably were Jack London, Zane Grey, and Rex Beach. The exposure of business and political corruption, a recurrent literary theme since the mid-sixties, grew in popularity during the days of the progressive movement. Upton Sinclair's *The Jungle* (1906), William Allen White's *A Certain Rich Man* (1909), and the later novels of Winston Churchill were reform documents in fictional form.

One of the most profitable opportunities open to authors was to write for the great juvenile public. A well-deserved early success was achieved by Louisa May Alcott's *Little Women* (1868), and a generation later the novels of Kate Douglas Wiggin, Gene Stratton Porter, and Eleanor H. Porter enjoyed huge sales. Stories of mischievous boys had a great vogue, not only with youngsters, but with adults. Mark Twain's *Tom Sawyer* (1876) and *Huckleberry Finn* (1885) belonged to a genre that included Thomas Bailey Aldrich's *Story of a Bad Boy* (1870), George W. Peck's *Peck's Bad Boy* (1883), and Booth Tarkington's *Penrod* (1914). The most spectacular exploit was that of Horatio Alger, Jr., who between 1867 and 1899 wrote 135 books for boys. His favorite formula of the poor but honest lad who rises by pluck and industry from rags to riches had universal appeal. According to one estimate the total sale of Alger books was about 17 million, but this can be little better than a guess. Even harder to estimate would be Alger's influence in sharpening the acquisitive instincts of several generations of American boys.

Youths who selected their own literature became enthusiastic readers of dime novels. The first of these to be published was Mrs. Ann S. Stephens's *Malæska, the Indian Wife of the White Hunter* (1860). Thousands followed, bringing wealth to the pioneer publisher Erastus F. Beadle. As Beadle's success drew competitors into the field, the tales became more and more lurid. The excitement began with the title and picture on the colored-paper cover and continued to the last paragraph. Moralists shook their heads gloomily, but the little books did not lack for stanch defenders, who pointed out that the tales always provided a bad end for evildoers and proper rewards for the virtuous. The authors, no longer remembered, were often picturesque characters in their own right like Colonel Prentiss Ingraham, Major Sam S. Hall, and Ned Buntline. Their literary style may have been crude, but their fertile imaginations never failed them, as a glance at their alliterative titles at once demonstrates. A bibliography of the works of Major Hall, for example, would include such alluring titles as *Double Dan, the Dastard; or, The Pirates of the Pecos* and *Ker-whoop, Ker-whoo!; or, The Tarantula of Taos.* Less ephemeral than the fame of the authors has been that of some of the dime-novel heroes like Deadwood Dick, Old Cap Collier, Nick Carter, and Frank Merriwell.

Emerging from the Architectural Dark Ages

In post-Civil War America architects and builders found lucrative opportunities. The growth of cities and the expansion of business required the erection of thousands of commercial buildings, and the newly rich were eager to display their wealth in ornate houses. But these conditions were hostile to the maintenance of any standards of architectural taste. Romanticism ran riot, finding its expression in capricious borrowings from any number of foreign styles. Houses were designated as Gothic, Italian, French, Queen Anne, and even Moorish—a veritable confusion of tongues. To later generations they seemed almost willfully ugly with their mansard roofs, colored window glass, and extraneous balconies, towers, and cupolas. The mechanical age left its most visible blemishes in a riot of jig-saw wooden ornament and cast-iron work.

Even in the tortured seventies, however, there were signs of better things to come. For the Vanderbilts and other rich clients, Richard Morris Hunt built great houses whose style was at least consistent—if somewhat ostentatious by later standards. The greatest force for architectural reform was Henry Hobson Richardson, a robust southerner well trained for his profession by study and travel in France. Given the commission to build Trinity Church in Boston in 1872, Richardson turned his back on the Gothic and developed an American Romanesque of sturdy dignity and beauty. The new style appealed to a generation weary of superficial detail, and Richardson became the most popular architect in the country, planning college buildings at Harvard, libraries and railroad stations for Massachusetts towns, residences in New York and Washington, and the great Marshall Field warehouse in Chicago. Other architects fell so much under the influence of his genial and vigorous personality that "Richardsonesque" became preeminently the architecture of the eighties.

But even in the hands of the master the Richardson style was oppressively massive, and his imitators usually lacked his saving instinct for composition. The nineties inevitably brought many changes. Heavy masonry was no longer necessary when steel frame construction had been developed to bear the weight of even the largest buildings. Commercial buildings hitherto limited to five or six stories—the height to which men could be reasonably expected to climb—were carried much higher after the invention of the elevator. Skyscraper architecture was first developed in Chicago, where Daniel H. Burnham and John W. Root were important pioneers. The problems of the new age were approached with the greatest originality by Louis H. Sullivan, another Chicago architect. Laying down the guiding principle that function should determine form, Sullivan sought to liberate architecture from slavish imitation of older styles and to adapt it frankly to the new materials and uses to which buildings were now being put. Skyscrapers, for example, should be so built as to accentuate their lofty, vertical lines—"every inch a proud and soaring thing." Sullivan's ideas had their most successful embodiment in the Wainwright Building, erected in St. Louis in 1890.

Not for many years, however, was Sullivan accepted as a major prophet. A revived classicism soon thrust aside both Richardson's Romanesque and Sullivan's functionalism. A skillful adaptation of Roman styles was already gaining favor in the East when the great Chicago World's Fair of 1893 gave its champions an unparalleled opportunity to impose their taste upon the country as a whole.

Visitors from every section were impressed by the classic beauty of Charles Atwood's Palace of the Fine Arts and other buildings of the Court of Honor. Classicism gained additional popularity through the fine designs provided by McKim, Mead and White of New York, who adapted Roman forms for such different uses as the Pennsylvania Station, the New York Post Office, and the

FIG. 45. Wainwright Building, St. Louis. Designed by Louis Sullivan and associates, 1890. The construction of this well-designed skyscraper represents a significant landmark in the development of functional architecture. (*Brown Brothers.*)

Columbia University Library. Although the classical style prevailed almost everywhere, Sullivan's able disciple Frank Lloyd Wright kept the idea of functional architecture alive with such buildings as the Larkin factory in Buffalo and Middle Western "prairie homes" with arresting horizontal lines.

Meanwhile, the skyscrapers were pushed ever higher, transforming the Manhattan skyline even before 1914. Although traditionalists found difficulty in accommodating these to the prevailing Roman style, their towerlike character did invite use of the Gothic. America's greatest architectural pride in pre-World

War I days was the 57-story Woolworth Building, a Gothic cathedral of commerce designed by Cass Gilbert and completed in 1912.

Painting and Sculpture

Families with newly acquired wealth collected works of art just as they built great houses or bought fine horses. Sometimes they bought genuine masterpieces, to the distress of sensitive souls pained to see these treasures in the hands of Philistines; sometimes they were the victims of unscrupulous foreigners who sold them second-rate works at first-rate prices. In either case art was regarded as primarily a European product, and native artists found it hard to win acceptance.

The natural result was to place a premium on European techniques. The aspiring young American artist was unhappy unless he could cross the Atlantic for study in France or Germany. He returned to America proud of his European training and determined to work within the European tradition. So strong, indeed, was this gravitational pull that some talented Americans preferred to live and work abroad—feeling like Henry James that only in England or on the Continent could they breathe civilized air.

The European apprenticeship of American art was by no means all loss. Studying the masterpieces of Old World galleries and the well-grounded techniques of Old World teachers, American painters became steadily more competent. The warmth of color and the idealistic unity of George Inness's landscapes brought enthusiastic acclaim, and Homer D. Martin and Alexander Wyant introduced some of the techniques of the French impressionists. John La Farge worked in stained glass and murals—mediums hitherto attempted by few Americans. The market for portraits, now more lucrative than ever before, gave employment to the considerable talents of such men as John W. Alexander, Frank Duveneck, and William M. Chase.

Among the American painters who elected to live abroad, three achieved outstanding places in the world of international art. James McNeill Whistler, born in Lowell, Massachusetts, and educated for a time at West Point, studied painting in Paris and eventually took up his residence in London, where he soon became notorious for his facility in what he himself called "the gentle art of making enemies." A great admirer of Japanese prints, he ventured far from the beaten path of artistic convention in paintings which he called "symphonies" and "nocturnes" since his purpose was to evoke moods through the use of subtle color tones. When John Ruskin described these as "a pot of paint flung in the public face," Whistler sued him for libel and won damages of one farthing. But despite his posturing and impudence Whistler was a man of great talent with challenging new ideas. John Singer Sargent, on the other hand, provoked little controversy and won acclaim through the soundness and brilliance of his work. Born in Italy of American parents, he was educated abroad and lived most of his life in England. His American connections were nevertheless intimate. Some of his finest portraits were of wealthy Americans, and he achieved conspicuous success with his murals in the Boston Public Library. Less in the public eye than Whistler and Sargent but a sensitive and highly talented artist was Mary Cassatt, the daughter of wealthy Pittsburgh parents. She spent most of her life in France, where she fell under the influence of the impressionists. Particularly successful were her paintings of mothers and children.

FIG. 46. *The Herring Net.* Painting by Winslow Homer. This fine artist found his best subjects in the sea and seafaring men. (*Courtesy of The Art Institute of Chicago.*)

Unique among the artists of their generation in being almost completely independent of European influences were Winslow Homer, Thomas Eakins,[1] and Albert Pinkham Ryder. Homer, a member of an old Boston family, began his career as an illustrator, contributing interesting material on Civil War soldier life to *Harper's Weekly.* But he discovered his real power when he turned to painting. He secluded himself in a cottage along the Maine coast, which he left only for occasional trips to the West Indies or to Florida. Wherever he worked, he achieved his greatest success in painting the surging sea and the strong men who braved it. Thomas Eakins spent his life, except for a brief period of study and travel in Europe, in Philadelphia, where he perfected a realistic style little appreciated by a public still wedded to romanticism. Eakins found subjects for his art in musicians bending over their instruments, athletes sculling on the Schuylkill, and doctors at work in their clinics. A contrast to the realism of Homer and Eakins was provided in the romanticism of Albert Ryder. Ryder, a

[1] See Fig. 43.

native of New Bedford, Massachusetts, was an eccentric recluse, often puttering for years over a single commission. He lived in a dream world of his own, which he transferred to canvas in paintings of eerie fascination.

The challenge to academic tradition implicit in these careers was carried farther by a younger generation who loudly asserted their independence and attempted a consciously American art. The great prophet of the rebels was Robert Henri, who in addition to being an accomplished artist himself was an influential teacher from 1900 to 1929. Henri and other young painters like John Sloan and George Luks found so many themes in the everyday life of New York City that they became known as the Ash Can School. Similar to this group in their robust realism were Jerome Myers and George Bellows.[1] The new art made a determined bid for recognition in the famous Armory show of 1913.

Most Americans had little contact with painting at its more pretentious levels, but they did like to have pictures in their books and magazines. This demand was met by the work of an unusually competent generation of illustrators. Thousands of readers visualized the characters of Shakespeare through the illustrations of Edwin A. Abbey, and sea stories found their perfect accompaniment in the drawings of Howard Pyle. Frederic Remington [2] caught the romantic spirit of the western plains, and Charles Dana Gibson delighted millions with his drawings of the "Gibson girl"—the feminine ideal of the pre-World War I generation. Few cartoonists in American history have exerted the power of Thomas Nast, whose vigorous caricature was equally potent against William M. Tweed, the Tammany boss, and James G. Blaine, the clay-footed idol of the Republicans.

Sculpture received generous, if undiscriminating, public support. Every self-respecting town had its war memorial; almost every city park and square was graced with an equestrian general. Although the public often seemed to take as much pride in mediocre statues as in good, a number of highly talented sculptors were at work. Of the older generation John Quincy Adams Ward was the most notable figure; of the younger Augustus Saint-Gaudens was clearly outstanding. Saint-Gaudens's most unusual creation was the shrouded figure which stood in Rock Creek Cemetery in Washington as a memorial to Mrs. Henry Adams. Highly gifted also were Daniel Chester French, William MacMonnies, and George Grey Barnard.

Music—Serious and Popular

America's musical taste in the sixties showed little improvement over that of the garish fifties. The favorite musical personality of the day was Pat Gilmore, an energetic band leader. At Boston in 1869 Gilmore staged a Great National Peace Jubilee, advertised as "the grandest musical festival ever known in the history of the world." An orchestra of 1,000 pieces and a chorus of 10,000 voices were assembled. Cannon, fired by electric buttons on the conductor's desk,

[1] See Figs. 41 and 54. [2] See Fig. 37.

marked the rhythm of the national airs, and 100 firemen in red shirts pounded real anvils to assure the authenticity of the "Anvil Chorus." This musical circus drew enthusiastic visitors from all parts of the country. Attendance by President Grant, cabinet officers, governors, and other celebrities, both civil and military, stressed the importance, if not the dignity, of the occasion. Three years later Gilmore out-Gilmored himself with the World Peace Festival in Philadelphia, which featured Johann Strauss, brought all the way from Europe to lead a chorus of 20,000 voices singing "The Blue Danube."

Music as music rather than as spectacle established itself with painful difficulty. The New York Philharmonic Society, founded in 1842, was still twenty years later a weak, struggling orchestra, attempting only a few concerts each year. Even so New York was better off than most of the country where symphonic music was scarcely known before Theodore Thomas and his orchestra began their tours in 1869. Thomas, who had entered the United States with his German parents as a boy of ten in 1845 and had helped to support the family by playing the violin at dances and weddings and in theaters and saloons, began to build his own orchestra in 1862. Convinced that poor ensemble playing would continue until musicians could be employed on a full-time basis, Thomas kept his orchestra busy with annual tours for almost twenty years. Visiting every part of the country, he had to contend with many annoyances—audiences that talked, laughed, and scratched matches, or that tried to hit the musicians with tobacco juice. He made some concessions to popular taste by interspersing his programs with short, melodious pieces, but he insisted that his audiences listen also to longer, serious works—even interrupting his performances to reprimand customers whose manners were too obnoxious.

Thomas's activities had many important results, both direct and indirect. He was invited to conduct civic music festivals like that organized in Cincinnati in 1873. By serving intermittent periods between 1877 and 1891 as conductor of the New York Philharmonic, he helped to improve that pioneer orchestra, and he inspired the organization of similar orchestras in other cities. The most important of these was the Boston Symphony Orchestra, founded in 1881. Generously subsidized by Major Henry Lee Higginson, banker and music lover, the Boston organization was the first orchestra in the country to attain an excellence which merited comparison with the best in Europe. The second American city to obtain a truly great orchestra was Chicago, where the necessary funds were raised in 1891 and Thomas himself was employed as conductor. Meanwhile, in New York the Philharmonic continued its somewhat erratic history, hampered by uncertain support and by the competition of a rival orchestra, the Symphony Society, organized in 1878 and led first by Leopold Damrosch and later by his son Walter. Neither orchestra could really rival the Boston and Chicago symphonies until 1907, when the Symphony Society secured the necessary subsidies for reorganization. A similar reform of the older Philharmonic occurred in 1909. The Philadelphia Symphony Orchestra was organized in 1902, but not until Leopold Stokowski became its director in 1912, did it too become a first-rate organization.

Unlike the symphony the opera appealed to many who were indifferent to music but enjoyed the exciting glitter of the opera house. Already well-established at the New York Academy of Music, opera became conspicuously fashionable after 1878, when Colonel James Henry Mapleson brought to the Academy some of the most famous European singers of the day. To occupy one's own box at the opera was considered an indispensable badge of social distinction. When William K. Vanderbilt and others became impatient because of the difficulty of securing boxes at the Academy of Music, they sponsored the building in 1883 of the great Metropolitan Opera House with its "diamond horseshoe"—two tiers of boxes in the very center of the house, where the rich had ample opportunity to display their jewels, gowns, and furs. On the eve of World War I the Metropolitan was at a peak of prestige. The fabulous Caruso headed the world's most brilliant company of singers, and Toscanini served as conductor.

The world of opera and symphony was largely a world of imported talent. In rare cases when American-born artists like Emma Eames rose to the top, they received unstinted adulation, but such distinction was not easily won. The native musician usually received serious consideration only if he had been trained abroad and had won acceptance with European audiences. American-born composers worked under similar handicaps, although it must be admitted that few of them merited more attention than they received. John Knowles Paine wrote symphonic music that was admired in its day but proved to be of little permanent significance. Horatio Parker composed choral music of real distinction and an opera *Mona,* good enough perhaps to have deserved more than the single performance it received at the Metropolitan in 1912. Ethelbert Nevin had a rare gift for creating attractive melody, but his talents were obviously for music in the minor forms—art songs like "The Rosary" and piano suites like "Water Scenes" and "A Day in Venice."

The most important figure in the American musical world was Edward MacDowell, born in New York in 1861. His parents, unlike many of the day, gave full support to his ambition for a musical career. At the age of fifteen he was sent to Europe, where he received instruction and encouragement from some of the leading masters of the day. When he returned to America at the age of twenty-seven, MacDowell was already regarded as a composer of great promise. For eight years he lived in Boston, teaching, composing, and playing as a concert pianist. In 1896 he moved to New York to become professor of music at Columbia. His career, hitherto happy and successful, now moved toward a tragic termination. Discouraged with the problems of teaching students of mediocre ability, disappointed in his projects for expanding art study at the university, and unable to work with Nicholas Murray Butler, who became president of Columbia in 1902, MacDowell resigned his post in 1904. The unnerving effects of the controversy with Butler and the cumulative fatigue which followed years of overwork brought on psychopathic symptoms. MacDowell brooded over his troubles, lost the ability to do creative work, and spent the last two years of his life staring vacantly out of windows. In 1908 he died. Although MacDowell composed piano sonatas, concertos, and symphonic suites, his most enduring work proved to be in the shorter forms—particularly in such piano suites as "Woodland Sketches" and "Sea Pieces."

Even in MacDowell America had scarcely produced a composer of first rank. The country's immaturity in music was more patent than in any of the other arts. Yet this deficiency was mostly in the realm of serious music. In less exalted spheres the Americans had a rich, although hardly recognized, tradition. Operetta had a great vogue in the late nineteenth and early twentieth centuries, and such composers as Reginald De Koven and Victor Herbert had conspicuous success in this medium. John Philip Sousa not only led the country's most popular band but composed a series of marches that exactly suited the average citizen's taste for strong melody and stirring rhythm. Sheet music publishers derived fortunes from such popular songs as "After the Ball," "On the Banks of the Wabash," and the "Sidewalks of New York."

Perhaps the most interesting American music of the day never achieved the dignity of written notation. The rough gangs who laid the western railroads did their work to the accompaniment of humorous and noisy songs whose authorship could rarely be traced and whose words and tunes were ever-changing. Other songs were sung by the lumberjacks of the northern forests, the cowboys on the western plains, and the poor farmers of the Appalachian highlands and the Ozarks. The richest folk-music tradition of all was that of the Negroes. Whites began to gain their first insight into the beauty of Negro spirituals through the tours of such organizations as the Fisk Jubilee Singers and the Hampton and Tuskegee quartets. The Negro's spontaneous feeling for music found many other avenues of release. There were cotton-picking and cotton-hoeing songs and appropriate chants for work on the river boats, the railroads, and the levees. For hours of relaxation the Negro had fiddle songs, cakewalks, and ragtime struts. When he was worried by his troubles, he found release in songs of haunting rhythm appropriately called "blues."

Negro music's most fateful contribution to American culture was jazz. After the Civil War many brass instruments from Confederate military bands fell into the hands of enthusiastic Negroes. Particularly in New Orleans Negro bands attained great popularity, finding at first their most characteristic activity in leading funeral parades to and from the cemeteries. These melancholy occasions did not inhibit the musicians from playing jaunty march tunes, in which they tried out all sorts of melodic and rhythmic experiments. The brass bands were brought indoors during the nineties to play in Negro dance halls and other palaces of pleasure. Here Negro jazz achieved its final form. During the so-called "classical" period which followed, Negro jazz players were notable for their freedom from written arrangements and other European musical conventions. Adapting patterns of rhythm which had originated in Africa and been perpetuated in Negro folk music, they took simple melodies—often of English, French, or Spanish origin—and used them as a basis for free improvisation, in which the musicians showed an astonishing virtuosity. Jazz devotees still speak in hushed tones of such New Orleans greats as "King" Bolden, "King" Oliver, Jelly-Roll Morton, and Bunk Johnson.

About 1900 white musicians also began to turn to jazz. The key figure in this development was Jack (Papa) Laine. A bustling organizer, he soon had not one but several "Dixieland bands" in the New Orleans area. Influenced by Negro jazz but soon developing distinguishing characteristics of their own, the white Dixielanders achieved great local popularity.

Peculiarly a product of the cosmopolitan culture of New Orleans, jazz began to appeal to a wider public when it was carried onto the Mississippi River excursion boats early in the twentieth century. But the sudden surge of popularity which was to carry jazz across the country did not begin until 1915, when one of the Dixieland bands transferred to Chicago.

Amusements in an Age of Business

More leisure and more money promoted the growth of vast amusement enterprises. In 1881 P. T. Barnum, whose name was already synonymous with shrewd showmanship, fortified his boast of having "the greatest show on earth" by joining his circus with that of his rival J. A. Bailey. The old-time minstrel show became more pretentious but lost ground to other forms of entertainment. The earliest important vaudeville house was Tony Pastor's in New York, but vaudeville's great popularity really dated from the introduction of continuous performances by B. F. Keith's in Boston in 1885. Since an enthusiastic masculine audience was available to producers who presented girls in tights or scanty attire, burlesque and musical shows became increasingly bold.

The legitimate theater appeared to be in vigorous health. In the seventies Edwin Booth was at the height of his fame, and Joseph Jefferson and Clara Morris were leading stars. In later decades the Shakespearean performances of Lawrence Barrett, Mary Anderson, Julia Marlowe, E. H. Sothern, and Richard Mansfield won wide applause, as did the acting of Mrs. John Drew, Ada Rehan, Fanny Davenport, Maude Adams, David Warfield, and Otis Skinner in lighter roles.

But in this age of clever acting most writing for the stage was mediocre or worse. For serious drama the old masterpieces usually sufficed. For lighter fare hack playwrights served up quantities of sentimental romance and farce. Excitement was at a premium, whether provided by adaptations of *Ben Hur* and other popular novels of the day or by melodramas like *Bertha, the Sewing-Machine Girl, The Turf Digger's Doom,* and *The White Slave.*

A few dramatists, however, provided work of a higher standard. During the

1880's Bronson Howard wrote social comedies based upon plausible American characters and scenes, and David Belasco's instinct for the theater gave his romantic dramas greater effectiveness than most contemporary works of the 1890's and early 1900's. James A. Herne's rustic comedies attained a popular success that was denied to his fine tragedy *Margaret Fleming* (1890), too grimly realistic for the day. Augustus Thomas and Clyde Fitch, both prolific writers, demonstrated a marked advance in technical competence and treated social and psychological themes with increasing realism. William Vaughn Moody's death in 1910 at the age of forty-one cut short a career that had gained unusual distinction both in poetry and in drama.

The theater showed the same tendency toward consolidation and concentration in the metropolis to be seen in the business world. New York managers found it less expensive and more popular to present famous stars with supporting casts than to maintain permanent stock companies. Traveling companies, taking advantage of improved methods of transportation, carried the star system into the smaller cities and provided fatal competition for the resident companies of the hinterland. A somewhat different problem arose out of the attempt of a few New York magnates to organize a theatrical trust which would control booking throughout the country. In a sharp struggle lasting from 1896 to 1910, the independents finally won out, but this victory was not enough to restore vitality to the provincial theater.

The competition of the moving pictures was just beginning to be felt. Edison's invention of the Kinetoscope, in which pictures could be watched by one person at a time, encouraged other experimenters to develop projectors which would throw the moving pictures on screens. A New York vaudeville theater presented this novelty as early as 1896, but the first films were only two or three minutes in length. After 1900, however, innovations were rapid. The filming of *The Great Train Robbery* in 1903 revealed the storytelling potentialities of the new medium, and the example of Harry Davis, who transformed a vacant Pittsburgh store into a crude theater, charging a 5-cent admission for a twenty-minute show, proved that the exhibition of movies could be very profitable. Similar nickelodeons were opened in thousands of cities, and communities too small to have regular theaters were served by traveling exhibitors.

The production of films was wildly competitive. In 1908 Edison and nine other leading producers pooled their interests in the Motion Picture Patents Company in an attempt to destroy their rivals. In the ensuing struggle between "The Trust" and the independents, many of the latter sought to escape enemy lawyers and detectives by transferring their studios to Los Angeles and Hollywood within convenient distance of the Mexican border. Western sunshine proved so advantageous for photography that most of the industry eventually moved there from New York. By 1914 the producers and exhibitors had learned the rudiments of their craft and were prepared to transform the amusement world with elaborate screenplays presented in pretentious theaters.

Before the Civil War foreign visitors had often commented on the curious indifference of the Americans to sports; a half century later such visitors were prone to accuse the Yankees of being "sports-crazy." Undoubtedly one cause of the great change was the growth of cities. In rural America there had been an abundance of outdoor exercise in men's daily tasks, and any need for recreation was readily met by hunting and fishing or by foot races and wrestling matches between local rivals. But as the villages grew into towns and the towns into cities, recreation more often took the form of organized sport.

The new trend was best exemplified by baseball. During the Civil War the game had been popular among the soldiers, and in the next few years thousands of local ball clubs were organized. Intercity games became numerous, and some of the best teams toured the country. Baseball's amateur status was soon more theoretical than actual. The more ambitious clubs offered a variety of inducements to secure outstanding players, and the practice of betting upon the games created many ugly scandals. In 1869 the Cincinnati Red Stockings were reorganized on a frankly professional basis, providing an example soon followed by such teams as the Chicago White Stockings, the Philadelphia Athletics, and the Washington Nationals. In 1876 four teams of the Middle West and four of the East joined in the formation of the National League with strict rules against betting, throwing games, and breaking contracts. Rival leagues were attempted, and between 1884 and 1890 the old American Association was strong enough to justify the playing of so-called "world series"—postseason games between the champions of the two leagues. But the National League dominated the professional field, and rival organizations were short-lived until after 1900, when the American League was formed. Three years of bitter conflict between the older circuit and its new rival were finally terminated by an agreement in 1903. The first of the modern world series was played in that year, and the game entered upon a period of popularity and prosperity. The newspapers gave it great publicity, and millions of Americans now debated the relative skill of such managers as John J. McGraw and Connie Mack and such players as Honus Wagner, Ty Cobb, and Christy Mathewson.

The great college game was football. Adapted from Rugby and similar English games, football in its primitive form became a matter of intercollegiate rivalry as early as 1869, when Princeton played Rutgers, and the famous series between Yale and Harvard began in 1875. But the important innovations which gave American football its distinctive character were made in the late seventies and eighties by pioneers like Walter Camp of Yale. So strongly did the East dominate the game in these days that when Camp selected his first "all-American" team in 1889, he chose his players exclusively from Yale, Harvard, and Princeton. But the game soon spread to other parts of the country, particularly to the large institutions of the Middle West. Football's popularity involved many problems. Since eligibility rules were lax or nonexistent, the teams used players who scarcely saw the inside of classrooms. The game, moreover, was so excessively rough that the death roll in 1903 reached a total of 44, and many were injured for life. So bad was the situation that Columbia dropped the sport from 1905 to 1915, and other institutions threatened to do so unless the game could be reformed. The football crisis was discussed at a White House luncheon arranged by President Roosevelt

FIG. 47. *Football.* Plaster group by John Rogers, 1891. Statuettes of familiar American scenes were popular home decorations for many decades of the nineteenth century. (*Courtesy of The New-York Historical Society.*)

in 1905 and at a special conference at New York in 1906. The result was the organization of a National Collegiate Athletic Association and the adoption of new rules intended to ban dangerous mass plays and to open up the game through innovations like the forward pass.

Professional boxing attracted increasing interest because of the popularity of such legendary figures as John L. Sullivan, the Boston "strong boy," who became heavyweight champion in 1882 by defeating Paddy Ryan and gained his greatest acclaim in 1889, when he defeated Jake Kilrain in a bloody 75-round battle at New Orleans—the last of the bare-knuckle bouts. Sullivan's reign of brute power was finally terminated by the boxing skill of Gentleman Jim Corbett, who held the crown from 1892 to 1897, to be followed by Fitzsimmons, Jeffries, Burns, and Johnson. But the brutality of the sport and its close affiliation with gamblers brought prize fighting under the attacks of moralists. Laws prohibiting such contests were common, and the records reveal that many of the famous contests were arranged on foreign territory or in out-of-the-way sections of the United States. Horse racing, popular since the opening of Jerome Park in Westchester County, New York, in 1866, fell into similar disrepute. Laws against race-track betting threatened to kill the sport between 1908 and 1911, but subterfuges were discovered through which both racing and betting survived.

Despite the trend toward the commercialization of sport not all Americans were reduced to the ranks of spectators. Play was no longer regarded as the exclusive province of children. Adults by the thousand turned to tennis or golf. Croquet attained an extraordinary popularity, and the craze for bicycling was at its height during the early nineties. By 1914 Americans had learned to play with the same energy with which they worked.

The world of sports, where this chapter has ended, seems far removed from the world of literature, where it began. Yet perhaps as much about American life was to be learned from the amusement pages of American newspapers as from its literary works. The unpleasant sides were reflected there—blatant commercialism which transformed even recreation into big business, dishonesty which threatened at times to ruin college football no less than other sports, an ambition to win so ruthless that it often led to the use of vicious tactics. But vividly illustrated also were other qualities—robust energy, instinct for fair play, and a passion for efficient performance—which were evidence of the basic health of American society.

IV. The Latest Age, since 1914

Chapter 28. Democracy on the Anvil

Since 1914 American democracy has been subjected to a succession of tremendous hammer blows. In World War I the nation was summoned by its President to fight to "make the world safe for democracy." The military effort was successful, but the permanent safeguarding of popular government proved elusive. During the great depression wholesale unemployment, bankrupt business, impoverished farmers, insolvent banks, and threatened foreclosures frightened the country and presented democratic statesmanship with one of its greatest challenges—all the more serious because such rival philosophies as communism and fascism were clamoring for converts. Then came World War II, a global conflict demanding a greater mobilization of energies than had been required of any earlier American generation. There followed, not the longed-for peace and stability, but an exasperating trial of strength between democracy and communism—the so-called "cold war" with its occasional flashes of heat.

How would American democracy react to this hammering of war and depression? Would it shatter and lose its identity? Or would the dross be pounded out, leaving on the anvil a purer and more resilient metal? Whatever the ultimate answer to this all-important question, the recurrent crises of the twentieth century compelled a restatement of democratic principles and their application to situations far different from those familiar to Thomas Jefferson.

Prelude to Crisis

Although World War I provided a dramatic initiation of American democracy into the problems of a new age, these problems seem, in retrospect, closely related to trends which had been in evidence for two decades or more.

From 1815 to 1890 the United States maintained a relatively high degree of isolation from the affairs of the rest of the world. When the nation's major agricultural and industrial expansion had been completed, however, the impulse to assert American interests in a wider sphere became insistent. Under pressure from active imperialists like Alfred Thayer Mahan, Whitelaw Reid, Henry Cabot Lodge, and Theodore Roosevelt, the United States developed a more active foreign policy—exerting its paramount influence in the Western Hemisphere and reaching out for colonies in the Pacific. Through the short but decisive Spanish-American War of 1898 American rule was extended not only over neighboring Puerto Rico but over the distant Philippines.

Anti-imperialists like Grover Cleveland, William Jennings Bryan, and Senator

George F. Hoar of Massachusetts attempted to halt the growth of the American empire but found only minority support throughout the nation. American involvement in world affairs increased rather than diminished with the pronouncement of the Open Door policy, Roosevelt's mediation in the Russo-Japanese War, the building of the Panama Canal, and American interventions in Cuba, the Dominican Republic, Nicaragua, Mexico, and Haiti.

Meanwhile, the nation's domestic affairs also appeared to be entering a new phase as the long alliance between the politician and the businessman was challenged by the rising progressive movement. Woodrow Wilson, campaigning for the presidency in 1912, said:

> Why are we in the presence, why are we at the threshold of a revolution? Because we are profoundly disturbed by the influences which we see reigning in the determination of our public life and our public policy. There was a time when America was blithe with self-confidence. She boasted that she, and she alone, knew the processes of popular government; but now she sees her sky overcast; she sees that there are at work forces which she did not dream of in her hopeful youth. . . . We are in a temper to reconstruct economic society, as we were once in a temper to reconstruct political society, and political society may itself undergo a radical modification in the process. I doubt if any age was ever more conscious of its task or more unanimously desirous of radical and extended changes in its economic and political practice.[1]

Theodore Roosevelt, also a candidate for the presidency in 1912, spoke in strikingly similar terms:

> Our task is to profit by the lessons of the past, and to check in time the evils that grow around us, lest our failure to do so may cause dreadful disaster to the people. We must not sit supine and helpless. We must not permit the brutal selfishness of arrogance and the brutal selfishness of envy, each to run unchecked its evil course. If we do so, then some day smouldering hatred will suddenly kindle into a consuming flame, and either we or our children will be called on to face a crisis as grim as any which this Republic has ever seen.[2]

The two aspirants for office agreed that the nation was in a bad way. Their principal disagreement was over which of them had been called upon to lead the work of salvation. The note of alarm might be explained as simply the traditional stock in trade of ambitious politicians, did it not coincide with a widespread feeling of discontent in the country at large.

Actually, of course, the movement of protest was not new. As we have seen, nineteenth-century writers like Henry George, Edward Bellamy, and Henry Demarest Lloyd had framed strong indictments of the old order, and the Knights of Labor, the Grangers, and the People's party had challenged basic tenets of conservative political philosophy.

To millions of Americans, however, these earlier criticisms of society had seemed a shocking form of heresy. Not until after 1900 did condemnation of pred-

[1] Woodrow Wilson, *The New Freedom* (Doubleday, Page, and Company, New York, 1913), 28–30.

[2] *The Works of Theodore Roosevelt* (Scribner, New York, 1925), XVII, 456.

atory business and special privilege become respectable. Influential in the transition in opinion were the writings of the group of journalists known as the muckrakers. Lincoln Steffens, investigating the causes of municipal corruption in a dozen cities, concluded that the blame should be placed not so much on the immigrant voter or the machine politician as upon the avarice of the businessman and the complaisance of the average citizen. Ray Stannard Baker, seeking the causes of labor violence, was equally shocked by the lawlessness of union leaders and that of employers. In her articles Ida M. Tarbell emphasized the Standard Oil trust's ruthless competitive methods and frequent evasions of the law. Muckraking became a journalistic vogue: *McClure's Magazine* revealed the possibilities of the field; other magazines like *Collier's* and *Everybody's* and newspapers like the New York *World* and the Kansas City *Star* helped to exploit it.

The composite picture that emerged from the efforts of the muckrakers was a shocking one. American democracy appeared to be threatened by the activities of irresponsible financiers who rigged the stock market, captured control of corporations, drove competitors to the wall, and cheated the public through high prices and adulterated products. Other enemies of the republic were bankers and insurance-company executives who speculated rashly with other people's money and political bosses who manipulated elections and legislatures in the interests of wealthy campaign contributors.

Jolted by these revelations, millions of middle-class citizens embraced the cause of reform with evangelical fervor. "Progressive" mayors were elected in a score of cities, and progressive governors pushed through ambitious programs of reform. As President from 1901 to 1909, Theodore Roosevelt promoted such causes as the conservation of natural resources, regulation of industry, and "trust-busting" suits. President Taft also tried to ride the galloping horse of reform but proved too inept a performer to please the public. Thus the stage was prepared for the political campaign of 1912, when the voter had an opportunity to choose his favorite from a field that included not only Taft, Roosevelt, and Wilson but the Socialist Debs.

Although the Socialists gained close to a million votes, the great majority of the voters indicated their support of less drastic programs. Progressivism—in both its Rooseveltian and Wilsonian versions—proposed that the state should protect the interests of the people, not by taking over the instruments of production, but by purifying politics and regulating business.

The progressives talked much of the rule of the people. Through primaries, initiative and referendum, recall, corrupt-practice laws, the direct election of senators, and woman suffrage, they hoped to construct a mechanism of direct democracy that would overthrow the bosses. They talked also of social justice. Through workmen's compensation acts, eight-hour laws, and minimum-wage regulations, they hoped to improve conditions for the laboring classes.

In their program for dealing with business, there was a nostalgic strain in progressive thought. The reformers looked back wistfully to the days of a simpler economy dominated by sturdy farmers, small businessmen, and honest artisans, where problems of monopoly, railroad abuses, and sharp clashes between capital and labor were unknown. Vigorous government action, it was hoped, would revive the healthy economic individualism and honest competition of the earlier age. Wilson struck the note with particular insistence. He rebuked Roosevelt's assumption that trusts were inevitable and that the only remedy was regulation. Through enforced competition Wilson hoped for utopian results:

> Are you not eager for the time when the genius and initiative of all the people shall be called into the service of business? When newcomers with new ideas, new entries with new enthusiasms, independent men, shall be welcomed? when your sons shall be able to look forward to becoming, not employees, but heads of small, it may be, but hopeful business, where their best energies shall be inspired by the knowledge that they are their own masters, with the paths of the world open before them? Have you no desire to see the markets opened to all? to see credit available in due proportion to every man of character and serious purpose who can use it safely and to advantage? to see business disentangled from its unholy alliance with politics? to see raw material released from the control of monopolists, and transportation facilities equalized for all? and every avenue of commercial and industrial activity levelled for the feet of all who would tread it? Surely, you must feel the inspiration of such a new dawn of liberty! [1]

Such was the philosophy of the "New Freedom," the domestic policy which Wilson as President pressed upon Congress with energy and persistence. To weaken monopoly and to encourage small business, Wilson obtained a reduction of the tariff, new antitrust laws, and a reform of banking. To benefit the farmer, he obtained new credit agencies and Federal aid for roads and extension services. To protect the workman, he obtained an exemption of labor-union activities from antitrust prosecution and an eight-hour law for railroad employees.

Impact of World War I

From the outbreak of war in Europe in 1914 progressives were sharply divided in their attitudes. Leaders from the Middle West like La Follette and Bryan strongly opposed any American involvement in the struggle. Very different was the position of Theodore Roosevelt and many eastern progressives. They saw the war as a struggle between right and wrong. They were convinced that autocratic Germany had deliberately begun the conflict in order to extend its domination over Europe. They were profoundly shocked by the German invasion of Belgium, stories of German atrocities, and German resort to poison gas, aerial bombardment, and ruthless submarine warfare. These conflicting attitudes toward the war were reflected in Wilson's personal reactions. Believing that involvement in war would endanger his program of domestic reform and hoping to play the role of neutral peacemaker, Wilson long clung to a policy of neutrality. Yet he believed that England and France had the better cause, and he was much disturbed by the

[1] Wilson, *op. cit.,* 270–271.

German submarine campaign, which he regarded as an inhumane violation of the law of nations.

It was characteristic of Wilson that when he finally decided to ask for a declaration of war, he stated American objectives in highly idealistic terms:

> Our object . . . is to vindicate the principles of peace and justice in the life of the world as against selfish and autocratic power and to set up amongst the really free and self-governed peoples of the world such a concert of purpose and of action as will henceforth insure the observance of those principles. . . . The world must be made safe for democracy. Its peace must be planted upon the tested foundations of political liberty. . . . It is a fearful thing to lead this great peaceful people into war, into the most terrible and disastrous of all wars, civilization itself seeming to be in the balance. But the right is more precious than peace, and we shall fight for the things which we have always carried nearest our hearts,—for democracy, for the right of those who submit to authority to have a voice in their own governments, for the rights and liberties of small nations, for a universal dominion of right, by such a concert of free peoples as shall bring peace and safety to all nations and make the world itself at last free. . . .[1]

Wilson sought to elevate the war from a sordid scramble for territory and indemnity to a crusade for international justice. In the speech in which he announced his famous "fourteen points," he assured the world that America had no selfish ends in view, that all it wanted was that the world should be made "fit and safe to live in; and particularly that it be made safe for every peace-loving nation which, like our own, wishes to live its own life, determine its own institutions, be assured of justice and fair dealing by the other peoples of the world as against force and selfish aggression." To crown the military victory which American arms helped to achieve, Wilson poured all his energy into organizing a League of Nations.

The ideal of internationalism which Wilson urged so eloquently was of course not original with him. European philosophers had long before argued for institutions that would substitute the rule of law for the use of force in dealings between nations. In America the reform had been agitated by William Ladd and many others. The United States government had set an example by submitting many particular disputes to arbitration and by offering general arbitration treaties to other powers. Theodore Roosevelt himself, despite his advocacy of military preparedness and occasional sword rattling, had won a Nobel peace prize for his support of the Hague Court. Roosevelt's Secretary of State, Elihu Root, had vigorously urged that this feeble tribunal should be supplanted by a more powerful permanent court of international justice. The outbreak of World War I had led to renewed demand for an organization of the nations.

The Senate's rejection of Wilson's League of Nations is one of the tragedies of modern history. Much of the blame must be assessed against Theodore Roosevelt and Henry Cabot Lodge, who conspired to defeat Wilson's project before it had even been given concrete form; some must be assessed against Wilson himself, since with the stubbornness of a sick man he refused to make the com-

[1] *Congressional Record,* LV, 103–104.

promises which the politics of the hour required. What was significantly lacking, however, was an overwhelming popular mandate. Weary of wartime excitement, the voters of 1920 renounced Wilsonian idealism and plumped for Harding's "normalcy."

Although the active participation of the United States in the war was brief, its influence on American life was profound. Almost five million men were enrolled in the armed services; two million of these saw service abroad. More than ever before, the nation's economic life was subjected to national control. The mobilization of thought was no less thorough. Official agencies poured out a torrent of propaganda. The most skillful illustrators of the country drew posters appealing to young men to enlist and older men to buy "Liberty bonds." Volunteer "minutemen" delivered patriotic speeches to audiences in churches, schoolhouses, and theaters. Plentiful information on the Wilsonian war objectives was supplied not only to Americans but to Europeans and Asiatics as well. Propaganda from the United States undoubtedly weakened the Germans' will to resist and helped to promote a revolution against the German monarchy. American ingenuity helped to develop the weapon of political warfare—a weapon that Americans were destined to fear greatly when it was taken up by the disciples of fascism and communism.

Dissenting opinion received scant tolerance. Debs and other socialists who opposed the war received long prison terms. The radical Industrial Workers of the World was crippled through the imprisonment of its leaders. Speeches and writings that threatened to interfere with the war effort were rigorously repressed. "When a nation is at war," said wise Justice Oliver Wendell Holmes, Jr., "many things that might be said in time of peace are such a hindrance to its effort that their utterance will not be endured so long as men fight. . . ." The habit of repression, once formulated, was not easily broken. Despite the attempts of Justices Holmes and Brandeis to limit curtailments of free speech to utterances creating "a clear and present danger," men were punished not merely for obstructing the war but for expressing criticisms of the existing political and social order. The worst infringements of civil liberties occurred after the war was over, when hundreds of alien radicals were arbitrarily arrested and deported from the country. Ironically, the war to make the world safe for democracy appeared to have weakened faith in democratic processes.

Although the war encouraged repression of free speech and otherwise crippled the movement for domestic reform, at least two causes were promoted by the conflict. Under the impact of war, sentiment for the prohibition of intoxicating liquors mounted rapidly. Brewers were regarded as German-Americans of dubious loyalty, and the diversion of scarce grains to the distillers weakened the war effort. Emergency prohibition measures were passed in 1917 and 1918; the Eighteenth Amendment, prohibiting the manufacture, sale, or transportation of intoxicating liquors throughout the United States, became part of the Constitution in 1919. Likewise hastened by the progressive movement and by the war was the triumph of woman suffrage. Male opposition, confronted on every side by evidence of women's competence and patriotism, suddenly crumpled, and the Nineteenth Amendment to the Constitution was ratified in 1920.

Recess on Reform

The demand for sweeping reform, so insistently heard between 1900 and 1914, quieted to a whisper during the 1920's. Already divided over American entry into the war, the progressives split even more bitterly on the issue of the League of Nations. In the opinion of Wilson and many other liberals this was the supreme democratic cause; domestic reform was illusory unless international relations were reformed to prevent war and aggression. But the League's bitterest opponents were western liberals like La Follette of Wisconsin, Norris of Nebraska, Borah of Idaho, and Johnson of California. They regarded with suspicion any commitment that the United States act with other nations in opposing aggression and gave their support only to such proposals as disarmament and the outlawry of war, which were consistent with American isolation. The American socialist movement, which had shown surprising strength in the election of 1912, was also crippled. First the Socialists lost support through their opposition to the war. Then they were bedeviled by the communist issue. The moderate majority rejected affiliation with the Third International and continued to work for the achievement of socialism through democratic processes, but a radical wing, impressed by the Bolshevik victory in Russia, seceded to form the American Communist party.

Neither progressivism nor socialism won many new converts during the 1920's. Most of the younger generation, captivated by apparent prosperity, accepted the existing order without serious misgivings. The minority, who resented the prevalent complacency, were more likely to display an attitude of cynicism than a zeal for reform. The idol of thousands of intellectuals was Henry L. Mencken, editor of the iconoclastic *American Mercury.* Mencken ridiculed the bombast of politicians and the antics of Klansmen, Rotarians, and other "boobs," "morons," and "yokels." Both in theory and practice he professed to consider democracy absurd:

I enjoy democracy immensely. It is incomparably idiotic, and hence incomparably amusing. Does it exalt dunderheads, cowards, trimmers, frauds, cads? Then the pain of seeing them go up is balanced by the joy of seeing them come down. Is it inordinately wasteful, extravagant, dishonest? Then so is every other form of government: all alike are enemies to laborious and virtuous men. Is rascality at the very heart of it? Well, we have borne that rascality since 1776, and continue to survive. In the long run, it may turn out that rascality is necessary to human government, and even to civilization itself—that civilization, at bottom, is nothing but a colossal swindle. I do not know: I report only that when the suckers are running well the spectacle is infinitely exhilarating. But I am, it may be, a somewhat malicious man: my sympathies, when it comes to suckers, tend to be coy. What I can't make out is how any man can believe in democracy who feels for and with them, and is pained when they are debauched and made a show of. How can any man be a democrat who is sincerely a democrat? [1]

Unchallenged by any overpowering demand for reform, conservatives enjoyed a more secure tenure of power than they had since McKinley's day. The tariff was raised, income and corporation taxes were reduced, and the trusts were left largely to their own devices. Such resurgences of progressivism as the La Follette third-party movement of 1924 and attempts to promote the public production of electrical power or to subsidize agricultural exports were successfully throttled.

Best spokesman for the dominant mood was Herbert Hoover, who believed sincerely that American progress was dependent on American individualism. He said:

[The American system] is founded upon a particular conception of self-government in which decentralized local responsibility is the very base. Further than this, it is founded upon the conception that only through ordered liberty, freedom, and equal opportunity to the individual will his initiative and enterprise spur on the march of progress. . . .

It is a false liberalism that interprets itself into the government operation of commercial business. Every step of bureaucratizing of the business of our country poisons the very roots of liberalism—that is, political equality, free speech, free assembly, free press, and equality of opportunity. It is the road not to more liberty, but to less liberty. Liberalism should be found not striving to spread bureaucracy but striving to set bounds to it. True liberalism seeks all legitimate freedom first in the confident belief that without such freedom the pursuit of all other blessings and benefit is vain. That belief is the foundation of all American progress, political as well as economic.[2]

The New Deal

The American voters were pragmatists. When Herbert Hoover preached his gospel of rugged individualism in the prosperous year 1928, they listened sympathetically. When he asserted that they were "nearer today to the ideal of the abolition of poverty and fear from the lives of men and women than ever before in any land," they readily believed that this was so. Four years later, when Hoover, running for reelection, repeated the same philosophy, he encountered hostile audiences. Rugged individualism seemed an inadequate slogan for a national emergency which had thrown millions of men out of work, sent banks and industries into receivership, deprived citizens of their homes through foreclosures, and impoverished millions of farmers through unmanageable surpluses and low prices. Even Hoover had conceded the need for fighting the depression with government funds, and such significant agencies as the Reconstruction Finance Corporation were organized while the champion of individualism still occupied the White House.

But the demand of the hour was for new leadership and bolder action. More and more Americans listened to the persuasive voice of Governor Franklin D. Roosevelt of New York, urging plans "that build from the bottom up and not

[1] Henry L. Mencken, *Notes on Democracy* (Knopf, New York, 1926), 211–212.

[2] *The New York Times,* Oct. 23, 1928.

from the top down, that put their faith once more in the forgotten man at the bottom of the economic pyramid." The mood of the proposed New Deal was frankly announced:

The country needs and, unless I mistake its temper, the country demands bold, persistent experimentation. It is common sense to take a method and try it. If it fails, admit it frankly and try another. But above all, try something. The millions who are in want will not stand by silently forever while the things to satisfy their needs are within easy reach.[1]

FIG. 48. President Roosevelt at the microphone. Democratic leadership in an age of mass communications. (*Brown Brothers.*)

Inaugurated President in March, 1933, Roosevelt promptly put his philosophy of bold experimentation to work. The activities of government were extended into a score of new fields. Millions of the unemployed were given temporary jobs. Attempts were made to stimulate economic recovery through the limitation of agricultural production, the curbing of cutthroat competition, the devaluation of the dollar, and the raising of prices. Fundamental reforms such as regulation of banking and the sale of securities, flood control and public-power projects, slum clearance, social security, protection of labor's right to organize, and national wage-hour standards were advanced.

[1] *The Public Papers and Addresses of Franklin D. Roosevelt* (Random House, New York, 1938), I, 646.

By 1936 an amazing number of New Deal proposals had been enacted into law. Friends and foes of the Roosevelt administration differed violently on the wisdom of the new measures, but none denied their significance as a departure from the individualism of the twenties. The President thus summarized his achievement:

> In March, 1933, I appealed to the Congress of the United States and to the people . . . in a new effort to restore power to those to whom it rightfully belonged. The response to that appeal resulted in the writing of a new chapter in the history of popular government. You, the members of the Legislative branch, and I, the Executive, contended for and established a new relationship between Government and people.
>
> What were the terms of that new relationship? They were an appeal from the clamor of many private and selfish interests, yes, an appeal from the clamor of partisan interest, to the ideal of the public interest. Government became the representative and the trustee of the public interest. Our aim was to build upon essentially democratic institutions, seeking all the while the adjustment of burdens, the help of the needy, the protection of the weak, the liberation of the exploited and the genuine protection of the people's property.[1]

Resistance to the new relationship was bitter. In the opinion of Hoover, who never ceased to insist that he and not Roosevelt was the true liberal, the New Deal was either "hit-and-run opportunism" or "a cold-blooded attempt by starry-eyed boys to infect the American people by a mixture of European ideas, flavored with our native predilection to get something for nothing."

Although conservatism was badly defeated at the ballot box in 1936, it was still firmly entrenched in the courts. Holding tenaciously to older concepts of the proper function of government, a majority of Supreme Court justices invalidated a dozen New Deal laws during the first Roosevelt administration. This situation led the President in 1937 to ask Congress to grant him authority to make new appointments to the Court for each judge who failed to retire upon reaching the age of seventy. This was necessary, he said, "to bring to the decision of social and economic problems younger men who have had personal experience and contact with modern facts and circumstances under which average men have to live and work. This plan will save our National Constitution from hardening of the judicial arteries."

Involved in the controversy over Roosevelt's "court-packing" bill was a sharp difference of constitutional interpretation that had divided the Supreme Court for thirty years. As early as 1905 Justice Oliver Wendell Holmes, Jr., had dissented from a decision invalidating a state maximum-hour law in these words:

> But a constitution is not intended to embody a particular economic theory, whether of paternalism and the organic relation of the citizen to the state or of *laissez faire*. It is made for people of fundamentally differing views, and the accident of our finding certain opinions natural and familiar, or novel, and even shocking, ought not to conclude our judgement upon the question whether statutes embodying them conflict with the Constitution of the United States.

[1] *Ibid.*, V, 13.

In 1923 the conflicting points of view were even more clearly developed in a case in which the majority of the Court held unconstitutional a law of Congress providing minimum wages for women workers in the District of Columbia. Justice George Sutherland expressed the conservative point of view when he said: "To sustain the individual freedom of action contemplated by the Constitution is not to strike down the common good but to exalt it; for surely the good of society as a whole cannot be better served than by the preservation against arbitrary restraint of its constituent members." But Justice Holmes once again dissented, pointing out that "pretty much all law consists in forbidding men to do some things that they want to do, and contract is no more exempt from law than other acts." The wisdom of such measures, Holmes believed, should be determined by the legislature. If the end of the law was constitutional and the means were such as reasonable men might think appropriate, the law should be upheld.

Although Holmes had retired from the bench before Roosevelt became President, his tolerant attitude toward social legislation had strongly influenced such justices as Brandeis, Cardozo, and Stone. But the majority was still strongly conservative. Justice Sutherland continued on the bench, and the philosophy of his opinion in the minimum-wage case still dominated the Court.

The reorganization bill by which Roosevelt hoped to swing the balance of power to the Holmes-Brandeis point of view was badly defeated. Nevertheless, the Presidential protest had far-reaching results. While the court fight was still in progress, the high tribunal upheld a state minimum-wage law, the Federal labor-relations act, and the Federal social-security law. The new liberal trend was made permanent when deaths and retirements provided Roosevelt with opportunities for new appointments.

Conservatives regarded Roosevelt's attack upon the Court as the most shameful episode of his administration. Far from acknowledging any sin, however, the President asserted that his policy had its justification in the changed attitude of the justices:

> I feel convinced . . . that the change would never have come, unless this frontal attack had been made upon the philosophy of the majority of the Court. That is why I regard the message of February 5, 1937, as one of the most important and significant events of my administration on the domestic scene. That is why I regard it as a turning point in our modern history. For unless the Court had changed, or unless some quick means had been found to give our democracy the power to work out its needs, there is grave doubt whether it could have survived the crisis which was bearing down upon it. . . .
>
> Democracy proved again that it had within it the power to function—the ability to furnish to its citizens the strength, the courage, the assistance, the instruments with which to meet their problems in an American way, in their continued effort to preserve and raise their American standard of living.[1]

[1] *Public Papers and Addresses of Franklin D. Roosevelt* (Macmillan, New York, 1941), VI, lxvi–lxxii.

War Against Fascism

While the American people and their government struggled with the problems of the depression, democracies everywhere were threatened by fascist aggression. Japan's path of conquest began with the extension of her control over Manchuria in 1931 and further encroachments against China that resulted in open war in 1937. Italy followed by crushing Ethiopia in 1935 and annexing Albania in 1939. Germany, most dangerous of all, absorbed Austria in 1938 and Czechoslovakia the next year, finally precipitating World War II by attacking Poland in September, 1939. Thereafter, German conquests followed in sickening succession. Poland, Denmark, Norway, Holland, Belgium, and France all fell to the Nazis before the summer of 1940. Great Britain, fighting alone, was racked by devastating air raids and feared invasion at any moment.

Where was all this to end? And what did it mean to the United States? During such a cyclone of aggression many Americans could think only in terms of storm shelters. The isolationism that had defeated Wilson's effort to commit the United States to a system of world order had been strengthened rather than weakened during the 1930's. On every hand could be heard assertions that America's entry into World War I had been a mistake, that we had been hoodwinked by British propaganda and the intrigues of the bankers and munition-makers, and that our insistence on the rights of neutrals had been foolhardy. Novels and plays depicted the futile horror of war. Church organizations, college student bodies, and countless individuals committed themselves to unconditional pacifism. Congress, responding to the prevailing mood, passed neutrality laws forbidding loans to the belligerents in any future conflict and prohibiting the sale of arms to either side. By placing aggressors and victims of aggression on the same basis, the new laws encouraged the dictators to believe that they could continue their conquests without fear of American intervention.

Roosevelt's most difficult feat of statesmanship was to convince the nation that it must abandon this course of folly and throw its strength into the scales against aggression. For the United States to stand aside and let fascist conquest run its course would be to make the nation "a lone island in a world dominated by the philosophy of force."

> Such an island may be the dream of those who still talk and vote as isolationists. Such an island represents to me and to the overwhelming majority of Americans today a helpless nightmare, the nightmare of a people without freedom—the nightmare of a people lodged in prison, handcuffed, hungry, and fed through the bars from day to day by the contemptuous, unpitying masters of other continents.[1]

By aiding the democracies, Roosevelt hoped to advance the cause of liberty everywhere. In words reminiscent of Wilson, he declared:

> In the future days, which we seek to make secure, we look forward to a world founded upon four essential human freedoms.

[1] *Ibid.,* IX, 261.

The first is freedom of speech and expression—everywhere in the world.

The second is freedom of every person to worship God in his own way—everywhere in the world.

The third is freedom from want—which, translated into world terms, means economic understandings which will secure to every nation a healthy peacetime life for its inhabitants—everywhere in the world.

The fourth is freedom from fear—which translated into world terms, means a world-wide reduction of armaments to such a point and in such a thorough fashion that no nation will be in a position to commit an act of physical aggression against any neighbor—anywhere in the world.[1]

In his struggle against isolationism Roosevelt could not have succeeded without the assistance of other Americans aroused by the totalitarian threat. Wendell Willkie, Republican candidate for President in 1940, directed his campaign against Roosevelt's highhanded methods and did not oppose the general proposition that the United States should assist victims of aggression by all means short of actual hostilities. After his defeat, moreover, Willkie became an even more ardent champion of aiding the democracies than Roosevelt himself. Henry L. Stimson and Frank Knox, lifelong Republicans, combated isolationism so vigorously that the President drafted them for key defense posts in his cabinet. Prominent Americans from both political parties associated themselves with the Committee to Defend America by Aiding the Allies, the Fight for Freedom Committee, and other anti-isolationist groups. Supported by this large segment of public opinion, Roosevelt was able to give increasing assistance to Britain, China, and Russia.

By authorizing the lend-lease policy, Congress clearly renounced the illusion of neutrality and committed itself to a policy of opposing aggression by all means other than overt force. This state of quasi war was transformed to full belligerency when Japan struck at Pearl Harbor on December 7, 1941. Soon American soldiers were fighting in every quarter of the globe—on the islands of the Pacific, in China and Burma, in North Africa, Italy, France, Belgium, and Germany.

World War II was a repetition of World War I magnified in extraordinary degree. In the earlier contest 5,000,000 Americans had served in the armed forces; in the later over 12,000,000 were required. The first war had cost 120,000 American lives; the second almost 400,000. The first had increased the national debt by 24 billion dollars; the second by 220 billion.

The war's most important result was to awaken the United States at long last to its international responsibilities. No Republican now cared to play the role of Lodge to Roosevelt's Wilson. On the contrary, Wendell Willkie, the defeated Presidential candidate of 1940, took the lead in crusading for world organization. In his best-selling book *One World* (1943), Willkie declared:

America must choose one of three courses after this war: narrow nationalism, which inevitably means the ultimate loss of our own liberty; international imperialism, which

[1] *Ibid.,* 672.

means the sacrifice of some other nation's liberty; or the creation of a world in which there shall be an equality of opportunity for every race and every nation. I am convinced the American people will choose, by overwhelming majority, the last of these courses. To makes this choice effective, we must win not only the war, but also the peace, and we must start winning it now.

To win this peace three things seem to me necessary—first, we must plan now for peace on a world basis; second, the world must be free, politically and economically, for nations and for men, that peace may exist in it; third, America must play an active, constructive part in freeing it and keeping its peace.[1]

Taking advantage of the decline of isolationism, Roosevelt cautiously laid the foundations for a new world organization. In his second inaugural of January 20, 1945, he declared: "We have learned that we cannot live alone. . . . We have learned to be citizens of the world, members of the human community." Striving to avoid Wilson's mistakes, the President gave senators and Republican leaders a prominent place in the American delegation to the conference which was to draft the Charter of the United Nations.

By the time that the San Francisco Conference actually convened in April, 1945, Roosevelt and Willkie were both dead. Yet their work had helped to prepare American opinion for active participation in the new world organization. An even greater influence had been history itself, which taught the futility of isolation and the need for cooperative measures to prevent aggression. When the United States Senate ratified the Charter of the United Nations by a vote of 89 to 2, America's acceptance of its new position in the world was impressively demonstrated.

The Problem of Communism

Democracy found no easy road ahead after World War II. Victory over the fascist states had been achieved through an alliance of the western nations with Soviet Russia—an alliance easy to establish when both were struggling with a common danger but difficult to continue after the war was over. The sudden collapse of Germany and Japan left a power vacuum over half the world, and into the empty space rushed communism. The Baltic states, Poland, Rumania, Bulgaria, Hungary, Czechoslovakia, and eastern Germany all fell under Soviet domination, as did most of China and half of Korea. Through the rise of aggressive Communist parties France and Italy stood in danger of the same fate.

Soon concluding that it was impossible to stabilize the world through agreement with the Russians, the Truman administration committed the United States to a policy of combating communist expansion through assistance to surviving democratic regimes. On March 12, 1947, President Truman declared:

I believe that it must be the policy of the United States to support free peoples who are resisting attempted subjugation by armed minorities or by outside pressures.

I believe that we must assist free peoples to work out their own destinies in their own way.

[1] Wendell Willkie, *One World* (Simon and Schuster, New York, 1943), 202.

The new policy began with the expenditure of 400 million dollars to stiffen Greek and Turkish resistance to Soviet pressure and was soon greatly expanded under the so-called "Marshall Plan," or European Recovery Program, under which over 5 billion dollars a year was expended to assist in the economic rehabilitation of 16 nations. It was assumed that communism could best be combated through an attack upon the hunger, poverty, desperation, and chaos on which revolutionary radicalism fed.

As it became obvious that economic aid might not be enough to halt the new aggression, the United States signed the North Atlantic Pact, an alliance of 12 nations committed to the principle that an attack upon one of them should be considered an attack against all of them. Having accepted a commitment without precedent in American history, the Truman administration secured appropriations from Congress to aid the rearmament of our allies.

Overt aggression, however, occurred in an area remote from that covered by the North Atlantic Pact. In June, 1950, the Communist state of North Korea invaded the territory of South Korea, which was governed by a regime elected under United Nations supervision. The challenge was clear-cut and the United States responded without hesitation, pledging full aid to the threatened state. Since the United Nations Security Council at once condemned the North Korean act of aggression, American intervention received immediate United Nations sanction. For the first time in modern history an act of armed aggression was met with prompt countersteps in the name of international security.

Fear of communism abroad inevitably increased fear of communism at home. The House Committee on un-American Activities and other Congressional committees conducted investigations into alleged communist infiltration of government bureaus, labor unions, and the moving-picture industry. Occasionally, charges were proved and situations that threatened the national security were uncovered. More often the investigations offered an opportunity for publicity-seeking legislators and witnesses to make unsupported charges—leaving to the unfortunate victims the burden of clearing themselves. The procedures of these committees raised the very serious question of whether democracy was not as greatly threatened by its overzealous defenders as by its communist enemies.

In the general revulsion against communism the President instituted procedures for investigating the loyalties of all Federal employees, and members of the Communist party or of Communist-front organizations were dismissed from positions in the teaching profession and in the moving-picture, radio, and television industries. Active in the unofficial purge of the entertainment world were self-appointed patriots who prepared black lists of persons suspected of radical sympathies. Congress and state legislatures were active in passing anticommunist laws.

American democracy was facing one of its most difficult problems. The democratic way of life was obviously threatened by communist totalitarianism. In combating this danger, how far was it wise or necessary to restrict the right of political association, the right of free speech, free press, and free assembly, and the right of individuals to practice their trades or vocations? How far could such restraints on liberty be carried without serious injury to American institutions?

The problem was not entirely new. During the Red scare that followed World War I, Justice Holmes had written one of his wisest pronouncements:

> Persecution for the expression of opinions seems to me perfectly logical. If you have no doubt of your premises or your power and want a certain result with all your heart you naturally express your wishes in law and sweep away all opposition. . . . But when men have realized that time has upset many fighting faiths, they may come to believe even more than they believe the very foundations of their own conduct that the ultimate good desired is better reached by free trade in ideas—that the best test of truth is the power of the thought to get itself accepted in the competition of the market, and that truth is the only ground upon which their wishes safely can be carried out. That at any rate is the theory of our Constitution. It is an experiment, as all life is an experiment.[1]

Even those who accepted Holmes's belief in the necessity of free trade in ideas were troubled as to how far this principle might safely be followed in the existing situation. In May, 1950, Supreme Court Justice Robert H. Jackson pointed out that there were "decisive differences between the Communist party and every other party of any importance in the long experience of the United States with party government." The goal of the party was "to seize powers of government by and for a minority rather than to acquire power through the vote of a free electorate." The party was dominated and controlled by a foreign government. Violent and undemocratic means were "the calculated and indispensable methods to attain the Communist party's goal." Every member of the Communist party was an agent to execute the Communist program. For these reasons Justice Jackson believed that Congress was acting within its constitutional powers in requiring officers of all unions claiming rights under the National Labor Relations Act to file affidavits stating that they were not members of the Communist party.

But security laws seeking to punish overt acts against the government were easily perverted to limitations on essential liberties. This realization prompted President Truman to veto the Internal Security Bill, passed by Congress in September, 1950. In the spirit of Holmes, Truman wrote:

> There is no more fundamental axiom of American freedom than the familiar statement: In a free country, we punish men for the crimes they commit, but never for the opinions they have. And the reason this is so fundamental to freedom is not, as many suppose, that it protects the few unorthodox from suppression by the majority. To permit freedom of expression is primarily for the benefit of the majority because it protects criticism, and criticism leads to progress.[2]

That few Congressmen shared these misgivings was evident by the overwhelming majorities by which both houses overrode the veto.

At least a portion of the public, however, believed that the best defense of

[1] Dissent in *Abrams v. United States,* 250 U.S. 624.

[2] *Congressional Record,* XLVI, 15674.

democracy was not a Maginot line of anticommunist laws but an aggressive campaign to demonstrate to the world that American popular government was thoroughly dedicated to the welfare of every social group within the nation. In the words of Justice William O. Douglas:

> Effective democratic government is the political antidote to Communism. Reactionary governments nurture the conditions on which Communism feeds. The kind of democratic government that will submerge the Communist influence is a liberal, progressive government that recognizes the human rights of all citizens, raises the standard of living at all levels of society, eliminates the insecurity of this industrial age, and wipes out the poverty that has plagued man from the dawn of history. Nothing short of this kind of political program will defeat the aims of the Communists.[1]

Democracy and the Negro

When the United States accepted the role of champion of democracy throughout the world, every divergence from democracy at home became a dangerously weak point in its armor. The position of the Negro in American society demanded particular attention. Did America's own Negro citizens possess the Four Freedoms we were proposing for the rest of the world? Did they have freedom from want and freedom from fear in a nation where discriminations in education, housing, and employment were widespread and where lynchings and unequal justice in the courts still persisted?

The increased discontent of the Negroes reflected the impact of new economic forces. So long as most of them lived in rural areas of the South, poorly educated and out of the main stream of American life, they tended to accept their inferior position with resignation. Two important forces disrupted this pattern: one was the increasing concentration of Negroes in cities; the other was migration to the North. Between 1900 and 1930 a million Negroes moved into southern urban communities like New Orleans, Memphis, Birmingham, and Atlanta and into smaller cities and towns. During the same period there was a growing migration to the North, stimulated particularly by the demand for unskilled labor during World War I. Drastic immigration restriction enlarged the opportunities for Negroes in the great cities of the North and West. By 1940 evidence of a major shift of population was clear. Almost 20 per cent of all Negroes in the United States now lived in New York, Pennsylvania, Illinois, Ohio, New Jersey, Michigan, California, and Indiana—eight states whose Negro inhabitants had amounted to only 6 per cent of the total Negro population in 1910. World War II provided another stimulus to migration: 250,000 Negroes were attracted to the war industries of the Pacific Coast, and others moved to great industrial centers like Detroit.

In moving to the North, the Negroes did not immediately pass into the prom-

[1] Quoted by permission of Justice William O. Douglas from his Freedom Train address at Denver, Colorado, May 20, 1948.

ised land. Although there were no Jim Crow laws, they were commonly excluded from all but the poorest paid jobs, either through the personnel policies of employers or the restrictive practices of labor unions. Since Negroes were kept from the better sections of northern cities through real-estate covenants and less formal devices, most of them were crowded into slum districts, where they paid exorbitant rents for ramshackle tenements. They were not even secure against occasional outbreaks of violence. Some of the worst race riots in American history occurred in northern cities: in the Chicago riot of 1919, 15 whites and 23 Negroes were killed; in the Detroit riot of 1943, 9 whites and 25 Negroes lost their lives.

Despite these evidences of prejudice and discrimination Negroes who moved to the North felt a distinct improvement in status. They enjoyed better educational opportunities than they had in the South. They were free from segregation in trains, stations, and public halls. Those with special talents had an opportunity to develop them. In many fields the record of Negro achievement was brilliant. The roster of great names included those of athletes like Joe Louis and Jackie Robinson, jazz musicians like Louis Armstrong and Duke Ellington, concert artists like Marian Anderson and Roland Hayes, actors like Paul Robeson and Todd Duncan, authors like James Weldon Johnson and Richard Wright, scholars like George Washington Carver and E. Franklin Frazier, and tireless crusaders for equal rights like W. E. B. Du Bois and Walter White.

In the North the Negro's right to vote and to hold office was accepted. In small but increasing numbers, Negroes obtained election as Congressmen, state legislators, and municipal judges. At first the Negro vote, both North and South, had been a monopoly of the Republican party, heir to Lincoln the Emancipator. This situation was radically altered during the 1930's, when many northern Negroes changed their allegiance to the party of Franklin D. Roosevelt. They believed that the President—and Mrs. Roosevelt even more—had a sincere interest in Negro problems. Moreover, they benefited by such New Deal programs as relief and public housing. As the Negro vote became more evenly divided between the two great parties, the bargaining position of Negro voters was greatly strengthened. Rival politicians competed in advocating measures that might be popular with them.

This situation together with the need for demonstrating democratic sincerity during a conflict with fascism resulted in substantial Negro gains during World War II. The Marine Corps and other services which had hitherto barred Negroes now accepted them. Negroes and whites were selected for officer training on the same basis and were sent to the same officer-candidate schools. Negro women served as Wacs and Waves. On the home front thousands of job opportunities were provided. At first the war industries were reluctant to abandon their traditional employment practices, but Negro resentment and the need for utilizing every human resource combined to force a change of policy. In the face of a threatened Negro march on Washington, President Roosevelt issued his famous

Executive Order 8802 on June 25, 1941, providing that "there shall be no discrimination in the employment of workers in defense industries or Government because of race, creed, color, or national origin. . . . And it is the duty of employers and of labor organizations . . . to provide for the full and equitable participation of all workers in defense industries, without discrimination. . . ." The President appointed a Fair Employment Practice Committee to investigate complaints of discrimination. Although the FEPC had no power to punish offenders, fear of unfavorable publicity caused thousands of employers and labor unions to modify their policies. Negroes were the principal beneficiaries, but Jews, Mexicans, Catholics, and other groups that had encountered discrimination were also helped.

After the war was over, Negroes hoped to hold the ground that they had won and to make new advances. President Truman showed his interest by appointing a committee to investigate the whole problem of civil liberties. In an impressive report this group pointed out the extent to which Negroes and other minority groups had been deprived of their rights. Immediate action was recommended, not only for moral and economic reasons, but also because of America's position in world affairs:

> The international reason for acting to secure our civil rights now is not to win the approval of our totalitarian critics. We would not expect it if our record were spotless; to them our civil rights record is only a convenient weapon with which to attack us. Certainly we would like to deprive them of that weapon. But we are more concerned with the good opinion of the peoples of the world. Our achievements in building and maintaining a state dedicated to the fundamentals of freedom have already served as a guide for those seeking the best road from chaos to liberty and prosperity. But it is not indelibly written that democracy will encompass the world. We are convinced that our way of life—the free way of life—holds a promise of hope for all people. We have what is perhaps the greatest responsibility ever placed upon a people to keep this promise alive. Only still greater achievements will do it.
>
> The United States is not so strong, the final triumph of the democratic ideal is not so inevitable that we can ignore what the world thinks of us or our record.[1]

President Truman urged upon Congress an ambitious civil rights program based in part on the recommendations of this committee—a program that would create a permanent Fair Employment Practices Commission, more adequately protect the right to vote, prohibit discrimination on interstate trains and buses, and make lynching a Federal offense. The civil-rights measures encountered strenuous opposition. Again and again decisive action was frustrated by filibusters of southern senators, and resentment over the Truman program was a principal factor in the "Dixiecrat" revolt of 1948 that resulted in the casting of 39 electoral votes for J. Strom Thurmond of South Carolina as states' rights candidate for President.

Although new Federal legislation was not forthcoming, progress was made

[1] *To Secure These Rights: The Report of the President's Committee on Civil Rights* (Washington, 1947), 148.

through other channels. In a series of significant decisions during the 1930's and 1940's, the Supreme Court upheld the right of Negroes to sit on southern juries, to vote in primary elections, and to secure graduate instruction equal in all respects to that provided for white students in the state universities. In several northern states like New York, New Jersey, Massachusetts, and Connecticut and in certain cities like Chicago, Milwaukee, Minneapolis, and Philadelphia, discrimination in employment was now prohibited by law. Labor unions also became much more liberal in admitting Negroes to membership.

Southerners, resentful of Federal interference in racial issues, insisted that the soundest progress was being made at the state level. They pointed to increased expenditures for Negro education, equalization in several states of the pay of white and Negro teachers, and the decline of lynchings as evidence that the South should be left alone to deal with a problem whose ramifications could not be understood by outsiders. Southern opinion was now divided between die-hard exponents of white supremacy and liberals who acknowledged the Negro's right to vote and to enjoy equality of economic opportunity. Even southern liberals, however, continued to believe that racial segregation was necessary to racial harmony.

The seriousness of the Negro problem in influencing both what foreigners thought of American democracy and what Americans thought of themselves was powerfully revealed in the study of the Swedish sociologist Gunnar Mrydal. This thoughtful critic concluded:

> America feels itself to be humanity in miniature. When in this crucial time the international leadership passes to America, the great reason for hope is that this country has a national experience of uniting racial and cultural diversities and a national theory, if not a consistent practice, of freedom and equality for all. What America is constantly reaching for is democracy at home and abroad. The main trend in its history is the gradual realization of the American Creed.
>
> In this sense the Negro problem is not only America's greatest failure but also America's incomparably great opportunity for the future. If America should follow its own deepest convictions, its well-being at home would be increased directly. At the same time America's prestige and power abroad would rise immensely. The century-old dream of American patriots, that America should give to the entire world its own freedoms and its own faith, would come true. America can demonstrate that justice, equality and cooperation are possible between white and colored people.[1]

[1] Gunnar Myrdal, *An American Dilemma: The Negro Problem and Modern Democracy* (Harper, New York, 1944), II, 1021.

Chapter 29. Crisis in American Capitalism

The American people expected much from their economy. In peacetime they demanded not only ample food, clothing, and shelter but automobiles, radios, vacuum cleaners, and hundreds of other modern conveniences. They also demanded wages and profits large enough to provide ample purchasing power and funds for investment. For war Americans required guns, shells, airplanes, tanks, and ships in quantities sufficient to give the United States speedy superiority over its enemies.

Although this was a large order, American industry and agriculture came close to filling it. The nation's great production effort of World War I was a decisive factor in Germany's defeat; the greater output of World War II turned the tide of battle against Germany, Italy, and Japan. Similarly impressive was the peacetime record of providing millions of Americans with automobiles and other mechanical marvels.

Across this page of economic achievement, however, fell the terrifying shadow of the Great Depression. Despite its unprecedented capacity to produce, the American economy did not escape a most serious breakdown, when millions of Americans searched hopelessly for jobs, family savings were wiped out, and homes were lost. In the midst of such disasters faith in economic individualism waned, and more and more people demanded government intervention to create employment, to prevent loss of savings, and to provide "freedom from want" and "freedom from fear."

Aftermath of World War I

Economic mobilization during World War I carried the government into business to an unprecedented degree. Thousands of plants received war contracts. The flow of critical raw materials was controlled through priorities and price fixing. Trade in food and fuel was carefully supervised to prevent hoarding and to assure adequate supplies. The Federal government was the owner of some two thousand ships built and purchased by the Shipping Board. The government, moreover, took over management of the nation's railroad, telegraph, telephone, cable, and wireless systems.

Some Americans hoped that the government would continue these economic activities after the war was over, but Congress was determined to get the government out of business as promptly as possible. Most of the great war agencies began a voluntary liquidation as soon as the armistice was signed. Those that did not were soon curtailed by cuts in their appropriations. The electrical communications system was returned to private management in July, 1919, and the railroads the following March. Congress stipulated that government-owned ships should be sold on easy terms to private corporations. The decision to return to private enterprise was confirmed by the conservative election victory of 1920.

With government controls removed economic trends were erratic. During the winter after the armistice there was hardship; cancellation of war contracts and discharges from the Army brought unemployment to a total of perhaps three million in February, 1919. But this phase soon ended as Americans began to spend their savings for automobiles and other goods that had been scarce during the war. Exports soared because of war-ravaged Europe's need for food and manufactured goods. The postwar boom drove prices up sharply: the general wholesale level of 1920 was over twice that of 1913.

The inflationary bubble broke during the second half of 1920, and the country suffered a short but severe depression. Europe's poverty curtailed the export market, bringing about a staggering fall in agricultural prices. Resistance of consumers to the high cost of living and overproduction caused thousands of factory shutdowns and serious unemployment.

Having plunged down, up, and down again, all within three years, American business now entered a famous period of prosperity. The upswing began in 1922 and continued with only minor interruptions until 1929.

The Automobile Age

Sustaining the good times of the twenties was the demand of millions of Americans for relatively new conveniences like automobiles, electrical appliances, and radios. Most important in its effect on the economy was the amazing growth of the automobile industry.

Although the early development of the motor vehicle had been almost entirely the work of Europeans, American mechanics entered the field with enthusiasm during the 1890's. After 1900 a score of small companies were engaged in manufacturing automobiles for customers wealthy enough to afford an expensive toy. A familiar figure in his cap, goggles, and linen duster, the automobilist stirred the dust of country roads, terrified horses, and provoked the taunts of urchins with frequent breakdowns. The period was still one of experimentation, when experts vigorously debated the rival merits of "steamers," "electrics," and gasoline models of two, four, six, or eight cylinders.

Henry Ford revolutionized the industry. Founding his own company in 1903, Ford at first manufactured in accordance with prevailing practice, supplying a small volume of cars in several different models and prices. But in 1909 he decided to concentrate on the production of "Model T." High, boxlike, and monotonously black, this primitive machine made no pretense to beauty. With its hand throttle, finicky spark adjustment, and pedal-gear shift, the Model T was awkward to drive, and its rudimentary springs transmitted every bump in the road. But its simplicity was its greatest virtue. Light in weight and high-slung in body, the Model T kept going over muddy or sandy roads that halted more fashionable cars. Parts were inexpensive and easily installed by the owner himself. Best of all, the Ford was cheap. In 1909 the Model T touring car sold for $950; almost annual reductions thereafter brought the price down to $290 in 1924.

FIG. 49. *Industry.* Painting by Edward Bruce. Twentieth-century artists began to discover beauty in the clean functionalism of the factory. (*Collection of Whitney Museum of American Art.*)

Ford's low prices reflected the extraordinary organization of his production. Through simplification of design, standardization of parts, and development of assembly-line techniques, manufacture was speeded amazingly. Ford also cut his costs by gaining control of raw materials, by making all necessary purchases at cash, and by avoiding bankers' charges through reinvesting a large share of his profits. Important though these economies were, Ford's most important discovery was the advantage of making a narrow margin of profit on a large volume of sales rather than a wide margin on a smaller volume. By trimming his prices to meet the consumers' needs, Ford expanded his market prodigiously. In 1909 he sold 18,000 cars; in 1917 over 785,000; in 1923, 1924, and 1925 about 2,000,000 each year.

The second great giant in the industry was the General Motors Corporation, an ambitious merger organized in 1908 by William C. Durant of Flint, Michigan. By acquiring control of the separate companies manufacturing the Buick, the Cadillac, the Oldsmobile, and several other less well-known cars, as well as numerous parts companies, Durant hoped to dominate the market for automobiles of every type and price range. The founder's Napoleonic policies soon plunged the new company dangerously into debt. The overgrown infant was rescued by New York bankers in 1910, but Durant was ousted from the management. He returned to power in 1915 but suffered a final fall during the depression of 1921. Thereafter, the great corporation was dominated by Morgan and Du Pont interests.

For over a decade Ford kept well ahead of General Motors. In 1917 he produced nearly four times as many cars as his rival. But during the twenties General Motors advanced rapidly. Although millions of motorists remained loyal to the beloved "Tin Lizzies," others began to prefer General Motors' Chevrolet with its better lines, conventional gearshift, foot throttle, and other features closely resembling those to be found in more expensive cars.

In 1927 an epoch of automobile history ended. After producing 15 million Model T's over a period of eighteen years, Henry Ford finally abandoned his famous money-maker—the car that had transformed the automobile from the rich man's toy to the poor man's servant. For several months the Ford plants were closed, while the public waited expectantly. When the new Ford—Model A—was finally exhibited in showrooms throughout the country in December, 1927, the event was heralded like the birth of a royal child. Model A was a good-looking car: it was offered in a variety of colors and trimmings; it was conventional in gearshift and other features. It sold well, yet Ford's preeminence in the industry was ended. If the Ford was handsome and relatively cheap, so was the Chevrolet. And so also was the Plymouth, introduced into the low-priced field by the Chrysler Corporation in 1929. The Ford, once unique as the common man's car, was now only one of several.

In 1929, *annus mirabilis* for the automobile industry, almost 4,800,000 cars were produced. The number of passenger cars registered in the country had climbed from 8,226,000 in 1920 to 23,122,000 in 1929. As this amounted to one automobile for every six inhabitants of the nation, it would have been possible for the entire population to have taken to the road at once with no more crowding than was considered normal in many family cars.

The mass distribution of automobiles was no less a tribute to American salesmanship than to American technology. Millions of families, unable to pay cash for cars, were induced to buy on the installment plan. Installment purchasing, infrequent and of dubious respectability before 1910, became all but universal during the 1920's. Having learned this painless method, the average citizen was induced to buy furniture, electric appliances, oil burners, and many other expensive items in the same way. In 1929 installment purchases totaled about 7 billion dollars. One school of economic opinion regarded the interest charges on these contracts as a heavy drain on household budgets and deplored the tendency of families to commit themselves to large monthly payments that would be impossible to continue if the wage earner lost his job. The opposing school hailed installment purchasing as fundamental to the prosperity of the "new era," since it widened the market for expensive goods to include millions of customers who could never have purchased on a cash basis.

Automobile dealers encouraged manufacturers to make annual changes in models. New cars were distinguishable at a glance from their older brothers of the same make. Thus were motorists encouraged to trade in their old automobiles for new ones long before they were worn out. "Our chief job in research," said Charles F. Kettering of General Motors, "is to keep the customer reasonably dissatisfied with what he has."

The automobile's contribution to prosperity was not confined to the industry's own 350,000 executives and workers. In every city and village of the country Americans found profit in selling and repairing cars, in lubricating them, and in filling their tanks with gasoline. Thousands were kept busy producing steel, glass, tires, and other products required by automobile manufacturers. Additional thousands were employed in constructing new hard-surface roads.

Other Boom Industries

The war had created a housing shortage, which provided golden opportunities for the postwar construction industry. In the suburbs—made more accessible to the cities by automobiles and buses—thousands of one-family dwellings were built. Promoters purchased large tracts of land, bestowed fancy names upon them, erected houses, and sold them to purchasers eager to own their own homes. In addition to making installment purchases on cars and furniture, many families were thus committed to heavy interest and principal payments on home mortgages.

Although the building of one-family dwellings reached its peak in 1925 and began to fall off, there continued to be a demand for large apartment houses and commercial buildings. For the building industry as a whole the banner year was 1928, when over 17 billion dollars' worth of materials were used—bringing good times to producers of lumber, hardware, plumbing supplies, and electrical fixtures.

The output of electrical power tripled between 1919 and 1929. From steam generating plants and dam sites current was carried to millions of homes and factories. Despite a large increase in the domestic use of electricity the most important development was in industry. In 1914 only about 30 per cent of factory machine equipment was run by electrical power; by 1929 about 70 per cent was electrified. By shifting from steam or water power to electricity, the factories rid themselves of cumbersome and dangerous systems of belts and pulleys and could organize their production more efficiently. With the increasing popularity of electric irons, vacuum cleaners, toasters, refrigerators, and washing machines, the manufacturing of such appliances naturally prospered.

The American chemical industry was enormously stimulated by World War I. The munitions orders of the Allies resulted in large expansion even before the United States entered the conflict. When imports from Germany were cut off, American chemical producers had their first opportunity to supply aniline dyes, medicines, and solvents in large quantities. Thousands of confiscated German patents were made available to American industry. To consolidate their wartime gains, the chemical companies obtained high protection in the Emergency Tariff of 1921 and the Fordney-McCumber Act of 1922. Still other opportunities for profitable expansion were found through the development of rayon, lacquers, plastics, and cheap fertilizers.

Net yet big business by American standards but challenging to the imagination was the aviation industry. Although Wilbur and Orville Wright had demonstrated the feasibility of flight in a heavier-than-air machine as early as 1903, airplanes had little practical importance until their military value was convincingly proved during World War I. Immediately after the war, interest was sustained by the establishment of the first air-mail service in the world between New York and Washington in 1918 and by the first transatlantic crossing—a feat achieved in 1919 by the United States Navy seaplane, the NC-4.

Thereafter, progress was slow until 1927, when Charles A. Lindbergh became a national hero through his flight in the *Spirit of St. Louis* from New York to Paris. This and several other highly publicized exploits focused attention on the still infant industry. Aviation stocks soared in price, and travel by air became for the first time something more than a stunt to prove the traveler's courage. By the end of 1928 there were 48 commercial airlines in the United States, serving 355 cities over 20,000 miles of routes. Even so, the industry was largely dependent upon government patronage. Between 1927 and 1933 over 50 per cent of the output of aircraft factories was purchased by the army and the navy, and over 80 per cent of the income of air-transport companies came from government mail contracts.

Concentration of Business

Big business became bigger during the era of prosperity. It was a period of mergers, when small firms were constantly falling under the control of larger. Much of this concentration was achieved through the organization of holding companies. Some of these effected economies of operation and management beneficial to the entire country. But others seemed to have little reason for existence except as devices for selling stock to the public and permitting insiders to gain control of huge economic empires with relatively small investment of their own. Through a pyramid of holding companies the Van Sweringen brothers of Cleveland, Ohio, dominated railroads having aggregate assets of 2½ billion dollars with an investment of less than 20 million dollars. By similar sleight of hand Samuel Insull of Chicago gained control of about 10 per cent of the electrical-power industry of the country. Through a bewildering network of interlocking companies Insull ruled over utilities companies serving 4,741 communities in 30 different states.

The trend toward concentration was also obvious in merchandising. The A & P and other grocery chains engaged in business on a nationwide scale. Establishing their own bakeries and factories and buying in huge quantities on the produce market, they were able to sell at prices that dismayed independent merchants. Woolworth, Kresge, and other "five and tens" appeared in every town, and chain drug and chain cigar stores became increasingly common. By 1929, 27 per cent of American food sales, 19 per cent of drugstore sales, and 93 per cent of variety-store sales were made through chains.

In cases where two or three giant corporations dominated an industry, the principle of "price leadership" was often accepted. Other gasoline companies followed the prices established by the Standard Oil Company; other steel producers fixed their prices to coincide with those of the United States Steel Corporation. The leading brands of cigarettes were always sold at the same price. Avoiding price competition, these industries sought to expand their sales through gigantic advertising campaigns cleverly contrived to make their brand names household words.

Trade associations had existed since the period of the Civil War, but they multiplied prodigiously during World War I and the postwar decade. The trade associations sponsored research, collected statistical information, simplified and standardized products. Because of these desirable features the movement received encouragement and practical assistance from the Department of Commerce during the period when Hoover was its head. The trade associations, however, easily lent themselves to activities of a different kind. They promulgated rules regarding conditions of sale and discount; they attempted to restrain competition and to maintain prices.

When the price-fixing activities of the great corporations or the trade associations became too flagrant, antitrust suits were sometimes instituted. But trust busting never achieved the vigor of earlier days. Courts and prosecutors distinguished between "reasonable" and "unreasonable" restraint of trade. Representatives of government and business often conferred on how the laws were to be interpreted in particular instances. In magazines and public discussions the idea was frequently expressed that the antitrust laws were antiquated and that businessmen should be given larger liberty to police their own affairs.

The age was one of free enterprise but not of free competition. The newcomer found it increasingly difficult to break into an established field of production.

There was little aggressive price cutting on manufactured products. If demand fell off, most businessmen preferred to meet the situation by curbing output rather than by cutting prices. Although methods of production were being steadily improved and unit costs reduced, most of the savings went into profits rather than lower prices.

American business became not only more highly concentrated but more intimately involved in a global economy. American imports rose from 1.9 billion dollars in 1914 to over 4 billion in 1928. To supply the American industrial machine, Japan sold us silk, Mexico and Colombia petroleum, the East Indies and Liberia rubber, the Malay States tin, and Canada wood pulp and nickel. American exports expanded even more—from 2.3 billion dollars in 1914 to 5.1 billion in 1928. Automobiles, radios, and other products of American factories became increasingly important items of export. Manufactured goods, only 31 per cent of American exports in 1914, composed 45 per cent in 1928.

The continued excess of exports over imports ceased to be a healthy symptom after World War I when the United States became for the first time a creditor nation. Before World War I a "favorable" balance of trade had enabled interest payments to be made to foreign holders of American railroad bonds and other securities. But the war had changed all this. The Allied governments had borrowed some 10 billion dollars from the United States and additional amounts from American bankers. Moreover, during the twenties large amounts of American capital were invested in foreign government bonds, in foreign industries, and in American-owned factories and plantations in all parts of the world. The amount of such investments was estimated to exceed 16 billion dollars in 1930. Throughout the twenties the nation showed a strange reluctance to adjust national economic policy to the new facts of life. The tariff was three times raised—in 1921, 1922, and 1930—and intimations from Europe that the United States should cancel the war debts were rejected with indignation.

Flaws in Prosperity

During a period when much economic activity was protected from the full impact of competition by production curbs and price agreements, producers who were genuinely individualistic encountered serious difficulties.

Such was the case in the bituminous coal industry. Here thousands of operators competed desperately. Despite the general boom in manufacturing and transportation the demand for coal tended to contract rather than to expand. Coal-produced power was used more efficiently than formerly, and it came increasingly into competition with hydroelectric power and power derived from petroleum. Coal fell in price from $3.75 per short ton in 1920 to $1.78 in 1929. Many mines operated at a loss; thousands of miners were unemployed or on short time. Northern mines using union labor found it particularly hard to compete with the nonunion mines of the South.

Also sick was the cotton textile industry. Changes in fashion—shorter dresses, fewer petticoats, the growing popularity of silk and rayon—restricted the domestic market, and the export market was disrupted by the growth of textile manufacturing in Japan, India, South America, and China. Prices fell with results particularly disastrous to New England. As great mills went bankrupt and thousands were thrown out of work, whole cities suffered paralyzing blows. But New England's difficulty was the South's opportunity. With their cheaper labor, proximity to raw material, favorable climate, ample power, new machinery, and infusions of northern capital, the textile factories of Virginia, North and South Carolina, and Georgia expanded their operations.

The nation's greatest individualists were its farmers. Millions of producers were competing under conditions that gave them no opportunity to control production or to fix prices. The competition, moreover, was not merely with other American farmers. Since one-third or more of American farm produce was exported, prices were dependent upon all the vagaries of a world market.

The depression of 1920–1921 fell with particular severity upon the farmers. Encouraged by high prices and unprecedented domestic and foreign demand, American agriculture had been greatly expanded during the war. As exports fell, supplies glutted the domestic market. Between December, 1919, and December, 1920, wheat dropped from $2.15 a bushel to $1.44, corn from $1.25 to $0.68, and cotton from $0.36 a pound to $0.14. Although farm prices improved somewhat during the period of recovery, the farmers were unhappy. The ratio of farm prices to other prices continued to be unfavorable; the farmer's dollar would buy less than in the days before the war.

Although the farm population declined by some three million during the years 1921–1928, improved agricultural methods kept production high. The number of tractors on American farms increased from 230,000 in 1920 to 920,000 in 1930. Wheat growing was radically influenced by the introduction of disk plows, power drills, and small combine harvesters. Every stage of corn growing was speeded by new laborsaving machines. Although the mechanization of cotton raising still lagged, production per acre and per laborer was greatly increased through the opening up of superior lands in Texas and Oklahoma. Modern science provided the farmer with better seed, improved breeds of livestock and poultry, new fertilizers, and new methods of controlling pests and disease.

That all this progress should fail to bring agricultural prosperity was exasperating. The farmer was plagued by high costs and low staple prices. He had to pay more for his purchases, higher wages to agricultural labor, higher taxes, higher freight rates, and higher distribution costs. Because of his wartime investment in more land and better equipment, he was likely to be heavily in debt. Large interest charges, therefore, were one of the farmer's most burdensome costs. Small farmers, usually tilling the less desirable land, were particularly burdened. Many lost their farms through foreclosure; others sold or abandoned them. Some now worked for wages as agricultural laborers or factory workers; others accepted the status of tenant farmers.

As more and more farmers found it difficult to make a living from the soil, the farm problem became a conspicuous issue in politics. The dominant Republican party attempted to assist agriculture through higher tariff rates, new credit facilities, regulation of the stockyards and produce markets, and encouragement of cooperatives. But none of these measures raised agricultural prices, and only higher prices would bring prosperity to the producers. Farm bloc leaders pushed through Congress the McNary-Haugen Bill—an ingenious measure designed to raise domestic prices through government purchase and sale abroad of agricultural surpluses; the losses incurred in these transactions were to be collected from the farmers through a special tax or "equalization fee." But such meddling with the market shocked President Coolidge. Vetoing the measure in 1927, he asserted: "Government price-fixing, once started, has alike no justice and no end. It is an economic folly from which this country has every right to be spared."

Still another drag upon the economy was the unemployed. Bad times in coal mining and cotton textiles threw thousands out of work. Even in prosperous industries the introduction of improved machinery or the consolidation of plants often deprived many workers of their jobs. Technological unemployment was understood to be the price of progress. In theory, those who lost their places through improved production methods would find new ones through the expansion of industry, but even in the prosperous twenties displaced workers often went months without jobs. Nor was their misfortune cushioned by any system of unemployment insurance.

Purchasing power was unevenly distributed. In 1929 there were over sixteen million families in the nation with less than $2,000 annual income. These composed nearly 60 per cent of all families, yet they received less than 24 per cent of the total national income. In the lowest income group—receiving less than $1,000 a year—were six million families, who constituted 21 per cent of the families of the nation but received only 4 per cent of the national income. Many of these were southern sharecroppers, living on a diet of fat pork, molasses, and corn, and consuming few of the products of American industry.

Speculation and Crash

Depressed industries, maldistribution of income, and technological unemployment were the concern only of those immediately affected. The attention of the rest of the country was riveted on the evidence of good times—sedans and trucks, skyscrapers and bungalows, radios and vacuum cleaners. Businessmen enjoyed their highest prestige. Magazines, which had once featured muckraking articles, now were filled with success stories. Newspaper reporters sought statements from industrialists and bankers on every conceivable subject.

Before 1917 the world of stocks and bonds had been a world apart from that of the average American. Millions made their first investment in such securities when they bought government bonds during World War I. That experience inspired many to put their savings into corporation stocks and bonds during the postwar decade. Similarly educational were the plans devised by numerous companies for selling stock on installments to their own employees. But the most active agents in creating new customers for securities were well-groomed young college graduates, specially trained to seek out prospective investors. The National City Company, an affiliate of the great National City Bank of New York, employed 350 salesmen, operating from offices in 58 different cities and connected with New York headquarters by 11,000 miles of private wire. Since many other investment houses were following similar tactics, it is little wonder that millions of small-town businessmen, doctors, and lawyers were honored with calls from strangers who extolled the merits of Radio Common or Peruvian bonds with the same fervor that other young salesmen lauded Hoover vacuum cleaners or Fuller brushes.

"Everybody Ought to Be Rich" was the arresting title of an article published in the *Ladies' Home Journal* in August, 1929. The magic formula, as explained by John J. Raskob, General Motors executive and chairman of the Democratic National Committee, was to save $15 a week, to invest it in good common stock, and to allow the dividends and rights to accumulate. At the end of twenty years the investor would have at least $80,000 and an income of $400 a month. "He will be rich. And because income can do that, I am firm in my belief that anyone not only can be rich, but ought to be rich."

To many Americans twenty years seemed a long time to wait for wealth. An enticing short cut was the practice of buying "on margin." Instead of paying cash for his stock purchase, the investor could put down about one-quarter of the market price and borrow the rest from his broker, leaving the stock with the latter as security. So long as stock prices continued to go up, buying on margin was immensely profitable. Investors could buy three or four times as much stock as they would have otherwise been able to afford and could pay for it painlessly out of their profits. Few saw the dangers involved. If the stocks declined in price, they would be subjected to repeated calls for more margin. If they were unable to raise the money, they would be wiped out—losing both their original investment and the pledged securities. The brokers obtained the funds for these transactions by borrowing from banks and corporations. In 1929 brokers' loans had mounted to a dangerous total of some 8 billion dollars.

Up to 1927 the performance of the market was not abnormal. Industry was expanding, profits were good, and stock prices bore a reasonable relationship to business prospects. For the next two years, however, the market soared into the stratosphere in seeming disregard of the laws of gravity. Business activity had leveled off, commodity prices tended to decline—but stocks continued to go up.

If there were clouds in the sky, they were too small to warn the millions who were eagerly "playing" the market. Nor were the optimists only foolish amateurs in investment. One widely respected industrial leader asserted, "There is no reason why there should be any more panics." Another announced, "We are only at the beginning of a period that will go down in history as a golden age."

The great bull market reached its peak on September 3, 1929. During the next six weeks there were tremors that worried some of the experts. Bad news from English financial circles and a suspicion that American stock prices were too high resulted in some selling by the cautious and a decline in the market. But the situation caused no real alarm. In October, prices advanced again, and there were optimistic statements from prominent authorities. On October 15, Professor Irving Fisher of Yale, a well-known economist, asserted that stock prices stood on "what looks like a permanently high plateau" and that he expected to see the market "a good deal higher than it is today within a few months."

There was little warning, therefore, of the catastrophic crash so near at hand. Prices fell badly from October 15 to 23. Suddenly terrified, thousands of investors offered their stocks for sale. Brokers made repeated calls on their customers for more margin. Panic captured the exchange on October 24: almost 13,000,000 shares of stock were traded; the ticker ran hours behind; prices dropped more rapidly than ever before in Wall Street history. A hastily organized bankers' pool served as an emergency dam, but the flood of selling again overwhelmed the market on October 29, when an all-time record of 16,410,030 transactions took place. After this second day of panic the liquidation proceeded in more orderly fashion, but heavy losses continued. In the seventy-one days between September 3 and November 13, the price of American Telephone and Telegraph stock fell from 304 to 197¼; General Electric from 396¼ to 168⅛; Radio Corporation from 101 to 28.

The Great Depression

Despite the pathetic plight of thousands who had lost all their savings, optimists asserted that the collapse of stock prices was for the best. The runaway boom had been unhealthy; liquidation of the speculators was a bitter but necessary remedy. The nation could now concentrate on the slower but more certain road to wealth—hard work and prudent investment.

It soon became apparent, however, that the nation was confronted by something much more serious than the market collapse. Manufacturers found it increasingly difficult to sell their products, and by 1932 industrial production had fallen to one-half its 1929 level. Even harder hit were contractors, as commercial and residential building was reduced to one-fifth its 1929 volume. At President Hoover's request employers attempted to sustain purchasing power by avoiding cuts in hourly wage rates. Actual take-home pay, however, fell sharply, as factories went on part time, closed down completely, or reduced personnel. Even these economies were inadequate to prevent eventual wage reductions. After September, 1931, wage and salary cuts were universal.

Thus was the country caught in a downward spiral of deflation. Reduced wages meant reduced purchasing power, and reduced purchasing power meant more factory shutdowns and unemployment. Particularly serious was the plight of debtors. Monthly payments that had seemed reasonable in 1929 were impossible to meet two years later. Automobiles and furniture had to be reclaimed by finance companies, and banks pondered the problem of defaulted mortgages. Foreclosure was a double-edged weapon, since real estate like stock certificates was often worth less than the loan it was supposed to secure. The nation's banks—none too sound even during the period of prosperity, when an average of about 700 had failed each year—now began to go under in alarming numbers: 1,326 closed their doors in 1930; 2,294 in 1931; and 1,456 in 1932. Frightened depositors began to withdraw and to hoard their money, adding to the banks' difficulties.

The most pitiable victims of the depression were the unemployed. Although no accurate government statistics were compiled, unofficial estimates placed the jobless at ten million or more in 1932 and as high as fifteen million in the spring of 1933. Men without work suffered a serious deterioration of morale. They saw their savings disappear; they cashed in their insurance policies; they gave up their flats and moved in with relatives or friends. Searching hopelessly for jobs by day, tossing restlessly by night, they often became the victims of what social workers described as "unemployment shock."

Sometimes unemployment dissolved all ties between a man and his family and community. Homeless wanderers took to the road. Unwelcome visitors in one community, they would be given temporary food and shelter and hurried on to the next. Railroad men reported that although their usual policy had been to remove transients from freight trains, the number became so great in 1932 that it was impossible to carry the policy out. There were an estimated 1,500 homeless men passing through Kansas City each day; 45,000 were said to have passed through El Paso in six months. Particularly shocking was the report that 200,000 homeless children were wandering through the country.

The seriousness of the unemployment problem was dramatized by the "bonus army"—a movement of jobless ex-soldiers which converged on Washington from all sections of the country in 1932. The men began to arrive in May and continued to come in large numbers over the next two months. Their hope was to convince Congress through parades and demonstrations that the Federal government should pay the bonus promised to World War I veterans immediately instead of waiting until 1945 as the law provided.

Considering that about 15,000 men—some of them accompanied by wives and children—had appeared in the capital city, there was remarkably little disorder. Some of the men were allowed to use vacant government buildings as barracks; more lived in pup tents and shacks erected across the Potomac at

Anacostia Flats. Food was contributed by charitable Washington residents or sent in by sympathizers from other parts of the country.

In July the bonus demonstration reached its crisis. When Congress adjourned without conceding the veterans' demands, a majority of the men gave up and went home—assisted by government loans for train fare. But five or six thousand stayed on, either because they were determined to continue their protest or because they had no place to go. On July 28, after a clash between the veterans and the police in which two lives were lost, orders were given to General Douglas A. MacArthur to use the regular army to restore order. Although tanks, cavalry, and infantry were moved in martial array against the demonstrators, no weapons more lethal than tear-gas bombs proved necessary. The men were evicted from their camps, and their shacks were burned to the ground.

Some of the bonus marchers went home; some returned to their wanderings; some attached themselves to ramshackle settlements in other cities. These shanty colonies—bitterly known as Hoovervilles—were to be found in many places. One, for example, was located in an abandoned reservoir in Central Park in the heart of New York City. From their packing-case homes these victims of the depression paid visits to the bakeries and markets in search of stale bread or overripe fruits and vegetables.

If homelessness and hunger were more common in the city than in the country, this did not mean that the country had escaped the depression. Quite the contrary. Unable to cut their production as the manufacturers had done, farmers glutted the market with unsalable surpluses. Agricultural prices fell 64 per cent between 1929 and the spring of 1933 as compared with a fall of 34 per cent in the price of manufactured goods. Farmers' cash income dropped from 11 billion dollars in 1929 to 5 billion in 1932.

For all but a few of the most efficient producers, 5-cent cotton, 33-cent corn, and 38-cent wheat threatened disaster. To find money for interest payments, taxes, and necessary purchases became all but impossible. Thousands of farmers lost their farms through foreclosure. In 1932 desperate agrarians, organized by Miles Reno as the Farmers' Holiday Association, attempted to force a rise in prices by blockading the roads leading into Sioux City, Iowa, and dumping on the ground the milk and produce of truck drivers who refused to turn back. Similar farmers' strikes were attempted elsewhere in Iowa and in neighboring states. There was a widespread demand not only for higher prices but for a halt on foreclosures and tax sales.

Proposed Remedies

The American economy was desperately sick. This was obvious, but there was no agreement on the cause of the disease or on how the patient might be restored to health.

President Hoover rejected all proposals for radical surgery. He believed that in its first phase the depression was like a score of earlier ones, which had been caused by overproduction and speculative mania and through which the nation had always passed safely after "a relatively short period of losses, of hardship, and adjustment." In 1931, according to Hoover's theory, there had been solid basis for hope that the worst was over and recovery was in sight. Then occurred the real disaster—"a blow from abroad of such dangerous character as to strike at the very safety of the Republic." This second phase of the depression was almost entirely European in its origins—caused by the great losses of World War I, gigantic national debts, heavy expenditures for armaments, and unwise experiments in subsidizing industry and employment. "Under these strains," said Hoover, "the financial systems of many foreign countries crashed one by one. . . . Thus . . . the worldwide storm rapidly grew to hurricane force and the greatest economic emergency in all history."

Since Hoover believed that it was Europe rather than America which had brought on the trouble, he saw little need for fundamental domestic reform. During the first phase of the depression he proposed simple palliatives; during the second he turned to stronger stimulants. Through the Hawley-Smoot Tariff of 1930, higher protection—that favorite home remedy of the Republicans—was administered despite warnings from economists that this would aggravate rather than relieve the situation. Immigration was all but completely halted. A cautious expansion of public works was permitted, while a new Federal Farm Board was authorized to encourage the organization of cooperative marketing through government loans. By means of White House conferences and the appointment of commissions, the President attempted to foster voluntary agreements to maintain wages, to spread work, to avoid strikes, and to coordinate the relief activities of private charities and local communities.

When the situation took its alarming turn for the worse in 1931, Hoover became bolder. His moratorium halted reparations and war-debt payments—thereby staving off complete financial collapse in Central Europe. His Reconstruction Finance Corporation prevented general bankruptcy of banks, insurance companies, and railroads. In an unsuccessful attempt to hold up farm prices, the Farm Board purchased 370,000,000 bushels of wheat and 1,300,000 bales of cotton over a period of three years.

Despite Hoover's faith in economic individualism the depression was obviously pushing his administration farther and farther in the direction of government intervention. Yet the things that Hoover refused to do were perhaps more significant than the things that he did do. Although the nation was already suffering from acute deflation, he persisted in attempts to balance the budget through reduction of government expenditures and the raising of taxes. Although prices had fallen so low that the whole credit structure was close to collapse, he opposed any departure from the gold standard. Despite the generally admitted fact that the farmers were being ruined by overproduction, he would sponsor no measure either for subsidizing exports or for eliminating the surplus through government-imposed production curbs.

Economic individualism's most obvious failure was in handling the problem of relief. During the first phase of the depression conservatives hoped that private charity would be enough. All the techniques of high-powered advertising were employed to induce voluntary contributions. But organized charities, adequate to meet the needs of normal times, were incapable of dealing with a major economic breakdown. More and more of the burden had to be accepted by local government. In every city could be seen long lines of unfortunates waiting to receive orders which they might exchange for groceries or fuel. The procedure was humiliating, and the dole was inadequate. Yet even to do this much threatened cities with bankruptcy. Several state governments took up the problem, but their resources were also limited.

Against the rising demand for a Federal relief program Hoover maintained stubborn opposition. "I am opposed to any direct or indirect government dole," he announced. "Our people are providing against distress in true American fashion." The greatest concession that he would make was to permit the Reconstruction Finance Corporation to make loans to states that had exhausted their own resources for relief.

As faith in the Hoover philosophy waned, any number of rival doctrines clamored for acceptance. At one extreme was communism. The Soviet Union was then engaged in its first Five-Year Plan. The contrast between this experiment and the planless muddle of the capitalist depression impressed many Americans. The example of Russia was more alluring than at almost any other time before or since, because the coercive features of the system were better concealed. Much was heard of the construction of giant dams and steel mills; little of purges, forced labor, or exploitation of the workers and peasants by the state. Naturally the American Communist party worked tirelessly to win new converts. Demonstrations of the unemployed were attributed—with varying accuracy—to Communist intrigue. The radical program made its greatest appeal to the jobless, to certain underpaid urban worker groups, and to intellectuals seeking the certainties of a new faith. The extraordinary thing was not that communism made gains but that these were so relatively small. Although Communist William Z. Foster received over twice as many votes for President in 1932 as he did in 1928, the total was only 103,000—which compared poorly not only with Roosevelt's 22,800,000 and Hoover's 15,700,000, but with the Socialist Norman Thomas's 880,000.

For another group of Americans who had lost faith in economic individualism, Mussolini's Italy suggested a way out. Talk was heard of the need for a dictator; attempts were made to organize Khaki Shirts, Silver Shirts, and other groups modeled on the Fascist or Nazi systems. Even less than communism, however, did overt fascism win a mass following.

American radicalism preferred to express itself through native channels. Favorite panaceas, almost forgotten since the 1890's, were again urged upon the country. Latter-day Populists called for greenbacks and free silver. Citizens who could not be stirred by these ancient slogans often responded to new programs. Technocracy was a nine days' wonder propounded by Howard Scott of New York, who demonstrated with charts and figures that if politicians and businessmen would only abdicate to engineers and technicans, the nation's economy could achieve full production, full employment, and abundance for all. Across the continent Upton Sinclair threw the West Coast into violent controversy with his EPIC (End Poverty in California) scheme. Longer lived were the later agitations led by Senator Huey Long of Louisiana, promising to "Make Every Man a King," by Dr. Francis E. Townsend of California, demanding $200 monthly pensions for all citizens over sixty years of age, and by Father Charles E. Coughlin of Royal Oak, Michigan, calling for radical inflation through his National Union for Social Justice.

Franklin D. Roosevelt, campaigning against Hoover in 1932, proposed no such magic formula for recovery. In a speech before the Commonwealth Club of San Francisco, he made no secret of the fact that he believed that the day of unrestrained individualism had passed:

> A glance at the situation today only too clearly indicates that equality of opportunity as we have known it no longer exists. Our industrial plant is built; the problem just now is whether under existing conditions it is not overbuilt. Our last frontier has long since been reached, and there is practically no more free land. . . .
>
> Clearly, all this calls for a re-appraisal of values. A mere builder of more industrial plants, a creator of more railroad systems, an organizer of more corporations, is as likely to be a danger as a help. The day of the great promoter or the financial Titan, to whom we granted anything if only he would build, or develop, is over. Our task now is not discovery or exploitation of natural resources, or necessarily producing more goods. It is the soberer, less dramatic business of administering resources and plants already in hand, of seeking to reestablish foreign markets for our surplus production, of meeting the problem of under-consumption, of adjusting production to consumption, of distributing wealth and products more equitably, of adapting existing economic organizations to the service of the people. The day of enlightened administration has come.[1]

The "mature economy" theory which Roosevelt propounded in this Commonwealth Club speech was greatly elaborated during the next few years. Many American economists, taking their lead from the English writer John Maynard Keynes, attributed the Great Depression to oversavings and underinvestment. The closing of the frontier, restriction of immigration, and the declining birth rate had, in their opinion, set limits to economic expansion. By 1930 the nation had all the railroads, all the automobile factories, all the skyscrapers, and all of many other capital investments that it needed for the time being. Funds lay idle, and the decline of real investment radically diminished the demand for steel, cement, and other basic products, causing unemployment and loss of purchasing power. Such a downward spiral could only be halted by bold government action: by tax policies that would discourage excessive corporate savings and by increased gov-

[1] *The Public Papers and Addresses of Franklin D. Roosevelt* (Random House, New York, 1938), I, 750–2.

ernment expenditures. Professor Alvin H. Hansen of Harvard, leading exponent of adjusting fiscal policy to meet the business cycle, wrote:

It is not possible to go back to the atomistic order. Corporations, trade-unions, and government intervention we shall continue to have. Modern democracy does not mean individualism. It means a system in which private, voluntary organization functions under general, and mostly indirect, governmental control. Dictatorship means direct and specific control. We do not have a choice between "plan and no plan." We have a choice only between democratic planning and totalitarian regimentation.[1]

Doctor New Deal

When Hoover was succeeded by Roosevelt in March, 1933, the most obvious contrast between the two physicians was in their bedside manner. Dr. Hoover had inclined toward glumness, and the sick economy had been as much frightened by his head shaking as by the ravages of disease. Dr. Roosevelt was nothing if not confident. Listening to his cheery optimism, the patient immediately felt better—even though the chart still showed serious symptoms.

The two doctors differed in another significant respect. Although Dr. Hoover gave occasional blood transfusions to save his patient from dying, he placed his principal reliance upon the curative processes of nature and avoided extensive medication. Dr. Roosevelt felt no such inhibitions. An enthusiast for experiment, he dosed his patient with almost every drug known to the profession. This procedure appeared to work. The economy, if not restored to full health, was soon convalescent. But as an experiment in science, the treatment provoked much debate. When so many pills had been given, which had cured the patient? Or was it true, as admirers of Dr. Hoover insisted, that the pills were all either worthless or actually harmful? Would the patient's recovery have been sounder and more complete without them?

Many New Deal measures were merely a bolder application of Hoover policies. Roosevelt's skillful handling of the banking crisis of March, 1933, depended on measures planned by the outgoing administration; the new President's greatest contribution was his effective radio appeal to depositors to abstain from runs upon the banks as they reopened. Hoover's Reconstruction Finance Corporation was retained and given vastly extended powers. Continuing Hoover's policy of propping up the sagging credit structure, Roosevelt developed programs for refinancing farm and home mortgages and for insuring bank loans for the construction of new dwellings and the repair of old ones.

More controversial was the New Deal's acceptance of direct Federal responsibility for the relief of the unemployed. The Civilian Conservation Corps took 300,000 jobless youths off the streets and put them to work in the national forests. The Civil Works Administration gave temporary employment to 4,000,000 men and women during the winter of 1933–1934. When large-scale

[1] Alvin H. Hansen, *Fiscal Policy and Business Cycles* (Norton, New York, 1941), 47.

unemployment persisted, the Works Progress Administration [1] was established in 1935. During the next five years the WPA created jobs for some 8,000,000 unemployed persons. Nearly 500 new airports were built and many old ones enlarged; over 500,000 miles of roads were constructed or improved. Schoolhouses and libraries were built and repaired; new sewers and culverts were laid; athletic fields, playgrounds, public parks, and swimming pools were provided. There were WPA projects for unemployed doctors, dentists, nurses, teachers, writers, actors, musicians, and artists. Critics of the WPA condemned the projects as a waste of money and a crude device for buying votes. Defenders praised the experiment as a great humanitarian effort creating purchasing power and saving the self-respect and skill of depression victims by giving work instead of a dole.

Although Roosevelt resisted the more radical schemes of the Greenbackers and free-silver crusaders, he showed scant reverence for the conventional gold standard. Private ownership of gold was prohibited by law; contracts to pay in gold were voided and made payable in currency. By progressive devaluation the dollar was eventually reduced to about 59 per cent of its former value in gold. The policy's effects were curiously indecisive. Departure from the gold standard certainly did not bring all the misfortunes predicted by Grover Cleveland and Herbert Hoover. Neither, however, did it bring all the benefits promised by inflationists since the days of William Jennings Bryan. Prices rose moderately—but perhaps as much in response to other New Deal measures as to this. The policy's most conspicuous result was to accumulate in the vaults of the United States government about 80 per cent of all the gold in the world.

In dealing with the farm problem, the new Agricultural Adjustment Administration shocked conservatives by developing a policy of planned scarcity. Farmers who would agree to reduce their acreage and their hog breeding were rewarded with benefit payments from the government. Although the AAA was temporarily hobbled by a Supreme Court decision, new legislation soon gave the agency ample powers. The details of the various mechanisms employed to assist the farmer through crop loans, marketing quotas, and parity and benefit payments were confusing, but their general tendency was clear. The policy of the Roosevelt administration was to raise farm income to what was considered an equitable level in relation to the income of other groups. To the rest of the nation the AAA meant higher prices and increased taxes; for the farmers it involved some restraint on traditional individualism. Against these debits the AAA could enter the credit items of restoring farm purchasing power, halting the liquidation of middle-class farmers as a healthy social group, assuring the nation ample food supplies, and fostering conservation of the soil—the nation's most essential resource.

[1] Not to be confused with the Public Works Administration, another major New Deal agency. The PWA attempted to stimulate recovery by advancing funds for the construction of dams, bridges, schoolhouses, and other major projects—many of them self-liquidating. Since most of the work was done by private contractors and at prevailing wages, it was not, properly speaking, a form of relief.

From the academic point of view a much better farm program would have been one which lowered the farmer's cost of production, reduced agricultural prices, and assisted millions of Americans, Europeans, and Asiatics to enjoy for the first time an adequate diet and decent clothing. A cautious experiment in this direction was made through the Food Stamp Plan—a device for enabling families on relief to increase their purchases of surplus commodities—but little else was done. To substitute an economy of abundance for the economy of scarcity was a task beyond the statesmanship of either political party.

Somewhat different was the New Deal approach to the special problems of tenant farmers and other small holders. Although handicapped by limited appropriations, the Farm Security Administration did much to rehabilitate its clients through emergency loans, instruction in diversification of crops and better care of property, and cooperative measures to provide proper medical care, tractors, and water for irrigation.

The New Deal's first great effort to revive business was through the National Recovery Administration. Each branch of industry was encouraged to formulate its own "code of fair competition." After approval by the President the codes had the force of law; violators could be prosecuted and punished through the Federal courts. Most businessmen at first supported the NRA, since it gave legal blessing to their trade associations, exempting their activities from the antitrust laws. The approval of labor was obtained by code provisions recognizing the right of collective bargaining, forbidding child labor, and fixing minimum wages and maximum hours. But NRA attempted too much. Even before the Supreme Court paralyzed its enforcement machinery, the agency was subjected to increasing criticism and defiance. Consumers protested that it sanctioned production controls and price fixing; small businessmen contended that it favored large corporations and hampered smaller competitors. After the demise of NRA the Roosevelt administration sought to achieve some of the same purposes through laws dealing with the special problems of the bituminous coal and oil industries.

Obviously, one New Deal tendency was to promote the philosophy of "live and let live." Businessmen in certain industries were encouraged, as were the farmers, to refrain from cutthroat competition and to share the market through government-sanctioned agreements on production and prices. This tendency was even stronger at the state level, where a variety of "fair trade" laws were enacted. Yet, with apparent inconsistency, the New Deal revived the antitrust philosophy of the old progressives. The Federal Trade Commission was restored to vigilant activity; the Department of Justice instituted numerous trust-busting suits; Congress authorized an extensive investigation of the monopoly problem through the Temporary National Economic Committee. New Deal confusion reflected that of the country; the American people could still not decide whether to stake their future on enforced competition or on regulated monopoly.

To some extent the New Deal renounced Hoover's dictum that the government must never compete with the economic activities of its own citizens. Although the

Tennessee Valley Authority was engaged in flood control, promotion of navigation, and other activities, its most publicized function was the production and distribution of electrical power to more than one hundred municipalities and cooperatives. Conservatives condemned this venture as socialism; liberals lauded it as one of the major New Deal successes, effective in reducing private utility rates throughout the country. Although public power was also generated at great dams in the Columbia Valley and at certain other points, conservative opposition prevented any bold extension of the TVA principle. Also subject to suspicion and held within modest bounds was the New Deal experiment in slum clearance and public housing.

The New Deal involved greatly increased government regulation of business. To old and new commissions were entrusted important powers over banking, the marketing of securities, public-utility holding corporations, motor trucks, water carriers, aviation, and radio.

As the thirties drew to a close, the causes of the Great Depression were still imperfectly understood, and the efficacy of the New Deal remedies was violently disputed. New Deal supporters pointed with pride to the restored morale of millions of Americans delivered from disaster: idle men put to work, home-owners saved from foreclosure, farmers no longer operating at a loss, rehabilitated tenants. Critics replied that no fundamental improvement had been achieved: the Federal debt had risen from 22 billion dollars to almost 43 billion; 7 million citizens were still unemployed; the country was still vulnerable to depressions—as the "recession" of 1937 had demonstrated.

Doctor Win-the-war

American achievement during World War II was most extraordinary. The war production of the United States, insignificant in 1940, was in 1942 as great as that of Germany, Japan, and Italy combined; in 1944 it was twice as great. To produce the steel, aluminum, rubber, gasoline, planes, tanks, and ships needed for victory, old factories worked day and night, and hundreds of new ones were built—many in previously underdeveloped sections of the South and West. Only the government could command the necessary funds for such an expansion. During the war the government owned 90 per cent or more of the facilities for producing synthetic rubber, aircraft, magnesium, and ships, 70 per cent of aluminum capacity, and substantial proportions of the plants producing machine tools, steel, and high-octane gasoline. Most of the plants were operated, however, by private companies to which they were leased.

The unemployment problem gave way to a manpower problem. With 12 million men and women in the armed services, where were the workers to be found to gather the nation's crops and to tend its machines? The 7 million unemployed of 1940 found jobs; in addition some 6½ million new wage earners were recruited. Two million of these were teen-age boys and girls, many of whom dropped out of high school to accept full-time employment. Four million were new women workers, deserting the kitchen for factory benches and clerical jobs. Additional manpower was also forthcoming from regular workers who put in many hours of overtime and older men who postponed their retirement.

The farm problem also changed. High prices and subsidies boosted farm income to unprecedented levels. In 1943, 1944, and 1945, farm income exceeded 20 billion dollars annually—four times its 1932 level. Despite shortages of labor and machinery the farmers produced the largest crops in American agricultural history—annual wheat crops of 1 billion bushels and corn crops of 3 billion bushels.

Economic mobilization required even more government direction than it had during World War I. Rationing and price control, which during the first contest had been applied mostly in wholesale transactions of basic commodities, were now extended to the consumer level. Rents, wages, and salaries were similarly regulated. Despite the inflationary pressure created by full employment and the large increase in take-home pay, the administration was remarkably successful in holding the brakes on rising prices. Heavy taxes, regular war-bond purchases, other forms of savings, and the reduction of debts siphoned off much of the extra money.

What would happen when the war was over, when government orders ceased and the veterans returned to civilian life? Fear of a new and more serious depression led to the formulation of numerous "full employment" plans by economists like Alvin Hansen and Stuart Chase and by politicians like Henry Wallace and Chester Bowles. All such plans accepted the capitalist system but attempted to modify American practice to prevent depressions. They called upon private business to enlarge its market by producing more efficiently and by reducing prices. During the immediate postwar period the government should continue price controls until the danger of serious inflation was passed; it should extend emergency credits to finance American exports to Europe; it should alter its tariff structure to permit greatly enlarged imports as a permanent policy. Above all, the advocates of full employment asserted, the government must anticipate economic trends and be ready to institute bold programs of public works and other forms of public investment when private investment declined and unemployment threatened.

Conservatives shuddered at this program. The planned economy and multitudinous controls of wartime were demons to be exorcised as quickly as possible once the war was over. They argued that prosperity could be best assured by allowing business to respond to the needs of a free market.

The controversy resulted in typically American compromises. Rationing was largely abandoned soon after the German and Japanese surrenders; price control was retained somewhat longer but became increasingly ineffective under peacetime conditions. Sweeping Republican victories in the elections of 1946 were interpreted as a mandate for allowing prices and wages to seek their own levels.

Only in the case of rents was a truncated form of control tolerated because of the acute housing shortage. Meanwhile, the government divested itself as quickly as possible of its war plants and surplus equipment.

A step of problematic significance was taken in 1946 when Congress passed the Maximum Employment Act. This law stated that it was the "continuing policy and responsibility of the federal government . . . to co-ordinate and utilize all its plans, functions and resources . . . to promote maximum employment, production and purchasing power." The Act created a Council of Economic Advisers to analyze and to interpret economic developments for the purpose of determining when a recession was in the making, to appraise the various programs and activities of the Federal government in relation to these trends, and to recommend to the President policies designed to avoid economic fluctuations. The President was required to present in January of each year an Economic Report to Congress; a joint Congressional committee was to review this report and consider what legislative action might be required.

Minor importance was attached to the early reports of the Council of Economic Advisers, because there was little evidence of an imminent depression. After a brief period of uncertainty the nation entered upon a "super boom." Industrial production achieved new records; from 57 to 60 million persons were gainfully employed, as compared with 45 million in 1940; corporate profits rose to record heights; farm income climbed above its wartime peak. Postwar prosperity received its initial impetus from the expenditure of wartime savings on automobiles, electrical appliances, and other goods that had been unavailable during wartime. Both residential and commercial types of construction rapidly expanded. There was a substantial rise in the real wages of the workers: between 1939 and 1948 average weekly wages increased 120 per cent while the cost of living was advancing only 70 per cent. The prosperity of 1946 was more widely distributed than that of the fabulous 1929: although the price level was about the same for the two years, families receiving an income of from $2,000 to $7,500 received an aggregate income of 111 billion dollars in 1946 as compared with 38 billion in 1929. Increased purchasing power clearly revealed itself in the excellent sales enjoyed by relatively high-priced goods. Television sets, far from being the luxury of the rich, were the proud possession of hundreds of thousands of the recently poor.

The boom, which at times seemed to be spending itself, was sustained by government expenditures incident to the struggle with Russia. To check the spread of communism abroad, Congress appropriated billions of dollars for foreign-aid programs—thus assuring a continuance of large American exports. The signing of the Atlantic Pact and the outbreak of hostilities in Korea resulted in increased expenditures to supply arms both to the United States Army and to various allies. The nation appeared to be returning to a quasi-war economy.

Enjoyment of good times was tempered by uncertainty regarding the future. What the effect of another great war would be few dared to speculate. And if war were averted, what then? In so far as the boom depended on grants abroad and war orders, it was obviously unhealthy. If through some miracle of statesmanship all issues between the Soviet Union and the United States were settled and a great program of international disarmament instituted, could the American economy adjust itself to the quieter demands of peace?

In three postwar elections the voters gave no clear mandate either for an extension of government intervention into the economy or a retraction. If the prevailing mood of the country could be ascertained, it appeared to cherish the advantages of capitalism but to hate its risks. Americans were deeply devoted to their freedom of choice in making investments or accepting jobs; they believed that the profit motive was essential to technological advance and increased productivity; they wanted economic activity to be primarily directed to meeting the needs of customers rather than objectives fixed by the state. But they insisted that their government must protect them against the evils of mass unemployment, catastrophic drops in prices, and wholesale insolvency. Would such a modification of capitalism work? This was one great problem confronting the nation as it entered the second half of the twentieth century.

Chapter 30. Militant Labor

Between 1915 and 1950 membership in American labor unions rose from 2½ million to 16 million. These statistics, impressive though they are, only begin to tell the story of organized labor's striking change of status. In industries concerned with steel, automobiles, electricity, and rubber, where there was scarcely any organization as late as 1932, the unions became strongly entrenched. Wages and conditions for millions of workers were fixed through industry-wide bargaining. Labor leaders like William Green, Philip Murray, John L. Lewis, and Walter Reuther were recognized as among the most powerful individuals in the country. Many Americans welcomed this trend as a broadening of American democracy; others feared big labor much as an earlier generation had feared big business.

Labor's World War I Offensive

Although union membership had tripled between 1900 and 1914, the great majority of American wage earners were still unorganized. Many workers—particularly recent immigrants—were grateful for wages that were high by European standards. The rapid expansion of American industry, moreover, still provided many opportunities for advancement. With a large proportion of their employees indifferent to unionization, employers in many fields found it possible to dominate the rest by using spies and by discharging and black-listing "trouble-makers." In hundreds of industrial towns this antiunion policy was supported by officials of local government and by general public opinion. Many Americans believed that the best labor relations were based upon individual "liberty of contract"—the employer offering wage-and-hour conditions which the worker was free to accept or reject without interference by any "walking delegate," or union representative. Yet critics of this assumption were numerous. In 1912 the House Committee on Labor reported:

> The body of workmen which would surrender its right to strike would, by virtue of the competition amongst themselves and their employers, be reduced to the lowest possible standard of living. A definite example is found in the iron and steel industry, where the unskilled workmen are unorganized and therefore have no power of collective resistance and have seldom in recent years engaged in a trade dispute. The wages in that industry are the lowest, the hours of labor the longest, and the conditions of employment the worst to be found in any large industry where men are employed in the United States.[1]

[1] Commission on Industrial Relations, House Report 726, 62d Cong., 2d Sess., 2–3.

American mobilization for World War I greatly increased the power and prestige of organized labor. So urgent was the need for uninterrupted production that the government intervened more and more actively to prevent strikes. Even before the United States became a belligerent, the trend was clear. In the summer of 1916 the preparedness drive was seriously threatened when the railroad brotherhoods demanded an eight-hour day and management refused either to agree or to arbitrate. Alarmed lest this dispute result in a nationwide transportation tie-up, President Wilson appealed to the employers to grant the eight-hour day, which had "the sanction of the judgment of society in its favor." When management still refused to yield, Congress passed the Adamson Act, establishing eight hours as the standard workday for all railroad employees. The great strike was averted, but conservatives were shocked both by this "surrender" to the threats of labor and by the precedent of a Federal maximum-hour law.

Samuel Gompers, president of the American Federation of Labor, strongly supported the war effort. He combated radical pressure to use the "capitalist war" as an opportunity for militant proletarian demands. He urged the workers to refrain from striking and to demonstrate their loyalty to the democratic cause. On the other hand, he made it clear that organized labor expected the government to enforce fair labor standards and to include labor representatives on all defense agencies. As Gompers took his place with leading industrialists upon the Council of National Defense, labor assumed in many middle-class eyes a new status and a new respectability.

If strikes were to be avoided in a period of rapidly advancing prices, a mechanism was needed for the peaceful adjustment of industrial conflicts. In March, 1918, a conference at Washington, attended by representatives of management, wage earners, and the public, recommended that the President create a National War Labor Board to make recommendations in disputes where direct bargaining had failed. To guide such a board the conference laid down principles of great significance: there should be no strikes or lockouts during the war; the right of workers to organize in trade-unions and to bargain collectively should not be denied or interfered with by employers; employers should not discharge workers for membership in trade-unions nor for legitimate trade-union activities; employers should have a similar right to organize and to bargain collectively.

In accordance with these recommendations President Wilson appointed a National War Labor Board, composed of five representatives of employers, five of labor, and two chairmen, former President William Howard Taft and Frank P. Walsh, well-known liberal, to represent the public. Over the next sixteen months the Board considered some twelve hundred cases. Although not legally binding, its awards were usually accepted. In a few cases the government obtained compliance by threatening to cancel the war orders of recalcitrant employers or the draft deferments of defiant employees. In addition to preventing many strikes and shortening those that did occur, the Board did much to establish the principle of collective bargaining. In its wage awards it strengthened the principle that labor should receive wages adequate to support families in decency and that wage rates should be increased as the cost of living rose.

Although prices went up sharply during the war period, workers' wages increased enough to result in a small rise in real wages. Labor benefited even more from full employment, overtime bonuses, and greater opportunities for advancement. In most industries the standard work week became forty-four hours—eight hours a day with a Saturday half holiday. Some of these gains were made through direct government intervention; more resulted from the general wartime situation involving shortages of labor and the willingness of employers to accept increased costs in return for maximum production.

For some time after the armistice it seemed as if labor would continue to make rapid gains. Union membership continued to grow, rising from 2½ million in 1915 to 5 million in 1920. No longer restrained by the promise not to strike, the workers vigorously contended for union recognition, better working conditions, and pay raises to meet the soaring postwar cost of living. Over 4 million workers were involved in strikes during 1919—a number that would not be exceeded until 1946, another postwar year.

Employers' Counter Offensive

Many of the strikes of 1919 succeeded. Important victories were won by New York clothing workers, New York harbor workers, New England textile employees, New England telephone operators, and New York actors. But union militancy alarmed both employers and the general public, and strong countermeasures were soon forthcoming.

Labor suffered because of widespread fear of radicalism. In 1917 the Communists had captured control of Russia; in 1919 they were dangerously strong in Hungary, Germany, Italy, and other war-ravaged countries. Although the American Communist party was small, many excited citizens feared that the Reds were in control of the labor unions and were awaiting their opportunity to paralyze the nation's economy. The Red scare resulted in a rash of state laws against criminal syndicalism, wholesale arrest and deportation of alien radicals, and frequent mob action against the I. W. W., the Communists, the Anarchists, and even the Socialists.

In such an atmosphere any large and bitterly fought strike was likely to be attributed to Red intrigue. In February, 1919, the nation was shocked by a general strike in Seattle, Washington, where 60,000 trade-unionists quit their jobs to support the demands of their fellow workers in the shipyards. Although there was little disorder and the men went quietly back to work after five days, Mayor Ole Hanson gained much publicity for his lurid description of this attempt at "revolution," foiled by his own boldness.

A nervous public was ready to proclaim as a hero any public official who took strong action against labor demonstrations. Governor Calvin Coolidge of

Massachusetts gained the fame that elevated him to the Vice-Presidency by his firmness during the Boston police strike. This crisis resulted from an attempt of the Boston policemen to affiliate their social club with the American Federation of Labor. Regarding this as a breach of discipline, Police Commissioner Edwin U. Curtis suspended 19 of the leaders. On the night of September 9, 1919, the entire police force went on strike in protest against the commissioner's action. Fortunately, the orgy of crime to be feared when a great city was left without police protection did not materialize. The first night of the strike passed with only minor acts of vandalism, and units of the state guard and volunteers began to patrol the city the next day. Governor Coolidge's intervention did not occur until the third day of the strike when he called out the rest of the state guard and appealed to the Secretary of War for a promise of Federal troops in case a general strike was attempted. The policemen were now willing to return to their posts but were prevented by Commissioner Curtis, who announced his intention of dismissing the strikers and recruiting an entirely new force. When Gompers tried to intercede for the men, Governor Coolidge upheld the commissioner with a terse telegram: "There is no right to strike against the public safety by anybody, anywhere, any time."

Even the Wilson administration, usually sympathetic to labor, resorted to repressive measures. When 425,000 bituminous-coal miners struck on November 1, 1919, they encountered a generally hostile public opinion. On November 9, the government secured from a Federal district court a sweeping injunction ordering officers of the United Mine Workers to cease all activities tending to encourage or to maintain the strike. Although spokesmen for labor protested against this exercise of the government's emergency war powers a year after the end of hostilities, the newspapers applauded. John L. Lewis, recently elected president of the United Mine Workers, announced that the workers would submit. "We are Americans," he explained. "We cannot fight our government." Defying a back-to-work order, however, the miners stayed away from the pits until the operators agreed to submit the dispute to a special commission.

The key battle between labor and management was the great steel strike which began on September 22, 1919. The antiunion policy, which had dominated most of the steel industry since the Homestead strike, had been strengthened by the creation of the United States Steel Corporation in 1901. Although it was popularly believed that steelworkers were well paid, high wages were enjoyed by only a small group of skilled employees. Almost 40 per cent of the workers were common laborers who received average annual wages of less than $1,400 in 1919; another 30 per cent were semiskilled workers who received less than $1,800. Hours were notoriously long: the average for the industry was almost sixty-nine hours a week; one-half the employees worked a twelve-hour day; one-quarter of them worked seven days a week. In transferring from one shift to another, laborers often stayed on the job eighteen, twenty-four, or even thirty-six hours.

Failure to organize the workers reflected not only the antiunion policy of the employers but weaknesses in the unions themselves. Except for the United Mine Workers and a few other industrial unions the AFL was organized along the lines of skilled crafts. Twenty-four different national unions thus claimed jurisdiction over some segment of the steelworkers. Moreover, the majority of unskilled workers in the industry had no close affinity with any of the established crafts. In an attempt to overcome this difficulty, the twenty-four unions agreed in 1918 to cooperate through a National Committee for the Organizing of the Iron and Steel Industry. As many steelworkers as possible were to be signed up by the National Committee. The new recruits would then be distributed among the locals of the cooperating unions.

This strategy met with striking initial success. By June, 1919, the National Committee had enlisted about 100,000 workers. Eager for material benefits, the new unionists urged their leaders to formulate demands. The National Committee several times requested a conference with Judge Elbert H. Gary, chairman of the United States Steel Corporation, but he refused to meet them on the grounds that they had no authority to speak for his employees.

Labor's sense of grievance and management's refusal to negotiate made a strike inevitable. Rejecting President Wilson's last-minute appeal to postpone action, about 300,000 steelworkers walked out on September 22, 1919. The strike affected nine states and involved plants of independent companies as well as those of the United States Steel Corporation.

From the beginning the employers' most effective device was to convince the nation and the strikers themselves that the issue was one of radicalism versus loyalty to the United States. Full-page advertisements in the Pittsburgh newspapers carried such messages as this:

> The steel strike can't win. It is uncalled for and un-American. It is led by men who apparently are trying to establish the "red" rule of anarchy and bolshevism in this land of opportunity and liberty. The American institution of majority rule is threatened by a malicious, radical group of agitators. They are trying to throw hundreds of thousands of wellpaid, prosperous workmen out of employment because of the whims of a very small minority.
>
> Don't be fooled any longer. Stand by America and all that America means. Stick to your job and keep up "good times."
>
> GO BACK TO WORK

In raising the cry of Bolshevism, management was mightily assisted by the fact that the most active strike leader was William Z. Foster, already identified in the public mind as an extreme radical. Another circumstance, easily twisted to make the movement appear un-American, was the large proportion of immigrants from eastern Europe among the strikers.

Confident of the support of government and the general public, United States Steel used all its influence and resources to break the strike. Antiunion local officials—especially in western Pennsylvania—forbade public meetings and other strike activities. The Pennsylvania State Constabulary rode their horses into groups of strikers, clubbed them, and subjected them to arbitrary arrest and detention. Federal troops, sent into Gary, Indiana, to maintain order, restricted picketing to a minimum.

Meanwhile, the Corporation was making shrewd use of its many plants. Mills where the strike was effective were closed down while production was shifted to other places. Strikebreakers were used to resume operations in one city and then shifted to another. The purpose of these maneuvers was to convince the strikers that their revolt had failed and that they should go back to work while there was still a place for them in the industry. Since the independent steel companies willingly followed the lead of United States Steel, management fought the battle with a united front. Among the workers solidarity was less evident. The prominence of Negroes among the strikebreakers reflected resentment against discriminatory union membership policies. Scarcely less divisive were the mutual jealousies of skilled and unskilled workers, of native Americans and immigrants, and of rival craft unions. A back-to-work movement steadily gained strength, and on January 8, 1920, the National Committee finally acknowledged complete defeat and declared the strike at an end. Twenty lives had been lost—all but two of them strikers'.

The genuineness of the workers' grievances, never adequately understood during the strike, eventually received impressive documentation from the report of the commission of inquiry appointed by the Interchurch World Movement to investigate the situation. This distinguished group of Protestant clergymen, headed by Bishop Francis J. McConnell of the Methodist Episcopal Church, concluded that the strike had been a mass movement of protest against long hours and arbitrary management and that charges of Bolshevism or of industrial radicalism in the conduct of the strike were without foundation. Not only did the commission publish a detailed report upon working conditions in the industry, but it revealed how U. S. Steel had combated the organization of its employees through labor spies, discharge of union members, black-listing, and playing off one group of workers against another. Although conservatives now turned the cry of radicalism against the clergymen themselves, the report had enough influence upon public opinion to hasten the final elimination of the twelve-hour day in 1923.

Local manufacturers' associations, chambers of commerce, and specially organized groups agitated for the "open shop." Defined as the right of a worker to seek and to hold a job without being compelled to join a union, this slogan met a sympathetic response from many liberty-loving Americans. Farmers and white-collar workers never clearly understood that the most aggressive champions of the open shop were employers who wanted to weaken the unions by favoring nonunion men and discriminating against union members.

The open-shop drive gained a most effective slogan in January, 1921, when the National Conference of State Manufacturers' Associations, meeting at Chicago, voted to support what it called "the American Plan," under which workers "have the right to work when they please, for whom they please, and on whatever terms are mutually agreed upon between employee and employer and without interference or discrimination on the part of others." Many of the supporters of the American Plan frankly renounced the idea of collective bargaining. A representative of the Indiana Manufacturers' Association asserted: "We will not employ an individual in any part of the plant that does not sign an individual contract in which it is expressed that he is not and will not become a member of a labor organization while in our employ."

National, state, and local manufacturers' associations promoted the American Plan by newspaper advertisements urging customers to patronize the open shop. Employers having labor troubles were often assisted to obtain special guards and strikebreakers. Employers defying the open-shop drive were sometimes subjected to pressure from their bankers or suppliers of materials.

Many of the unions suffered crippling blows. When the Amalgamated Meat Cutters, goaded by successive wage cuts, went on strike against the great packing houses, they were badly defeated and lost all the ground that they had gained during the war. Following another unsuccessful strike, the Seamen's Union shrank to one-fifth its former size. In both conflicts the antiunion victories of the employers were aided by the depression of 1921, which created a situation far less favorable for labor solidarity than that during the war and postwar inflation. Also defeated in an attempt to protect their gains during hard times were the railroad shopmen. In 1922, when the Railroad Labor Board, which had been created by the Transportation Act of 1920, approved a second wage cut within twelve months, the shopmen rebelled in a nationwide strike, involving about 400,000 men. After the contest had continued throughout the summer, Attorney General Harry Daugherty obtained from a Federal district-court judge in Ohio a sweeping injunction forbidding union officers from engaging in activities that had, even in the remotest degree, any connection with the strike. The order failed to halt the struggle, but the strikers soon found it necessary to accept what terms they could get. Eleven of the roads signed agreements, but the others—including the great Pennsylvania Railroad—refused further recognition of the shopmen's union.

The Daugherty injunction was one more incident confirming labor leaders in the belief that the courts were hopelessly prejudiced against them. Supreme Court decisions between 1917 and 1923 upheld "yellow-dog contracts," [1] ruled that secondary boycotts were not protected by the Clayton Act, upheld the power of the courts to restrict picketing, invalidated state laws limiting the power of state courts to grant labor injunctions, and denied the power of Congress to pass

[1] A yellow-dog contract was one which an employer compelled an employee to sign as a condition of employment and in which the employee promised that he would not join a labor union or otherwise participate in concerted action.

a minimum-wage law for women and children in the District of Columbia. This series of defeats combined with other factors to overcome the AFL's traditional avoidance of third-party movements. In the 1924 election Gompers and other labor leaders supported the La Follette Progressive candidacy with its platform demanding popular election of all Federal judges, a constitutional amendment empowering Congress to pass laws over judicial vetoes, abolition of labor injunctions, and legal protection for labor's right to organize and to bargain collectively. Although La Follette received nearly five million votes, the AFL returned to more conservative political tactics after the election.

The drive for the American Plan was in its most aggressive phase between 1920 and 1923. During these years labor-union membership fell from 5,000,000 to 3,600,000. Heaviest losses were suffered in industries like packing, shipbuilding, and water and rail transportation, where the unions had expanded abnormally under government protection during the war. Although the building trades were hard hit in Chicago and San Francisco, the older craft unions were generally successful in holding their ground.

Union losses during the depression of 1921 were to be expected. The most unusual feature of the twenties was the failure of the unions to revive during the period of prosperity. In 1929 their total membership was less than 3,450,000—a shrinkage of 150,000 since 1923. The United Mine Workers lost ground as production shifted to nonunion fields in West Virginia, Kentucky, and Alabama. Attempts to unionize southern textile workers precipitated violent but unsuccessful strikes in Tennessee and South Carolina. Union defeats reflected not only the hostility of employers but weaknesses in the labor organizations themselves. The craft unions proved themselves incapable of organizing the mass-production industries, where workers were quickly trained on the job for assembly-line techniques. Yet the AFL continued to obstruct the growth of new unions composed of all the workers in particular industries. Samuel Gompers died in 1924, but William Green, who succeeded him, was equally conservative. The issue was unfortunately complicated by Communist attempts to bore from within the labor movement. Since William Z. Foster and other Communist agitators had adopted the industrial-union slogan, all attempts to adapt AFL organization to new conditions fell under suspicion.

Welfare Capitalism

Although employers continued to combat union organization through labor spies, arbitrary discharge, black-listing, and company police, their most effective device was to convince their employees that the latter's welfare was best secured through cooperation with management.

Companies now prided themselves on the clean and healthful working conditions that they provided and on their excellent cafeterias and recreation halls.

Many offered their employees group life- and disability-insurance policies and developed old-age pension plans. The foreman's arbitrary power was curbed, and responsibility for hiring, firing, and upgrading employees was vested with personnel departments, staffed with experts in labor relations. To encourage workers to think of themselves as partners in a joint enterprise, many corporations sold stock to their employees on the installment plan.

Such management devices might have been regarded with skepticism by the workers had they not been accompanied by a liberal wage policy. Many employers acted from no other motive than a desire to keep their employees reasonably contented. Others developed a more elaborate philosophy. They acknowledged that labor was entitled to higher pay as superior techniques increased productivity. They also recognized that increases in mass purchasing power expanded the market for automobiles, radios, and similar products. The real wages of American workers increased about 32 per cent between 1914 and 1928. Not all this gain was to be attributed to employer generosity. Many pay raises were wrested from unwilling managements by union action. The laborer's improved standard of living, moreover, rested to some extent on the farmer's misfortunes. Food prices lagged behind wages, thus contributing to the purchasing power of workers.

Among the most useful mechanisms of welfare capitalism were the so-called company unions. One of the best known of these was the Rockefeller Employee Representation Plan, adopted by the Colorado Fuel and Iron Company following serious labor strife in 1915. During American participation in World War I a great variety of company unions were established with the general approval of the War Labor Board. In 1919 about 500,000 workers were covered by such plans; in 1924 about 1,250,000; in 1928 about 1,500,000.

Company unions operated under a variety of names—employee-representation plans, employees' associations, industrial-relations plans, shop councils, work councils, industrial assemblies, company brotherhoods, good-will clubs, protective associations, industrial democracies. All had certain common features. They were subject to direct or indirect employer control; they were limited in membership to the workers in one company or plant. As a means of bringing grievances to the attention of management and of enlisting employee cooperation with management, they were very useful. As bargaining agents for the workers, they exercised little power. Usually financed by management, the company unions were impotent to conduct strikes and rarely negotiated contracts.

In order to prevent further losses, many old-line unions also emphasized cooperation with management. Under the widely copied Baltimore and Ohio plan the railroad management agreed to have as much work as possible done by union labor, and the union pledged to make the work as efficient and economical as it could. Management-union cooperation received another notable demonstration in the men's clothing industry, where the Amalgamated Clothing Workers were strong.

Restriction of Immigration

Fear of radicalism and "un-Americanism," which handicapped organized labor in many ways, nevertheless helped it to obtain one of its major goals—the drastic reduction of immigration. Although a literacy test had been enacted in 1917 over Wilson's veto, this dam was not trusted to hold back the flood of foreigners expected to pour out of war-ravaged Europe. In their demand for new legislation the AFL and other workers' groups received a great deal of support from employers' associations, whose desire for an ample supply of workers was now outweighed by fear of alien radicalism. Belief that the new immigration carried with it dangerous thought germs also permeated the Daughters of the American Revolution and other patriotic orders.

Restrictionists demanded a quota system to place rigid limits on the number of immigrants who might enter from any particular European country. They gained their first victory in 1921, when Congress passed the Emergency Immigration Act, limiting the number of aliens who might be admitted from any non-American country each year to 3 per cent of the foreign-born population of that nationality according to the census of 1910. The effect of this was to curb the new immigration very sharply and the old immigration not at all.

The Emergency Act was twice extended, and Congressional restrictionists, urged on by organized labor and patriotic societies, planned new curbs. The Immigration Act of 1924 reduced the quotas to 2 per cent of the foreign-born of each nationality according to the census of 1890—thus reducing the total number from about 350,000 to 164,000 while discriminating still more drastically against southern and eastern Europe. The new immigration, which had contributed 75 per cent of the total between 1901 and 1910, was now restricted to less than 13 per cent. Anti-Japanese prejudice resulted in a clause excluding all aliens ineligible for citizenship. Since Japanese immigration was already controlled under the gentleman's agreement and since the quota would have been only 100 in any case, the exclusion clause was a gratuitous insult which seriously injured Japanese-American relations.

The most extraordinary provision of the Immigration Act of 1924 was a section that provoked little discussion at the time. The quotas based upon the 1890 census were to be only temporary. The law went on to state:

> The annual quota of any nationality for the fiscal year beginning July 1, 1927, and for each fiscal year thereafter, shall be a number which bears the same ratio to 150,000 as the number of inhabitants in continental United States in 1920 having that national origin . . . bears to the number of inhabitants in continental United States in 1920, but the minimum quota of any nationality shall be 100.

To make such an analysis of the American population was obviously impossible. For three hundred years immigrants had come to America, intermarried, and bred children. How could the "national origins" of any one American be scientifically determined, to say nothing of those of 100 million? Senator Reed of Missouri characterized the formula as "idiotic, nonsensical, ridiculous, and absurd." The idea appears to have originated with Captain John B. Trevor, a wealthy former intelligence officer who had made a specialty of the immigration problem. Lobbying industriously, he had converted key legislators to the plausible contention that quotas should be based not on the number of foreign-born alone but upon the entire population. The real motivation of the proposal is suggested by Captain Trevor's estimates of quotas under his plan: the quota for Great Britain and Northern Ireland would be raised from 34,000 to 85,000, that for the Irish Free State would be reduced from 28,000 to 8,000, that for Germany would be cut from 51,000 to 20,000.

Captain Trevor's estimates were of course unofficial. Congress delegated the unenviable task of fixing the official quotas to the Secretaries of State, Commerce, and Labor. That these gentlemen disliked their assignment was soon apparent. In January, 1927, they transmitted to the President the preliminary report of a subcommittee of experts with the comment that "the statistical and historical information available raises grave doubts as to the whole value of these computations." In 1927 and 1928 Congress agreed to a postponement of the new quotas to give the secretaries more time to study the problem.

Meanwhile, publication of the preliminary findings of the experts gave the country its first real understanding of the issue. Although the official reports were somewhat less drastic than Captain Trevor's estimates had been, still it became obvious that the national-origins formula would reduce German and Irish quotas by almost one-half and Scandinavian quotas by two-thirds. Legislators with large Irish, German, and Swedish constituencies began to demand repeal of the national-origins provision, and this step was advocated by both Hoover and Smith during the presidential campaign of 1928.

Common sense, however, had little chance to operate. "Keep America American" was the slogan of an effective pressure group called The American Coalition, supported by dozens of patriotic organizations. Congress refused to repeal the provision, and Hoover reluctantly put the national-origins quotas into effect on July 1, 1929. The victory for "one-hundred percent Americanism" was complete: the Italians and the Poles had been strongly discriminated against in the laws of 1921 and 1924; the Germans and the Irish, in the policy of 1929.

For American social history the drastic restriction of immigration marks a decisive turning point. One of the principal forces influencing the composition of American society was all but terminated. Although considerable numbers of Canadians, Mexicans, Puerto Ricans, and other nonquota nationalities might still be added to the American melting pot, their effect could never be the equivalent of that of the large influx from Europe. Since the nation could hardly continue to absorb immigration at the prewar rate of 1 million a year, some control had been necessary. The actual form of restriction, however, was based upon unfortunate racial assumptions. That an immigrant from England was ten times as desirable as an immigrant from Italy or Poland was an absurd premise. All American history contradicted the assumption. Capacity for good citizenship was an individual quality, not an attribute of certain groups.

A New Deal for Labor

The great depression created serious suffering among workers. Unemployment, short hours, and pay cuts reduced earnings and threw millions of families on relief. On the whole, these disasters were met with remarkable fortitude. Radical demonstrations of protest seldom occurred. But quieter evidence of disillusionment was not lacking. Election returns indicated that the workers no longer believed that a vote for the Republican party was a vote for the full dinner pail. Nor did welfare capitalism seem to offer the final answer to the workers' aspiration for security.

Despite the changing mood labor unions were for the time being powerless to extend their influence. With 15 million unemployed few workers dared to risk their jobs by choosing this time to join a union. For the first time since 1916 total labor-union membership dropped below the 3 million mark in 1933. AFL leadership continued to be conservative. For the problems of the day it offered such unimaginative remedies as share-the-work movements and agitation for a thirty-hour week. Not until 1932 did the Federation reverse its earlier stand and endorse the principle of unemployment insurance.

Union conservatism had at least the merit of diluting the widespread suspicion of organized labor that characterized the early twenties. The Railroad Labor Act of 1926, abolishing the unsatisfactory Railroad Labor Board and substituting mediation machinery, recognized the right of the railroad workers to organize and to bargain collectively. Even more significant was the Norris-LaGuardia Anti-Injunction Act of 1932, declaring it to be the public policy of the United States that the worker should have "full freedom of association, self-organization, and designation of representatives of his own choosing" and that he should be "free from the interference, restraints, or coercion of employers." Yellow-dog contracts, being contrary to this declared policy, were no longer enforceable in Federal courts, and the conditions under which labor injunctions might be issued were strictly limited.

Labor's right to organize received still more effective protection under the New Deal. Section 7–A of the National Industrial Recovery Act of 1933 provided that every code of fair competition should contain the following conditions: (1) employees should have the right to organize and to bargain collectively through representatives of their own choosing without coercion from employers; (2) no employee should be required to join any company union or to refrain from joining a labor organization of his own choosing; (3) employers should comply with maximum hours of labor, minimum rates of pay, and other conditions of employment approved or prescribed by the President.

For the first time in many years unions dropped their defensive tactics and entered upon a spirited organizing campaign. John L. Lewis, whose United Mine Workers had suffered many defeats during the 1920's, took advantage of Section 7–A to increase membership in his organization from 150,000 to 400,000 between 1933 and 1935. In many industries the workers needed no propaganda from the national unions. In a grass-roots movement unparalleled since the days of the Knights of Labor, hundreds of local unions were organized without outside help, leaving to the AFL leadership the problem of how these new bodies would be accommodated within the old framework. Particularly significant was the eagerness with which auto and rubber workers now defied the traditional antiunion policy of their employers.

Industrialists were not disposed to surrender meekly to this assault. Still hostile to the whole idea of collective bargaining, the Ford Motor Company refused to accept the NRA automobile code. Other corporations accepted the codes but put their own interpretation upon Section 7–A. The number of company unions more than doubled between 1933 and 1935, and the number of employees covered by such plans increased from 1,263,000 to 2,500,000. A sinister development was the increasing patronage of detective agencies by management and the building up of private arsenals. A Senate Civil Liberties Committee, headed by Senator Robert M. La Follette, Jr., reported that from 1934 to 1936 General Motors spent almost a million dollars on private-detective services and that the Youngstown Sheet and Tube Company prepared for industrial warfare by purchasing 8 machine guns, 369 rifles, 190 shotguns, 109 gas guns, and 13,000 rounds of ammunition.

Since labor was restless and management defiant, the country was subjected in 1934 to over eighteen hundred strikes, involving almost 1½ million workers. NRA officials were caught between two fires. Employers accused them of creating trouble through their prolabor policies; workers, disgusted by NRA toleration of company unions and other evasions of the spirit of Section 7–A, ridiculed the agency as the "National Run Around." In an attempt to deal with the situation, President Roosevelt appointed a National Labor Board, but neither this body nor the first National Labor Relations Board, authorized by Congress in 1934, possessed adequate powers to make its rulings effective.

The situation was clarified in 1935, when the Supreme Court invalidated the NRA and Congress enacted the National Labor Relations Act—the so-called Wagner Act. To implement a general guarantee of labor's right to organize and to bargain collectively, the Wagner Act now specified a list of unfair labor practices. It was, for example, an unfair labor practice for an employer to dominate any labor organization or to contribute financial support to it, for him to encourage or to discourage membership in any labor organization, or for him to refuse to bargain collectively with the representatives of his employees. The law provided for the appointment of a new National Labor Relations Board with wide powers to compel testimony and to issue orders enforceable through the Federal courts. In case of dispute as to which representatives were the choice of a majority of employees, the National Labor Relations Board was authorized to take a secret ballot of the workers.

Relying on a belief that the Supreme Court, which had invalidated so many New Deal laws, would hold the Wagner Act unconstitutional also, many employers deliberately defied it. Company unions were fostered, antiunion propaganda was distributed, and workers were discharged for union activities. The inevitable result was a new wave of strikes in 1937, more serious than the conflicts of 1934.

Events soon proved that the industrialists had been badly advised by their lawyers. Not only was the constitutionality of the Wagner Act upheld by the Supreme Court, but the National Labor Relations Board was permitted to exercise broad powers. Employers who had followed the old tradition of discharging union members found themselves required to reinstate some 300,000 men with back pay totaling 9 million dollars. Company unions were liquidated or completely reorganized to make them genuinely independent. Between 1935 and 1945 the NLRB conducted some 24,000 elections through which about 6,000,000 workers had an opportunity to choose their bargaining representatives.

Although old-age pensions and unemployment insurance had been common for many years in Europe, Americans had shown little interest in such plans. The thrift and forethought of the individual were depended upon "to put something aside for a rainy day." The great depression proved how inadequate such savings might be to protect the individual against modern economic forces. Thousands of savings accounts were wiped out overnight by bank failures; thousands more were dissipated during months of unemployment. During the thirties all kinds of pension plans were eagerly agitated.

Congress responded to the new mood by passing the Social Security Act of 1935, providing for Federal-state cooperation in providing old-age pensions, unemployment insurance, public assistance to the needy aged, the blind, and dependent children, and an extension of additional aid for maternal and child welfare and public-health facilities. The law was essentially conservative, covering only certain groups in the population and providing rather niggardly benefits. But the principle was all-important. Government had accepted a responsibility to provide a cushion of protection against contingencies that had hitherto been left to individual responsibility or to charity. Subsequent legislation widened the coverage of the law and increased its benefits.

Old theories of individualism received another rude shock in 1938, when Congress passed the Fair Labor Standards Act. Applying to employees engaged in interstate commerce or producing goods for interstate commerce with certain specified exceptions, the act provided for wages of not less than 25 cents an hour and hours of not more than forty-four a week. These standards were to be gradually raised until a minimum wage of 40 cents an hour was reached in 1945 and maximum hours of forty a week in 1940. When the employee worked more than the maximum, he was entitled to time and a half for overtime. The act also forbade the employment of children under the age of sixteen in industries producing goods for interstate commerce.

AFL versus CIO

An aggressive minority within the AFL, led by John L. Lewis of the United Mine Workers, believed that the opportunity presented by the New Deal could only be effectively met by the establishment of new industrial unions in the mass-production industries. The issue came to an angry showdown at the Atlantic City convention of the AFL in 1935. The progressives attempted to secure approval for a resolution stating that

> . . . in those industries where the work performed by a majority of the workers is of such a nature that it might fall within the jurisdictional claim of more than one craft union, or no established craft union, it is declared that industrial organization is the only form that will be acceptable to the workers or adequately meet their needs.

But this proposal was voted down in favor of a conservative resolution emphasizing the need "to protect the jurisdictional rights of all trade unions organized upon craft lines."

In November, 1935, soon after this defeat, the minority leaders organized the Committee for Industrial Organization with Lewis as chairman. Professing to work for "educational and advisory" ends within the framework of the AFL, the new CIO planned an aggressive campaign to unionize the steelworkers. Green and other conservative leaders condemned this as an act of rebellion, and in 1936 the AFL voted to suspend 10 unions which were supporting the movement. A year later the unrepentant rebels were formally expelled. In 1938 the CIO, keeping its initials but changing its name to the Congress of Industrial Organizations, adopted its own constitution and elected Lewis president. Eventually, some forty national unions became affiliated with this branch of the labor movement.

Bitter strife resulted from CIO attempts to organize the automobile, rubber, electrical, meat-packing, and steel industries against stubborn employer resistance. Particularly controversial were the "sit-down strikes" of 1936 and 1937, in which the strikers remained in the plants instead of walking off the job and establishing picket lines. First used in the packing and rubber industries, the sit-down strategy received its most provocative trial in the CIO's battle for recognition from the General Motors Corporation. For six weeks in 1937 strikers remained in occupation of key plants in Flint, Michigan. Police attempting to interfere with the strikers were driven off with streams of water from the fire hoses and a barrage of bolts and door hinges. Determined to avoid bloodshed, Governor Frank Murphy refused to order the National Guard to evict the sit-downers, even after the corporation obtained a court order directing the strikers to evacuate company property. Through Murphy's mediation a settlement was finally reached, whereby General Motors agreed to accord limited recognition to the union, to rehire all the strikers, and to refrain from further discrimination against union members.

This widely publicized struggle and similar ones precipitated bitter controversy over the legitimacy of labor's new weapon. Those who defended sit-down tactics stressed management's notorious defiance of the Wagner Act and its wholesale resort to spies and company police. But most Americans were nevertheless shocked by labor's flouting of property rights. The Senate resolved that sit-down strikes were "illegal and contrary to public policy," and the Supreme Court condemned them in 1939. By this time, however, the CIO had largely abandoned the sit-down weapon in favor of strike tactics less likely to antagonize the public.

In the steel industry the CIO experienced both its sweetest victory and its bitterest defeat. The victory came in March, 1937, when the United States Steel Corporation announced the negotiation of contracts by all its subsidiary companies with the Steel Workers Organizing Committee. The most famous citadel of antiunionism in the country had been conquered without a strike through a skillful organizing campaign led by Philip Murray of the United Mine Workers. So eager to enlist were the steelworkers that many of the company unions themselves had been captured.

Although most of the other steel companies followed the lead of "Big Steel," the group of corporations known as "Little Steel"—Republic, Youngstown Sheet and Tube, Inland, and Bethlehem—elected to fight. In Tom M. Girdler, president of Republic Steel, the CIO encountered an old-fashioned captain of industry prepared to combine the strike-breaking tactics of Frick, Pullman, and Gary. Assisted by local officials and "citizens' committees," the steel companies broke up picket lines and organized back-to-work movements. Violence reached a peak on Memorial Day, 1937, when police killed 10 strikers and wounded more than a hundred outside Republic Steel's South Chicago plant. Lacking the support of the public, which had become frightened by CIO aggressiveness, the Steel Workers Organizing Committee eventually had to admit defeat. Little Steel's victory was short-lived. In 1941 the Supreme Court upheld a NLRB order requiring the companies to reinstate all employees who had been discharged because of union activity and to accept collective bargaining.

During the months before Pearl Harbor organized labor stood in a position of unprecedented strength. Compliance with the Wagner Act had been required by the courts in spite of management resistance. The unions had obtained contracts from scores of companies which had never before accepted the principle of collective bargaining. Even Ford negotiated a union-shop contract in 1941. Although the CIO was most often in the headlines, the AFL enjoyed a no less remarkable growth. Total union membership in 1941 rose to 10½ million—three and one-half times that of 1933.

The armies of labor continued to resist unified command. Numerous efforts to heal the AFL-CIO schism failed. As time went on, personal and institutional rivalries became more important than the old clash between craft and industrial unionism. Indeed, after the AFL had chartered new industrial unions to compete with those of the CIO and the CIO had retaliated with the organization of new craft unions, the old issue dividing the rival federations was largely obscured. One unfortunate result was an increase in jurisdictional conflicts. Most Americans were now willing to concede the legitimacy of strikes for recognition, higher wages, or shorter hours, but they were baffled and annoyed by work stoppages caused by disputes between rival unions.

Labor factionalism was intensified by the strong-willed individualism of John L. Lewis. Although originally a Republican, the CIO head gave Roosevelt strong backing in the election of 1936. But a succession of incidents soon broke up this alliance. Lewis blamed Roosevelt for not supporting the CIO more vigorously during the strikes of 1937. He criticized the President for not giving union men key posts in government and—so at least it was alleged—for not supporting Lewis's own aspiration for the Vice-Presidency. An outspoken isolationist, Lewis condemned Roosevelt's policy of aiding Britain and France after the outbreak of World War II. The climax came during the election of 1940, when the burly leader attempted to deliver the CIO vote to Willkie and the Republicans. Regarding the election returns as proof that most unionists had ignored his advice, Lewis resigned the CIO presidency and withdrew his United Mine Workers from the organization. For the next six years the Lewis union remained a powerful independent, threatening to create a third great labor empire through extension of District No. 50, a catchall for enlisting thousands of workers who had never seen a mine. In 1946 Lewis took the United Mine Workers back into the AFL; at the end of 1947 he pulled them out again. Although his leadership seemed arbitrary and dangerous to most outsiders, the nation's coal miners followed him without serious protest in gratitude for the many gains which he won for them.

Meanwhile, the CIO continued vigorously alive. Lewis was succeeded in the presidency by Philip Murray—once Lewis's lieutenant in the miners' union but now widely respected for his leadership of the steelworkers. Of equal prestige in CIO ranks was Sidney Hillman, the head of the Amalgamated Clothing Workers and leader of the powerful Political Action Committee, which was at the height of its effectiveness in the election of 1944.

Labor on the Defensive

The National Association of Manufacturers and other employer spokesmen never ceased to attack the Wagner Act as essentially unsound in that it prohibited the unfair practices of employers without condemning those of unions. At every session of Congress measures that would modify the law were proposed. A new wave of strikes in 1941—resented because they threatened the defense effort—

resulted in increasing public support for such proposals. Several states enacted measures regulating union activities, and a similar bill passed the national House of Representatives early in December, 1941.

Pearl Harbor postponed a showdown on the issue. Leaders of every faction of labor pledged their support in the great emergency. In many ways the pattern of developments repeated that of World War I. Once again a White House labor-management conference agreed on the principles of no strikes or lockouts and the submission of unsettled disputes to a National War Labor Board. Once again prominent labor leaders took their place beside leading industrialists in the war-production agencies.

Labor's war record was on the whole excellent. The great stream of production necessary for victory was made possible by many hours of overtime work. Aiding government efforts to curb inflation, employees put a large proportion of their extra earnings into war bonds. Despite certain misgivings on the part of employers fearful of losing their prerogatives, some five thousand labor-management committees were organized to increase production.

The National War Labor Board was one of the busiest war agencies. About 415,000 voluntary wage agreements received its approval, and some 20,000 disputes were referred to it for decision. Although it had no power to enforce its rulings, there were relatively few cases of noncompliance. In the most serious of these the President ordered government seizure of the struck plants in order to maintain production. Many of the NWLB decisions were of great importance as precedents for future labor relations. One of their most significant long-range results was to encourage nationwide wage patterns for different industries.

As in World War I, labor's no-strike pledge was not completely effective. In 1942 there were almost 3,000 work stoppages; in 1943 about 3,750; in 1944 almost 5,000. Reading these statistics, the general public was likely to get a picture of seriously interrupted war production. Actually, most of the strikes were local, involving relatively few workers, and were quickly settled. National union officers devoted much of their time to smoothing these local situations, trying to dissuade hotheaded workers from striking and to get those who had quit their benches to go back to work while their grievances were being adjusted through conference.

But patriotic Americans—especially parents with boys in the service—were distressed that there should be any wartime strikes. They were particularly indignant at the tactics of John L. Lewis, who defied the authority of the War Labor Board and treated President Roosevelt himself with scant respect. For six months during 1943 Lewis played a dangerous and provocative game, alternately calling his men out of the mines and sending them back again just in time to forestall drastic measures. In the end, he won most of the points that he had been contending for.

The coal strikes and other work stoppages that captured the headlines resulted in a new demand for curbs on labor. In June, 1943, Congress passed the Smith-

Connally War Labor Disputes Act, overriding the veto of President Roosevelt, who warned that the new law would make the situation worse rather than better. Increased powers were given to the National War Labor Board; thirty days' notice was required before a union could conduct a strike vote; government seizure of strike-bound war industries was authorized; criminal penalties were provided for persons who promoted a strike in government-operated plants or mines; and union contributions to political campaign funds were prohibited. Several states in the South and West passed laws restricting union activities still more stringently.

After the surrender of Japan in August, 1945, the country experienced a period of labor turmoil somewhat similar to that of 1919. The unions with membership now risen to 14½ million were determined to consolidate their gains; employers wanted to halt what they regarded as a dangerous trend toward union interference in matters that concerned only management. The unions demanded large increases in basic wage rates in order to maintain take-home pay after the loss of war overtime. They argued that such increases were necessary because of the increased cost of living and that employers could afford to pay them out of profits. Employers resisted these demands as excessive and claimed that they could not grant them without increasing prices and thereby contributing to inflation. An unhappy third party to all these disputes was the government, which was still trying to control wages and prices but received scant support from a public impatient with the continuance of wartime controls.

The postwar strikes of 1946 differed from those of 1919 in their closer adherence to a national pattern and in their lack of violence. Typical of the new day was the General Motors strike, which dragged on from November 21, 1945, to March 13, 1946, before a settlement was finally reached. Although almost 200,000 employees in 20 different states were involved, there was little disorder. The strikers, intelligently led by Walter Reuther, made no attempt to occupy corporation property. Instead they based their demands upon the persuasive slogan, "Open the Books"—contending that investigation of company profits would prove that wage raises could be made without increasing automobile prices. The corporation, in turn, made no attempt to operate its plants with strikebreakers but appealed for the support of public opinion in advertisements denouncing labor's threat to the free-enterprise system. Similar tactics were employed by 300,000 meat packers, 200,000 electrical workers, and 750,000 steelworkers, who struck for pay increases during January, 1946. The disputes were eventually settled on the basis of raises of about 18½ cents an hour—raises facilitated by government consent to a "bulge in the line" of price control. Despite this peaceful outcome the public was disturbed by these industry-wide work stoppages involving almost 2 million workers.

Antiunion feeling rose more menacingly in May, 1946. One storm center was the now familiar figure of John L. Lewis, who almost paralyzed the nation's industry and transportation with a bituminous-coal strike which lasted six weeks before Lewis consented to a "truce." A second storm center hovered over the Brotherhoods of Locomotive Engineers and Railroad Trainmen. Rejecting both the recommendations of a fact-finding board acting under the Railroad Labor Act of 1926 and a compromise suggested by President Truman, the two unions went out on strike on May 23, almost completely halting railroad transportation across the country. On the afternoon of May 25 the President made a dramatic appearance before a joint session of Congress to ask for drastic emergency legislation under which the government might proceed by injunction against union leaders in any emergency threatening the public welfare and might draft workers striking against the government in such disputes into the army. Interrupted by a special messenger during the reading of his address, the President announced that the union chiefs had accepted his recommendations and called off the strike.

For a time John L. Lewis avoided drastic government action by a policy of strategic retreat. From May to November, 1946, the bituminous-coal mines remained under the nominal control of the government, and the miners worked under a contract negotiated between Lewis and Secretary of the Interior Krug. In the end, however, the aggressive mine chief terminated the contract, which the government had refused to reopen, and the miners under the principle of no contract-no work left the pits on November 21. Their action was in direct defiance of an injunction issued by Federal District Court Justice T. Alan Goldsborough. On December 4 Justice Goldsborough found Lewis and the United Mine Workers guilty of contempt of court and imposed fines of $10,000 upon Lewis and $3,500,000 upon the union. In his protest against this return to strikebreaking by injunction, Lewis had the support of most of organized labor. But the Supreme Court ruled that the Norris-La Guardia Act did not bar the government from seeking an injunction in a situation in which the government had taken over an industry and in which the strike threatened the national welfare and security. The Court stipulated, however, that the fine against the union should be reduced to $700,000 on condition that Justice Goldsborough's restraining order was obeyed. Lewis complied in typical fashion. Although the strike was officially called off, he took advantage of a shocking mine disaster at Centralia, Illinois, to call upon the workers to halt work for one week as a period of mourning.

Government crackdowns on the railroad brotherhoods in May and on the miners in December gave warning of the seriousness of public resentment over what was regarded as wanton union disregard of the general welfare. The Republican election victory of November, 1946, was widely interpreted as another rebuke to labor. The new Congress proceeded to pass over President Truman's veto the Taft-Hartley Labor-Management Relations Act of 1947. To restore equality of bargaining between employers and employees, the basic rights guaranteed labor in the Wagner Act were now balanced by provisions protecting employers against such union practices as coercion of employees, refusal to bargain collectively, excessive membership fees, secondary boycotts, and jurisdictional strikes. Particularly drastic were provisions banning closed-shop contracts and permitting union-shop contracts only under rigid restrictions. Unions were required to give sixty days' notice for the termination of any agreement and might be sued for breach of contract. They were forbidden to make any expenditures for political purposes. Union officials were required to file affidavits certifying that they were not members of the Communist party.

The Taft-Hartley Act became a center of political controversy over the next several years. Employers' associations praised the law as a long-overdue reform. All branches of organized labor joined to denounce it as a diabolical scheme intended to hamstring their legitimate activities. The public gave no clear mandate on the issue. The Democratic election victory of 1948 was interpreted in some quarters as a repudiation of the Taft-Hartley Act, but when the new Congress failed to repeal or to amend the law, the voters showed no signs of resentment. On the contrary, Senator Taft's sweeping reelection victory in 1950 seemed to indicate that the voters of Ohio were not disposed to punish the principal author of the controversial measure. Meanwhile, there was evidence of growing support for a middle-of-the-road policy which would retain much of the Taft-Hartley Act but amend certain unfair and unworkable features.

Despite the hated Taft-Hartley Act the unions appeared to be holding their lines after World War II much better than they had after World War I. In 1949 total union membership was estimated to be about 16,000,000, including 8,000,000 in the AFL, 6,000,000 in the CIO, 600,000 in the United Mine Workers, and 1,400,000 in other unaffiliated unions. Although still centering their energies upon the traditional goals of higher wages and shorter hours, the unions now attempted a much broader program. They participated more vigorously in politics. In negotiating with employers, they placed much greater emphasis on pension plans and group-insurance benefits. Many innovations of welfare capitalism were now extended through union contracts rather than through unilateral action by management. The unions developed more ambitious educational and social programs for their own members and devoted more effort to improving their public relations.

Labor unions had at last won acceptance as basic American institutions. Open-shop drives of the 1921 pattern now had little chance of success. On the other hand, the public appeared unwilling to submit indefinitely to union policies that were regarded as antisocial.

Intelligent labor leaders realized that they could best avoid additional regulation by energetic housecleaning on their own part. In 1949 the CIO expelled the United Electrical Workers on the grounds that the union had become dominated by Communists; this step was immediately followed by an attempt to win over the rank and file of the old union to a new International Union of Electrical, Radio and Machine Workers that would be free of Communist influence. By this and similar steps Philip Murray and other CIO leaders attempted to purge their organization of a Communist minority that had attached itself to the movement during the thirties. Another needed reform was the expulsion from the labor movement of racketeers and other criminal elements who used local unions to extort protection money from unhappy businessmen. Although not characteristic of the union movement as a whole, these labor crooks seriously injured organized labor's reputation—especially when their activities were exposed by antiunion newspapermen like Westbrook Pegler. Friends of unionism hoped and believed that when unions no longer had to expend their strongest efforts in defending their right to exist, they would evolve toward more democratic internal organization, more interest in increasing productivity, and greater appreciation of the underlying community of interest between labor and all other groups in the nation.

Chapter 31. Search for Moral Anchors

Reading of atomic bombs and biological warfare, of concentration camps and the liquidation of entire social groups, of increasing suicide and insanity, religious people were sometimes skeptical of contemporary reform movements. Could men really win security from the hazards of twentieth-century civilization through improved technology, larger armies, old-age pensions, or world government? Was not the underlying crisis a moral one? Unless men renounced hate and learned to love, unless they rejected falsehood and spoke the truth, unless they conquered their selfishness and practiced benevolence, could the world be saved?

Challenges to Faith

Statistically the churches made a very satisfactory showing. The number of members reported by the various denominations increased more rapidly than the population—rising from 42 million in 1916 to 82 million in 1950. The statistics, however, are not entirely convincing. Returns for the earlier year appear to have been much less complete than for the later. Figures, moreover, give no indication of the quality of religious life or even of regularity of church attendance.

Ministers, priests, and rabbis expressed alarm at the rising secularism of American life. Without any formal revolt against religion many individuals lapsed into religious indifference. If they practiced their faith at all, the performance was perfunctory. Their real Sunday interests were golf and movies; their real weekday passions were making money and amusing themselves. Religionists were distressed by the cynicism and corruption that often seemed to pervade political and business life. Even more alarming was the decay of morals reflected in the statistics of divorce and juvenile delinquency.

In the case of many intellectuals the rejection of religion became explicit. So vast was the universe described by astronomers and physicists that it became difficult to believe that human destiny, either individual or collective, had any cosmic importance. "Astronomically speaking," wrote Harry Elmer Barnes in *The Twilight of Christianity* (1929), "man is almost totally negligible." To James Branch Cabell man seemed "a parasite infesting the epidermis of a midge among the planets," to Henry L. Mencken, "a sick fly" taking a dizzy ride on the whirling cosmos. Clarence Darrow felt that the most satisfactory part of life was the time spent in sleep, when one was utterly oblivious to existence, and the next best was the time when one was so absorbed in activities that he was altogether unmindful of self. The pessimism of the 1920's received its most uncompromising development in Joseph Wood Krutch's *The Modern Temper* (1929).

Some of the most disturbing ideas were derived from the relatively new science of psychology. Traditional concepts of the soul were challenged by theories that assumed that the mind was merely a function of the physical organism. In the simple system of John B. Watson's *Behaviorism* (1925) the mind was little more than a central switchboard for the nervous system, receiving stimuli and sending out automatic responses. Since men were completely conditioned by their early training and environment, the idea of moral choice—of men consciously deciding between good and evil—became an absurdity. Behaviorism was popularized through many channels. Novelists depicted their characters as the helpless creatures of their environment. Clarence Darrow took the idea into the courtroom in eloquent defenses of murderers on the ground that they were not responsible for their deeds.

In its more extreme statements behaviorism was a short-lived fad. Much more influential were the ideas associated with Dr. Sigmund Freud of Vienna, Austria. As early as 1900 Freud had developed a technique for the treatment of neurotic patients by what he called "psychoanalysis." This assumed that conscious mental activity constituted only a small portion of normal mental processes. Underlying the conscious was the "unconscious"—a chaotic reservoir of instinctive impulses. Emotional disturbances occurred when these unconscious instincts were repressed; psychoanalytic treatment assisted the patient to discover the source of conflict—often an episode in infancy—and to replace the unconscious mental act with a conscious one. Freud believed that the strongest of these instincts and the one most likely to suffer repression was the libido, or sexual impulse. The great Austrian's influence on American thought began in 1909 with an invitation to lecture at Clark University in Worcester, Massachusetts, and was soon extended through the efforts of A. A. Brill, who translated Freud's writings into English and founded the New York Psychoanalytical Society in 1911. After World War I Freud's ideas became the subject of eager discussion among American intellectuals. The talk of the sophisticated was now liberally salted with references to the libido, the id, the ego, and the superego. College students talked knowingly of Oedipus complexes, wish fulfillments, and phobias. Particularly alarming to moralists was popular Freudianism's emphasis on the sex impulse and on the danger of repressing it.

Modernists and Fundamentalists

Protestant liberals undertook to meet skeptics on their own ground. They accepted evolution as proved and went on to study the newer theories in physics and psychology. None of these, they contended, conflicted with essential religion. Dr. Harry Emerson Fosdick stated the liberals' central affirmations in seemingly orthodox terms—"the living God, the divine Christ, the indwelling Spirit, forgiveness, spiritual renewal, the coming victory of righteousness on earth, the life everlasting." But he insisted that the ancient truths must be stated in new terms:

> Liberalism is not a negative movement; it is a positive campaign to maintain vital religion in the face of materialistic and paganizing influences of our time. Instead, however, of barricading ourselves in the citadel of pre-scientific theology, we are convinced that the only way to victory is to take the field. If we are to persuade this younger generation, we must meet materialistic philosophy on its own ground, fight it with its own intellectual weapons, beat it at its own game. We must make Christianity intelligible to people of the twentieth century, as our Protestant forefathers made their Christianity intelligible to people of the sixteenth century. . . .[1]

In making religion more acceptable to the new generation, the modernists challenged many of the older ideas. They discarded "man-sized representations" of God—of a God who walked in the garden at the cool of the day, made woman from man's rib, and decreed a flood to drown humanity. They offered natural explanations or gave symbolic interpretations for miracles. They rejected the idea of the inerrancy of the Scriptures. The Bible, wrote Dr. Fosdick, is "the supreme Book of spiritual life." It gives a valid revelation of the character and the will of God. But to use it as a scientific textbook is "perilous nonsense which does far more harm to religion than to anything else."

Modernism was particularly strong in the great theological seminaries of the East and Middle West. Inevitably the youthful graduates of these institutions carried the new teachings to thousands of churches—often to the bewilderment of their parishioners.

Even before World War I religious conservatives had been aroused by these modern trends. In Chap. 25 the influence of Bible conferences, Bible institutes, and the publication of *The Fundamentals* has been described. World War I stimulated the conservatives to new militancy. Many earnest religionists regarded the great conflict as a fulfillment of Biblical prophecies and a sign of the imminent second coming of Christ. The war, moreover, encouraged suppression of unorthodox opinions, whether political or intellectual. Higher criticism was particularly vulnerable, since it could be traced to German origins. "We ought to make war," declared the Reverend Courtland Myers, "against foreign innovation into our religious world. . . . Go back to the fountain head and you will find that your crimson stream has its source in the rank German theology that has been forcing its way into the veins and arteries of all our religious life. We ought to fight it to the finish."

In 1919, 6,000 enthusiastic fighters for old-time religion met in convention at Philadelphia and organized the World's Christian Fundamentals Association. For the next decade the Association remained active, organizing national and regional

[1] Harry Emerson Fosdick, *Adventurous Religion and Other Essays* (Harper, New York, 1926), 246–247.

conferences and sending out speakers to sound the alarm against the enemies of orthodoxy. The fundamentalists called for a purging of modernist professors from colleges and seminaries, for more careful scrutiny of the theological beliefs of men sent into the missionary field, and for stricter standards of orthodoxy within the several denominations.

FIG. 50. *Baptism in Kansas.* Painting by J. S. Curry. Captures the spirit of simple piety in rural religion. (*Collection of Whitney Museum of American Art.*)

Among the Baptists were to be found outstanding leaders of both the modernist and fundamentalist factions. Harry Emerson Fosdick and Shailer Mathews, dean of the University of Chicago Divinity School, represented liberal Protestantism at its best; William B. Riley of Minneapolis and John Roach Straton of New York were tireless fighters for the old ideas. Throughout the early twenties the annual sessions of the Northern Baptist Convention were enlivened by clashes between the two camps. The conservatives tried to impose a strict creed upon the denomination but were voted down—not because they were necessarily in a minority, but because their demand ran counter to such historic Baptist principles as the complete autonomy of local churches and the right of individual interpretation of the Scriptures.

The Presbyterians were disturbed by somewhat different issues. Doctrine had already been defined in the historic Westminister Confession. But conservatives and liberals differed on the extent to which literal acceptance of the creed should be forced upon the ministers. One center of controversy was Dr. Harry Emerson Fosdick, who, although a Baptist, was serving as minister of the First Presbyterian Church of New York City. In 1922 Fosdick aroused excited controversy by a sermon entitled "Shall the Fundamentalists Win?" in which he disclaimed the dogma of the inerrancy of the Bible, regretted the stress being laid upon the virgin birth and the second coming of Christ, and pleaded for a policy of Christian tolerance. For the next two years the Fosdick case divided the denomination. The conservative presbytery of Philadelphia denounced Fosdick's preaching as heretical; the liberal presbytery of New York defended him. In 1924 the judicial commission of the church ruled that Fosdick must take the vows of a Presbyterian minister or vacate his pulpit. Declining to subscribe to the Westminister Confession because it would be "a violation of conscience and a moral surrender," Fosdick resigned his Presbyterian pastorate and became minister first of the liberal Park Avenue Baptist Church and later of the beautiful new Riverside Church, built through the generosity of the Rockefellers.

Presbyterian modernists and fundamentalists continued to clash on many issues. Up to 1925 the conservatives had the upper hand, but after that date a more liberal spirit prevailed. The fundamentalists lost one of their most cherished strongholds in 1929, when Princeton Theological Seminary was reorganized over their objections. As a result, Professor J. Gresham Machen, the most scholarly of fundamentalist leaders, resigned from Princeton and founded the rival Westminister Theological Seminary in Philadelphia.

In varying forms the controversy was carried into other denominations. Dr. Percy Stickney Grant, an Episcopal rector of New York City, was rebuked by Bishop William T. Manning for his denial that Jesus Christ had the power of God. But bishops themselves might harbor modernist ideas, as was made evident by the publication of *Fifty Years* (1923), in which Bishop William Lawrence of Massachusetts questioned the doctrines of the virgin birth and the bodily resurrection of Christ. A pastoral letter issued by the Board of Bishops in 1923 reasserted the doctrinal authority of the historic creeds, but liberalism was too strongly entrenched among the Episcopal clergy to permit drastic disciplining of individual modernists.

The fundamentalists gained their greatest popular support for a crusade to drive the teaching of evolution from the schools. William Jennings Bryan, seasoned campaigner against the gold standard, imperialism, war, and rum, fought his last vigorous battle against modern science. In his demand for state laws to prohibit the teaching of evolution in the public schools, he had the enthusiastic support of William B. Riley, John Roach Straton, and other leading fundamentalists.

In March, 1925, the Tennessee legislature passed a law making it a criminal offense for "any teacher in any of the universities, normals and all other public schools of the State, which are supported in whole or in part by the public school funds . . . to teach any theory that denies the story of the Divine creation of man as taught in the Bible, and to teach instead that man has descended from a lower order of animals." John Thomas Scopes, a young high-school teacher of Dayton, Tennessee, obligingly violated the law to provide the grounds for a test case. Assisting the prosecution when the trial opened in July, 1925, was the great Bryan in person; assisting the defense were such well-known lawyers as Clarence Darrow, Dudley Field Malone, and Arthur Garfield Hays, dispatched to the front by the American Civil Liberties Union. Scopes became a forgotten man at his own trial, while the courtroom audience cheered the passages at arms between Darrow and Bryan. By putting Bryan on the stand as an expert on the Bible, Darrow tried to demonstrate the absurdity of fundamentalist ideas. But militant rationalism was not popular in rural Tennessee. Judge, jury, and audience sympathized with the champion of the Bible. Scopes was convicted and fined $100. In an anticlimactic decision the following year the Tennessee Supreme Court upheld the constitutionality of the antievolution law but reversed the conviction on a technicality.

For the moment fundamentalism seemed to be strengthened by the Dayton trial. Not only did the conservatives win a victory, but they gained a martyr. The sudden death of Bryan was attributed to overexertion in his great battle for the Lord. Almost a million dollars was pledged for a most appropriate memorial—a university in Dayton, Tennessee, to bear the great Commoner's name and constitute a citadel of fundamentalist education. The drive for antievolution laws was carried to a score of states by the Flying Fundamentalists, a group that included Riley and Gerald Winrod of Kansas. Within four years of Bryan's death antievolution laws were enacted in Mississippi, Arkansas, and Texas.

Yet the fundamentalist victory at Dayton had not been as complete as the conservatives liked to believe. Millions of church members had been painfully impressed by the spectacle. Religion had been made to look ridiculous—and on issues that had little to do with essential Christianity. Quietly but effectively moderates in each denomination insisted that the controversy be quieted and that the churches devote their energies to more fruitful activities. Depression and war soon presented problems of such urgency that the old quarrel was largely forgotten. Fundamentalism's most obvious legacies were a crop of Bible schools where ministers could be trained without going to the suspected seminaries and a number of independent foreign missionary organizations founded by conservatives who disapproved the larger missionary boards.

Ku Klux Klan

The fear of dangerous ideas, which had given force to the campaigns to suppress radicalism, to restrict immigration, and to combat the theory of evolution, found its most sinister embodiment in the Ku Klux Klan.

This was not the Klan of Reconstruction days, long since extinct, but a new organization founded on Thanksgiving night, 1915, when Colonel William Joseph Simmons, salesman, preacher, and promoter of fraternal orders, administered the oath of the "invisible empire" to a group gathered on Stone Mountain near Atlanta, Georgia. Although Imperial Wizard Simmons dedicated his Knights to such persuasive ideals as protection of the home and the chastity of women, maintenance of white supremacy, and conservation of pure Americanism, the organization at first grew slowly. In 1920, when the Klan had only about five thousand members, mostly in the southern states, Simmons engaged the services of Edward Y. Clarke, a publicity man of wide experience. The new "imperial kleagle" organized a membership drive of extraordinary effectiveness. Local kleagles recruited energetically out of enthusiasm not only for 100 per cent Americanism but for the $4 which they were permitted to pocket out of each $10 initiation fee. The balance provided a good income for the miscellaneous kleagles, goblins, and wizards, who composed the higher echelons of the empire. Unfavorable publicity and internal friction led to a reorganization in 1922, through which Simmons and Clarke were ousted and Hiram Wesley Evans, a Texas dentist, became imperial wizard. But this palace revolution did not shake the loyalty of the rank and file. The Klan continued to grow, attaining an estimated 4½ million members in 1924. Although fiery crosses burning on hillsides, hooded figures parading through city streets, and other signs of Klan activity were to be seen in every section of the country, the invisible empire had its greatest strength in the South, in the Middle West, and on the Pacific Coast.

The Klan appealed to natural joiners—Americans of a familiar type, easily recruited to any fraternal order and particularly attracted by one so liberally endowed with mysterious titles, secret passwords, and outlandish costumes. The movement also attracted the superpatriots—those inflamed against German spies and Reds during the war and now easily convinced that the nation was gravely threatened by other forms of un-Americanism. Above all, the Klan took advantage of deep-seated prejudices against Negroes, Jews, and Catholics.

In 1921 the New York *World* accused the Klan of responsibility for 4 killings, 1 mutilation, 1 branding with acid, 41 floggings, 27 tar-and-featherings, 5 kidnapings, and 43 persons driven into exile. Klan spokesmen denied that their order sanctioned such acts of violence. Whether or not this was so, both Klan propaganda and the Klan practice of donning robes and hoods for midnight demonstrations encouraged terrorism. Self-righteous local groups took it upon themselves to discipline bootleggers, loose women, labor agitators, and Negroes who forgot "their place."

Such crude acts of violence, however, were less characteristic of the Klan than other activities. Catholic and Jewish businessmen were boycotted; Catholic and Jewish workers found it difficult to obtain jobs. Schoolteachers and ministers bold enough to criticize the secret order were ostracized or ousted from their positions. Ambitious politicians accepted Klan membership cards and welcomed Klan election support. Politically powerful in a dozen states, the Klan almost completely dominated the Indiana state government and was overthrown only after the local Klan boss Daniel C. Stephenson landed in prison on conviction of abducting and murdering a girl.

The Stephenson scandal and similar revelations of crime and graft greatly damaged the Klan's reputation as the champion of law and morality. The best elements in the movement—those who had joined out of an honest, if confused, sense of patriotism—dropped out. Many others deserted the order, because they believed that they had been bilked by avaricious promoters or because the novelty and excitement had worn off. In 1928 Imperial Wizard Evans tried to revive the movement by ordering the Knights to unmask, but as an open society the Klan had still less appeal.

To compete with the declining order, several similar societies sprang up. Former Imperial Kleagle Clarke attempted to promote The Supreme Kingdom, dedicated to combating evolutionary ideas and modernism; Gerald Winrod sought the same ends in his Defenders of the Christian Faith. Borrowing both from the Klan and from foreign fascist agitations, William Dudley Pelley's Silver Shirts were organized in 1933. The new mood was more conducive to anti-Semitism than to anti-Catholicism. So far in this direction had the wheel of intolerance turned by 1938 that the Klanlike Christian Front, followers of Father Charles E. Coughlin of Royal Oak, Michigan, appealed mostly to Irish Catholics. Youthful hoodlums in eastern cities wrote anti-Jewish slogans on sidewalks and walls, assaulted Jewish schoolboys, and overturned tombstones in Jewish cemeteries.

The Noble Experiment

Evangelical Protestants greeted with fervent thanksgivings the news that the Eighteenth Amendment had been declared in effect January 16, 1920. National prohibition, they were convinced, would destroy the evil influence of the saloon, save millions of men from crime and insanity, and improve the lot of women and children. Few doubted that the decision was final. Whatever their personal sentiments, politicians displayed awesome respect for the political power of the Anti-Saloon League, the Woman's Christian Temperance Union, and other dry organizations. Although the antisaloon forces had their strongest support in the churches, they found willing allies among employers eager to increase production and to solve the problem of Monday hang-overs and among progressives disgusted by the close alliance between the liquor trade and corrupt politics.

It soon became obvious, however, that the problem of enforcement was much more complex than anyone had realized. Along the great stretches of Atlantic, Pacific, and Gulf coasts it was easy for liquor vessels to hover just outside American territorial waters and to deliver their cargoes to speedy motorboats; for the Coast Guard to intercept the rumrunners was difficult. Similarly arduous was the task of patrolling thousands of miles of Canadian and Mexican border. Liquors manufactured within the United States for sale as medicine on doctors' prescriptions were easily diverted to illicit channels. Industrial alcohol was—with more or less success—freed of its nauseous additions and flavored for sale as "rye" or "gin." Since near-beer—beer with less than 0.5 per cent alcoholic content—had to be produced by dealcoholizing real beer, further opportunities for evading the law were provided. Largest of all and most difficult to eliminate was the manufacture of liquor in clandestine establishments ranging in size from the basement still to the distillery or brewery that filled a lonely barn, an empty warehouse, or an abandoned factory.

Bootleggers delivered mysterious packages to individual customers and whole truckloads of intoxicants to speak-easies and private clubs. Despite their usual tawdriness the speak-easies possessed a fascination for their clientele. To know the secret address, to pass the scrutiny of the sharp-eyed doorman, to wonder whether the establishment might be raided at any moment surrounded drinking with an atmosphere of excitement and adventure. Observers disputed vigorously whether there was more or less consumption of liquor under prohibition than there had been in earlier days. What could not be denied was that the drinking of the twenties represented a much greater degree of moral revolt. To drink became something more significant than the mere gratification of an appetite; it became a conscious gesture of protest against what was regarded as an unwarranted interference with personal liberty.

Prohibition's most alarming result was to foster the growth of organized crime. Law-defying gangs had operated in American cities for many years, plundering the community through robbery, extortion, and the operation of gambling rooms, houses of prostitution, and other illegal establishments. But conditions in the twenties offered criminals an opportunity to greatly extend their operations. Bootlegging constituted a multimillion-dollar business unsanctioned by the law and perfectly adapted for gangster control. Automobiles and trucks provided vehicles capable of transporting members of the underworld and wholesale lots of whisky and beer across the countryside at breakneck speed. Most sinister of all were the deadly weapons—revolvers, sawed-off shotguns, and machine guns—readily procured by desperate men.

Organized crime found its capital in Chicago, where "Scarface Al" Capone amassed a fortune estimated at 20 million dollars. Some 10,000 Chicago speak-easies contributed to Capone's profits. He commanded a private army of several hundred henchmen, ready at an instant's notice to bomb the premises of a recalcitrant customer or to assault or kill rival gangsters trying to "muscle in" on Capone's territory. Some five hundred gang murders occurred in Chicago during the twenties, and most of them went unpunished. New York and other large cities struggled with crime problems scarcely less serious.

The immunity which gangsters seemed to enjoy gave eloquent testimony to the close tie-up between organized crime and corrupt politics. Out of crime's huge profits came large sums to bribe policemen, prosecutors, mayors, and judges. Earnest citizens' committees agitated for reform but hardly knew where to begin the housecleaning. Not until the G men of the Federal Bureau of Investigation took up the problem in the early thirties were effective steps taken to curb the reign of lawlessness. Capone himself was finally arrested and sent to prison for evading—of all things—the Federal income tax.

Prohibition, still politically secure in 1928, suffered a catastrophic drop in popular support during the next four years. Millions of moderates, who had been supporting the drys because they believed that prohibition would improve social conditions and increase industrial efficiency, now decided that the experiment had created more problems than it had solved. The reversal of opinion was hastened by the Great Depression, which provided plausible reasons for legalizing the liquor business to provide a market for the farmers' grain and a source of revenue for the deficit-harassed government. More important than any specific argument arising out of hard times was a loose identification of prohibition with the Republican party, welfare capitalism, and other idols of prosperity. Liberally provided with money by the Du Ponts and other wealthy industrialists, the Association Against the Prohibition Amendment defeated the Anti-Saloon League at its own game—carrying on a ceaseless agitation and lining up votes in Congress and the state legislatures. Two weeks before Roosevelt's inaugural Congress approved the Twenty-first Amendment, providing for the repeal of the Eighteenth. On December 5, 1933, the thirty-sixth state ratified the new amendment, and the prohibition experiment came to an inglorious end.

The wet victory was so complete that the victors felt little need to fulfill their pledge against the return of the old evils. The new tavern looked much like the old saloon—unless the disappearance of sawdust from the floor and the appearance of stools before the bar were to be counted as major reforms. Distillers conducted great advertising campaigns to convince readers that men of distinction drank their products, and brewers assailed the ears of radio listeners with enthusiastic descriptions of the mellowness of their beers and ales.

Drys hoped that such excesses would swing the pendulum toward prohibition again. The Woman's Christian Temperance Union agitated for restrictions on liquor advertising and other regulatory devices. Without winning any spectacular success, the drys were able to stabilize their lines and to gain back a little lost ground through state and local action.

A growing body of American opinion held that alcoholism was a serious national problem but that prohibition was not the answer. In 1938 the Research Council on Problems of Alcohol was organized in an attempt to apply scientific method to an issue long obscured by emotionalism. The Council approached alcoholism as a public-health problem rather than as a question of morals or crime. It pointed out that of 50,000,000 Americans who used alcoholic beverages, approximately 6 per cent became excessive drinkers and that of the excessive drinkers about 25 per cent became chronic alcoholics. This meant about 750,000 chronic alcoholics in the United States—more than the number of active cases of tuberculosis. About 13,500 of these developed alcoholic psychosis, or alcoholic insanity. Yet society scarcely recognized alcoholism as a disease. Hospital provisions for treatment were almost nonexistent. The Council recommended research, more adequate hospital services and other facilities for treatment, education concerning the nature, treatment, and prevention of alcoholism, and control measures based on accurate scientific data.

During the forties the new approach to the old problem appeared to be making progress. At the Yale School of Alcohol Studies and at similar institutions intensive research was instituted. The legislatures of New Jersey, Connecticut, New Hampshire, and Alabama provided modest appropriations for the rehabilitation of alcoholics. Most effective in meeting the problems of individual victims was Alcoholics Anonymous, an organization founded in 1938 through which former alcoholics gave each other moral support in maintaining abstinence and helped other unfortunates to straighten out their lives.

Any assumption that the organized crime problem would be automatically cured by repeal soon proved erroneous. Despite the legalization of the liquor trade and FBI arrests of prominent gangsters, the country continued to pay heavy tribute to the professional criminal. The full extent of the situation was not widely recognized until the spring of 1951, when millions of Americans watched the televised hearings of a Senate crime-investigating committee, headed by Senator Estes Kefauver of Tennessee. Through the testimony of a procession of reluctant witnesses the general public could piece together a picture of great crime syndicates with capitals in New York and Chicago and branches throughout the whole country. With the same organizing genius that other men applied to legitimate business, members of the underworld accumulated fortunes through the consolidation of chains of gambling resorts, houses of prostitution, abortion rings, and racketeering labor unions. Many key figures were revealed to be not scar-faced thugs with prison records but respectable-looking men living in quiet neighborhoods and maintaining close acquaintainceships with businessmen and politicians.

Although an aroused public might obtain the passage of increased appropriations for law enforcement and stricter legislation, it seemed unlikely that the crime situation could be materially improved until the average citizen decided to use his ballot to support honest city administrations. He would also have to curb the instinct to try to get something for nothing through placing bets on the horses or trying to guess the figures in the United States Treasury balance—or some other occult number selected for the "policy racket"—thus supporting the big gambling syndicates.

Morals and the Family

Throughout the twenties the "revolt of youth" was a favorite topic of discussion. Magazines and newspapers published sensational articles, and popular novelists presented the theme in fictional form. Ministers, priests, and rabbis deplored the trends of the times.

Many things causing distress to the moralists were of secondary importance. Skirts, which had long trailed in the dust or hung about the ankles, became shorter and shorter until in 1927 they scarcely covered the knees. Short sleeves and low necks came into vogue; evening gowns were often sleeveless and almost backless. Beneath these dresses much less was worn than had formerly been considered proper. Petticoats and corsets were abandoned; stockings were often rolled. Bobbed hair—considered prima facie evidence of radicalism or eccentricity before 1918—became increasingly popular. Rouge and lipstick, long regarded as the badges of the hussy, were now liberally applied by women of all classes.

Even more difficult for conservatives to accept was women's increasing use of cigarettes and liquor. Before World War I only the most sophisticated and the most rustic women smoked. Now the habit was boldly adopted by other groups. To drink was considered more daring than to smoke, yet an increasing proportion of the bootlegger's product was imbibed by women. At private parties and at speak-easies wives drank with their husbands and unmarried women with their male escorts. College authorities worried over the pocket flasks freely passed among students of both sexes at football games and dances.

Youth's passion for dancing to the sound of moaning saxophones and throbbing drums also caused concern. To many elders the new music itself seemed immoral, and the close embrace of couples dancing cheek to cheek was shocking in the extreme. One sensation gave way to another. Youths already adept in the fox trot were presently learning the complicated contortions of the "Charleston" and the "black bottom." The culminating inanity was marathon dancing, in which weary couples shuffled around dance floors for days and weeks in pursuit of notoriety and prizes.

Parental authority was visibly slackening. The one or two children of the typical middle-class family were indulged in a way that would have been impossible in the larger and poorer families of an older generation. Younger children had more toys, older children more privileges. Many teen-age boys demanded and had the use of the family car. Worried fathers and mothers were left at home to spend restless nights wondering what their children were doing and at what hour of the morning they would come in. They knew only too well how tragically juvenile mixtures of alcohol and high speed sometimes ended. Equally a cause for anxiety was the popularity of the "petting party." Girls now sallied forth on "dates" without the encumberance of chaperons and often spent much time parked on secluded lanes. Petting developed its own code of unwritten rules. Girls who would not kiss at all and girls who permitted themselves to be kissed too easily were both subject to male disapproval. On the girls, moreover, was placed the principal responsibility for keeping a potentially dangerous game within bounds.

In many of its manifestations the moral revolt of the twenties was merely another chapter in the story of the emancipation of women. In earlier generations women had gained equality in property rights, in educational opportunities, in the professions, and in the right to vote and to hold office. Now they had abbreviated their dress, bobbed their hair, and adopted rouge and lipstick in defiance of older conventions. Men had long reserved a right to sow their wild oats—to smoke, to drink, and to make love. Women were now demanding similar privileges.

Underlying this transition in manners and customs were more serious moral issues. In an earlier generation talk about sex was unthinkable in mixed groups. Men told other men off-color stories or boasted of their exploits, but nice women never referred to such subjects except among themselves and then in the most indirect manner. Girls received sex information only from their mothers, and such explanations were usually vague and embarrassed. All was different among the sophisticated young people of the "jazz age." To talk about sex frankly was to demonstrate one's modernity. To display familiarity with the language and point of view of Freud was even smarter.

Just how much of this preoccupation with sex was mere talk and how much found outlet in actual experiment no one really knew. Optimists asserted that there were no more irregular sexual relations than there had always been; the only difference was that such affairs were kept less secret. Pessimists painted a lurid picture of a complete breakdown in morals. The truth obviously lay somewhere between. Probably the most significant change was the erasure of the sharp distinction that had formerly existed between "nice" women and "bad" women. The double standard tended to disappear as women claimed the right to be judged no more harshly than men for the same offense.

The morals of the married aroused controversy no less serious than did those of the unmarried. The trend toward smaller families, already well established during the nineteenth century, was still strong. The birth rate, which had declined to 27 per thousand population in 1910, dropped to less than 24 in 1920 and less than 19 in 1930. In 1933, during the Great Depression, the rate dropped to 16.6. Although the declining number of births reflected such factors as the separations of wartime, the increasing number of divorces, and later marriages, the most important cause was indisputably the more general practice of birth control.

Religious leaders differed sharply on the moral issues involved. In an encyclical on *Christian Marriage* issued in 1931 Pope Pius XI strongly condemned the limitation of families by any other method than continence. Before World War I Protestant ministers also censured birth control; during the next decade many of them gave the practice cautious approval. In 1931 the Committee on Marriage and Home of the Federal Council of Churches issued a statement on *Moral Aspects of Birth Control.* A majority concluded that "the careful and restrained use of contraceptives by married people is valid and moral," but a minority held to the opinion that abstinence was the only moral method of family limitation.

Despite much opposition reformers carried on an aggressive campaign to extend birth-control information among the lower income groups and to secure the repeal of Federal and state laws that stood in the way of this practice. It was argued that the proper spacing of pregnancies would save the lives and health of mothers, assure better care for children, and prevent the poverty created by excessively large families. Birth control's most aggressive crusader was Mrs. Margaret Sanger, who founded the American Birth Control League in 1921. A permanent clinic was established in New York City in 1923, and others were soon founded elsewhere. In 1930 there were 81 free clinics; in 1944 there were 783. Except in Massachusetts and Connecticut, where Catholic influence was particularly strong, the laws were liberalized to recognize the right of physicians to give out birth-control information and materials. Several states went beyond neutrality to give the movement active support. In 1938 North Carolina began to organize birth-control clinics as a part of its public-health program for low-income families, and six other southern states soon followed.

Interestingly enough, with the birth-control fight all but won, there was some shift of emphasis toward encouraging larger families for those able to afford them. Increasing attention was given to the problem of married couples who wanted children but had not been able to have them. Through medical advice and treatment many of these were helped. In 1942 the Birth Control Federation changed its name to Planned Parenthood Federation of America. During the forties babies appeared to be increasing in popularity. The birth rate, depressed by war separations to an all-time low of 10.6 per thousand in 1944, shot up after the war to 25.8 in 1947—the highest rate in over thirty years.

Moralists also debated the issues presented by the continued increase in divorce. The 1914 divorce rate of 100 per 100,000 inhabitants had been regarded as a national scandal; yet this was only a beginning. At the peak of prosperity in 1929 the rate stood at 170. It fell somewhat during the worst years of depression but then climbed again to reach 200 in 1940. The hasty marriages, unfortunate separations, and other tensions of war lifted the rate to a fantastic 430 in 1946. Although this situation was abnormal, the rate was still 280 per 100,000 in 1948. About one marriage in four now ended in divorce.

Since there had been very little change in the laws over a period of sixty or seventy years, the increase in divorce had to be attributed to other factors. Family-relations experts pointed out the influence of the transition from rural to urban society. In the cities couples who married knew less about each other and had fewer common elements in their backgrounds. People had more money to meet the expense of divorce proceedings; women were not so frequently deterred by fear that they could not earn a living. The fewer children of the modern family made divorce easier. Above all, the increasing number of broken homes was attributed to the nervous tension of people living in an increasingly complex society, to exaggerated expectations of romantic bliss, and to the increasing tolerance with which divorce was regarded by the general public.

As in earlier generations, reformers bewailed the confusion of 48 different systems of divorce law and urged uniformity. But they could not agree on whether the national code should approach the laxity of the Nevada laws or the rigidity of those of South Carolina and New York. Perhaps the most intelligent approaches to the problem were in communities where domestic-relations courts set up procedures for counseling unhappy couples and attempting to effect reconciliations before granting final divorce decrees.

The Church and the Social Order

Widespread unemployment and misery during the depression increased the appeal of the social gospel. Revising its social creed in 1932, the Federal Council of Churches went beyond the principles laid down in its historic statement of 1908. It now urged that speculation and the profit motive be subordinated to the "creative and cooperative spirit," that there be "social planning and control of the credit and monetary systems and economic processes for the common good," that there be "a wider and fairer distribution of wealth," that the right of employers and employees to organize and bargain collectively be protected, and that there be "social insurance against sickness, accident, want in old age and unemployment." Obviously these ideas had more in common with Roosevelt's proposed New Deal than with Hoover's rugged individualism. In its bold blueprint for a reformed social order the Federal Council was marching far in advance of most of the Protestant army. Neither ministers nor laymen were ready to embrace unanimously the ideal of the welfare state. Nevertheless, a generation of Protestant agitation for social justice undoubtedly helped to prepare the American mind for New Deal departures from laissez-faire capitalism.

Similar in influence were the pronouncements of other religious bodies. In 1931 the Central Conference of American Rabbis drafted a "Program of Social Justice." The same year Catholic discussion of economic issues was stimulated by Pope Pius XI's encyclical *Quadrigesimo Anno,* issued to commemorate the fortieth anniversary of the great *Rerum Novarum.* The Pope renewed the condemnation of communism and socialism but urged the reconstruction of the social order on Christian principles. The encyclical received rather irresponsible exploitation in Father Coughlin's radio speeches and a more temperate statement in the writings of Monsignor Ryan. Defenders of the economic *status quo* found little comfort in Father Ryan's explanation that "the industrial system proposed by the Pope would occupy a middle ground between capitalism and Communism, between individualism and Socialism." It would organize occupational groups composed of both employers and employees and empowered by law to fix wages, interest, dividends, and prices, to determine working conditions, to adjust industrial disputes, and to carry on whatever economic planning was thought feasible. Although Father Ryan opposed complete economic regimentation by the state, he advocated nationalization of public utilities, mines, and petroleum deposits, and "government competition with great corporations in any industry when this is the only effective means of preventing monopoly."

Thorniest of all social issues was the Christian's duty in time of war. A few

Protestant clergymen like John Haynes Holmes, Norman Thomas, and Episcopal Bishop Paul Jones opposed America's participation in World War I. But they were a small and exceedingly unpopular group. The great majority of ministers supported the war wholeheartedly. Some of the harshest denunciations of the Germans came from Protestant pulpits. "Thou knowest, O Lord," prayed the evangelist Billy Sunday, "that no nation so infamous, vile, greedy, sensuous, blood-thirsty, ever disgraced the pages of history. Make bare thy mighty arm, O Lord, and smite the hungry, wolfish Hun, whose fangs drip with blood, and we will forever raise our voices to thy praise."

Ashamed that so much hatred had been preached during these years, many Protestant ministers swung over to extreme pacifism during the next decade. Typical of the new pronouncements was one prepared by an interdenominational conference at Columbus, Ohio, in 1929, which declared that

> . . . war means everything that Jesus did not mean and means nothing that he did mean. We therefore hold that the churches should condemn resort to the war system as sin, and should henceforth refuse as institutions to sanction it or to be used as agencies in its support. . . . We hold that the churches should support and sustain with moral approval individuals who, in the exercise of their right of conscience, refuse to back up any war or military training.

Despite the rising menace of fascist aggression many ministers held to their new position. In March, 1939, a hundred prominent clergymen signed an *Affirmation of Christian Pacifist Faith,* stating that "the gospel of God as revealed in Jesus Christ" left them no other choice "but to refuse to sanction or participate in war." This attitude was a powerful support to American isolationism right up to Pearl Harbor.

When the United States finally became involved in World War II, pacifism still persisted in many quarters. Although two-thirds of the inmates of conscientious objectors' camps professed the Quaker, Mennonite, or some other historic pacifist creed, there were also many young Methodists, Baptists, Presbyterians, Catholics, Jews, and others who convinced their draft boards that they had sincere scruples against bearing arms. But this position was not sufficiently widespread to interfere with the war effort. The great majority of Protestants, Catholics, and Jews accepted the conflict as just and necessary. Religious idealism could only cherish the hope that the struggle would not be in vain and that a peace of justice and an effective world organization would somehow be achieved after the war was over.

Although most Protestants continued to have faith that peace and social justice were achievable goals, a number of thinkers, haunted by the world's grim troubles, came to conclusions strikingly different from the optimistic assumptions of nineteenth-century liberal Christianity. American scholars studied with approbation the works of the contemporary German theologian Karl Barth, who emphasized the doctrine of a transcendent God, high and lifted up, "totally other" than man. God was not interested in society; his concern was to attend and to assist the individual soul "through time into eternity," because God's victory was achieved "not in history but beyond history." Christian pessimists of the Barthian school regarded the social gospel with its aspiration for social justice and world peace as both futile and presumptuous.

The most thoughtful theologian of the period, Reinhold Niebuhr of Union Theological Seminary, rejected the extreme position of Barth but nevertheless condemned the shallowness of recent liberalism. Old-fashioned enough to believe that all men were sinners but modern enough to be a resolute crusader for social reform, Niebuhr embodied the paradox which to him was at the heart of Christianity. "An adequate religion," he wrote, "develops only where the ethical impulse is set in vivid juxtaposition to the forces of nature in man; and man is forced both to seek after an impossible victory and to adjust himself to an inevitable defeat." [1]

Varieties of Religion

Americans continued to worship through a bewildering number of denominational channels. In 1950 there were about 49,000,000 Protestants, 27,700,000 Roman Catholics, 5,000,000 Jews, and 700,000 Eastern Orthodox Christians in the country. Although the Protestants were distributed among more than 200 different religious bodies, more than two-thirds of them belonged to 10 large denominations.[2] Over one-half of American Protestants were affiliated with some Baptist or Methodist group.

Although the rate of Roman Catholic growth was somewhat reduced by drastic immigration curbs, large Catholic families and conversions gave the Church a gain of over 50 per cent between 1916 and 1949. Vigorous life was also evident in the erection of thousands of churches, schools, and colleges. The American church's increasing prestige in the general Catholic world was symbolized by the splendid pageantry of the International Eucharistic Congress held in Chicago in 1926 and by the inclusion of four American churchmen among the thirty-two new cardinals appointed by Pius XII in 1945. A number of prominent Americans, unhappy in the frustrations of modern life, found the stability they longed for in the historic church. Among the Catholic converts were Heywood Broun, well-known liberal journalist, Clare Boothe Luce, popular playwright and politician, Henry Ford II, leading industrialist, Louis Budenz, ex-Communist editor, and Senator Robert F. Wagner of New York. Instrumental in bringing

[1] Reinhold Niebuhr, *Reflections on the End of an Era* (Scribner, New York, 1934), 14.

[2] Protestant denominations claiming more than 1,000,000 members in 1950 were: The Methodist Church 8,900,000, Southern Baptist Convention 6,700,000, National Baptist Convention, U.S.A. 4,300,000, National Baptist Convention of America 2,500,000, Presbyterian Church, U.S.A. 2,400,000, Protestant Episcopal Church 2,300,000, Evangelical Lutheran—Missouri Synod 1,700,000, Disciples of Christ 1,700,000, American Baptist Convention 1,500,000, Congregational Christian Church 1,200,000.

about most of these conversions was Monsignor Fulton J. Sheen of Catholic University, one of the most persuasive Catholic spokesmen in American history.

Although the postwar years witnessed a rising interest in all religious books, Catholic authors enjoyed a particularly striking success. Thomas Merton, a Catholic convert who joined the Trappist order, wrote persuasively of his experiences in *The Seven Storey Mountain* (1948) and *The Waters of Siloe* (1949). Monsignor Sheen's *Peace of Soul* was a best seller in 1949, and Henry Morton Robinson's novel *The Cardinal* led the list in 1950.

Catholicism's rising prestige did not go unchallenged. Although crude anti-popery of the Ku Klux Klan variety became less evident, a more intellectual hostility to the Roman Church gained ground. Many liberals were seriously disturbed by the increasing activity of the Vatican in world politics, by the aggressiveness of American Catholic spokesmen on the education issue, and by Catholic attempts to impose on the rest of the community their ideas on birth control and the censorship of books and motion pictures. Leading critic of the Catholic Church on such issues as these was Paul Blanshard, whose *American Freedom and Catholic Power* (1949) caused heated controversy.

Much of the narrow denominationalism of American Protestantism was conquered during the twentieth century. In smaller communities there was an increasing trend toward community or federated churches. In the cities denominational organization was usually kept, but ministers worked in close harmony through councils of churches and other agencies. At the national level the Federal Council of Churches maintained a vigorous existence despite occasionally sharp criticism from fundamentalists and conservatives who disliked the Council's emphasis on the social gospel. During the forties plans went forward for a more comprehensive organization that would include not only the Federal Council but the Foreign Missions Conference, the Council of Church Boards of Education, the United Council of Church Women, and other interdenominational bodies. On November 29, 1950, the National Council of Churches of Christ in the United States of America was officially constituted in an impressive ceremony at Cleveland, Ohio. Through this new organization 25 Protestant and 4 Eastern Orthodox bodies with a total membership of over 31,000,000 planned to coordinate their missionary, educational, and welfare activities. The movement toward Protestant unity was also demonstrated in such important mergers as that which established the United Lutheran Church in 1918, the Congregational Christian Church in 1931, the Evangelical and Reformed Church in 1934, and the Methodist Church in 1939.

Fearful of all things Catholic, old-time Protestants had insisted on severely plain church interiors dominated by their pulpits. Many ministers now felt the need for more dignity and beauty in Protestant worship. In the construction of new churches and the remodeling of old ones chancel fronts were frequently provided. Both preacher and choir occupied less prominent places, and altar, cross, and candles appeared in the central position. Choirs were robed, and ministers forsook the long coats of an earlier generation in favor of gowns.

These innovations together with the introduction of a more liturgical mode of worship often disturbed Protestants brought up in a different tradition. They smelled a whiff of Rome in candles and clerical vestments; they missed the vigorous exhortations and loud "Amens" of the old-time religion. Equally distasteful to them were sermons replete with references to evolution, recent Biblical scholarship, and the latest teachings of psychology and sociology. To many simple souls this was not religion at all but some strange new cult that they did not understand and could not love. Although a majority learned to reconcile themselves to the new ways, a significant minority sought some other form of religious outlet. Evangelical emotionalism found expression in Youth-for-Christ mass meetings, in crowded Gospel Tabernacles, and in the energetic preaching of Billy Graham and other popular evangelists. Among the economic groups hardest hit by depression and war, religious sects that emphasized redemption from sin and the second coming of Christ had a rapid growth. The Assemblies of God reported a membership of 275,000 in 1950, the various Churches of God aggregated 274,000, and the Church of the Nazarene had 248,000.

In the opinion of many, the queerest workers in the Lord's vineyard were Jehovah's Witnesses. After Pastor Russell's death in 1916 the movement was carried vigorously forward under the leadership of "Judge" J. F. Rutherford. Convinced that the rule of Christ had already begun and that the Battle of Armageddon, the destruction of the wicked, and the final establishment of the theocracy were imminent events, the faithful published the glad tidings through a variety of activities likely to perplex and to annoy the unregenerate. They sold their pamphlets on street corners, canvassed from house to house, spoke over the radio, and blared out their teachings from sound trucks. Bewildered Catholics who had incautiously allowed strangers to enter their houses might have to listen to the playing of phonograph records abusing the pope.

Among the numerous legal issues arising out of the activities of Jehovah's Witnesses, the most significant was whether children of this faith might be required by law to salute the flag in public schools. According to "Judge" Rutherford's somewhat turgid explanation the Witnesses believed

> . . . that for them to indulge in the formalism or ceremony of saluting any flag is a violation of God's specific commandment as set forth in Exodus 20:3–5 and emphasized in many other scriptures. The reason that such flag saluting is a violation of that commandment is that the salute attributes salvation to the state which the flag represents, thus making the state a mighty one or a god, whereas salvation belongeth alone to Jehovah, and violation of God's commandment would mean their certain destruction.

First confronted with this problem in 1940, the Supreme Court upheld the right of the state to require the salute. But the expulsion of children from school for refusing on religious grounds to pledge allegiance to the state shocked Americans proud of the nation's tradition of toleration. In 1943 the Supreme Court reversed its position in order to respect the scruples of the Witnesses. This did not save the sect from many petty acts of local tyranny nor from much more serious persecution in Nazi Germany and other totalitarian states where they ventured to witness.

Out on religion's eccentric fringe were a score of other sects and cults. During the twenties the adroit showmanship of Aimee Semple McPherson attracted thousands to Angelus Temple in Los Angeles. In the hospitable climate of southern California flourished the still more fantastic "I Am" movement of Guy and Emma Ballard, which claimed a million members during the late thirties and early forties. Psychiana was a highly successful mail-order religion, carried on by Dr. Frank B. Robinson of Moscow, Idaho, who advertised in leading magazines: "I TALKED WITH GOD. SO CAN YOU—IT'S EASY . . . If your life lacks anything good, be it financial, domestic, or spiritual, or otherwise, . . . the Power of which we speak can supply that lack and supply it NOW. . . ." Most of the cultists were content to be regarded as God's favorite prophets, but New York's Father Divine enjoyed a unique kind of homage. Thousands of enthusiastic followers, most of them Negro but many white, sang:

> Father Divine is God
> Father Divine is God Almighty
> He is God, is God, is God.

By purchasing a number of former resort hotels and private estates and by organizing highly successful cooperatives, Father Divine was able to establish many of his Peace Mission followers in the comfort of earthly "heavens."

Although most cults drew their following from low-income groups eager to be saved from a hostile world, the Oxford Group movement enjoyed its greatest success among the well-to-do. The movement grew out of the activities of Frank Buchman, an American Lutheran minister who underwent a profound religious experience in an English church during a visit abroad. First at a house party in China in 1918, then at similar parties at Oxford University in England in 1921, Buchman undertook to "share" his experience with other people. Thus evolved a unique device for reviving Christian faith. Gathering at house parties, earnest individuals conversed about religion, gave personal testimony, engaged in quiet meditation, cleared their consciences through confession to others, and were thereby "changed." Renamed Moral Re-Armament in 1937, the movement gained its greatest influence in England, where university students and professors, members of Parliament and cabinet officers, writers and prominent businessmen participated. In the United States Moral Re-Armament had less success but gained a respectable following, particularly among Episcopalians.

Both the growth of the historic denominations and the appearance of new cults demonstrated that men's religious impulse was still strong. Indeed, many Christian optimists were convinced that the trend toward irreligion had been checked and that a countermovement had begun. They pointed to statements by

Albert Einstein, Robert Millikan, and Arthur Compton as indicating that the new physics supported a belief in God. Prominent psychologists were quoted to prove that religious faith was necessary to a well-organized and adjusted personality.

But if a return to religion had begun, many Americans were as yet untouched by it. For millions faith in the old certainties seemed no longer possible. A few intellectuals sought some well-defined substitute. Their problem in Walter Lippmann's analysis was "how mankind, deprived of the great fictions, is to come to terms with the needs which created those fictions." But the type of conscious humanism propounded in Lippmann's *A Preface to Morals* (1929) found little explicit acceptance. Millions of Americans ordered their lives by the rule of mundane experts. Parents sought the counsel of pediatricians and psychologists; they worried much over whether their children knew that they were wanted and loved, whether they were unduly frustrated, or whether they had adequate opportunity for self-expression. In their own search for success and happiness adults proved good customers for an unending stream of marriage manuals and books on winning friends, achieving peace of mind, and gaining maturity.

The great demand for works on popular psychology was a symptom of the increasing number of Americans who were harassed by the anxieties of twentieth-century life and felt a need for guidance. Much more alarming evidence of such conditions was available. In 1910 about 110 of each 100,000 of the population were under treatment in state mental hospitals; by 1948 the rate had risen to over 300 per 100,000. Some part of this disquieting increase might be explained by the circumstances that a larger proportion of the insane were now hospitalized and that the statistics of insanity—principally an adult malady—reflected the larger proportion of adults in the population and the longer life span. Even allowing for such corrections as these, however, experts believed that mental disorders were becoming much more frequent. The layman's suspicion that this increase was related to the fast pace and worries of modern life appeared to be confirmed by statistical evidence that the rate of admissions to mental institutions was higher for the urban population than for the rural and also higher for the large cities than for the small.

It was obvious that cases of mental disorganization diagnosed as insanity constituted only one part of the problem. Psychiatrists, psychoanalysts, and physicians all testified to an increasing number of patients requiring private treatment for miscellaneous neuroses, psychosomatic disturbances, and "nervous breakdowns."

Although treatment of such disorders both inside and outside institutions became increasingly skillful, many authorities believed that satisfactory conditions of mental health could only be achieved through preventive measures. In 1909 the National Committee for Mental Hygiene was established. Through this and other agencies much was done to promote more intelligent guidance of children both at home and in school and better personal adjustments to life at all ages.

The best of the popular works on psychology served a useful purpose in familiarizing the general public with means toward these same ends.

Rationalists and religionists naturally differed in their explanations for the increasing evidence of anxiety and unhappiness. Rationalists found the cause in the conflicts of modern American life: in the contradictions between competition and success, on the one hand, and brotherly love and humility, on the other, between the stimulation of needs by advertising and the possibility of their complete fulfillment, between the alleged freedom of the individual and all his factual limitations.

> These contradictions embedded in our culture are precisely the conflicts which the neurotic struggles to reconcile: his tendencies toward aggressiveness and his tendencies toward yielding; his excessive demands and his fear of never getting anything; his striving toward self-aggrandizement and his feeling of personal helplessness.[1]

Religious Americans had their own explanation. Modern man's restlessness, they were certain, arose out of his loss of faith; only in God would he find the peace and happiness for which he yearned.

[1] Karen Horney, *The Neurotic Personality of Our Time* (Norton, New York, 1937), 288.

Chapter 32. New Prestige for the World of Scholarship

American faith in education was demonstrated anew after World War II. Veterans, taking advantage of the "GI bill of rights," crowded the colleges. In many institutions they had to be housed along with their wives and children in reassembled barracks that had lately stood in army posts, while they attended classes in temporary buildings also furnished by the government. Probably a majority of the new students came from homes where the parents had received no more than a high-school education and the grandparents less than that. No elaborate statistics were necessary to demonstrate that each generation of Americans was receiving substantially more education than its predecessor.

Despite these impressive gains the progress of the schools and colleges hardly sufficed to meet the vital needs of American society. In a world of jet-propelled planes and atom bombs the nation's very existence obviously depended on training an adequate corps of scientists and engineers. Even more important, though not so clearly understood, was the need for more social intelligence and a sharper sense of values.

Bull Market in Education

At every level in the educational system a larger proportion of children were going to school in 1949 than in 1900. The increase was particularly impressive for the older groups. In 1900 about 700,000 students—only about 11 per cent of the population between the ages of 14 and 17—were enrolled in high schools. In 1949 almost 6,800,000, or 81 per cent of this age group, were in school. College enrollments also increased rapidly. In 1900 fewer than 250,000 students—about 4 per cent of the population between the ages of 18 and 21—attended various institutions of higher learning. By 1940 enrollment had risen to 1,500,000—almost 16 per cent of the college age group. In 1948 the presence of over 1,000,000 veterans on college campuses brought total enrollment to an unprecedented 2,400,000.

The rise in school attendance reflected more than growing faith in education. New laws and changing economic conditions prevented youngsters from taking jobs that had been open to them in earlier generations. In 1910 almost 2,000,000 American children between the ages of ten and fifteen were gainfully employed.

This number declined to 667,000 by 1930 and was still further reduced during the next decade under the influence of hard times and new Federal legislation. Even for sixteen- and seventeen-year-olds there were progressively fewer job opportunities under twentieth-century industrial conditions.

In many sections of the country the school equipment of 1950 was vastly superior to that of 1914. Buses and better roads made it possible to close one-room schools and bring children together in well-constructed buildings with separate classrooms, laboratories, shops, domestic-science rooms, gymnasiums, auditoriums, and cafeterias.

Even with the consolidation of school districts rural education still lagged behind urban. In 1942 there were over 100,000 one-teacher schools in the nation. Such schools were not necessarily poorly taught. As in earlier generations many of the district teachers were women of fine character, who gave more individual attention to their pupils than was possible in overcrowded urban systems. Despite their good qualities, however, most of the village teachers were poorly paid and inadequately trained, and the schoolhouses were meagerly equipped.

Some sections of the country were less able than others to support good schools. Although $88 per pupil was the national average for 1940, three states—Mississippi, Arkansas, and Alabama—spent less than $40 per pupil, and five other southern states spent between $40 and $50. The poor record of the South reflected, not willful neglect, but regional poverty. New York with a per capita income of $863 in 1940 could obviously afford to spend far more on education than Mississippi with a per capita income of only $202. The educational problem was further complicated by the larger ratio of children to adults in the poorer states. In 1945, 31 per cent of the population of South Carolina was between five and seventeen years of age, while only 18 per cent of the population of California was in this age group.

Inequalities in educational opportunity—between city and country, rich states and poor, whites and Negroes—called for reform. Although increasing state aid helped to some extent, Federal aid seemed to promise the only really adequate solution to the problem.

A trend toward increasing Federal activity in education had been in progress for some time. The support given to higher education in agriculture and the mechanical arts by the Morrill Act of 1862 was extended to the secondary level by the Smith-Hughes Act of 1917. This provided permanent annual appropriations for cooperation with the states in the promotion of vocational education in agriculture, trades and industries, and home economics. Later legislation provided for training in transportation, trade, and clerical work. By 1940 annual Federal expenditures for vocational education amounted to approximately 22 million dollars.

Federal educational activities multiplied under the New Deal. In 1938 about 230,000 young men were enrolled in the classes of the Civilian Conservation Corps, and 1,416,000 persons attended adult education classes sponsored by the

Works Progress Administration. By part-time employment the National Youth Administration helped 225,000 elementary and secondary-school pupils and 101,000 college students to continue their education. During World War II the Federal government spent millions of dollars in sending soldiers and sailors to various colleges and schools for special courses. After the war the government assisted over a million veterans each year to attend public and private schools of every description.

At each session of Congress after World War II bills were introduced providing for regular educational grants to the states. The legislators found it difficult to enact any of these proposals into law. Supporters of states' rights were eager for Federal funds but balked at Federal supervision. Negro spokesmen warned that unless safeguards accompanied the grants, minority groups might not share equitably in their benefits.

Most troublesome of all was the religious issue. Separation of church and state persisted as a basic American principle, but its application became increasingly subject to controversy. Although sectarian schools were everywhere barred from direct benefit from state or local government, different policies were followed in regard to indirect benefits. One of the reforms by which Huey Long had gained support for his Louisiana machine was a measure to provide free textbooks for every child, whether in public or private school. Challenged as an unconstitutional grant in support of religious education, the Louisiana law was upheld by the United States Supreme Court in 1930 on the ground that the aid was granted to the children and not to the schools.

On the basis of this decision Catholics soon requested other benefits. They argued with particular insistence that parochial-school children should be provided with the same free transportation to and from school that public-school children enjoyed. Many Protestants vigorously opposed this contention in the belief that the use of public revenues to transport pupils to sectarian schools violated the First Amendment of the Constitution. The New Jersey school-bus case of 1947 found the United States Supreme Court sharply divided on the issue: five justices considered legislation on free-bus transportation to be public-welfare legislation, from whose benefits members of no religious group should be excluded; four justices considered it unconstitutional as a "reimbursement of expense to individuals for receiving religious instruction and indoctrination." By 1947, 19 states had specifically authorized the transportation of parochial-school pupils at public expense; several others had specifically prohibited it. Proposals for Federal aid to education inevitably became involved in the controversy: one faction believed that Federal grants should be for the exclusive benefit of public schools; another would refuse Federal aid to any state that failed to provide free transportation and other benefits to parochial-school children; a third would make grants to the states and allow them to administer the funds as they saw fit.

Debate over Objectives

Americans agreed much better on the importance of going to school than on what the schools should teach. Some educators believed that the purpose of education was to provide moral and mental discipline; these considered that the content of courses was less important than the habits of industry and obedience that good schools inculcated. Others emphasized content; these believed that their principal responsibility was to transmit a certain body of knowledge whose truth and usefulness had been established by time.

Both of these schools of thought were challenged by new philosophies of education that developed during the twentieth century. The rethinking of educational problems was stimulated by the rise of teachers colleges and schools of education. The rapid expansion of high schools created a great demand for college graduates to teach in them. Whether prospective teachers needed courses in methods of teaching was a matter of controversy, but the proponents of such courses had more and more success in imposing their views. In 1879 the University of Michigan employed a professor of the science and art of teaching, and similar appointments were soon made at the University of Wisconsin, Johns Hopkins, and other institutions. First there were individual professors of education, then departments of education, and finally separate schools of education. Teachers College, founded in 1888, became affiliated with Columbia University in 1893. A School of Pedagogy was organized at New York University in 1899, and the University of Chicago School of Education was founded in 1901. Meanwhile, the state normal schools, hitherto largely concerned with the training of elementary school teachers, began to organize four-year programs for the preparation of high-school instructors. In 1890 the Albany Normal School was reorganized as the Albany State Teachers College. A similar metamorphosis was soon to be observed in the normal schools of Michigan, Illinois, and other states.

Education now became a field for research. Psychologists explored the learning process and devised new methods of testing the abilities and accomplishments of students. The school curriculum was critically examined: new courses were suggested and the combination or revision of old ones was advocated. Various methods of teaching were evaluated. Edward L. Thorndike instilled in professional educators a passion for statistical method—for tests and measurements of ever-increasing ingenuity. John Dewey inspired innumerable experiments in "progressive education." The great philosopher's disciples differed on many points, but they at least agreed in their dislike for the formalism of traditional educational method. Dewey explained the matter thus:

> If one attempts to formulate the philosophy of education implicit in the practices of the newer education, we may, I think, discover certain common principles amid the variety of progressive schools now existing. To imposition from above is opposed expression and cultivation of individuality; to external discipline is opposed free activity; to learning

from texts and teachers, learning through experience; to acquisition of isolated skills and techniques by drill is opposed acquisition of them as means of attaining ends which make direct vital appeal; to preparation for a more or less remote future is opposed making the most of the opportunities of present life; to static aims and materials is opposed acquaintance with a changing world.[1]

Progressive education had its most thorough trial in certain private schools, where organized course work was entirely discarded. Children were encouraged to explore problems that aroused their interest. The young learner's aspiration to build a birdhouse might provide motivation for him to learn to use tools, to perform the arithmetical functions necessary to calculate the lumber that he would need, to study the habits of the birds, to read and to write about birds and houses—perhaps even to study the history of architecture! Such radical applications of progressive theory were rarely possible in the public schools, but in attenuated form many of the same ideas were at work. Learning through memorization and drill was in disrepute; learning through projects and activity was held in high esteem. Teachers who talked too much were condemned; those who conducted socialized recitations and employed motion pictures and other forms of audio-visual aids were praised.

The new methods encountered much conservative opposition. Employers often protested that high-school graduates spelled badly, wrote and spoke ungrammatically, and seemed unfamiliar with the multiplication table. At the mid-century, educators were divided between those who wanted to push forward in the revolt against traditional methods and those who advocated a strategic retreat through reemphasis upon the basic tools of learning.

Many educational changes reflected the logic of events more than they did the planning of theorists. In 1870 two out of three high-school graduates went on to complete four years of college: it was therefore logical that the high-school curriculum should be largely devoted to Latin, algebra, geometry, and other college-preparatory subjects. By 1938 the situation had fundamentally altered. Despite the large increase in college enrollment only one high-school graduate in seven went on to complete four years of college. The high school was a terminal institution for millions of young people who would become bookkeepers, stenographers, sales girls, garage mechanics, factory workers, salesmen, and farmers. Inevitably the curriculum changed to meet the needs of this new student body. The minority who expected to go to college studied the traditional subjects. The rest took English, American history, and a few other required courses and filled out their schedules with nonacademic subjects like home economics, industrial arts, agriculture, bookkeeping, typewriting, art, and music.

The increasing number of subjects offered by the high schools was both good and bad. Education became more democratic as it adapted itself to meet the needs of all its pupils. Recognizing that individuals differed greatly in interests and abilities, the new high schools sought to provide something for every type

[1] John Dewey, *Experience and Education* (Macmillan, New York, 1938), 5–6.

of mind. But in adjusting themselves so thoroughly to vocational needs, the schools tended to lose sight of the fact that they were training citizens as well as breadwinners. Many educational reformers at mid-century were appealing for a restoration of balance by the introduction of courses that all students should take in order to gain a common body of knowledge and the ability to think effectively.

Debated with equal energy was the question of what a student ought to study in college. The growing complexity of American economic life was reflected in the multiplication of colleges within the great universities. To the older professional schools of medicine, law, engineering, and agriculture were now added colleges of business administration, forestry, library science, optometry, and journalism. Some of these required two, three, or four years of preparatory work in a liberal-arts college; others accepted students directly from high school.

The trend toward vocational specialization invaded the liberal-arts college itself. It was possible for two graduates of the same college to take not more than one or two of the same courses. The major in chemistry might not recognize the name of Thoreau or Garrison; the major in French might not know the difference between an atom and a molecule; the major in economics might never have heard of Emily Brontë. Attempts to remedy this situation by requiring a distribution of courses during the freshman and sophomore years afforded only a partial solution.

Chancellor Robert M. Hutchins of the University of Chicago was a particularly sharp critic of the colleges. In 1936 he wrote:

> The college of liberal arts is partly high school, partly university, partly general, partly special. Frequently it looks like a teacher-training institution. Frequently it looks like nothing at all. The degree it offers seems to certify that the student has passed an uneventful period without violating any local, state, or federal law, and that he has a fair, if temporary, recollection of what his teachers have said to him. . . .[1]

Hutchins suggested a reorganization of the whole educational system to provide for four years of general education to follow the sophomore year of high school. The content should be rigidly prescribed since "the heart of any course of study designed for the whole people will be, if education is rightly understood, the same at any time, in any place, under any political, social, or economic conditions." Graduating from college at the age of nineteen or twenty, students with an aptitude for research should be admitted to the specialized work of the university.

At the University of Chicago some of Chancellor Hutchins's ideas were carried out. Students were admitted after only two years of high school; those who came with four years of preparation might with sufficient application complete their college work in two years. Abandoning the customary system of credit hours, the University of Chicago bestowed its bachelor's degree on those who could pass comprehensive examinations in broad areas of knowledge.

[1] Robert M. Hutchins, *The Higher Learning in America* (Yale University Press, New Haven, Conn., 1936), 2.

A more thorough testing of Chancellor Hutchins's ideas was made at St. John's College at Annapolis, Maryland. Students with only two years of high-school preparation were admitted to a rigidly prescribed four-year course. During their first year these fifteen-year-olds sharpened their intellectual teeth by reading and discussing Plato, Aristotle, Euclid, and other Greek classics; during the second year they read ancient and medieval Latin authors like Vergil, Livy, St. Augustine, and St. Thomas Aquinas; during the last two years they studied such later writers as Rousseau, Pascal, Kant, Hegel, and Marx. During his college career the St. John's student read over one hundred great books in their entirety. Although most of his reading was done in English translations, he had some opportunity to study Greek, Latin, French, and German with his tutors. Mathematics and science were taught through the ancient texts; the experiments of Galileo and Faraday were repeated with duplicates of the original equipment.

Although St. John's was a small college, its experiment in basing education entirely on the so-called "great tradition" attracted keen interest. Strongly supporting the St. John's idea were President Hutchins, Mortimer Adler, Stringfellow Barr, and other "neo-Thomists," who adopted St. Thomas Aquinas's theory that the purpose of education was to inculcate the timeless concepts of morality, truth, and beauty. The critics of St. John's included, of course, all the disciples of John Dewey, who emphasized the cultivation of individuality and adaptability to a changing world. They denied the relevancy to modern life of many of the classics so carefully read at St. John's. They pointed out that only three of the authors studied were American and that there was little in the curriculum to help a twentieth-century man make his way through the complexities of contemporary economic and political life. Probably unjustly, the neo-Thomists were charged with hostility to democracy and sympathy for authoritarianism.

Moving in the opposite direction from the University of Chicago and St. John's were Sarah Lawrence, Bennington, and other small liberal-arts colleges which endeavored to build individual programs of study planned by the students themselves in close cooperation with faculty advisers. The courses might be broadly cultural or directed toward some specific vocational objective. Ample opportunity was provided for studying art, music, the dance, and the theater. Showing her sharp disagreement with the "great tradition" faction, President Constance Warren said: "We learn by proceeding gradually from the familiar to the unfamiliar, moving from our lives and environments into the lives and environments of others. . . . Thus at Sarah Lawrence, the point at which the student starts her quest for higher learning is not the Age of Pericles, but her own orbit of experiences and interests." Obviously, at Sarah Lawrence and Bennington higher education was built on the pragmatic philosophy of William James and John Dewey rather than on the eternal verities of St. Thomas Aquinas.

Most American colleges attempted to steer between the Scylla of St. John's and the Charybdis of Sarah Lawrence. They neither required all students to take an identical course nor permitted each to follow a special one of his own devising. Instead, they struggled to build a curriculum that would give all students some common elements of higher education and at the same time recognize their divergent interests and ambitions.

During the twenties and thirties many colleges required all freshmen to take not only the traditional English composition course but one or more "orientation courses." One of the earliest of these was Columbia's course in contemporary civilization, first given in 1919. A cooperative effort of the history, economics, government, and philosophy departments, contemporary civilization undertook to provide both a historical background for an understanding of modern society and an introduction to present-day problems. Similar experiments were attempted elsewhere: interdepartmental courses under such names as "responsible citizenship," "western civilization," and "introduction to the social sciences" became required freshman or sophomore courses in many institutions. Orientation courses in the humanities and the sciences also appeared.

During the thirties and the forties the term, "general education," was used with increasing frequency in the discussions of college faculties. Its meaning was thus explained by a committee of distinguished Harvard professors:

> Education is broadly divided into general and special education. . . . The term, general education, is somewhat vague and colorless; it does not mean some airy education in knowledge in general (if there be such knowledge), nor does it mean education for all in the sense of universal education. It is used to indicate that part of a student's whole education which looks first of all to his life as a responsible human being and citizen; while the term, special education, indicates that part which looks to the student's competence in some occupation.[1]

The need for general education was underlined by the challenging international and domestic problems of World War II and its aftermath as well as by the greatly expanded postwar college enrollments. Harvard, Yale, and scores of other institutions appointed faculty committees to study curriculum requirements. Typical of the new trends were the recommendations of the Harvard committee, which urged more emphasis on general education at both the high-school and college levels. Of 16 courses required for a bachelor's degree at Harvard, it was recommended that at least 6 should be in general education.

The general-education vogue appeared likely to influence both college teaching methods and graduate training. Reformers condemned excessive dependence on lectures and textbooks and urged that instruction be organized around problems or cases that would stimulate the student's interest and require him to collect data, to assess their value, and to arrive at reasoned judgments. Graduate schools fell under increasing criticism. In 1947 the President's Commission on Higher Education reported:

[1] *General Education in a Free Society: Report of the Harvard Committee* (Harvard University Press, Cambridge, Mass., 1945), 51.

Since less than a third of the holders of Ph.D. degrees are primarily engaged in research—in educational institutions, industry, or government—it is unrealistic to confine graduate programs to the kinds of experience that contribute in the main to proficiency in research. . . .[1]

Howard Mumford Jones of Harvard urged separate programs for graduate students who wished training in research and those who wished to prepare for college teaching.

The Doctors and the Public

Medical science continued to advance along the front so dramatically opened during the nineteenth century. To the simple anesthetics of the earlier period were now added new ones, both general and local in effect, each with its special advantages for certain types of cases. The work of leading surgeons like Dr. Harvey Cushing of Boston and Dr. George W. Crile of Cleveland became increasingly bold and skillful. The exacting demands of the American College of Surgeons, founded in 1913, did much to improve the equipment and practices of the nation's hospitals.

The great germ discoveries had seemed to promise that most human ailments would soon be conquered. As enemy bacteria were one after another identified under the microscope, the development of vaccines and serums for the prevention and cure of each disease inevitably followed. During the twentieth century this process went forward. For most American children, receiving "shots" became a part of growing up. Vaccination against smallpox was usually required by law; injections to prevent diphtheria, tetanus, whooping cough, and measles became increasingly common. Millions of newly inducted soldiers during World War II were inoculated against influenza, typhus, yellow fever, and other diseases likely to be encountered in overseas service.

But the microbe hunters encountered many difficulties. Even when the causative bacteria had been discovered, not all diseases could be prevented or controlled. Tuberculosis continued to be a stubborn foe. Some types of pneumonia responded to serum treatment; others did not. To complicate the doctor's problems still further, many diseases were attributed to viruses so small that they passed through the finest filters and could not be seen through any instrument until the electron microscope was developed during the late thirties. Although vaccines and serums were developed to combat some virus infections, others defied this line of attack.

The slow process of developing a specific defense against each disease was short-circuited during the thirties and forties by the discovery of new drugs which proved effective against a wide range of infections. Sulfanilamide, developed by German chemists between 1908 and 1917, was valued at first as a synthetic dye compound. Its potency in destroying bacteria, although early noted,

[1] *Higher Education for American Democracy: A Report of The President's Commission on Higher Education* (Harper, New York, n. d.), I, 89.

was not scientifically tested until the thirties, when German, French, and British investigators reported remarkable success. American clinical testing began at Johns Hopkins University in 1936. Soon sulfanilamide and other related sulfa drugs were revolutionizing medical practice. They proved effective against many infections that had resisted all other forms of treatment. The death rate from types of meningitis, hitherto almost 100 per cent fatal, was cut in half, and that from the common forms of pneumonia was reduced from 30 to 10 per cent. The sulfa drugs, however, proved to have limitations: some patients reacted badly to their use, and most viruses were beyond their reach.

Fortunately, the discovery of penicillin provided a remedy even more effective than the sulfa products and without their toxic effects. The penicillin story began in 1928, when Sir Alexander Fleming, a London scientist, observed the unusual way in which a plateful of bacteria was destroyed when one of his cultures was accidentally contaminated by a spot of greenish mold. He carefully saved the mold, grew it in a proper medium, and experimented with the substance which appeared in the medium during the process. This product, which he named penicillin, proved to be effective against various types of bacteria. Although Fleming announced his findings to the scientific world in 1929, no important results followed for over a decade. Penicillin was too difficult to produce to be medically useful. In 1939 a new round of experiments began in the Oxford laboratories of Howard Florey and Ernest Chain. In two years they obtained enough penicillin to experiment on 75 mice and 5 human patients. The results were decidedly encouraging, but large-scale production of the drug was impossible in wartime England. In 1941 Florey brought his problem to the United States and succeeded in enlisting the interest of the wartime Committee on Medical Research. Through the cooperation of government laboratories and leading pharmaceutical firms, the tremendous difficulties involved in the large-scale production of penicillin were eventually conquered. In April, 1943, shipments began to American troops overseas. A year later enough of the product was available for a strictly rationed distribution to hospitals for the treatment of civilians. By March, 1945, production had reached the point where all restrictions could be removed. Doctors could now freely prescribe a drug which proved strikingly effective against wound infections, pneumonia, meningitis, gonorrhea, syphilis, and many other ailments.

Even more important than the immediate results of the use of sulfa drugs and penicillin was the impetus given to the whole field of chemotherapy—the science of treating diseases with drugs. Laboratories all over the country concentrated on the discovery of new curatives. Streptomycin was a postwar sensation offering new hope to tuberculosis sufferers and others. Also in the stage of clinical testing were such new drugs as aureomycin, neomycin, and terramycin.

Medical science advanced along other lines as well. In the intricate functioning of the human organism, the minute secretions of ductless glands were proved to play a vital role. John J. Abel of Johns Hopkins was a pioneer in isolating adrenaline at about the turn of the century. In 1910 Walter B. Cannon of Harvard demonstrated the way in which fear and anger increase the flow of adrenaline into the blood stream, thus raising the blood pressure and the fighting vigor of the animal. The development of synthetic adrenaline provided a lifesaving stimulant for emergency use. In 1914 E. C. Kendall of the Mayo Clinic isolated thyroxine and opened the way for treatment of cretins and other victims of faulty metabolism. Few episodes in the history of medicine were more dramatic than the delivery from death provided for diabetics through the discovery of insulin by Dr. F. G. Banting of the University of Toronto in 1922. The isolation of various sex hormones aided in treating abnormal physical development and in relieving the unpleasant symptoms of growing old. In 1949 sufferers from such crippling ailments as arthritis, rheumatic fever, and rheumatic heart disease gained new hope through the discovery of the powerful hormones, cortisone and ACTH.

The study of nutrition also made significant progress. Early in the century the emphasis was on measuring calories and testing the energy content of various foods. But the assumption that food was nothing more than fuel to be burned in the human furnace was soon disproved. Since the eighteenth century sea captains had known that scurvy could be prevented by rations of lime juice, and late in the nineteenth century Japanese and Dutch scientists learned that a polished-rice diet would bring on attacks of beriberi. In 1911 Casimir Funk, a Polish investigator working in London, coined the word "vitamins" to describe the minute chemical factors in food that were essential to life. Preeminent in identifying various vitamins and demonstrating their importance was Elmer V. McCollum of Johns Hopkins University, who discovered Vitamin A in 1914, Vitamin B in 1916, and Vitamin D in 1922.

The general public took keen interest in these discoveries. Eager mothers forced more fruit and vegetables into their children's diet. Since there were also vitamins in sunlight, the younger generation—and many of the older—exposed as much skin to the summer sun as the law allowed. Vitamins became an American fad and shrewd entrepreneurs were not slow to reap a profit. Cereal manufacturers and other food processors made extravagant claims for their products, and vitamin pills and capsules flooded the market.

While the death rate from infectious diseases—especially those of children—was being sharply reduced, that from the degenerative diseases of middle age was climbing. Heart ailments took a heavier toll than any other cause of death. This appeared to be a penalty imposed by the fast tempo of modern life with its excitements and anxieties. The doctor's favorite prescription was rest and relaxation, but few breadwinners found it possible to take this in large doses. Meanwhile, new drugs and methods of treatment relieved the heart sufferers' symptoms and prolonged many lives. Despite intensive research the cause of cancer remained obscure, but encouraging progress was made in its diagnosis and treatment. Skillful surgery, radium, and X-ray therapy cured many patients, and new hope for others was offered in the development of radioactive isotopes and new drugs and hormones. Since early diagnosis was still of paramount importance, earnest efforts were made to educate the public in the importance of regular examinations.

Something of the enthusiasm which had been aroused in earlier generations by crusades against the evils of slavery, rum, and male domination was now forthcoming for organized campaigns to conquer specific diseases. The work of the National Tuberculosis Association pointed the way for later organizations. Poliomyelitis, or infantile paralysis, was particularly feared by the general public as a ruthless killer and crippler of children. In 1938 President Franklin D. Roosevelt, himself the veteran of a long struggle with polio, founded the National Foundation for Infantile Paralysis. Through the March of Dimes, an annual campaign during the last two weeks of January, the Foundation raised millions of dollars for research and assistance to victims unable to afford proper medical care. The latter was particularly important, since expenses for treatment were heavier than for any other disease—averaging $2,000 a case in 1949. Similar national drives against cancer, heart disease, cerebral palsy, and arthritis were eventually organized.

The prestige of the medical profession fluctuated violently. During the twenties the doctor was a popular hero. Novelists and dramatists portrayed the "men in white" as selfless benefactors of mankind, and the books of Paul de Kruif and other popularizers of medical research fascinated a wide public.

During the thirties and the forties, doctors found themselves targets for increasing criticism. Patients complained that the general practitioner was becoming extinct. Urban practice was so highly specialized that the sick often found themselves shunted from office to office while one doctor tested them for allergies, another for cardiovascular ailments, and a third for diseases of the nose and throat. Specialists' fees were usually high, and the patient sent to the hospital for major surgery was likely to spend all his savings and to go into debt.

Most doctors were conscientious in fixing their charges. They tried to scale their fees, charging wealthy patients more than poor. Both in their individual practice and in clinics, they often gave free service to the destitute.

But these policies did not go far enough. The Committee on the Costs of Medical Care, whose 50 members were drawn from private practice, medical institutions, the fields of public health and the social sciences, and the general public, reported in 1932 after five years of study of the problem:

> The predominant economic institution in medical practice today—private individual practice—dates back to ancient times. Under this system medical services are now so provided that many persons either cannot and do not receive the care they need, or are heavily burdened by its costs. At the same time, many of the practitioners and the agencies which provide medical service are inadequately occupied and poorly remunerated. A barrier—in large part economic—stands between practitioners, able and eager to serve, and patients who need the service but are unwilling or unable to pay for it.[1]

[1] *Medical Care for the American People: The Final Report of the Committee on the Costs of Medical Care* (University of Chicago Press, Chicago, 1932), 3.

A majority of the committee recommended that medical practice should be furnished largely by organized groups of physicians, dentists, and nurses and that the costs of medical care should be placed on a group-payment basis, "through the use of insurance, through the use of taxation, or through the use of both of these methods."

Spokesmen for the American Medical Association condemned this program. Group practice and prepayment were regarded as threatening the individual relationship of doctor and patient and opening the way to government control of the profession. Some local medical societies denied membership and the use of hospital facilities to physicians who served in the voluntary group-practice plans of the thirties.

The doctors soon found it necessary to shift ground. Proposals for compulsory health insurance so alarmed them that they dropped their hostility to voluntary prepayment plans. By 1943 there were in the country about 113 industrial plans providing comprehensive medical coverage for employees of large corporations on a prepayment basis. After receiving the blessing of the American Medical Association in 1933, the Blue Cross plan for the prepayment of hospital expenses grew with great rapidity. In 1949 the Blue Cross had almost 33 million members, and 9½ million belonged to the Blue Shield and similar voluntary plans for the prepayment of medical and surgical expenses.

The demand for more thoroughgoing measures persisted. President Truman advocated extension of the Federal social-security system to include compulsory health insurance. Supporters of this proposal asserted that it was an essential step toward social justice to provide adequate medical care for the entire population, but most doctors condemned it as "socialized medicine," threatening to ruin the medical profession through political interference and encouragement of malingering.

The Challenge of the Atom

America's scientific coming of age, presaged before 1914 by the researches of Gibbs, Michelson, and Morgan, was dramatically demonstrated during World War II. The development of the atomic bomb was a triumph of intensive research, imaginative thought, and practical engineering skill.

Yet nationalists who used this achievement to demonstrate the intellectual superiority of Americans could find scant support in the history of science. The atomic bomb was the final result of a series of discoveries that had been revolutionizing the field of physics for half a century. In the earlier phases of that revolution Americans played only a modest part.

The observation of data that could not be explained by the older theories of matter and energy began in the laboratories of Germany and France, when Roentgen discovered X rays in 1895, Becquerel observed the radioactivity of uranium in 1896, and the Curies found radium in 1898. Meanwhile, the Cavendish Laboratory of Experimental Physics at Cambridge, England, had become the center of highly significant experiments that completely altered the conception of the atom. In 1897 J. J. Thomson proved that the atom was not the ultimate unit of matter and that within the atom were electrons—minute particles charged with negative electricity. In 1911 Ernest Rutherford, Thomson's associate, propounded the theory that each atom contained also a heavy central nucleus, charged with positive electricity.

The nucleus was not an ultimate unit. In 1919 Rutherford announced that within the nucleus he had found protons—positively charged particles. Even more important than the discovery itself was the method which Rutherford had employed in making it. By bombarding nitrogen with the alpha particles emitted by radium, he had detached protons from the nucleus and changed nitrogen into oxygen. The artificial transformation of elements—the ancient dream of the alchemists—had been proved a possibility. Physicists valued the demonstration, however, not as a means of getting rich, but as providing a technique whereby further secrets about atomic structure could be learned. The bombardment of atoms by various ingenious methods became a favorite laboratory activity. In 1932 James Chadwick of the Cavendish group demonstrated that the nucleus contained not only protons but uncharged particles called neutrons. These neutrons proved the most effective bullets yet used for the bombardment of atoms. With this new weapon Enrico Fermi of Rome, Italy, began important studies of uranium in 1934.

The development of the new physics was watched with fascinated interest in American scientific circles. Following the leads suggested by European research, Americans began to make contributions of increasing significance. First at the University of Chicago and then at the California Institute of Technology, Robert A. Millikan carefully measured the electrical charge of electrons. From this problem he turned to the study of cosmic rays, bewildering his countrymen with researches that involved sending balloons into the stratosphere, setting up equipment on mountain tops, and lowering instruments deep into California lakes. A friendly rival was Arthur Compton of the University of Chicago, whose study of cosmic rays involved a round-the-world tour and the accumulation of data from 60 fellow observers in different countries.

Other American scientists explored the problem of isotopes—varieties of the same element having identical chemical properties but different atomic weights. In 1932 Harold C. Urey of Columbia University discovered deuterium, or heavy hydrogen. Three years later Arthur Dempster of the University of Chicago demonstrated that natural uranium contained three isotopes—U-234, U-235, and U-238.

Americans were challenged in particular by the engineering problems involved in devising machines to generate the high voltages necessary for further progress in atomic research. One type of "atom smasher" was the electrostatic generator, first built by Robert van de Graaff of the Massachusetts Institute of Technology in 1933; another was the cyclotron, first constructed by Ernest O. Lawrence of the University of California in 1932 and steadily improved by him.

The harsh intolerance of fascist nations helped to strengthen the position of the United States in the new physics. Albert Einstein, the world's most brilliant theorist, transferred his activities from Germany to the Institute for Advanced Study at Princeton, New Jersey. Einstein's importance had been emphasized by every new discovery. The vast store of energy locked in the heart of each atom was measurable by his famous formula of 1905, $E = mc^2$ (energy equals mass multiplied by the square of the speed of light). Another leading theorist, Niels Bohr of Denmark, presently joined Einstein at Princeton. Meanwhile, Enrico Fermi had left Mussolini's Italy to work at Columbia University. Three of the world's greatest physicists were thus on American soil in 1939, an *annus mirabilis* for science.

Experimenting at the Kaiser Wilhelm Institute in Berlin with Fermi's technique of bombarding uranium with neutrons, Otto Hahn and Lise Meitner had most unexpected results. Somehow their procedure produced barium, an element with only about half the atomic weight of uranium. Forced into exile as a non-Aryan, Miss Meitner had a fascinating subject for speculation. She soon concluded that the neutron bombardment had actually split the uranium nucleus, producing two other elements and transmuting a minute quantity of matter into energy of breath-taking magnitude. She transmitted her exciting news to her scientist nephew, Otto Frisch of Copenhagen, who promptly cabled a report to his father-in-law, Niels Bohr, in America. On January 27, 1939, Bohr created a tremendous sensation by announcing the discovery to a group of leading American physicists in Washington. Soon experiments in nuclear fission were in progress in all the important research centers of the country.

Fermi, Einstein, and other scientists pointed out the possible importance of atomic energy to the United States armed services. Before the end of 1939 President Roosevelt appointed an Advisory Committee on Uranium, and the army and the navy made small grants of money to encourage research. But really energetic steps were not taken until the uranium committee was placed under the new National Defense Research Committee in June, 1940. American scientists now began an intensive study in cooperation with British and Canadian colleagues. On November 6, 1941, the experts reported:

> *A fission bomb of superlatively destructive power will result from bringing quickly together a sufficient mass of element U-235.* This seems to be as sure as any untried prediction based upon theory and experiment can be. . . .[1]

The nub of the problem was that of obtaining adequate quantities of U-235, since only this isotope was known to produce the chain reaction necessary for a bomb. Uranium itself was a rare metal, extracted with difficulty from its ore.

[1] Quoted in James Phinney Baxter 3d, *Scientists against Time* (Little, Brown, Boston, 1946), 427.

Even in pure uranium, however, there was only one part of U-235 to 140 parts of U-238. The separation of the vital isotope in quantities large enough to make bombs was a problem of staggering difficulty—a problem in experimental science, in engineering, and in business organization.

The scientists eventually provided not one but three methods of separating U-235 from natural uranium: by gas diffusion, by centrifuge, and by an electromagnetic process. In addition their experiments led to the discovery of plutonium, a new element with the fissionable character of U-235. Plutonium might be produced from a controlled chain reaction of uranium—an hypothesis proved in 1942 in the famous uranium-graphite pile under the stands of Stagg Field at the University of Chicago.

Next it was necessary to apply the new knowledge in large-scale production. In 1942 the army organized the "Manhattan District" with Brigadier General Leslie R. Groves in charge. Large plants for the production of U-235 were built some 18 miles west of Knoxville, Tennessee, where the boom town of Oak Ridge soon sprang up. Although a small plutonium plant was also built in this area, major production of the material was organized at Hanford, Washington, on the Columbia River. From these widely separated production areas priceless U-235 and plutonium were rushed to Los Alamos, New Mexico, where the best equipped physics research laboratory in the world had been built. Here a remarkable team of physicists under the direction of J. Robert Oppenheimer of the University of California developed the actual atomic bomb.

On June 16, 1945, the first atomic bomb was exploded at a lonely spot in New Mexico. Two months later the surrender of Japan was hastened by use of the new weapon. The destruction of Hiroshima dramatized the magnitude of the power which the scientists had unleashed. A single plane dropping a single bomb had done as much damage as a thousand planes could have inflicted with their heaviest loads of ordinary explosives. Almost 100,000 persons had been killed; 30,000 or 40,000 more had been injured; buildings were leveled over an area of 4 square miles. Yet the Hiroshima bomb was reported to be a crude early model; larger and far more terrible applications of nuclear fission were possible.

American scientists, frightened by the danger of an atomic war that might destroy civilization, did their best to educate the public. They declared that the United States could not long enjoy a monopoly of the new knowledge, that other nations would develop atomic weapons, and that defense against them was impossible. They argued that human survival demanded the organization of effective international control of atomic energy. The American government proposed such a plan to the United Nations in 1946, but Soviet suspicion prevented its acceptance. The results were most unfortunate. Spurred on by the announcement that Russia too had the bomb, the United States felt it necessary to spend vast sums of money in the continued production and stock-piling of atomic weapons. Research, which had been enormously advanced by the free exchange of data before World War II, was now handicapped by the necessity for secrecy. Atomic power, which might be harnessed for the benefit of mankind, was valued almost exclusively for its ability to destroy some future enemy.

The Study of Government and Society

Debate over the atomic bomb served to emphasize a fact already obvious: the health and welfare of the individual was becoming steadily more dependent on forces that were beyond his direct control. Total war killed the warmonger and the pacifist without discrimination; economic depressions ruined both the industrious and the lazy. If social scientists knew what caused war and peace, prosperity and depression, good citizenship and crime, or rational and irrational social behavior, it was high time that their knowledge be translated into social action.

The study of government changed its orientation. Political theory received less attention, political practice more. Recognition of the complexity of the new problems with which governments had to deal led to the intensive study of public administration by pioneers like Frank Goodnow and W. F. Willoughby. Universities organized courses to train professional administrators for civil-service posts in local, state, and Federal agencies of government. The decisive importance of political parties was at last given adequate recognition when M. Ostrogorski, Charles E. Merriam, and other scholars explored their actual structure and function.

In the study of the effect of public opinion on government an obvious point of attack was an investigation of the character and influence of propaganda—a force the impact of which was strikingly demonstrated during World War I and in the rise of communist and fascist dictatorships. The techniques of organized pressure groups and propaganda artists were studied by men like Harold D. Lasswell and Peter H. Odegard.

Public-opinion research led to attempts at scientific poll taking. Dr. George Gallup, although only one expert among many, was the figure best known to the general public. Newspapers provided wide publicity for his findings, and politicians gave serious weight to his announcements of what the public wanted. Unfortunately for the experts, the American voters confounded all predictions by reelecting President Truman in 1948. The incident illustrated a major difficulty besetting the students of social science. The consequences of bringing together a certain quantity of U-235 could be safely predicted; those of assembling 48 million voters at the polls could not. Even in the individual, human behavior was capricious; in the mass it was influenced by factors still imperfectly understood by social psychologists.

The pragmatic approach which dominated research in government also profoundly influenced the study of law. On the Supreme Court of the United States, Justices Oliver Wendell Holmes, Jr., Louis D. Brandeis, and Benjamin Cardozo set an example of interpreting the law in the light of the changing conditions of society. Sociological jurisprudence, as taught by Dean Roscoe Pound of Harvard and others, greatly altered legal education.

Economists also had to come to grips with stubborn reality. The perfect competition which they had posited in economic theory had less and less existence in economic fact. Adopting at length the methods of pragmatism, the economists assembled and studied vast quantities of data about the contemporary economy—an undertaking in which they were aided by the greatly expanded statistical services of the government. The practical quality of the investigations of the twenties is suggested by Wesley C. Mitchell's studies of the business cycle, Edwin R. A. Seligman's inquiries into the results of installment buying, and Paul Douglas's calculations of the real wages of American workers.

The Great Depression presented problems of the utmost urgency. In its attempts to create employment by government spending, the Roosevelt administration was at first motivated by humanitarian instinct more than by any well-formulated economic philosophy. Theoretical justification for New Deal policies was sought only in feeble suggestions that work relief might "prime the pump" of private business. By the end of the decade, however, deficit spending gained respectability through the growing vogue of the so-called "Keynesian economics," based upon the writings of the famous English theorist John Maynard Keynes.

The application of the Keynesian theories to the American situation was made by Alvin H. Hansen of Harvard and other American economists, who asserted that the closing of the frontier, restriction of immigration, decline in the birth rate, and completion of the great railroad- and factory-building process had created a "mature" economy with fewer opportunities for profitable investment. By reducing interest rates and taxing idle money, the government should attack the propensity of corporations and wealthy individuals to "oversave"; by deliberately increasing its expenditures and reducing its revenues, it should create employment and expand the national income. Public investment should be increased through road building, public housing for low-income groups, rural-rehabilitation loans, and the construction of hospitals and schools.

To conservatives repudiation of the ideal of an annually balanced budget, deliberate deficit spending, and national economic planning were all heresies. Many insisted that the nation's business would prosper if only the New Dealers and Fair Dealers would leave it alone. Beset by rival theorists, Congress tended to follow a middle-of-the-road course.

The patient fact finding of political scientists and economists was paralleled in sociology. The modern American city provided any number of challenging problems. University of Chicago sociologists assembled statistics and compiled case histories on almost every significant group in the Middle Western metropolis. Robert S. Lynd of Columbia University and his wife, Helen, attempted to investigate the behavior and attitudes of an entire community. Choosing for their study Muncie, Indiana, an industrial city with some 40,000 inhabitants, the

Lynds found out how businessmen and their employees felt toward each other, how Negro, Jewish, and immigrant groups were treated, what young people thought about love and marriage, who went to church and why, how life was influenced by radio and the movies. The resulting book, *Middletown* (1927), gave a fascinating cross section of American life during the twenties.

A community study of a different type was represented by the "Yankee City" series of W. Lloyd Warner of the University of Chicago and his associates. Warner was convinced that realistic description of American society required recognition of its class structure. Despite the ideal of equality and relatively great social mobility, Warner concluded that social class "is a major determinant of individual decisions and social actions; that every major area of American life is directly and indirectly influenced by our class order; and that the major decisions of most individuals are partly controlled by it." The three classes of popular terminology were expanded by Warner to six: upper-upper, lower-upper, upper-middle, lower-middle, upper-lower, and lower-lower.

Extremely useful in helping Americans to understand their own times was *Recent Social Trends in the United States* (1933), a cooperative study undertaken at the initiative of President Hoover. Another cooperative work of great significance was *Studies in Social Psychology in World War II* (1950)—a four-volume report on the American soldier's reactions to the experiences of training, combat, and demobilization. Regional studies made notable advance under such scholars as Howard Odum of the University of North Carolina.

Negro-white relations and other racial-minority problems engaged the attention of many sociologists. Since objectivity was particularly difficult in this field, Americans welcomed the careful analysis of Gunnar Myrdal, a distinguished Swedish scholar, in the two-volume study entitled *An American Dilemma* (1944). Many pseudoscientific assumptions about racial characteristics were disproved by the careful researches of Franz Boas, Aleš Hrdlička, Otto Klineberg, and other cultural anthropologists.

Historians felt the full impact of twentieth-century intellectual currents. In 1912 James Harvey Robinson published an influential volume entitled *The New History*. History, he said, should not be narrowly political and military; it should give ample attention to economic and intellectual development, borrowing materials and methods from the fields of economics, sociology, and anthropology. Although the new history was less new than Robinson implied, the historians' changing interests were clearly evident during the next three decades.

Best known of American historians during the twenties and the thirties was Charles A. Beard. His challenging monographs *An Economic Interpretation of the Constitution of the United States* (1913) and *Economic Origins of Jeffersonian Democracy* (1915) inspired a generation of younger scholars to seek the explanation for every important political event in the conflict of economic groups. Beard himself realized the danger of oversimplification and in later books emphasized the interplay of other social and intellectual forces. *The Rise of Amer-*

ican Civilization (1927), written by Beard in collaboration with his wife, Mary, was the most discussed American historical work of the decade. The Beards wrote in the spirit of the new realism, reexamining the whole course of American history and rejecting many traditional interpretations.

Scholars paid increasing respect to the influence of ideas in history. James Harvey Robinson stimulated interest in intellectual history through his teaching at Columbia and through such popular books as *The Mind in the Making* (1921). Carl Becker of Cornell wrote essays on the history of thought—particularly that of the eighteenth century—which few of his contemporaries could match for clarity of exposition and felicity of style. Ralph Gabriel of Yale, Merle Curti of Wisconsin, and Henry Steele Commager of Columbia also contributed important studies in the history of ideas.

Meanwhile, other historians were exploring the vast field of American social history. Between 1926 and 1948 were published 13 volumes of *A History of American Life,* in which such able historians as Thomas Jefferson Wertenbaker, James Truslow Adams, Allan Nevins, and Arthur M. Schlesinger described life in America in all its fascinating variety, stressing the influence of changing religious concepts, new inventions and technological progress, immigration and the rise of cities, the founding of schools and colleges, and organized efforts for humanitarian reform.

Interest in ideas and social trends did not destroy respect for the role of the individual in history. On the contrary, American biography reached a high level of excellence in Albert J. Beveridge's *The Life of John Marshall* (1916–1919), Douglas S. Freeman's *Robert E. Lee* (1934), and Allan Nevins's *Grover Cleveland* (1933) and *Hamilton Fish* (1937).

The achievements of social science lacked the quality of high drama. No discovery by an economist or sociologist challenged the imagination as did penicillin or nuclear fission. Human relations were governed by factors too complicated to be captured in a formula. Yet the newer theories of social evolution emphasized the importance of purposeful action. Optimistic Americans did not believe that a better society could be achieved overnight, but they did have faith that more realistic knowledge both of present conditions and of the past would help men solve their problems.

Chapter 33. The Artist Becomes a Democrat

In the surge of American material progress the sensitive individual who tried to express himself in literature, in art, or in music often felt himself an outsider. Many such people lived in Europe because they felt that the native environment was stultifying to the artist. Others lived in the United States but never felt spiritually at home. This situation reached its culmination during the 1920's, when American intellectuals were unusually severe in their condemnation of the society that had bred them. During the thirties and the forties most of these expatriates—spiritual as well as physical—came home. America beset by depression and war called forth more affection than America prosperous and complacent. Intellectuals who had doubted the validity of the democratic philosophy now loudly championed it. American themes were emphasized in literature, art, and music. Meanwhile, inventions like the movies, the radio, and the phonograph made the world of literature and art more accessible to the American people than it had ever been before.

Renaissance of Poetry

A new interest in poetry became evident about 1912. In that year Harriet Monroe, a Chicago poet of minor talent but great enthusiasm, convinced a group of wealthy patrons that they should underwrite the expenses of a new periodical called *Poetry: A Magazine of Verse.* Intelligently edited by Miss Monroe, this "little magazine"—the prototype for scores of subsequent "little magazines"—exerted an influence out of all proportion to its circulation, which never exceeded 3,000. New poets found a medium through which their efforts could be brought to the attention of a discriminating audience; critics contributed essays and reviews provocative of controversy; new movements were promoted and attacked. Poetry—which had recently seemed to have little value except for magazine editors in need of filler for half pages—suddenly became material for excited discussion.

Particularly spirited was the controversy over the "imagists." The first highly articulate champion of a new poetry which would be free of the strait jacket of conventional verse forms and diction was Ezra Pound, a precocious native of Idaho who had forsaken America to live abroad, where he was brilliantly successful in his early experimentation. His post as commander-in-chief of the imagists, however, was soon usurped by Amy Lowell, who inherited not only the wealth of a famous New England family but also its will to achieve and to dominate. Her own work, exhibited in such volumes as *Sword Blades and Poppy Seed* (1914), occasionally achieved striking results, but her greatest importance lay in her energetic fight to secure greater sympathy and tolerance for poetic experimentation.

While some persons fought the battle on the intellectual front, others provided a practical demonstration of the striking variety which modern poetry could achieve—among them a group of Middle Western poets. Vachel Lindsay, born in Springfield, Illinois, spent the early years of the century wandering about the country, reciting poetry to any individual or group who would listen to him. His philosophy was well expressed in the title of the little pamphlet he gave out, *Rhymes to Be Traded for Bread.* Not until he developed a bold new technique for capturing the rhythms of revival songs, jazz melodies, and folk music did Lindsay enlist a wide public for such works as *General William Booth Enters Heaven and Other Poems* (1913) and *The Congo and Other Poems* (1914).

Edgar Lee Masters was a Chicago lawyer whose early attempts at poetry rarely rose above the commonplace. But in 1915 he published *Spoon River Anthology,* a book of epitaphs laying bare the secret lives of real and imaginary persons in a southern Illinois village. Although there were occasional flashes of heroism and nobility in these Spoon River characters, there was more of meanness and hypocrisy. Masters's book provided matter for excited controversy, a faction of traditionalists denying the truth of this unflattering picture of village life while modernists enthusiastically cheered the lawyer-poet for the accuracy of his insights and the effectiveness of his style.

A third bold experimenter of the Chicago school was Carl Sandburg, a curious mixture of toughness and tenderness, whose career and point of view had many interesting parallels with Walt Whitman. Sandburg had learned about America from personal experience in a score of jobs. He had been a milk-delivery boy, a sceneshifter in a theater, a dishwasher, a harvest hand, a soldier in the Spanish-American War, a college basketball player, a Socialist organizer, a salesman, and a newspaper reporter. Whether he was also a poet was an issue on which readers differed violently after reading his *Chicago Poems,* published in 1916. Even for literary liberals it was hard to accept the credentials of a poet who apostrophized a city as:

> Hog Butcher for the World,
> Tool Maker, Stacker of Wheat,
> Player with Railroads and the Nation's Freight Handler;
> Stormy, husky, brawling,
> City of the Big Shoulders. . . .

But those who dismissed Sandburg as a roughneck missed his underlying feeling for beauty. Whitman himself had not loved America more deeply or with a firmer faith in the essential goodness and wisdom of the people. Long after the vogue of Lindsay and Masters had spent itself, Sandburg was making a memorable contribution to American culture with his poems, his collections of folk songs, and his extensive prose works: *Abraham Lincoln: The Prairie Years* (1926) and *Abraham Lincoln, The War Years* (1939).

The Muse's unexpected descent upon Chicago did not mean that the Northeast was lacking in literary talent. Acclaimed by many as the most important poet of the day was Edwin Arlington Robinson, native of Maine and for many years a resident of New York. Although Robinson's *The Children of the Night,* a brilliant volume including such memorable character creations as Richard Corey and Miniver Cheevy, had been published as early as 1897, the poet's first great success was won with *The Man Against the Sky* (1916). Some of his later works like *Tristam* (1927) outsold popular novels. Robinson not only had the ability to breathe life into material as apparently hackneyed as the Arthurian legends, but he could use traditional meters and verse forms to express highly original twists of thought and expression. Despite the wide range of his poetry—from short character studies to long narratives and from medieval romances to modern murder mysteries—a certain characteristic mood pervaded all his work. Almost obsessively aware of the omnipresence of evil and tragedy in the world, Robinson yet clung to a ray of hope—to the glimmer of "the Light" seen faintly through the pervading gloom.

Even slower than Robinson in winning recognition was Robert Frost. For twenty years, while he supported his growing family by schoolteaching, shoemaking, country journalism, and farming, Frost wrote poetry—most of which no one would publish. Despairing of support in America, he sold his New Hampshire farm in 1912 and sailed to England, accompanied by his wife and four children. There the freshness and originality of the poems contained in *A Boy's Will* (1913) and *North of Boston* (1914) were warmly praised. Fortunately, Frost bore America no ill will for its long neglect, and in 1915 he returned to the northern New England area which he loved and understood so well. In such fine later books as *New Hampshire* (1923) and *West Running Brook* (1928) Frost caught the beauty of the New England countryside at all seasons. He echoed the rhythms of Yankee speech and recorded its humor and intelligence. Despite his almost unvarying choice of regional themes he conveyed universal meanings: mending walls and swinging on birches became symbolic acts in Frost's kindly wisdom.

The exciting first course spread out between 1912 and 1920 aroused expectations of a feast of poetry that were not entirely satisfied. During the twenties magazines devoted to poetry multiplied, and many expert practitioners entered the field. Yet the frustration and discontent lying close to the surface of American life permitted few writers to achieve the poise and philosophic unity of Robinson and Frost. Edna St. Vincent Millay, who had won fame with "Renascence," published in 1912 while she was still an undergraduate at Vassar, maintained an extraordinary popularity. With the college generation her most widely quoted verses were those expressing lighthearted impudence and casual love—a kind of posturing that delighted a generation seeking to defy convention. More serious readers deplored these flippancies but applauded her fine sonnets and other lyrics.

T. S. Eliot, one of the most gifted poets of the day, found himself at home neither in his native St. Louis nor at Harvard University, where he earned bachelor's and master's degrees. Moving to London in 1914 and eventually becoming a naturalized British subject, Eliot nevertheless exerted a far-reaching influence on American poetry. He believed that in an exceedingly complex civilization poetry must become correspondingly complex. This was certainly true of his own work published in such volumes as *Prufrock and Other Observations* (1917) and *The Waste Land* (1922). Eliot's readers had to struggle with quotations in Greek, German, Latin, French, and Hebrew, with allusions to classical mythology and anthropology, with bewildering juxtapositions of slang and exalted diction. But the reward for this mental effort was to experience an exciting kind of poetry, technically brilliant and intellectually provocative. Eliot found his way out of the waste land by becoming, in his own words, "Anglo-Catholic in religion, royalist in politics, and classicist in literature." But few of his admirers followed him to these affirmations.

During the restless twenties poetry took many forms. E. E. Cummings, rebelling against capital letters and punctuation marks, wrote effective lyrics without them. Robinson Jeffers, isolating himself on the California coast, turned out poetry of unusual passion and violence. At Nashville, Tennessee, a Vanderbilt University group led by John Crowe Ransom and Allen Tate produced work distinguished by polished style and intellectual depth. Hart Crane, dissipated and unhappy, attempted to telescope all American experience into one long poem, *The Bridge* (1930)—a work of uneven merit but strikingly effective in parts.

Affection for the nation and the people—somewhat unfashionable during the early twenties—found more frequent expression in the thirties and forties. This was the theme of Hart Crane's most ambitious work; it was the note struck ever more firmly by Carl Sandburg. Archibald MacLeish had once written:

> A poem should not mean
> But be.

During the age of crisis, however, MacLeish abandoned this attitude of detachment and plunged into the strife of the day with such works as *America Was Promises* (1939). In essays and speeches he urged other literary people to follow his example. No exhortation was necessary in the case of Stephen Vincent Benét. Deep affection for America ran through all his work from his long narrative Civil War poem, *John Brown's Body* (1928), to his epic of colonization, *Western Star,* published after his death in 1943.

Novelists of the Twenties

Theodore Dreiser, whose early efforts had been obstructed by timid publishers and self-appointed custodians of public morals, came into his own during the twenties. In *An American Tragedy* (1925), his longest and most ambitious novel, Dreiser explored all the environmental factors that caused an ambitious young man to murder his sweetheart in order to be free to marry another woman of superior social position. Judgments differed sharply: one school of opinion proclaimed this to be a triumph of naturalism—not only Dreiser's masterpiece but one of the greatest of American novels; another, complaining of the author's tedious detail, his slovenly style, and the essential weakness of his principal character, rated the novel a pretentious failure. But scarcely to be denied was Dreiser's profound influence on scores of younger writers.

Another earnest exponent of naturalism was Sherwood Anderson. A moderately successful small-town businessman, Anderson once left his office and his job in the middle of dictating a letter. His restless subsequent career reflected a dissatisfaction with modern life which Anderson repeatedly delineated in his literary work. He was most successful in his short stories—a medium that he helped to emancipate from artificial plots and trick endings. In *Winesburg, Ohio* (1919) he wrote feelingly of the emotional problems of strong-willed individuals caught in the web of small-town society. Like Dreiser, Anderson insisted on exploring the impact of sex on the lives of his characters.

The extent to which literature might deal with sex became one of the liveliest controversies of the twenties. State and Federal laws prohibited the transportation and sale of obscene books, but what was obscene? Did the same ban apply to obviously pornographic material and to serious works of literature which offended not because of their effect as a whole but because of the frank language of some of their passages? The issue was clearly raised by the case of James Branch Cabell's *Jurgen* (1919). Cabell was a wealthy Virginian who for years had been writing urbane fantasies which had little in common with the naturalism of Dreiser and Anderson. Cabell's skepticism, irony, and literary skill had appealed to only a small audience until a new generation of sophisticated readers suddenly proclaimed *Jurgen* a modern masterpiece. The much-discussed novel dealt with the fantastic adventures of Jurgen, a middle-aged pawnbroker, who was given back his youth by the goddess of disillusion and visited heaven, hell, and numerous way stations in search of justice. The sexual aspect of many of Jurgen's experiences was scarcely concealed by the symbolic language which Cabell employed. For two years the New York Society for the Suppression of Vice was able to prevent the open sale of the book, but a New York judge finally ruled that it was "of unusual literary merit and contains nothing 'obscene, lewd, lascivious, filthy, indecent or disgusting' within the meaning of the statute. . . ." Although this victory heartened opponents of censorship, their long struggle was just beginning. The Boston Watch and Ward Society was successful in preventing the sale not only of Dreiser's *An American Tragedy* but of books as reserved in their treatment of forbidden subjects as Upton Sinclair's *Oil* and Sinclair Lewis's *Elmer Gantry*. In New York, censorship was less successful, and by the end of the decade the champions of frankness had gained an almost complete victory.

But—although the fact seemed sometimes to be forgotten—there were subjects other than sex which needed to be treated with greater honesty and realism. Sinclair Lewis, a native of Sauk City, Minnesota, satirized skillfully the cultural poverty, complacency, and noisy go-getting of small towns and provincial cities of the Middle West. His earlier writing had aroused little interest, but *Main Street* (1920) made him famous—or at least notorious, since many Americans were provoked to wrath against the author of so unflattering a description of small-town life. Equally fertile in controversy was *Babbitt* (1922), a novel which delineated with devastating sharpness a familiar American type—one who "made nothing in particular, neither butter nor shoes nor poetry," but was "nimble in the calling of selling houses for more than people could afford to pay." Babbitt was proud of his membership in the Boosters' Club, proud of the bustling city of Zenith and its 35-story skyscraper, proud of his "altogether royal bathroom of porcelain and glazed tile and metal sleek as silver." In *Arrowsmith* (1925) Lewis turned his attention to the medical profession. Once again he found many things that provoked his scorn, but he also found much to admire in the scientist's honest search for truth and desire to serve humanity. The most savage of Lewis's portraits was *Elmer Gantry* (1927)—an overdrawn picture of a hypocritical, high-pressure evangelist. Readers who assumed that Lewis had nothing but contempt for the American middle class were surprised by *Dodsworth* (1929), in which a businessman struggling to establish his independence from a domineering wife was sympathetically portrayed. Lewis was in reality far less hostile to American society than many of his literary contemporaries. His spirited assaults upon the artificial and the false derived their vigor from his basic affection for his country.

In 1920 when *Main Street* was arousing so much discussion, F. Scott Fitzgerald's *This Side of Paradise* also created excitement. The young people of this novel lived in an urban society far removed from Lewis's Gopher Prairie. Cynical and pleasure-loving, they sought to escape boredom with all-night parties, heavy drinking, and casual love-making. That Fitzgerald found in the revolt of youth a profitable theme is obvious from a mere listing of such titles as *Flappers and Philosophers* (1920), *Tales of the Jazz Age* (1922), *The Beautiful and Damned* (1922), and *All the Sad Young Men* (1926). Yet Fitzgerald did not need to rely on sensationalism. He had the sensitive perceptions and the literary skill to become a great writer. Among the finest novels of their day were *The Great Gatsby* (1925) and *Tender Is the Night* (1934). *The Last Tycoon* (1941), although only a fragment posthumously published, was a brilliant treatment of the fantastic world of Hollywood.

Fitzgerald was one of a sizable company of young American writers and artists who elected to reside abroad during the twenties. They deserted the homeland for many reasons. Prohibition and censorship aroused their resentment; the prevailing complacency and worship of material success exasperated them; to live in France was sometimes cheaper than to live in America. More strongly felt than anything else was a difference in the intellectual atmosphere; in Europe, as one writer expressed it, he was "able, spiritually, to breathe." The self-appointed ruler of this expatriate colony was Gertrude Stein, a wealthy American who had lived in Paris since 1903. Despite the artfully unintelligible character of her own writing Miss Stein's forceful personality made a deep impression on the young Americans who crowded her apartment. It was she who was reputed to have described her young admirers in a phrase of penetrating insight: "You are all a lost generation."

The best known description of the "lost generation" was Ernest Hemingway's *The Sun Also Rises* (1926). The central character was an American newspaperman whose life had been ruined by a war injury. He and his friends, disillusioned and bored, sought pleasure abroad in bouts of drinking, love-making, and attendance at bullfights. Hemingway himself was a husky young native of Illinois, who liked to box, to play football, and to hunt. During World War I he served as an ambulance driver on the Italian front; after the war he became a reporter in Paris. Both as a short-story writer and a novelist, Hemingway demonstrated exceptional ability. Rebelling against all high-flown language, he developed a style of extreme simplicity in which the narrative was largely developed by unadorned dialogue. Hemingway's short sentences and monosyllabic vocabulary established a pattern which many younger writers endeavored to imitate. Also influential was Hemingway's complete disillusionment with the romantic idealism which had pervaded World War I propaganda. The demoralizing chaos of modern war was depicted with unforgettable vividness in Hemingway's *A Farewell to Arms* (1929). Distrustful of all ideas, Hemingway glorified raw experience.

Disillusionment with World War I pervaded much of the literature of the twenties. Its earliest memorable statement was in John Dos Passos's *Three Soldiers* (1921). Dos Passos, a typical intellectual of the day, had studied at Harvard, served in the war, and traveled in Spain. In his later novels he attempted ambitious experiments both in subject matter and technique. His *Manhattan Transfer* (1925) reflected the complexity of urban society by introducing a score of characters, developing several parallel stories, and jumping rapidly from one to another. Still more grandiose was Dos Passos's attempt to portray the development of America for a whole generation in his trilogy *U S A*, composed of *The 42nd Parallel* (1930), *1919* (1932), and *The Big Money* (1936). Some readers believed *U S A* to be a uniquely comprehensive study of twentieth-century America; others contended that it was a gigantic distortion, magnifying American greed and shallowness and showing little of American idealism and intelligence.

Dos Passos's virtuosity was surpassed by that of William Faulkner, the author of somber tragedies with scenes almost invariably laid in his native Mississippi. One of the most interesting experiments in technique during the twenties was Faulkner's *The Sound and the Fury* (1929) in which the author first developed his grim story through the almost unintelligible stream of consciousness of an idiot and then from the points of view of two other characters. Thus was gradually disclosed the degeneration of the Compson family, a typical Faulknerian clan, once proud members of the Mississippi aristocracy and now fallen on evil days. Although Faulkner received international recognition with a Nobel prize in 1950, his difficult style and preoccupation with incest, insanity, suicide, and other horrors precluded any wide popularity for his novels.

While the male authors of the twenties were largely committed to naturalism, disillusionment, and satire and were struggling with new techniques, the leading women authors were finding it possible to write fine novels within the framework of an older tradition. Eldest of these was Edith Wharton, author of the stark New England tragedy *Ethan Frome* (1911) but best remembered for penetrating studies of New York society like *The Age of Innocence* (1920). In the same intimate way that Mrs. Wharton understood New York, Ellen Glasgow knew the aristocracy of Virginia. Miss Glasgow had no use for the old romanticism that had distorted southern literature; she was a realist seeking to tell the exact truth about her section, whether in historical novels like *The Battle-Ground* (1902), in novels of a declining agriculture like *Barren Ground* (1925), or in sensitive character studies like *The Sheltered Life* (1932). But she was no naturalist; even when her characters were defeated by forces too strong for them, they maintained their courage and integrity of character. Willa Cather, also born in Virginia, passed her childhood and youth in frontier Nebraska, where she listened with fascination to the talk of immigrant settlers. This was the scene of her first sensitive novels: *O Pioneers* (1913), *The Song of the Lark* (1915), and *My Antonia* (1918). Throughout the twenties Miss Cather continued to delight readers who appreciated fine writing and the sympathetic understanding of character. Widely praised as her masterpiece was *Death Comes for the Archbishop* (1927)—a warm recapturing of Catholic civilization in the Southwest.

Response to Depression and War

When American smugness was shattered by hard times and the revolt of youth was no longer news, literature had to turn to new themes. The novels of the thirties dealt more often with the evils of society than with the problems of individuals. Many of them were proudly proletarian—discovering heroes in workers and labor-union leaders and plots in strikes and acts of protest. To judge literature by aesthetic standards was no longer fashionable; its significance derived from its degree of social awareness.

John Dos Passos' *U S A* strongly reflected the new trends, as did other novels devoted to narrower themes. James T. Farrell, a naturalist strongly influenced by Dreiser, depicted with grim thoroughness the vice and brutality of the lower middle-class Irish section of Chicago where his own youth had been spent. His Studs Lonigan trilogy—*Young Lonigan* (1932), *The Young Manhood of Studs Lonigan* (1934), and *Judgment Day* (1935)—was a somber study in degeneracy. Equally depressing was Richard Wright's *Native Son* (1940)—a powerful account of the forces that made a murderer of a boy brought up in the Black Belt slums of Chicago. Erskine Caldwell's novels of poor-white life in the South achieved popularity by their grotesque humor, but a serious purpose seemed to underlie the burlesque of such works as *Tobacco Road* (1932), *God's Little Acre* (1933), and *Trouble in July* (1940).

John Steinbeck, only twenty-seven years old when the Great Depression began, dealt with the problems of the new period with conspicuous success. *In Dubious Battle* (1936) showed the bitterness of the strife between striking migrant fruit pickers and the vigilantes who opposed them. *The Grapes of Wrath* (1939) made vivid the plight of a family which was driven from Oklahoma by the great dust storms of the thirties and made the long trip to California, only to become tragically involved in the troubles of the migrant workers of that state.

Even the novelists, whose choice of subject and mood had set the style for the twenties, revealed new influences at work. Sinclair Lewis warned his readers of the possibilities of an American fascism in *It Can't Happen Here* (1935). Twelve years later the veteran novelist took up the explosive Negro question in *Kingsblood Royal* (1947). Ernest Hemingway's *For Whom the Bell Tolls* (1940) gave a balanced picture of the Spanish Civil War, showing its heroism and its brutality, its idealism and its stupidity. Hemingway's rejection of the anarchic individualism of the twenties was implicit in the very title of his novel, derived from a striking quotation from John Donne:

> No man is an Iland, intire of it selfe; . . . any man's death diminishes me, because I am involved in Mankinde; and therefore never send to know for whom the bell tolls; It tolls for thee.

Thomas Wolfe, the most unusual literary figure of the thirties, presented his publishers with manuscripts of such bulk that they could only be published after laborious editorial pruning. The first of these, *Look Homeward, Angel* (1929), told of the North Carolina boyhood and youth of Eugene Gant, a character easily identified as Wolfe himself. The autobiographical element was equally dominant in Wolfe's second novel, *Of Time and the River* (1935), which carried Elmer Gant's story through a period of graduate study at Harvard, life among the literary elite of New York City, and travel abroad. In his later novels Wolfe grew out of excessive preoccupation with his personal experiences into a more mature interest in the whole American environment. Wolfe's prose was interspersed with passages so lyrical that they were sometimes republished as poetry.

Many of these were exuberant expressions of Wolfe's love for his country and faith in its mystical destiny.

But greater literary appreciation for democratic ideals did not preclude the appearance of a crop of post-World War II books even more extreme than the works of the twenties in their disillusionment with war and the life of the soldier. Typical of these were the widely read novels *The Naked and the Dead* (1948), by Norman Mailer, and *From Here to Eternity* (1951), by James Jones. A better balanced description of the life of men at war was contained in Herman Wouk's fine novel, *The Caine Mutiny* (1951).

Battle of the Critics

While poets and novelists produced works which exhibited contrasting attitudes toward life and society, serious students of literature debated the underlying issues involved. During the second and third decades of the twentieth century literary radicalism became a vogue. Van Wyck Brooks in *America's Coming-of-Age* (1915) stated a theme that was to be heard with variations over the next several years. American cultural life was criticized as thin and bloodless; the inhibiting factors were the Puritan tradition, provincialism, and academic narrowness. During the twenties Brooks undertook to demonstrate this thesis with case studies of Mark Twain and Henry James. Not until the 1930's did this pioneer radical turn from his attack on false gentility to such mellow appreciations of American literary achievement as *The Flowering of New England, 1815–1865* (1936).

H. L. Mencken applied the pickax most vigorously to the clay feet of national idols. As Baltimore newspaperman, as editor of *Smart Set* and the *American Mercury*, and as author of several volumes of *Prejudices*, Mencken delighted the irreverent and outraged the pious with slashing attacks on clericals, local boosters, politicians, and professors. Although most influential in his role as iconoclast, the Baltimore critic contributed to the formulation of literary taste during the twenties through his enthusiasm for the unpolished naturalism of Dreiser and the sophisticated fantasy of Cabell. To the student of American culture, Mencken's most useful work was *The American Language*—a labor of love first published in 1919 and several times expanded.

The point of view of the literary radicals, represented not alone by Brooks and Mencken but by Randolph Bourne, Ludwig Lewisohn, and many other writers, soon provoked a countermovement. In several thoughtful volumes W. C. Brownell condemned the sensational naturalism of the day and appealed for finer values. The so-called "new humanism" became particularly associated with the teaching and writing of Irving Babbitt at Harvard and Paul Elmer More at Princeton. The new humanists condemned both religious orthodoxy and scientific determinism. Insisting upon the unique qualities of man—his reason, his freedom of will, and his ability to formulate ideals—the conservative critics condemned with equal vigor nineteenth-century romanticism and twentieth-century naturalism, calling instead for a return to classical literary standards of harmony and restraint.

During the thirties many of the radicals went beyond attack upon the old orthodoxies to the formulation of new ones of their own. Marxism provided a particularly inviting framework of ideas for many intellectuals: it purported to be scientific and realistic; it appeared to explain the economic and social dislocations of the Great Depression; above all, it represented the ultimate in defiant revolt against the existing order. Donning Marxist spectacles, critics like V. F. Calverton and Granville Hicks reassessed American literature, both past and present, in terms of economic determinism and class struggle. Earnest radicals of the day even divided into Stalinist and Trotskyist factions. Shocked by the Hitler-Stalin Pact of 1939, Granville Hicks repudiated Communism and became a fervent champion of traditional American values. Many of the other literary Marxists experienced a similar disenchantment during the forties.

Even critics untouched by Marxism tended during the thirties to judge literature largely on the basis of the social and political ideas which it reflected. This trend, natural enough under the conditions of the period, was strongly accelerated by the success of Vernon Louis Parrington's *Main Currents in American Thought* (1926–1930). Brilliantly written, provocative in its judgments, and sturdy in its democratic faith, Parrington's great work was a potent intellectual force, weakening the influence of the Hamiltonian ideal and strengthening that of Jefferson.

But emphasis on the sociological interpretation of literature brought in turn a reaction toward aestheticism. There was a striking revival of interest in Henry James both as theorist and practitioner of literary art. Study of structure and style was also stimulated by the writings of the two later expatriates, Ezra Pound and T. S. Eliot. The so-called "new critics"—men like Edmund Wilson, Kenneth Burke, and R. P. Blackmur—analyzed literature with a sharp eye both to its technical competence and the integrity of its moral ideas. Some of the exponents of aestheticism were friendly to experiments with style inspired by Freudian psychoanalysis, the study of semantics, and the like. Others rejected these innovations and called for a return to older standards. John Crowe Ransom, Allen Tate, and others of the regionalist school condemned the literature and civilization of industrial America and urged southern authors to take their stand on the aristocratic agrarian tradition both in art and life.

The lively battle of the critics gave evidence that a growing number of Americans took a serious interest in the world of poetry and fiction.

Literature for the Market

The market for books and magazines expanded with the population and the increasing number of Americans who received at least elementary schooling. Its levels of taste could be measured by the various types of magazines. For the simplest minds there were numerous periodicals devoted to western stories, crime stories, the "real life" of the movie actors, and "true" romances and confessions. For the vast middle class of business people and housewives there were magazines of huge circulation like the *Saturday Evening Post, Collier's, Ladies' Home Journal, Woman's Home Companion,* and *McCall's,* all hardy perennials planted in an earlier period, to which were now added the fabulously successful *Reader's Digest, Time, Newsweek,* and *Life.* For readers seeking stimulating ideas, there were magazines of smaller circulation but great influence like the venerable *Nation,* the younger *New Republic*, and the vigorously mature *Atlantic Monthly* and *Harper's.* During the twenties the *American Mercury* was the particular delight of sophisticated readers who enjoyed the sharp comment of H. L. Mencken and George Jean Nathan. Of more permanent influence was *The New Yorker,* founded in 1925 and destined to create a more subtle American humor. Finally, there were innumerable "little magazines," which had small circulation and short lives but served a useful function in encouraging new talent and in exploring the intellectual stratosphere.

For each level of readers there was not only a type of magazine but a type of book. Several new marketing devices greatly influenced the publishing business. Since regular bookstores were only to be found in the larger cities, an enormous market awaited entrepreneurs shrewd enough to organize the large-scale sale of books by mail. Two such ventures, the Book-of-the-Month Club and the Literary Guild, were successfully launched in 1926. By offering various book premiums, each club was able to enroll thousands of subscribers committed to buy a minimum number of books each year from selections made monthly by a board of experts. By 1939 the Book-of-the-Month Club had pushed its membership to 200,000. The most remarkable period of growth was during the forties. Despite the war—or perhaps because of it—the Book-of-the-Month Club achieved a membership of one million in 1946. The Literary Guild lagged behind its rival during the early thirties but grew prodigiously after 1937 when the selection of books was placed in the hands of John Beecroft, who possessed an uncanny knowledge of what his subscribers would like. By catering to the general demand for a simple type of fiction with easily followed plot, the Literary Guild was able to attract a membership of 1,250,000 by 1946. The success of the two pioneer clubs encouraged imitation. Clubs were tailored to fit every variety of interest and every pocketbook. Some fifty were in the field in 1947.

The book-club vogue reflected the willingness of thousands of subscribers to defer to the judgment of "experts" in selecting what they ought to read. Although the "book-of-the-month" was often a volume of little enduring importance, the clubs assured wide distribution for many thoroughly worthy books which might otherwise have had a much smaller sale. One of the first great book-club successes was Pearl Buck's fine novel *The Good Earth* (1931), and the clubs gave a well-deserved popularity to the satires of John Marquand. They also opened up a large market for serious works of nonfiction; one of their most extraordinary exploits was to make a best seller of a one-volume condensation of Arnold Toynbee's erudite *A Study of History.*

Books which had exhausted the market in their original editions often achieved excellent sales when reprinted in cheaper bindings and distributed through department stores and drugstores. The economics of the situation was obvious. Every reduction in price opened a new market. The ultimate achievement was the quarter book—a reprint bound in a stiff, glazed paper cover with an arresting design to catch the eye of the newsstand customer. Pocket Books, Inc., began to exploit this market in 1939 with amazing results. By the summer of 1946 the pioneer company had printed 420 different titles and had sold an aggregate of 1½ million books.

Since the pocket-book publishers paid royalties of only 1 cent a copy to be divided equally between author and original publisher, this business was more important in stimulating the reading habits of the population than in increasing the rewards of authorship. But writers fortunate enough to have their work selected for distribution by the larger book clubs collected handsome profits. Hollywood offered another source of wealth to the lucky few. Hungry for good stories, the producers often bought motion-picture rights at fancy figures even before a novel's publication. Skillful writers were also much in demand in Hollywood to supply dialogue and to develop story ideas.

Any book achieving phenomenally large sales was likely to be followed by many others attempting to gain success by the same formula. During the thirties two long historical novels—Hervey Allen's *Anthony Adverse* (1933) and Margaret Mitchell's *Gone With the Wind* (1936) [1]—dominated the best-seller lists for many months. Historical romances thereafter appeared with monotonous regularity, each attempting to outdo its rivals in picturesque derring-do and amorous adventure. The adroit mixture of earnest moral lesson with interesting story, which had brought success to General Lew Wallace, Charles M. Sheldon, and Harold Bell Wright in an earlier day, still possessed magic power. The Reverend Lloyd C. Douglas, writing his first novel at the age of fifty-one, gained great popularity with *Magnificent Obsession* (1929). His *Green Light* (1935) led the best-seller lists in the year of its publication, and *The Robe* (1943) sold almost two million copies.

Busy people, looking for fast-moving fiction that would help them to forget momentarily their own problems and those of the world, were likely to become mystery-story addicts. Erle Stanley Gardner, who learned about courts and crime as a lawyer in California, exploited this market most skillfully. Able to compose so rapidly that he kept from three to five secretaries busy transcribing dictaphone records, Gardner produced one best seller after another. Seven of his stories in their original editions and cheap reprints achieved sales of over 1,200,-

[1] By selling about three million copies, *Gone With the Wind* became the most popular novel in American publishing history, even surpassing *Uncle Tom's Cabin.*

000 each. Other conspicuously successful practitioners in this field were "S. S. Van Dine," Earl Derr Biggers, Dashiell Hammett, and "Ellery Queen."

Though the literature of escape represented by historical romances, religious novels, and crime stories had great popularity during this age of troubles, many readers were eager to study books that discussed the serious issues of the day. Pierre van Paassen's *Days of Our Years* was a best seller in 1939, William L. Shirer's *Berlin Diary* in 1941, and Wendell Willkie's *One World* in 1943.

Although the size of the American market increased the rewards for authors who could establish themselves, the problems of newcomers tended to increase rather than to diminish. The costs of publishing mounted steadily with the rising price of paper, higher wages, and greater advertising expenses. Consequently, publishers became more and more reluctant to place books on the market unless they could be sure that their sales would at least cover printing costs.

Changing Styles of Architecture

The prosperity and optimism of the twenties encouraged the construction of thousands of buildings. The entire country took pride in New York's towering skyscrapers. Five buildings now topped the Woolworth Tower. The new champion was the Empire State Building with 102 stories, soaring 1,250 feet above the sidewalk. Although the skyscraper had less justification in cities not so restricted in area, the tall office building became a matter of local pride throughout the country. Chicago had nine skyscrapers of 500 feet or more, and Cincinnati, Cleveland, Detroit, Kansas City, Philadelphia, Pittsburgh, and Seattle all had one or more such giants. Most of the great towers were office buildings, but the skyscraper form was adapted for city halls in Philadelphia and Los Angeles, for the state capitol of Louisiana, and for the University of Pittsburgh.

The hand of tradition lay heavy on most American architecture. In the classicism of Henry Bacon's Lincoln Memorial in Washington or in the Gothic churches and college buildings designed by Ralph Adams Cram, the general public found a comfortable standard of beauty that even the simplest could appreciate. Modernists who demanded greater boldness and originality were voices crying in the wilderness. The issue was sharply defined in 1922, when architects from all over the world were invited to submit their designs for the Chicago Tribune Tower. The competition attracted 260 plans from 23 different nations; most of the drawings were eclectic horrors, but a few were strongly prophetic of new trends. The prize design, submitted by John Mead Howells and Raymond Hood, disappointed the modernists by its resort to Gothic detail and flying buttresses. But the design which received the second prize, the work of the Finnish architect Eliel Saarinen, delineated what was perhaps the most famous building never actually built. Its simplicity and cleanness of outline revealed new possibilities of beauty in the skyscraper, were it once to be emancipated from extraneous ornamentation. The

FIG. 51. Eliel Saarinen's design for the Chicago Tribune Tower. Although awarded only second prize in the competition, Saarinen's beautiful design had great influence on American skyscraper architecture. (*Courtesy of Mrs. Eliel Saarinen.*)

influence of Saarinen's plan was to be seen in many of the buildings erected during the late twenties.

Modernism invaded skyscraper design with less opposition than it did other areas where tradition had established itself more firmly. Intellectuals admired the buildings planned by the French architect Le Corbusier and other Europeans, but most Americans were repelled by their coldness and excessively geometrical design. Modernism in architecture, like many other artistic vogues of the day, seemed to be an expatriate growth without vital American roots. Yet in this field also there was a spiritual homecoming during the thirties and forties. American architects rediscovered many sturdy regional styles where form had followed function for generations. Pennsylvania barns, western ranch houses, and California residences had been adapted to climate, topography, and available materials in various ways which were of interest to designers seeking fresh modes of expression. Moreover, a prophet, long neglected in his own country, came at last into his own. Frank Lloyd Wright had the artist's touch necessary to clothe the functional house in romantic beauty. Leaving to others the exploitation of the vertical architecture of the skyscraper, Wright became a master of the horizontal—spacious homes that seemed to cling to the earth and made the most of natural settings. The influence of Wright was to be seen increasingly in the residential construction of the thirties and forties. By then modernism was also invading other strongholds of traditionalism—college, school, and public-building architecture.

Painters' America

Admirably equipped to bridge the gap that had long existed between American art and American society was George W. Bellows,[1] whose brilliant career was cut short by death in 1925. Once a star shortstop for the Ohio State University baseball team, Bellows had a typically American love for sports. In virile paintings and drawings of the prize ring, he demonstrated his ability to transmit the rough vigor of one side of American life. But he showed equal talent in tender portraits and scenes of everyday activity.

Art in the hands of a brilliant group of Middle Westerners became a means of interpreting regional patterns of American life. After studying in Europe and experimenting in the fads of the day, Grant Wood came to the sudden realization, so he said, that all his really good ideas had come to him when he was milking a cow. So he went back to Iowa to spend the rest of his life teaching art at Iowa State University and painting pictures rich in understanding of the hardy farm folk of his native state. In neighboring Missouri Thomas Hart Benton developed a highly individual style based on humorous recapture of the frontier spirit. Kansas was no less fortunate in its artist-interpreter. John Steuart Curry[2] faithfully recorded the simple piety of frontier baptisms, the awful power of prairie storms, and the fierce fanaticism of such historic Kansans as John Brown.

Other regionalists were not so closely associated with particular states. Charles Burchfield developed a unique ability to invest the commonplace with nostalgic beauty. Even in ugly Victorian Gothic houses on drab streets Burchfield's sensitive art discovered a kind of poetry. A close observer of New York City and the Atlantic Coast was Edward Hopper, who found subjects among such unlovely scenes as run-down mansions, shabby streets, and cheap hotel rooms. Other

[1] See Figs. 41 and 54. [2] See Fig. 50.

painters devoted themselves to the interpretation of every variety of American landscape and every facet of American society.

Of course, regional art was susceptible to overemphasis—to the crowding out of the painter's legitimate interest in the study of people as individuals, and in the exploration of impressions and ideas without consideration of their social importance. American art retained its balance through the work of many craftsmen of sharply individual interests. Eugene Speicher and Leon Kroll painted portraits of exceptional sensitivity. John Carroll developed his own dreamy imaginative style, and Max Weber, John Marin, and Georgia O'Keeffe sought through the use of symbols to express ideas of great subtlety.

FIG. 52. *Arts of the West.* Mural by Thomas Hart Benton. Representative of the artist's discovery of lively subjects in the life and traditions of various American regions. (*Collection of Whitney Museum of American Art.*)

Perhaps the most significant development of the thirties was the greatly increased interest of the general public in art. More commonly than ever before the walls of government office buildings were decorated with interesting murals. The practice spread to thousands of local post offices and school buildings. Much of this work was made possible through the Federal Art Project, organized under the Works Progress Administration to provide employment for artists hard hit by the depression. Thousands of easel paintings were loaned by the project for display in schools, libraries, and hospitals. Not many of these were great art, but they served to educate a much wider public in the interesting world of color and imagination.

Music and the Machine

The phonograph, invented by Thomas A. Edison in 1877, had achieved a place of honor in thousands of American living rooms by 1914. Although reproduction was thin and lifeless, the machines made the names of the great operatic and concert artists of the day household words. The records of Caruso, McCormack, Schumann-Heink, and Paderewski sold in huge volume and added materially to the rewards of musicianship.

During the twenties most families relegated the phonograph to the attic to make room for the new radio. It was commonly assumed that hearing records could never hold its own against the thrilling experience of listening to music transmitted from the actual concert hall. Radio did indeed offer rich opportunities. Concerts by the great symphony orchestras, complete operas, and recitals by famous performers were now regularly available to those who enjoyed serious music. When sound was added to motion pictures, another mass medium was provided. In occasional movies the leading musical personalities of the day were now to be heard; in others the life and work of some great composer served as theme.

But the phonograph's eclipse proved temporary. During the thirties and forties music lovers discovered that the older machine was better adapted for their pleasure than its younger rivals. Through new electrical techniques of recording and reproducing the quality of the original performance could now be recreated with a minimum of loss. Record collecting became the hobby of thousands of Americans, who thus insured that they would always have music to suit their mood without dependence on the rigid programs of radio or on Hollywood's starvation diet.

Although the various devices for mechanical reproduction enormously increased the audience which could listen appreciatively to music, their influence was not entirely good. In the glare of fame now enveloping the best known musicians, many artists scarcely less talented were thrown into the shade. Especially threatened by the encroachments of the machine were thousands of local musicians. When the movies began to carry their own sound track, local theater orchestras were largely disbanded. Smaller groups of musicians who played in restaurants and dine-and-dance resorts often lost their jobs to gaudy jukeboxes. Insecurity drove the musicians' union to countermeasures that annoyed the general public.

Signs of a new birth of community interest in music presently appeared. In the public schools music escaped from the status of exotic intruder to a more respected place in the curriculum. Children enjoyed a sense of achievement in performing together in school bands and orchestras. During the depression large audiences heard the free concerts of WPA orchestras and learned to listen with respect to civic groups which played interesting music often neglected by the great symphony organizations. After the WPA program was terminated, an increasing number of cities supported local civic orchestras.

America's dependence on foreign performers was still great but less complete than in earlier days. Among the great singers of the new generation were such native artists as Gladys Swarthout, Grace Moore, Eleanor Steber, Marian Anderson, Helen Traubel, Lawrence Tibbett, Jan Peerce, and Leonard Warren. Although American-born instrumentalists of comparable rank were fewer, they included master violinists like Albert Spalding and Yehudi Menuhin. The immaturity of American music was most obvious in the scarcity of native conductors: the top-ranking orchestras of the country were almost as dependent on Europeans in 1950 as they had been in 1900.

Opera repertoires, symphony and concert programs, and record catalogues all testified to the fact that American listeners still accepted the work of European composers as their staple diet. On the stage of the Metropolitan Opera Company the works of Americans like Deems Taylor and Howard Hanson were occasionally presented, and the Boston Symphony Orchestra under the direction of Serge Koussevitzky was more likely than most major orchestras to play the work of Aaron Copland, Roy Harris, Leonard Bernstein, and other talented young Americans. But these were regarded by the general public as novelties, hardly to be compared with the compositions of contemporary Europeans like Strauss, Stravinsky, and Sibelius, to say nothing of the older masters. One of the boldest American pioneers, Charles Ives, wrote music so difficult that it was seldom to be heard at all.

Many intellectuals refused to regret America's failure to contribute more to the world's literature of operas, symphonies, and concertos—old bottles ill shaped to hold effervescent New World wine. Jazz, which had broken out of its New Orleans chrysalis during World War I, flourished mightily in Chicago, New York, London, and other new habitats.

Hitherto the creation of small dance bands, the new music soon attempted more pretentious forms. Paul Whiteman, acclaimed the "King of Jazz" by his astute publicity agents, assembled a large orchestra and played elaborate "symphonic arangements" in the largest theaters of the country. In 1924 Whiteman attempted to command the attention of serious music lovers by presenting an all-jazz concert at Aeolian Hall in New York City. Loud applause greeted Whiteman's performance of the "Rhapsody in Blue," especially written for the occasion by George Gershwin, already famous as a composer of hit tunes for Broadway shows. Introducing Gershwin's "Concerto in F" in 1925, the veteran conductor Walter Damrosch paid tribute to the composer and to Lady Jazz. "He is the Prince who has taken Cinderella by the hand and openly proclaimed her a princess to the astonished world, no doubt to the fury of her envious sisters." Gershwin's happiest venture in symphonic composition was "An American in Paris" (1928), and his "Porgy and Bess" (1935) proved to be an interesting experiment in "folk opera."

Jazz appealed to many serious composers as a new and original way of saying things musically. Americans like Aaron Copland and Marc Blitzstein experimented with jazz ideas, and Europeans like Stravinsky, Milhaud, and Ravel showed the American influence in some of their work.

But the notion that jazz needed to marry "serious music" in order to become an honest woman brought howls of rage from lovers of "pure" jazz. Whiteman was dismissed as a mere promoter; Gershwin was characterized as a song-writing genius whose attempts at pretentious composition never quite came off. Indeed, many purists looked with suspicion on all attempts to write jazz and regarded improvisation as its essence. Jazz fundamentalists had to hear their jazz on old records, since the music they loved was essentially a lost art that had flourished in New Orleans and Chicago and then been contaminated by the commercialization of the twenties. Jazz liberals regarded jazz as a continuing development and accepted as legitimate heroes such later jazz men as Louis Armstrong, "Fats" Waller, "Duke" Ellington, "Count" Basie, and—with some reservations—Benny Goodman. Although the "sweet" music of the early thirties was regarded with horror, the rise of "swing" and "bebop" was acclaimed as a return to sound principles.

Recognized neither by the lovers of symphony and opera nor by the specialists in jazz were the commercial song writers who ground out tunes for Tin Pan Alley. Most of their product was indeed insipid and soon forgotten. A few of the tunesmiths, however, created songs in the Stephen Foster tradition—simple melodies that millions of Americans continued to hum years after they were published. Irving Berlin contributed such memorable songs as "Alexander's Ragtime Band," "Easter Parade," and "White Christmas," Cole Porter the haunting melody "Night and Day," and Hoagy Carmichael the sentimental "Star Dust."

Entertainment for the Millions

Although the production and projection of moving pictures had become highly profitable by 1914, the business was still dominated by unfortunate assumptions. Movie audiences were visualized as predominantly composed of the poor and the ignorant—groups that had provided most of the patronage for the nickelodeons. Stories designed for these customers, it was believed, had to be short and exceedingly simple. Cheaply and unintelligently made, most American films were less original and interesting than the contemporary product of European studios.

During the years 1914 to 1919 this situation was radically altered. The motion-picture audience multiplied and became predominantly middle class in composition. Pictures became longer and more ingenious in plot. Suddenly spurting ahead of European competition, the American industry captured some 90 per cent of the world market. Many factors combined to produce this revolution. The closing of European studios during World War I provided American movie makers with a golden opportunity. Experimentation was encouraged by circumstances within the industry: since the so-called "movie trust" controlled the nickelodeon market, the independents were encouraged to produce more ambitious films for the pretentious moving-picture theaters now being built. Finally, these years saw the emergence of imaginative directors, who could sense the larger possibilities of the medium, and of talented stars, who could arouse the enthusiasm of the customers.

Boldest of the directors was David Wark Griffith, who began making pictures for Biograph in 1908. A restless experimenter, Griffith eventually organized his own company in order to be free to work out his ambitious ideas. On *The Birth of a Nation* (1915) Griffith spent a sum sufficient to make six ordinary movies of the day. The picture was a vast epic of the Civil War and Reconstruction, based upon the Reverend Thomas Dixon's novel, *The Clansman.* Not only was the film much longer and more pretentious than any predecessor, but it displayed for the first time the full technical possibilities of the screen. Griffith's camera was a restless eye following the action of the story—now compassing an entire battlefield, now focusing on the expression of a single face, flashing from one scene to another and back and forth in time. First shown in New York, *The Birth of a Nation* drew capacity audiences despite the $2 admission price. Eventually exhibited to crowded theaters all over the United States and abroad, the Griffith film was the most sensational success in the history of the movies. It demonstrated the dangers of mass entertainment as well as its profits. By exaggerating Negro crime and brutality, *The Birth of a Nation* did incalculable harm to race relations; by glorifying the original Ku Klux Klan, it helped to fasten on the nation the vicious Klan of the twenties.

The movies' great leap in popularity was more to be attributed to hero worship than to any other factor. In 1909 when Griffith gave sixteen-year-old Gladys Smith an acting job, the Biograph Company little realized that it had acquired a golden asset. Believing that its actors should remain inconspicuous, the company refused to answer inquiries written in by customers captivated with the sweet girl with golden curls who played the part of "our Mary." But the day of anonymity was brief. Gladys Smith was soon known to millions of Americans and Europeans as Mary Pickford—"America's Sweetheart." When Mary fell in love with Douglas Fairbanks, who had fascinated movie audiences by his high spirits, flashing smile, and athletic grace, the country was delighted. The princess of the American fairyland had found her prince.

In 1913 Charlie Chaplin, an English vaudeville performer specializing in pantomime, began to act in Mack Sennett's Keystone Comedies. Chaplin's talents were particularly well adapted to the silent screen. His toothbrush mustache, derby hat, baggy pants, and cane made him a figure more immediately recognized than any other personality of his generation. Although he fitted well into the slapstick comedy world, his extraordinary ability to convey an idea through a simple gesture and his subtle blending of pathos and hilarious farce gave his acting an artistry that delighted many intellectuals ordinarily contemptuous of Hollywood products.

Other stars became famous for their romantic ardor. The "vamp," a fascinating type of wicked woman, became familiar to movie audiences through the acting of Theda Bara and her imitators. The "great lover" of the twenties was Rudolph Valentino, star of *The Sheik, The Four Horsemen of the Apocalypse,* and *Blood and Sand.* When Valentino died in 1926, hysterical women mobbed his funeral service.

FIG. 53. *Twenty Cent Movie.* Painting by Reginald Marsh. Moralists sometimes had as much to worry about in the lurid theater billboards as they did in the movies themselves. (*Collection of Whitney Museum of American Art.*)

The popularity of vamps, sheiks, and other creatures of dubious morality alarmed many parents and clerics. Fear that the movies would make virtue seem dull and vice alluring created a widespread demand for censorship. The campaign for control gained impetus from several unfortunate personal scandals in the movie colony during the early twenties. Frightened movie makers attempted to set their house in order by organizing the Motion Picture Producers and Distributors of America, Inc. Postmaster General Will H. Hays was induced to resign from Harding's cabinet to head the organization. Under the guidance of the Hays office the studios pledged themselves to eliminate from films overpassionate love scenes, the ridicule of any religious group, or the portrayal of crime or sin in which the culprit escaped just retribution.

Up to 1926 the silence of the films was their most important characteristic.

Although this factor burdened the movies with exaggerated gestures and absurd subtitles, there were compensations. With no sound to record, the cameramen were free to experiment with ingenious techniques of photography, and directors could improvise episodes on the inspiration of the moment, uninhibited by a rigid script. In the great movie palaces of the cities the films were shown to the accompaniment of orchestras or pipe organs, often playing musical scores especially composed for the pictures. In rural movie halls pianists developed facility in accompanying the film stories with their own selection of appropriate music. Juvenile audiences amused themselves by shouting warnings or advice to the screen characters, whistling at the heroines, hissing the villains, and supplying appropriate bits of dialogue.

Those who enjoyed the amiable chaos of the old movie houses could not regard the development of talking movies as clear gain. But the difficult problems of synchronizing picture and sound were at length solved. Short sound films featuring famous musicians of the day were exhibited in 1926, and the first full-length sound picture, *The Jazz Singer,* starring Al Jolson, was released in 1927. During the next two years every branch of the business grappled with serious problems. Thousands of theaters had to purchase expensive new equipment and be wired for sound. Producers had to build sound studios, secure carefully written scripts, hire actors who could speak distinctly, and fire those who could not. The movie fans followed these developments with intense interest. Even in the days of the catastrophic Wall Street crash the principal worry of many Americans was whether Garbo could talk. When the great Swedish star strolled into a waterfront saloon in *Anna Christie* (1930) and demanded in a throaty voice, "Gif me a visky," a sigh of relief rolled across the land.

The transition to sound brought the movies to a peak of popularity in 1929, when an estimated 95 million customers a week crowded the theaters. Although attendance dropped during the depression, interest in the transformed medium helped to cushion the shock of bad times.

Under pressure on one side from church and parent organizations for stories that would not offend against good morals and on the other from intellectuals for realistic films that would come to grips with fundamental issues, Hollywood walked a precarious tightrope. The flood of gangster films during the early thirties was condemned by some critics for glorifying crime and defended by others as a healthy warning to the nation. Particularly disturbing to many was the misconception of normal American life fostered in foreign countries through the wholesale export of crime pictures and stories of the antics of the idle rich. Hollywood producers who attempted to warn the nation of the Nazi threat were subjected to Congressional accusations of warmongering. During the forties the producers showed greater courage in dealing with serious problems like racial intolerance, juvenile delinquency, alcoholism, and insanity.

The impact of the screen on American life was undeniable. Since Americans of every section saw the same pictures, the movies had a nationalizing influence.

Provincial accents and idiom tended to give way to the spoken language heard from the screen; indeed, the popularity of Hollywood films in England threatened to modify the mother tongue. Americans became better groomed by copying the dress and hair styles of their favorite stars. Whether the movies made the nation happier might well be doubted. Frequent excursions into a world of imagination probably made it harder to live in the world of hard reality where husbands seldom looked like Clark Gable nor wives like Hedy Lamarr. The publicity attending the frequent marriages and divorces of the idolized stars combined with other factors to undermine the stability of American family life.

The competition of the movies applied the *coup de grâce* to the old-style provincial stock companies, already weakened by earlier developments. The decay of the theater was regretted in many quarters, and there were frequent attempts at revival. College students often gave excellent amateur performances; earnest "little-theater" groups wrote and performed experimental plays. During the thirties the WPA theater project revived interest in stage plays in many communities, and in the forties summer stock companies were highly successful in rural vacation centers. Despite these local efforts, however, only New York could count on a rich annual offering of plays. Other cities were largely dependent on the occasional visits of road companies.

Notwithstanding these difficulties, writing for the stage attained an excellence unknown in earlier days. Most gifted of the new dramatists was Eugene O'Neill, whose plays were first presented in 1915 by the Provincetown Players—one of the pioneer little-theater groups. Although O'Neill rejected all the established formulas, his dramas played to crowded theaters during the twenties. *Desire under the Elms* (1924) was a New England tragedy involving the struggle of a stern patriarch and his son for the same farm and the same woman. In *The Great God Brown* (1926), dealing with the problem of genius frustrated by mediocrity, the actors wore masks to symbolize the pretenses of modern life. *Strange Interlude* (1928), a play on a Freudian theme and three times the usual length, used long soliloquies to reveal the secret thoughts of its characters. *Mourning Becomes Electra* (1931) was a trilogy, transferring one of the great themes of Greek tragedy to an American setting. The acclaim of these grim tragedies reflected the contemporary eagerness to applaud revolts against convention.

The New York stage offered a variety of fare during the thirties and forties. Maxwell Anderson wrote effective tragedies in verse like *Elizabeth the Queen* (1930) and *Winterset* (1935). S. N. Behrman provided comedies witty and wise enough to delight the sophisticated. Clifford Odets devoted his considerable talents to proletarian appeals like *Waiting for Lefty* (1935). William Saroyan exhibited his optimistic exuberance in *The Time of Your Life* (1939). Deservedly popular were the well-written plays of Robert E. Sherwood and Thornton Wilder.

Musical comedies, long favorites with the American public, also gained in maturity. Jerome Kern's melodious *Show Boat* was a hit of the twenties and the Gershwin brothers' *Of Thee I Sing* dealt entertainingly with American politics during the early thirties. The finest musical plays of the next decade resulted from the partnership of Oscar Hammerstein II and Richard Rodgers. Their *Oklahoma* (1943) pioneered in the use of ballet to enrich musical comedy, and *South Pacific* (1949), which enlisted the talents of Ezio Pinza, famous Metropolitan Opera Company artist, achieved an extraordinary success.

After a generation of experimental work regular radio broadcasting began from Westinghouse station KDKA, Pittsburgh, on November 2, 1920. The Harding-Cox election returns provided the first program material. As the radio fad swept the country, bringing receivers into 10 million homes by 1929, the full commercial implications of the situation became evident. The broadcast of programs sponsored by advertisers began in 1922. The advertising possibilities were enormously increased through the coast-to-coast hookups provided by the National Broadcasting Company, organized in 1926, the Columbia Broadcasting Company, organized in 1930, and later chains.

American radio differed significantly from that of most foreign countries, where the governments owned the stations and levied a tax on receiving sets to pay the expenses of broadcasting. The weakness of the American system was its annoying flood of "commercials" and the shallowness of many of its programs. American radio, however, was in less danger than foreign of becoming an agency for government propaganda, and its programs had at least the merit of popularity with the mass of the population, whose listening habits were regularly checked through polls. Even under the American system some government regulation proved necessary when the existence of over seven hundred stations threatened chaos on the air waves. A Federal commission was established to grant licenses, to assign wave lengths, and to fix hours of operation.

By 1949 there were radio sets in 42 million American homes. Although many critics were disappointed by the industry's failure to assign more time to programs of an educational type, there could be no doubt that the invention had contributed to the happiness of millions of persons. To invalids the radio brought the consolation of regular religious services and stories that helped to pass the weary days. To isolated farms it brought market reports and entertainment for the hours after the completion of chores. Housewives cooked and dusted to the accompaniment of innumerable soap operas—radio serials carrying favorite characters through lugubrious trials and tribulations. Millions of Americans placed more reliance on the broadcasts of "commentators" and "newscasters" than on the newspapers. Political campaigning was revolutionized by the radio, and the electoral success of Franklin D. Roosevelt was believed to result in part from his skill in the new medium.

An extraordinary demonstration of both the latent power of the radio and the neurotic credulity of the American public was provided by the Orson Welles *War of the Worlds* broadcast of 1938. Intended merely as a vivid dramatization of one of H. G. Wells's fantasies, the broadcast terrified at least a million Americans, who were convinced that the New Jersey countryside was being ravaged by a rocket-borne invasion from Mars.

Long anticipated as the next logical step, television became a commercial reality after World War II. Although the first receivers were expensive, high postwar earnings resulted in larger sales than had been expected. By 1950 about eight

FIG. 54. *Dempsey and Firpo.* Painting by G. W. Bellows. An exciting moment in the sports history of the 1920's, when Firpo knocked Dempsey, the champion, out of the ring. Dempsey came back to win by a knockout. (*Collection of Whitney Museum of American Art.*)

million sets were in use and over one hundred stations were sending out programs. Supported by advertising, television seemed destined to inherit both the virtues and vices of American radio.

The fact that some of the most popular television offerings were baseball, football, and wrestling contests emphasized the sports-mindedness of the American public. During the twenties the extraordinary prowess of Babe Ruth, who hit 54 home runs for the New York Yankees in 1920, 59 in 1921, and 60 in 1927, helped to bring big-league baseball to a peak of popularity. During the same decade professional boxing attracted unparalleled crowds, eager to see the crushing attacks of Jack Dempsey. On September 22, 1927, Dempsey's unsuccessful attempt to win back his heavyweight championship from Gene Tunney attracted 104,000 customers, who paid a record gate of $2,658,000.

Interest in college football was no longer confined to undergraduates and alumni. The general public clamored for tickets, and many colleges were able to support their entire athletic program on the profits of the football season. To accommodate these eager crowds, many institutions built huge stadiums—some of them large enough to hold 70,000 or 80,000 spectators. Despite the popularity of college football there was growing patronage for professional sports of all kinds.

Although many Americans preferred to watch hired athletes rather than to participate in sports themselves, millions found a new interest in games. Golf, once the pastime of the rich, was democratized through the opening of thousands of municipal golf courses. Tennis became a favorite playground sport. Swimming and hiking gained new popularity through the improvement of state and national parks during the depression. Hunting and fishing—once vital to frontier subsistence—now provided recreation for thousands of business and professional men, who escaped from the cities to renew their spirits by stalking game through the Maine forests or casting flies into quiet Minnesota lakes.

Americans, picnicking or watching baseball games, winning jackpots on radio give-away shows or reading detective stories, were Americans as they liked to be. Jefferson's famous phrase "the pursuit of happiness" still described a basic aspiration of American society. It was an ideal liable to be misunderstood. It might be perverted to mere restlessness and search for excitement. But wisely followed, the pursuit of happiness could lead to worthier things. It could lead Americans to the contentment and security of religious faith, to the widened horizons of liberal education, to the affection for other people that would strengthen family and community life.

American civilization might in many areas fall short of the achievements of earlier civilizations. No American sculptor ranked with Phidias and Michelangelo, no American philosopher with Aristotle and Plato, no American soldier with Julius Caesar and Napoleon, no American poet with Dante and Shakespeare, no American theologian with Augustine and Calvin, no American composer with Bach and Beethoven. The glory of American civilization was less in its peaks of genius—although these were not lacking—than in its high plateaus. To have formed a nation from a mosaic of different nationalities, to have provided ever-widening opportunities for education, to have lightened the age-old toil of women, to have shortened the working hours and increased the rewards of human labor, to have provided inspiration and recreation for people of every background and temperament—in a word to have created a democratic culture was American civilization's most legitimate claim to greatness.

Suggestions for Further Reading

Books are listed for each major chronological division and also for each chapter. Publisher's name, place, and date of publication are given only in the first citation of the work. Names of publishers are usually omitted for books published before 1900.

I. COLONIAL FOUNDATIONS, 1607–1776

GENERAL. The most comprehensive coverage of American social and cultural history is to be found in A. M. Schlesinger and D. R. Fox, eds., *A History of American Life* (13 vols., Macmillan, New York, 1927–1948); volumes dealing with the colonial period are H. I. Priestley, *The Coming of the White Man, 1492–1848*; T. J. Wertenbaker, *The First Americans, 1607–1690*; J. T. Adams, *Provincial Society, 1690–1763.* Excellent surveys are C. P. Nettels, *The Roots of American Civilization* (Crofts, New York, 1938); H. J. Carman, *Social and Economic History of the United States* (2 vols., Heath, Boston, 1930); Harvey Wish, *Society and Thought in Early America* (Longmans, New York, 1950); and L. B. Wright, *The Atlantic Frontier: Colonial American Civilization, 1607–1763* (Knopf, New York, 1947).

REGIONAL STUDIES. T. J. Wertenbaker, *The Old South: The Founding of American Civilization* (Scribner, New York, 1942), and W. F. Craven, *The Southern Colonies in the Seventeenth Century, 1607–1689* (Louisiana State University Press, Baton Rouge, La., 1949) represent excellent recent scholarship. The Puritan founders of New England are most sympathetically portrayed in S. E. Morison, *Builders of the Bay Colony* (Houghton Mifflin, Boston, 1930). For a more critical view see J. T. Adams, *The Founding of New England* (Atlantic Monthly, Boston, 1921), and T. J. Wertenbaker, *The Puritan Oligarchy* (Scribner, New York, 1947). T. J. Wertenbaker, *The Middle Colonies* (Scribner, New York, 1938), is excellent for that area.

SOURCES. Important contemporary accounts of the founding of the colonies are to be found in L. G. Tyler, ed., *Narratives of Early Virginia* (Scribner, New York, 1907); William Bradford, *History of Plymouth Plantation (1620–1647)*, ed. by W. C. Ford (2 vols., Houghton Mifflin, Boston, 1912); J. K. Hosmer, ed., *Winthrop's Journal, "History of New England" 1630–1649* (2 vols., Scribner, New York, 1908); J. F. Jameson, ed., *Johnson's Wonder-working Providence, 1628–1651* (Scribner, New York, 1910). Interesting descriptions of colonial life by travelers and diarists are Carl Bridenbaugh, ed., *The Itinerarium of Dr. Alexander Hamilton, 1744* (The University of North Carolina Press, Chapel Hill, N. C., 1948); L. B. Wright and Marian Tinling, eds., *The Secret Diary of William Byrd of Westover, 1709–1712* (2 vols., Dietz Press, Richmond, Va., 1941); and J. R. Williams, ed., *Philip Vickers Fithian: Journal and Letters, 1767–1774* (Princeton University Press, Princeton, N. J., 1900). A good anthology of contemporary descriptions of early New England life is Barrows Mussey, ed., *Yankee Life: By Those Who Lived It* (Knopf, New York, 1947).

Chapter 1. Early Americans

GENERAL. The best survey of immigration is Carl Wittke, *We Who Built America: The Saga of the Immigrant* (Prentice-Hall, New York, 1940); it does not, however, cover the coming of the English and the Negroes. Excellent, particularly for its descriptions of European causes, is M. L. Hansen, *The Atlantic Migration, 1607–1860* (Harvard University Press, Cambridge, Mass., 1940).

SPECIAL STUDIES. On migration to New England, see Morison, Wertenbaker, and Adams, cited above; also George F. Willison, *Saints and Strangers* (Reynal and Hitchcock, Inc., New York, 1945), and C. E. Banks, *The Winthrop Fleet of 1630* (Houghton Mifflin, Boston, 1930). On the southern colonies see the works of Craven and Wertenbaker, cited above; also T. J. Wertenbaker, *The Planters of Colonial Virginia* (Princeton University Press, Princeton, N. J., 1922); P. A. Bruce, *Economic History of Virginia in the Seventeenth Century* (2 vols., New York, 1895); and the same author's *Institutional History of Virginia in the Seventeenth Century* (2 vols., New York, 1910). On the indentured servant traffic consult A. E. Smith, *Colonists in Bondage: White Servitude and Convict Labor in America* (The University of North Carolina Press, Chapel Hill, N. C., 1947).

The following works dealing with particular groups of immigrants are recommended. For the Negroes, J. H. Franklin, *From Slavery to Freedom: A History of American Negroes* (Knopf, New York, 1948), and U. B. Phillips, *American Negro Slavery* (Appleton, New York, 1918). For the Dutch, Priestley, *The Coming of the White Man*; Wertenbaker, *The Middle Colonies*; and E. L. Raesly, *Portrait of New Netherland* (Columbia University Press, New York, 1945). For the Swedes and Finns, Amandus Johnson, *The Swedish Settlements on the Delaware* (2 vols., University of Pennsylvania Press, Philadelphia, 1911); A. B. Benson and Naboth Hedin, eds., *Swedes in America, 1638–1938* (Yale University Press, New Haven, Conn., 1938); and J. H. Wuorinen, *The Finns on the Delaware, 1638–1655* (Columbia University Press, New York, 1938). For the Irish, M. J. O'Brien, *A Hidden Phase of American History* (Dodd, Mead, New York, 1919). For the Scotch-Irish, C. A. Hanna, *The Scotch-Irish* (2 vols., Putnam, New York, 1902); H. J. Ford, *The Scotch-Irish in America* (Princeton University Press, Princeton, N. J., 1916); and W. F. Dunaway, *The Scotch-Irish of Colonial Pennsylvania* (The University of North Carolina Press, Chapel Hill, N. C., 1944). For the Germans, A. B. Faust, *The German Element in the United States* (2 vols., New York, 1909), and Ralph Wood, ed., *The Pennsylvania Germans* (Princeton University Press, Princeton, N. J., 1942).

Chapter 2. Conquering the Soil

GENERAL. Good surveys of American economic history are H. U. Faulkner, *American Economic History* (Harper, New York, 1943); E. C. Kirkland, *A History of American Economic Life* (Crofts, New York, 1941); and F. A. Shannon, *America's Economic Growth* (Macmillan, New York, 1940).

SPECIAL STUDIES. Interesting interpretations are contained in Joseph Schafer, *The Social History of American Agriculture* (Macmillan, New York, 1936). Lyman Carrier, *The Beginnings of Agriculture in America* (McGraw-Hill, New York, 1923) is a valuable monograph. Detailed information on crops and methods may be found in P. W. Bidwell and J. I. Falconer, *History of Agriculture in the Northern United States, 1620–1860* (Carnegie Institution, Washington, D. C., 1925), and L. C. Gray, *History of Agriculture in the Southern United States* (2 vols., Carnegie Institution, Washington, D. C., 1933). On plantation agriculture see Bruce, *Economic History of Virginia*; U. B. Phillips, *Life and Labor in the Old South* (Little, Brown, Boston, 1929); and A. O. Craven, *Soil Exhaustion as a Factor in the Agricultural History of Virginia and Maryland, 1606–1860* (University of Illinois, Urbana, Ill., 1926). A good description of the New England land system is in Wertenbaker, *Puritan Oligarchy*; see also C. M. Andrews, *The River Towns of Connecticut* (Johns Hopkins, Baltimore, Md., 1889). Useful material may be found in Wertenbaker, *Middle Colonies*; W. F. Dunaway, *A History of Pennsylvania* (Prentice-Hall, New York, 1935); and Irving Mark, *Agrarian Conflicts in Colonial New York, 1771–1775* (Columbia

University Press, New York, 1940). F. J. Turner, *The Frontier in American History* (Holt, New York, 1920) contains important essays on the colonial frontier.

CHAPTER 3. ARTISANS AND MERCHANTS

GENERAL. See the economic histories cited for Chap. 2.

SPECIAL STUDIES. Extensive information is to be found in V. S. Clark, *History of Manufactures in the United States* (3 vols., Carnegie Institution, Washington, D. C., 1929), and R. M. Tryon, *Household Manufactures in the United States, 1640–1860* (University of Chicago Press, Chicago, 1917). A simple description of domestic industry is in A. M. Earle, *Home Life in Colonial Days* (New York, 1898). Important studies of the status of artisans and laborers are M. W. Jernegan, *Laboring and Dependent Classes in Colonial America* (University of Chicago Press, Chicago, 1931); R. B. Morris, *Government and Labor in Early America* (Columbia University Press, New York, 1946); and Carl Bridenbaugh, *The Colonial Craftsman* (New York University Press, New York, 1950). W. T. Baxter, *The House of Hancock: Business in Boston, 1724–1775* (Harvard University Press, Cambridge, Mass., 1945) is an excellent study of the colonial merchants. Carl Bridenbaugh, *Cities in the Wilderness* (Ronald, New York, 1938) provides a wealth of information on the colonial towns. On the rise of a colonial aristocracy see L. B. Wright, *The First Gentlemen of Virginia* (Huntington Library, San Marino, Calif., 1940), and Dixon Wecter, *The Saga of American Society* (Scribner, New York, 1937).

CHAPTER 4. WORSHIPING GOD

GENERAL. The most satisfactory survey of American religious life is W. W. Sweet, *The Story of Religion in America* (Harper, New York, 1939). Interesting interpretative chapters may be found in W. L. Sperry, *Religion in America* (Macmillan, New York, 1946).

SPECIAL STUDIES. W. W. Sweet, *Religion in Colonial America* (Scribner, New York, 1943) contains much useful information. Important in understanding the European background are T. C. Hall, *The Religious Background of American Culture* (Little, Brown, Boston, 1930), and R. H. Tawney, *Religion and the Rise of Capitalism* (Harcourt, Brace, New York, 1926). For Anglicanism see G. M. Brydon, *Virginia's Mother Church* (Virginia Historical Society, Richmond, Va., 1948), and A. L. Cross, *The Anglican Episcopate and the American Colonies* (Longmans, New York, 1902). On Congregationalism see Perry Miller, *Orthodoxy in Massachusetts, 1630–1650* (Harvard University Press, Cambridge, Mass., 1933); R. B. Perry, *Puritanism and Democracy* (Vanguard, Inc., New York, 1944); and Perry Miller, *Jonathan Edwards* (William Sloane Associates, New York, 1949). On other denominations consult R. G. Torbet, *A History of the Baptists* (Judson Press, Philadelphia, 1950); L. J. Trinterud, *The Forming of an American Tradition: A Re-examination of Colonial Presbyterianism* (Westminster Press, Philadelphia, 1949); Elbert Russell, *The History of Quakerism* (Macmillan, New York, 1942); C. H. Smith, *Story of the Mennonites* (Mennonite Book Concern, Berne, Ind., 1941). The standard authority on the Roman Catholic Church in early America is J. G. Shea, *History of the Catholic Church in the United States* (4 vols., New York, 1886–1892). Briefer accounts are Theodore Roemer, *The Catholic Church in the United States* (Herder, St. Louis, Mo., 1950), and Theodore Maynard, *The Story of American Catholicism* (Macmillan, New York, 1942). The rise of rationalism may be traced in Max Savelle, *Seeds of Liberty: The Genesis of the American Mind* (Knopf, New York, 1948), and in H. M. Morais, *Deism in Eighteenth Century America* (Columbia University Press, New York, 1934).

CHAPTER 5. THE WORLD OF THE SCHOLAR

GENERAL. The most important American intellectual histories are V. L. Parrington, *Main Currents in American Thought* (3 vols., Harcourt, Brace, New York, 1927–1930), and Merle Curti, *The Growth of American Thought* (Harper, New York, 1943)—both Pulitzer prize books. Excellent cooperative histories of American literature are *The Cambridge History of American Literature* (4 vols., Macmillan, New York, 1917–1921) and *Literary History of the United States* (3 vols., Macmillan, New York, 1948).

COLONIAL EDUCATION. Elementary and secondary education are competently treated in E. P. Cubberley, *Public Education in the United States* (Houghton Mifflin, Boston, 1919), and Paul Monroe, *Founding of the American Public School System* (Macmillan, New York, 1940). C. F. Thwing, *A History of Higher Education in America* (Appleton, New York, 1906) is not very satisfactory. For an adequate understanding of the colonial colleges it is necessary to consult the histories of particular institutions. S. E. Morison, *The Founding of Harvard College* (Harvard University Press, Cambridge, Mass., 1935), and the same author's *Harvard College in the Seventeenth Century* (Harvard University Press, Cambridge, Mass., 1936) are exceptionally readable and informative. Also useful are Edwin Oviatt, *The Beginnings of Yale (1701–1726)* (Yale University Press, New Haven, Conn., 1916), and T. J. Wertenbaker, *Princeton, 1746–1896* (Princeton University Press, Princeton, N. J., 1946).

PURITAN SCHOLARSHIP. A sympathetic introduction to Puritan culture is S. E. Morison, *The Puritan Pronaos: Studies in the Intellectual Life of New England in the Seventeenth Century* (New York University Press, New York, 1936). A profound work of scholarship, brilliantly presented, is Perry Miller, *The New England Mind: The Seventeenth Century* (Macmillan, New York, 1939). On important individuals see Kenneth Murdock, *Increase Mather* (Harvard University Press, Cambridge, Mass., 1925); C. H. Faust and T. H. Johnson, eds., *Jonathan Edwards: Representative Selections* (American Book, New York, 1935); and Miller, *Jonathan Edwards.*

EIGHTEENTH-CENTURY TRENDS. In the pages of Carl Van Doren, *Benjamin Franklin* (Viking, New York, 1938) eighteenth-century America comes to life. See also Savelle, *Seeds of Liberty;* Michael Kraus, *The Atlantic Civilization: Eighteenth Century Origins* (Cornell University Press, Ithaca, N. Y., 1949); and T. J. Wertenbaker, *The Golden Age of Colonial Culture* (New York University Press, New York, 1942). The progress of medicine may be studied in F. R. Packard, *History of Medicine in the United States* (2 vols., Hoeber, New York, 1931), and M. B. Gordon, *Aesculapius Comes to the Colonies* (Ventnor Publishers, Ventnor, N. J., 1949). The colonial historians are evaluated in Michael Kraus, *A History of American History* (Farrar & Rinehart, Inc., New York, 1937).

NEWSPAPERS AND MAGAZINES. An indispensable guide is C. S. Brigham, *History and Bibliography of American Newspapers, 1690–1820* (2 vols., American Antiquarian Society, Worcester, Mass., 1947). See also F. L. Mott, *A History of American Magazines, 1741–1885* (3 vols., Appleton, New York, 1930–1938), and the same author's *American Journalism: A History of Newspapers in the United States* (Macmillan, New York, 1941).

CHAPTER 6. ARTS AND AMUSEMENTS IN COLONIAL AMERICA

GENERAL. O. W. Larkin, *Art and Life in America* (Rinehart, New York, 1949) is a brilliant survey of all the arts, emphasizing the influence of social forces. See also D. M. Robb and J. J. Garrison, *Art in the Western World* (Harper, New York, 1942).

ARCHITECTURE. Useful surveys are T. F. Hamlin, *The American Spirit in Architecture* (Yale University Press, New Haven, Conn., 1926), and Fiske Kimball, *American Archi-*

tecture (Bobbs-Merrill, Indianapolis, Ind., 1928). Fiske Kimball's *Domestic Architecture of the American Colonies and of the Early Republic* (Scribner, New York, 1922) is a well-illustrated study. Eighteenth-century trends may be studied in Carl Bridenbaugh, *Peter Harrison, First American Architect* (The University of North Carolina Press, Chapel Hill, N. C., 1949).

PAINTING. A standard work, conservative in its judgments, is Samuel Isham and Royal Cortissoz, *The History of American Painting* (Macmillan, New York, 1927). More recent trends of criticism are reflected in Vergil Barker, *American Painting* (Macmillan, New York, 1950), and Alan Burroughs, *Limners and Likenesses* (Harvard University Press, Cambridge, Mass., 1936). J. T. Flexner, *American Painting: First Flowers in Our Wilderness* (Houghton Mifflin, Boston, 1947) is a beautifully illustrated history of colonial painting.

MINOR ARTS. Colonial taste in home furnishings may be studied in R. T. H. Halsey and Elizabeth Tower, *The Homes of Our Ancestors* (Doubleday Page, Garden City, N. Y., 1925). See T. H. Ormsbee, *Early American Furniture Makers* (Crowell, New York, 1930), and G. S. and Helen McKearin, *American Glass* (Crown, New York, 1941). On folk art see E. O. Christensen, *The Index of American Design* (Macmillan, New York, 1950), and Frances Lichten, *Folk Art of Rural Pennsylvania* (Scribner, New York, 1946).

MUSIC. The most convenient survey is J. T. Howard, *Our American Music: Three Hundred Years of It* (Crowell, New York, 1931). Important in clarifying an often-misunderstood matter is P. A. Scholes, *The Puritans and Music in England and New England* (Oxford, London, 1934).

AMUSEMENTS. F. R. Dulles, *America Learns to Play* (Appleton-Century, New York, 1940) is an interesting history of popular recreation. Arthur Hornblow, *A History of the Theatre in America from its Beginnings to the Present Time* (2 vols., Lippincott, Philadelphia, 1919) is a standard authority.

II. THE NEW NATION, 1776–1861

GENERAL. Volumes in *A History of American Life* covering this period are Greene, *The Revolutionary Generation*; J. A. Krout and D. R. Fox, *The Completion of Independence, 1790–1830*; C. R. Fish, *The Rise of the Common Man, 1830–1850*; and A. C. Cole, *The Irrepressible Conflict, 1850–1865.* A pioneer venture in social history, still useful for reference, is J. B. McMaster, *A History of the People of the United States from the Revolution to the Civil War* (8 vols., New York, 1883–1913). Still stimulating are the brilliantly written chapters on social and intellectual developments in Henry Adams, *History of the United States during the Administrations of Jefferson and Madison* (9 vols., New York, 1889–1891). R. E. Riegel, *Young America, 1830–1840* (University of Oklahoma Press, Norman, Okla., 1949) provides a colorful picture of an interesting period. Allan Nevins, *Ordeal of the Union* (2 vols., Scribner, New York, 1947), and the same author's *Emergence of Lincoln* (2 vols., Scribner, 1950) contain excellent material on social and intellectual trends. Light but highly entertaining is E. Douglas Branch, *The Sentimental Years, 1836–1860* (Appleton-Century, New York, 1934). See also Wish, *Society and Thought in Early America,* and Carman, *Social and Economic History of the United States,* Vol. 2.

SOURCES. This is the period when the American republic was a subject of eager European curiosity. Excellent samplings of travelers' descriptions are provided in H. S. Commager, ed., *America in Perspective: The United States through Foreign Eyes* (Random House, New York, 1947); Allan Nevins, *America through British Eyes* (Oxford, New York, 1948); and Oscar Handlin, *This Was America* (Harvard University Press, Cambridge, Mass., 1949). Classic interpretations of the American character are St. Jean de Crèvecoeur, *Letters from an American Farmer*, ed. by W. P. Trent (Boni, New York, 1925), and Alexis de Tocqueville, *Democracy in America,* ed. by P. Bradley (2 vols., Knopf, New York, 1945). Particularly interesting are Frances Trollope, *Domestic Manners of the Americans,* ed. by D. Smalley (Knopf, New York, 1949); Michel Chevalier, *Society, Manners and Politics in the United States* (Boston, 1839); Harriet Martineau, *Society in America* (3 vols., London, 1837); Charles Dickens, *American Notes* (London, 1842); and Alexander Mackay, *The Western World* (2 vols., London, 1849).

Chapter 7. Independence and Nationhood

THE REVOLUTION. Modern investigation of the causes is well represented by C. H. Van Tyne, *Causes of the War of Independence* (Houghton Mifflin, Boston, 1922); C. M. Andrews, *Colonial Background of the American Revolution* (Yale University Press, New Haven, Conn., 1931); C. H. McIlwain, *The American Revolution: A Constitutional Interpretation* (Macmillan, New York, 1923); Philip Davidson, *Propaganda and the American Revolution, 1763–1783* (The University of North Carolina Press, Chapel Hill, N. C., 1941); J. C. Miller, *Origins of the American Revolution* (Little, Brown, Boston, 1943); and Vol. 3 of Edward Channing, *History of the United States* (6 vols., Macmillan, New York, 1905–1925). The social results of the period are treated in J. F. Jameson, *The American Revolution Considered as a Social Movement* (Princeton University Press, Princeton, N. J., 1926); Allan Nevins, *The American States during and after the Revolution, 1775–1789* (Macmillan, New York, 1924); Merrill Jensen, *The New Nation* (Knopf, New York, 1950); and Greene, *The Revolutionary Generation.*

DECLARATION OF INDEPENDENCE AND CONSTITUTION. Carl Becker, *The Declaration of Independence* (Knopf, New York, 1922) is a brilliant contribution to the history of political ideas. Edward Dumbauld, *The Declaration of Independence and What It Means Today* (University of Oklahoma Press, Norman, Okla., 1950) analyzes the meaning of each phrase of the famous document. The drafting of the Constitution is described in a number of excellent studies: Max Ferrand, *The Framing of the Constitution* (Yale University Press, New Haven, Conn., 1913); Charles Warren, *The Making of the Constitution* (Little, Brown, Boston, 1928); A. C. McLaughlin, *Constitutional History of the United States* (Appleton, New York, 1935); and Carl Van Doren, *The Great Rehearsal* (Viking, New York, 1948). C. A. Beard, *An Economic Interpretation of the Constitution of the United States* (Macmillan, New York, 1913) skillfully presents a controversial point of view.

SOURCES. The classic documents are to be conveniently found in H. S. Commager, ed., *Documents of American History* (5th ed., Appleton-Century-Crofts, New York, 1949). Excellent selections from contemporary political thought are found in B. F. Wright, Jr., *A Source Book of American Political Theory* (Macmillan, New York, 1929); A. T. Mason, ed., *Free Government in the Making* (Oxford, New York, 1949); and F. W. Coker, ed., *Democracy, Liberty, and Property* (Macmillan, New York, 1942).

Chapter 8. Agriculture and the Frontier

GENERAL. Robert Riegel, *America Moves West* (Holt, New York, 1947), and R. A. Billington, *Westward Expansion* (Macmillan, New York, 1949) are well-written surveys. F. J. Turner, *Rise of the New West, 1819–1829* (Harper, New York, 1907), and the same author's *The United States, 1830–1850* (Holt, New York, 1935) represent the work of the first great specialist in frontier history. Land policy is surveyed in R. M. Robbins, *Our Landed Heritage: The Public Domain, 1776–1936* (Princeton University Press, Princeton, N. J., 1942).

SPECIAL STUDIES. On migrations from New England, L. K. Mathews, *The Expansion of New England* (Houghton Mifflin, Boston, 1909) was a pioneer study; a recent popular account is S. H. Holbrook, *The Yankee Exodus* (Macmillan, New York, 1950). Famous routes to the West are described in R. L. Kincaid, *The Wilderness Road* (Bobbs-Merrill, Indianapolis, Ind., 1947); P. D. Jordan, *The National Road* (Bobbs-Merrill, Indianapolis, Ind., 1948); and Jay Monaghan, *The Overland Trail* (Bobbs-Merrill, Indianapolis, Ind., 1947). A Pulitzer prize-winning study is R. C. Buley, *The Old Northwest: Pioneer Period, 1815–1840* (2 vols., Towers, Inc., LaGrange, Ill., 1950); see also B. W. Bond, *Civilization of the Old Northwest* (Macmillan, New York, 1934). On the Old Southwest T. P. Abernethy, *From Frontier to Plantation in Tennessee* (The University of North Carolina Press, Chapel Hill, N. C., 1930), and Everett Dick, *The Dixie Frontier* (Knopf, New York, 1948) are interesting. On the influence of the fur trade excellent studies are H. M. Chittenden, *The American Fur Trade of the Far West* (2 vols., R. R. Wilson, Inc., New York, 1936), and K. W. Porter, *John Jacob Astor, Business Man* (2 vols., Harvard University Press, Cambridge, Mass., 1931). Bernard De Voto, *Across the Broad Missouri* (Houghton Mifflin, Boston, 1947), and the same author's *The Year of Decision, 1846* (Little, Brown, Boston, 1943) are brilliant accounts of the opening up of the Far West.

AGRICULTURAL REFORM. See the standard accounts in Bidwell and Falconer, and Gray cited for Chap. 2. Agricultural journalism is studied in A. L. Demaree, *The American Agricultural Press, 1819–1860* (Columbia University Press, New York, 1941).

SOURCES. A unique treasure house is R. G. Thwaites, ed., *Early Western Travels, 1748–1846* (32 vols., A. H. Clark Co., Cleveland, 1904–1907). Francis Parkman, *The Oregon Trail* (Boston, 1849) is an American classic. See also Daniel Drake, *Pioneer Life in Kentucky, 1785–1800,* ed. by E. F. Horine (Henry Schuman, New York, 1948); J. R. Commons and others, eds., *A Documentary History of American Industrial Society* (10 vols., Arthur H. Clark Co., Cleveland, 1911), Vols. 1 and 2; and H. J. Carman, ed., *Jesse Buel, Agricultural Reformer: Selections from His Writings* (Columbia University Press, New York, 1947).

Chapter 9. The Old South

GENERAL. A 12-volume work, *A History of the South,* ed. by W. H. Stephenson and E. M. Coulter, is now in progress of publication by the Louisiana State University Press; among the volumes already published, C. W. Sydnor, *The Development of Southern Sectionalism, 1819–1848* (Baton Rouge, La., 1948) deals with this period. Good general surveys are W. B. Hesseltine, *A History of the South, 1607–1936* (Prentice-Hall, New York, 1936); Clement Eaton, *A History of the Old South* (Macmillan, New York, 1949); and F. B. Simkins, *The South, Old and New* (Knopf, New York, 1947).

SOCIAL STRUCTURE. Phillips, *Life and Labor in the Old South* and *American Negro Slavery* discuss slavery from the southern-white point of view; Franklin, *From Slavery to Freedom,* and E. Franklin Frazier, *The Negro in the United States* (Macmillan, New York, 1949) from the Negro position. The neglected majority of the southern population is described in Frank Owsley, *The Plain Folks of the Old South* (Louisiana State University Press, Baton Rouge, La., 1949).

INTELLECTUAL TRENDS. Among the many attempts at interpreting the antebellum southern mind, the following are outstanding: J. T. Carpenter, *The South as a Conscious Minority, 1789–1861* (New York University Press, New York, 1930); W. S. Jenkins, *Pro-slavery Thought in the Old South* (The University of North Carolina Press, Chapel Hill, N. C., 1935); Clement Eaton, *Freedom of Thought in the Old South* (Duke University Press, Durham, N. C., 1940); W. J. Cash, *The Mind of the South* (Knopf, New York, 1941); R. G. Osterweis, *Romanticism and Nationalism in the Old South* (Yale University Press, New Haven, Conn., 1949).

SOURCES. For contrasting first-hand descriptions of the slave system compare S. D. Smedes, *Memories of a Southern Planter* (Baltimore, Md., 1887), and F. A. Kemble, *Journal of a Residence on a Georgia Plantation* (New York, 1863). F. L. Olmsted, *The Cotton Kingdom* (2 vols., New York, 1861) records the observations of a northerner who traveled extensively through the South in the 1850's. For the contemporary southern defense of their society consult *The Pro-slavery Argument; As Maintained by the Most Distinguished Writers of the Southern States* (Charleston, 1852).

Chapter 10. Revolution in Industry

GENERAL. Changes in manufacturing methods are described in the economic histories by Faulkner, Kirkland, and Shannon, cited for Chap. 2. For a more detailed study consult Clark, *History of Manufactures in the United States.* L. M. Hacker, *The Triumph of American Capitalism* (Simon & Schuster, New York, 1940), and T. C. Cochran and William Miller, *The Age of Enterprise: A Social History of Industrial America* (Macmillan, New York, 1942) provide stimulating interpretations. The impact of new conditions on the workers is treated in J. R. Commons, ed., *History of Labour in the United States* (4 vols., Macmillan, New York, 1918–1935), Vol. 1, and in F. R. Dulles, *Labor in America: A History* (Crowell, New York, 1949).

SPECIAL STUDIES. Important phases of the industrial revolution are treated in A. H. Cole, *The American Wool Manufacture* (2 vols., Harvard University Press, Cambridge, Mass., 1926); L. D. Baldwin, *Pittsburgh; the Story of a City* (University of Pittsburgh Press, Pittsburgh, Pa., 1937); and Norman Ware, *The Industrial Worker, 1840–1860* (Houghton Mifflin, Boston, 1924).

Chapter 11. Transportation and the Rise of the Cities

GENERAL. See appropriate chapters in Faulkner, Kirkland, and Shannon, cited for Chap. 2. An extensive work of uneven quality is Seymour Dunbar, *History of Travel in America* (4 vols., Bobbs-Merrill, Indianapolis, Ind., 1915). Brief but good is A. B. Hulbert, *The Paths of Inland Commerce* (Yale University Press, New Haven, Conn., 1921). Although limited to New Jersey, W. J. Lane, *From Indian Trail to Iron Horse* (Princeton University Press, Princeton, N. J., 1939) is excellent.

OCEAN TRANSPORTATION. A. H. Clark, *The Clipper Ship Era* (Putnam, New York, 1910) is a classic study. Excellent later works are S. E. Morison, *Maritime History of Massachusetts, 1783–1860* (Houghton Mifflin, Boston, 1921); R. G. Albion, *The Rise of New York Port (1815–1860)* (Scribner, New York, 1939); R. G. Albion, *Square-riggers on Schedule* (Princeton University Press, Princeton, N. J., 1938).

INLAND WATERWAYS. S. L. Clemens (Mark Twain), *Life on the Mississippi* (Harper, New York, 1903) is a classic description of the steamboat age; an excellent recent study is L. C. Hunter, *Steamboats on the Western Rivers* (Harvard University Press, Cambridge, Mass., 1949). For an earlier phase consult L. D. Baldwin, *The Keelboat Age on Western Waters* (University of Pittsburgh Press, Pittsburgh, Pa., 1941). Popular in style and unusually comprehensive is A. F. Harlow, *Old Towpaths: The Story of the American Canal Era* (Appleton, New York, 1926).

RAILROADS. Popular accounts are S. H. Holbrook, *The Story of American Railroads* (Crown, New York, 1947); A. F. Harlow, *The Road of the Century: The Story of the New York Central* (Creative Age, New York, 1947); A. F. Harlow, *Steelways of New England* (Creative Age, New York, 1946); and Edward Hungerford, *The Story of the Baltimore and Ohio Railroad* (2 vols., Putnam, New York, 1928). Outstanding works of scholarship are P. W. Gates, *The Illinois Central Railroad and Its Colonization Work* (Harvard University Press, Cambridge, Mass., 1934); R. C. Overton, *Burlington West:*

A Colonization History of the Burlington Railroad (Harvard University Press, Cambridge, Mass., 1941); and E. C. Kirkland, *Men, Cities and Transportation, a Study in New England History, 1820–1900* (2 vols., Harvard University Press, Cambridge, Mass., 1948).

TELEGRAPH. R. L. Thompson, *Wiring a Continent: The History of the Telegraph Industry in the United States, 1832–1866* (Princeton University Press, Princeton, N. J., 1947) is an excellent study. See also Carleton Mabee, *American Leonardo: A Life of Samuel F. B. Morse* (Knopf, New York, 1943).

CITIES. Good accounts of urban development are scarce. Somewhat unique are B. L. Pierce, *A History of Chicago* (2 vols., New York, 1937–1940), and Blake McKelvey, *Rochester, the Water-power City, 1812–1854* (Harvard University Press, Cambridge, Mass., 1945). Much concerning life in New York and Philadelphia may be gleaned from Allan Nevins, ed., *Diary of Philip Hone, 1828–1851* (2 vols., Dodd, Mead, New York, 1927); E. C. Mack, *Peter Cooper: Citizen of New York* (Duell, Sloan & Pearce, New York, 1949); J. F. Watson, *Annals of Philadelphia and Pennsylvania* (2 vols., Philadelphia, 1843).

Chapter 12. Coming of the Foreigners . .

GENERAL. The best accounts are those by Wittke and Hansen, cited for Chap. 1. See also G. M. Stephenson, *A History of American Immigration, 1820–1924* (Ginn, Boston, 1926).

SPECIAL ACCOUNTS. W. F. Adams, *Ireland and Irish Emigration to the New World from 1815 to the Famine* (Yale University Press, New Haven, Conn., 1932) is a thorough study. On the Germans see Faust, *The German Element in the United States,* and A. E. Zucker, ed., *The Forty-eighters: Political Refugees of the German Revolution* (Columbia University Press, New York, 1950). On the Scandinavians consult Benson and Hedin, *Swedes in America,* and T. C. Blegen, *The Norwegian Migration to America* (Norwegian American Historical Association, Northfield, Minn., 1930). On the problems of assimilation see Oscar Handlin, *Boston's Immigrants, 1790–1865* (Harvard University Press, Cambridge, Mass., 1941), and Robert Ernst, *Immigrant Life in New York City, 1825–1863* (King's Crown Press, New York, 1949). Native hostility to the immigrants is thoroughly treated in R. A. Billington, *The Protestant Crusade, 1800–1860: A Study of the Origins of American Nativism* (Macmillan, New York, 1938).

SOURCES. Indispensable collections are Edith Abbott, ed., *Historical Aspects of the Immigration Problem: Select Documents* (University of Chicago Press, Chicago, 1926), and Edith Abbott, ed., *Immigration: Select Documents and Case Records* (University of Chicago Press, Chicago, 1924). See also *The Reminiscences of Carl Schurz* (3 vols., New York, 1907–1908).

Chapter 13. The Rise of Democracy and Nationalism

GENERAL. See excellent discussions in Parrington, *Main Currents in American Thought,* and in Ralph Gabriel, *The Course of American Democratic Thought: An Intellectual History since 1815* (Ronald, New York, 1940). A general survey is F. G. Wilson, *The American Political Mind: A Textbook in Political Theory* (McGraw-Hill, New York, 1949). Richard Hofstadter, *The American Political Tradition and the Men Who Made It* (Knopf, New York, 1948); W. E. Binkley, *American Political Parties: Their Natural History* (Knopf, New York, 1943); and B. F. Wright, *The Growth of American Constitutional Law* (Reynal & Hitchcock, Inc., New York, 1942) are stimulating interpretations. Much of interest is also to be found in Joseph Dorfman, *The Economic Mind in American Civilization* (3 vols., Viking, New York, 1946–1949).

STUDIES OF INDIVIDUALS. A recent impartial biography is Nathan Schachner, *Alexander Hamilton* (Appleton-Century, New York, 1946). Dumas Malone, *Jefferson the*

Virginian (Little, Brown, Boston, 1948) is the first volume of an extended work on *Jefferson and His Time* now being prepared by an unusually competent scholar. See also the following studies: Adrienne Koch, *The Philosophy of Thomas Jefferson* (Columbia University Press, New York, 1943), and the same author's *Jefferson and Madison: the Great Collaboration* (Knopf, New York, 1950). A. J. Beveridge, *The Life of John Marshall* (4 vols., Houghton Mifflin, Boston, 1916–1919) is a work of unusual distinction. A. M. Schlesinger, Jr., *The Age of Jackson* (Little, Brown, Boston, 1945) is a brilliant interpretation that has provoked much controversy. On southern political thought see C. M. Wiltse, *John C. Calhoun* (2 vols., Bobbs-Merrill, Indianapolis, Ind., 1944–1949); E. T. Mudge, *The Social Philosophy of John Taylor of Caroline* (Columbia University Press, New York, 1939); and Harvey Wish, *George Fitzhugh, Propagandist of the Old South* (Louisiana State University Press, Baton Rouge, La., 1944). J. G. Randall, *Lincoln the President* (2 vols., Dodd, Mead, New York, 1945) is the most important recent study of the Civil War President.

SOURCES. See the books of readings edited by Wright, Mason, and Coker, cited for Chap. 7, and also the collected works of Hamilton, Jefferson, Adams, Calhoun, Webster, and Lincoln.

Chapter 14. Religious Ferment

GENERAL. The best surveys are those by Sweet and Sperry cited for Chap. 4. E. S. Bates, *American Faith: Its Religious, Political, and Economic Foundations* (Norton, New York, 1940) contains interesting material.

SPECIAL STUDIES. For most denominations useful histories have been cited for Chap. 4. Other competent studies are Peter Guilday, *The Life and Times of John Carroll* (2 vols., Encyclopedia Press, New York, 1922); Gerald Shaughnessy, *Has the Immigrant Kept the Faith? A Study of Immigration and Catholic Growth in the United States, 1790–1920* (Macmillan, New York, 1925); H. E. Luccock and Paul Hutchinson, *The Story of Methodism* (Methodist Book Concern, New York, 1926); W. E. Garrison and A. T. DeGroot, *Disciples of Christ: A History* (Bethany Press, St. Louis, Mo., 1948); G. W. Cooke, *Unitarianism in America* (American Unitarian Association, Boston, 1902); E. T. Clark, *The Small Sects in America* (Cokesbury Press, Nashville, Tenn., 1938); M. F. Melcher, *The Shaker Adventure* (Princeton University Press, Princeton, N. J., 1941); F. M. Brodie, *No Man Knows My History: The Life of Joseph Smith, the Mormon Prophet* (Knopf, New York, 1945); Nels Anderson, *Desert Saints: The Mormon Frontier in Utah* (University of Chicago Press, Chicago, 1942). For Deism consult G. A. Koch, *Republican Religion: The American Revolution and the Cult of Reason* (Holt, New York, 1938). For the conservative reaction see J. K. Morse, *Jedidiah Morse, a Champion of New England Orthodoxy* (Columbia University Press, New York, 1939).

CHURCH AND STATE. A. P. Stokes, *Church and State in the United States* (3 vols., Harper, New York, 1950) is an important work of scholarship. See also E. B. Greene, *Religion and the State: The Making and Testing of an American Tradition* (New York University Press, New York, 1941).

SOURCES. A rich variety of materials is collected in W. W. Sweet, ed., *Religion on the American Frontier, 1783–1830*: Vol. 1. *The Baptists*; Vol. 2. *The Presbyterians*; Vol. 3. *The Congregationalists*; Vol. 4. *The Methodists* (Holt and University of Chicago Press, New York and Chicago, 1931–1946). See also W. P. Strickland, ed., *Autobiography of Peter Cartwright, the Backwoods Preacher* (New York, 1856).

Chapter 15. Humanitarian Reform

GENERAL. The best account is A. F. Tyler, *Freedom's Ferment: Phases of American Social History to 1860* (University of Minnesota Press, Minneapolis, Minn., 1944). See also Fish, *The Rise of the Common Man;* Branch, *Sentimental Years;* and Riegel, *Young America.*

CRIMINALS AND INSANE. Informative, although poorly written, is O. F. Lewis, *The Development of American Prisons and Prison Customs* (Prison Association of New York, Albany, N. Y., 1922). See also Blake McKelvey, *American Prisons* (University of Chicago Press, Chicago, 1936). J. K. Hall, G. Zilboorg, and H. A. Bunker, eds., *One Hundred Years of American Psychiatry* (Columbia University Press, New York, 1944) is a cooperative work of great value. H. E. Marshall, *Dorothea Dix, Forgotten Samaritan* (The University of North Carolina Press, Chapel Hill, N. C., 1937) is good.

UTOPIAN SOCIALISM. Although it covers the period only to 1828, A. E. Bestor, Jr., *Backwoods Utopias* (University of Pennsylvania Press, Philadelphia, 1949) is the standard authority on the subject. W. A. Hinds, *American Communities and Co-operative Colonies* (Chicago, 1908) gives a brief account of a large number of communal experiments. R. W. Leopold, *Robert Dale Owen* (Harvard University Press, Cambridge, Mass., 1940) is a good biography.

TEMPERANCE AND ANTISLAVERY. J. A. Krout, *The Origins of Prohibition* (Knopf, New York, 1925) is a scholarly account of the pre-Civil War temperance movement. The abolition movement is best described in G. H. Barnes, *The Anti-slavery Impulse, 1830–1844* (Appleton-Century, New York, 1933), and in D. L. Dumond, *Antislavery Origins of the Civil War in the United States* (University of Michigan Press, Ann Arbor, Mich., 1939). Interesting biographies are W. P. and F. J. Garrison, *William Lloyd Garrison, 1805–1879* (4 vols., New York, 1885–1889); R. V. Harlow, *Gerrit Smith, Philanthropist and Reformer* (Holt, New York, 1939); and B. P. Thomas, *Theodore Weld, Crusader for Freedom* (Rutgers University Press, New Brunswick, N. J., 1950).

WOMEN'S RIGHTS AND PEACE. A storehouse of poorly digested materials is E. C. Stanton, S. B. Anthony, and M. J. Gage, *The History of Woman Suffrage* (3 vols., New York, 1881–1886). I. H. Irwin, *Angels and Amazons: A Hundred Years of American Women* (Doubleday, Doran, Garden City, N. Y., 1934) is a popular account. E. C. Stanton, *Eighty Years and More* (New York, 1898) is an interesting autobiography. Scholarly accounts of the peace movement are Merle Curti, *The American Peace Crusade* (Duke University Press, Durham, N. C., 1929), and W. F. Galpin, *Pioneering for Peace* (Bardeen Press, Syracuse, N. Y., 1933).

Chapter 16. The Passion for Learning

GENERAL. Curti, *Growth of American Thought* is indispensable, both for its careful analysis of trends and its excellent bibliographies.

ELEMENTARY AND SECONDARY SCHOOLS. The rise of the public schools is described in Cubberley, *Public Education in the United States*; Monroe, *Founding of the American Public School System*; and Sidney Jackson, *America's Struggle for Free Schools* (American Council on Public Affairs, New York, 1941). The influence of economic and social trends is given particular emphasis in N. Edwards and H. G. Richey, *The School in the American Social Order* (Houghton Mifflin, Boston, 1947). On individual educators see Merle Curti, *The Social Ideas of American Educators* (Scribner, New York, 1935); Harry Warfel, *Noah Webster, Schoolmaster to America* (Macmillan, New York, 1936); and Harvey Minnich, *William Holmes McGuffey and His Readers* (American Book, New York, 1936).

COLLEGES. For an over-all view Thwing, *A History of Higher Education in America,* and D. G. Tewksbury, *The Founding of American Colleges and Universities before the Civil War* (Teachers College, Columbia University, New York, 1932) are useful. On particular institutions see Wertenbaker, *Princeton*; L. B. Richardson, *History of Dartmouth College* (2 vols., Dartmouth College, Hanover, N. H., 1932); Howard Coon, *Columbia:*

Colossus on the Hudson (Dutton, New York, 1947); Archibald Henderson, *The Campus of the First State University* (The University of North Carolina Press, Chapel Hill, N. C., 1949); R. S. Fletcher, *A History of Oberlin College from Its Foundation through the Civil War* (2 vols., Oberlin College, Oberlin, Ohio, 1943).

NEWSPAPERS AND MAGAZINES. In addition to Mott, *American Journalism,* and Mott, *A History of American Magazines* see Allan Nevins, *The Evening Post* (Boni & Liveright, New York, 1922); W. H. Hale, *Horace Greeley, Voice of the People* (Harper, New York, 1950); and J. A. Isely, *Horace Greeley and the Republican Party, 1853–1861* (Princeton University Press, Princeton, N. J., 1947).

SCIENCE. Excellent recent studies are D. J. Struik, *Yankee Science in the Making* (Little, Brown, Boston, 1948), and Thomas Coulson, *Joseph Henry: His Life and Work* (Princeton University Press, Princeton, N. J., 1950). On medical progress the most thoughtful work is R. H. Shryock, *The Development of Modern Medicine* (Knopf, New York, 1947); see also H. B. Shafer, *The American Medical Profession, 1733–1850* (Columbia University Press, New York, 1936), and Victor Robinson, *Victory over Pain: A History of Anesthesia* (Schuman, New York, 1946).

Chapter 17. Literary Nationalism

GENERAL. Indispensable not only for its discussion of trends and important figures but for its unusually comprehensive bibliography in Vol. 3 is the *Literary History of the United States.* Perennially stimulating are the pertinent chapters in Parrington, *Main Currents in American Thought.*

SPECIAL STUDIES. Van Wyck Brooks has written a sparkling series: *The World of Washington Irving* (Dutton, New York, 1944); *The Flowering of New England, 1815–1865* (Dutton, New York, 1936); *The Times of Melville and Whitman* (Dutton, New York, 1947). On an earlier period Leon Howard, *The Connecticut Wits* (University of Chicago Press, Chicago, 1942) is valuable. F. O. Matthiessen, *American Renaissance* (Oxford, New York, 1941) is an outstanding work in American literary criticism; a brief but suggestive discussion of the same period is Lewis Mumford, *The Golden Day* (Boni & Liveright, New York, 1926). Excellent studies of fiction are Carl Van Doren, *The American Novel: 1789–1939* (Macmillan, New York, 1940); Alexander Cowie, *The Rise of the American Novel* (American Book, New York, 1948); and H. R. Brown, *The Sentimental Novel in America, 1789–1860* (Duke University Press, Durham, N. C., 1940). Constance Rourke, *American Humor* (Harcourt, Brace, New York, 1931) is a brilliant contribution.

HISTORICAL WRITING. Useful discussions are found in Kraus, *A History of American History,* and in J. S. Bassett, *The Middle Group of American Historians* (Macmillan, New York, 1917).

STUDIES OF INDIVIDUAL WRITERS. An excellent biography of Emerson is now available: R. L. Rusk, *The Life of Ralph Waldo Emerson* (Scribner, New York, 1949). H. S. Canby, *Thoreau* (Houghton Mifflin, Boston, 1939) is an appreciative study. The same author's *Walt Whitman, an American* (Houghton Mifflin, Boston, 1943) is the most comprehensive critical work on this figure. Excellent works of scholarship are W. E. Sedgwick, *Herman Melville: The Tragedy of Mind* (Harvard University Press, Cambridge, Mass., 1944), and Newton Arvin, *Herman Melville* (William Sloane Associates, New York, 1950).

Chapter 18. The American Spirit in Arts and Amusements

GENERAL. Chapters of fascinating interest will be found in Larkin, *Art and Life in America.* See also H. Cahill and A. H. Barr, Jr., eds., *Art in America* (Reynal & Hitchcock, Inc., New York, 1935).

ARCHITECTURE, PAINTING, SCULPTURE. Talbot Hamlin, *Greek Revival Architecture in America* (Oxford, New York, 1944) is an exceptionally fine study, beautifully illustrated. Isham and Cortissoz, *A History of American Painting;* Barker, *American Painting*; and Burroughs, *Limners and Likenesses* are all useful. See also J. T. Flexner, *America's Old Masters* (Viking, New York, 1939). Lorado Taft, *The History of American Sculpture* (Macmillan, New York, 1930) is a standard authority.

MUSIC. Howard, *Our American Music* is the most useful survey. Special phases are treated in Sigmund Spaeth, *A History of Popular Music in America* (Random House, New York, 1948); I. W. Ford, *Traditional Music of America* (Dutton, New York, 1940); and J. T. Howard, *Stephen Foster, America's Troubadour* (Crowell, New York, 1948).

AMUSEMENTS. Dulles, *America Learns to Play,* and Hornblow, *History of the Theatre* are useful. On manners see A. M. Schlesinger, *Learning How to Behave: A Historical Study of American Etiquette Books* (Macmillan, New York, 1947).

III. TRIUMPH OF THE BUSINESSMAN, 1861–1914

GENERAL. The following volumes of *A History of American Life* deal with this period: A. C. Cole, *The Irrepressible Conflict, 1850–1865*; Allan Nevins, *The Emergence of Modern America, 1865–1878;* I. M. Tarbell, *The Nationalizing of Business, 1878–1898*; A. M. Schlesinger, *The Rise of the City, 1878–1898*; and H. U. Faulkner, *The Quest for Social Justice, 1898–1914.* E. P. Oberholtzer, *A History of the United States Since the Civil War* (5 vols., Macmillan, New York, 1917–1937), covers in detail the period from 1865 to 1901. Among the several one-volume histories of this period L. M. Hacker and B. B. Kendrick, *The United States Since 1865* (Crofts, New York, 1936) is outstanding for its treatment of economic and social developments.

FOREIGN ESTIMATES. Unsurpassed in keenness and balanced judgment is James Bryce, *The American Commonwealth* (new ed., 2 vols., Macmillan, New York, 1904). Other works of interest include: W. H. Russell, *My Diary North and South* (Boston, 1863); Matthew Arnold, *Civilization in the United States* (Boston, 1888); E. A. Freeman, *Some Impressions of the United States* (New York, 1883); and Hugo Münsterberg, *The Americans* (McClure, Phillips & Co., New York, 1904).

AUTOBIOGRAPHIES. Justly most famous among American autobiographies and particularly important for the student of American culture is *The Education of Henry Adams* (Modern Lib., New York, 1931). Of exceptional interest is *The Autobiography of Lincoln Steffens* (Harcourt, Brace, New York, 1931). Also recommended are *The Autobiography of William Allen White* (Macmillan, New York, 1946); H. L. Mencken, *Happy Days, 1880–1892* (Knopf, New York, 1940); H. S. Canby, *The Age of Confidence: Life in the Nineties* (Farrar & Rinehart, Inc., New York, 1934).

Chapter 19. Upheaval in the South

CIVIL WAR. On the causes of the conflict compare Charles and Mary Beard, *The Rise of American Civilization* (2 vols., Macmillan, New York, 1927); Channing, *History of the United States,* Vol. VI; A. O. Craven, *The Coming of the Civil War* (Scribner, New York, 1942); R. F. Nichols, *The Disruption of American Democracy* (Macmillan, New York, 1948); Nevins, *The Emergence of Lincoln*; and Randall, *Lincoln the President.*

The impact of war on the South is skillfully described in E. M. Coulter, *The Confederate States of America, 1861–1865* (Louisiana State University Press, Baton Rouge, La., 1950), and in three studies by Bell I. Wiley: *Southern Negroes, 1861–1865* (Yale University Press, New Haven, Conn., 1938); *The Life of Johnny Reb* (Bobbs-Merrill, Indianapolis, Ind., 1943); *The Plain People of the Confederacy* (Louisiana State University Press, Baton

Rouge, La., 1944). A convenient source is M. B. Chesnut, *A Diary from Dixie* (Houghton Mifflin, Boston, 1949). On the war's effects on the North see E. D. Fite, *Social and Industrial Conditions in the North during the Civil War* (Macmillan, New York, 1910).

RECONSTRUCTION. The standard authority is W. A. Dunning, *Reconstruction, Political and Economic* (Harper, New York, 1907). A brief useful account is W. L. Fleming, *The Sequel of Appomattox* (Yale University Press, New Haven, Conn., 1921). Recent trends in southern scholarship are reflected in E. M. Coulter, *The South during Reconstruction, 1865–1877* (Louisiana State University Press, Baton Rouge, La., 1947), and F. B. Simkins and R. L. Woody, *South Carolina during Reconstruction* (The University of North Carolina Press, Chapel Hill, N. C., 1932). The Negro point of view is given radical expression in W. E. B. Du Bois, *Black Reconstruction* (Harcourt, Brace, New York, 1935), and more moderate development in Franklin, *From Slavery to Freedom.*

THE NEW SOUTH. See Simkins, *The South, Old and New*; Holland Thompson, *The New South* (Yale University Press, New Haven, Conn., 1919); and H. W. Grady, *The New South* (New York, 1890). For the expansion of the tobacco industry consult J. C. Robert, *The Story of Tobacco in America* (Knopf, New York, 1949).

Chapter 20. Last Frontier

GENERAL. Useful accounts are Riegel, *America Moves West*; Billington, *Westward Expansion*; D. E. Clark, *The West in American History* (Crowell, New York, 1937); and L. R. Hafen and C. C. Riser, *Western America* (Prentice-Hall, New York, 1941). F. L. Paxson, *The Last American Frontier* (Macmillan, New York, 1910), and Emerson Hough, *The Passing of the Frontier* (Yale University Press, New Haven, Conn., 1921) concentrate on this period.

THE MINING FRONTIER. California during gold rush days is described in R. G. Cleland, *A History of California: The American Period* (Macmillan, New York, 1922). On Nevada see G. D. Lyman, *The Saga of the Comstock Lode* (Scribner, New York, 1934). Good contemporary descriptions are Bayard Taylor, *Eldorado; or Adventures in the Path of Empire* (New York, 1856), and S. L. Clemens (Mark Twain), *Roughing It* (Harper, New York, 1924).

WESTERN TRANSPORTATION. Le Roy Hafen, *The Overland Mail, 1849–1869* (A. H. Clark Co., Cleveland, 1926), and R. E. Riegel, *The Story of the Western Railroads* (Macmillan, New York, 1926) are competent studies. For contemporary accounts of travel in prerailroad days consult Samuel Bowles, *Across the Continent* (Springfield, Mass., 1865), and A. D. Richardson, *Beyond the Mississippi* (Hartford, 1867).

THE CATTLE FRONTIER. An unusual study in the influence of geographical and climatic conditions is W. P. Webb, *The Great Plains* (Ginn, Boston, 1931). E. S. Osgood, *The Day of the Cattleman* (University of Minnesota Press, Minneapolis, Minn., 1929); E. E. Dale, *The Range Cattle Industry* (University of Oklahoma Press, Norman, Okla., 1930); E. E. Dale, *Cow Country* (University of Oklahoma Press, Norman, Okla., 1942); and Louis Pelzer, *The Cattleman's Frontier, 1850–1890* (A. H. Clark, Glendale, Calif., 1936) are excellent works. A contemporary memoir, originally published in 1885, is C. A. Siringo, *A Texas Cowboy, or Fifteen Years on the Hurricane Deck of a Spanish Pony* (William Sloane Associates, New York, 1950).

THE FARMER'S FRONTIER. F. A. Shannon, *The Farmer's Last Frontier: Agriculture, 1860–1897* (Farrar & Rinehart, Inc., New York, 1945) contains much information, vigorously presented. Unusually comprehensive is Everett Dick, *The Sod-house Frontier, 1854–1890* (Appleton-Century, New York, 1937).

INFLUENCE OF THE FRONTIER. Turner's famous essay may be found in his *The Frontier in American History.* Some significant criticisms of the Turner thesis have been conveniently brought together in G. R. Taylor, ed., *The Turner Thesis Concerning the Role of the Frontier in American History* (Heath, Boston, 1949). L. L. Hazard, *The Frontier in American Literature* (Crowell, New York, 1927) is a scholarly study.

CHAPTER 21. RISE OF BIG BUSINESS

GENERAL. See Faulkner, *American Economic History*; Kirkland, *A History of American Economic Life*; Shannon, *America's Economic Growth*; Hacker, *Triumph of American Capitalism*; Cochran and Miller, *Age of Enterprise*; Clark, *History of Manufactures in the United States*. Tarbell, *The Nationalizing of Business* is particularly useful. Roger Burlingame, *Engines of Democracy* (Scribner, New York, 1940) is a thoughtful discussion of inventions and their social impact.

ECONOMIC EMPIRE BUILDERS. Gustavus Myers, *History of the Great American Fortunes* (Modern Lib., New York, 1936) is an indictment of big business, based on much patient research. Hostile also is the highly readable Matthew Josephson, *The Robber Barons: The Great American Capitalists, 1861–1901* (Harcourt, Brace, New York, 1934). A sympathetic, but superficial, treatment is T. J. Grayson, *Leaders and Periods of American Finance* (Wiley, New York, 1932). Allan Nevins, *John D. Rockefeller; The Heroic Age of American Enterprise* (2 vols., Scribner, New York, 1940) is a fine biography, sympathetic to its subject but without special pleading. For more hostile discussions of Rockefeller consult two famous works: H. D. Lloyd, *Wealth Against Commonwealth* (New York, 1894), and I. M. Tarbell, *The History of the Standard Oil Company* (2 vols., McClure, Phillips & Co., New York, 1904). B. J. Hendrick, *The Life of Andrew Carnegie* (2 vols., Doubleday, Doran, Garden City, N. Y., 1932) is a friendly biography. Vague on many important episodes but interesting as a self-portrait is the *Autobiography of Andrew Carnegie* (Houghton Mifflin, Boston, 1920). F. L. Allen, *The Great Pierpont Morgan* (Harper, New York, 1949) is a brilliant interpretation. Excellent also is the account of high finance in F. L. Allen, *The Lords of Creation* (Harper, New York, 1935). Other key figures are depicted in W. J. Lane, *Commodore Vanderbilt* (Knopf, New York, 1942); J. G. Pyle, *The Life of James J. Hill* (2 vols., P. Smith, New York, 1936); J. B. Hedges, *Henry Villard and the Railways of the Northwest* (Yale University Press, New Haven, Conn., 1930); F. E. Leupp, *George Westinghouse* (Little, Brown, Boston, 1918); George Kennan, *E. H. Harriman* (2 vols., Houghton Mifflin, Boston, 1922); F. B. Copley, *Frederick W. Taylor, Father of Scientific Management* (2 vols., Harper, New York, 1923). John Moody, *The Truth About the Trusts* (Moody, New York, 1904) is the classic contemporary discussion of the problem of monopoly.

CHAPTER 22. PROTESTS FROM LABOR

GENERAL. The standard authority is Commons, *History of Labour in the United States*; briefer and more readable is Dulles, *Labor in America*. P. S. Foner, *History of the Labor Movement in the United States* (International Publishers, New York, 1947) contains much interesting information but should be used with caution because of its radical orientation. Controversial also are the interpretations of C. A. Madison, *American Labor Leaders* (Harper, New York, 1950).

SPECIFIC MOVEMENTS. The best discussion of the National Labor Union and the Knights of Labor is N. J. Ware, *The Labor Movement in the United States, 1860–1895* (Appleton, New York, 1929). Ware's unfavorable estimate of Powderly should be compared with the latter's own account in T. V. Powderly, *Thirty Years of Labor, 1859 to 1889* (Columbus, Ohio, 1890), and with *The Path I Trod: The Autobiography of Terence V. Powderly* (Columbia University Press, New York, 1940). L. L. Lorwin and J. A. Flexner, *The American Federation of Labor* (Brookings, Washington, D. C., 1933) is a standard account; see also Samuel Gompers, *Seventy Years of Life and Labor* (2 vols., Dutton, New

York, 1925). An interesting contemporary account of the railroad strikes of 1877 is J. D. McCabe (Edward Winslow Martin), *The History of the Great Riots* (Philadelphia, 1877). Almont Lindsay, *The Pullman Strike* (University of Chicago Press, Chicago, 1942) is a thorough study.

RADICALISM. The confused skein of the post-Civil War radical movement is skillfully unraveled in Henry David, *The History of the Haymarket Affair* (Farrar & Rinehart, Inc., New York, 1936). See also C. M. Destler, *American Radicalism, 1865–1901* (Connecticut College, New London, Conn., 1946); P. F. Brissenden, *The I. W. W.: A Study of American Syndicalism* (Columbia University Press, New York, 1919); Morris Hillquit, *History of Socialism in the United States* (Funk, New York, 1910); Ray Ginger, *The Bending Cross: A Biography of Eugene Victor Debs* (Rutgers University Press, New Brunswick, N. J., 1949); *Bill Haywood's Book, The Autobiography of William D. Haywood* (International Publishers, New York, 1929).

GEORGE AND BELLAMY. A reading of Henry George, *Progress and Poverty* (Modern Lib., New York, 1938), and Edward Bellamy, *Looking Backward, 2000–1887* (World Publishing, Cleveland, 1945) may be supplemented with Henry George, Jr., *The Life of Henry George* (Doubleday, Doran, Garden City, N. Y., 1930); L. F. Post, *The Prophet of San Francisco* (Vanguard, Inc., New York, 1930); and A. E. Morgan, *Edward Bellamy* (Columbia University Press, New York, 1944).

Chapter 23. Protests from the Farmer

GENERAL. Conditions in agriculture are discussed in the economic histories of Faulkner, Kirkland, and Shannon. A more detailed account is Shannon, *The Farmer's Last Frontier.*

SPECIAL STUDIES. Brief but excellent is S. J. Buck, *The Agrarian Crusade* (Yale University Press, New Haven, Conn., 1920). Authoritative, detailed studies are S. J. Buck, *The Granger Movement* (Harvard University Press, Cambridge, Mass., 1913), and J. D. Hicks, *The Populist Revolt: A History of the Farmers' Alliance and the People's Party* (University of Minnesota Press, Minneapolis, Minn., 1931). Populism in the South has been studied in a number of competent works: F. B. Simkins, *Pitchfork Ben Tillman, South Carolinian* (Louisiana State University Press, Baton Rouge, La., 1944); C. V. Woodward, *Tom Watson, Agrarian Rebel* (Macmillan, New York, 1938); A. M. Arnett, *The Populist Movement in Georgia* (Columbia University Press, New York, 1922); Stuart Noblin, *Leonidas Lafayette Polk, Agrarian Crusader* (The University of North Carolina Press, Chapel Hill, N. C., 1949).

SOURCES. For the point of view of an important participant see W. J. Bryan, *The First Battle* (Chicago, 1898), and *The Memoirs of William Jennings Bryan: By Himself and His Wife, Mary Baird Bryan* (Winston, Philadelphia, 1925). W. H. Harvey, *Coin's Financial School* (Chicago, 1894); W. H. Harvey, *A Tale of Two Nations* (Chicago, 1894); and Ignatius Donnelly, *The American People's Money* (Chicago, 1895) are interesting specimens of silverite propaganda.

Chapter 24. Problems of the City

GENERAL. Schlesinger, *The Rise of the City, 1878–1898* is the indispensable account.

IMMIGRATION. The best general survey is still Wittke, *We Who Built America.* See also Stephenson, *History of American Immigration*; M. R. Davie, *World Immigration: With Special Reference to the United States* (Macmillan, New York, 1936); F. J. Brown and J. S. Roucek, *One America: The History, Contributions, and Present Problems of Our Racial and National Minorities* (Prentice-Hall, New York, 1945); and Louis Adamic, *A Nation of Nations* (Harper, New York, 1945). Notable immigrants tell their own stories and develop their own philosophies in Mary Antin, *The Promised Land* (Houghton Mifflin, Boston, 1912); Mary Antin, *They Who Knock at Our Gates* (Houghton Mifflin, Boston, 1914); Edward Bok, *The Americanization of Edward Bok* (Scribner, New York, 1921); Michael Pupin, *From Immigrant to Inventor* (Scribner, New York, 1923); and Jacob Riis, *The Making of an American* (Macmillan, New York, 1924). See also documents in Abbott, *Historical Aspects of the Immigration Problem*, and Abbott, *Immigration: Select Documents and Case Records.*

THE CITY. Allan Nevins and J. A. Krout, eds., *The Greater City: New York, 1898–1948* (Columbia University Press, New York, 1948) contains useful chapters. A muckraking classic is Lincoln Steffens, *The Shame of the Cities* (McClure, Phillips & Co., New York, 1904). The ceaseless fact finding and crusading of a great reporter is reflected in the books of Jacob A. Riis: *How the Other Half Lives* (New York, 1890); *The Children of the Poor* (New York, 1892); *The Battle with the Slum* (New York, 1902). Important also is R. W. De Forest and Lawrence Veiller, *The Tenement House Problem* (2 vols., Macmillan, New York, 1902). Josiah Strong, *The Challenge of the City* (Eaton & Mains, New York, 1907), and F. C. Howe, *The City: The Hope of Democracy* (Scribner, New York, 1905) are important contemporary discussions.

REFORM MOVEMENTS. The evolution of systematic methods in charity and welfare work may be traced in S. P. Breckenridge, ed., *Public Welfare Administration in the United States: Select Documents* (University of Chicago Press, Chicago, 1927), and in F. D. Watson, *The Charity Organization Movement in the United States* (Macmillan, New York, 1922). Jane Addams, *Twenty Years at Hull House* (Macmillan, New York, 1910) is a fine memoir. On the temperance movement see E. H. Cherrington, *The Evolution of Prohibition in the United States* (American Issue Press, Westerville, Ohio, 1920). On prison reform see F. H. Wines, *Punishment and Reformation* (Crowell, New York, 1910). The women's rights movement may be traced in Stanton, Anthony, and Gage, *History of Woman Suffrage*; Irwin, *Angels and Amazons*; Stanton, *Eighty Years and More*; and I. H. Harper, *The Life and Work of Susan B. Anthony* (3 vols., Indianapolis, 1898–1908). On the changing family, material may be found in A. W. Calhoun, *A Social History of the American Family* (3 vols., A. H. Clark, Cleveland, Ohio, 1917–1919).

Chapter 25. Religion's Response to the Industrial Age

GENERAL. Sweet, *Story of Religion in America* may be supplemented by the more detailed discussions of G. G. Atkins, *Religion in Our Times* (Round Table, New York, 1932), and W. E. Garrison, *The March of Faith: The Story of Religion in America since 1865* (Harper, New York, 1933).

RELIGIOUS GROWTH. For histories of the various denominations see the works cited for Chaps. 4 and 14. See also Ismar Elbogen, *A Century of Jewish Life* (Jewish Publication Society of America, Philadelphia, 1945), and A. L. Lebeson, *Pilgrim People* (Harper, New York, 1950). Valuable for understanding Catholic problems are James Cardinal Gibbons, *A Retrospect of Fifty Years* (2 vols., John Murphy Co., Baltimore, Md., 1916), and A. S. Will, *Life of Cardinal Gibbons, Archbishop of Baltimore* (2 vols., Dutton, New York, 1922). The founder of Christian Science is sympathetically treated in L. P. Powell, *Mary Baker Eddy: A Life Size Portrait* (Macmillan, New York, 1930); E. F. Dakin, *Mrs. Eddy: The Biography of a Virginal Mind* (Scribner, New York, 1929) is critical. H. R. Niebuhr, *The Social Sources of Denominationalism* (Holt, New York, 1929) provides useful interpretation. The revolt against formal religion is treated in Sidney Warren, *American Freethought, 1860–1914* (Columbia University Press, New York, 1943).

NEW RELIGIOUS TRENDS. On the impact of science and higher criticism see F. H. Foster, *The Modern Movement in American Theology* (Revell, New York, 1939). On the social gospel consult C. H. Hopkins, *Rise of the Social Gospel in American Protestantism,*

1865–1915 (Yale University Press, New Haven, Conn., 1940), and H. F. May, *Protestant Churches and Industrial America* (Harper, New York, 1949).

CHAPTER 26. THE NEW AGE OF SCIENCE

GENERAL. Trends and influences are analyzed in great detail in Curti, *Growth of American Thought*, and Gabriel, *The Course of American Democratic Thought.* H. S. Commager, *The American Mind: An Interpretation of American Thought and Character since the 1880's* (Yale University Press, New Haven, Conn., 1950) is stimulating and provocative in its judgments.

PROGRESS IN SCIENCE. Bernard Jaffe, *Men of Science in America* (Simon & Schuster, New York, 1944) is a successful effort to explain the work of the scientists in language that the layman can understand; see also J. G. Crowther, *Famous American Men of Science* (Norton, New York, 1937). The best account of medical progress is Shryock, *Development of Modern Medicine.* An excellent biography of a key figure is Simon and J. T. Flexner, *William Henry Welch and the Heroic Age of American Medicine* (Viking, New York, 1941). Muriel Rukeyser, *Willard Gibbs* (Doubleday, Doran, Garden City, N. Y., 1942) is a brilliant interpretation.

SOCIAL SCIENCE. An outstanding study is Richard Hofstadter, *Social Darwinism in American Thought, 1860–1915* (University of Pennsylvania Press, Philadelphia, 1945). L. L. and Jessie Bernard, *Origins of American Sociology* (Crowell, New York, 1943) is a comprehensive work, useful in tracing the origins of all the social sciences. See also Howard Odum, ed., *American Masters of Social Science* (Holt, New York, 1927), and H. E. Barnes and Howard Becker, *Social Thought from Lore to Science* (2 vols., Heath, Boston, 1938). J. S. Clarke, *The Life and Letters of John Fiske* (2 vols., Houghton Mifflin, Boston, 1917) is a standard work. Very useful is Joseph Dorfman, *Thorstein Veblen and His America* (Viking, New York, 1935). See also Dorfman, *Economic Mind in American Civilization*, Vol. III.

PHILOSOPHY. A distinguished scholar surveys this period in R. B. Perry, *Philosophy of the Recent Past* (Scribner, New York, 1926). An excellent more detailed discussion is Philip Wiener, *Evolution and the Founders of Pragmatism* (Harvard University Press, Cambridge, Mass., 1949). One of the finest American biographies is R. B. Perry, *The Thought and Character of William James* (2 vols., Little, Brown, Boston, 1936). See also the discussion of James and Royce in George Santayana, *Character and Opinion in the United States* (Scribner, New York, 1921). Sidney Hook, *John Dewey, an Intellectual Portrait* (John Day, New York, 1939), and P. A. Schlipp, ed., *The Philosophy of John Dewey* (Northwestern University, Evanston, Ill., 1939) are valuable.

EDUCATION. On elementary and secondary schools Cubberley, *Public Education in the United States*, and Edwards and Richey, *The School in the American Social Order* may be supplemented with the older C. F. Thwing, *A History of Education in the United States since the Civil War* (Houghton Mifflin, Boston, 1910). Excellent for this period is Curti, *Social Ideas of American Educators.* A useful contemporary survey of higher education is E. F. Slosson, *Great American Universities* (Macmillan, New York, 1910). Many general trends are reflected in S. E. Morison, ed., *The Development of Harvard University since the Inauguration of President Eliot, 1869–1929* (Harvard University Press, Cambridge, Mass., 1930). On the adult education movement see J. T. Adams, *Frontiers of American Culture* (Scribner, New York, 1944).

CHAPTER 27. FROM ROMANTICISM TO REALISM

GENERAL. The most useful work is the *Literary History of the United States.* Parrington, *Main Currents in American Thought,* Vol. 3, contains some brilliant chapters, but the author's untimely death left the work uncompleted. Van Wyck Brooks, *New England: Indian Summer: 1865–1915* (Dutton, New York, 1940), and Alfred Kazin, *On Native Grounds* (Reynal & Hitchcock, Inc., New York, 1942) are excellent.

MAJOR WRITERS. Van Wyck Brooks, *The Ordeal of Mark Twain* (Dutton, New York, 1933) is a highly controversial interpretation; for later judgments see Bernard De Voto, *Mark Twain's America* (Little, Brown, Boston, 1932); De Voto, *Mark Twain at Work* (Harvard University Press, Cambridge, Mass., 1942); J. D. Ferguson, *Mark Twain: Man and Legend* (Bobbs-Merrill, Indianapolis, Ind., 1943). Important works are D. G. Cooke, *William Dean Howells: A Critical Study* (Dutton, New York, 1922); F. O. Mathiessen, *Henry James: The Major Phase* (Oxford, New York, 1944); John Berryman, *Stephen Crane* (William Sloane Associates, New York, 1951). A useful study is W. F. Taylor, *The Economic Novel in America* (The University of North Carolina Press, Chapel Hill, N. C., 1942). The impact of European ideas is brilliantly analyzed in Oscar Cargill, *Intellectual America: Ideas on the March* (Macmillan, New York, 1948).

POPULAR LITERATURE. F. L. Mott, *Golden Multitudes: The Story of Best Sellers in the United States* (Macmillan, New York, 1947) is an interesting study in popular taste. Albert Johannsen, *The House of Beadle and Adams, and Its Dime and Nickel Novels* (2 vols., University of Oklahoma Press, Norman, Okla., 1950) is authoritative; see also the entertaining Edmund Pearson, *Dime Novels* (Little, Brown, Boston, 1929).

THE ARTS. See the works cited for Chaps. 6 and 18. Important works for this period are Hugh Morrison, *Louis Sullivan, Prophet of Modern Architecture* (Norton, New York, 1935), and Frank Lloyd Wright, *An Autobiography* (Longmans, New York, 1932).

AMUSEMENTS. In addition to the works cited for Chaps. 6 and 18, see J. A. Krout, *Annals of American Sport* (Yale University Press, New Haven, Conn., 1929), and A. H. Quinn, *A History of the American Drama from the Civil War to the Present Day* (Crofts, New York, 1936).

IV. THE LATEST AGE, SINCE 1914

GENERAL. The following volumes in *A History of American Life* deals with this period: P. W. Slosson, *The Great Crusade and After, 1914–1928,* and Dixon Wecter, *The Age of the Great Depression, 1929–1941.* Well-written surveys are Gerald Johnson, *Incredible Tale: The Odyssey of the Average American in the Last Half Century* (Harper, New York, 1950), and Lloyd Morris, *Postcript to Yesterday; America: The Last Fifty Years* (Random House, New York, 1947).

SPECIAL PERIODS. Still unsurpassed as a description of the 1920's is F. L. Allen, *Only Yesterday* (Harper, New York, 1931); for the thirties see the same author's *Since Yesterday* (Harper, New York, 1940). To compare trends of the twenties with those of the thirties, read two collections of critical essays on American civilization: H. E. Stearns, ed., *Civilization in the United States* (Harcourt, Brace, New York, 1922), and H. E. Stearns, ed., *America Now* (Literary Guild, New York, 1938). Trends may also be studied by comparing R. S. and H. M. Lynd, *Middletown: A Study in Contemporary American Culture* (Harcourt, Brace, New York, 1929), and R. S. and H. M. Lynd, *Middletown in Transition: A Study in Social Conflicts* (Harcourt, Brace, New York, 1937). A storehouse of valuable information is President's Research Committee, *Recent Social Trends in the United States* (2 vols., McGraw-Hill, New York, 1933). R. B. Perry, *Characteristically American* (Knopf, New York, 1949) is an interesting attempt to define the national character.

FOREIGN ESTIMATES. For the twenties André Siegfried, *America Comes of Age: A French Analysis* (Harcourt, Brace, New York, 1927) is recommended. The best recent appraisal is Denis Brogan, *The American Character* (Knopf, New York, 1944).

CHAPTER 28. DEMOCRACY ON THE ANVIL

GENERAL. One-volume histories dealing with political developments for this period are O. T. Barck, Jr., and N. M. Blake, *Since 1900* (Macmillan, New York, 1947); F. R. Dulles, *Twentieth Century America* (Houghton Mifflin, Boston, 1945); D. L. Dumond, *America in Our Time* (Holt, New York, 1947); and Harvey Wish, *Contemporary America* (Harper, New York, 1945).

PROGRESSIVISM. The best study of the muckrakers is Louis Filler, *Crusaders for American Liberalism* (Harcourt, Brace, New York, 1939). On both literary and political aspects see John Chamberlain, *Farewell to Reform: The Rise, Life and Decay of the Progressive Mind in America* (John Day, New York, 1933). Controversial in its judgments is Matthew Josephson, *The President Makers . . . 1896–1919* (Harcourt, Brace, New York, 1940). Good biographies are H. F. Pringle, *Theodore Roosevelt* (Harcourt, Brace, New York, 1931); R. S. Baker, *Woodrow Wilson, Life and Letters* (8 vols., Doubleday Doran, Garden City, N. Y., 1927–1938); A. S. Link, *Wilson, The Road to the White House* (Princeton University Press, Princeton, N. J., 1947); A. T. Mason, *Brandeis: A Free Man's Life* (Viking, New York, 1946).

WORLD WAR I AND AFTERMATH. The most useful extended treatment is F. L. Paxson, *American Democracy and the World War* (3 vols., Houghton Mifflin, Boston, 1936–1948). On American propaganda see J. R. Mock and Cedric Larson, *Words That Won the War* (Princeton University Press, Princeton, N. J., 1940). D. F. Fleming, *The United States and the League of Nations, 1918–1920* (Putnam, New York, 1932) is strongly pro-Wilson; more critical is T. A. Bailey, *Woodrow Wilson and the Great Betrayal* (Macmillan, New York, 1945). For the political atmosphere of the twenties see Karl Schriftgiesser, *This Was Normalcy* (Little, Brown, Boston, 1948), and the excellent characterization of Coolidge in W. A. White, *A Puritan in Babylon* (Macmillan, New York, 1938). Herbert Hoover, *American Individualism* (Doubleday Page, Garden City, N. Y., 1922) well states the political philosophy of its author. Alfred Lief, *Democracy's Norris* (Stackpole, Harrisburg, Pa., 1939), and Max Lerner, *The Mind and Faith of Justice Holmes* (Little, Brown, Boston, 1945) describe two sturdy independents.

THE NEW DEAL. S. I. Rosenman, comp., *The Public Papers and Addresses of Franklin D. Roosevelt* (9 vols., Random House and Macmillan, New York, 1938–1941) is valuable, not only for Roosevelt's speeches, but for his later comments in the introductions and notes. Basil Rauch, *The History of the New Deal* (Creative Age, New York, 1944) is the most detailed account; C. A. and Mary Beard, *America in Midpassage* (Macmillan, New York, 1939) provides interesting interpretation. R. E. Sherwood, *Roosevelt and Hopkins* (Harper, New York, 1948), and Frances Perkins, *The Roosevelt I Knew* (Viking, New York, 1946) are outstanding among many recent memoirs. Herbert Hoover, *The Challenge to Liberty* (Scribner, New York, 1934) is a sharp indictment of the early New Deal.

CONTEMPORARY PROBLEMS. The new internationalism received its most eloquent statement in Wendell Willkie, *One World* (Simon and Schuster, New York, 1943). Most recent writing on serious issues has been excited and ephemeral. More thoughtful and substantial are the discussion in Max Ascoli, *The Power of Freedom* (Farrar, Strauss, New York, 1949), and A. M. Schlesinger, Jr., *The Vital Center* (Houghton Mifflin, Boston, 1949).

DEMOCRACY AND THE NEGRO. Gunnar Myrdal, *An American Dilemma: The Negro Problem and Modern Democracy* (2 vols., Harper, New York, 1944) is the most thorough and objective study. For the Negro point of view see Roi Ottley, *"New World A-Coming": Inside Black America* (Houghton Mifflin, Boston, 1943). *To Secure These Rights: The Report of the President's Committee on Civil Rights* (U. S.

Government Printing Office, Washington, D. C., 1947) is an important, although controversial, document.

CHAPTER 29. CRISIS IN AMERICAN CAPITALISM

GENERAL. See the economic histories cited for Chap. 3; also Broadus and L. P. Mitchell, *American Economic History* (Houghton Mifflin, Boston, 1947), and C. W. Wright, *Economic History of the United States* (McGraw-Hill, New York, 1949). More detailed accounts are George Soule, *Prosperity Decade: From War to Depression: 1917–1929* (Rinehart, New York, 1947), and Broadus Mitchell, *Depression Decade: From New Era through New Deal, 1929–1941* (Rinehart, New York, 1947). For a contemporary discussion of trends during the twenties see *Recent Economic Changes in the United States* (2 vols., McGraw-Hill, New York, 1929).

SPECIAL STUDIES. A. A. Berle and G. C. Means, *The Modern Corporation and Private Property* (Commerce Clearing House, New York, 1932) is a realistic interpretation of the economic and social function of the corporation; see also the excellent discussion in Peter Drucker, *The New Society: The Anatomy of the Industrial Order* (Harper, New York, 1950). David Lynch, *The Concentration of Economic Power* (Columbia University Press, New York, 1946) is a convenient summary of the findings of the Temporary National Economic Committee. A vigorous but exaggerated picture of the consolidation of economic power is given in Ferdinand Lundberg, *America's 60 Families* (Vanguard, Inc., New York, 1937). Interesting analyses of the contemporary economy, steering a middle course between New Deal and Old Deal philosophies, are H. G. Moulton, *The State of the American Economy* (Haynes Foundation, Los Angeles, Calif., 1949), and the same author's *The Nineteen Fifties Come First* (Holt, New York, 1951).

NEW INDUSTRIES. Readable popular accounts of the automobile industry are in D. L. Cohn, *Combustion on Wheels* (Houghton Mifflin, Boston, 1944), and Lloyd Morris, *Not So Long Ago* (Random House, New York, 1949). Henry Ford, *My Life and Work* (Garden City Publishing Company, Inc., Garden City, N. Y., 1922) is an interesting memoir. On aviation see F. C. Kelly, *The Wright Brothers* (Harcourt, Brace, New York, 1943), and E. E. Freudenthal, *The Aviation Business: From Kitty Hawk to Wall Street* (Vanguard, Inc., New York, 1940).

CHAPTER 30. MILITANT LABOR

GENERAL. The most useful brief survey is that of Dulles, *Labor in America.* Selig Perlman and Philip Taft, *History of Labor in the United States, 1896–1932* (Vol. 4 of Commons, *History of Labor in the United States*) is the most detailed discussion of the pre-New Deal period. A good general discussion is Herbert Harris, *American Labor* (Yale University Press, New Haven, Conn., 1939).

SPECIAL STUDIES. P. H. Douglas, *Real Wages in the United States, 1896–1926* (Houghton Mifflin, Boston, 1930) is very useful. For realistic accounts of labor organization see three works by Robert R. R. Brooks: *When Labor Organizes* (Yale University Press, New Haven, Conn., 1938); *Unions of Their Own Choosing* (Yale University Press, New Haven, Conn., 1939); *As Steel Goes . . . Unionism in a Basic Industry* (Yale University Press, New Haven, Conn., 1940). On the rise of the CIO consult J. R. Walsh, *C. I. O., Industrial Unionism in America* (Norton, New York, 1937); Edward Levinson, *Labor on the March* (Harper, New York, 1938); Herbert Harris, *Labor's Civil War* (Knopf, New York, 1940). J. A. Wechsler, *Labor Baron, a Portrait of John L. Lewis* (Morrow, New York, 1944) discusses a highly controversial figure. Some of the serious implications in the new status of labor unions are explored in Wellington Roe, *Juggernaut: American Labor in Action* (Lippincott, Philadelphia, 1948), and C. W. Mills, *The New Men of Power: America's Labor Leaders* (Harcourt, Brace, New York, 1948). Useful reference works are Florence Peterson, *American Labor Unions: What They Are and How They Work* (Harper, New York, 1945), and *How Collective Bargaining Works: A Survey of Experience in Leading American Industries* (Twentieth Century Fund, New York, 1942).

Chapter 31. Search for Moral Anchors

GENERAL. Useful surveys of trends are found in Sweet, *Story of Religion in America*; Sperry, *Religion in America*; Atkins, *Religion in Our Time*; and Garrison, *The March of Faith.*

CHALLENGES TO FAITH. Post-World War I skepticism is set forth in Walter Lippmann, *A Preface to Morals* (Macmillan, New York, 1929), and J. W. Krutch, *The Modern Temper* (Harcourt, Brace, New York, 1929). On the influence of Freud in America see Gregory Zilboorg and G. W. Henry, *A History of Medical Psychology* (Norton, New York, 1941), and *One Hundred Years of American Psychiatry.* A somewhat different psychological interpretation is suggested by Karen Horney, *The Neurotic Personality of Our Time* (Norton, New York, 1937). A contemporary discussion of changing standards of conduct is J. H. Tufts, *America's Social Morality* (Holt, New York, 1933).

MODERNIST-FUNDAMENTALIST CONTROVERSY. Although poorly organized, S. G. Cole, *The History of Fundamentalism* (Richard R. Smith, New York, 1931) is the most useful account. See also Foster, *The Modern Movement in American Theology.* H. E. Fosdick, *Adventurous Religion* (Harper, New York, 1926), and Shailer Mathews, *The Faith of Modernism* (Macmillan, New York, 1924) are representative of the thought of leading modernists. An interesting source is L. H. Allen, ed., *Bryan and Darrow at Dayton: The Record and Documents of the "Bible-Evolution Trial"* (A. Lee & Co., New York, 1925).

PROHIBITION. Hostile accounts are Charles Merz, *The Dry Decade* (Doubleday Doran, Garden City, N. Y., 1931); Herbert Asbury, *The Great Illusion: An Informal History of Prohibition* (Doubleday, Garden City, N. Y., 1950); Virginius Dabney, *Dry Messiah: The Life of Bishop Cannon* (Knopf, New York, 1949); and Peter Odegard, *Pressure Politics, the Story of the Anti-saloon League* (Columbia University Press, New York, 1928). For defenses of prohibition see Irving Fisher, *Prohibition at Its Worst* (Macmillan, New York, 1926), and Herman Feldman, *Prohibition, Its Economic and Industrial Aspects* (Appleton, New York, 1927).

OTHER STUDIES. J. A. Hutchison, *We Are Not Divided: A Critical and Historical Study of The Federal Council of the Churches of Christ in America* (Round Table Press, New York, 1941), and Shailer Mathews, *New Faith for Old* (Macmillan, New York, 1936) deal largely with the social gospel. Catholic social thought is represented by J. A. Ryan, *A Better Economic Order* (Harper, New York, 1935). C. C. Morrison, *Can Protestantism Win America?* (Harper, New York, 1948) is an argument for Protestant unity. C. S. Braden, *These Also Believe: A Study of Modern American Cults and Minority Religious Movements* (Macmillan, New York, 1949) deals sympathetically with the smaller sects.

Chapter 32. New Prestige for the World of Scholarship

GENERAL. Curti, *Growth of American Thought*; Commager, *The American Mind*; and Gabriel, *The Course of American Democratic Thought* are the leading intellectual histories.

EDUCATION. Thoughtful surveys of the American system are H. C. Morrison, *American Schools: A Critical Study of Our School System* (University of Chicago Press, Chicago, 1943), and J. D. Russell and C. H. Judd, *The American Educational System* (Houghton Mifflin, Boston, 1940). On the troublesome religious issue see A. W. Johnson and F. H. Yost, *Separation of Church and State in the United States* (University of Minnesota Press, Minneapolis, Minn., 1948), and R. F. Butts, *The American Tradition in Religion and Education* (Beacon Press, Boston, 1950). Representative of the extensive literature on the goals and methods of higher education are the following: R. F. Butts, *The College Charts Its Course* (McGraw-Hill, New York, 1939); R. L. Kelly, *The American Colleges and the Social Order* (Macmillan, New York, 1940); R. M. Hutchins, *The Higher Learning in America* (Yale University Press, New Haven, Conn., 1936); H. D. Gideonse, *The Higher Learning in a Democracy: A Reply to President Hutchins' Critique of the American University* (Farrar & Rinehart, Inc., New York, 1937); Benjamin Fine, *Democratic Education* (Crowell, New York, 1945); W. B. Donham, *Education for Responsible Living* (Harvard University Press, Cambridge, Mass., 1944); Harvard Committee, *General Education in a Free Society* (Harvard University Press, Cambridge, Mass., 1945).

SCIENCE. Trends during the thirties may be traced in Bernard Jaffe, *Outposts of Science: A Journey to the Workshops of Our Leading Men of Research* (Simon and Schuster, New York, 1935), and in G. W. Gray, *The Advancing Front of Science* (McGraw-Hill, New York, 1937). An excellent account of the role of science in World War II is J. P. Baxter, 3d, *Scientists against Time* (Little, Brown, Boston, 1946). On nuclear research see George Gamow, *Atomic Energy in Cosmic and Human Life: Fifty Years of Radioactivity* (Macmillan, New York, 1946), and Daniel Lang, *Early Tales of the Atomic Age* (Doubleday, New York, 1948).

SOCIAL SCIENCE. An excellent recent study is M. G. White, *Social Thought in America: The Revolt against Formalism* (Viking, New York, 1950). Glenn Hoover, ed., *Twentieth Century Economic Thought* (Philosophical Library, New York, 1950) is a useful cooperative work.

Chapter 33. The Artist Becomes a Democrat

GENERAL. The most convenient works are the *Literary History of the United States*, and Larkin, *Art and Life in America.* A stimulating criticism of the thirties was W. A. Orton, *America in Search of Culture* (Little, Brown, Boston, 1933).

LITERATURE. Stimulating critical discussions are Kazin, *On Native Grounds*; Regis Michaud, *The American Novel Today* (Little, Brown, Boston, 1928); Maxwell Geismar, *The Last of the Provincials: The American Novel, 1915–1925* (Houghton Mifflin, Boston, 1947); Maxwell Geismar, *Writers in Crisis: The American Novel, 1925–1940* (Houghton Mifflin, Boston, 1942); Harry Hartwick, *The Foreground of American Fiction* (American Book, New York, 1934); J. D. Adams, *The Shape of Books to Come* (Viking, New York, 1944). A good historical survey of trends in poetry may be found in the preface to Louis Untermeyer, ed., *Modern American Poetry* (6th rev. ed., Harcourt, Brace, New York, 1942). Irene and Allen Cleaton, *Books and Battles: American Literature, 1920–1930* (Houghton Mifflin, Boston, 1937) is an entertaining account of publishing high lights and literary trends.

THE ARTS. R. L. Duffus, *The American Renaissance* (Knopf, New York, 1928) surveys museums, community theaters, and other agencies of art education. Suzanne La Follette, *Art in America* (Harper, New York, 1929), and Homer Saint-Gaudens, *The American Artist and His Times* (Dodd, Mead, New York, 1941) cover both earlier and recent art history. *Contemporary American Painting: The Encyclopaedia Britannica Collection* (Duell, Sloan & Pearce, New York, 1945) offers a representative cross section. Sheldon Cheney, *The New World Architecture* (Longmans, London, 1930), and F. L. Wright, *Modern Architecture* (Princeton University Press, Princeton, N. J., 1931) are stimulating discussions. David Ewen, *Music Comes to America* (Crowell, New York, 1942) is an interesting account of recent influences like phonograph and radio. Representative of a growing literature on jazz are Rudi Blesh, *Shining Trumpets: A History of Jazz* (Knopf, New York, 1946), and Sidney Finkelstein, *Jazz: A People's Music* (Citadel, New York, 1948).

MOVIES, RADIO, TELEVISION. The most stimulating recent discussion is Gilbert Seldes, *The Great Audience* (Viking, New York, 1950). Excellent for both movies and radio is Morris, *Not So Long Ago.* Popular works on the movies are Lewis Jacobs, *The Rise of the American Film* (Harcourt, Brace, New York, 1939), and Frederic Thrasher, *Okay for Sound: How the Screen Found Its Voice* (Duell, Sloan & Pearce, 1946). L. C. Rosten *Hollywood: The Movie Colony, The Movie Makers* (Harcourt, Brace, New York, 1941) is an interesting sociological study.

Index

A

I

M

N

T